# RAPID APPLICATION DEVELOPMENT
## BY JAMES MARTIN

### Television Series

In conjunction with the writing of this book, a television series has been made or training courses on the same subject. Nine 40-minute tapes were made on RAD (Rapid Application Development) with a total viewing time of 6 hours, and eight similar tapes were made on RAD in an information-engineering environment, with a total viewing time of 5 hours, 20 minutes. The tapes are available from Applied Learning International, Naperville, Illinois (tel: 708-369-3000).

The tapes complement the book because they contain sequences from a variety of project managers describing their experiences with RAD. We selected practitioners who have learned how to build systems *repeatedly* at exceptionally high speed, often achieving productivity levels of 100 function points per person-month or more.

Over 30 hours of television interviews were recorded with these practitioners. Their experience helped me write this book, and I would like to express my gratitude.

Particularly impressive were the development activities of:

STEVE ALLWORTH, Vice President, Consulting, Westpac Banking Corp.

GRAEME FAIRLEY, Application Division Manager, JMA, London

MARK FILTEAU, Vice President, ISD, BDM International, Inc.

CHARLES GEE, Business Product Manager, IPS&S, United Data Services, Inc.

SAMUEL B. HOLCMAN, President, C.E.C.

DENNIS MINIUM, Manager, Product Planning and Methodology, Texas Instruments, Inc.

PETER B. PRIVATEER, Director, Product Programs, KnowledgeWare, Inc.

SCOTT SCHULTZ, Manager, DuPont Information Engineering Associates

THOMAS SCHWANINGER, Director, Planning and Control, The Bekins Company

SCOTT THOROGOOD, Director, Strategic Development, Information Technology Group, Texas Instruments, Inc.; previously Manager, Consulting Services, Fourth Generation Technology.

STEVE R. WATSON, Director, A&A Computing, Washington State University

DAVID L. WELLS, Application Development Manager, Washington State University.

JOHN W. WHITE, Senior Vice President and Director, Information Technology Group, Texas Instruments, Inc.

STEVE K. WIGGINS, Vice President, Information Systems, BC/BS of South Carolina.

Rapid Application Development

# Rapid Application Development

James Martin

MACMILLAN PUBLISHING COMPANY
NEW YORK
COLLIER MACMILLAN CANADA
TORONTO
MAXWELL MACMILLAN INTERNATIONAL
NEW YORK   OXFORD   SINGAPORE   SYDNEY

Editor: Ed Moura
Technical Editor: Lillian Larijani
Production Supervisor: Ron Harris
Production Manager: Nick Sklitsis
Text & Cover Designer: Sheree Goodman
Cover Illustration: York Graphic Services, Inc.

This book was set in Berkeley Old Style by Waldman Graphics, printed and
bound by Halliday Lithograph. The cover was printed by Lehigh Press.

Macmillan Publishing Company
866 Third Avenue, New York, New York 10022

Collier Macmillan Canada, Inc.

**Library of Congress Cataloging in Publication Data**
Martin, James, 1943–
    Rapid application development / James Martin.
        p.    cm.
    Includes bibliographical references.
    ISBN 0-02-376775-8
    1. Computer software—Development.    I. Title.
QA76.76.D47M365    1991
005.1—dc20                                             90-6117
                                                       CIP

Printing: 1 2 3 4 5 6 7 8        Year: 1 2 3 4 5 6 7 8 9 0

To Corinthia

# Preface

One of the most urgent concerns in enterprises today is the need for I.S. organizations to create and modify applications *much* faster than with the traditional development lifecycle. If applications take two or three years to build and the application backlog is several years, businesses cannot create and react to competitive thrusts quickly enough. The vital ability for dynamic change is lost.

Critical success factors for every I.S. department are:

- *speed of development of high-quality applications;*
- *speed of application change (maintenance);*
- *speed of cutover of new applications.*

Some I.S. organizations have mastered (or partially mastered) the techniques for building applications fast; most, however, are stuck in a tarpit of old and slow methods.

There are many diverse aspects to achieving fast application development. This book discusses them and shows how they can be used together in new application development lifecycles. It is essential to emphasize high quality in development. Poor quality wastes money. The techniques described here use people and automation to achieve much higher quality applications than those built with the traditional lifecycle.

While doing the researching for this book, a television series of training courses was created, containing comments from a variety of project managers who repeatedly build systems at high speed with a high success rate. The difference between the development illustrated in these tapes and development in the average I.S. organization, mired in manual COBOL, PL/I or FORTRAN programming, is astonishing.

The author hopes that the techniques and lifecycles described in this book become widely adopted so that I.S. can move into a new era of fast development that facilitates dynamic changes in the way corporations operate.

## What Is RAD?

RAD (Rapid Application Development) refers to a development lifecycle designed to give much faster development and higher-quality results than those achieved with the traditional lifecycle. It is designed to take maximum advantage of powerful development software that has evolved recently.

There are variations on the RAD lifecycle, depending on the nature of the system and the tools being used.

RAD has been demonstrated in many projects to be so superior to traditional development that it seems irresponsible to continue to develop systems the old way.

J. M.

# Brief Contents

# Methodology Charts                                          413

# Appendixes                                                  509

# Contents

# APPENDIXES

# INTRODUCTION

# CHAPTER 1

# Executive Overview

## The Best Application Development

Today there is an astonishing difference between the best application development and that in the majority of Information Systems (I.S.) departments. Some I.S. organizations have acquired the capability of building high-quality applications fast. Most are taking two or three years to build applications of questionable quality. This book examines the techniques used to build applications, including complex applications, strategic applications and mission-critical applications, in *months* rather than *years*.

All of the examples and techniques in this book are based on real organizations that build systems fast and can do so repetitively. As with scientific experiments, the success must be repeatable in order to be interesting. Throughout the book we emphasize measurements so that different developers and techniques can be compared.

The best development teams have 10 times the productivity of the average. They can help give their enterprise a major competitive edge. The examples we provide do not depend on magic or genius. They use tools and techniques that are transferable to all I.S. organizations, given appropriate management. It seems astonishing that the majority of I.S. organizations are still building systems so painfully slowly.

## What Is RAD?

RAD (Rapid Application Development) refers to a development lifecycle designed to give much faster development and higher quality results than the traditional lifecycle. It is designed to take maximum advantage of powerful development software that has evolved recently, like that from KnowledgeWare, Texas Instruments, the AD Cycle tools of IBM and COHESION tools of DEC.

There are variations on the RAD lifecycle, depending on the nature of the system and the tools being used. RAD has been demonstrated in many projects to be so superior to traditional development that it seems irresponsible to continue to develop systems the old way. The development lifecycle described in this book applies to the building of the I.S. applications that are essential for every large enterprise. It would not apply to the building of chess-playing programs, complex operating systems, software tools such as Lotus' 1-2-3 or the software for the space shuttle. These unique and highly complex programs cannot be created with code generators and cannot, today, be built quickly (although some of the techniques in this book are applicable to them). They are hand-crafted, typically with a productivity level of around 10 lines of code per person-day. Such systems often consist of hundreds of thousands of lines of unique code and require the management of over 100 person-years of development effort. Commercial data-processing systems of hundreds of thousands of lines of code, on the other hand, are being built by small teams with I-CASE tools in six months or so. The book and its affiliated videotapes give you detailed examples of such systems.

## Lower Cost

The techniques for fast application development almost always result in lower-cost development. A key aspect of fast development is to use small teams rather than large teams. Small teams can be made highly productive if they use methodologies for rapid analysis and use power tools that generate code. A shortening of the development time is thus combined with a reduction in the number of people needed.

The power tools for application development are referred to as *CASE* tools. CASE stands for "Computer-Aided Systems Engineering." Just as engineers in other fields use computer-aided design tools, so should software engineers. The CASE tools on the market vary greatly in their capability. With some of them, little improvement in productivity occurs. It is critical to select tools of appropriate power that generate program code. Chapter 3 discusses the tools.

The best of the tools needed are quite expensive, but not compared with the cost of large teams of I.S. professionals using the old techniques.

Some I.S. organizations introducing CASE tools have not improved productivity, lowered costs or shortened the development time. A small proportion of CASE users have learned how to achieve dramatic improvements, cutting the development time to a quarter of what it was before, lowering the cost by a greater factor and greatly improving system quality. Some I.S. executives achieve these improvements on virtually every project.

The press sometimes quotes the *average* improvements from CASE usage. The best is dramatically better than the average because "average" includes the many organizations that are groping, with no RAD methodology in place. It is of little interest that the average building in New York is 4.2 stories high. What is of interest are the skyscrapers that dominate the skyline. The same is true with CASE usage. The lifecycle described in this book produces results many times higher than the average. The book discusses I.S. organizations that are achieving those results repetitively.

## Quality

Fast development does not mean "quick and dirty." It is necessary to build applications of high quality. Indeed, much higher quality is needed than is found in many of the applications built with traditional methodologies.

There should not be a compromise between speed of development and quality. It is sometimes thought that speed is inversely proportional to quality. That is not the case here. Some chapters of this book are concerned with meeting user needs and business needs better, creating excellent human factoring, building systems that can evolve continuously, building systems that fit into an information-engineering framework, and building systems of great complexity.

Fortunately, today's CASE tools, code generators and prototyping tools provide us with the means of ensuring higher quality when employed with an appropriate methodology. They enable us to:

- Meet business needs better.
- Fit user capabilities better.
- Enforce technical integrity in complex analysis and design.
- Create bug-free systems.
- Create systems with excellent human factoring.
- Create systems that are easy to maintain.
- Create systems that can evolve continuously, becoming rich in functionality.
- Create systems of great complexity.

Most organizations define software quality in an inappropriate way. They define it as:

**conforming to the written specifications as effectively as possible.**

In the traditional system development lifecycle, user specifications are frozen before the technical design, coding and testing are done. Often, they are frozen eighteen months before the system becomes operational. During this time, the business needs change substantially; so, the system does not meet these needs when it becomes operational. The users have to "make do" with an inadequate system.

A more appropriate definition of **quality** is:

**meeting the true business (or user) requirements as effectively as possible at the time the system comes into operation.**

The shorter the elapsed time between *user design* and *cutover*, the more likely will the system be satisfactory. Fast application development techniques require that users be thoroughly involved in the design of a system and that the design be in a computerized form that can be driven into code as quickly as possible.

In addition to avoiding a situation where specifications become obsolete, rapid development requires several factors that improve the quality of the delivered system (as summarized in Figure 1.1):

- thorough involvement of the end user in the design of the system;
- prototyping, which helps the users visualize and make adjustments to the system;
- use of an integrated CASE toolset, which enforces technical integrity in modeling and designing the system;
- a CASE repository that facilitates the reuse of well-proven templates, components or systems;
- an integrated CASE toolset that generates bug-free code from a fully validated design;
- user involvement in the Construction Phase, allowing the details of the prototype to be adjusted if necessary.

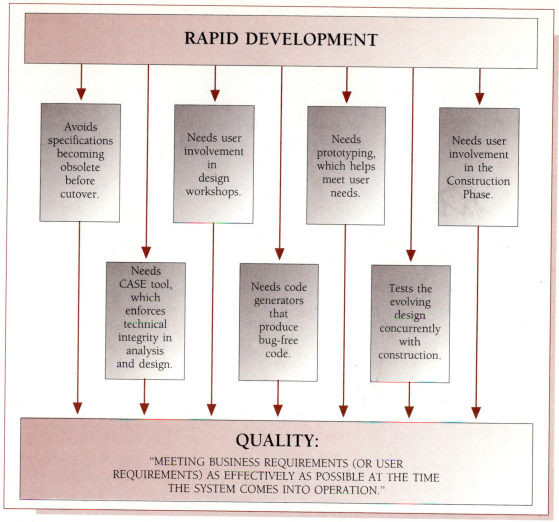

**RAPID DEVELOPMENT**

Avoids specifications becoming obsolete before cutover.

Needs user involvement in design workshops.

Needs prototyping, which helps meet user needs.

Needs user involvement in the Construction Phase.

Needs CASE tool, which enforces technical integrity in analysis and design.

Needs code generators that produce bug-free code.

Tests the evolving design concurrently with construction.

**QUALITY:**

"MEETING BUSINESS REQUIREMENTS (OR USER REQUIREMENTS) AS EFFECTIVELY AS POSSIBLE AT THE TIME THE SYSTEM COMES INTO OPERATION."

FIGURE 1.1 The techniques for high-speed application development lead to higher-quality systems.

# RAD

*High quality, lower cost and rapid development*, thus, go hand-in-hand if an appropriate development methodology is used (Figure 1.2).

This is truly a win-win situation. Systems so developed *meet the needs of the users better and have lower maintenance costs* (Figure 1.3).

This book discusses such a methodology. The accompanying video series has many interviews with I.S. executives who have achieved this interrelated set of advantages [ALIa][ALIb].

We use the term **RAD**, **Rapid Application Development**, to refer to such a meth-

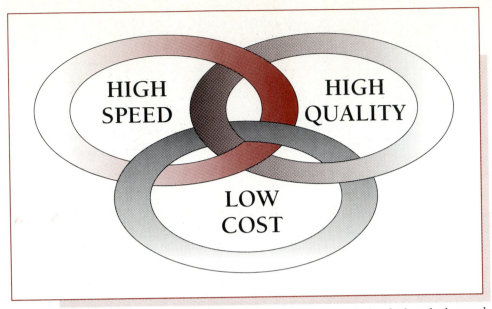

FIGURE 1.2 High quality, fast development and low costs go hand in hand when the best tools and techniques are used.

odology. We use the three-ring diagram of Figure 1.2 as a symbol of RAD to emphasize that quality is a vital ingredient.

**It is important to distinguish between techniques and methodologies.**

A **technique** is a means of carrying out one operation. Data flow diagramming, for example, is a technique. A systems development **methodology** refers to the set of tasks that have to be accomplished in order to develop a system. There are many tasks, employing many techniques. The output from one task is often the input to another task. In applying computers to system development, it is desirable to automate whatever tasks can be automated and to make others computer-assisted. The flow of knowledge from one task to another should be within the computerized tools whenever possible. The RAD methodology uses computerized tools and human techniques in a tightly interwoven fashion to achieve the goals of high speed and high quality.

It is necessary to describe in detail the set of tasks in a computerized methodology and train the practitioners how to proceed as effectively as possible [MARTIN90].

## Complex Systems

As indicated in Figure 1.4, complexity of large applications is steadily increasing. It is desirable to have fast development lifecycles for highly complex applications.

Fast development of complex systems can be achieved by modeling the system with

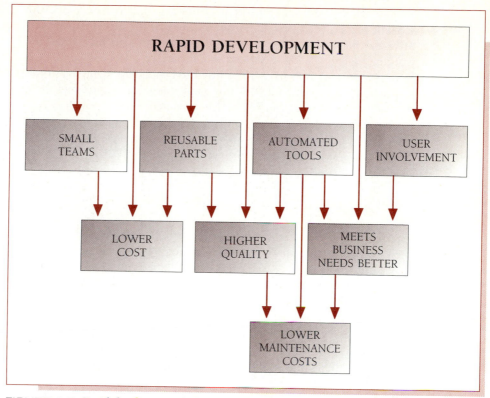

FIGURE 1.3 Rapid development, high quality and lower costs go hand in hand if an appropriate development methodology is used.

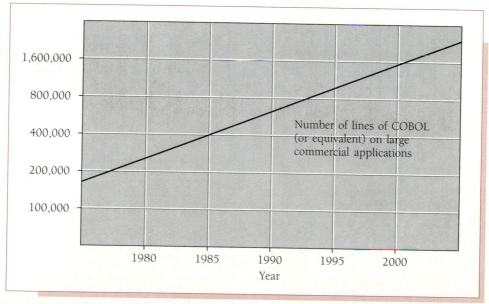

FIGURE 1.4 The complexity of large commercial applications is increasing.

an integrated CASE tool and then splitting it into pieces that can be developed by separate teams. The CASE tool must ensure that the pieces fit with computer-enforced precision into a coordinating model so that they can be integrated into a correctly working system. This is described in Chapter 12.

Expert-system tools have frequently been applied to complex problems. These tools provide a simple way to deal with complex logic by expressing the business logic as independent rules that can be directly executed.

Complex systems development can sometimes be achieved with a methodology for assembling reusable components. Analysis and design for reusability has achieved spectacular results in certain corporations (Chapter 22).

# The Need for Speed

The pace of business is increasing. To stay competitive, corporations are shortening their manufacturing lifecycles. They are increasingly under pressure to design new goods quickly (Figure 1.5) [FORTUNE89] and to shorten the time from receiving an order to fulfilling the order (Figure 1.6) [FORTUNE89]. Factories are striving to lower their inventory by adopting *just-in-time* inventory control. In many situations, the time-window available for decision-making is shortening.

To a large extent, this speeding up is caused by the use of networks of computers, immediate access to data and powerful decision-support tools on the desktop.

Mail, which used to be delivered in days, has been replaced by facsimile and electronic mail. Funds move between banks on opposite sides of the earth in seconds. Executive travel is sometimes replaced by video conferencing. In the days of movies like *Doctor Strangelove* and *Fail-Safe,* nuclear bombers took half a day to reach their destination. Now a submarine-launched missile could reach Washington in five minutes. If SDI space-based interceptors are launched, they will have 150 seconds in which to shoot down a missile during its launch phase.

When a customer ordered a car in a dealer's office, it used to be delivered in months. Now the order may go on-line to a computerized factory and be delivered in days. It used to take a year to design and produce the first working version of a new microchip. Now some vendors can design and produce a customized chip in days.

| FASTER PRODUCT DEVELOPMENT | | | |
|---|---|---|---|
| COMPANY | PRODUCT | EARLY 1980s | NOW |
| Honda | cars | 5 years | 3 years |
| AT&T | phones | 2 years | 1 year |
| Navistar | trucks | 5 years | 2.5 years |
| Hewlett-Packard | printers | 4.5 years | 22 months |

FIGURE 1.5 The time taken to develop new products is shrinking [FORTUNE89].

| FASTER PRODUCTION (from order to finished goods) | | | |
| --- | --- | --- | --- |
| COMPANY | PRODUCT | EARLY 1980s | NOW |
| GE | circuit-breaker boxes | 3 weeks | 3 days |
| Motorola | pagers | 3 weeks | 2 hours |
| Hewlett-Packard | electronic testers | 4 weeks | 5 days |
| Brunswick | fishing reels | 3 weeks | 1 week |

FIGURE 1.6  The time taken to produce products is shrinking [FORTUNE89].

Increasingly, corporations are looking for ways to outdo their competition by beating them to the marketplace with new goods or services. American Airlines increased its market share by building SABRE, a complex system to put on-line terminals in travel agents' offices. United Stationers grew much faster than its competition by guaranteeing its customers 24-hour delivery of orders placed with terminals in the customer location. Canon devised computerized techniques for designing innovative lenses and cameras faster than competing companies. An innovative design could capture a large segment of the market quickly. First Boston in New York devised a way to create new financial vehicles and develop the computerized processing for them faster than its competition on Wall Street.

# A Battle of Technology

Having succeeded spectacularly with the SABRE system in the United States, American Airlines proceeded to move into Europe, putting European travel agents on-line to the reservation center in Dallas. European airlines fought back by forming two consortia to create two competing systems, Amadeus and Galileo, both of formidable complexity.

Increasingly, business is becoming a battle of high technology, often a battle of competing computer systems. In such a world, the corporation that can create the necessary computer applications fastest can win the battle. If a corporation takes three years to build and debug a complex application while its competition can do it in six months, the competition runs away with the business.

In DuPont, a top management document describing future information systems strategy [DUPONT] makes the following comment:

It is speed that is the deciding factor in most competitive situations—in identifying a new end use, in getting products to the market, in implementing new services, in resolving problems that reduce waste, in responding to fashion trends, in designing better processes, in making effective organizational changes, in controlling inventories and distribution, and in scenario simulations to optimize the machine/product mix. . . . *A top criterion for I.S. is that information systems should never interfere with the business' ability to seize an opportunity.*

It is necessary to create new systems quickly and modify existing systems quickly. In a society with a worldwide mesh of intercorporate computer networks, electronic decision-making, electronic funds transfer, computers in one organization placing orders on-line with computers in other organizations, where robot-operated factories build the goods overnight, it seems an anachronism to take three years to hand-craft computer applications.

# Four Essential Ingredients

To create applications rapidly, tools are needed such as code generators, CASE tools, prototyping tools and fourth-generation languages. The tools are only part of the story. It is necessary to devise methodologies for using the tools as effectively as possible.

To make the tools and techniques as effective as possible for the enterprise as a

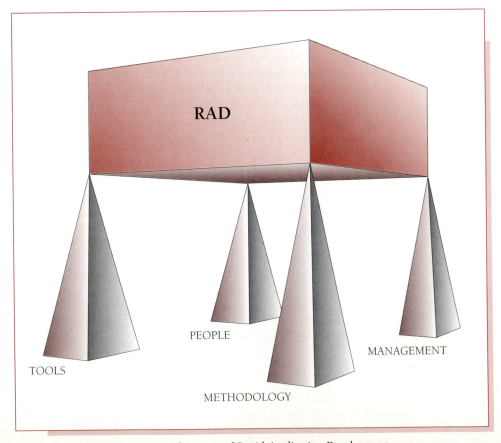

FIGURE 1.7 The Four Essential Aspects of Rapid Application Development

whole, it is desirable to create an infrastructure within which fast development of complex applications can take place. Chapters 20, 21 and 22 describe development within a planned infrastructure, as opposed to development of isolated systems.

An essential part of fast development is having people with the right skills and talents. The people need to be well selected, highly trained and appropriately motivated. The roles played by end-user management are critical. There must be strong, well-planned end-user participation at all stages of the lifecycle.

Systems will not be developed and deployed rapidly if bureaucracy or political obstacles are in the way or if appropriate end-user actions are not taken. Management has to have its act together to facilitate fast system building.

There are four essential aspects of fast development—tools, methodology, people and management (Figure 1.7).

The book describes development lifecycles in which these aspects are woven together. To develop applications as fast as possible, attention has to be paid to many different types of factors. Chapters 3 through 6 respectively discuss tools, methodologies, people and management.

# Lifecycle Management

RAD needs a methodology that spells out the tasks to be done. Just as on a building site, the tasks to be done must be well defined and planned; the players must be moved into action to perform them with no schedule slippage. The management of this activity is sometimes referred to as **process management** or **lifecycle management**. The players must be appropriately trained. The I.S. professionals should be experienced in the techniques. Management should know what tasks have to be accomplished and, for each task, what the inputs are and what deliverables are required.

The tasks are described in detail in a computerized methodology designed for use in conjunction with this book. This is called *RAD Expert* [JMA]. It indicates what is needed for each task, how to succeed with it, what can go wrong and how to avoid the dangers. The *RAD Expert* is a complex hyperdocument that operates on the same personal computer as the tools for accomplishing RAD.

Hyperdocument software provides an appropriate vehicle for describing the complex set of tasks to be performed. The user of a hyperdocument reads it on a computer screen and can navigate through it at high speed, opening or closing parts of the document at the touch of a mouse key, linking to explanations, guidelines, diagrams, CASE screens, project management tools and, possibly, expert-system modules, computer-based training, and so on.

A methodology in hyperdocument form is fluid; it can be added to or adapted as required. Project managers or skilled professionals can add their own knowledge or recommendations to it as appropriate. It can be adapted to the circumstances of a particular implementation.

The tasks can be selected or adapted to the circumstances in question. In some installations, they are part of an information-engineering environment (Chapter 21); in others, they relate to development of an isolated system. They can be adapted to different development toolsets.

# RAD Cells

It is not practical to convert a large I.S. organization to RAD overnight, but it should be done as quickly as is practical. The best way to proceed is usually to establish a small **RAD cell**—a small group of professionals committed to the methodology and its toolset. This startup group makes RAD work and applies it to the first projects. It measures what is achieved and fine-tunes the methodology. The RAD cell can then grow, taking on more projects and more people and improving its skills. A large I.S. organization may set up more than one RAD cell.

As the RAD group demonstrates the practicality and effectiveness of its methods, a standard selection of tools and diagramming conventions should be made and the methodology (like RAD Expert) adjusted as appropriate and adopted throughout the I.S. organization.

# The Need for Integration

It is often tempting to use RAD techniques to build stand-alone systems—to solve a given business problem in isolation. In practice, most business applications are strongly related to other applications and share databases with them. Because of this, a common infrastructure is necessary. The infrastructure requires a common network and standards. Particularly important, it requires commonality of data structure, which is represented in a data model. Commonality of process models facilitates reusable code.

An essential measure of the quality of I.S. development is its capacity to merge, synthesize and summarize information up and down the management hierarchy and to pass information from one system to another along the value chain (i.e., from *ordering* to *marketing, selling and manufacturing*, from *production scheduling* to *inventory and purchasing*, from *manufacturing* to *customer support*, from *ordering and manufacturing* to *financial planning*, and so on). It is the integration of information resources that enables very fast delivery of information and, thus, rapid decision-making. Users can access information in the form they need.

A statement of the DuPont strategy document referenced earlier is:

A fundamental objective of information technology architecture is to make integration as easy as possible, so that time-based competitive advantages can be realized.

# RAD Within a Planned Infrastructure

In order to achieve the level of integration that has a direct effect on profits, RAD techniques should be employed within a planned infrastructure. As illustrated in Figure 1.8, there needs to be a technological framework and an information framework into which the RAD techniques fit.

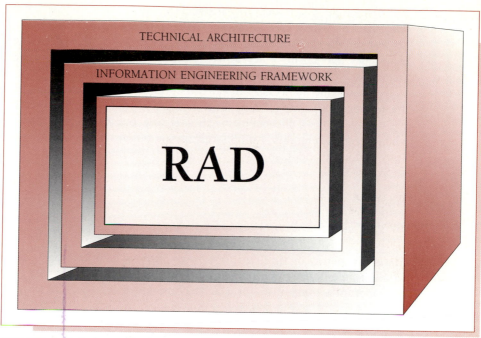

FIGURE 1.8 To be as effective as possible, RAD techniques should fit into a well-planned infrastructure, which includes an architecture for connectivity and interoperability and an architecture for information engineering, designed to integrate systems with shared data and reusable designs. The infrastructure takes time to evolve. Once it exists, application development can proceed more rapidly and effectively than with isolated RAD.

Sometimes RAD techniques are used in isolation; sometimes they are used for development within a planned infrastructure. The infrastructure takes a long time to build. It evolves over the years. However, if it is built in an appropriate fashion, applications can be built more quickly within the infrastructure than they could be without it. The reason for this is that part of the work has already been done. Stable data models exist; process models exist for a business area; naming conventions have been established; application standards and tools may be well established. Sometimes most important, the infrastructure facilitates development with reusable code and reusable design. The infrastructure should be designed with the goal of fast application development and maintenance.

Chapter 20 (as well as Chapters 21 through 25) discusses RAD within a planned infrastructure.

## Getting the Act Together

There are many factors that contribute to high-speed development of high-quality systems. Different organizations have used different techniques. This book describes the different techniques and shows how they can be built into the development life-cycle. The author could find no example of a development organization that does *everything* right; when analyzing the success stories, there always seemed to be *something* that could have been done even better. Integrating the entire family of techniques for fast development is a complex act to get together. It is desirable to list all the techniques and create a development organization and methodology that integrate them to achieve the maximum benefits.

If we ask why a cheetah can catch its prey faster than any other animal on earth, the answer is not simple. Many different capabilities have to be beautifully integrated. It is complex to be a cheetah racing after its prey, but the cheetah can repeat its success whenever it feels hungry. An I.S. organization ought to integrate the set of capabilities described in this book so that it can build the systems its enterprise needs faster than the competition.

# Retooling the I.S. Factory

At certain points in time, major industry sectors have to retool. Their technology, dating from an earlier era, has slipped into obsolescence so that they are ill equipped to support new competitive thrusts. If a corporation fails to retool when its competition

---

**Box 1.1**
**Vital Actions for Retooling the I.S. Organization**

- Implement information engineering across the enterprise with a growing I.E. repository. (See Chapter 21.)
- Establish a RAD environment throughout the entire I.S. organization.
- Establish a culture of reusability throughout I.S. (Chapters 15 and 22).
- Establish a program for replacing the core I.S. systems with the most effective new technology.
- Drive for an environment of open interconnectivity and software portability across the entire enterprise.
- Establish intercorporate network links to most trading partners.
- Determine how to give all knowledgeworkers a high level of computerized knowledge and processing power.
- Conduct a technology impact study to determine how the basic business of the enterprise should change to maximize the opportunities presented by rapid technological change.
- Evaluate how the corporation itself should be re-engineered to take advantage of new technology.
- Determine the changes in management structure needed to take full advantage of innovative systems.

A corporation taking these actions ahead of its competition will gain a major competitive advantage.

is doing so, eventually its competition will become much stronger. Failure to retool when needed slowly puts corporations out of business.

The core computer applications in most corporations are obsolete and fragile. They cannot be maintained easily. They were created with third-generation languages before modern design techniques were understood. They were built for an era of dumb terminals or batch processing, not for an era of powerful desktop machines connected by local area networks to powerful servers, requiring worldwide connectivity. It is appropriate to think of an enterprise's I.S. systems collectively as an information factory. The information factory in most enterprises is badly in need of retooling. Box 1.1 lists some of the actions needed in retooling the I.S. organization.

Some enterprises have developed a top-level strategy for retooling their information facilities. Some have driven hard to evolve a RAD environment. Many, however, have no such strategy and are building non-integrated systems with slow and obsolete methodologies. This failure to retool will eventually cause severe damage to their ability to be competitive.

# Productivity Reports for the CEO

Fast application development is so critical for business success that Chief Executive Officers (Managing Directors) ought to demand to see measurements of the productivity and performance of their I.S. organization. The author worked with one large bank in which a set of charts are submitted to the CEO quarterly, giving measurements of development speed and productivity.

Some of the lowest development productivity is that in some government departments. It seems desirable that metrics and goals for development speed be established for government organizations.

The I.S. executive and project managers should be measured in terms of results delivered, not in terms of how many people they manage. Fast development emphasizes the use of small teams with power tools, not large teams. There may be some bullets to bite in downsizing bureaucracies (both inside and outside I.S.).

Measurements of development capability, including those that should go to the CEO, are discussed in Chapter 2.

# References

[ALIa] *RAD: Rapid Application Development*, a training series with 9 video tapes from Applied Learning, Inc., Naperville, Illinois (708–369–3000).

[ALIb] *Information Engineering: Design and Construction*, a training series with 8 video tapes on RAD in an Information-Engineering environment, from Applied Learning, Inc., Naperville, Illinois (708–369–3000).

[DUPONT] "A New Strategy for the Selection, Assimilation and Utilization of Information Technology for Fibers," Fibers Department, E. I. duPont de Nemours and Company, Inc., Wilmington, Delaware, 1989. This document was given to selected computer vendors and industry leaders to encourage evolution of Open standards and software.

[FORTUNE89] "How Managers Can Succeed through Speed," *Fortune*, February 13, 1989, p. 56.

[JMA] *RAD Expert*, a methodology in hyperdocument form adaptable to different toolsets, available from James Martin Associates, Reston, Virginia (703–620–9504).

[MARTIN90] James Martin, *HYPERDOCUMENTS and How to Create Them*, Prentice-Hall, Inc., Englewood Cliffs, New Jersey, 1990 (201–592–2261).

# CHAPTER 2

# Metrics

## Reasons for Metrics

A vital goal in today's I.S. organizations is to develop systems:

- faster;
- with higher quality;
- at lower cost;
- with fewer people.

Ongoing improvement of these capabilities is desirable. To help achieve ongoing improvements, it is vital that measurements be made. Only with well-designed measurements can we be sure that we are improving. The performance of all development efforts should be measured and recorded.

Appropriate measurements enable management to set goals for developers and motivate developers. They make possible the comparison of tools and techniques. They enable management to detect, examine and, possibly, replicate examples of excellence.

---

**Box 2.1   Reasons for Needing Metrics**

Metrics are needed to:

- facilitate estimating and planning.
- set goals for projects.
- motivate the developers.
- reward the best developers.
- compare the effectiveness of tools.
- compare the effectiveness of techniques.
- establish quality standards.
- detect, and possibly replicate, examples of excellence.
- identify areas where improvement is needed.
- establish an ongoing program for improvement.
- achieve top-management measurement of overall I.S. efficiency and responsiveness.

They facilitate estimating and planning. In a few organizations, the head of I.S. has to submit periodic reports to the CEO, giving measurements of development costs, speed and productivity. This makes sense because I.S. speed, efficiency and responsiveness comprise a critical success factor of the enterprise.

# What Metrics Are Needed?

Measurements of I.S. productivity are sometimes complex and often not very precise. It is desirable for any organization to establish practical metrics and apply them to all projects.

There should be metrics for each project and metrics for the I.S. department as a whole. The critical set of metrics should be:

- small;
- graphical;
- easily computed;
- as reliable as possible;
- objective, in that they measure the external characteristics of the system;
- a basis for estimating;
- a basis for taking corrective action when needed.

Where the main objective is *speed of development*, the primary metric is total elapsed time. This is easy to measure.

# Cycle Time

The total elapsed time for the entire development lifecycle is sometimes referred to as **cycle time**. We will use that term throughout this book. An objective of developers should be to *minimize cycle time*.

The cycle time may be subdivided into the times taken in sections of the development process; for example:

| Initiation & Requirements Planning | User Analysis & Design | Technical Design, Coding & Testing | Cutover & Fan-out |
|---|---|---|---|

Sometimes measurements are made of only coding and testing. This is especially so for lifecycles with manual coding in third-generation languages, where coding and testing is the longest segment of the lifecycle. Business planners are more concerned with the *total* time for development. The time measurements quoted in this book refer to *total* cycle time.

# Cycle Time vs. Complexity

Cycle time varies greatly with the complexity of projects. Large projects take years; spreadsheet or report generation projects may be finished in days. To be meaningful, cycle time needs to be related to the complexity of the project.

For multiple projects, cycle time may be plotted against complexity.

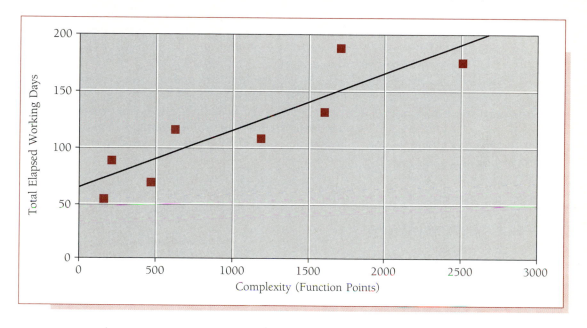

A major challenge with today's tools is to learn how to achieve a low cycle time with projects of substantial complexity.

# Complexity Measurements

All meaningful measurements of development productivity need to relate to project complexity. In I.S. organizations, it is valuable to plot various measurements of productivity against project complexity. How do we measure complexity?

In the days when all projects were built with COBOL (or PL/I, FORTRAN or other third-generation languages), complexity was usually measured by counting the number of lines of code. This metric cannot be used for direct comparison of fourth-generation-language (4GL) projects with COBOL projects because a 4GL may require an order of magnitude fewer lines of code.

Sometimes people ask, "How many lines of code would it have needed if it had been programmed in COBOL?" and use this estimate as a complexity metric. Many CASE methodologies use COBOL generators. With these, the number of lines of COBOL generated gives a metric for project comparison.

Lines of COBOL need to be counted with caution. The count should include executable lines of code and the Data Division lines but should not include comments. Large segments of code that are used repetitively may be counted only once.

Development cost, number of person-days or cycle time may be plotted against number of lines of COBOL (or its equivalent). Using lines of COBOL as a metric, overall speed of development is measured in terms of **lines of COBOL per day**, and **lines of COBOL per person-day** can be calculated. When used with caution, these metrics can be informative.

Lines of COBOL per person-day vary greatly from one I.S. organization to another, depending on the tools, techniques and people. Some large projects average fewer than 5 lines of COBOL per person-day; some projects, tightly managed with integrated CASE tools that generate code, average over 1000 lines of COBOL per person-day. As we shall see, many different factors contribute to this wide variance. High-speed development requires highly trained people, powerful tools, a methodology that takes maximum advantage of power tools, and a management focused on moving fast. Overall development speed typically varies from 50 lines of COBOL per day to over 5000 lines of COBOL per day, depending on how many developers work on the project.

# Language-Independent Complexity Measurements

It is desirable to have a measure of project complexity that is independent of any particular computer language. It should be complexity in terms of external characteristics of the system rather than in terms of internal mechanisms. The complexity metric in most common use is **function points**. This was developed at IBM and improved in GUIDE, the IBM users' organization. Appendix I gives details of how to calculate function points. Appendix II is the GUIDE paper on productivity measurements using function points.

The function-point method lists and counts the elements of a system, including:

- inputs (screens, messages, batch transactions);
- outputs (screens, reports, messages, batch transactions);
- system data stores (logical files);
- data stores shared with other systems (external interface files);
- inquiries.

The method applies a weight to each of these, based on its complexity, totals the result, and then adjusts the result for factors estimating the internal processing complexity and general system complexity. (See Appendix I.)

GUIDE analyzed hundreds of programs to isolate the critical variables that determine programming productivity. Based on this research, Albrecht [ALBRECHT83] introduced **function-point evaluation**. His technique was used extensively, first at IBM and later throughout the computer industry. It has proven a useful technique for estimating and for measuring productivity. In other research, Rudolph found that 1 function point was equivalent to 114 lines of COBOL [RUDOLPH84]. This is so for systems of average complexity with the user dialog typical of the mid-1980s. When complex user dialogs are employed (such as those with a mouse, icons, an action bar and pull-down menus), more code is required, and there is a larger number of lines of code per function point.

Function-point metrics are generally not appropriate for scientific or engineering computing or for systems in which complex algorithms must be coded.

It would be possible to remove some of the subjectivity from function-point calculation, and devise a somewhat more precise complexity metric, by having CASE tools compute complexity automatically. It would be useful to do further research on refining function-point computation. Having said that, we note that function points computed as in Appendix I are useful metrics and are widely used.

Overall values of function points per day and function points per person-day can be calculated for a project or for an I.S. department as a whole. For multiple projects, *development cost, number of person-days* and *total elapsed time* may be plotted against complexity measured in function points.

Box 2.2 lists types of measurement of I.S. development that use function points.

## Box 2.2
## Examples of Measurements of I.S. Development

*Note:* This list refers to function points as the basic metric of complexity. Alternative complexity metrics, such as equivalent-lines-of-COBOL, could be used throughout.

### Speed of Development

- project cycle time;
- project cycle time subdivided into lifecycle stages;
- cycle time for multiple projects plotted against complexity (in function points);
- cycle time for multiple projects (subdivided into lifecycle stages) plotted against complexity (in function points).

### Cost of Development

- development cost per function point;
- defect-removal cost per function point;
- development cost per function point plotted against complexity (in function points).

### Development Productivity

- function points per person-month;
- function points per person-month plotted against complexity (in function points).

Box 2.2    Continued

## Quality Measurements

- number of defects per function point categorized by type of defect;
- number of defects per function point categorized by time of detection of defect (after module is handed over, after cutover, etc.);
- number of bugs per function point plotted against complexity (in function points);
- number of failures per month of installed system;
- monthly failures plotted against complexity (in function points);
- number of user change requests within four weeks after cutover.

## Overall Measurement of I.S. Development

- net function points delivered per year;
- net cost per function point;
- average function points per person-month;
- function points per person-month plotted against complexity (in function points);
- average cycle time;
- cycle time plotted against complexity (in function points);
- number of bugs per function point plotted against complexity (in function points);

## Maintenance Efficiency

- number of maintenance staff per total development staff;
- total function points in portfolio per number of maintenance staff;
- function points of maintained code per maintenance person.

*Note:* When all systems have been built with RAD techniques, maintenance changes into ongoing, evolutionary RAD projects.

# Measures to Remember

It is useful for an individual to have units of measure that he personally remembers in order to compare different projects, estimates or vendors' claims. He may translate different units into the units he remembers. Some individuals remember **equivalent-lines-of-COBOL per person-day**, relating this perhaps to their own experience in programming. Other individuals remember **function points per person-month (FPPM)**. We recommend that I.S. executives measure and remember **function points**

**per person-month**. We quote this measurement throughout the book so that different case examples can be compared.

For systems of average complexity without elaborate user interfaces, one function point per person-month is equivalent to about five equivalent-lines-of-COBOL per person-day. (Assuming that one function point is equivalent to 114 lines of COBOL and one person-month is 22 days; 114/22 = 5.18. As there is no point in being precise to two decimal places, people remember the ratio 5.) For systems with elaborate human interfaces (e.g., mouse, icons, pull-down menus, etc.), the ratio becomes higher than 5. (Code for the point-and-click human interface should be *generated*.)

It is useful to remember a metric for the cost of development. **Dollars per function point** is appropriate—the cost being that for the entire lifecycle. Some organizations calculate hours per function point and relate it to dollars per function point.

## Typical Achievements

The U.S. average is 5 function points per person-month [BOULDIN89] (and this relates to systems most of which are of dubious quality compared to RAD-built systems).

Many organizations developing systems with COBOL, database tools and the traditional I.S. lifecycle average about 40 lines of COBOL per person-day (about 8 function points per person-month). Some have used productivity aids with otherwise manual COBOL development and have pushed their productivity up to about 60 lines of COBOL per person-day (about 12 function points per person-month). The objective of today's power tools and techniques is to drive to substantially higher productivity numbers.

Figure 2.1 shows experience in the Marine Midland Bank. COBOL development

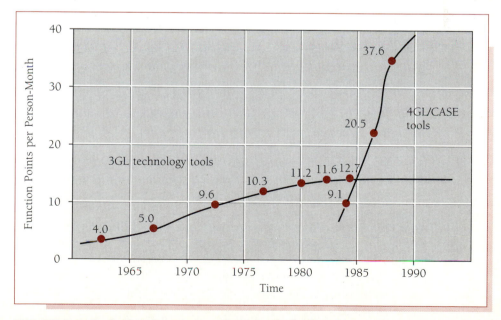

FIGURE 2.1 Productivity Experience at the Marine Midland Bank.

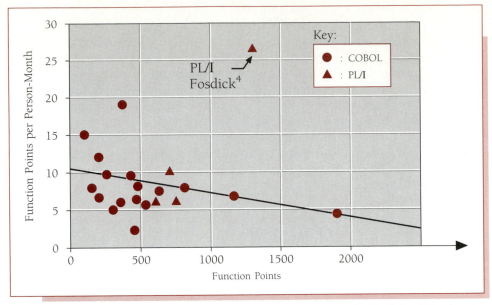

FIGURE 2.2 Measurement of Productivity in Typical Projects Using the Traditional Development Lifecycle with COBOL or PL/I [RUDOLPH84]

had reached a plateau of about 12 function points per person-day. The first introduction of CASE tools gave slightly lower productivity, but the staff rapidly climbed a learning curve, building to about 40 function points per person-day. This is a fairly typical number for well-managed use of a CASE tool with a code generator. Using an integrated CASE (I-CASE) environment and a tighter methodology, the productivity figures are likely to climb higher.

Rudolph [RUDOLPH84] measured productivity in 21 COBOL and PL/I projects that were regarded as typical. The results are plotted against complexity in Figure 2.2.

Fosdick [FOSDICK82] described an application in which exceptional productivity was achieved with PL/I using good management practices combined with development productivity tools (not CASE tools) to create what he described as an optimal IBM MVS, IMS environment. This group achieved 6 hours per function point (26.7 function points per person-month), writing 84,000 lines of PL/I in 44 person-months (95 lines of code per person-day, on average). Fosdick's result is the top point plotted in Figure 2.2. This level of productivity is rarely achieved in non-CASE developments.

Highly trained specialized teams using I-CASE tools with the techniques described in this book can achieve much higher productivity figures. Some small highly-skilled teams regularly achieve 1000 equivalent-lines-of-COBOL per person-day (or 200 function points per person-month) on projects of moderate complexity. This number does not incorporate the cost of end-user time, which is substantial on RAD projects. Almost no I.S. organization has measured this.

Measurements in the DuPont Fibers division shows skilled developers averaging 13.8 hours per function point with Yourdon methodology while DuPont was averaging 2 hours per function point with its "timebox" RAD methodology described in Chapter 11 [DUPONT].

```
┌─────────────────────────────────────────────────────────────┐
│              FUNCTION POINTS PER PERSON-MONTH                 │
└─────────────────────────────────────────────────────────────┘

  ▪ Some large government projects:                         2
  ▪ Average for traditional COBOL lifecycle:                8
  ▪ Well-managed 3GL lifecycle with productivity aids:     13
  ▪ Typical well-managed 4GL/CASE lifecycle:               35
  ▪ Reasonable target for RAD lifecycle:                  100*
  ▪ Some of the best examples of RAD:                     200*
  NOTE:  RAD projects have a high level of end-user involvement. The figures quoted
         throughout this book relate to I.S. professional work days, not end-user
         time. Almost no I.S. organization measures the end-user time. This makes
         the figure for function points per person-month somewhat artificially high.
```

FIGURE 2.3  Typical Figures for I.S. Development Productivity
There is a startling difference between average development with the traditional lifecycle and high-quality development with the techniques described in this book.

Figure 2.3 summarizes these productivity achievements, providing a framework to help the reader put the numbers given in this book into perspective.

Some large and bureaucratic application development projects cost over $1000 per function point. Some software development companies charge more than $1000 per function point. Many I.S. organizations average around $500 per function point. A reasonable target for RAD project is about $100 per function point (corresponding to 100 function points per person-month). Figure 2.4 summarizes typical development costs.

Cycle time is only indirectly related to the numbers in Figures 2.1 through 2.4. To a limited extent, cycle time for a complex project can be shortened by putting more people on the project. This has to be done within a carefully structured framework; otherwise, the separate developers create incompatible fragments and cause time delays in modifying and integrating their work. It is often said that putting more developers on a late project makes it later [BROOKS75].

Figure 2.5 shows typical figures for cycle time with traditional lifecycles and RAD lifecycles. The numbers vary over a wide range, depending on the number of developers and how well simultaneous development activities are managed. Appallingly, about a

```
┌─────────────────────────────────────────────────────────────┐
│                 DOLLARS PER FUNCTION POINT                   │
└─────────────────────────────────────────────────────────────┘

  ▪ Some large government projects:                      $1500
  ▪ Average for traditional COBOL lifecycle:              $800
  ▪ Well-managed 3GL lifecycle with productivity aids:    $500
  ▪ Typical well-managed 4GL/CASE lifecycle:              $250
  ▪ Reasonable target for RAD lifecycle:                  $100
  ▪ Some of the best examples of RAD:                      $50
  NOTE:  The figures do not include the cost of end-user time, which is substantial
         on RAD projects. Almost no I.S. organization has measured this.
```

FIGURE 2.4  Typical Figures for Cost of Development (including tools; not including training or cost of the system hardware)

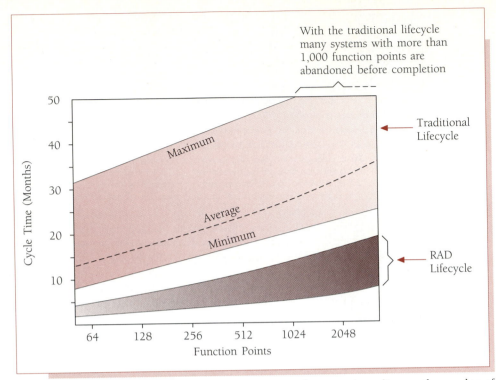

With the traditional lifecycle many systems with more than 1,000 function points are abandoned before completion

FIGURE 2.5 Total development time varies over a wide range, depending on the number of developers and how well simultaneous development activities are controlled. These are typical figures.

quarter of systems over 1000 function points are abandoned before completion; many are more than a year late. Many systems of more than 1000 function points fail to meet the needs of their users when they are delivered—not surprisingly because of the long cycle time. Business procedures can change substantially in a 2- or 3-year period.

Throughout this book are other examples that quantify experience with rapid development lifecycles.

# Quality

It is desirable to create systems of higher quality than those of the past. To do so, we need measurements of quality. This is especially important as we aim for high-speed development. If not managed well, fast development might result in systems of poor quality.

**Quality** is often assessed by counting the number of defects found. We can count defects:

- after a software module is handed over;
- after the application is claimed to be complete;
- after cutover;
- after delivery to customers.

The defects may be divided into six categories.

1. *Bugs.* These are programming errors that cause a malfunction.
2. *Failures.* These are bugs or problems sufficiently severe to cause the system to fail.
3. *Design Defects.* These are problems caused by inappropriate design or errors in design.
4. *Human Interface Flaws.* These are faults in the design of the human interaction with the system.
5. *Specification Defects.* These are flaws in the understanding and specification of user needs.
6. *Failures to Meet User Needs.* These include changes in system design needed after cutover (reflecting either specification defects or changes in requirements since specification).

These defects vary greatly in their severity. To take severity into account, the cost of correcting the defects may be estimated. Requirements defects are often the most expensive to correct because part of the system has to be respecified and recoded.

In general, the earlier a defect is found, the less time-consuming and expensive it is to correct. Figure 2.6 illustrates this fact.

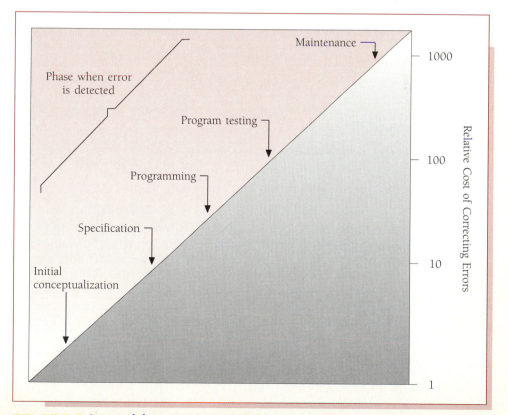

FIGURE 2.6 It is much less expensive to catch the error early.

Wherever possible, requirements defects should be found at the specification stage, design defects should be found at the design stage, and coding bugs should be found during the coding stage. There is a danger that, in the rush to develop systems fast, defects may go undetected until a later stage. In the long run, this makes the development process slower. Tools, techniques and controls should be used, as part of the lifecycle, to help catch all defects at the earliest possible stage.

The efficiency of debugging may be measured by calculating the ratio of defects removed in development to total defects.

# Cutover Quality

As indicated in Chapter 1, the most important measure of quality is how well a system meets its users' needs at cutover. This is quite different from how well a system meets its specifications because the users' needs change while the system is being developed. Defects of type 6 in the preceding list should be minimized.

To do this, the ultimate users should be involved during the construction until cutover (as described later), and automated techniques are needed to adapt the design, as required, during the code generation phase. The tools and techniques for doing this will be described.

An appropriate measure of this type of quality is the number of change requests from users during the four weeks after cutover.

# Defect Density

Measurements should be made of the quality of work of the development team. These measurements may be:

- bugs or other defects per 1000 lines of code;
- bugs or other defects per 1000 equivalent-lines-of-COBOL;
- bugs or other defects per function point.

Such measures are sometimes referred to as the **defect density**.

When traditional lifecycle techniques are used, the more complex the application, the greater the defect density. See Figure 2.7. With powerful and partially automated quality-control techniques, the defect density is lower and does not rise with complexity as rapidly.

There are many ways to lower the defect density; these are discussed in subsequent chapters.

Fourth-generation languages give a lower defect density per function point than COBOL or PL/I (usually at the expense of machine performance), and good code generators generally give a lower defect density than fourth-generation languages. It is desirable to take any possible steps to lower the defect density because defects slow down the development process.

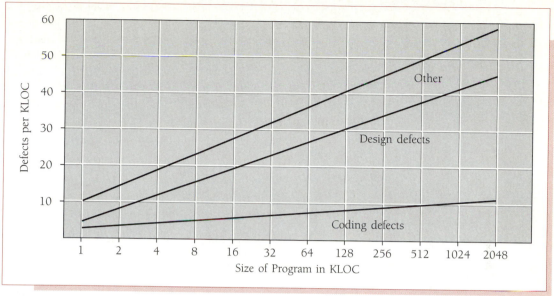

FIGURE 2.7 Defects per 1000 Lines of Code for COBOL Development with the Traditional Life-cycle. (Source: Statistics compiled by Capers Jones.)

The number of defects per 1000 lines of code tends to rise with the size of the program when the traditional development lifecycle is used. The defect density varies greatly from one project to another, depending on the techniques used to control defects. The use of automated tools and human techniques to improve quality can hold the defect density down so that it rises little with complexity.

# The CEO's I.S. Productivity Report

We commented that a corporate president should monitor I.S. productivity because of its vital effect on corporate capabilities. Box 2.3 lists types of measurements that should go to a concerned CEO (Managing Director).

The CEO report should have five types of measurements:

1. Speed of Development
2. Development Costs
3. Development Productivity
4. Quality of Delivered Systems
5. Maintenance Costs

When this type of report is requested on a quarterly basis by the CEO, I.S. management is motivated to strive vigorously for the most efficient use of powerful development techniques.

Box 2.3 suggests what information should be included in a quarterly report to the CEO on I.S. development efficiency.

# I.S. DEVELOPMENT SUMMARY REPORT

■ Total function points delivered by I.S. this quarter = 6050.

■ Number of developers = 21.

---

## 1. SPEED OF DEVELOPMENT

■ Cycle time for new systems exceeding 100 function points

Average in 1991 = **168 working days**
(Cycle time is the elapsed time from initiation to cutover.)

## 2. DEVELOPMENT COSTS

■ Cost per function point for new systems

Average in 1991 = **$98**

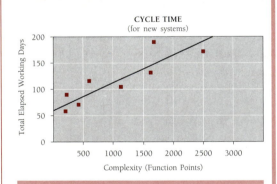

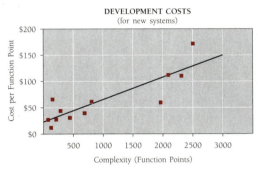

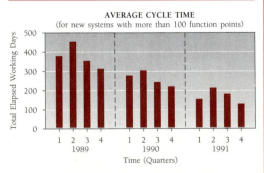

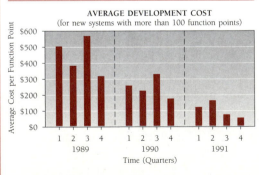

## 3. DEVELOPMENT PRODUCTIVITY

■ Function points per person-month for new systems.

Average in 1991 = 78

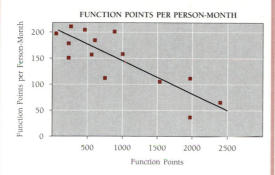

**FUNCTION POINTS PER PERSON-MONTH**

## 4. QUALITY OF DELIVERED SYSTEMS

■ Number of technical defects and user change requests per 100 function points recorded within 4 weeks after cutover

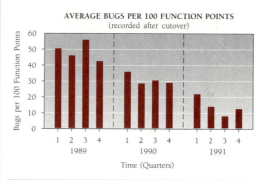

**AVERAGE BUGS PER 100 FUNCTION POINTS**
(recorded after cutover)

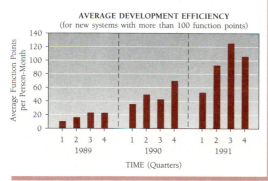

**AVERAGE DEVELOPMENT EFFICIENCY**
(for new systems with more than 100 function points)

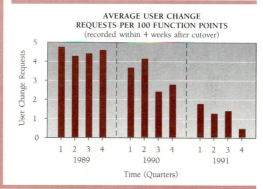

**AVERAGE USER CHANGE REQUESTS PER 100 FUNCTION POINTS**
(recorded within 4 weeks after cutover)

## 5. MAINTENANCE

■ Ratio of maintenance costs to development costs = **22**

■ Average maintenance function points per person-month = **189**

**RATIO OF MAINTENANCE COSTS TO DEVELOPMENT COSTS**

BOX 2.3 *Continued*

# References

[ALBRECHT83] Allen Albrecht, "Measuring and Estimating Application Development and Maintenance," *Guide 57.0 Conference Report*, Session No. DP-7234 A, Guide International, Inc., Chicago, Illinois, October 1983.

[BOULDIN89] Barbara M. Bouldin "CASE: Measuring Productivity," *Software Magazine*, August 1989.

[BROOKS75] Fred P. Brooks, Jr., *The Mythical Man-Month*, Addison-Wesley Publishing Co., Reading, Massachusetts, 1975.

[DUPONT] Information from W. Robert White, Information Engineering Associates, E. I. duPont de Nemours and Company, Inc., Wilmington, Delaware, 1989.

[FOSDICK82] H. Fosdick, "Productivity in a Database Environment," *Datamation*, August 1982.

[RUDOLPH84] E. E. Rudolph, *Productivity in Computer Application Development*, University of Auckland, Auckland, New Zealand, 1984.

# Bibliography

B. W. Boehm, *Software Engineering Economics*, Prentice-Hall, Inc., Englewood Cliffs, New Jersey, 1981.

GUIDE International Information Publications, *Estimating Using Function Points Handbook*, GUIDE Publication #GPP-134, Chicago, Illinois, 1985.

GUIDE International Information Publications, *Maintenance Productivity Improvement through Matrices and Measurement*, GUIDE Publication #GPP-130, Chicago, 1985.

GUIDE International Information Publications, *Process of Managing Productivity Improvement*, GUIDE Publication #GPP-88, Chicago, Illinois, 1982.

GUIDE International Information Publications, *Measurement of Productivity*, GUIDE Publication #GPP-65, 1981.

GUIDE International Information Publications, *Structured Analysis Methodologies*, GUIDE Publication #GPP-57, Chicago, Illinois, 1980.

GUIDE International Information Publications, *Productivity in the Maintenance Environment*, GUIDE Publication #GPP-29, Chicago, Illinois, 1978.

GUIDE International Information Publications, *Productivity in the Systems Life Cycle*, GUIDE Publication #GPP-24, Chicago, Illinois, 1977.

AD/M Productivity Measurement and Estimate Validation, *GUIDE Doc No. CIS and A Guideline 313*, GUIDE Information, Chicago, Illinois, November 1984.

M. H. Halstead, *Elements of Software Science*, Elsevier Science Publishing Co. The Netherlands 1977.

Arthur Jay, *Measuring Programmer Productivity and Software Quality*, John Wiley & Sons, Inc., New York, 1985.

Arthur Jay, *Programmer Productivity: Myths, Methods and Murphy's Law*, John Wiley & Sons, Inc., New York, 1983.

Information from Capers Jones; presented at James Martin Seminar.

T. C. Jones, "Measuring Programming Quality and Productivity," *IBM Systems Journal*, Vol. 17, No. 1, 1978.

Girish Parikh, *Programmer Productivity*, Reston Publishing Co., Reston, Virginia, 1984.

Howard A. Rubin, Hunter College, "Art and Science of Software Estimation. Where Are We Heading?" *SHARE 62 Proceedings*, Anaheim, California, March 1984.

# CHAPTER 3

# Tools

RAD lifecycles are dependent on automated tools. The development process should have the maximum degree of automation. Toolsets such as integrated CASE (Computer-Aided Systems Engineering) tools came into existence towards the end of the 1980s.

This chapter gives an overview of the tools. The following three chapters relate to management, development-process and people issues, which are fundamentally changed by the higher level of automation inherent in the best tools.

## Inadequate Tools

The tools must have certain characteristics in order to be usable and effective in fast development lifecycles. This chapter summarizes the important characteristics that are necessary. It is important to observe that many of the toolsets on the market are inadequate for fast development lifecycles. Many CASE tools, for example, look spectacular at first glance; they have flashy graphics but lack some of the most important features for fast development. Many fourth-generation languages are inadequate for high-quality development. One CASE toolset is advertised as "The World's Most Powerful CASE Tool" although it lacks most of the features that make CASE tools truly powerful. The author never ceases to be amazed at how software salesmen can sell hopelessly inferior software.

The manager of systems development must select the right tools; otherwise, development efficiency is low. The toolset should support the techniques described throughout this book. All of the techniques in the book (described in detail in the associated *RAD Expert* methodology [JMA]) are based on actual experience of high-speed development with existing tools. In doing the research for the book, we found many development efforts using inadequate CASE tools and achieving relatively low gains in productivity. The tool buyer must understand the characteristics of the RAD methodology.

## The Mess in Data Processing

*The Wall Street Journal* lamented that software is one of the two principal obstacles to economic progress. A former U.S. Pentagon chief commented, "If anything kills us before the Russians, it will be our software" [ATHERTON87].

Much has been written about what is wrong with data processing today. There are backlogs of several years. It takes too long to build systems, and the cost is too high.

The difficulties of maintenance are outrageous. Management cannot obtain information from computers when needed. Tape and disk libraries are a mess of redundant, chaotic data. Many programs are made up of fragile spaghetti code. When management needs to change business procedures or introduce new products and services, data processing cannot make the required modifications.

Today computers are assuming more important roles in business, government and the military. We have entered the age when computing and information systems are strategic weapons, not a backroom overhead. The terms **mission-critical systems** and **strategic systems** have become popular. There are many examples of corporations growing faster than their competition because they had better information systems. In certain cases, corporations have been put out of business by competitors with better computing resources. As computing becomes critical to competitive thrusts, it becomes vital to both develop applications quickly and to be able to modify them quickly. Many of today's competitive business thrusts require application software far more integrated and complex than that of the past. It is necessary to build—*in a short time, without excessive cost*—applications that are *highly complex, of high quality* and that *truly meet the needs of end users*. These applications must be *easy and quick to modify* (maintain).

The problems of software development can be solved. It is important for executives to realize that there are solutions. A sweeping revolution has begun in the methodologies of putting computers to work. This revolution depends on **power tools**. The methodologies of the past used pencils and templates; the new methodologies use design-automation techniques linked to code generators, along with computer-aided planning and analysis.

# The Need for Power Tools

It would not be possible to build today's cities or microchips or jet aircraft without power tools. Our civilization depends on power tools; yet, the application of computing power to corporate systems is often done by hand methods. Design of the interlocking computer applications of a modern enterprise is no less complex than the design of a microchip or a jet aircraft. To attempt this design by hand methods today is ridiculous.

The use of power tools changes the methods of construction. Now that such tools exist, it is desirable that the entire application development process be re-examined and improved. Advanced power tools give rise to the need for an engineering-like discipline.

Important from the business point of view is that power tools change *what can be constructed.*

These changes need to be understood by management at every level. Making the changes is a *business* critical success factor. Top management needs to ensure that its I.S. organization is adopting the new solutions as quickly as possible.

# A Variety of Tools

A variety of different tools have been created to help make I.S. development faster, cheaper and of higher quality.

Some tools are simple; some are complex. When building a simple system, a complex tool may slow down development. It is desirable to *use simple tools for simple systems*. For some needs, a report generator or a spreadsheet tool is sufficient. Most of the examples in this book relate to systems more complex than this, which need sophisticated tools.

In the early 1980s, **fourth-generation languages** were invented [MARTIN85]. Non-procedural languages gave ways to express what result was required rather than how to achieve it. SQL became a standard and provides a nonprocedural way to access relational databases. Other, more user-friendly, query languages and report generation languages proliferated.

**Prototyping tools** became important, enabling developers to build prototypes quickly and see how end users react to them. Prototyping languages gave rise to iterative development in which a prototype was successively refined.

**CASE (Computer-Aided Systems Engineering) tools** provided graphically oriented ways of expressing plans, models and designs [JMPSa].

**Code generators** were created that could generate COBOL or other languages from high-level constructs [JMPSb].

Expert-system shells provide an easy way to capture and modify application functionality within a powerful and flexible rule language. Hybrid shells combine this with object-oriented programming facilities, providing what is, in essence, direct execution of specifications.

The tools really started to look powerful when these facilities were integrated. CASE tools for planning, for data and process modelling, and for creating designs were integrated with code generators. Prototyping capability was linked into the design tools. Nonprocedural languages, including SQL and report generators, were integrated into the CASE environment. The term I-CASE came into use to describe integrated CASE products. Most important in I-CASE was the ability to generate code directly for the CASE design tool.

The integrated toolsets are the basis for RAD.

IBM introduced its AD Platform and Repository, setting standards for how tools from different vendors should work together in IBM's environment (Figure 3.1).

IBM's Repository and resources for linking to it comprise IBM's AD Platform at the bottom of Figure 3.1. In the middle of the diagram are tools from various vendors for portions of the lifecycle. These plug into the AD Platform. At the top of the diagram are multivendor cross-lifecycle tools, which relate to the entire lifecycle, such as project management and methodology guidance tools.

IBM's AD Cycle can be used with many methodologies, but the most valuable and powerful are those that employ information engineering and RAD.

## CASE and I-CASE

The systems analyst interacts with a CASE tool by means of diagrams (Figure 3.2).

Diagrams are used to represent planning information, an overview of systems, data models and data flows, detailed designs and program structures. A principle of CASE is that, whenever appropriate, diagrams are used as an aid to clear thinking. The figures in this book show examples of the types of diagrams that I.S. professionals create on a workstation screen with CASE tools.

A critical characteristic of an I-CASE tool (as opposed to merely CASE) is that it generates executable programs. A code generator is driven by the design workbench.

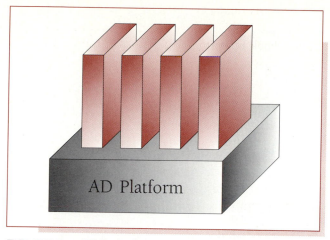

FIGURE 3.1 IBM's Application Development Cycle (AD Cycle), provides an OPEN framework into which the tools of many vendors fit to provide an integrated CASE environment. Essential to this is IBM's Repository with its precise model of the types of objects in the Repository and the rules that apply to them. The Repository Services and Tool Services ensure integrity and consistency among information stored in the model. IBM's standard end-user interface (CUA, Common User Access) applies to the diverse tools, making them appear similar and easy to use. Common workstation services also apply to all the tools. The equivalent of this from DEC is their COHESION architecture.

The tight integration of the analysis and design tools with a code generator gives much higher productivity than the use of tools that are not coupled.

In the past, systems analysts drew their diagrams with pencils and erasers (Figure 3.3). Often, hand-drawn diagrams became very large, straggling across white boards or pasted on large sheets of paper. A design often had binders of nested data-flow diagrams and structure charts. These binders contained numerous errors, inconsistencies and omissions that were not caught. Often, the diagrams themselves were sloppy and the diagramming technique casual or ill-thought-out.

CASE tools enforce precision in diagramming. A good CASE tool employs diagram types that are precise and computer-checkable. Large, complex diagrams can be handled by means of zooming, nesting, windowing and other computer techniques. The computer quickly catches errors and inconsistencies even in very large sets of diagrams. Today, business, government and the military need highly complex, integrated computer applications. The size and complexity of these applications are too great for there to be any hope of accurate diagramming without the aid of a computer. The magnitude of the diagrammatic requirements for *information engineering* dictates that automated tools be used.

It is the *meaning* represented by the diagram, rather than its graphic image, which is valuable. A good CASE tool stores that meaning in a computer-processable form. The tool helps build up a design, data model or other deliverable segment of the development process in such a way that it can be validated and then used in a subsequent development stage.

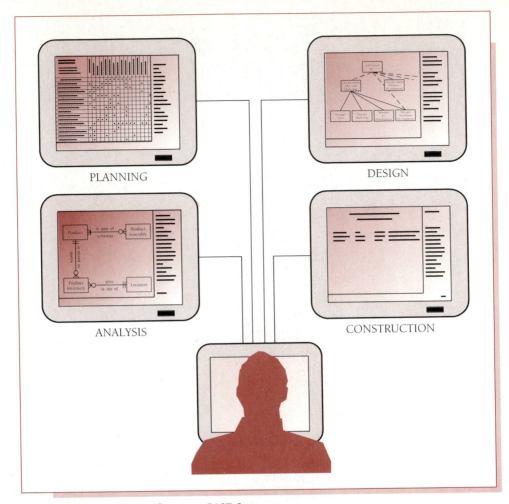

FIGURE 3.2 Analyst Working at a CASE Screen

An article in *Fortune* [FORTUNE89] attempted to describe why software is so difficult to create:

Software is "pure thought stuff," so conceptual that designers cannot draw explicit, detailed diagrams and schematics—as creators of electronic circuits can—to guide programmers in their work. Consequently, routine communication among programmers, managers and the ordinary people who use software is a chore in itself.

It is vital to understand that this popular wisdom is *wrong* today. Explicit, detailed diagrams and schematics are drawn, analogous to those used by electronic circuit designers, with the I-CASE tools, and code is generated from them. Much testing can be done at the diagram level. These diagrams are very effective for routine communications among programmers, analysts, managers and end users. To attempt to build software without them is irresponsible management.

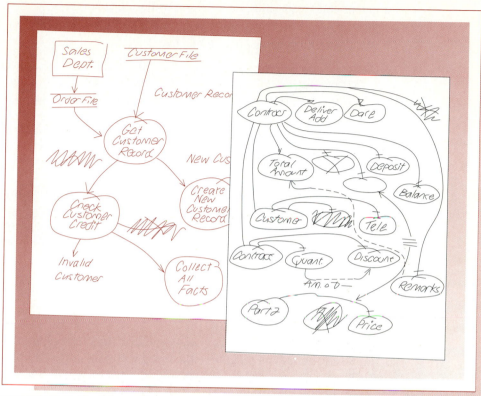

FIGURE 3.3 Hand-drawn diagrams usually contain inconsistencies, errors and omissions, which a CASE tool could detect. They are slow to draw and cumbersome to revise; so they inhibit experimenting with design changes. Hand-drawn diagrams are entirely inadequate as a basis for complex systems or for an information-engineering approach.

# Objects and Associations

Many CASE diagrams show **objects** and **associations among objects**. The objects are drawn as boxes on a diagram, and the associations are drawn as lines connecting the boxes.

Examples of **objects** are:

- an entity type;
- a process;
- a data store;
- a program module;
- a department;
- a business goal.

Examples of **associations** are:

- a relationship between two entity types;
- a data flow on a data-flow diagram;

- a parent-child association on a decomposition diagram;
- a line showing how a procedure is dependent on other procedures;
- a line connecting events on a PERT chart.

Figure 3.4 shows diagrams with objects and associations.

The CASE software may ask the user for detailed information about each object and each association. When needed, this information is entered or displayed in **windows**.

Figure 3.5 shows an example of a window appearing on a CASE diagram.

The CASE software uses such windows to collect a complete set of data so that it can check the integrity of models and designs, do design calculations and accumulate the information it needs for code generation.

Sometimes the relationships among objects are best displayed with a **matrix diagram**, as shown in Figure 3.6.

Again, details may be entered or displayed using windows. If the user points to a cell in the matrix, a window may appear that shows the details known about that intersection or the details that must be entered.

# Diagrams of Programs

A particularly important form of diagram is one that shows the structure of programs. It should represent optimal program structuring and show loops, nesting, conditions, case-structures, escapes, database accesses, subroutine calls and other program structures.

Curiously, in the early evolution of structured techniques, no such program diagram was used. Perhaps because of this, some of the early CASE tools also did not support program diagramming techniques. A program structure can be made clear by representing it visually in such a way that any portion of it can be either contracted on the screen to examine an overview or expanded to show detail. Detail can be added to the structure one step at a time.

Figure 3.7 shows an **action diagram** used for representing program structures. The action diagram can be drawn independently of any programming language or can be set to a particular language. Figure 3.8 shows an action diagram set to COBOL.

An action diagram can be specified in the language of a code generator. Commands representing programming constructs need not be typed; they can be selected from a mouse menu. When the computer adds them to the action diagram, it automatically inserts relevant END statements and utilizes correct case-structures. It can insist that ELSE actions be filled in when a condition is used. It can enforce optimal code structuring.

Action diagrams are also used to show specifications in a structured form [MARTIN&MCCLURE89].

A box representing a procedure on a decomposition diagram, data flow diagram or other diagram can be expanded in the form of an action diagram, as shown in Figure 3.9.

The action diagram shows the data types that are the inputs and outputs of the procedure.

Appendix V describes action diagrams.

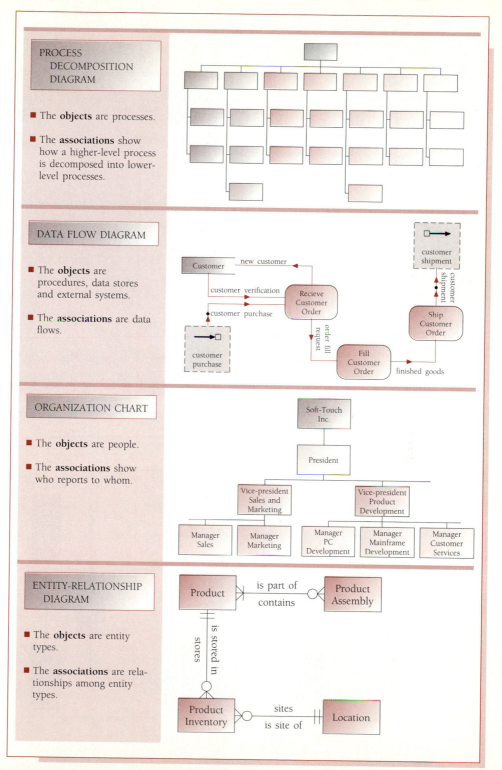

**PROCESS DECOMPOSITION DIAGRAM**

- The **objects** are processes.

- The **associations** show how a higher-level process is decomposed into lower-level processes.

**DATA FLOW DIAGRAM**

- The **objects** are procedures, data stores and external systems.

- The **associations** are data flows.

**ORGANIZATION CHART**

- The **objects** are people.

- The **associations** show who reports to whom.

**ENTITY-RELATIONSHIP DIAGRAM**

- The **objects** are entity types.

- The **associations** are relationships among entity types.

FIGURE 3.4  Diagrams with Objects and Associations

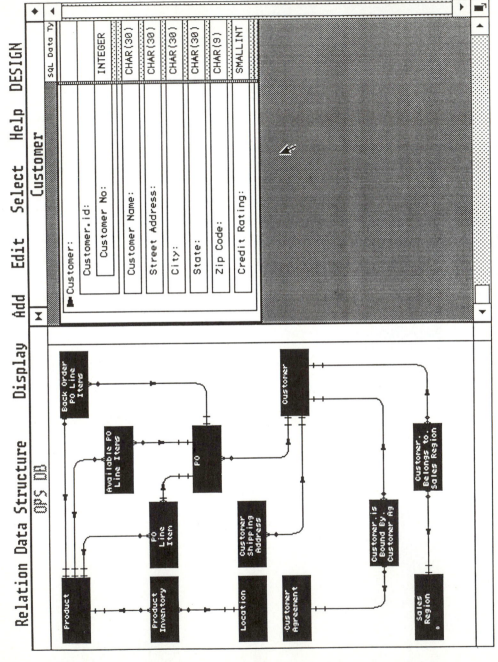

FIGURE 3.5 Picture of a Window on a CASE Screen Prompting for Specific Details

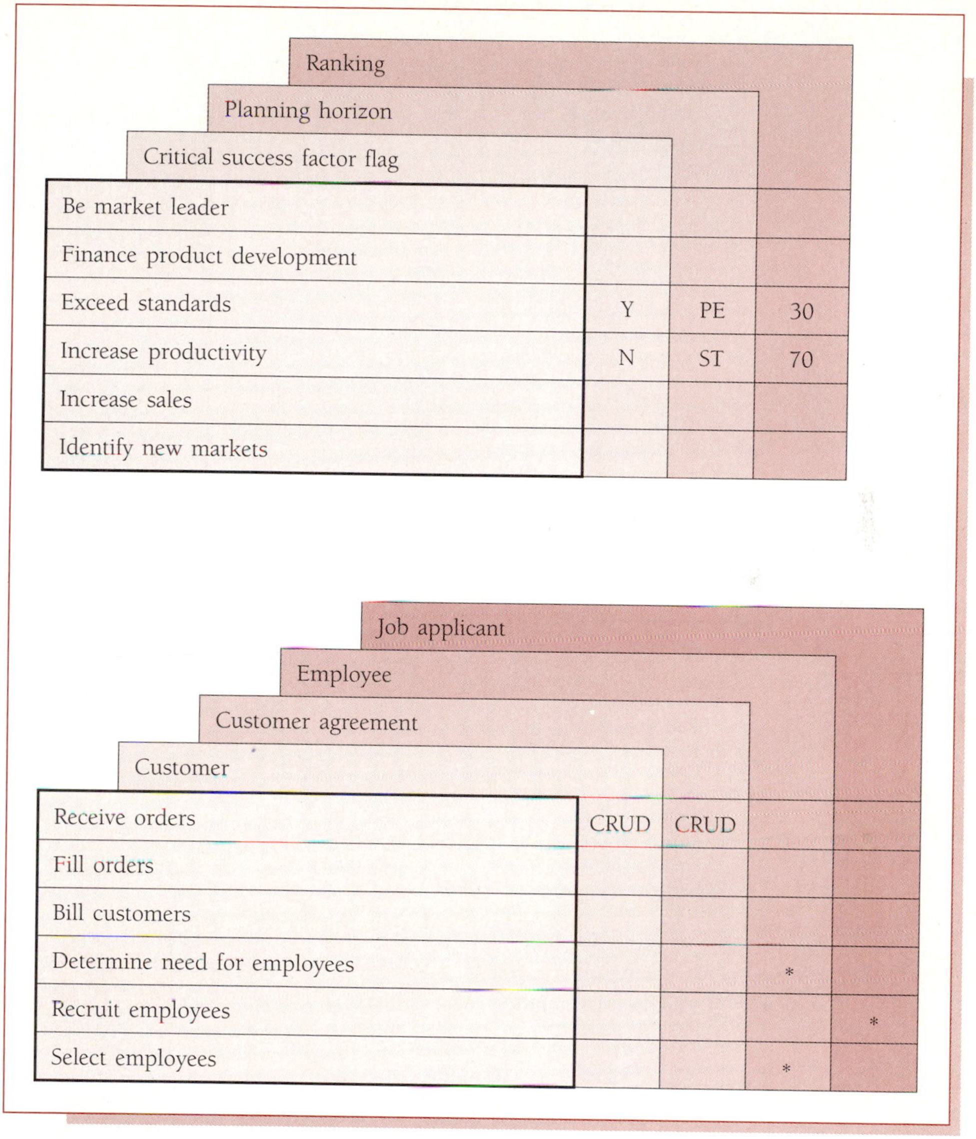

| | Critical success factor flag | Planning horizon | Ranking |
|---|---|---|---|
| Be market leader | | | |
| Finance product development | | | |
| Exceed standards | Y | PE | 30 |
| Increase productivity | N | ST | 70 |
| Increase sales | | | |
| Identify new markets | | | |

| | Customer | Customer agreement | Employee | Job applicant |
|---|---|---|---|---|
| Receive orders | CRUD | CRUD | | |
| Fill orders | | | | |
| Bill customers | | | | |
| Determine need for employees | | | * | |
| Recruit employees | | | | * |
| Select employees | | | * | |

FIGURE 3.6  Two Matrix Diagrams

# The Language of Diagrams

The diagrams and their manipulation by computer are a form of thought processing. The analyst, designer, programmer, user and executive need a family of diagram types to assist in clear thinking. These diagram types should be as clear and simple as possible. Although there are multiple diagram types, a minimum number of icons should have to be learned, and their meanings should be as obvious as possible.

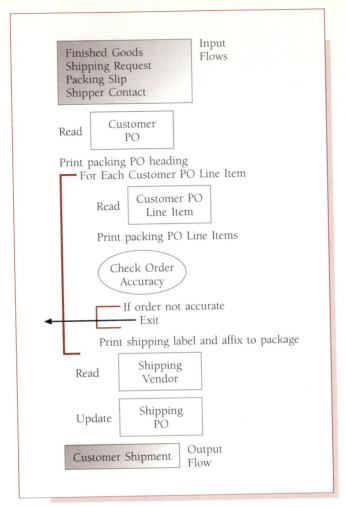

FIGURE 3.7  Action Diagram

   The diagrams must be complete enough and rigorous enough to serve as a basis for code generation and for automatic conversion of one type of diagram into another. The diagrams of the early "structured revolution" are not good enough for this purpose. The analyst and designer had to use human intelligence to bridge gaps between one type of diagram and another, and they often made mistakes in doing so. I-CASE needs a complete, integrated, rigorous set of diagramming standards.

   Given appropriate diagramming techniques, it is much easier to describe complex activities and procedures in diagrams than in text. A picture can be much better than a thousand words because it is concise, precise and clear. Computerized diagrams do not allow the sloppiness and woolly thinking common in textual specifications. Engineers of different types all use formal diagrams that are precise in meaning—mechanical drawings, architects' drawings, circuit diagrams, microelectronics designs and

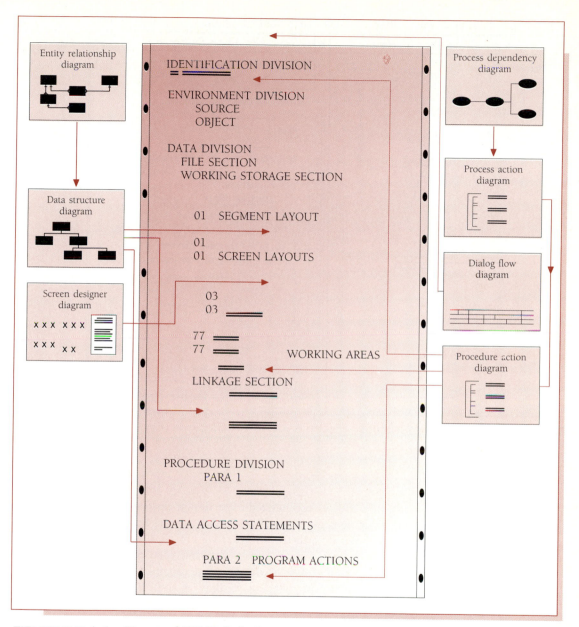

FIGURE 3.8 Action Diagram of COBOL Code (Source: Texas Instruments, IEF.)

so on. Software engineering and information engineering also need formal diagrams with standardized diagramming constructs.

As in other branches of engineering, the diagrams become the documentation for systems (along with the additional information collected in the repository when the diagrams are drawn). When changes are made to systems, the diagrams are changed

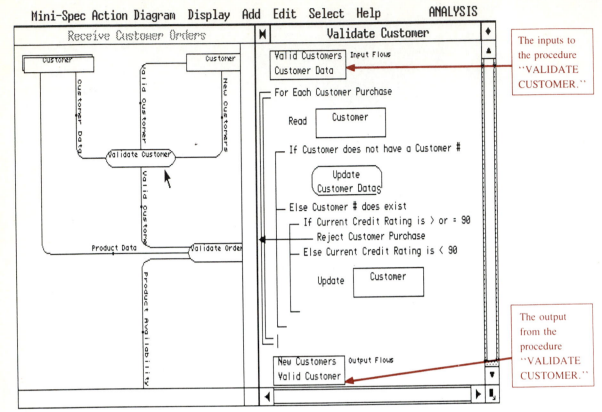

FIGURE 3.9 Action Diagram Window Showing Details of a Block on a Data-Flow Diagram (Source: Knowledgeware, Inc., IEW.)

on the screen, and the code is regenerated. The design documentation is generated automatically and, thus, does not slip out of date as changes are made.

Philosophers have often described how what we are capable of thinking depends on the language we use for thinking. When mankind used only Roman numerals, ordinary people could not multiply or divide. That capability spread when Arabic numbers became widely used. The diagrams we draw of complex processes are a form of language. With computers, we may want to create processes more complex than those we would perform manually.

Appropriate diagrams help us visualize and invent those processes.

- *For an individual developing a system design or program, the diagrams used are aids to clear thinking.* A poor choice of diagramming technique can inhibit thinking. A good choice can speed up work and improve the quality of the results.
- When *several people work on a system or program, the diagrams serve as an essential communication tool.* A formal diagramming technique is needed to enable the developers to interchange ideas and make their separate components fit together with precision.

- *When systems are modified, clear diagrams are an essential aid to maintenance.* They make it possible for a new team to understand how the program works and to design changes. When a change is made, it often affects other parts of the program.
- *Clear diagrams of the program structure enable maintenance programmers to understand the consequential effects of changes they make.* When debugging, clear diagrams are also highly valuable tools for understanding how the programs ought to work and for tracking down what might be wrong.

Diagramming, then, is a language, essential both for clear thinking and for human communication. An enterprise needs standards for its I.S. diagrams, just as it has standards for engineering drawings.

# Hyperdiagrams

A diagram and its associated information in a CASE tool can be very different from that on paper. Paper constrains the diagram to what can be drawn in a two-dimensional space. Analysts are used to building designs with two-dimensional drawings. With a computer, many different representations can be linked together logically. A block on a data-flow diagram may be the same as a block on a decomposition diagram. A data access on an action diagram must relate to information on an entity-relationship diagram or data model. The inputs and outputs to a procedure represented by an action must be the same as those on the corresponding data-flow diagram.

The analyst using the screen of a CASE tool may point at a block or line and display details of that block or line. The details may be displayed in the form of another diagram, sometimes a diagram of a different type. They may be displayed in the form of text or fill-in-the-blanks panels. The analyst may have multiple windows on the screen at one time showing different aspects of a design, as presented in Figure 3.10. He may have a "DISPLAY" menu (like that in Figure 3.11) with which to display different aspects of a design.

The term **hyperdiagram** or **hyperchart** describes a representation of plans, models or designs in which multiple two-dimensional representations are logically linked together. A simple hyperdiagram is a diagram in which the details of objects may be displayed in windows. A more complex hyperdiagram uses multiple types of two-dimensional diagrams. A block or a line may be displayed in a window as text, as a fill-in-the-blanks form, an action diagram, a matrix, a different type of diagram and so on.

Figure 3.12 shows a family of screen windows that are part of one hyperdiagram. The hyperdiagram can be explored by pointing to objects or associations and displaying details of them. There can be diagrams within diagrams within diagrams; there can be details within details within details.

A system is generally too complex to draw as one single type of diagram. Its components may be summarized with a decomposition diagram, or their interdependencies may be shown with a data-flow diagram. The detailed logic may be depicted with an action diagram. The system may use a database structure, and individual views of data are derived from that structure. The action diagram may refer to screen designs or report designs. All of these may be stored in a computable form, with explanatory text,

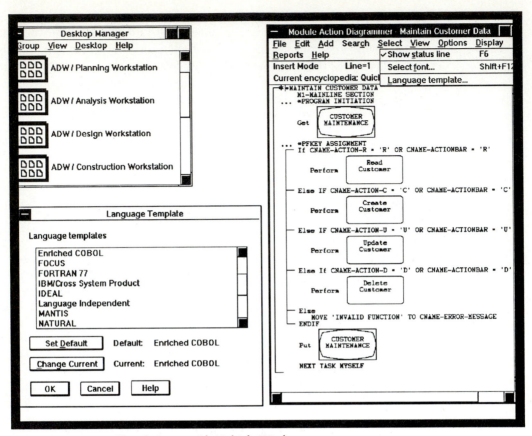

FIGURE 3.10 Workbench Screen with Multiple Windows
  Each window can be scrolled or expanded to fill the screen to show more detail than is shown here.

in a hyperdiagram. An I-CASE toolkit gives the implementor the facilities to explore or to build the hyperdiagram. *The tool should enforce consistency within the hyperdiagram.*

  Figures 3.13 through 3.15 provide illustrations of diagrams that are linked to form hyperdiagrams. Because the hyperdiagram contains logical linkages between different types of representations and enforces consistency among these representations, it is a major advance relative to paper-oriented methods of analysis and design.

# The Repository

The meaning represented by diagrams and their detail windows is stored in a **repository**. The repository steadily accumulates information relating to the planning, analysis, design, construction and, later, maintenance of systems. IBM defined a standard repository that many vendors use. Some vendors sell their own integrated family of CASE tools with their own unique repository [IEF, IEW, ADW]. The early repositories

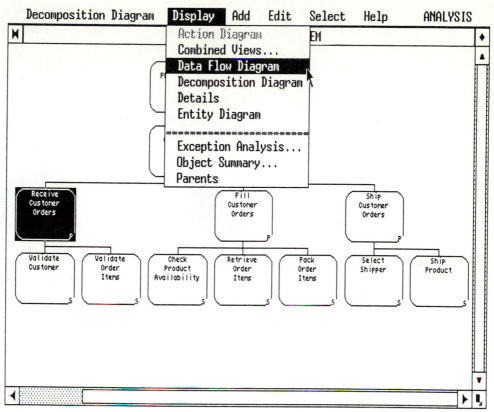

**Decomposition Diagram    Display    Add    Edit    Select    Help    ANALYSIS**

FIGURE 3.11  DISPLAY Menu on a workbench screen offers the analyst the choice of different ways of displaying objects or designs.

have been in practical use for several years now. *The repository is the heart of an I-CASE system.*

The repository is essential to the RAD lifecycle. Early in the lifecycle, information already in the repository is extracted and put to use. While *planning* is being done, information is stored in the repository that is later used in *design*. While *design* is done, information is stored in the repository that is later used in the *construction* of the application. The I-CASE repository steadily collects information that will drive the code generator. Critical to fast development is the employment of reusable templates, structures, models and designs. These are stored in the repository and can be modified to fit the application in question.

Some repositories are "dumb" and some are "intelligent." A dumb repository is like a database management system; it does not in any way process or "understand" the information stored in it.

Some repositories are object-oriented. They store information about object-types such as those in Figure 3.4 and associations among the objects. They know the properties and behavior of each object-type and association. The toolset asks the analyst for information about the object or association, and code associated with the repository carries out validity checks.

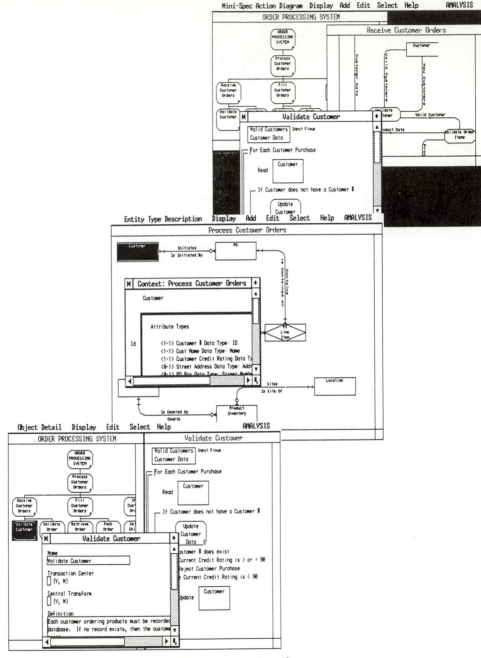

FIGURE 3.12 Separate Diagrams Forming One Hyperdiagram

All of these are parts of a logically consistent whole. By selecting blocks (or links between blocks) and displaying them in detail windows, an analyst may obtain more information about this hyperdiagram. Each window can be scrolled or expanded to show more detail. Consistency within the hyperdiagram and among different hyperdiagrams is enforced by the computer.

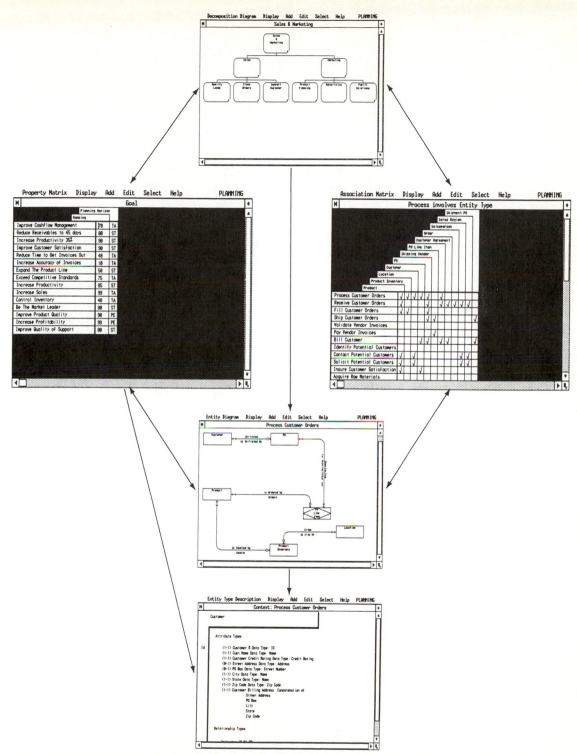

FIGURE 3.13 Sample of a Complex Hyperdiagram

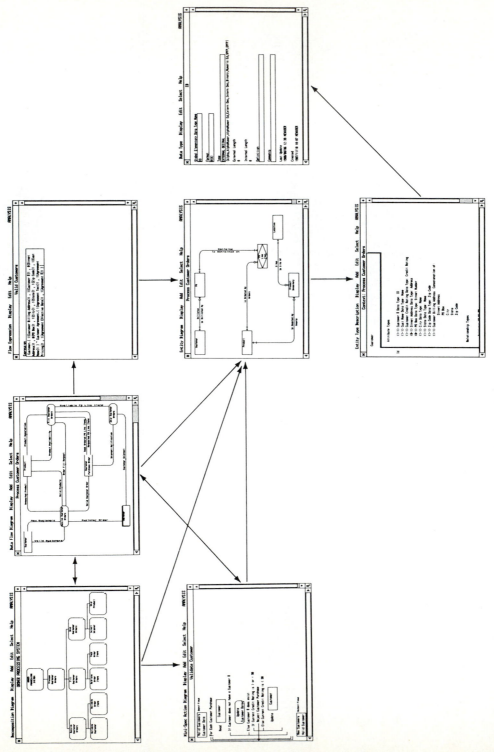

FIGURE 3.14 Examples of Logical Connections in a Complex Hyperdiagram

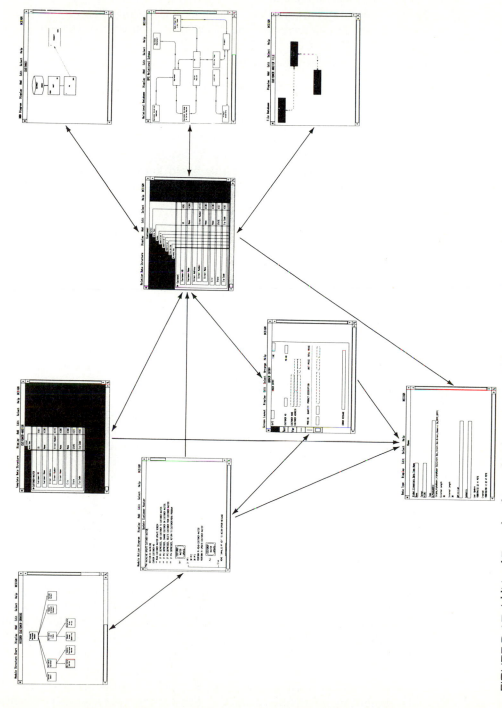

FIGURE 3.15 Additional Examples of Logical Linkages Between Different Types of Representations in a Complex Hyperdiagram

The highest level of repository contains coded representations of the plans, models and designs with tools for cross-checking, validating and coordinating this knowledge. This level of repository is sometimes called an **encyclopedia**. The encyclopedia "understands" the entire plans, models and designs, and can enforce consistency across the representation [IEF, IEW, ADW].

There are thus three levels of repository:

1. **Dictionary**. This contains names and descriptions of data items, processes, variables and so on.
2. **Repository**. This contains knowledge about the objects in the system, their properties and behavior. It validates the information about objects.
3. **Intelligent Repository**. This contains knowledge about plans, models and designs and their objects. It uses a rule-based **knowledge coordinator** to apply rule-based processing to the entire collection of knowledge.

# Use of a Repository

A repository is essential for RAD. The more intelligent the repository, the better. The repository-based I-CASE tools help enforce technical quality and greatly lessen the integration testing needed to interlink the work of different developers or to interlink reusable components. The more complex the system, the more the repository **knowledge coordinator** is needed. The repository contains many rules relating to the knowledge it stores and may employ rule processing, the artificial intelligence technique, to help achieve accuracy, integrity and completeness of the plans, models and designs. The repository is thus a knowledge base, which not only stores development information but helps control its accuracy and validity.

To emphasize that the repository is *intelligent*, we draw it with an icon like a skull, as in Figure 3.16.

Any one diagram on a CASE screen is a facet of a broader set of knowledge that may reside in the repository. The repository normally contains far more detail than is on the diagram. This detail can be displayed in windows by mouse navigation around a hyperdiagram.

In an I-CASE tool, the repository drives a code generator. The goal of the design workbench is to collect sufficient information so that code for the system can be generated. The generator should also generate database description code and job control language. It should generate a comprehensive set of documentation so that designers and maintenance staff can understand the system clearly.

Figure 3.17 shows the repository accumulating information from the planning, analysis, design or construction toolkits and generating code, database descriptions and documentation. Structured code is usually not as efficient as highly optimized code. The code may, therefore, be fed into an optimizer to make it as machine-efficient as possible (bottom, Figure 3.17). Figure 3.18 encapsulates the nature of an I-CASE toolset.

In a complex enterprise using I-CASE development, the repository will grow large, steadily accumulating information about the enterprise and its systems, its data models, data flows, process models, rules, specifications, screen designs and so on.

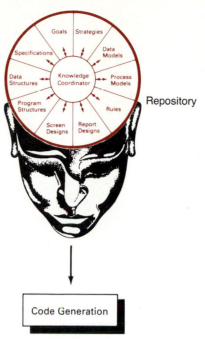

Repository

Code Generation

FIGURE 3.16 A **dictionary** contains names and descriptions of data items, processes, variables, etc.

A **repository** contains complete coded representations of plans, models and designs with tools for cross-checking, correlation analysis and validation. Graphic representations are derived from the repository and are used to update it. The repository contains many rules relating to the knowledge it stores, and employs **rule-processing**, the artificial intelligence technique, to help achieve accuracy, integrity and completeness of the plans, models and designs. The repository is thus a **knowledge base** that not only stores development information but helps control its accuracy and validity.

The repository should be designed to drive a code generator. The toolset helps the systems analyst build up in the repository the information necessary for code generation. For the purpose of this book, to emphasize that the repository is an *intelligent* facility, it is drawn with the icon above.

# Views and Hyperviews

A common term in database technology is **view**. A view of a database is a representation of data that is perceived by one person or program. The structure of the database may be far more complex than the structure of the view. The view shows only those fields in which the user is interested at the time. The view is a subset of the overall database structure.

A CASE repository contains many objects and associations among objects. A workstation normally displays some of those objects and associations at one time. It displays a *view* from the repository contents. An analyst or designer creates a view when he works at the screen. When this view is entered into the central repository, it becomes part of a much larger representation. The view may have a name and may be referred to in the repository index so that it can be quickly retrieved.

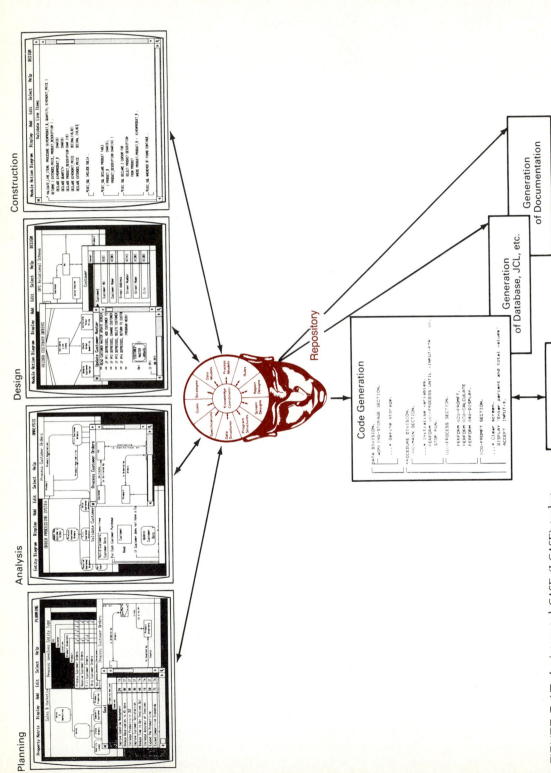

FIGURE 3.17 An integrated CASE (I-CASE) toolset needs to link the various facilities with computerized consistency checking.

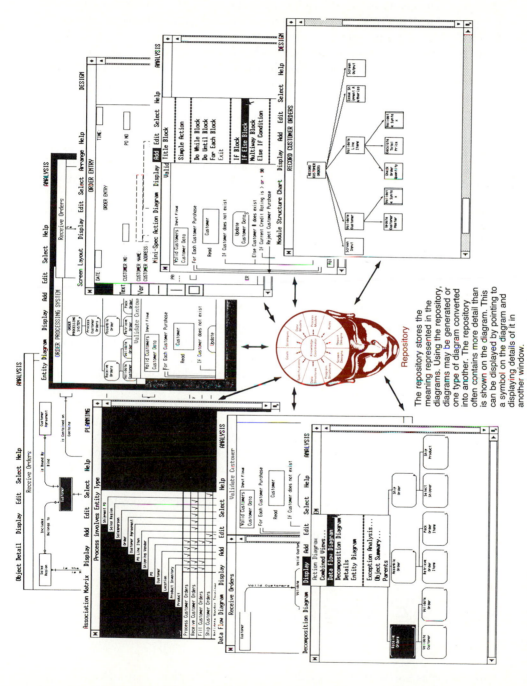

FIGURE 3.18 The repository stores the *meaning* represented in the diagrams. Through use of the repository, diagrams may be generated, or one type of diagram may be converted to another. The repository often contains more detail than is shown on the diagram. These can be displayed by pointing to a symbol on the diagram and displaying details in another window.

Repository

The repository stores the meaning represented in the diagrams. Using the repository, diagrams may be generated or one type of diagram converted into another. The repository often contains more detail than is shown on the diagram. This can be displayed by pointing to a symbol on the diagram and displaying details of it in another window.

Many views may be logically linked to form a **hyperview**, just as many diagrams are logically linked to form a hyperdiagram. A hyperview is a collection of knowledge about a given activity or group of activities and the data these activities use. It can be represented with multiple, logically related screen displays. A hyperview has sometimes been referred to as a **perspective**. A hyperview is given an identification number and, possibly, a name and is one of the formal objects tracked by the repository.

The central repository contains many hyperviews. The different hyperviews overlap; in other words, they use common objects and employ data derived from a common data model.

One implementor (or sometimes a team) works on one hyperview at a time. The hyperview contains multiple objects, associations, diagrams, notes and text that can be manipulated in the workstation called its **owner**. Many people may look at the hyperview but not modify it. These people are called **users** of the hyperview. The hyperview may record the **knowledge source**—an end user, end-user group, JAD (Joint Application Design) workshop, Construction Team and so on.

## Consistency Among Diagrams

Different types of diagrams show different manifestations of the same information. These diagrams are linked together into hyperviews. Data may be entered in one type of diagram and displayed with a different type of diagram. The repository tools ensure that the different diagrams reflect a consistent meaning. If a procedure block is added to a data-flow diagram, that procedure must appear on the equivalent decomposition diagram, and vice versa.

If the analyst has two windows on the screen with different diagram types of the same information, when he changes one diagram, the change needed to ensure consistency should appear automatically on the other diagram. The analyst may add a process block to a decomposition diagram, for example, and the equivalent block appears on a data-flow diagram. Because the software does not know how to link it to the other blocks on the data-flow diagram, it asks for that information. In this way, one type of diagram can be converted into another or used as a component of another diagram.

For example, knowledge "X" may be best entered into the repository by Mr. Jones via a data flow diagram. Ms. Smith then requests the same information from the repository, reinterpreted automatically, as an entity-relationship diagram. This logically interconnected family of diagrams constitutes a **hyperview** with which the implementor can explore and add to an integrated set of knowledge.

## Consistency Among Different Analysts

Large projects are worked on by different teams of implementors. Designs done by different people need to work together with absolute precision. It is very difficult to achieve this with manual methods. A good I-CASE tool enforces consistency among the work of different analysts and implementors. One of the major benefits of using I-CASE tools is this computerized enforcement of consistency among the different parts of the design as they evolve. The larger and more complex a project, the more it needs precise computerized coordination of the work of different implementors.

# Consistency Among Different Projects

A computerized corporation has many different databases and systems. It is necessary to achieve consistency among different systems because they interact with one another in complex ways. Systems in different plants and locations transmit information to one another. Data are often extracted from multiple systems and aggregated for purposes of business management. Different locations need commonality of management measurements. Sometimes the term **corporate transparency** is used to mean that detailed information in all locations is accessible in a computerized form by a central management group for decision-support and control purposes.

CASE tools make it practical to achieve consistency among multiple projects. Designs for different systems are derived from common data models and process models, which are available to implementors from the repository.

# The Knowledge Coordinator

An integral part of repository-based systems is a **knowledge coordinator**. The knowledge coordinator ensures consistency among the different pieces of knowledge that reside in the repository. It applies rule-based reasoning to the information that is checked into the repository. When a person using a workstation enters new information, the knowledge coordinator checks that it obeys the rules and is consistent with what is already in the repository. In IBM AD Cycle tools, this checking is done by the **Repository Services** and **Tool Services** components.

A person using a CASE toolset builds his own model or design. This is represented in a local hyperview. The knowledge coordinator enforces consistency within that hyperview. The local hyperview is built with objects that are extracted from a central repository and use the detail that is centrally stored. There is, thus, consistency between the local hyperview and the central representation.

The person using the toolset may create new objects, new associations or new detail. This will eventually be entered into the central repository. The knowledge coordinator then has the task of ensuring that the local hyperview is consistent with the central information. It will indicate any inconsistencies, and these must be corrected. The local workstation user will normally correct the inconsistencies arising from his work. Sometimes a central administrator has to resolve conflicts about how objects are designed or described.

Two implementors may create two separate hyperviews. The knowledge coordinator has the task of examining them in combination to ensure complete consistency between them. In this way, consistency is achieved even in a multi-person project or in a multi-project environment.

It is difficult or impossible to achieve consistency among the work of many analysts or implementors with manual techniques. A computer with CASE representations can enforce consistency. Achieving consistency becomes a human problem of resolving different opinions rather than a technical problem of detecting inconsistencies. The computerized corporation of the future cannot be built without computerized enforcement of consistency among its many information systems.

# Layers of Integrity Checking and Analysis

The axioms and rules that a computer can apply to the work of the designers and planners are built up in layers, as shown in Figure 3.19. First, they can be applied to a single diagram to make it complete and consistent. Then, they can be applied to the combination of information from multiple diagram types that form a hyperview. The hyperview is made complete and consistent in its own right. Next, the information in the hyperview is coordinated with that of other hyperviews. At each of these stages, rule-processing techniques can be applied. A "dialog" with the designer takes place in which the computer asks for information it needs to complete its knowledge of a hyperview or deal with inconsistencies.

A variety of analysis tools are required for the synthesis of different data views, different hyperviews and different types of planning information. The outer layer of Figure 3.19 relates to the types of analysis applied to the knowledge in the repository.

# Distributed Architecture

Coordinating the computerized knowledge across a large development project requires substantial computing and is likely to be done on the machine that controls the central repository. The analysts using CASE tools, however, need a fast response from their desktop machine; so, there should be a repository and knowledge coordinator in that desktop machine. A distributed architecture is thus desirable.

Figure 3.20 shows a typical distributed I-CASE environment.

There is a central repository, which is usually on a mainframe. Developers have an I-CASE toolset on their desk with its own repository. With the desktop tools, they can do planning, analysis, design and code generation. The developers may be many miles from the mainframe, connected to it by telephone lines. They download a subset of the central repository into their desktop machine and work with it locally. A desktop knowledge coordinator checks the integrity of what they build. Periodically, the changes and additions they have made to the subset are sent back to the mainframe, where a central knowledge coordinator goes to work, detecting any discrepancies among the work of different analysts, which must then be resolved.

Normally, no one individual or design team is familiar with the entire set of designs in the central repository. When the individual starts to create a design, he will extract

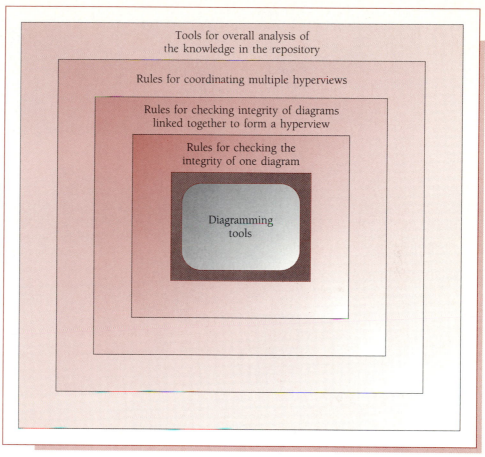

FIGURE 3.19 Axioms and rules are used for checking first a single diagram, then the group of diagrams that combine to create a hyperview and, finally, the coordination of multiple hyperviews across the enterprise. A variety of analysis tools is needed to help build the combinations of hyperviews and aid planners in developing the information resources of the enterprise.

whatever information in the central repository relates to the design. For example, he may extract a portion of a data model. The individual may be designing the detail of a process that is already shown in a higher-level representation. He then works on the design, largely independently of the central repository. When the design is ready for review, it can be coordinated with the knowledge already in the central repository. When the design is coordinated and approved, it will reside in the central repository and may affect the work of other designers.

## Code Generation on the Desktop

Some code generators are on a mainframe; some are on personal computers. Today's personal computers are powerful enough to do complete development, code generation and compiling of programs that will eventually be executed on a mainframe. I-CASE

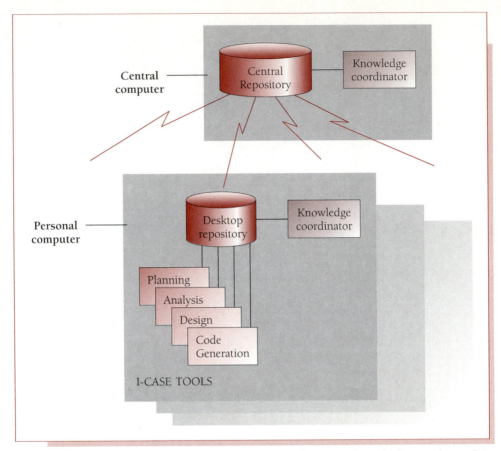

**FIGURE 3.20** The central repository is often on a mainframe. Analysts check out subsets of the repository to their desktop computers. The desktop knowledge coordinator coordinates what is in the local designs as they evolve. Periodically, the results are uploaded to the central repository, where central coordination takes place and discrepancies among different developers are resolved.

tools with desktop code generators generally enable a developer to work faster than when he needs to access a mainframe for code generation and compiling. It is desirable that the developer be able to design a system (or subsystem), generate code for it, test it, modify it and regenerate it as quickly as possible (Figure 3.21). He should be able to do this on a desktop machine, completely debugging the logic on that machine, generating the linkages to the mainframe databases, network and operating system. When fully tested on the personal computer, the code is handed over for execution and testing on the mainframe or machine where it will eventually run.

# The Information Systems Pyramid

It is useful to draw a pyramid to describe corporate I.S. activities.

Figure 3.22 illustrates the I.S. pyramid.

At the top of the pyramid is strategic *planning*. This needs to be anchored firmly in

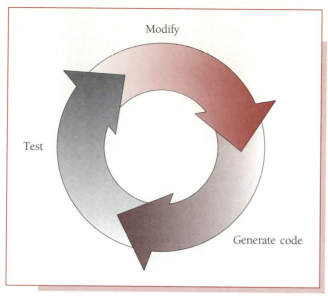

FIGURE 3.21 The RAD developer needs to go through the fastest possible cycle of designing a system, generating code, testing it, modifying it and regenerating it. This is faster if a desktop construction workbench is used. The code generator and compiler should be on the personal computer. The finished code can then be uploaded for execution and testing on the mainframe or machine where it will eventually run.

the strategic plans of the business itself. The next level down is *analysis*. A model is built of the fundamental data and processes needed to operate the enterprise. From this analysis, the need for systems is determined. The third level is *design*. Designs are expressed in rigorous detail. The bottom level is *construction*, where the code is generated and tested. The tools should make it possible to build and test a backbone system quickly and make successive refinements to the backbone with the involvement of end users.

On the left side of the pyramid are **data**; on the right are **activities**. Both data and activities are managed from a high-level, management-oriented view at the top through implementation at the bottom (Figure 3.23).

At the *strategic* level on the data side, an overview of the information needed to run the enterprise is created with an entity-relationship diagram. At the *analysis* level, this is extended into a normalized data model. At the strategic level on the right-hand side, an overview model of the enterprise is created, and planning tools are used to relate its goals, problems, critical success factors and so on, to the functions in the enterprise. At the analysis level, a model of the processes is created and linked to the data model.

At the *design* level, specifications for procedures are created and filled out in enough detail to drive a code generator. Tools required at this level include a screen painter,

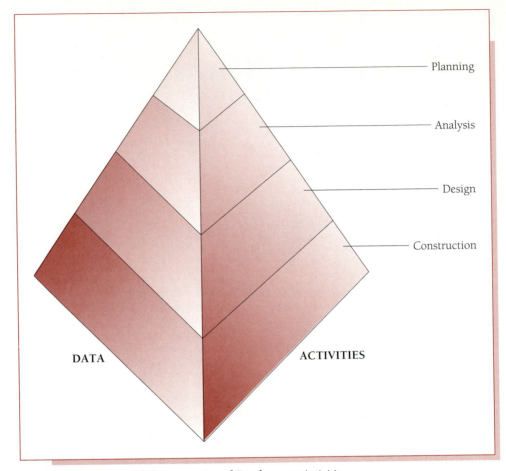

FIGURE 3.22 Pyramid Representation of Development Activities

report generator, data structure diagrammer and tool for showing program structures. At the *construction* level, program code, database code and job control code should be generated.

# Categories of CASE Tools

It is desirable to have CASE tools for each of the four stages of I.S. development— *planning, analysis, design and construction.*

Some vendors sell separate workbenches for these sets of activities. It is desirable that such toolsets be fully integrated and employ a common repository. Work should evolve from the *planning* phase to *construction*, with the knowledge acquired in one phase being used in the next phase. There should be a seamless interface between the phases.

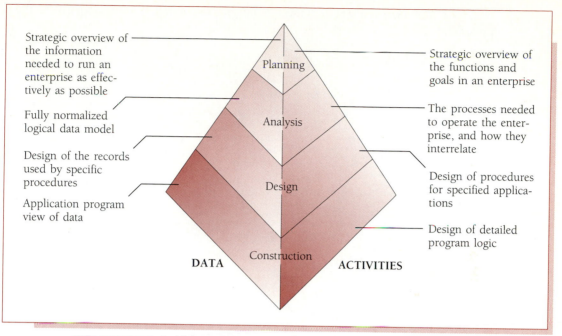

Strategic overview of the information needed to run an enterprise as effectively as possible

Fully normalized logical data model

Design of the records used by specific procedures

Application program view of data

Strategic overview of the functions and goals in an enterprise

The processes needed to operate the enterprise, and how they interrelate

Design of procedures for specified applications

Design of detailed program logic

**DATA**   **ACTIVITIES**

FIGURE 3.23 Activities and Data Required at Each Level of System Development

- Some case tools are for system design and contain no planning and analysis components.

- Some are code generators with separate planning, analysis or design tools.

- Some analysis and design toolkits have a process-oriented view of development, with no data modeling capability.

- Some provide data modeling tools without process analysis or design.

An **I-CASE environment** provides an *integrated* set of tools for *all* parts of the pyramid.

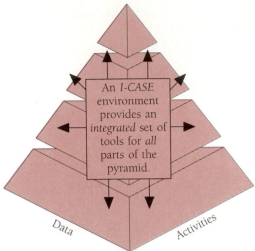

An *I-CASE* environment provides an *integrated* set of tools for *all* parts of the pyramid.

Data    Activities

Some vendors have specialized in building code generators without front-end design and analysis tools. Other vendors have built planning, analysis and design tools without a back-end code generator. Many attempts have been made to couple front-end analysis and design tools loosely to back-end code generators. This is not a fully satisfactory solution because much manual work is still needed to complete the code generator function. What is needed is full integration between the CASE front-end tools and the generator so that code is automatically generated from the front-end tools.

The term **I-CASE** should be used only to relate to products with this full integration. This implies that the front-end tools and the code generator use the same repository. The repository should generate program code, database code and documentation, as illustrated in Figure 3.18.

## Summary of Tool Characteristics

### Box 3.1    Summary of Functional Characteristics of CASE Tools

CASE software should perform the following functions:

- Enable the user to draw diagrams for planning, analysis, design and code-generation phases on a desktop screen.
- Solicit information about the objects in the diagram and relationships among the objects so that a complete set of information is built up.
- Store the *meaning* of the diagram, rather than the diagram itself, in a repository.

- Check the diagram for accuracy, integrity and completeness. The diagram types used should be chosen to facilitate this.
- Enable the user to employ multiple types of diagrams representing different facets of an analysis or design.
- Enable the user to draw program procedures with diagrams, showing conditions, loops, case structures and other constructs of structural programming.
- Enforce structured modeling and design of a type that enables accuracy and consistency checks to be as complete as possible.
- Coordinate the various types of information on multiple diagrams, checking that they are consistent and, *together*, have accuracy, integrity and completeness.
- Store the information built up on the desktop machine in a central repository shared by all analysts and designers.
- Coordinate the information in the central repository, ensuring consistency among the work of all analysts and designers.

## Box 3.2  Summary of Functional Characteristics of I-CASE Tools

I-CASE software incorporates the following:

- The toolkit incorporates the characteristics of CASE tools listed in Box 3.1, "Summary of Functional Characteristics of CASE Tools."
- The activities of planning, analysis, design and construction each have a software workbench with multiple tools. These tools are fully integrated so that one tool directly employs the information from another.
- A repository stores the knowledge from the multiple tools in an integrated manner.
- The knowledge stored in the repository is checked automatically and meticulously (to ensure integrity, consistency and completeness). This may be done with rule-based inferential reasoning (using thousands of rules).
- A code generator is fully integrated with the design toolset (as opposed to having a bridge to a separate code generator with its own separate syntax).
- The generator generates the requisite database statements and job control language.
- Code should be generated and compiled on the desktop machine, with facilities for testing so that it will run correctly in the target environment with the requisite operating system, database management system, and so on.
- The desktop toolset should enable the developer to go through the cycle of design, modify, generate code, test, modify, generate code, test, and so on as quickly as possible.

## Box 3.2    Continued

- Tool services check the knowledge created when tools are being used to ensure its integrity, consistency and completeness of that knowledge before it is stored in the repository.
- The toolset supports rapid prototyping, including screen painting, dialog prototyping, report generation, and full transaction prototyping. (See Methodology Chart 9.)
- The prototype need not be thrown away; it becomes part of the final system.
- The output of the generator may be fed into an optimizer, which adjusts the code and database accesses to give optimal machine performance.
- The tools support all phases of the project lifecycle in an integrated manner.
- In addition to supporting project lifecycles, an I-CASE toolkit supports enterprisewide planning, data modeling and process modeling to create a framework into which many project lifecycles fit. In other words, the toolkit is designed for information engineering rather than merely software engineering.
- System design employs entity-relationship models and data models with full normalization.
- The planning, analysis and design workbenches can support user workshops such as JRP (Joint Requirements Planning) and JAD (Joint Application Design).
- The design workbench employs a screen designer, dialog designer and report designer, each of which is integrated with the repository.
- Code structures are represented graphically (by action diagrams or similar diagrams).
- Technical documentation is generated automatically.
- The toolkit enables highly complex systems to be subdivided into less complex systems that can be developed by separate small teams. The interface between the separate systems is defined with precision in the repository.

A tool should not be referred to as CASE if it lacks any of the basic characteristics listed in Box 3.1.

The simplest CASE tools are little more than diagramming aids. They might be thought of as word processors for diagrams. (They do not have all the characteristics listed in Box 3.1.) These tools simplify the drawing of diagrams and enable them to be modified quickly and kept tidy.

CASE tools have a productivity effect comparable to that achieved by the introduction of word processors in a lawyer's office. Lawyers' word processors often result in far more text being created; diagramming tools often result in far more diagrams being created.

A more valuable effect of good CASE tools is the removal of errors and inconsistencies at the design stage. The designs are of higher quality, leading to fewer problems in subsequent time-consuming removal of errors from code.

Code generators enable implementors to produce working programs quickly. However, if the generator is not linked to a repository, data model or design tools, the programs generated may be incompatible fragments, ill-designed and not linked together.

To maximize productivity and quality, the tools for design need to be tightly coupled to the code generator. The design tools should employ a data model and should enable the design to be represented in a powerful, visual, easy-to-modify form from which code is generated directly. The programs should be quickly executable so that the designer can observe what they do, adjust or add to the design, rerun the programs, enhance the design and so on, until a comprehensive system is created. Many design errors are detected only by testing the programs. The principle "What you see is what you get" should apply to the combination of visual design tool and code generator. The need for manual coding of procedures should be removed, and reusable structures and designs should be employed to the maximum extent.

The generator first produces structured code that relates to the design screens. This code may be used for prototyping and debugging. Structured code does not give optimal machine performance; so, for heavy-duty applications, the code may be fed into an optimizer (as shown at the bottom of Figure 3.17), which creates code with optimal machine performance. This code will never be touched by maintenance programmers; all maintenance is performed at the specification level.

The designer-generator tool should facilitate the rapid building and designing of prototypes. It should generate test data and provide testing tools. It should generate database code and job control code so that the program can be quickly executed when design changes are made.

Substantial skills and training are needed to use a code generator. A person who masters these skills can create defect-free code much faster than with conventional programming.

# Prototyping

Prototyping has become an important part of development lifecycles. It is almost essential to show the users what they will get and allow them to think about it and react to it. The RAD toolset must include the prototyping capability to create screens and dialogs quickly and to modify them while interacting with users.

The ability to generate code, test it and modify it quickly and regenerate it, as shown in Figure 3.21, provides the ability to operate in a prototyping-like fashion. The difference from conventional prototyping is that what is evolving is not a throw-away prototype but is part of the final system. That is critical for RAD. *The prototype should become the final system,* which should have the machine performance, reliability and other features that the final system requires. RAD, thus, uses evolutionary development, with prototypes evolving quickly to the final system.

Chapter 9 discusses prototyping and the characteristics of tools for doing it.

# Fourth-Generation Languages

Some I-CASE toolsets incorporate fourth-generation languages (4GLs). Many make use of SQL, for example. Some 4GLs have been upgraded to become I-CASE toolsets. On the other hand, some I-CASE toolsets generate COBOL, largely ignoring the concepts of 4GLs.

Even if 4GLs are not used by the RAD development team, it is often worthwhile to build a system in which the end users employ 4GLs. The end users may employ a report generator. This gives the system more flexibility because they can extract the reports they want. They may extract data for a spreadsheet tool or Executive Information System software. They may employ a 4GL with which they can do programming or perform sophisticated calculations on the data in the systems.

This flexibility lessens the amount of work the system developers have to do. They do not need to anticipate every reporting need in advance and design the report, for

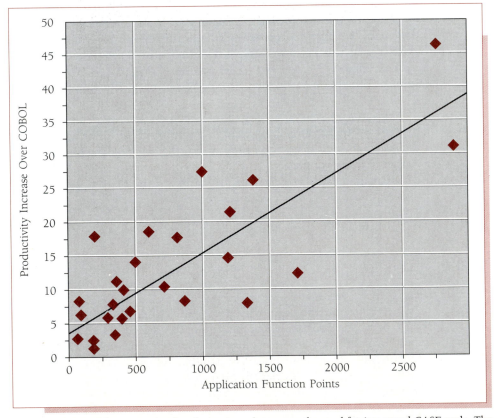

FIGURE 3.24 The more complex the project, the greater the need for integrated CASE tools. The traditional lifecycle can result in low productivity for complex projects. This chart illustrates measurements made on 30 projects built with RAD techniques, showing the ratio of the productivity achieved to the productivity estimated for traditional COBOL development. The measurements are for a diverse set of applications built on the DEC VAX using the CORTEX toolset [PICARDI86]. The productivity improvement tends to increase as application function points increase.

example. It makes sense for I.S. developers to build systems with an I-CASE toolset and RAD lifecycle and for end users to be trained to access the system with an end-user language.

## Complexity and I-CASE

The more complex the project, the greater the need for I-CASE tools. Figure 3.24 shows the results of measurements made of 30 applications built with an early version of the CORTEX toolset [PICARDI86]. The productivity increase over the traditional COBOL lifecycle gets larger as the number of function points increases.

Complex projects have many components that need to be integrated; so, the integrating capability of the repository and knowledge coordinator becomes especially important. As we will see later, the key to building complex systems is to have *small*, autonomous teams working simultaneously with powerful I-CASE tools, their work being coordinated with a model that is in the common I-CASE repository.

People who have learned to manage RAD lifecycles with I-CASE tools look back on the earlier methodologies with horror and say that the use of them is irresponsible. There is no way that systems of quality can be built quickly with the traditional methodologies being used by many enterprises.

## References

[ADW] *Application Development Workbench* (Specific to the AD Cycle), repository-based I-CASE toolset covering all phases of the lifecycle (KnowledgeWare, Inc., Atlanta, Georgia).

[ATHERTON87] *White Paper*, Atherton Technology, Sunnyvale, California, August 1987.

[FORTUNE89] "How Managers Can Succeed through Speed," *Fortune*, February 13, 1989, p.56.

[JMA] *RAD Expert*, a methodology in hyperdocument form adaptable to different toolsets, available from James Martin Associates, Reston, Virginia (703-620-9504).

[IEF] *Information Engineering Facility*, I-CASE toolset covering all phases of information engineering (Texas Instruments, Plano, Texas). In the *IEF*, the repository is referred to as the encyclopedia.

[IEW] *Information Engineering Workbench*, repository-based I-CASE toolset covering all phases of the lifecycle (KnowledgeWare, Inc., Atlanta, Georgia).

[JMPSa] *The James Martin Productivity Series*, Volume 6, *Computer-Aided Software Engineering*, The Martin Report, Inc., 22 Bessom Street, Marblehead, Massachusetts 01945 (617–639–1958).

[JMPSb] *The James Martin Productivity Series*, Volume 4, *Application Generators for End Users*, and Volume 5, *Application and Code Generators for I.S. Professionals*, The

Martin Report, Inc., 22 Bessom Street, Marblehead, Massachusetts 01945 (617–639–1958).

[MARTIN85] James Martin, *Fourth-Generation Languages* (three volumes), Prentice-Hall Inc., Englewood Cliffs, New Jersey, 1985 (201–592–2261).

[MARTIN&MCCLURE89] James Martin and Carma McClure, *Action Diagrams* (2nd edition), Prentice-Hall Inc., Englewood Cliffs, New Jersey, 1989 (201–592–2261).

[PICARDI86] Anthony C. Picardi, "Productivity Increases with the CORTEX Application Factory: Empirical Survey Results," DECUS Northeast Regional Conference, Boston, Massachusetts, June 5–6, 1986.

# Methodology

## RAD Methodology

We now have powerful tools for improving I.S. productivity. A study of corporations using them makes it clear that there is an enormous difference between what one I.S. organization and another has achieved using the same toolset. Some I.S. organizations using CASE tools are achieving over 100 function points per I.S. person-month; others with the same tools are achieving 10.

To make sure that it achieves good results, an I.S. organization needs a methodology that has been adapted to the toolset in question. The methodology specifies the *process* of development. It states the *tasks* that must be accomplished, how they are done and how they relate to one another. It should specify a PERT chart of tasks and, for each task, show the inputs and deliverables. It gives guidelines in the accomplishment of each task. Most tasks result in information being added to the I-CASE repository. The tasks should be based on experience and should describe what must be done to make the lifecycle as effective as possible.

For decades, development has been done by systems analysts using plastic templates and paper to create a binder of specifications. The specifications are used by programmers who do line-by-line coding with a third-generation language such as COBOL, FORTRAN, PL/I and so on. The code they produce requires extensive debugging.

Development in such an environment is very different from development by people trained to use modern toolsets, which integrate:

- prototyping;
- graphical computer-aided modeling and design;
- a repository of design information and reusable components;
- automation for enforcing design integrity;
- an integrated code generator, testing tools;
- thorough end-user interaction with developers, aided by tools.

Because of the difficulties in application development, methodologies were created to guide the developers. These methodologies were refined over the years and resulted in large binders of paperwork, which became corporate standards manuals or purchasable methodologies. Some became as large as 24 three-ring binders.

The methodology is used to train and guide the practitioners. The best techniques are written down and are steadily improved with experience. When things go wrong, warnings are incorporated in the methodology to help avoid stumbling into the same problems again.

---

### The New Fast-Development Techniques Need Methodologies.

These must specify:

- the sequence of tasks to be done;
- inputs to and deliverables from each task;
- a description of how to do the task, the people needed, the training needed;
- guidelines about how to succeed and what pitfalls to avoid.

---

### Box 4.1    Reasons for Needing a Recorded Methodology

- The best techniques are written down.
- The methodology forms the basis of training courses.
- All the developers are trained in the same methodology so that there is mutual understanding.
- The developers become highly skilled with the methodology.
- The methodology is steadily refined as experience in its use grows and as new ideas are tested.
- The methodology informs the developers about the best techniques.
- The methodology warns the developers of pitfalls that need to be avoided.
- The methodology can leverage the key resource: people, especially developers of exceptional ability.
- The methodology accumulates and refines the ideas of many creative people.
- In a computer, the methodology can be adapted to specific circumstances.
- The methodology encourages evolution of the toolset to aid or automate aspects of the methodology.
- An expert system may be built to guide the developers.

---

## Computerized Methodologies

Methodologies of the past have been on paper. Methodologies today should be in a computerized form. Box 4.2 lists reasons for computerizing methodologies.

As indicated elsewhere, the RAD methodology discussed in this book is presented in task-oriented detail in the *RAD Expert* tool, which runs on the same personal computer as the CASE tools used for RAD. This computerized methodology can be adapted to different tools and circumstances. Many development organizations are likely to add their experience, knowledge, standards and procedures to the computerized methodology [JMA].

**Box 4.2    Reasons for Computerizing Methodologies**

- It is convenient to have the methodology on the screen of the development workbench in hyperdocument form.
- Developers or I.S. managers may add their own techniques, guidelines or standards to the methodology or may change components of the methodology.
- The methodology should be tuned and improved as experience is gained.
- There may be many methodology variants, depending on the tools used.
- The methodology may be adapted to the installation standards.
- The methodology may be edited for the system in question.
- Project-management tools may be built into the computerized methodology (for example, estimating tools and PERT chart tools).
- The methodology may be an integral part of a CASE toolset.
- Parts of the methodology may be automated.
- The methodology may have built-in computer-based training.
- The methodology may have a built-in expert system.

# The Best Combinations of Techniques

Some authorities advocate *prototyping;* some advocate *reusable design and code;* some advocate *end-user workshops for planning and design;* various authorities advocate *fourth-generation languages, CASE tools, code generators, reverse engineering,* a *repository, automatic rule-based validations and coordination, data modeling, process modeling,* specialized *implementation teams,* and so on.

Any one of these is valuable if used correctly. However, in synergistic combinations, they become more powerful and bring a revolutionary change to the development process. To be as valuable as possible, the combination ought to fit under the umbrella discipline of information engineering; otherwise, uncoordinated, redundant systems will proliferate.

Modern development methodologies should connect all of the preceding techniques into the most effective combinations. Toolsets exist that support and automate the combinations. The methodology should guide the practitioners in the best use of the combined techniques. Such methodologies are evolving rapidly as the toolsets and experience with them evolve.

# Good and Bad Methodologies

While it is essential to have a methodology that spells out the RAD lifecycle, it is important to say that, in much I.S. development, the Methodology (with a capital *M*) is the problem.

The Methodology used in many I.S. organizations is a set of paperwork binders occupying a foot or more of shelf space. It specifies a rigid set of tasks that the developers must carry out. The tasks are often boring and time-consuming. Often, they require the creation of much paperwork. Many of the tasks may be irrelevant to the particular circumstances.

The Methodology creators assume that they know better than the developers. The developers, they suppose, are not very bright and must be told, blow by blow, what to do. In reality, the best development is often accomplished by skilled teams that know exactly what to do. They resent having to follow a slow and rigid methodology when they can build high-quality systems faster. There is a demotivating message in the Methodology: Management thinks that the developers are so uncreative that they must be told exactly what paperwork to fill in.

In the film *The Magnificent Men in Their Flying Machines*, there is a funny scene in which Kurt Frobe, a high-level German officer, explains that you operate the flying machine the way you do everything in the German Army—"by reading ze Book!" The German General Staff model of management does not work well for the RAD lifecycle. Instead, the developers are highly trained in the tools and techniques and are then expected to use their own initiative and creativity to build a quality system, while interacting with the users to ensure that it meets their needs.

Box 4.3 lists good and bad properties of a methodology. The RAD methodology should have the properties on the right-hand side of the box. It guides the development team in what has been proven to work best; it steers them away from pitfalls; it lists things that they might forget; but it does not impose a rigid bureaucracy on them. It assumes that they will use their own creativity within the limits of the guidelines. This form of methodology is particularly important and effective with today's I-CASE tools.

---

### Box 4.3   Good and Bad Properties of a Methodology

| BAD | GOOD |
|---|---|
| • Rigid. | • Fully adaptable to circumstances. |
| • Work-intensive. | • Minimizes manual work. |
| • Bureaucratic. Assumes that developers are not smart enough to do their own thinking. | • Assumes that the developers are intelligent and creative. |
| • Represented by a shelf of paperwork binders. | • Computerized. Designed to be adapted. May contain expert-system segments. |
| • Gives an inflexible set of tasks. | • Gives proven guidelines for success, warnings of pitfalls and checklists so that vital actions are not forgotten; developers apply these intelligently and flexibly. |
| • Developers do not understand why certain tasks are really necessary. | • Makes good sense to the developers. |

The most effective I.S. organization is constantly improving its methods. This will surely be true of the RAD lifecycle. The methodology must be alive, fluid and constantly improving.

The last act of a dying regime is to create a vast, unchangeable procedures manual.

# Ease of Change

Businesspeople in most corporations would like to change their procedures or move quickly into new competitive thrusts, but the necessary computer applications cannot be built and put into operation in time. Boxes 4.4a and 4.4b summarize the problems of computing as seen by users and management, and the technical problems that cause those concerns. A goal of RAD methodology must be to tackle all of these problems and solve them.

As well as making new development fast, the methodology should create systems that can be changed rapidly. The maintenance cycle time should be shrunk as much as the development cycle time. Most systems cost more to maintain over their lifetime than to build (Figure 4.1). Most large, old I.S. organizations have three quarters of their staff working on maintenance.

---

### Box 4.4a    Problems of Computing as Seen by Users and Managers

- Users cannot obtain applications when they want them. There is often a delay of years.
- It is difficult or impossible to obtain changes that managers need in a reasonable amount of time.
- Because of the long time taken to obtain results, systems important to the business are not implemented. I.S. development is a bottleneck that prevents management from changing the business in ways that would increase its competitiveness.
- The programs have errors or sometimes do not work.
- Systems delivered often do not match the true user requirements.
- It is difficult to understand I.S. professionals and to communicate precise requirements.
- Specifications, on which users have to sign off, are difficult to check and are usually full of inconsistencies, omissions and errors.
- Requirements change after the specifications are frozen.
- Systems cost much more to develop and to maintain than anticipated.
- The development process is not dynamic, as in the real world.

All of these problems can be solved by the RAD methodology.

## Box 4.4b   Technical Problems Causing Concerns Listed in Box 4.4a

- Programming in conventional languages takes too long.
- Program testing takes too long.
- After testing, too many subtle errors remain.
- Vendors' software is often of poor quality.
- Programs do not match specifications. There are misinterpretations.
- Specifications do not match requirements. There are misinterpretations.
- Requirements are always changing—even after the specifications are frozen.
- Users do not check and understand the details of specifications before coding begins.
- Specifications are verbose, ambiguous, incomplete, unspecific, inconsistent or incorrect.
- When programs are maintained, the specifications are not updated correspondingly.
- Structured techniques have not improved productivity by enough.
- Different programmers have different ideas of structured programming.
- The design of programs is not rigorous.
- Usage and modification of variables are not traceable.
- Seemingly small changes to programs set off chain reactions of problems.
- Maintenance successively degrades code quality.
- The design tools and languages are not integrated.
- Development techniques are not integrated.
- There are many interface problems among separately developed systems and even between modules within programs.
- There is excessive redundancy in program function.
- There is no organizationwide data planning.
- The same data are represented incompatibly in different systems.
- Programs are not transferable.
- Different programmers use different forms of user dialog, making systems unnecessarily difficult to use.
- There is resistance to new methodologies and adherence to obsolete ones.
- The I.S. standards manual enforces old, inappropriate methods.
- An excessive bureaucracy has grown up around old-fashioned methods.
- Management operates constantly in fire-brigade mode because of the preceding problems.
- Management tied down by detail is unable to plan better ways of operating.

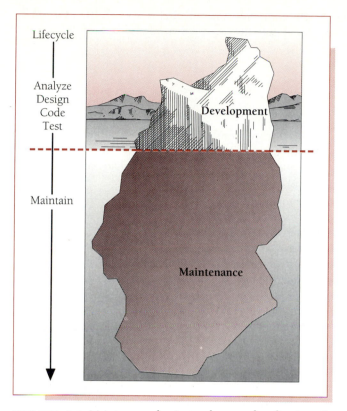

Lifecycle

Analyze
Design
Code
Test

Development

Maintain

Maintenance

FIGURE 4. 1  Maintenance dominates the cost of applications. In many organizations, software maintenance activities consume three quarters of the total lifecycle expenditures and I.S. personnel resources. The RAD methodology must lower the cost and time for maintenance as much as for new development.

The enterprise of the future needs systems that constantly evolve. They should be architected so that they can be added to and changed again and again, growing richer in functionality. Data models and process models stored in an I-CASE repository, along with standard templates for screens and dialogs, make practical an ongoing, orderly evolution.

Sometimes the requirements change unpredictably before a system is cut over. The techniques that make maintenance quick and easy make it possible to produce last-minute changes before cutover.

Nykredit, an organization that does computing for many Danish banks, built a system for processing foreign currency loans. It was a complex system with 70 IMS transactions. At the time the system was cut over, the Danish government changed the banking regulations, severely affecting the system. However, the system was built with a sound data model, using the Texas Instruments I-CASE tool, the *IEF* (Information Engineering Facility). The new legislation was enacted on Friday, February 24, 1989. The changes were incorporated into the design, and new code was generated over that weekend. On Monday morning, February 27, the system ran with the changes. Nykredit claimed that this gave them a "significant lead over our competitors" [LEE].

## Lifecycle Goals

The high-level goals of a lifecycle designed to take advantage of today's tools should be those of the three-ring diagram presented in Figure 4.2.

Some of the items in Box 4.5 go beyond the immediate goals of fast development. They include, for example, enterprisewide planning.

Enterprisewide planning and the creation of an I.E. infrastructure take time. However, once in place, an enterprise is likely to develop more valuable applications and be able to build them quickly. Application development can be greatly speeded up by having a rich set of reusable designs of data and processes in the repository of an integrated-CASE tool. An enterprisewide approach to data modeling, object-oriented design and reusable components may take two or three years to evolve but, once in place, it enables many applications to be built very rapidly.

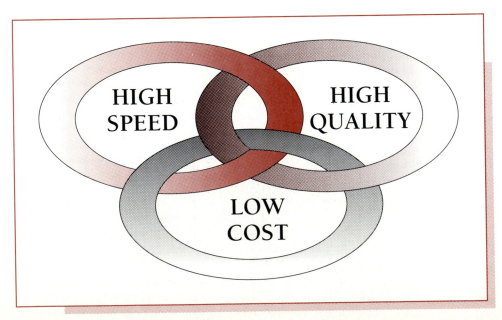

FIGURE 4.2 High-Level Goals of RAD

# Users Involved at Every Stage

One of the most important differences between a lifecycle designed for modern development tools and the classical lifecycle is that, today, the intended users of the system should be involved at every stage. The lifecycle needs to be designed to incorporate this involvement in a thorough way. It is only by involving the users throughout the development that we can achieve *high quality*, defining quality, as in Chapter 1, as "meeting the true business (or user) requirements as effectively as possible *at the time the system is cut over*." This measure of quality relates to the number of change requests from users in the period (say, eight weeks) after cutover. This number should be as low as possible, with a target of zero.

An objective of the RAD process is to get the user to assume "ownership" of the product before the product is complete. This ensures the proper partnership and helps generate functional quality.

# Four Phases

To help ensure that developers build what the users really need, the RAD lifecycle has four phases:

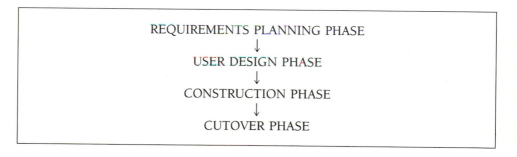

REQUIREMENTS PLANNING PHASE
↓
USER DESIGN PHASE
↓
CONSTRUCTION PHASE
↓
CUTOVER PHASE

### Requirements Planning Phase

The Requirements Planning Phase requires that high-level or knowledgeable end users determine what the functions of the system should be. There should be structured discussion of the business problems that need to be solved. This is done with the guidance of I.S. professionals. Requirements planning is usually best done in a workshop with well-structured procedures. It can usually be done quickly when the right users and executives are involved.

Chapter 7 describes the **Joint Requirements Planning (JRP)** workshop.

### User Design Phase

The User Design Phase requires that end users participate strongly in the nontechnical design of the system, under the guidance of I.S. professionals. User design is done in a **Joint Application Design (JAD)** workshop similar to the **Joint Requirements Planning (JRP)** workshop. There should be a smooth transition from the planning work-

## Box 4.5    What Do We Need in I.S. Methodologies?

- *Speed.* Techniques are needed that obtain results very quickly, with high-quality design and implementation.
- *Changeability.* Techniques are needed that enable programs to be changed quickly, without the cost and slowness of traditional maintenance.
- *Verification of Correctness.* All syntax errors and all possible internal semantics errors should be caught automatically. Maximum assistance should be provided in catching external semantics errors easily.
- *Quality.* Quality is defined as "meeting the true user needs as effectively as possible at the time the system is cut over."
- *Avoidance of a Specification Freeze When Requirements Are Changing.* The time between the end of *User Design* and delivery of the system should be as short as possible. The *Construction* Phase should allow user modifications to screens and transactions if necessary.
- *Creativity.* The methodology should encourage and aid creative thinking about possible system functions.
- *Avoidance of Hand Programming.* Hand programming is too slow, clumsy and error-prone. The maximum use should be made of code generators.
- *Bug-Free Operation.* The debugging of hand-written code is slow and expensive, does not catch all errors and should be replaced with automated code generation.
- *Techniques That Facilitate Communication with End Users.* The knowledge of the users must be harnessed and their needs responded to flexibly. Users should be able to check every stage of system evolution.
- *User-Driven Computing.* Users should be able to employ their own query and update languages, report generators, decision-support languages and specification languages.
- *Identification of Business Needs.* There should be formal interaction with high-level users that encourages identification of the ways in which new systems can improve the business.
- *Enterprisewide Planning.* An information-engineering approach should be taken to enterprisewide strategy, planning, data modeling and process modeling.
- *Enterprisewide Data Modeling.* Data should be modeled to avoid the Tower of Babel effect of different analysts creating the same data incompatibly.
- *Enterprisewide Process Modeling.* Processes should be analyzed across the enterprise to lessen the creation of unrelated versions of the same objects and to maximize the application of reusable design.
- *Overview Planning.* Complex organizations need overview planning for streamlining on-line procedures.
- *Stable Database Design.* Automation of data modeling is necessary, linked to techniques to make the databases a stable foundationstone.

- *Fast Database Languages*. Languages should be adopted that enable new information to be extracted from the databases for management immediately upon need.

- *Reusability*. Object-oriented planning and design should be done to achieve the maximum degree of reusable data structures, procedures, components, templates and designs that are used to generate code. High-quality applications or shells should be designed for reusability.

- *Modularity*. Systems should be divided into easily comprehensible modules. Changes should be able to be made locally within a module. Any effect of changes outside a module should be *rigorously* traceable.

- *Control of Interoperability*. A formal, rigorous, computerized technique is needed to ensure that separately developed systems and modules operate together correctly.

- *Automated Change Control*. When changes are made, the consequences of these should be revealed automatically, and the complete set of consequential corrections should be represented in the library.

- *Evolving Power*. The methodology should encourage an evolving set of more powerful mechanisms built with lower-level mechanisms. The mechanisms should be designed for reusability.

- *Evolutionary Growth of Systems*. Systems should be designed so that they can be added to, in a rigorously controlled fashion, by different people in different places at different times, so that they steadily evolve more comprehensive sets of capabilities.

- *Repository or Encyclopedia*. All systems information should be stored in a repository or encyclopedia that is on-line to the development tools. The repository or encyclopedia mechanisms should enforce integrity and consistency in all of the information stored.

- *Truly Usable Library Control*. There should be an ever-growing collection of reusable systems objects and components, with a methodology for making these known to and usable by all developers.

- *Expert System*. An expert system may be used to guide the practitioners and help them find and employ reusable components.

- *Integrated Set of Tools*. Tools that achieve the preceding objectives should work together and avoid manual bridges that introduce errors. They should use common syntax and graphics where possible.

- *Metrics*. There should be ongoing measurements of the effectiveness of I.S. development (Chapter 2).

- *Computer Representation of Methodology*. The methodology should be represented in a computer so that it can grow, evolve and be linked to computerized tools for the developers.

- *Fun*. The tools and techniques should be fun to use so that the developers' jobs are as enjoyable and creative as possible.

shop to the design workshop. Some of the users in the planning workshop should be present in the design workshop (Chapter 8).

In these first two phases, users of the application and user executives should play a larger role than I.S. professionals. Planning and user design should be done, to a large extent, by users, with I.S. providing a firm hand to guide them.

The User Design Phase uses I-CASE tools and prototyping. The users interact with the prototypes and help I.S. professionals create the CASE design specifications. The output of the User Design Phase should be not mere paperwork but rather *a design represented in an I-CASE tool, which will be taken directly into the Construction Phase, using a code generator* so that it progresses as quickly as possible.

The users do not sign off on a binder of paper specifications. Instead, they sign off on a design in an I-CASE tool. The Executive Owner of the system releases funds for its construction on the basis of the I-CASE design. Basing this commitment on the I-CASE design rather than on a binder of paperwork has several major advantages:

- The user design has computerized precision.
- The user design has more detail than is usual with paper-based specifications.
- The I-CASE tool can fully cross-check the integrity of the design.
- The user design can be done much faster than the traditional I.S. authoring of specifications.
- Particularly important, the I-CASE tool facilitates extension of the user design into technical design and code generation. This can be done relatively quickly.

When the end users and user executives agree to the user design, it should meet their needs well. It can be taken into code generation quickly; so, the needs are unlikely to change much before the system is cut over. There might be a 3-month gap between user sign-off and cutover rather than an 18-month gap, which is common with the traditional lifecycle. During 18 months, the business can change fundamentally.

## Construction Phase

In the traditional development lifecycle, detailed design is a separate phase from programming. First, specifications are written, then detailed design is done, then the code is written and, finally, substantial time is taken to debug the code. With an I-CASE toolset, the relationship between design and coding changes. A detailed design is built on the screen of an I-CASE tool, and code is generated from it. The code should be free from coding errors (though it often has design errors). It can be run immediately, then adjusted as desired.

In the traditional lifecycle, a team of analysts may design the application, and a separate team of programmers may code and debug it. In the RAD Construction Phase, I.S. professionals do the detailed design and code generation of one transaction after another, using the I-CASE toolset. They may show each transaction, as it is built, to end users and make adjustments to it. The computerized coordination of the I-CASE toolset integrates the separate transactions.

End users are closely involved during the Construction Phase. They validate the screens and design of each transaction as it is built. If there is a serious change in requirements during the Construction Phase, the end users make it known. Testing of the generated system is done throughout the process. In this way, construction can proceed quickly, with ongoing user involvement to ensure that the delivered product meets the needs of the users when it is cut over. There should be no surprises for the users when the system is installed because they have participated in its construction.

The I-CASE toolset should generate the coded database descriptions, as well as executable program code. It should also generate technical documentation, thus ensuring that the documentation exactly describes the generated system. A final stage of the Construction Phase may be to perform database optimization and use a code optimizer to enhance the run-time performance of the code. When this is done, good code generators give about the same run-time performance as skilled programmers. (See Chapters 9 and 10.)

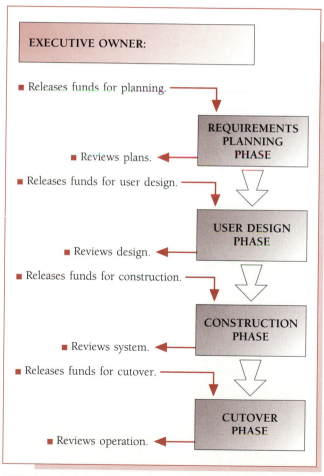

FIGURE 4.3 System implementation with automated tools should proceed in four phases, as shown, with approval from the Executive Owner (Executive Sponsor), who controls the system budget, prior to each phase.

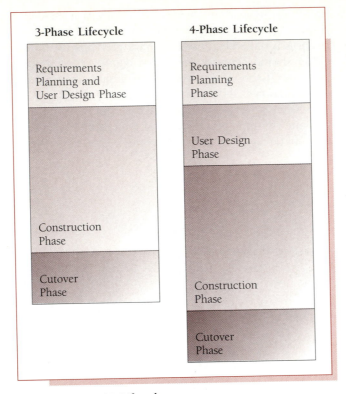

FIGURE 4.4 RAD Lifecycles
In the four-phase lifecycle, Requirements Planning and User Design are separate phases. In the three-phase lifecycle, they are combined. The three-phase lifecycle is used when system requirements
are already well known or obvious.

## Cutover Phase

When the system is cut over, a variety of actions is needed, including comprehensive
testing, training the end users, organizational changes and operation in parallel with
the previous system until the new system settles in. Because the Construction Phase
is relatively rapid, planning and preparation for cutover must begin early. Some of this
planning is done in the Requirements Planning Phase, and detailed preparation is
begun in the User Design Phase. (See Chapters 18 and 19.)

At the start of each of these phases, there should be approval from the user executive
whose money is going to be spent—the Executive Owner, as shown in Figure 4.3.

Where the requirements are simple or obvious, the Requirements Planning and
User Design Phases are combined, as shown in Figure 4.4.

# Timing

Figure 4.5 shows typical elapsed times for the four phases of fast development lifecycles. It shows 3-month and 6-month lifecycles.

Figure 4.6 breaks down the activities of a 5-month lifecycle into more detail.

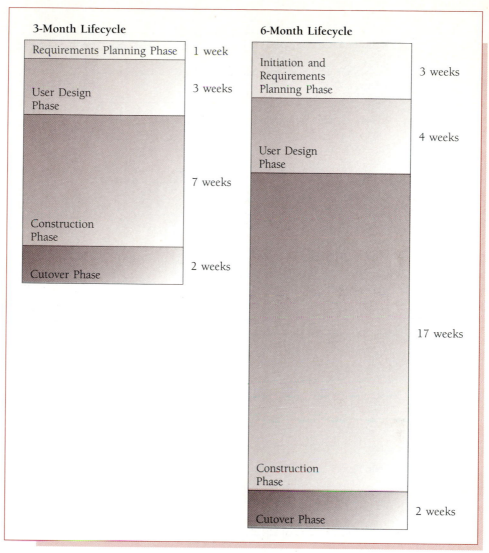

**3-Month Lifecycle**

| | |
|---|---|
| Requirements Planning Phase | 1 week |
| User Design Phase | 3 weeks |
| Construction Phase | 7 weeks |
| Cutover Phase | 2 weeks |

**6-Month Lifecycle**

| | |
|---|---|
| Initiation and Requirements Planning Phase | 3 weeks |
| User Design Phase | 4 weeks |
| Construction Phase | 17 weeks |
| Cutover Phase | 2 weeks |

FIGURE 4.5  Typical Times for the Four Phases of Fast Development
A 5-month lifecycle is shown in more detail in Figure 4.6.

Figure 4.7 shows the person-days worked on building a system of 1300 function points in a large insurance company and compares this experience with the estimates used for traditional development with a well-managed COBOL lifecycle.

Figure 4.7 is fairly typical of RAD experience. Many RAD projects achieve more than the 85 function points per person-month of Figure 4.7, and most traditional development achieves fewer than this organization's estimated 13.3 function points per person-month.

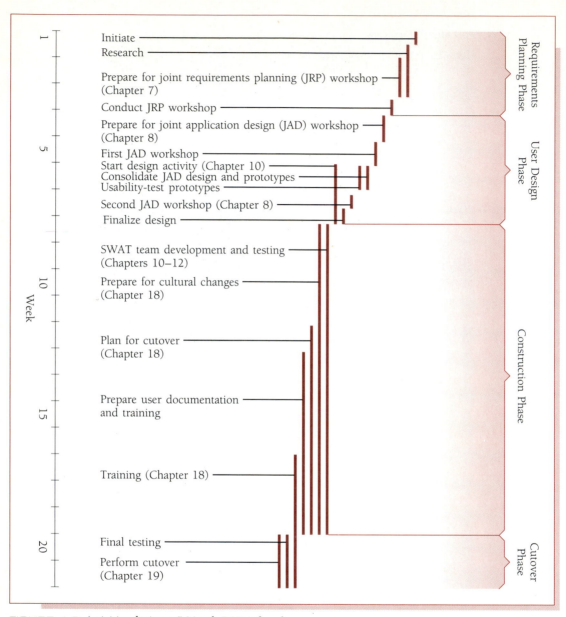

FIGURE 4.6  Activities during a 5-Month RAD Lifecycle

# Parallel Operations

Very fast supercomputers need parallelism. Complex problems are broken into many pieces that are executed simultaneously. To achieve fast development of complex systems, we need parallel development. The development needs to be broken into separate tasks that can be carried out simultaneously. The RAD lifecycle is not a relay

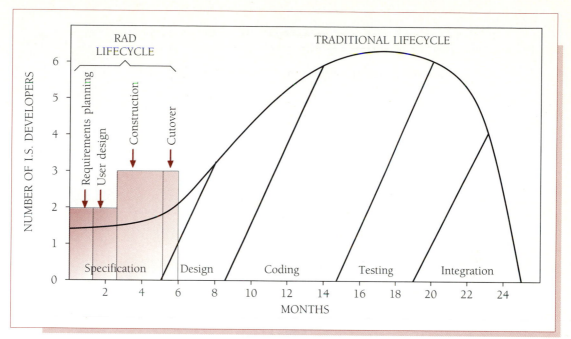

FIGURE 4.7 Actual RAD Lifecycle and Traditional Lifecycle for a System of 1300 Function Points in a Large Insurance Company

*Actual* function points per person month = 85 (counting I.S. staff only, not end users). *Estimated* function points per person month for the traditional lifecycle = 13.3.

race, but a race in which the runners are running alongside each other where possible.

Some parallel activities are shown in Figure 4.6. Figure 4.8 shows a lifecycle with a higher degree of parallelism. In practice, there is more parallelism in the Construction Phase than this figure shows because individual developers work on different transactions simultaneously.

A serious concern with parallel development is that the separately developed pieces may not fit together. Resolution of interface problems can be time-consuming. I-CASE tools help solve this problem. A coordinating model of the system is created, consisting of a rigorously normalized data model linked to a detailed process model. The system is divided into subsystems that all fit into the coordinating model. The I-CASE tool enforces correctness of the interfaces so that the subsystems fit together with computer-controlled precision. Small teams, and sometimes an individual developer, can then create the subsystems quickly, using the I-CASE code generator.

Parallel development is discussed in Chapter 12. The coordinating model is discussed in Chapters 13 and 14.

## Small Teams

A characteristic of RAD lifecycles is that they avoid large teams of developers. A team of two or three people can move rapidly; a large team bogs down and has problems with human communication. A small team can consist of people carefully selected,

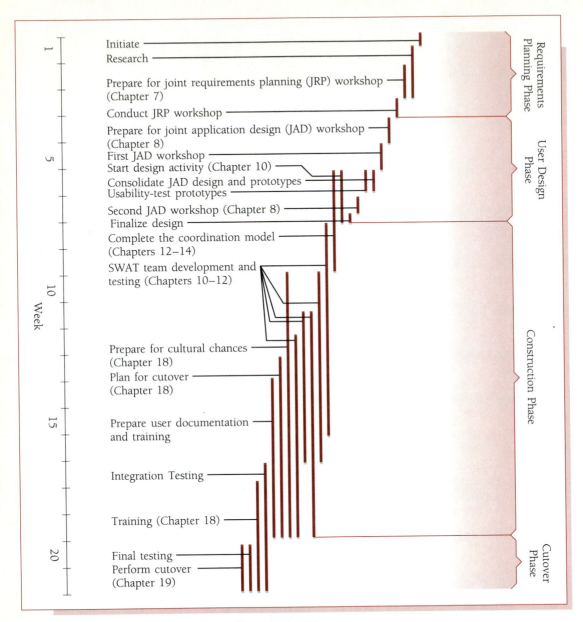

FIGURE 4.8 A RAD Lifecycle Similar to That in Figure 4.6
In this example, a higher degree of parallel operation is used to build a more complex system.

well trained, highly focused and well motivated. The small team should use the most powerful toolset so that it can move quickly. Figure 4.7 is a typical example of small-team RAD. The management and use of small, skilled teams are discussed in Chapters 10 and 11.

| APPLICATION | WORK EFFORT (person-days) | WORK PRODUCT (function points) | PRODUCTIVITY (function points per person-month) |
|---|---|---|---|
| Payroll | 146 | 995 | 150 |
| Bill of Materials | 84 | 673 | 176 |
| General Ledger | 57 | 384 | 148 |
| Parts Distribution | 39 | 387 | 218 |
| Order Entry | 1266 | 1765 | 31 |
| Telephone System | 60 | 349 | 128 |
| | | | Average 164 |

FIGURE 4.9 Productivity Measurements Made at the UNISYS LINC Customer Support Center, Atlanta, of Skilled UNISYS Developers Creating Applications with LINC [UNISYS85]

## Scaling Up

Some types of tool usage and methodology do not scale up well. They provide high productivity for small systems but do not work well for large systems. Figure 4.9 shows a set of measurements of developments using the UNISYS tool, LINC. Productivity, shown in the right-hand column, is high for systems of up to 1000 function points but falls off for the Order Entry system, which is more complex. The problem of larger team size is slowing down the development [UNISYS85].

It is desirable to have methodologies that scale up well for complex systems. This requires the computerized coordination of separate small-team efforts, as described in Chapter 12.

Large projects should be subdivided so that separate small teams work in parallel with precise, computerized coordination (Chapter 12). When several people or multiple teams work on a project, the tools need to be "groupware," which allows developers to share a repository, coordinating with precision the changes made by different developers.

## Reusability

One of the most important aspects of RAD methodology is the extent to which components that already exist can be used. The I-CASE repository can contain reusable templates, structures, data models, objects (entity-types with described properties and behavior) and applications. These preexisting designs can be modified as required, linked together and used to generate code. The more reusable design that can be employed, the greater the productivity and speed of development. The I-CASE toolset, with its repository and ability to enforce consistency among complex sets of designs, provides the support software needed for reusability on a large scale.

Figure 4.10 compares building a computer application with building a house.

| | BUILDING A HOUSE | BUILDING A COMPUTER APPLICATION |
|---|---|---|
| PRIMITIVE | Hand-cut trees. Use clay and sticks. | Hand-code a program in COBOL. |
| FASTER | Custom design and construct from bricks and lumber. | Custom design and generate code with an I-CASE tool. |
| HIGH SPEED HIGH QUALITY | Adapt existing designs and build using a catalog of existing panels, doors and components. | Adapt existing designs and build, using a repository of existing templates and components. |

FIGURE 4.10 Modern construction methods use existing designs and components to the fullest extent.

Hand-coding COBOL is a primitive way to proceed, like hand-cutting trees in order to build a house. I-CASE provides the application builder with power tools but, like a house builder with bricks and lumber, he has to do the design and construction from scratch. It is more efficient to use existing designs, templates and building blocks, which can be assembled and modified quickly, as with prefabricated panels, doors, windows and so on. The house builder can select components from catalogs; the application builder can select components from the I-CASE repository.

Systems may be built from reusable components that are *purchased*, or an I.S. organization may create its own collection of reusable components. The collection of reusable components tends to grow with time if the I.S. organization is managed for reusability.

Achieving a high level of reusability needs substantial management control. The I-CASE tool should facilitate this control. From the developers' point of view, the toolset must make it *easier to reuse components than to reinvent them.*

Chapters 15 and 22 discuss reusability.

# The Bigger Picture

When an application is needed urgently, the I.S. organization will often build it in the fastest way as an isolated project. With planning on a much larger scale, however, development can be made faster and more satisfactory.

An enterprise should set standards for its application architecture and create reus-

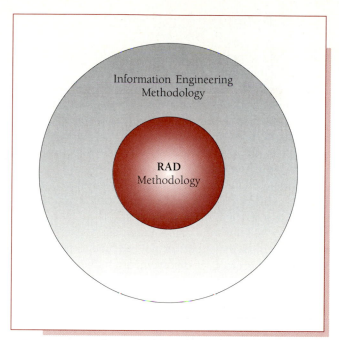

FIGURE 4.11 The methodology for rapid development should fit into the broader methodology for information engineering [MARTIN90].

able structures for transactions, database updating, sign-on, security and so on. It should perform data modeling across the enterprise and create an information-engineering framework. The RAD methodology then fits into the broader methodology of information engineering [MARTIN90].

Figure 4.11 depicts RAD in a broader I.E. methodology.

Some of the case examples we describe in other chapters are ones in which the broader framework has been established. Where this has been done with reusability and fast development as a major objective, the results are the most impressive of the case examples we studied.

An I.S. organization, thus, has one of three choices:

1. Establish a methodology that will facilitate fast development of applications *today*.
2. Establish an information-engineering environment that will facilitate fast development *in the future*.
3. Do *both* of these.

Almost always, the third choice is the best. An enterprise should select an I-CASE toolset with which it can do fast development now and also, with the same toolset, build a long-term infrastructure that will facilitate even faster development in the future. Chapters 20 through 22 discuss the long-range option.

# Avoiding Obsolete Methodologies

Realizing the seriousness of the problems in Box 4.4, many organizations have undertaken to create and sell "methodologies" for system planning and development. Methodologies are sold by consultants, accounting firms and new companies formed for this purpose. Many of these methodologies are utterly obsolete, including some with high prices, voluminous documentation and an impressive sales force. To use them guarantees low productivity, high maintenance costs and the inability to evolve the applications. They formalize the ways of the past, fail to automate system development, and encourage excessive, unnecessary bureaucracy.

The I.S. executive should be aware that application development is going through the greatest changes in its history and should meticulously avoid methodologies that fossilize the manually oriented techniques of the past.

What should a manager look for in new methodologies? Above all, *automation*. We must automate the lifecycle in an integrated fashion, as fully as possible. Second, better communication with the end users, user involvement at all stages of the lifecycle and

---

**Box 4.6   Methodology Charts at the End of This Book**

MC 7:      Requirements Planning Phase
MC 8:      The User Design Phase
MC 9:      Prototyping
MC 10–1: The Management of SWAT Teams
MC 10–2: Construction Phase
MC 11:     Timebox Development
MC 12:     Parallel Development
MC 13:     Data Modeling
MC 14–1: Procedure for Creating a Process Model
MC 14–2: Creation of the Coordinating Model
MC 15:     Actions Taken to Achieve Generic Reusability
MC 18–1: Preparing for Cultural Changes
MC 18–2: Perform Cutover
MC 19:     Cutover Phase
MC 21–1: I.E. Procedure for Information Strategy Planning (ISP)
MC 21–2: I.E. Procedure for Business Area Analysis (BAA)
MC 22:     Identifying Reusable Modules
MC 23:     Rapid Maintenance
MC 24:     Migration and Reverse Engineering
MC 25–1: Timetable for 13-Week RAD Lifecycle (around 1000 function points)
MC 25–2: Timetable for 21-Week RAD Lifecycle (around 3000 function points)
MC 25–3: Timetable for 26-Week RAD Lifecycle (around 5000 function points)
MC 25–4: Essentials for Maximum Success

flexible adaptation to their changing needs. These goals fit together because the automated tools enable us to work with the users in a prototype-evolution fashion, rather than freeze them out while we code COBOL.

Box 4.6 lists the Methodology Charts associated with other chapters, each of which is one window into a broader methodology hyperdocument [JMA]. These are provided at the end of the book.

# References

[JMA] *RAD Expert*, a methodology in hyperdocument form adaptable to different toolsets, available from James Martin Associates, Reston, Virginia (703–620–9504).

[LEE] Detail of the Nykredit experience is from Michael Lee, a consultant from James Martin Associates, who worked on the system.

[MARTIN90] James Martin, *Information Engineering* (a trilogy), Prentice-Hall, Inc., Englewood Cliffs, New Jersey, 1990 (201–592–2261).

[UNISYS85] Figures are from the UNISYS Customer Support Center, Atlanta, Georgia, 1985.

# CHAPTER 5

# People

Fast application development, like ocean racing, is highly dependent on people. There are certain critical players who must know their role and perform it well. In ocean racing, it is necessary to have an excellent sailing boat, but this alone would not win the race. The people must be a special and highly trained team. For fast development, excellent tools are needed, but people must know how to use the tools and work together as closely knit teams trained to use a well-designed methodology.

| Box 5.1 Key Players in the RAD Lifecycle |
| --- |

This cast of characters will be referred to throughout the book.

**From the I.S. Community:**

- **Project Manager.** The person responsible for the overall development effort.
- **Construction Team (SWAT Team).** A small team of implementors, highly skilled with the toolset, who build the system—typically two, three or four people (Chapter 10).
- **RAD Workshop Leader.** A specialist who organizes and conducts the workshops for Joint Requirements Planning (Chapter 7) and Joint Application Design (Chapter 8).
- **Scribe.** The person who records what is decided in the JAD sessions.
- **Human-Factors Expert.** Specialist in human factoring who is responsible for usability testing (Chapter 17).
- **Data Modeling Expert.** A specialist with experience in data modeling who can create data models rapidly and competently (Chapter 13).
- **Repository Manager.** Executive responsible for the I-CASE repository and its integrity. He may control what reusable constructs are in the repository. The Repository Manager is particularly important in an environment of Information Engineering (Chapter 21) reusable design. (See Chapters 15 and 22.)

---

**From the User Community:**

- **Executive Owner**. Sometimes called **Executive Sponsor**; a high-level user executive who funds the system and "owns" it. This executive must be *committed* to achieving results quickly.
- **System Champion**. Person who perceives the value of the system and becomes determined to introduce it into the organization. Ideally, the system champion is an end user, an I.S. person knowledgeable and enthusiastic about particular applications or improved procedures; sometimes, it is the Executive Owner.
- **User Coordinator**. A user appointed by the Executive Owner to oversee the project from the users' viewpoint. (Sometimes this individual is the Executive Owner or a person appointed by the Executive Owner.)
- **Requirements Planning Team (JRP Team)**. The team of high-level users who participate in the requirement planning workshop (Chapter 7).
- **User Design Team (JAD Team)**. The team of users who participate in the design workshop. Some of these may be members of the Requirements Planning Team. Others should be able to participate in more detailed design (Chapter 8).
- **Construction Assistance Team**. Certain end users are selected to provide this help to the I.S. Construction Team. They are called the Construction Assistance Team (CAT).
- **User Review Board**. The team of users who review the system after construction and decide whether any modifications are needed before cutover; they also deal with user decision deadlocks along the way.
- **Training Manager**. Person responsible for training users in how to use the system.

---

# Executive Owner

Perhaps the most important player is the **Executive Owner**. Some organizations use the term **Executive Sponsor**. This person is a high-level user executive who wants the system and who is committed to it. The Executive Owner makes the business decision that the system is needed and provides the money for it. He "owns" the system and is, ultimately, responsible for it.

The Executive Owner must be committed to fast development of the system. He should understand the procedures of the RAD lifecycle and should read this book.

The Executive Owner is responsible for cutting through any bureaucracy or politics that may slow down the building of the system. Any questions about the requirements or design that cannot be resolved at a lower level should be taken to the Executive Owner. (See Appendix III.)

# Funding the System

The Executive Owner should release the funds for the system in four stages, as shown in Figure 5.1. First, funds are released for Requirements Planning. This has a relatively small budget. The last act of the Requirements Planning Phase is to make a presentation to the Executive Owner. If satisfied that the requirements are well thought out, he releases the funds for the User Design Phase.

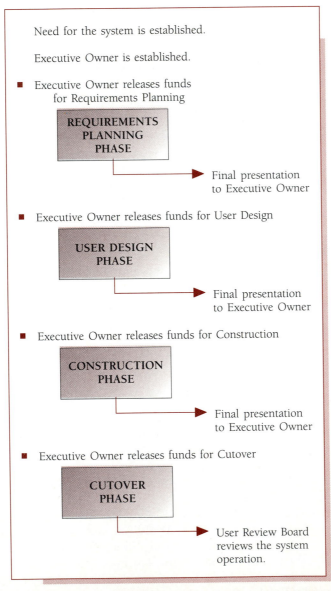

Need for the system is established.

Executive Owner is established.

■ Executive Owner releases funds
    for Requirements Planning

**REQUIREMENTS
PLANNING
PHASE**

→ Final presentation
   to Executive Owner

■ Executive Owner releases funds for User Design

**USER DESIGN
PHASE**

→ Final presentation
   to Executive Owner

■ Executive Owner releases funds for Construction

**CONSTRUCTION
PHASE**

→ Final presentation
   to Executive Owner

■ Executive Owner releases funds for Cutover

**CUTOVER
PHASE**

→ User Review Board
   reviews the system
   operation.

FIGURE 5.1  Releasing the Funds for the Four Phases of RAD
(See Figure 5.2.)

The last act of the User Design Phase is, again, to make a presentation to the Executive Owner. If he is convinced that the users are happy with the design, he releases funds for the Construction Phase.

The last stage of the Construction Phase is a review by a User Review Board. When the Review Board is convinced that the system should be put into operation, the Executive Owner releases funds for the Cutover Phase.

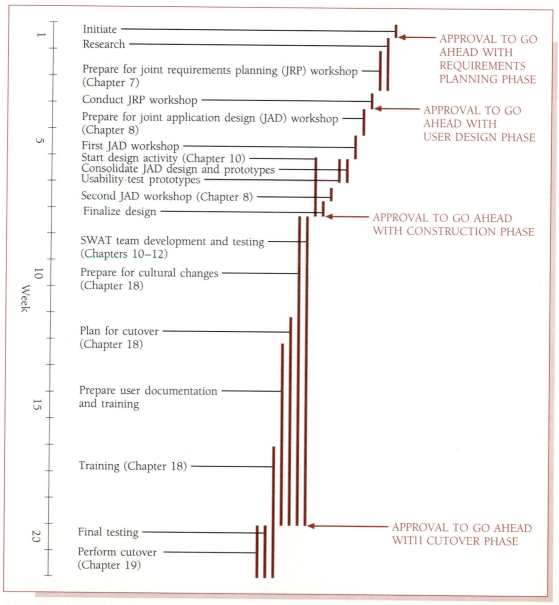

FIGURE 5.2 At the start of each phase, the Executive Owner (Sponsor) gives the approval to go ahead and releases the funds.

Figure 5.2 depicts a timetable for the approval of phases and the release of funds for subsequent phases.

# System Champion

A *champion* of an idea is the person who perceives the value of that idea and becomes determined to introduce it into an organization. The champion relentlessly pursues the idea, persuading people of its value, until it becomes reality.

The **champion of a system** is sometimes the Executive Owner of that system, sometimes not. The champion may persuade a different executive that he needs the system.

It is generally best if the system champion is an end user. Sometimes it is an I.S. person who is knowledgeable and enthusiastic about a particular application or who can see a way to improve procedures.

# End Users

We have commented that a characteristic of the RAD lifecycle is that users are involved at every stage. Because the lifecycle is short, they can see the results of activities they start. They are, therefore, more interested and more committed. In the lengthy traditional lifecycle, users see the specifications for a system and then forget about it for 18 months or more.

With traditional development, the managers who initiate the system often will have left by the time it is cut over. If it fails or appears ill-thought-out, the new managers can happily blame the previous regime. Sometimes they surreptitiously want it to fail so that they can demonstrate that they know better. With the RAD lifecycle, the managers who start a project are more easily held *accountable* for it because they will probably be there when it becomes operational. They have a strong incentive to make it succeed. They make whatever adjustments to the system are needed to make it as useful as possible. If the beginnings are far back in the forgotten past, this accountability is lost. The accountability of the System Champion and Executive Owner are important for ensuring success.

To ensure that the users are fully involved, groups of key users are selected to participate in every phase. They may form the following groups:

- Requirements Planning Team;
- User Design Team;
- Construction Assistance Team;
- User Review Board;
- Cutover Team.

To a large extent, the same users play successive roles in this activity; so, it does not require a large number of people.

# Requirements Planning Team (JRP Team)

The team of high-level users who participate in the requirement planning workshop (Chapter 7) is referred to as the **Requirements Planning Team**.

Requirements planning is done in a user Joint Requirements Planning (JRP) workshop (Chapter 7). A team of high-level users participates in this workshop and identifies the requirements under the guidance of a workshop leader. The Executive Owner may be part of the Requirements Planning Team and may (or may not) be its leader. Members of the Requirements Planning Team need to be able to think creatively about how operations could be changed by using the system. They need to be able to make business judgments about the value of possible system features.

# User Design Team (JAD Team)

The **JAD Team** is the team of users who participate in the design workshop. Some of these may be members of the Requirements Planning Team. Others should be able to participate in more detailed design (Chapter 8).

A workshop similar to the Joint Requirements Planning (JRP) workshop is used in the User Design Phase (Chapter 8). The team of users who participate in the design usually includes some of those who were in the Joint Requirements Planning workshop. In this phase, decisions are made about finer detail in the design of the system. This requires talents somewhat different from those of requirements planning. Users who will work with the eventual system should be part of the User Design Team.

Members of the User Design Team will monitor the evolution of the system during the Construction Phase, ensuring, for example, that transaction screens are easily usable and do not omit important items.

The Requirements Planning Team may nominate the users who participate in the User Design Team. A final selection will be made by the RAD Workshop Leader when doing the JAD preparation.

# Construction Assistance Team (CAT)

Construction is performed by creating prototypes or building transactions that can be quickly reviewed by key users. The transactions are adjusted during construction to ensure that they meet the user needs. The system, as it evolves, may be usability-tested with end users to minimize difficulties that could be encountered in using the system.

Certain end users are selected to provide this help to the I.S. Construction Team. They are called the **Construction Assistance Team (CAT)**. They should be available, if needed, for a short time every day during the Construction Phase. These users may be the same ones involved in the User Design Phase.

# User Review Board

The **User Review Board** is the team of users who review the system after construction and decide whether any modifications are needed before cutover.

At the end of the Construction Phase, a User Review Board should examine the system and determine whether it is suitable for cutover. It may decide that minor modifications or additions are needed before cutover. The Review Board reports to the Executive Owner, who decides whether to cut over the system.

The Review Board may consist of the same individuals as the Requirements Planning Team. If there are different individuals, they may be appointed by the Requirements Planning Team. (See Appendix III.)

# Cutover Team

Many activities have to occur in order to implement the system, including training, creating user documentation and, possibly, changing people's jobs. Much planning and preparation are needed for this, and time is short because the RAD lifecycle is short. The bottleneck with RAD is often not system development but *the rate at which the user organization can adapt to the system*. Users, rather than I.S., are on the critical path.

The cutover tasks must be reviewed at the start of the lifecycle, and people should be assigned responsibility for the tasks.

# Project Manager

This is the person responsible for the overall development effort.

The **Project Manager** is the I.S. person responsible for development of the system and is sometimes responsible for more than one project simultaneously. In a project with a single Construction Team, the Project Manager may be the leader of the Construction Team. He manages the RAD lifecycle to ensure that its phases are well planned and executed on time, with no essential component missing.

# RAD Workshop Leader

This is a specialist who organizes and conducts the workshops for Joint Requirements Planning and Joint Application Design (Chapters 7 and 8).

The workshop technique for Joint Requirements Planning and Joint Application Design is highly dependent on the skills of the workshop leader. We refer to this person as the **RAD Workshop Leader**. The skills he needs are discussed in Chapter 7.

The RAD Workshop Leader should be regarded as a professional in this activity. It is his job to conduct workshops repeatedly for Joint Requirements Planning and Joint Application Design. The more workshops he conducts, the more skilled he becomes at it.

# Scribe

The **Scribe** is the person who records what is decided in the JAD sessions.

In the early JAD sessions, the Scribe produced paper documentation. Predesigned forms were available for recording much of the documentation [IBM84].

With RAD JAD, the Scribe uses an I-CASE toolset and, wherever possible, records the planning and design information in I-CASE format. The medieval word "Scribe" now describes a person skilled with a computerized tool.

The Scribe uses the I-CASE tool during the session to document and validate the design, remove inconsistencies, generate screen and report designs, and illustrate the design to the participants as it emerges. During breaks or in the evening, he may polish it, possibly adding to it or raising questions for further discussion.

# Construction Team (SWAT TEAM)

Construction is done by a small team of implementors, highly skilled with the toolset, who build the system; typically two, three or four people (Chapter 10).

For large projects, there will be multiple Construction Teams (Chapter 12).

Fast development should be done by *small teams* of implementors. These teams are described in Chapter 10. The team members are carefully selected so that they *work well together* and *move fast*. The Construction Team should consist of *excellent, highly motivated professionals* who are *well trained and skilled* with the tools.

With a powerful I-CASE tool, small systems may be constructed by one person. Medium-sized systems (say, 400 to 2000 function points) may be constructed by one Construction Team of the type described in Chapter 10. Large systems (over 2000 function points, say) may be subdivided so that they can be built by more than one team working simultaneously (Chapter 12). The preceding numbers vary with the power of the toolset and the experience using it. Where more than one team work on different parts of a system, there needs to be computer-controlled coordination of their work so that the pieces fit together. They build with a common coordinating model in the I-CASE repository (Chapters 12, 13 and 14).

The **Construction Team Leader** is often a different person from the I.S. Project Manager. This person uses the I-CASE toolset to build the system and guides the other builders on the team. The Construction Team Leader is a master builder, skilled at using the tools, rather than an administrator. The I.S. Project Manager is more administrative, pulling the act together, ensuring that the resources are available and ensuring that every activity in the RAD lifecycle happens on time.

The members of the Construction Team must be highly trained with the I-CASE toolset and able to move fast with it. The design of the workshops for training in tool use is critical. Mentor-based training works particularly well. As in the medieval craft guilds, an **Apprentice Builder** should work with an experienced builder to learn the skills. A **Masterbuilder** is expert and fast at all aspects of construction with the toolset, including the use of reusable components and knowing what reusable components are available. A **Journeyman Builder** may work with the Masterbuilder to improve his skills.

The titles Apprentice Builder, Journeyman Builder and Masterbuilder have been used in some organizations for the new breed of RAD professionals.

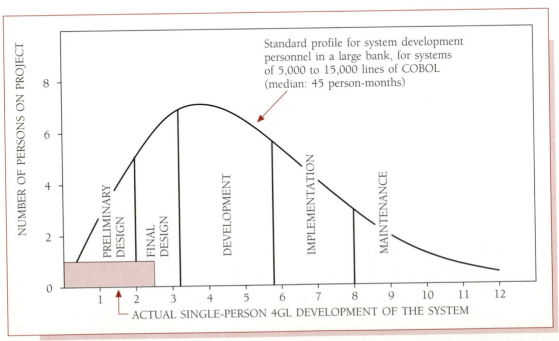

FIGURE 5.3 The highest development productivity is often achieved on one-person projects, where that person has made himself skilled with a powerful development tool. This example is from a large New York bank.

A small Construction Team generally has much higher productivity than a large team because there are difficulties in controlling communications within a large team. The highest productivity often occurs with one-person construction, especially if that person is bright and highly skilled with a powerful tool. Figure 5.3 shows an example.

Careful attention is needed in building the team, in selecting bright people who complement each other and work well together and in motivating the team. The team members should be thoroughly trained on the toolset and should know how to achieve speed and quality with it.

# Human-Factors Expert

This is the person responsible for ensuring that systems are well human-factored.

Usability testing should be done to ensure that systems are as easy to learn and use as possible. A **Human-Factors Expert** may be responsible for guidance in screen and dialog design and for usability testing. This professional may operate a usability testing facility that serves many projects (Chapter 17).

# Data Modeling Expert

The **Data Modeling Expert** is a specialist with experience in data modeling; he can create data models rapidly and competently (Chapter 13).

A data model is an important part of the system design, especially in complex systems built by multiple teams and in systems that link into a shared database environment. Some professionals have experience in data modeling, are highly skilled at it and can create correct models quickly.

The Data Modeling Expert may be a data administrator or part of the data administration staff. Because of the importance of data modeling, the availability of a skilled data modeler is desirable. This individual may be called upon for many separate projects.

# Repository Manager

The executive responsible for the I-CASE repository and its integrity is called the **Repository Manager**.

A repository is the heart of an I-CASE environment. Many projects share information from a central repository. The coordinating model is essential for projects with development by multiple teams (Chapter 12). In an environment of information engineering or reusable designs, the repository has a broader set of objectives (Chapters 21 and 22). A person is needed to manage the repository and coordinate the information in it. (See Appendix III.)

# Training Manager

The **Training Manager** is the person responsible for training users in how to use the system.

Users of new systems must be trained. A Training Manager arranges for the design and creation of training materials and plans the training process (Chapter 19). On some systems, user staff members are responsible for training; on others, training is done by the I.S. staff. (See Appendix III.)

# Chief Information Engineer

The best examples of fast development are often found in an information-engineering environment, especially one designed to maximize reusable design. In such an environment, an executive is needed to take charge of the overall I.E. effort and of the central repository for I.E. Sometimes he has the title **Chief Information Engineer** and reports to the Chief Information Officer.

# Key Players at Each Stage

At each phase of a project, there are certain activities that need to move fast. The people who can make this happen should be highly motivated. They must have deadlines and be motivated to meet the deadlines.

The people who need to act with speed are different at different stages of the lifecycle. At the start, it is critical that management, including the Executive Owner, initiate the project quickly, cutting through any potential political delays or bureaucracy. At the Requirements Planning stage, the key end users must participate in the Joint Requirements Planning workshop and, following that, users must move quickly in Joint Application Design. When the system is being constructed, the I.S. team that uses the I-CASE toolset to do detailed design and code generation must be geared to move fast. At the end of the lifecycle, the team that does training and cutover must move quickly.

Nobody should be under pressure all the time, and high-speed development does not require that anyone should be. In the Requirements Planning and early User Design Phases, the users should be under pressure to think out their needs and convert them into a design quickly. At the Construction stage, the pressure moves to the Construction Team. During cutover and preparation for cutover, user executives responsible for bringing about the system need to move with appropriate speed.

To avoid delays at any part of the lifecycle, each phase needs to come into play on time, like a well-produced stage show. The players for each phase need to be ready to play their role and highly motivated to move fast and work hard for their part of the project. Skilled planning needs to be coupled with careful human motivation. Figure 5.4 shows the critical players at each stage of the five-month lifecycle illustrated in Chapter 4.

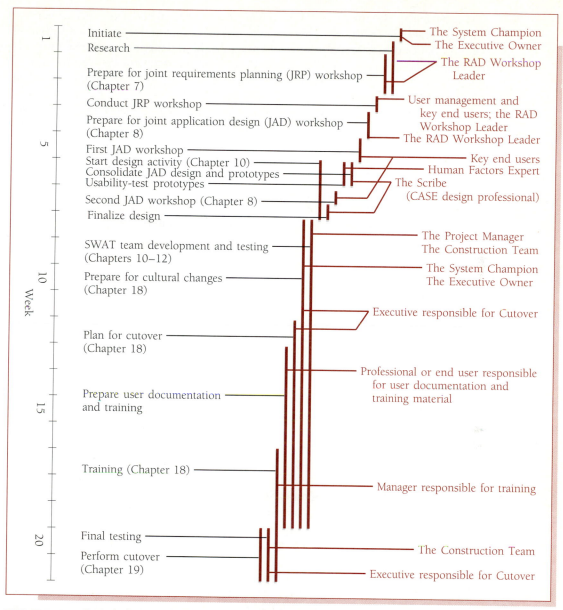

FIGURE 5.4  Critical Players at Each Stage of a 5-Month Lifecycle

# One-Person Development

While we have described a substantial cast of characters, there are many examples of one person doing the entire development of a system—sometimes a complex system. One person plays all of the I.S. RAD roles. Today's toolsets are powerful enough to make this possible.

A spectacular example occurred at the Security Pacific Bank. The bank decided to enter the asset sales business. This involves selling corporate loans to such buyers as regional banks, domestic subsidiaries of foreign banks and large institutional investors like insurance companies and brokerage firms. Top management decided to capture this market with an all-out assault which has been described as being like the Allied invasion of Normandy.

In 1986, when Security Pacific made its first asset sale, Bankers Trust Company and Citibank were two of the entrenched market leaders. By 1988, the new Security Pacific group was ahead of the former front runner, Bankers Trust. Its gross sales were twice those of Bankers Trust. It sold $400 billion worth of corporate loan assets in 1988, earning $100 million for the bank, with a staff of about 50.

This activity needed complex computer applications. Medium-term (one- to five-year) asset sales required different computing from short-term asset sales. They include leveraged buyout financing and recapitalizations, loan syndications and restructurings. The legal requirements are very complicated and are constantly changing. Each deal is unique and requires a dedicated application to support it, often with as little as 10 days' advance notice.

The Operations Vice President, Joseph Holliday, retained a consultant, Mike Joblin, to build the applications, and it was critical that they be built quickly. Joblin was free to use the bank's computers, which included various VAXes. Joblin started with a fourth-generation language, but as the complexities grew, it proved too unwieldy. He switched to an I-CASE toolset, *CorVision* from Cortex, which generates code. Joblin built his own family of reusable structures from which he could create new asset loan applications quickly. In slightly over two years, Joblin created more than 900,000 lines of code with *CorVision*. His system for medium-term asset sales had over 500 menu choices and 250 reports and dealt with a wide array of regulatory requirements. He also built billing and sales-lead tracking systems.

Holliday states that Security Pacific has a reputation for having more accurate data than its competitors, and that helps its salespeople get more business [CORTEX89]. The sales and front-office staff can make any deal they want because they know that the requisite computer application can be built quickly.

In complex, one-person development, that person (Joblin, in the cited Security Pacific Bank case) can create a large collection of reusable designs from which new applications can be created quickly with a code generator. If there are multiple developers, a challenge is to manage reusability so that all of them can select and modify the reusable components and add to the repository of components.

What the one person in the Security Pacific case built in two years would have taken hundreds of person-years with the traditional development lifecycle. Like some of the other examples in this book, the rapid development was strategically vital for the business. Without it, Security Pacific could not have moved with such spectacular success into the new business area.

## Turnover

When key developers leave, development productivity is harmed. In one typical organization with about 50 professionals, the recruitment of a new, skilled developer was likely to cost two months' salary, and building his skill level took about three

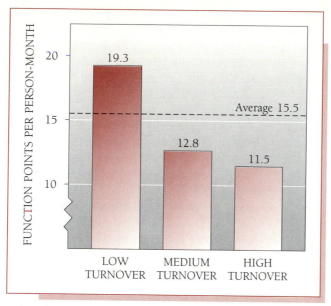

FIGURE 5.5 Having a high turnover of developers lowers the development productivity, as shown in this summary of 41 projects using a traditional lifecycle with some use of 4GL tools [DUPONT].

months. In addition, there were training costs and moving costs. The accountants calculated that a turnover of 20 per cent in the organization cost about $150,000 a year. However, the real cost was much higher because development productivity suffered.

Figure 5.5 shows the impact of turnover in the organization, which was a well-organized development shop using a traditional development lifecycle with productivity tools and use of fourth-generation languages [DUPONT]. The organization spent about $3 million per year on this development; so, the difference between the development costs with "high turnover" (11.5 function points per person-month) and those with "low turnover" (19.3 function points per person-month) represents about $1 million per year.

The hidden costs were even higher because slow development caused by high development turnover impeded the introduction of new efficiency measures and competitive business thrusts. This may have affected earnings by another $1 million per year.

*It is important to understand that high developer turnover is much more expensive than the accountants' calculations show.*

Turnover tends to be lower among developers who are excited about their jobs. We observed this excitement in well-managed RAD projects. Developers enjoy using powerful tools and creating results fast enough to see their effect. Morale is often lowest in long, drawn-out traditional lifecycles where a target delivery date is not achievable. High turnover on such projects makes a bad situation worse.

With a three-month lifecycle, there is a smaller chance of developers leaving in mid-project than with a two-year lifecycle. Developers who are members of a small, highly motivated Construction Team are likely to avoid leaving in mid-project so that they do not let their fellow team members down.

An important function of management in a RAD organization is to ensure that developers are excited about their jobs. Give them encouragement, rewards, stimulation and pleasant working conditions. Make them feel proud of what they do. Nurture them. Have a victory celebration at the end of each successful project. Make them feel that they are more respected here than they would be elsewhere. Make them feel a bond to the organization and to their development team.

Some I.S. organizations have very high turnover. Tom DeMarco and Timothy Lister, authorities on "peopleware," comment that typical turnover figures they encounter are in the range of 80 per cent to 33 per cent per year, implying an average employee longevity of from 15 to 36 months [DEMARCO&LISTER87]. In a healthy RAD development shop, there is a conscious management effort to have much lower turnover than these figures.

Some I.S. organizations treat analysts and programmers as disposable parts. ("Nobody is indispensable around here.") Because of this, the analysts and programmers have no sense of loyalty; they have no feeling of long-term involvement in the job. They believe that the route to high salaries is job hopping. In such an environment, turnover engenders turnover. People leave quickly, so management believes it is not worth spending money on training. Such organizations have had difficulty introducing an I-CASE environment and tuning it for high-speed development.

A RAD organization makes investments to build a high skill level in its teams and should keep the teams together. It has a professional career path allowing the Masterbuilders to rise to high salaries. It should recruit developers who expect to stay. It should make them feel that they are a special part of the organization and probably could not be as special elsewhere.

# Brilliant People

Brilliant developers achieve higher productivity than average developers. One of the characteristics of the programming profession is that good programmers can create three times as much bug-free code as the average programmer; genius programmers create ten times as much. The worst programmers are much worse than the average. The good programmer often creates far more elegant program designs than the average; the worst makes an unholy mess.

When innovative code has to be created quickly, it helps to use brilliant programmers. However, genius programmers are in short supply, and they tend to have problems, such as not doing documentation, writing code that others cannot maintain and, sometimes, turning into prima donnas who view the world in strange ways.

I-CASE tools change this situation. They enforce well-structured design. A new developer can easily understand and modify someone else's design. The design is highly graphic, easy to understand and easy to modify. There is less scope for a genius to do something special; so, some brilliant programmers do not want to work with I-CASE tools. I-CASE tends to have a leveling effect: the brilliant developer does better than the average developer, but not ten times better. Most intelligent analysts can become highly skilled with I-CASE tools and usually find them fun to use.

If programming is an art, I-CASE development is an engineering discipline. The art and creativity in I-CASE development are not in devising code structures but in thinking about how to improve the world of the end user, sometimes fundamentally restructuring how information is handled. This rethinking of procedures requires intelligent designers.

Where innovative procedures must be developed and built quickly, it pays to have brilliant developers, their brilliance applied more to business problems than to coding. Many examples of fast development are fast because the developers are much better than average. It pays to put the best developers on the most urgent systems.

In general, for fast development, the best people should be trained to use the best tools and organized into small teams that can move with speed.

The end users who help should be bright people with good communication skills. There should be careful selection of users who are likely to innovate and avoid the types of argument or bureaucracy that slow things down.

The RAD lifecycle needs to avoid people who have retired on the job. Many people strive for promotion, reward and success up to a certain point but, eventually, they realize that the difference between ''busting their guts'' and taking it easy is about $1000 a year before taxes. They reach a switch-off point. Instead of aiming at the maximum possible, they aim at the minimum excusable. They avoid rocking the boat and keep out of the way of the storms of enthusiasm that periodically blow by. The RAD players are often younger people, excited by the technology, striving for accomplishment.

The RAD lifecycle is highly dependent on the quality of the RAD Workshop Leader and the Construction Team. These individuals need to be chosen with care. We describe their qualities in Chapters 7, 8 and 10. Training is very important to develop the requisite skills, and the individuals will grow on the job but, as with an ocean racing team, you could not train just *anybody* to win; you must pick the *right* people. The human qualities needed are there when you select the person. You cannot change the raw material. If you make a mistake in the selection, you will have to correct it.

Teams are very important in the RAD lifecycle. The Requirements Planning Team and the User Design Team stay together for a short period. The Construction Team, if it works well, should stay together for many projects. Each of these teams should be greater than the sum of its parts. The creative interaction among the team members should be an enjoyable experience and should generate better results than those that would have been achieved without team interaction. The players in each team need to be selected such that the interaction is as positive as it can be. The membership of the Construction Team may be adjusted if necessary to increase its effectiveness.

As we make machines increasingly easy to communicate with (the good I-CASE systems are user-friendly), the work of building systems becomes more of a sociological problem and less of a technical problem. Many of the components of RAD methodology are intended to improve the facility for human communication. Increasingly, the choice of people to participate in the lifecycle needs to focus on their skills in human interaction.

# References

[CORTEX89] Quoted in a press release about Security Pacific's Asset Sales Group from Cortex, Inc., Waltham, Massachusetts, August 23, 1989.

[DEMARCO&LISTER87] T. DeMarco & T. Lister, *Peopleware, Productive Projects and Teams*, Dorset House, New York, 1987.

[DUPONT] Plotted from development statistics for 41 projects over a 5-year time period in the Fibers Department, E. I. duPont de Nemours and Company, Inc., Wilmington, Delaware, 1989. Fourth-generation languages FOCUS and NATURAL were employed, as well as COBOL and PL/I.

[IBM84] IBM Overview Pamphlet, *JAD, Joint Application Design*, IBM, White Plains, New York, 1984.

# CHAPTER 6

# Management

## Getting the Act Together

In doing the research for this book and the associated video series, we examined many enterprises that have achieved fast development of applications, in some cases very complex applications. The results were frequently impressive, sometimes achieving more than 200 function points per person-month. The techniques used are the basis for RAD methodologies. Nevertheless, we found no enterprise that we thought was doing *everything* right. All of the examples, although impressive, could have been even better. We often felt the desire to take a technique from one installation to another installation.

Achieving high-speed development is a complex act to get together. We felt that no enterprise had the whole act together. To operate a jumbo jet passenger service is a complex act. If part of the act is missing, the result will not be good. Some attempts at fast development were mediocre because inadequate CASE tools were used. Some misfired because of user problems. Some did not emphasize quality. One of the most powerful approaches to fast development involves *reusable design*, as described in Chapters 15 and 22. Most of the organizations we studied were not employing reusable design. Some that *were* did not have a code generator; some did not have a CASE repository. Reusability has a long-term payoff, giving steadily better results as more reusable items are built. Reusability is at its most powerful when it fits into an information-engineering environment. Some organizations have done this with excellent results, but most have not.

Some projects did not employ end users in JRP and JAD workshops. Some did not have a high-level Executive Owner to "grease the wheels." Some did not have users' help in developing the prototypes. Some projects slipped because of inadequate cutover planning. Complex projects need parallel development activities coordinated with computer precision. Some projects we examined could have been faster if they had had a higher degree of parallelism (Chapter 12).

To be as effective as possible, an I.S. organization should identify all the good techniques and combine them. It should employ *all* the techniques that can improve a fast development lifecycle and try to make *all* of them work. The RAD methodology is an attempt to do this. Box 6.1 summarizes what is required.

## Box 6.1    Factors Contributing to Realization of RAD Lifecycle Goals

*TOOLS*

- *I-CASE.* Ensure that an efficient, graphically oriented I-CASE toolset is used, one that integrates data modeling, process modeling, system design, prototyping, screen painting, dialog generation, report generation, database code generation, efficient code generation and testing tools.

- *Repository.* Use an I-CASE repository on-line to all developers. The repository should be "intelligent," comprehensively coordinating the knowledge stored in it.

- *Knowledge Coordinator.* Employ a facility for comprehensively validating and checking the consistency of the information stored in the repository.

- *Desktop Environment.* Use tools that allow desktop development, giving the fastest possible cycle of design-generate-test. There should be distributed repository control, allowing a subset of the repository to be extracted to the desktop of the developer, with full integrity control when the developed system is checked back into the control repository.

- *Error Catching.* Use a toolset designed to automatically catch all the errors and inconsistencies possible to catch.

- *4GLs.* Employ end-user query language, report generator, fourth-generation languages, spreadsheet tool and so on, so that end-user interaction with the system increases its flexibility and lessens the I.S. workload.

- *Code Optimizer.* Use a code optimizer where appropriate to give the most efficient code possible.

- *Testing Tools.* Use a test-data generator and efficient testing tools.

- *Open Architectures.* Use tools with Open architectures to achieve portability of the resulting systems where possible.

- *Technology-Independent Design.* Use tools that create designs that are as independent of technology as possible so that they remain valid when technology changes.

- *Reverse Engineering.* Use tools to capture information about existing systems. Use tools that restructure the code and data of existing systems as automatically as possible and feed the result into the I-CASE environment.

*END USERS*

- *Executive Owner.* Ensure that a high-level user executive is responsible for the system, is financially committed to it and is determined to move fast. The executive must be briefed on the events and timetable of the RAD lifecycle.

- *End-Users' Commitment.* Ensure that the end users want the system and are committed to help in establishing its functions and design. Ensure that all users know the role they should play in the development lifecycle.

- *End Users in Planning and Design.* Ensure that the right users (the most knowledgeable) are present at the Requirements Planning and User Design workshops.

- *Prototype Reviewers.* Select appropriate end users to review the prototypes as the system evolves.

- *User Report Generation.* Ensure that users can generate reports or employ end-user languages directly with the database (to increase flexibility and lessen the amount of development work).

- *Development of User Skills.* Pay careful attention to the training of end users and to building them up to higher levels of computer skill.

- *User Motivation.* Pay careful attention to the motivation of end users and user management.

- *Job Changes.* Pay careful attention to job changes, minimizing social disruption. Ensure that planning and education for job changes are done early in the lifecycle.

## I.S. PEOPLE

- *Project Manager.* Ensure that the Project Manager understands the RAD lifecycle and, if possible, is experienced with it. Select a Project Manager who is a leader, leading the others in using the methodology correctly.

- *RAD Workshop Leader.* The RAD Workshop Leader, who organizes and conducts the user JRP and JAD workshops, should be professional at this task, doing it continuously and building up a high level of expertise at it. This is critical to RAD success.

- *Construction Teams.* Create Construction Teams that are small, highly trained and skilled with a powerful toolset and that are able to build systems rapidly from the I-CASE design output of the JAD workshop (Chapter 10).

- *Data Modeling.* Employ a person experienced and skilled in data modeling to build or validate both the data model used (Chapter 13) and the coordinating model for parallel development (Chapter 12).

- *Tool Specialist.* Employ a person skilled and fast with the toolset to build the computerized design and prototypes in the JAD workshop.

- *Repository Manager.* Ensure that the repository is well managed. A Repository Manager should resolve conflicts where different developers want to represent the same item in different ways. He should control what reusable constructs are stored in the repository.

- *Motivation.* Use all appropriate forms of motivation to help create a striving for excellence in the Construction Teams. Pay strong attention to the motivation of everybody involved.

- *Pride.* Build an environment where the Construction Teams have the maximum sense of pride in achieving the RAD objectives.

## LIFECYCLE

- *Methodology.* The RAD methodology should be represented in hyperdocument form on the personal computer of each developer. It should give guidelines and a warning of pitfalls for each stage.

Box 6.1    Continued

- *Lifecycle Customized to Toolset.* The lifecycle and methodology should be customized to make the best possible use of the toolsets selected. Aspects of the methodology vary from one toolset to another.
- *Lifecycle Customized to Circumstances.* The lifecycle should be customized to the circumstances. It will be somewhat different for different levels of system complexity.
- *Phases.* The lifecycle should have the following phases:

  Requirements Planning ⎫
  User Design           ⎬   These may be combined.
                        ⎭

  Construction
  Cutover

- *Requirements Planning Phase.* This phase should be done with a user Joint Requirements Planning (JRP) workshop (Chapter 7).
- *User Design Phase.* This phase should be done with a user Joint Application Design (JAD) workshop (Chapter 8) with prototyping and I-CASE tools.
- *Construction Phase.* This output of the User Design Phase should be in an I-CASE toolset so that it can be used directly in the Construction Phase, where the design is done in detail and used to drive a code generator (Chapters 10, 11 and 12).
- *Cutover.* Ensure that the planning and preparation for cutover starts early enough and that no essential component is forgotten. Preparation for cutover should proceed in parallel with the other development phases (Chapters 18 and 19).
- *Avoidance of Paperwork Specifications.* Build the specifications and design with the I-CASE tool as far as possible so that the toolset can check their integrity and consistency and so that they can be used directly with the Construction Phase tools. Avoid the hand-drawn diagrams and English text of traditional specifications because a computer cannot check these and they are usually full of inconsistencies, omissions and errors.
- *Specifications and Design in User Workshops.* Create the specifications and design in user workshops. This is faster than the traditional process of analysts writing specifications, and it meets the user needs much better (Chapters 7 and 8).
- *Computer-Generated Documentation.* Print documentation wherever possible from the I-CASE toolset. Some such tools generate development workbooks.
- *Usability.* Employ standards and guidelines for human factoring. Employ a person with skill in human factoring to check the evolving system for usability. (There may be one such person for the entire location.) Test the system for usability, possibly with a usability testing laboratory (Chapter 17).

# Large Differences Among I.S. Organizations

Even without the relatively new tools and techniques, such as CASE tools, code generators, the repository and reusable building blocks, there is a surprising difference in productivity among development organizations. Harlan Mills found a 10-to-1 difference among different development organizations [MILLS71][JAY]. DeMarco and Lister, conducting experiments to measure coding productivity in 92 different organizations, found that the organization with the best average performance worked 11.1 times faster than those with the the the worst performance.

This large difference does not relate to higher productivity tools. It relates to people and management. DeMarco and Lister comment:

> This is more than a little unsettling. Managers for years have affected a certain fatalism about individual differences. They reasoned that the differences were innate, so you couldn't do much about them. It's harder to be fatalistic about the clustering effect. Some companies are doing a lot worse than others. Something about their environment and corporate culture is failing to attract and keep good people or is making it impossible for even good people to work effectively. [DEMARCO&LISTER87]

If good management had this large an effect with conventional programming, it makes an even larger difference with the new power tools. Poor management is not adopting the new tools and techniques. Good management is adopting them and is learning how to achieve the many changes needed to make them as effective as possible. Many of the changes needed relate to people and how to manage them. Many of the lessons in DeMarco and Lister's classic book, *Peopleware*, are directly applicable to the RAD lifecycle.

# Preoccupation with Being the Best

The I.S. organizations that we found most noteworthy for high productivity and fast development were constantly striving to improve. In meetings and in casual conversations, there was a preoccupation with being the best. Striving to be the best was a common goal.

Believing that they were the best was a great source of pride. In many other I.S. organizations, there was no such preoccupation. The development organization seemed to operate as an unmotivated body shop where interchangeable programmers came and went. They quoted the computer industry's self-appointed pseudoauthorities who say that CASE tools do not improve productivity.

The best I.S. managements invested heavily in training and improving the developers, and they worked actively to keep turnover to a minimum. The developers knew that they were expected to be loyal to the organization and usually stayed with it. In other I.S. organizations, the developers never planted trees in their home gardens because they did not expect to be around to see them grow.

# Managing a Change in Culture

It is difficult to change the culture of a large I.S. organization. I.S. managers and professionals are often surprisingly reluctant to change the techniques they use. The introduction of a RAD lifecycle is alarming and threatening to professionals comfortable with an older and slower methodology.

An efficient I.S. organization today needs to have an environment of information engineering, RAD and reusability. All of these need I-CASE tools with a well-managed repository. There must be a lifecycle with a precise set of tasks with well-defined deliverables. The lifecycle (the "process" of system building) must be well managed. Some I.S. shops have none of these. To introduce them represents a revolutionary change in the way the I.S. organization functions.

The first essential in managing such a change is having the top I.S. executive totally committed to it. This executive needs to understand fully the methodologies described in this book and drive hard to implement them. The top I.S. executive should have an excellent rapport with the CEO. The CEO should understand that business needs the retooling of I.S. summarized in Box 1.1 and should make the rest of top management understand the urgency of this retooling.

Some of the retooling provides no short-term improvement in profits; its results are long-term. The payoff from the introduction of RAD techniques, however, can affect the current year's profit.

# Adapters and Resisters

When new tools and methodologies become available in I.S., some professionals become immediately enthusiastic about them and want to try them; others resist and want to delay their introduction. It is useful for management to categorize the professionals into groups:

- experimenters;
- early adapters;
- pragmatists;
- late adapters;
- resisters.

Figure 6.1 shows the percentages of these types in some I.S. organizations and the relative time they take to adapt to the new methodology.

Most I.S. organizations have some **experimenters** who like to try anything new but do not necessarily stick with it. The **early adapters** see the value of a new methodology and lead the way in making it practical. They adjust the methodology to make it work well in their environment. The **pragmatists** are the middle-of-the-road developers, not anxious to experiment, cautious of failure, reluctant to spend time learning new methods until they are sure this will be a good investment of their time. They adopt a new methodology only when the early adapters have demonstrated that it is significantly better than what currently exists and have had repeated success with it. The **late**

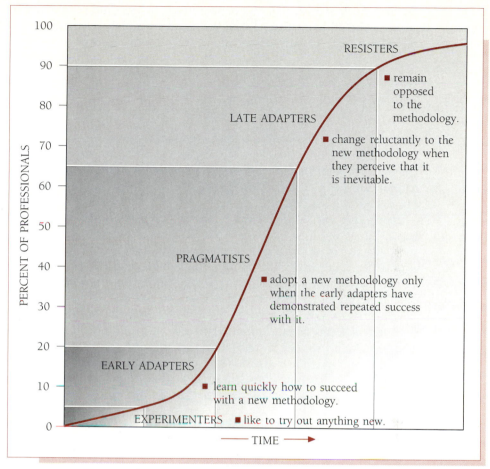

FIGURE 6.1  The Mix of Personalities When a New Methodology Is Introduced
Management should identify the early adapters who learn how to succeed with the methodology.

**adapters** are reluctant to change; they are the old dogs who do not want to learn new tricks. The **resisters** consciously oppose the new methodology, sometimes disguising their negativism with intellectual arguments. Resisters are present in most I.S. organizations and sometimes voice their opposition vigorously from the beginning. The champion of a new methodology has to know how to deal with the resisters. The worst resisters may be modern-day Luddites, searching for subtle ways to sink the methodology before it takes hold.

The late adapters or resisters are sometimes the older people in an organization, who are dignified, influential and, sometimes, powerful. A gardener putting colorful new plants into perennial beds finds that the old plants try to choke them.

The champion of new techniques needs to identify the early adapters. He needs early successes, and these come from energetic people excited about learning a new skill and putting it to work to achieve something special. He needs to form organizational structures appropriate for the early adapters and needs to motivate them well and protect their potential achievement from the opposition of the resisters. The early adapters should know that, if they fail the first time, there will be no penalty. People often learn from an early failure and convert it into repetitive success.

# Motivation

When we change the world too fast for human comfort, we need to pay careful attention to human motivation. This is true with the introduction of the RAD lifecycle. The champion of RAD should work out how to best motivate the users involved and how to motivate the I.S. staff. This is especially important when old methodologies are bureaucratically entrenched.

Individuals can be motivated by money, prestige, pride, fear and excitement. Of these, fear is the least effective in the long run. Money is the most expensive. The most effective is probably a sensitive combination of all of them. Construction Teams should be encouraged to be proud of their superior performance. Individuals should be encouraged to have pride in achieving superior results with superior tools. There should be prestige motivations that encourage non-RAD developers—or non-CASE developers—to want to switch to the new environment.

Different forms of motivation work with different individuals. The leaders of the RAD revolution should identify the most effective motivations for each person involved. Every individual asks himself, "What's in it for me?" A manager should put himself inside that individual's head and explore how he thinks. He should set the rules so that the individual decides that there is "plenty" in it for him if he succeeds with RAD.

Perhaps the most powerful motivation is excitement. When people are excited about something, they work hard for long hours and enjoy it. RAD leaders should generate a sense of excitement that fundamental changes are occurring. It should be exciting to be part of the RAD revolution. It should be exciting to build a mission-critical system that will change the enterprise in a relatively short time.

The **experimenters** are usually excited but sometimes do not convert their excitement into solid construction. The **early adapters** who build real systems need to be infected with excitement. *Excitement and pride are often the most effective motivators of the early adapters.*

A high level of prestige should be associated with the achievements of the **early adapters**. Management needs to make their successes very visible, with measurements believable to the **pragmatists**. The prestige attached to the early accomplishments should be used to persuade the **pragmatists** to learn the RAD methods.

Money is a universal motivator. Developers should know that *all* development is being measured and that the measurements are related to the individuals involved. Salary raises should be based on measured performance in achieving high speed, high productivity and high quality. Some organizations say that they are not allowed to use financial incentives as a motivation. It should be made clear that this is a bureaucratic attitude that will inevitably result in lower performance.

The **late adapters** might be seduced out of their cave with financial incentives. The **resisters** are the most difficult to motivate. Resistance is a symptom of an underlying

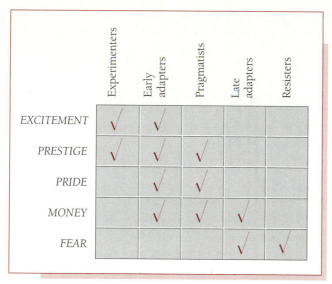

FIGURE 6.2 Management should analyze the type of motivation most effective for each individual.

problem which needs to be unearthed and dealt with. Management should find out what lies behind an individual's resistance. Resistance is a symptom of something deeper that can often be corrected. The problem may be fear of the unknown, mistrust or blind faith that the tried-and-true methods of the past work best. The problems causing the resistance may be solved by rational argument. Management should listen to and probe the resister, finding out the cause for the resistance and attempting to change the resister's views if they are wrong. The resister may express some valid concerns. Where the resister obstructs progress and refuses to change, he should have his power and prestige removed. Permanent resisters should be put into a position where they cannot assert negative influence.

Management should evaluate the best forms of motivation for everyone involved (Figure 6.2).

Different types of motivation are appropriate for different people. There is extensive literature on human motivation.

# Measurements

It is essential to establish measurements so that estimates can be made, results can be compared and developers can be motivated to achieve better results. Some or all of the metrics in Box 2.3 should be used. No software development metrics are perfect, but without metrics everyone is in the dark about what is actually being accomplished, and emotional arguments prevail.

Sometimes developers oppose being measured and are hostile to any metrics program. Mark Filteau, Vice President of Information Systems at BDM in Kettering, Ohio, managed an evolution to development with CASE tools with a precise program of

measurements. He found that developers initially objected to the measurements. "People said it was senseless, a bureaucratic hassle. The project managers thought they would be judged, and they were right. I was called the Darth Vader of BDM" [ALIa]."
In fact, the measurements were vital in enabling him to push successfully for higher speed and higher-quality results.

Developers who are achieving *good* results generally like being measured. With measurements, their success can be appreciated better by management. The measures of speed, quality and productivity translate into financial figures, which show how valuable the successful RAD developers are.

> If there are no measurements, there cannot be good management of the evolution toward RAD.

# Quality

There are three main aspects of quality:

- technical quality;
- ease of use;
- effectiveness in improving the business.

*Technical quality is greatly improved* by the use of code generators and I-CASE tools with rule-based validation of the integrity of the design. It is improved when there is reuse of building blocks or subsystems that have been well designed and perfected with experience.

*Ease of use* is improved by employing standards for dialog design (which may incorporate vendors' standards such as IBM's SAA, Systems Application Architecture, or DEC's AIA, Application Integration Architecture). Ease of use is improved by having user involvement in the design and construction, with prototyping and employment of usability testing (Chapter 17).

*Effectiveness in improving the business* depends upon involving the right business-people in the Requirements Planning and User Design Phases and by having a short lifecycle with ongoing user involvement during the Construction Phase.

Management should drive explicitly for all three types of quality improvement.

# Trapped in Obsolescence

Obsolescence becomes a self-reinforcing trap. A professor with 4-foot-high piles of paper in a messy office is slowed down because he cannot find items he needs, but he does not have the time to organize the office because of the ever-growing backlog of work he must finish. Much of I.S. is similar because I.S. executives are under pressure to keep the core applications running and maintain existing systems that are critical to the business. This consumes so much of their effort and manpower that they feel barely able to consider a major change in the I.S. development culture. They do not have any spare staff with which to take risks. However, there is a growing demand for rapid development of new applications. They are in the squeeze shown in Figure 6.3.

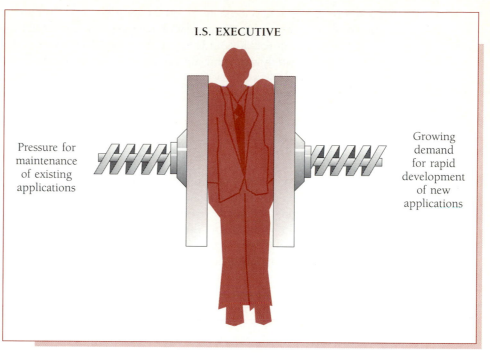

## I.S. EXECUTIVE

Pressure for maintenance of existing applications

Growing demand for rapid development of new applications

FIGURE 6.3 Mounting Pressures on the I.S. Executive: Maintenance, Backlog and Demand for New Applications

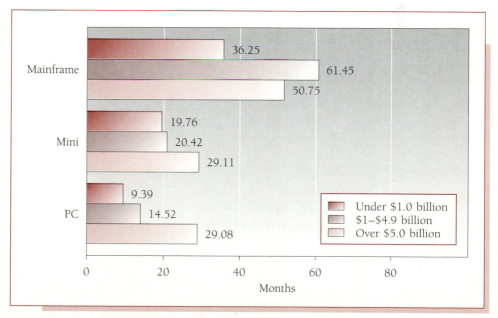

Mainframe — 36.25, 61.45, 50.75
Mini — 19.76, 20.42, 29.11
PC — 9.39, 14.52, 29.08

Under $1.0 billion
$1–$4.9 billion
Over $5.0 billion

Months

FIGURE 6.4 Application Development Backlog by Size of Company. (Source: *Software News*, April 1988)

Because I.S. has slow development lifecycles, and because maintenance of the old systems is difficult, there are large application backlogs. Figure 6.4 shows a survey on the extent of application backlogs in U.S. corporations. If I.S. has backlogs like those in Figure 6.4, it is severely damaging the ability of a corporation to adopt new computerized business procedures. In order to compete effectively, it is critical that a RAD lifecycle be introduced.

# A Foot in the Door

Rather than attempt to change the entire I.S. organization, the best way to introduce RAD techniques may be to start small. A small group should be charged with selecting the tools and techniques for fast development. One or more small, specialized Construction Teams should be set up and their members highly trained with the tools and techniques. A goal should be to make the brightest and most capable developers as skilled as possible with the most powerful tools. These special teams of two, three or four people should be put to work on some real but noncritical projects (not "laboratory experiments").

A computerized methodology should be used [JMAa]. The methodology should be customized to the specific toolset. As experience is gained, the methodology may be enhanced to reflect what the developers think works best.

Some organizations have set up **high-productivity cells** in an otherwise low-productivity I.S. department. Some have called such a group an **advanced technology group**. It is important to *measure* the results from such a group. The goal is to achieve productivity and cycle time dramatically better than those of the rest of I.S. while creating systems of high quality. If this is achieved, the methods should be spread. The high-productivity group should describe its successes and train others to use the same techniques.

To make a high-productivity cell work, the most capable **early adapters** should be identified. The most powerful toolset should be used and RAD methodology employed that is tailored to the toolset. The developers should be encouraged to learn everything they can about the toolset and the methodology, making themselves as competent as possible with them. A high-quality, thoroughly trained RAD unit should be established.

# Attitude

The attitude of the developers is extremely important. Scott Shultz, who introduced rapid development into DuPont with impressive results, describes how he was involved with two separate projects with a similar application, laboratory management, using the same tools. One group demonstrated that their new toolset from Cortex was 300 per cent more productive than COBOL; the other demonstrated that COBOL was enormously more productive than the Cortex tools. The difference lay in the attitude; the latter group did not want to learn new techniques [ALIb]. It is important, therefore, to choose members of the development team who have a very positive attitude and who are excited about the opportunity to become skilled with advanced tools.

There have been many examples of subtle sabotage of new techniques by developers firmly wedded to old techniques. Reluctant developers can only too easily demonstrate that new tools do not work. They can scuttle new methodologies by adopting a work-to-rule attitude. Many organizations have achieved low productivity figures with CASE tools because the developers have, basically, not wanted to use them. They are comfortable with their existing techniques and do not want to climb a new learning curve.

A skilled, well-motivated Construction Team can demonstrate the value of the RAD lifecycle and can tune the methodology to make it as effective as possible. More such teams can be added. Productivity, cycle time and quality are measured, and the teams are compared with the other developers. It should be made clear that salary raises and promotions relate to measured achievements. The RAD techniques should then spread from the **early adapters** to the **pragmatists**.

Sometimes a first attempt at RAD fails even though the attitudes are good. When this happens, the cause of the failure should be identified, the situation corrected and another attempt made. The developers should never be penalized because of one initial failure; on the contrary, they should be rewarded for a good try and encouraged to try again, correcting the problem.

The problem may be an *inappropriate choice of tool*. In this case, it is important to find a toolset that does what is wanted and switch to it. There are many unfortunate examples of I.S. organizations becoming committed to an inadequate toolset. The switch to a different toolset is painful; if it is needed, it should be done as early as possible, before many people have climbed the learning curve with the inadequate tools. Nonintegrated CASE tools should be avoided like the plague.

Sometimes the reason for failure is *inadequate training*. Many I.S. organizations have underestimated the training needed for building an I-CASE environment. The powerful toolsets are rich in functionality, and the developers have much to learn. The commitment to good training is vital. The training should be oriented to fast development.

Having good training on tools that are exciting for I.S. professionals has a strong effect on the attitude of the professionals. The training should be well thought out, with skillfully designed "learner packs" that give practice in using the I-CASE product. Training with the learner packs should be followed immediately by initial projects designed to solidify the learning with experience.

# First Applications

The first applications should be ones that fit comfortably within the capabilities of the toolset. They should be applications that can be accomplished by *one small, skilled Construction Team* in three months or so. Within these constraints, the applications should be appropriately complex—say, 500 to 1000 function points. A purpose of the first projects is not only to build systems but to demonstrate that the methodology works well.

It is useful to categorize two types of initial projects:

- **Proof-of-Concept Projects**

  *Proof-of-concept* projects are intended to demonstrate that the tools and methodology work. They should be noncritical systems that are not too large. They should be buildable in 60 days or less by a small Construction Team.

They should engender confidence and credibility in the RAD lifecycle and enable its productivity to be compared with the traditional lifecycle.

To demonstrate the true capability of the methodology, it may pay to have a skilled consultant lead or participate in the proof-of-concept project.

- **Pathfinder Projects**

*Pathfinder* projects are projects of discovery. They help train the team in the use of the tools, adjust the methodology and establish standards, templates and the initial reusable building blocks that will greatly speed up the development of subsequent systems. The timeframe is flexible on a pathfinder project. Important are discovery and education, rather than a demonstration of speed or productivity. There should be no time pressures.

Some corporations have used throw-away systems for proof-of-concept or path-finder projects. This should be avoided. Noncritical systems that are real and that meet a minor business need are more appropriate. Concepts like JRP (Joint Requirements Planning) and JAD (Joint Application Design) cannot be tested adequately on nonreal projects.

# Work Environment

The RAD team needs a work environment that encourages them to work hard during the period of fast development and that makes work as enjoyable as possible. The rooms where they work should be private and pleasant to be in. They should be accessible at all hours to encourage those who work later or earlier than regular office hours. They should have plenty of desk space and a white board for discussions. Every developer should have his own computer with the I-CASE toolset. There should be chairs so that two or more people, including end users, can discuss what is on the screen. Printing and copying should be quick and easy.

Particularly important, fast development requires freedom from interruption. There should be no unnecessary visitors or meetings other than those that are part of the lifecycle. The telephone should be silenced by using an answering machine, facsimile machine and electronic mail. There should be peripheral support—secretarial, phone answering and so on.

It has been demonstrated repeatedly that a good work environment more than pays for itself in increased productivity. A RAD work environment is discussed in Chapter 10.

# Management of the User Roles

In a RAD lifecycle, the end-user roles are critical. Users must play their roles in a well-orchestrated fashion. A suitably high-level user executive is needed to ensure that this happens.

The user executive is usually the Executive Owner who is paying for the system. The Executive Owner must interact with a counterpart in I.S.—the Project Manager or a higher manager. This person explains the lifecycle procedure to the Executive Owner when the project is initiated and makes clear the roles of the end users (Box

6.1). The Executive Owner must make sure that the necessary users assume their roles, commit the time and are motivated appropriately. I.S. should ensure that the user participants are given the requisite training (Chapter 8).

In the traditional lifecycle, most of the work consists of programming and testing. With code generators, most of the work is in the planning and design. The design should be done in such a way that automatic code generation can be used. Planning and design should be done with workshops and with prototyping efforts that involve the users. Techniques such as JRP and JAD need to harness the knowledge of the users and business managers. There is, thus, more work for users at the front of the lifecycle, but the system is built more quickly. Figure 6.5 illustrates this.

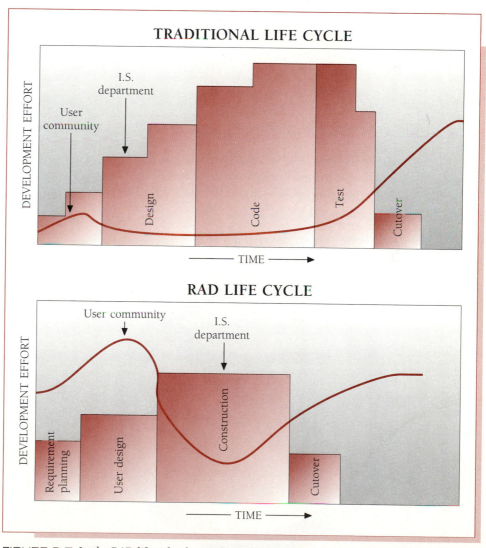

FIGURE 6.5 In the RAD lifecycle, the involvement of the user community is greater and must be well managed.

# Clear Responsibilities

It is important to establish clear responsibility for what has to happen, with defined deadlines for when it has to happen. If something delays the project, it should be clear who is responsible. Fitzhugh, when Secretary of the Army, gave the following description of the Pentagon:

> Everybody is somewhat responsible for everything and nobody is completely responsible for anything. So there's no way of assuming authority, or accountability. There is nobody you can point your finger to if anything goes wrong, and there is nobody you can pin a medal on if it goes right, because everything is everybody's business.... They spend their time coordinating with each other and shuffling paper back and forth, and that's what causes all the red tape and big staffs ... nobody can do anything without checking with seven other people [WARD70].

RAD is the opposite.

> Each person knows exactly what he is expected to achieve, by when, and must act quickly and concisely.

# Avoidance of Bureaucracy

To develop systems fast, it is essential to bypass bureaucratic delays. Bureaucracy insists on formal procedures. Rather than use intelligence to select the actions that get the job done quickly and effectively, you have to fill in the right forms, go through the right channels, get the right approvals and hone the status of the authorities.

Bureaucracy is the enemy of speed. Indeed, it is the enemy of the three main goals of RAD: speed, high quality and low cost:

Many attempts to create new computer applications quickly have ground to a halt because of career bureaucrats or managers motivated by politics rather than speed. In a healthy competitive corporation, the enemy is on the outside. In a bureaucratic organization, the enemy tends to be internal, in other departments. This is one reason why successful entrepreneurs have difficulty transferring their executive skills from business to government. They expect loyalty from a staff seeking common goals for the enterprise but, instead, they find that predominant goals relate to internal politics. Instead of hostile external forces, they find hostile internal forces.

In Chinese writing, the ideogram for a bureaucrat

shows "a man puffed up with contentment and a full stomach, sleeping siesta-style"

under a roof

The character was written first as and finally as .

The operation of small, specialized Construction Teams, with good measurements, will bypass bureaucratic tendencies in the I.S. organization. The Executive Owner and his I.S. counterpart have to agree that rapid action is essential in the user community and that, if bureaucracy threatens to impede it, the Executive Owner will cut the red tape. As in I.S., the players from the user community should be early adapters determined to act quickly to make the new system work.

# Reusability

Once a RAD methodology is well established, a factor that has a major effect on speed of development is the extent to which reusable designs and building blocks are used (Chapters 15 and 22).

David Henry, Vice President of Technology at BancA, Dallas, achieved 6000 lines of code per person-month with CASE tools (several times higher than the productivity of the average I.S. organization), but by building a set of reusable code modules, this was increased until it leveled off at 50,000 lines of code per person-month. Of 2 million lines of code built, only 200,000 were unique. Employing reusable code lessens the debugging effort. BancA projected 4500 bugs in the 2 million lines of code, but in actuality there were 800 to 900, almost all related to the unique code rather than the reusable code [BOULDIN89].

Reusability requires *management*. There are many examples of teams doing rapid development of an isolated project, not relating it to systems already built or that will be built in the future. On the other hand, some I.S. executives say that every project should use designs already in existence or create designs that may be used in the future. The designs are input to a code generator. The development team needs to be managed so that it is discouraged from re-creating designs that already exist. It should have easy access to designs that can be easily modified.

For reusability to succeed and be generally accepted by developers, it must be *easier to find and adapt existing designs than to create new designs*. To achieve this ease of reuse, the designs must reside in the I-CASE repository and be well catalogued. They should be in CASE format so that they can be quickly modified and linked to other components. An appropriate way of organizing reusability on a large scale is needed.

NASA is using an expert system implemented in *ART-IM* (Automated Reasoning Tool for Information Management) from Inference Corporation to provide intelligent assistance in the selection and composition of software modules from a library of reusable specifications and corresponding Ada code. The expert system retrieves components that have specifications close to the requirements and supports combining submodules into modules. *ART-IM*'s support for constraint propagation automatically modifies submodule interfaces at the code level [ALLEN89].

A culture of reusability is more difficult to introduce and manage than a culture of simple rapid development.

# Avoidance of Customization

Many code generators generate a particular pattern of system—one with a certain style of user dialog, for example. The users may say that they want something different. To build systems fast, it is desirable to use existing structures or generatable structures wherever possible. It should be explained to the user management that a different, customized structure will cost more, take longer to create and possibly not work out as well as the structure that can be demonstrated.

Conforming to a fixed style of user interface has another advantage—the system looks and feels familiar. It is likely to be easier for users to learn and to use to obtain quick results. It is better to have a well-thought-out, off-the-shelf result than an ill-thought-out, customized one. We should select generatable structures that are as well-thought-out as possible.

The same argument applies to reusability. An I.S. organization with a rich library of reusable modules can often create new systems quickly. The users may want a system different from those that can be assembled from reusable components. Again, they should be encouraged to accept the proven solution, which can be built fast, unless there is a clear reason why it is unsatisfactory. A goal should be to avoid unnecessary customization of unique solutions. Usually, if the cost and time arguments are explained to management, they opt for the quick, low-cost (but still high-quality) solution.

# Creating an Infrastructure

In practice, most business applications are strongly related to other applications. They move data to and from other applications and share databases with them. Because of this, a common infrastructure is necessary. The infrastructure requires a common network and standards. Particularly important, it requires commonality of data that is represented in a data model. To achieve this commonality, a **masterplan** is needed. The masterplan specifies an architecture within which many applications can evolve.

Setting up high-productivity cells for fast development is relatively easy and achievable, but doing so does not create the masterplan necessary to achieve reusable design. Some of the most spectacular successes in changing an organization and building new applications rapidly has occurred in an *information-engineering* environment with *reusable data and processes*. The evolution to information engineering may be a fundamental change in culture in an I.S. organization. It usually provides a high return on investment if done comprehensively [MARTIN90] but takes substantial time before the full benefits are achieved.

The infrastructure of information engineering should consist of object-oriented data models and process models. These evolve over years. However, if they are built in an appropriate fashion, applications can be built more quickly within the infrastructure than they could be without it. The reason for this is that part of the work has already been done. Stable data models exist; naming conventions have been established; application standards and tools may be well established. Sometimes most important, the infrastructure facilitates reusable code and reusable design.

In order to build applications quickly and modify applications quickly, which is so important for business, the infrastructure should be designed with the goals of fast application development and maintenance.

For an enterprise without information engineering, it makes sense to introduce information engineering in conjunction with high-speed development techniques. Both can use the same toolset with the same repository. They tend to reinforce one another. Good designs from fast-development teams can reside in the information-engineering repository and be used elsewhere. The data models and process models of information engineering help speed up developments, especially with systems complex enough to require a coordinating model.

The *RAD Expert* giving methodology guidance on the personal computer screen is affiliated with the *IE Expert* giving similar detailed guidance in the accomplishment of information engineering [JMAa][JMAb].

# Repository Management

Information engineering and the widespread application of reusable design are dependent on the I-CASE repository. The repository has to be well administered. Just as a data administrator needs to manage the use of a data dictionary, so does a repository administrator need to manage the contents of the repository. He is concerned with how it is updated, how inconsistencies are resolved and how subsets and version control are managed.

In an environment of information engineering, the contents of the repository steadily grow, becoming an extremely valuable corporate resource containing knowledge of the data, processes and systems. It should be managed so that the amount of reusable design steadily grows and steadily increases the ability to assemble applications rapidly from what already exists.

These subjects are explored in more detail in Part II of this book.

# Reverse Engineering

In older enterprises, large numbers of applications exist that need to be rebuilt. Many of these are badly designed and have spaghetti code, and their data are ill-structured. It would be useful to restructure the old applications as automatically as possible and feed them into an I-CASE toolset that can regenerate them in an easily maintainable form. This process is referred to as **reverse engineering**.

When a RAD methodology has been made to work well, the cost of modifying and restructuring old applications should be compared with the cost of scrapping and rebuilding them. Rebuilding with a RAD lifecycle is often cheaper and faster and usually gives higher-quality results.

The toolkit used should be able to capture the data descriptions or data dictionary of the old systems and incorporate them in the I-CASE repository. Tools are available that automatically restructure spaghetti code and analyze it to help a developer decide what pieces of it could be reused in a new system. Usually, the functions of the old system need major improvements; that is why it is being rebuilt. The JAD (Joint Application Design) workshop with end users may examine the data and process structure of the old system to decide what should be kept, what should be rebuilt and what entirely new functions should be added. Often, the best action to take with old systems is to capture and restructure what is valuable in them and use that in a RAD lifecycle to fundamentally rebuild them.

Chapter 24 discusses migration and reverse engineering.

# Variations in Results

There is a big difference between development with third-generation programming and development with I-CASE tools. However, with modern tools, there is a large difference between what is achieved by one organization and another. *This difference relates to management.*

Dr. A. Picardi made a detailed study of applications developed with the Cortex toolset [PICARDI86]. He studied 30 diverse applications at 22 sites. The applications are plotted in Figure 6.6. He measured productivity and compared it with estimates from a commonly used estimating technique for the traditional COBOL lifecycle (which gave estimates averaging 5 function points per person-month).

Figure 6.7 gives the productivity increase over COBOL. The worst system had twice the productivity of COBOL; the best, 45 times the productivity of COBOL. The average was 13.2 times better than COBOL.

These figures indicate that the toolset is useful. However, *different teams achieved widely different levels of productivity with it.* This is shown in Figure 6.8. For both small and large systems, the productivity (hours per function point) varied over a wide range. This result has been found with most productivity tools. It is the task of management to drive the points on a chart like Figure 6.8 to the lower end of the range. This can be done by applying an appropriate RAD methodology and carefully selecting and motivating the people involved.

- Job quotation and interface to order entry system
- International purchase order tracking
- Consultant job and time tracking and reporting
- Software maintenance contract tracking and renewal letter production
- Integrated inventory, accounts receivable/payable and payroll for an offshore wholesaler
- Hotline call tracking and bug reporting
- Medical office management, patient registration, scheduling, insurance and billing
- Manufacturing material tracking, inspection and quality control weighing, packing, labeling, storage, history for plants in a variety of industries
- Inventory and reorder for a municipal water department, an electric company and various manufacturing companies
- Order entry, inventory and production scheduling for a variety of industries
- Student registration, student and teacher scheduling, and reporting
- Sample testing and quality control for beverages and pharmaceuticals
- Field service database for scheduling software and hardware maintenance, billing, phone call documentation
- Travel club membership, mailing list, trip discount tracking
- Commodities daily price tracking, market analysis and reporting
- Commodity contract tracking integrated with shipping and receiving
- Document tracking for large engineering firms
- Customized payroll packages for universities or foreign countries
- Health club membership, checking, billing and dietary analysis
- Manufacturing cost and price volume analysis
- Remote automatic teller application for bank customers, including cash management query, cable payments/receipts
- Publisher subscription tracking, billing, mailing labels, notices
- Work order control for building maintenance cost control, reporting cost center allocation
- Installment loan tracking status query, approval and reporting
- Sales cycle tracking from quote request to proposal, maintenance of prospect and competitor information data
- Professional Services time and billing, office and individual performance measurement, financial reporting

FIGURE 6.6  The Applications to Which Figures 6.7 and 6.8 Refer

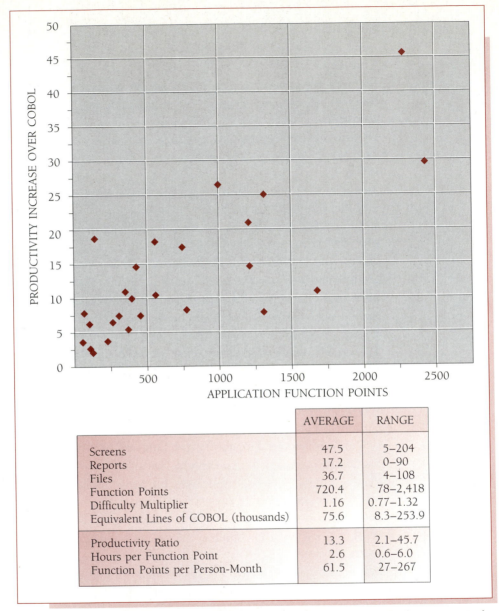

| | AVERAGE | RANGE |
|---|---|---|
| Screens | 47.5 | 5–204 |
| Reports | 17.2 | 0–90 |
| Files | 36.7 | 4–108 |
| Function Points | 720.4 | 78–2,418 |
| Difficulty Multiplier | 1.16 | 0.77–1.32 |
| Equivalent Lines of COBOL (thousands) | 75.6 | 8.3–253.9 |
| Productivity Ratio | 13.3 | 2.1–45.7 |
| Hours per Function Point | 2.6 | 0.6–6.0 |
| Function Points per Person-Month | 61.5 | 27–267 |

FIGURE 6.7 Measurements of a Diverse Set of Applications Built with the Cortex Toolset [PICARDI86]. (See Figure 6.6.)

"Productivity Increase over COBOL" refers to the ratio of productivity (function points per person-month) achieved in practice with the Cortex toolset to the productivity estimated, with a common estimating technique, for traditional COBOL development.

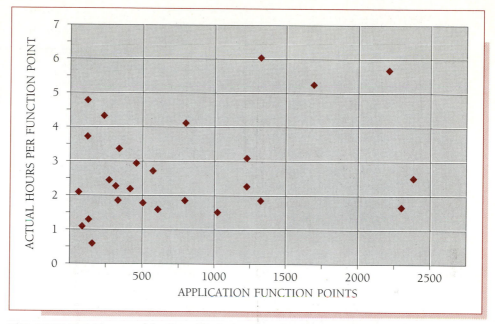

FIGURE 6.8 A Measure of the Hours Worked per Function Point on 30 Diverse Applications Using the Cortex Toolset [PICARDI86]

The scatter between high and low productivity is great for applications at all levels of complexity (function points). Project managers have the challenge of driving the points on a chart like this to the lower end of the range by using an appropriate RAD methodology with good "people management."

Eight of the 30 projects in Figures 6.6 through 6.8 achieved more than 100 function points per person-month. There seems to be nothing special about the ones that did except that *they had their act together*. Probably all 30 projects could have been built with more than 100 function points per person-month. Two of the projects exceeded 200 functions points per person-month. It is interesting to speculate how many could exceed this productivity level with good management.

The Cortex tools are now more powerful than they were when this study was done. Other tools and techniques that are more powerful have also become available. The employment of reusable restructures, reusable code (Chapters 15 and 22) and information-engineering code generators (Chapter 21) is providing examples of development exceeding 200 function points per person-month. However, the more powerful the toolkit, the greater the need for good methodologies and management if its potential is to be fully realized. It is important to identify the management factors that give the best results.

As we commented, the most effective RAD is a complex act to get together. Although we found impressive examples of the techniques we describe, we could find no project using all of the techniques from which it could benefit. Few I.S. organizations have the "whole act" together. Box 6.1 lists the factors that help make a RAD lifecycle achieve its goals. I.S. executives should try to achieve all of them.

# References

[ALLEN89] B. P. Allen and S. D. Lee, "A Knowledge-Based Environment for the Development of Software Parts Composition Systems," *Proceedings*, Eleventh International Conference on Software Engineering, IEEE, May 1989.

[ALIa] Mark Filteau describes this in the Applied Learning series of training tapes on *RAD: Rapid Application Development*, from Applied Learning, Inc., Naperville, Illinois, 1989 (708–369–3000).

[ALIb] Scott Shultz tells this story in the Applied Learning series of training tapes on *RAD: Rapid Application Development*, from Applied Learning, Inc., Naperville, Illinois, 1989 (708–369–3000).

[BOULDIN89] Barbara M. Bouldin, "CASE: Measuring Productivity," *Software Magazine*, August 1989.

[DEMARCO&LISTER87] T. DeMarco and T. Lister, *Peopleware, Productive Projects and Teams*, Dorset House, New York, 1987.

[JAY] Arthur Jay, *Measuring Programmer Productivity and Software Quality*, John Wiley & Sons, Inc., New York, 1983.

[JMAa] *RAD Expert*, a methodology in hyperdocument form adaptable to different toolsets, available from James Martin Associates, Reston, Virginia (703–620–9504).

[JMAb] *IE Expert (Information Engineering Expert)*, a detailed methodology in computerized form, available from James Martin Associates, Reston, Virginia (703–620–9504) & London.

[MARTIN90] James Martin, *Information Engineering (a trilogy)*, Book I: *Introduction*, Ch. 7, "How Do You Justify the Expenditure on Information Engineering?" Prentice-Hall, Inc., Englewood Cliffs, New Jersey, 1990 (201–592–2261).

[MILLS71] Harlan Mills in Courant Institute of Technology (N.Y.U.) Publication, Randall Rustin, Ed., *Debugging Techniques in Large Systems*, Prentice-Hall, Inc., Englewood Cliffs, New Jersey, 1971 (201-592-2261).

[PICARDI86] Anthony C. Picardi, "Productivity Increases with the CORTEX Application Factory: Empirical Survey Results," DECUS Northeast Regional Conference, Boston, Massachusetts, June 5–6, 1986.

[WARD70] Fitzhugh on the Pentagon, quoted by Just Ward, "Soldiers—Part II," *The Atlantic Monthly*, November 1970.

# PART 2

# IMPLEMENTATION

# CHAPTER 7

# The Requirements Planning Phase (JRP)

## User Workshops

When systems are built by I.S. professionals, it is vital to harness the end users to the processes of requirements planning and design. The RAD lifecycle does this to a far greater extent than the traditional lifecycle, with the objective of improving quality as well as decreasing cycle time. This chapter and the next describe twin techniques for doing this:

- **JRP**, Joint Requirements Planning
- **JAD**, Joint Application Design

These techniques have been particularly successful and have spread in many corporations. They have speeded up the requirements analysis and design process and have resulted in designs that meet the end users' needs much better.

The basic idea of JRP and JAD is to select key end users and conduct workshops that progress through a structured set of steps for planning and designing a system. At the start of the workshop, the users are encouraged to do most of the talking. The I.S. staff in the session translates what the users want into structured specifications and design in such a way that the users can understand and discuss the results.

The success of JRP and JAD is highly dependent on the person who organizes and conducts the workshop. This is a skilled task. The same person usually conducts both the JRP and JAD workshops. We shall refer to this person as the **RAD Workshop Leader**. This should be a full-time position so that the person can develop his skill in managing JRP and JAD to the fullest.

JRP and JAD in a RAD lifecycle are different from those conducted in some corporations because they use I-CASE and prototyping tools to collect knowledge about the system in a structured format, which is taken directly into the Construction Phase. The workshops do not generate paperwork; they generate a computerized design that directly feeds the construction process. The users sign off on the computerized information in the I-CASE toolset.

IBM has produced literature on how JAD should be conducted [IBM84]. It is important to understand that JRP and JAD in a RAD lifecycle are very different. The IBM

---

JAD. *First generation (1982–1985)*

• Flip charts; paper; no computerized tools.

---

JAD. *Second generation (1986–1989)*

• Prototyping tools.
• CASE tools.
• Large-screen monitor so that workshop members could see the evolving design.

---

JAD. *Third generation (1990–     )*

• JAD is an integral part of the RAD lifecycle.
• The *repository* provides input to the JAD workshop.
• Output from the workshop is in the *repository* in a form that can be taken directly into code generation.
• End-users sign off on a computer-validated design in the *repository*.

---

FIGURE 7.1  Three Generations of JAD

JAD produces paperwork; the RAD JAD uses knowledge from the I-CASE repository and creates a design in that repository that is direct input to the Construction Phase. This gives faster and higher-quality implementation.

Some JAD workshops have used nonintegrated CASE tools effectively, but these tools cannot drive a code generator. In RAD, it is vital that the toolset used in the JAD workshop is the front end of the code generator used in the Construction Phase. This requires a fully integrated CASE toolset.

JAD techniques have evolved through three generations (Figure 7.1):

1. JAD without CASE tools (as described in IBM literature [IBM84]).
2. JAD with CASE tools and prototyping.
3. JAD as an integral part of the RAD lifecycle (which requires I-CASE tools).

# Should JRP and JAD
# Be Separate?

Sometimes Joint Requirements Planning and Joint Application Design are combined into one activity; sometimes they are separate. RAD lifecycles often have a **Requirements Planning Phase**, using a JRP workshop, separate from the **User Design Phase**, which uses a JAD workshop. For systems where the requirements are already well known or obvious, JRP and JAD may be combined into one workshop. The RAD lifecycle then has three phases, as shown in Figure 7.2.

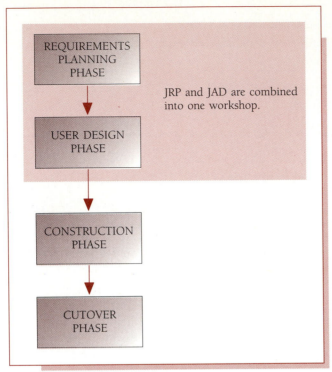

FIGURE 7.2 Where system requirements are already well known or obvious, JRP (Joint Requirements Planning) and JAD (Joint Application Design) are combined into one workshop. The Requirements Planning and User Design Phases of the lifecycle are combined.

Compared to a JAD session, a JRP session is usually shorter and without technical detail. It often involves higher-level managers and is sometimes held at the top-management level. A JRP session establishes the requirements and justification for a system and the detailed functions the system will perform. It should be done before there is a go-ahead decision to build the system. The JAD session establishes the detailed design of the system. It establishes the data model and process model for the system, detailed specifications, the screen designs, report designs and, possibly, rough prototypes.

The main reason for JRP and JAD workshops being separate is that different players participate. The JRP workshop often has higher-level participants with an understanding of the overall business requirements and the power to influence them. The JAD workshop has users who will own or work with the system when it is built. If the players are the same in the planning and design workshops, these activities should be combined into one workshop (which is usually called JAD).

Sometimes a JRP workshop is conducted at a high management level to determine whether, or how, technology can change the enterprise. This may be done before any detailed vision exists of a specific system. On the other hand, users may have an urgent need for a new system, possibly to replace an existing system, and they know in detail what tasks it should perform. In the latter case, requirements planning is the start of the JAD workshop. For many systems, JRP and JAD are combined, as shown in Figure 7.2.

# Benefits

A major benefit of JRP is that it makes business executives think creatively about how information systems can help them. The workshop causes an examination of the goals, problems, critical success factors and strategic opportunities that may have been analyzed in a separate study [MARTIN90] or may be examined for the first time in the JRP workshop. Business executives and end users brainstorm the possible functions of the system, identify the most useful functions and eliminate or defer those of questionable value.

Boxes 7.1a and 7.1b list the benefits of JRP and JAD, respectively. These are impressive lists of benefits, and those organizations that have learned to do JRP and JAD well do not want to go back to the older, time-consuming, inadequate techniques of the traditional lifecycle.

# The Executive Owner

Particularly critical to JRP, and indeed to the entire RAD lifecycle, is the **Executive Owner**, sometimes called the **Executive Sponsor**. (We prefer to call this person the Executive *Owner* to emphasize that he has a financial commitment to the system.) Establishment of this end-user executive, at a suitably high level, who is *committed* to the system, should happen before the JRP activity proceeds.

Because this executive is financially committed, he is entitled to kill the system after the JRP workshop if the planning does not indicate that the system will meet his needs with a high enough return on investment. (See Appendix III.)

---

**Box 7.1a   Benefits of JRP**

- JRP harnesses top business executives to the system-planning process.
- JRP links system planning to the top-level analysis of goals, problems, critical success factors and strategic systems opportunities [MARTIN90].
- JRP encourages brainstorming of what the most valuable system functions are likely to be.
- JRP eliminates functions of questionable value.
- JRP encourages creative business executives to think about how they can use information systems to enhance business opportunities.
- JRP helps get the requirements right the first time. It is expensive and harmful to change the requirements after a system has been designed or implemented.

> ### Box 7.1b    Benefits of JAD
>
> - With JAD sessions, the specification and design of systems take a much shorter elapsed time than with traditional system analysis.
> - JAD substantially improves productivity of the development process.
> - JAD harnesses the end users to the design process and helps avoid dissatisfaction.
> - JAD replaces voluminous paper specifications with live screen designs, report designs, prototypes, concise structures and design diagrams that are easily edited. These, especially when created with rigorous design tools, give much more help to the programmers or system implementors.
> - JAD results in systems that often have higher quality and greater business value.
> - JAD helps produces a user community with greater computer literacy. It often causes users to be imaginative and inventive about creating better procedures.
> - JAD saves money by avoiding the need to preprogram or modify systems of inadequate design. Maintenance expenses are less.
> - JAD helps integrate and unify the needs of different parts of the organization.
> - JAD removes the I.S. analyst from being trapped in a situation of having to resolve political conflicts between end users. End users in potential conflict resolve their differences in the JAD workshop.
> - JAD results in user satisfaction. Because the users designed the system, they take an interest in it, feel ownership of it and help in the Construction Phase.
> - RAD JAD is done with an I-CASE toolset so that the design uses the data models and knowledge already in the repository and so that the toolset can enforce consistency and rigor in the design. It can link precisely to other systems designed with the toolset.
> - RAD JAD produces a computerized design that directly feeds into the Construction Phase. The implementation then employs the JAD output directly. If the implementors have to deviate from the JAD output, they can discuss that with the users directly. Computerized coupling of the User Design and Construction Phases makes implementation faster.
> - JAD helps get the design right the first time. It is expensive and harmful to change the design after a system is built. The earlier the design errors are caught, the lower the cost.

# The RAD Workshop Leader

The skills of the person who organizes and presides over the workshop are particularly critical to the success of JRP and JAD. As we commented, this person should be employed full time conducting such workshops in order to become highly proficient at the task. Usually, one person conducts both JRP and JAD workshops. He is often referred to as the **JAD Leader**; here we use the term **RAD Workshop Leader**.

Being a RAD Workshop Leader should be regarded as a profession, needing professional skills that take time to develop. The RAD Workshop Leader should stay in that job full time until he is promoted or moves, and then a new RAD Workshop Leader should work with him early enough to learn the skills. A RAD Workshop Leader is not likely to do a perfect job on his first JAD session. After the third or fourth, the RAD Workshop Leader builds up the confidence and skill to make the activity as effective as possible. When JRP or JAD fails, it is almost always because of the RAD Workshop Leader; more skilled leadership could have made it work. Some organizations appoint different RAD Workshop Leaders for each project; they are part of the project team. This often results in unskilled leadership and inadequate results.

The RAD Workshop Leader should be chosen mainly for his human communication skills and could come from either the end-user or I.S. community. In practice, most come from I.S. Some RAD Workshop Leaders have been information-center staff. Some have a marketing background. In some cases, they are external consultants.

The RAD Workshop Leader needs to be diplomatic and not associated with any politics that affect the session. Above all, the RAD Workshop Leader must be *impartial*. It is his job to prepare the session, orchestrate the session, make discussions occur within a structured framework, and make the session move reasonably quickly to the required conclusions. The RAD Workshop Leader acts as the focal point for tying together the views of management, the end users and I.S. professionals (Figure 7.3).

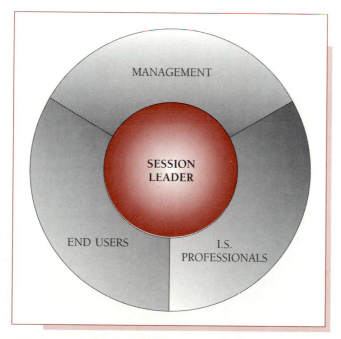

FIGURE 7.3 A JRP or JAD session needs the commitment of management and the partnership of management, end users and I.S. professionals. Their cooperation is facilitated and coordinated by an impartial session leader.

Thorough preparation is extremely important. The RAD Workshop Leader needs to do his research and prepare the meeting well, providing the participants with a suitable level of printed detail.

The RAD Workshop Leader needs to be comfortable standing in front of a group of people. He needs to be confident in his task and have the ability to direct the discussion and fact-finding activity. He needs to command the respect of all parties at the session. To do so, he must be well prepared, knowledgeable about the business area and competent in the techniques that are used. He needs to be able to control controversies and stay flexible.

A good session leader can eliminate the effects of politics, power struggles and communication gaps. He puts I.S. and end users on equal terms and establishes them as partners. He assumes the role of a referee at times, arbitrating debates. He should constantly elicit questions. He should encourage the quieter members to participate, ask questions, and respond when the more aggressive members take a position. He needs to prevent domineering participants from overpowering the meeting and to draw out shy participants. He needs to redirect participants who have a hidden agenda. He should have his own agenda well thought out and should stick to it.

A good RAD Workshop Leader knows that certain goals must be accomplished by a given time. He moves the session forward until the requisite designs are completed, along with screens, reports and, possibly, prototypes. He obtains concurrence of the users on these designs. The goal is to discuss the ideas fully and reach agreement as a group without too much delay or haggling. It is important for the session leader to be enthusiastic about JRP or JAD and to convey his excitement to the participants about how well it can work.

# RAD Workshop-Leader Training

An organization that incorporates JRP and JAD into its development methodology should train one or more RAD Workshop Leaders and make this their job for two years or more. JAD Leaders become skilled at the task with experience.

The RAD Workshop Leader should be trained in areas listed in Box 7.2. He should have had on-the-job training in other JRP and JAD sessions. A mock-up session to put him in a variety of problematical situations and to videotape and critique his performance is desirable. He should have thorough practice with the automated tools used. The RAD Workshop Leader should have management skill, business savvy and a good reputation because credibility will make his job much easier when working with a variety of end users, executives and I.S. staff.

A RAD Workshop Leader might be regarded as a trainee until his fourth JRP or JAD session. In the first, he works as an apprentice with an experienced leader. He observes the initiation, research and preparation, as well as the final workshop, and helps the RAD Workshop Leader. In the second and third, he co-leads with an experienced leader to build his skill and confidence. In the fourth, he is on his own.

If a corporation is doing its first JRP or JAD workshops, it may employ an outside consulting firm to run them until its own RAD Workshop Leader becomes experienced.

Some cities have organized JAD user groups. A RAD Workshop Leader may improve

---

## Box 7.2     Characteristics of a Good RAD Workshop Leader

- Excellent human communication skills.
- Impartial, unbiased, neutral.
- Good negotiating skills; sensitive to corporate politics; diplomatic.
- Good at conducting a meeting; has meeting leadership qualities like those of a good Board Chairman; makes the meeting move quickly to conclusions and avoids tangents; can turn a floundering meeting into a productive session; can summarize what has been said.
- Understands group dynamics and can excite the participants, getting them to work hard on items that need detailing.
- Something of a "ham" in front of an audience.
- Capable of organizing the research, documents and people.
- Not an expert on the applications but capable of researching and learning quickly.
- Fully familiar with the diagramming techniques used in the workshop; familiar with data modeling and process modeling.
- Fully familiar with the RAD lifecycle; familiar but not necessarily skilled with the tools used.
- A professional who has become skilled at the job by practice in other JRP and JAD sessions.

(See Appendix III.)

---

his skills by discussing experience with other RAD Workshop Leaders. When doing so, it should be remembered that RAD JAD is different from how JAD is conducted in many organizations.

# The Scribe

As described in Chapter 5, the Scribe records what happens in the workshop. With RAD JAD, the Scribe uses an I-CASE toolset and, wherever possible, records the planning and design information in I-CASE format. The Scribe may also create prototype screens during the session.

The planning process may use decomposition diagrams and flow diagrams recorded in the I-CASE tool. The design process uses more detailed diagrams, as shown in the next chapter. Where lists and text are created, these should be in a personal computer because they are likely to be modified and edited as the session progresses.

Because the I-CASE toolset correlates information with knowledge it already has and indicates discrepancies, the Scribe may interrupt the meeting frequently (especially in the JAD workshop) and say that what has just been said is inconsistent with something already decided or already in the repository. The Scribe is thus an active, not a passive, participant. (See Chapter 8.)

# Who Attends the JRP Workshop?

Selecting the best user participants is particularly important. The participants should have the right mix of knowledge about the business. They should have the authority to make decisions about the design. All should be people who communicate well. There is often one or more key people who are critical to creating the design and having it accepted. *If the key players are not available, the workshop should not be run.*

JRP and JAD are particularly valuable for projects that span user organizations or for applications that affect multiple locations or disciplines. The workshops are useful for resolving operational, organizational or procedural differences. The end users or managers in the workshop confront each other under the guidance of a session leader trained in negotiating skills and must sign off on a design that both sides accept. The systems analyst is not trapped in the middle of political conflicts. Conflicts are brought into the open in a constructive planning or design session.

Often, contentious political issues are known about before the workshop. They should be dealt with by appointing an executive sponsor at a suitably high level and having him meet with the parties in question, seeking consensus on the issues or motivating the parties to achieve consensus during the workshop. The workshops attempt to achieve consensus among participants with different experiences, needs or visions.

A goal of the workshop is to get the planning or design *right the first time* or, at least, as close as possible to the final system. It is expensive and time-consuming to have to change the requirements of the system after it has been designed or to change the design after it has been constructed. To get it right at the workshop, those end users and managers who really understand the requirements *must* be present.

Increasingly today, Electronic Document Interchange (EDI) systems are being built that transmit data electronically among enterprises. Corporations are placing workstations in the locations of agents, wholesalers, retailers, buyers, suppliers or dealers. On-line cooperation between organizations is important for minimizing inventory costs and improving service. It can be valuable to have representatives of the external organization present at the JRP or JAD session when such systems are designed.

# A Jelled Team

Teams play an important part in the RAD lifecycle. A team has to "jell." Team members have to develop respect for one another, know each other's talents and like to call on each other's talents to address a situation collectively. The members of a jelled team have a common goal. A task of the RAD Workshop Leader is to establish the goal with clarity and make sure that all team members are motivated to drive hard for the same goal. Any hidden agendas of the participants should be temporarily set aside. When a jelled team of talented people are hellbent to achieve a single, clear goal, they can do so with great energy.

An important principle is that all members of the JAD/JRP team are equal; however, various individuals in the team may provide leadership, taking charge temporarily when dealing with subjects relating to their expertise. Except for the RAD Workshop Leader, no individual should be dominant for more than periodic bursts; otherwise, the contributions of the others may be lost, and the team unjells. The RAD Workshop Leader must preserve the right balance.

A jelled team usually has fun. It enjoys its ability to address problems in concert, with different team members peeling off periodically to prepare a presentation, invent a chart or create a segment of a design. In some cases, JRP or JAD teams have a wonderful time working on tasks that could otherwise be dull. The skilled RAD Workshop Leader knows how to help the team jell and build up momentum so that it attacks problems like a cavalry charge.

It usually takes two days for the JRP/JAD team to jell. JAD teams spend much of the first two days becoming comfortable with one another. If the first JAD workshop lasts five days, the real work is usually done on days 3, 4 and 5, when the team has jelled.

## Group Dynamics

JRP and JAD sessions work because of the group dynamics. The session leader needs to know how to use group dynamics as constructively as possible. The participants are shut away in a workshop knowing that they have a given task to accomplish by a given time, with a given agenda. This task-oriented environment helps participants concentrate on sharing ideas and achieving the established goals. It helps to ensure that the information provided is complete. When appropriately motivated, such groups tend to police themselves and avoid politics. Bickering and pettiness are seen for what they are and tend to disappear.

The leader may follow the agenda by asking questions of the users at each stage:

*What functions do you perform here?*

*What information do you need to make better decisions here?*

*How can this step be done more effectively if information is available from the customer database?*

*Could this step be eliminated or done by machine?*

*Shouldn't this decision be made in a different place?*

The answers and discussions should be made as tangible as possible by quickly generating and displaying screens or reports that future users could employ. As new flows or structures are designed, these should be printed by the design tool so that session members can study them and make notes on them.

The main participants of the workshop must attend *full-time*. If they miss a day, they cannot contribute fully. The others waste time updating them on what they missed. They may cause earlier decisions to be reexamined, which wastes time. Each day in a workshop builds upon the previous day. One has to be there today to understand what will happen tomorrow. Each person is dependent on what others contribute; so, part-time attendance should be banned.

Some JRP and JAD workshops have "observers" who come in to see what is happening. This practice should be discouraged. If it is not practical to keep out observers, they should be kept quiet and not allowed to interrupt the meeting. The group dynamics depend upon intense, full-time participation.

The number of participants varies from one system to another. The session should not be too big. Large groups tend to argue too much or to waste the time of participants. The most effective sessions usually have fewer than eight people.

The group should follow a structure with agreed-upon stages, goals and deliverables. In this way, time-wasting ad-hoc debate is avoided.

# Open Issues

JRP or JAD should move along at a rapid clip. When an issue comes up that cannot be resolved, the meeting should not be bogged down in discussion of it. It should be declared an open issue, and the Scribe should make a note of it, listing the following:

Issue Number:

Issue Name:

Person Assigned to Resolve the Issue:

Date for Resolution:

Description:

The Scribe may have forms or computer screens for recording open issues.

# Five-Minute Rule

When arguments threaten to slow down the progress, the RAD Workshop Leader should stop them and declare them an open issue. Some RAD Workshop Leaders impose a five-minute rule: *No argument is allowed to go on for longer than five minutes.* If it cannot be resolved within five minutes, it is declared an open issue.

Open issues will be reexamined at the end of the day. If an issue still cannot be resolved, the person to whom the issue has been assigned will try to produce a solution. If there are major disagreements among participants, the issue may be taken to the *Executive Owner* for resolution.

# JRP Outputs

The Scribe is responsible for producing the outputs of the JRP workshop. Box 7.3 lists appropriate outputs.

The results of the JRP session should be recorded in the repository of the I-CASE tool, ready to be used directly in the JAD workshop. The paper version of the outputs

## Box 7.3    Output from a JRP Workshop

- List of which departments and locations are served by the system.
- List of system objectives.
- Details of possible system functions;
  - List of possible system functions;
  - List of benefits of each function (tangible and intangible);
  - Rough estimate of the return on investment of the function (possibly indicated as HIGH, MEDIUM, LOW and ZERO);
  - Prioritization of the functions (using three or more categories of priority);
    - Which functions *must* be present in the first version of the system;
    - Which functions *might* be present in the first version if they can be built quickly;
    - Which functions *ought to be saved* for a subsequent version of the system.
- A process decomposition diagram of the system.
- A process flow diagram of the system.
- A flow diagram showing interfaces with other systems.
- Listing of unresolved issues.
  - Unresolved issue.
  - Responsibility and deadline for unresolved issue.
  - Details of Issue:
    - Issue:
    - Person assigned to resolve the issue:
    - Assign date:
    - Date to be resolved by:
    - Resolution:
- Implementation target dates.
- What happens next.

should be printed from the repository. The items included in this documentation vary from one JRP session to another.

The documentation should be in the repository of the I-CASE tool. Box 7.3 lists what should be included in the documentation.

# A JRP/JAD Room

JRP and JAD workshops need an appropriately equipped room. Box 7.4 lists facilities that should be in the room. Often, hotel rooms with these facilities are used. Some I.S. organizations have created their own JAD rooms.

---

**Box 7.4     Facilities in the JRP/JAD Room**

- Large white board with colored pens.
- Flip-chart board, colored pens and space to display multiple flip charts.
- Overhead projector and screen, with preprepared and blank transparencies; colored pens.
- Possibly, a magnetic or felt board with a kit for building diagrams.
- PC with the prototyping and I-CASE toolset.
- Large-screen monitor or projector so that all participants can see and discuss what is on the screen of the prototyping and I-CASE toolset.
- Printer so that I-CASE designs can be printed for the participants.
- Portable copier so that all participants can be given copies of information created.
- Polaroid camera to record white-board drawings or wall charts.
- Slide projector if the RAD Workshop Leader has prepared slides.
- Videotape player and television monitor if the RAD Workshop Leader has planned to use videotapes.
- Coffee and refreshments.
- Name cards and stationery for participants.
- *No telephone!*

---

The I-CASE and prototyping tools should be used by the Scribe in the workshop. The participants should be able to see, periodically, what is on the toolset screen and discuss it. The personal computer should, therefore, have a large-screen monitor or projector. This is not permanently switched on because the Scribe wants to build the design in private some of the time.

The projector may project onto a white board so that participants can scribble on the design that is projected. The workbench tool has a printer so that parts of the design, specifications, agenda and so on can be printed and distributed to the users.

Figure 7.4 shows a typical layout of a JRP/JAD room.

There should be large white boards, to create sketches and lists, and flip charts that remain visible throughout the session. An overhead projector is used to make prepared presentations and sketch diagrams during the session. There may also be a slide projector or videotape player. The session leader may arrange for slides or videotapes to be available of the processes that need automating. A PC printer and a copying machine should be available.

Refreshments are available in the room, but there is no telephone. An important aspect of the workshop is the isolation from the interruptions of daily business.

A permanently established JAD room may be designed to serve other functions also, such as other meetings, training, demonstrations and sales presentations.

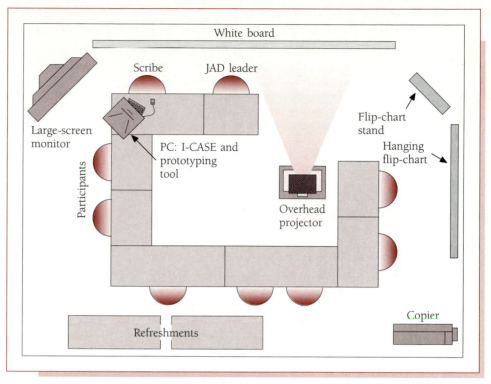

FIGURE 7.4 An Appropriate Layout of a JRP/JAD Room

## JRP Procedure

The five stages in the JRP procedure, as shown in Figure 7.5, are:

1. Initiate.
2. Research.
3. Prepare the workshop.
4. Conduct the workshop
5. Finalize.

A vital first step in the **Initiate Stage** of the procedure is the establishment of the Executive Owner. Also during the Initiate Stage, a decision should be made on whether the **RAD Planning Phase** is to be separate or whether it will be combined with the **User Design Phase** (i.e., whether JRP and JAD will be combined).

During the **Research Stage**, the RAD Workshop Leader makes himself familiar with (but not expert in) the application. He may look for information from similar applications elsewhere. He should find out what is in the repository that can be used in the application. One of the goals of an advanced RAD environment ought to be to establish a high degree of reusability, as described in later chapters.

*Initiate.*

- Establish the need for a system.
- Determine the scope of the system.
- Establish the Executive Owner (Executive Sponsor).
- Establish the JRP Leader.
- Determine the key user executives.
- Determine whether the JRP and JAD procedures should be combined.

*Research.*

- Identify overall objectives.
- Become familiar with the current system (if any).
- Find what relevant information exists in the I-CASE repository.
- Research similar systems that might offer guidance or ideas.
- Create a tentative overview of the new system in the I-CASE repository.

*Prepare the workshop.*

- Select the workshop participants.
- Prepare the materials.
- Customize the JRP agenda.
- Hold the kick-off meeting.
- Prepare the room.

*Conduct the workshop.*

- Stage the opening speech.
- Conduct an initial review.
- For the system as a whole, determine its functions.
- Examine each process.
- Create the documentation.
- Establish appropriate user expectations.

*Finalize.*

- Complete the documentation.
- Present the results to the Executive Owner of the system.
- Obtain a decision from the Executive Owner whether to give the go-ahead for the User Design Stage and release the funds for it.

FIGURE 7.5  Five Stages of the JRP Procedure

Information established in previous strategic planning studies [MARTIN90] may be used in establishing the opportunities and scope of the proposed system.

# Determining Opportunities and Scope

- Examine strategic business opportunities that may be relevant to this system.
- Establish management's objectives for the project.
- Determine which locations are involved.
- Determine which departments are involved.
- Examine relevant goals, problems and critical success factors.
- Determine what business assumptions are to be made by the planning group.
- Determine which business processes are involved.

> If the project is in an information-engineering environment, much planning material may already exist in the I.E. repository. (See Chapter 21.) In preparing the material prior to the JRP workshop, this information should be used. Goals, problems, critical success factors and strategic opportunities relevant to the system may be established prior to or at the start of the JRP workshop.

## Steps to Take If the Project Is in an I.E. Environment

- Extract relevant information from the I.E. encyclopedia.
- List possible strategic opportunities.
- List relevant critical success factors.
- Print matrices from the encyclopedia, mapping goals, problems, critical success factors and others, with corporate functions, locations, executives and so on.
- Add detailed comments to the above matrices where necessary.

The RAD Workshop Leader should prepare a tentative list of system functions prior to the workshop and decompose these into a tentative process decomposition diagram. A tentative process flow diagram (process dependency diagram) should be created, showing the flow of work in the new system and its relationship to other systems.

During the Preparation Stage, the RAD Workshop Leader works with the Executive Owner to select the appropriate workshop participants. He prepares material for the participants and prepares his own presentation.

After the workshop, the documentation is finalized in the I-CASE repository and printed from the repository. A presentation is made to the Executive Owner, who should then decide quickly whether to proceed to the User Design Stage described in Chapter 8.

# Summary

Box 7.5 lists ten essentials for the Requirements Planning Phase.

Box 7.5, like all similar boxes, is part of a hyperdocument representation of RAD methodology. These boxes represent one view of a much more complex and interlinked body of knowledge [JMA].

Everyone involved should heed these ten essentials, except where the system is well understood and no creativity is needed in requirements planning—in which case JRP should be part of the JAD activity.

Methodology Chart MC 7 gives a detailed JRP procedure. This should be adjusted to the situation in question, and a detailed agenda should be prepared.

At the end of the workshop, it is desirable to give the participants realistic expectations of what will happen next and how long it might take to build the system.

---

**Box 7.5    Ten Essentials for the Requirements Planning Phase**

These apply to nontrivial requirements planning. Where the requirements are fairly obvious or simple, JRP should be combined with JAD.

1. A suitably high-level end-user executive ("Executive Owner") must be committed to having the system and must be determined to move fast.
2. The Requirements Planning Phase must be conducted by an experienced, skilled, unbiased, full-time JAD professional who organizes a JRP workshop (sometimes combined with the JAD workshop).
3. The workshop must be attended by suitably high-level user executives who can brainstorm the potential functions of the system and its deployment across the enterprise.
4. The participants attend the workshop full time.
5. There should be thorough preparation prior to the workshop to identify the potential benefits and negatives of the proposed system. All such material should be treated as a proposed basis for brainstorming.
6. During the workshop, all participants are treated as equals.
7. The possible functions of the system should be prioritized, understanding that not all of them can be implemented in the first version of the system.
8. Any cultural changes, or changes in people's jobs, must be identified and planned for.
9. The workshop room should have no telephone; there should be no interruptions; an off-site location works best. The sessions should start on time. The participants should be committed to work in the evening for the duration of the workshop.
10. Technical jargon should be avoided.

# References

[IBM84] IBM Overview Pamphlet, *JAD, Joint Application Design*, IBM, White Plains, New York, 1984.

[JMA] *RAD Expert*, a methodology in hyperdocument form adaptable to different toolsets, available from James Martin Associates, Reston, Virginia (703–620–9504).

[MARTIN90] James Martin, *Information Engineering* (a trilogy), Book II: *Planning and Analysis*, Prentice-Hall, Inc., Englewood Cliffs, New Jersey, 1990. (201–592–2261).

# CHAPTER 8

# JAD—Joint Application Design

Joint Application Design is the heart of the User Design Phase. It produces results faster than does the traditional writing of specifications. More important, it creates a design that is much better from the users' point of view. The design is in I-CASE format and, hence, can be taken into construction with a code generator *quickly*. The I-CASE design is steadily refined and extended into detail during the Construction Phase.

JAD is a natural follow-on from JRP and, as previously stated, the two are combined when the requirements are already fairly clear. Some of the same people are involved in JRP and JAD. The users in a JRP workshop tend to be higher-level and more business-oriented; the users in a JAD workshop must have the time and knowledge to take the design into an adequate level of detail.

A JAD session uses a top-down approach to system design. The diagrams used and the systems representations must be as easy as possible for the end users to understand. The session is highly visual. Overhead projectors are used. Often a design is built up on white boards or on walls hung with flip charts. A large-screen monitor should be employed so that users can see the designs on the I-CASE screen as they evolve. The system design evolves with cooperative discussion. The users take printouts of the design away with them in the evening and mark them up, ready for the next day's discussion.

The Executive Sponsor or a top-level review board should release the project for the User Design Phase after examining the JRP results and should release the project for the Construction Phase after examining the JAD results. The budget is thus released in stages, as shown in Figure 4.4. The JRP and JAD phases together should not last longer than seven weeks. On smaller projects, less time is needed. On some very large projects, JAD has been done with separate workshops being conducted simultaneously (**parallel JAD**).

When management examines the results of JRP or JAD, it may request certain changes. This *feedback* should be built into the JRP and JAD procedures, as shown in Figure 8.1.

## Benefits of JAD

JAD recognizes that I.S. professionals have difficulty understanding the subtleties of the user requirements. The traditional methods of interviewing users and writing text specifications have proven inadequate for this purpose. At the same time, users cannot

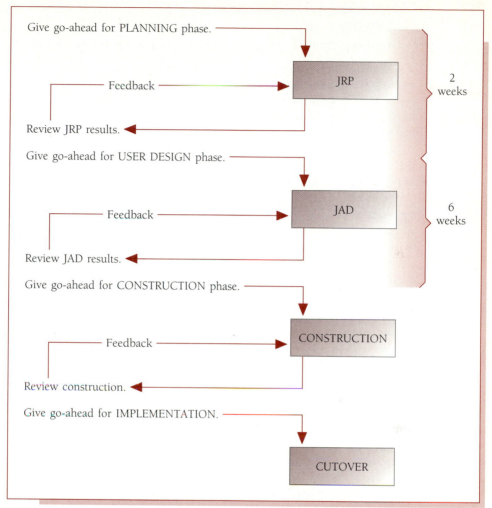

Give go-ahead for PLANNING phase.

JRP

Feedback

Review JRP results.

2 weeks

Give go-ahead for USER DESIGN phase.

JAD

Feedback

Review JAD results.

6 weeks

Give go-ahead for CONSTRUCTION phase.

CONSTRUCTION

Feedback

Review construction.

Give go-ahead for IMPLEMENTATION.

CUTOVER

FIGURE 8.1  Approval Actions by the Executive Sponsor or Top-Level Review Board
The project progresses in stages, with the money being committed a stage at a time. The first two stages should not take longer than eight weeks.

design complex procedures without professional help.
We have stressed that there are three vital aspects to *quality*:

- functional quality;
- technical quality;
- usability.

JAD helps in all three.

- The *functions* of the system are well thought out because creative end users are involved in the process.

- *Technical quality* is enforced by the (complex) integrity checking built into the I-CASE toolset.
- *Usability* should be ensured by prototyping and usability testing.

The elapsed time of the design process can be much faster than with traditional I.S. analysis techniques. Any corporation well organized to conduct JAD workshops can prepare for a workshop in about 3 weeks and complete the JAD in another 2 or 3 weeks. The initial 3 weeks may include the requirements planning and may include a JRP workshop.

JRP and JAD often take about one fifth of the elapsed time of traditional techniques [RUSH85]. One large insurance company, CNA in Chicago, compared the productivity of JRP and JAD with conventional planning, analysis and design, using function points (Appendix I) as a measurement [ALBRECHT79]. It was found that the user-workshop approach took 2.5 person-hours per function point; conventional requirements analysis and design took 8 person-hours per function point. In the JAD approach, more people worked on the analysis and design. Productivity improved by 300 per cent, but total elapsed time shrank to less than one fifth. More important, the overall design met the business needs much better. (See Box 7.1b of Chapter 7, "Benefits of JAD.")

# Who Attends the JAD Workshop?

*The key players are the end users who want the system.* End users should be chosen who are easy to work with, who know the business area well and who express their opinions easily.

As with the JRP session, getting the right user participants is critical. In selecting them, the RAD Workshop Leader should ask the users who they think ought to attend. There are usually some good choices whom only the end users know about.

Certain individuals are knowledgeable and vocal about the proposed system. A final step in the JRP workshop should be to suggest the names of participants who would be effective in the JAD workshops.

Different types of personnel should be involved in a JAD session.

- *The Executive Owner (Executive Sponsor). This person has made a commitment to have the system built.* He should kick off the session but may not stay long. He should visit periodically to lend support and examine the design as it evolves.
- *The RAD Workshop Leader.* This individual does the preparation, directs the session, encourages the players to participate and moves the session along to meet its goals. A session leader who, like a good board chairman or TV moderator, can direct the human dialog constructively and avoid squabbles is essential.
- *I.S. Professionals.* There should be one or more I.S. professionals who build the design and ensure that it is good technically. Part of this task is the building or extraction of the requisite normalized data model.

- *Scribe.* The Scribe is responsible for the documentation. He builds the design as it emerges on the screen of the I-CASE tool, adding comments as needed. He should be skilled with the tools that are used to build and edit the diagrams, create the design, extract repository information, build screen designs and reports, and create prototypes. He should be fast and competent with the I-CASE toolset and is responsible for the final I-CASE representation.
- *Visiting Specialists.* Specialists may attend the session part-time to give advice on specific areas.
- *The Project Manager.* The manager responsible for implementing the project may be present at a JAD session. He should not be the session leader because RAD JAD depends upon having an experienced, impartial, full-time, professional RAD Workshop Leader.

To provide continuity from the JRP to the JAD session, some of the participants should be the same—the RAD Workshop Leader, Scribe, some end-user executives and, possibly, others.

(See Chapter 5 and Methodology Chart 8.)

# Automated Tools

Some primitive JAD workshops are conducted without automated tools. Experience has shown that JAD produces far better designs when I-CASE and prototyping tools are used. The workshop should be linked tightly to the repository, using information from the repository and building up design knowledge in it.

The **Scribe** should operate the tools, building up the design in an I-CASE repository as the workshop progresses. This gives more rigorous design, anchored into existing data models, from which code can be produced more quickly. A screen generator, report generator and prototype generator should be used by the Scribe or by another I.S. expert, who can obtain results with such tools quickly and competently, to present the most realistic view of the design to the end users and have it discussed in the session. The participants examine the screens painted, the sample reports generated, the screen dialog and the structured design represented in decomposition diagrams, data flow diagrams and action diagrams. Periodically, parts of the design are printed for the users to review or take with them in the evening. Participants may examine or modify parts of the design on their personal computers.

The RAD Workshop Leader leads the participants through a preplanned set of steps. The Scribe records the results with the I-CASE tool and periodically interrupts when the tool detects inconsistencies or ambiguities. The tool helps ensure that the deliverables from the workshop are rigorous, consistent and complete.

When he has cleaned up the design, the Scribe shows it to the participants on the large-screen monitor. This helps in the discussion of designs and prototypes. Some JAD sessions employ an I-CASE tool without this large-screen projection facility. The Scribe builds the design with the CASE tool as it evolves on the white boards and periodically prints parts of it.

# Duration of the Sessions

JAD sessions vary in their duration and pattern of involvement. Most common are sessions that last about a week. Sessions for very complex systems may last longer. The session may take place in a hotel to isolate the users from business distractions. There should be a firm goal of having a design in an I-CASE tool and, possibly, rough prototypes by the end of the period. Often, excellent creative designs come together in a pressure-cooker environment with a firm deadline. The time pressure encourages the participants to work hard and cooperate. Many JAD sessions go on until late at night.

Some designs evolve in multiple sessions of a few days at a time. Some sessions employ the users for half of each day, and the I.S. professionals build design models, screens, reports and prototypes during the other half of each day. The most productive form of workshop is usually an unbroken session of a week in a room with no telephones.

For RAD we recommend full-time, not half-day, participation. The workshop should usually last five days because the participants tend to spend the first two days getting to know and respect one another, finding out each other's ability to contribute. As noted earlier, in a five-day workshop, the real work is often accomplished in the last three days.

*Very* large applications need to be broken into subsystems with a design tool that ensures consistent data models and precise interfaces among the subsystems. Separate, one-week JAD sessions may then be used for the separate subsystems. Often, very large systems should be *implemented* as separate, smaller systems.

The most effective procedure for most systems is to have two workshops. At the first, the initial design is done. After that workshop, the design is solidified and cleaned up by I.S. professionals. Prototypes are built. The users examine the design documents and work with the prototypes. At the second workshop, the experience with the prototypes is reviewed, and enhancements to the design are discussed. Substantial design improvements or additions may be made. Before the first workshop, there is a period of preparation, and a kickoff meeting is held. After the second workshop, the design is further solidified and then finalized.

Figure 8.2 shows the stages of the JRP workshop followed by a two-workshop JAD activity.

Figure 8.3 shows this fitting into a seven-week timetable. Systems of substantial complexity (500,000 lines of COBOL) have been designed in seven weeks with such a timetable, where the Executive Owner ensures that the right users are available when needed and the I.S. participants are appropriately skilled.

# JAD and Prototyping

JAD and *prototyping* fit together naturally. They should be used in conjunction with one another. Many valuable prototypes emulate part of a system, not all of it. Some partial prototypes can be created very quickly. For example, a person skilled with a

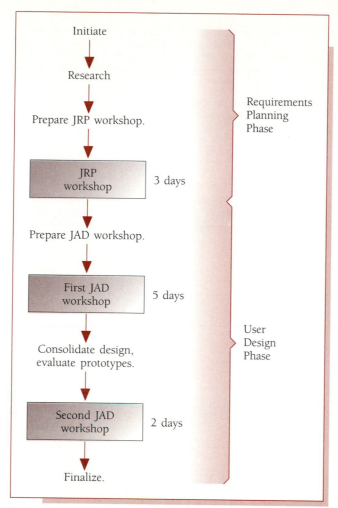

FIGURE 8.2 Planning and User Design Done with a JRP Workshop and Two JAD Workshops

For simpler systems, one or two workshops suffice. (See Figure 8.3.)

screen painter can generate the screens used in dialogs quickly. These screens can be linked together to simulate a dialog. Reports can be designed and generated very quickly. If end users see simulated dialog, menus and reports, they begin to form a good idea of what the system will be like. This level of prototyping should be done during the workshops. More elaborate prototyping may require the time interval between workshops. The Scribe or another I.S. professional should be able to use the prototyping tool rapidly and may work late at night during the session in order to build prototypes for the following day.

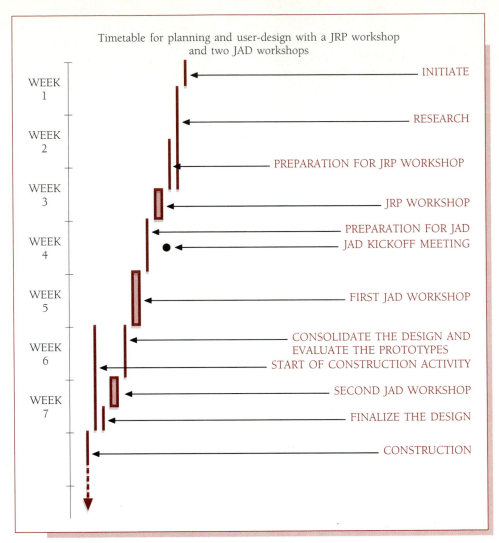

FIGURE 8.3 Timetable for Planning and User Design with a JRP Workshop and Two JAD Workshops

# Phasing in Construction

Preparation for the Construction Phase should overlap the end of the JAD activity. In Figure 8.3, the Construction Team becomes involved after the first JAD workshop, when the design is being consolidated and the prototypes are evaluated. Members of the Construction Team are present at the second JAD workshop (even though the Executive Owner's go-ahead for construction is not given until the end of the second workshop).

End users should be involved during the Construction Phase. These may be the users present at the second JAD workshop; so they will have had a chance to get to know Construction Team members.

# The Language of Business

The language used throughout the session and the language on the diagrams should be the language of business, the language of the application or the language of the user, not technical language. The diagrams should be populated with business or application terms, not technical terms.

It is often necessary to define the application terms used. Group consensus should be achieved about the definitions, which should be stored in the design tool.

# The Diagrams Used

More than a JRP workshop, a JAD workshop depends upon diagrams. The goal is to achieve with a graphically based I-CASE tool, a design that the tool checks for consistency and correlates with existing data models, process models and system interfaces, and which can be taken directly into the Construction Phase, using the same I-CASE toolset.

Four types of diagrams should be understood by the participants in the JAD workshop:

1. *Entity-Relationship Diagram.* Through use of this diagram, the participants can understand and discuss the data model used.
2. *Decomposition Diagram.* With decomposition diagrams, the participants can add detail by decomposing functions, processes or procedures.
3. *Dependency or Data Flow Diagram.* A dependency diagram shows how one process (or procedure) is dependent on another, i.e., cannot be executed until the other has been executed. A data flow diagram is special form of dependency diagram. This diagram shows that one process (or procedure) is dependent on another because it requires certain data from the other.
4. *Action Diagram.* An action diagram shows a list of programmable actions with the conditions, loops, escapes and so on that control those actions. It shows the logic of a procedure.

The users and the RAD Workshop Leader draw and discuss the diagrams on the white board or flip charts. The Scribe enters them into the I-CASE toolset. The toolset shows how the diagrams relate to one another and shows details of the objects in the diagrams. The participants examine these linkages and details on the large-screen monitor, adjusting the I-CASE design as the workshop progresses.

# Training the Participants

The participants in a JAD workshop may need some training prior to the workshop. They need to be able to read and think constructively about the types of diagrams used. The four types of diagrams in Figures 8.4 through 8.7 can be taught to end users in a half-day training course. In some organizations, two half-day training sessions are used to ensure that the diagrams are correctly understood.

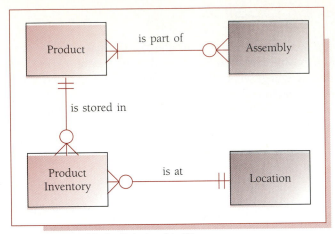

FIGURE 8.4 Entity-Relationship Diagram

Users who have not participated in JAD before need to be familiarized with what it is and what they are expected to contribute. The author has made a set of four videotapes with Advanced Learning, Inc., to teach JAD [ALI]. These tapes show a live JAD session, with the Scribe using an I-CASE tool. In many corporations, these tapes are viewed by the participants prior to the JAD session.

## Wall Charting

It is common for groups discussing complex subjects to use wall charts. Participants stand in front of white boards or pin many flip charts to the wall. Kits especially

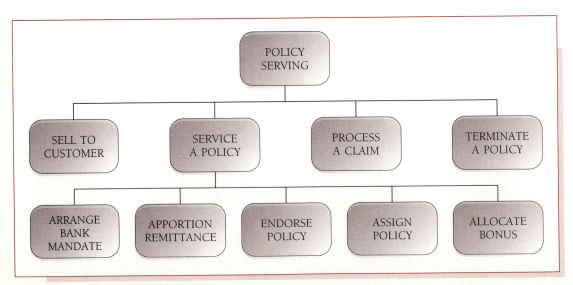

FIGURE 8.5 Decomposition Diagram

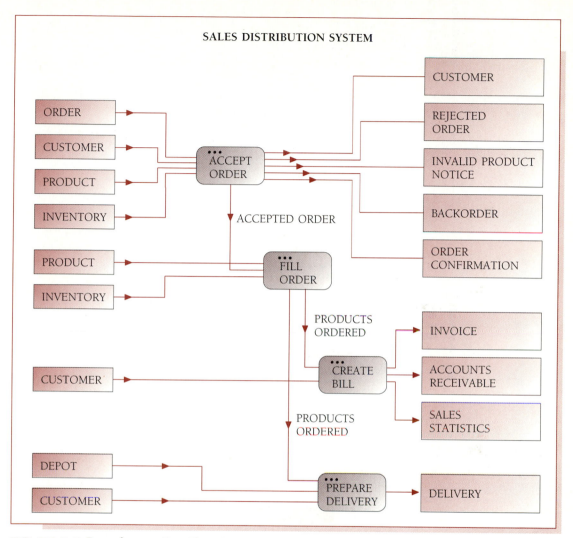

FIGURE 8.6 Dependency or Data-Flow Diagram

designed for wall charting are available. Blocks of different shapes can be written on with an erasable pen and stuck to a wall to create a chart such as a decomposition diagram, flow chart or entity-relationship diagram. With some kits, the blocks are stuck on a metal board with magnets; with others, pieces of cardboard are stuck to a wall with chewing-gum-like adhesive. It is desirable for the JAD room to have a wall-charting facility on which charts are easy to change.

When viewed from a distance, a large wall chart gives an overview of the subject; when viewed up close, it gives details. The Scribe or RAD Workshop Leader may have a Polaroid camera so that temporary wall charts can be recorded. The Scribe enters information from the wall-chart discussions into the I-CASE tool (Figure 8.8).

```
┌ Policy Serving
│  ┌ Sell to Customer
│  │     Prepare Proposal
│  │  ┏━ Select Benefit
│  │  ┣
│  │  ┃  Decide # Units
│  │  ┣
│  │  ┃  ┌ Calculate Premium
│  │  ┗
│  │     ┌ IF age > 40
│  │     │  ┌ Assess Risk
│  │     │  │     Arrange Medical Exam
│  │     │  │  ┌ Revise Premium
│  │     │  └
│  │     └
│  │     ┌ IF Accepted
│  │     │  ┌ Establish Policy
│  │     │  │     Offer Policy
│  │     │  │  ┌ Draw Up Contract
│  │     │  └
│  │     └
│  │     ┌ IF Services Used
│  │     │     Pay Brokerage
│  │     └
│  ┌ Service a Policy
│  │     ┌ IF Bank Mandate Needed
│  │     │     Arrange Bank Mandate
│  │     └
│  │  ┏     Apportion Remittance
│  │  ┣━ Accept Premium
│  │  ┃
│  │  ┣  Accept Loan Interest
│  │  ┃
│  │  ┗     Pay Commission
│  │  ┏━ Endorse Policy
│  │
│  │     ┌ IF Loan Needed
│  │     │  ┌ Assign Policy
│  │     │  │     Consider Loan
│  │     │  │     IF Credit OK
│  │     │  │        Offer Loan
│  │     │  │  ┌ Draw Up Contract
│  │     │  └
│  │     └
│  │     ┌ IF Bonus Due
│  │     │  ┌ Allocate Bonus
│  │     └
│  ┌ Process a Claim
│  │  ┌
│  ┌ Terminate a Policy
│  │     ┌ Close Mature Policy
│  │     │  ┌
│  │     ┌ Close Lapsed Policy
│  │     │  ┌
│  │     ┌ IF canceled
│  │     │  ┌ Surrender the Policy
│  │     │  │     Calculate Value
│  │     │  │     Advise Customer
│  │     │  │  ┌ If Payment Due
│  │     │  │        Pay Customer
│  │     │  └
│  └
└
```

FIGURE 8.7 Action Diagram

166

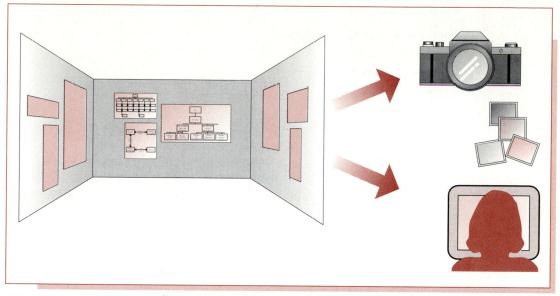

FIGURE 8.8 Information on wall charts, flip charts and white boards may be photographed with a Polaroid camera. The information is entered into the I-CASE tools by the Scribe. The tool detects inconsistencies and helps build a design with overall integrity.

## The JAD Procedure

Figure 8.9 shows stages in the JAD procedure. Methodology Chart 8 shows the procedure in more detail.

The Initiation Stage is, basically, what happens at the end of the JRP workshop. The Executive Owner gives the go-ahead for the User Design Phase, and the participants are tentatively selected.

## Preparation for JAD

To prepare for a JAD session, it is necessary to select the participants carefully and obtain their time commitment, prepare the materials, create the agenda and prepare the participants. The Executive Owner must agree to what is planned.

```
┌ JAD Procedure
│  ...Initiate.
│  ...Prepare.
│  ...Hold kickoff meeting.
│  ...Conduct the first design workshop.
│  ...Extend the prototypes and solidify the design.
│  ...Conduct the second design workshop.
└  ...Finalize.
```

FIGURE 8.9  The JAD Procedure

**Prepare.**

- Select the workshop participants.
- Prepare the materials.
- Customize the JAD agenda.
- Prepare the participants.
- Hold the kickoff meeting.

As we have stressed, obtaining the right participants is critical. The session should not proceed until the key end users are available.

The kickoff meeting reviews with the participants what is going to happen. The participants are given materials to study prior to the first workshop. Considerable enthusiasm should be generated in this session. The Executive Owner should make a motivating speech.

When the materials are being prepared, there may be much information in the I-CASE repository that should be used. The repository contains the JRP plans. It may contain reusable templates or designs. The results of a Business Area Analysis may be in the repository. The repository may contain a relevant data model. In general, the more thoroughly the Business Area Analysis has been done, the faster the design activity is likely to proceed (Chapter 21). A subset of such information should be extracted from the repository for the design of this system. Appropriate parts of it should be printed to create the binder of materials that the JAD participants must study before the first workshop.

The session leader creates the JAD agenda, editing a hyperdocument of a JAD procedure such as that in Methodology Chart 8. He ensures that the participants have the basic knowledge necessary to take part in the session.

# The Design Procedure

The initial design of the system is done in the first workshop. To begin, the scope and objectives are reviewed, along with the output of the JRP workshop. Relevant information from the repository is reviewed. It may be shown "live" on the large-screen monitor from the I-CASE tool. Adjustments may be made and comments added. The data model may be discussed and modified.

The RAD Workshop Leader should have a well-prepared agenda and should make sure that it is followed.

Each process, represented by a process block on the process flow diagram, is then examined in detail. This may be done in five stages:

**For each process block:**

- Determine what the steps are in the procedure.
- Build an initial data flow diagram showing the steps.
- Examine each procedure step in more detail.
- For each procedure step, create a partial prototype (Chapter 9).
- Address unresolved issues.

The workshop participants should be shown screen designs and prototypes of the dialog. They should examine and comment on specimens of the reports the system will produce.

Between the two JAD workshops, the design is solidified by the I.S. I-CASE-tool users. The users work with the prototypes to become comfortable with them and modify them as desired. Unresolved issues are dealt with.

The Construction Team (described in Chapter 9) typically becomes involved after the first JAD workshop. The Construction Team examines the output of the workshop and is involved in solidifying the prototypes. The Construction Team starts to work with the end users who will participate in the Construction Phase.

The Construction Team may be able to adjust the design so that it can be built more quickly. They should examine it to see where reusable designs and constructs can be applied. This adjustment of the design is reviewed in the second JAD workshop and, if practical, during the user interaction with the prototypes.

The Construction Team should make estimates of the amount of work required in the Construction Phase. The estimates should be based on function points (Appendix I). They may indicate that the system should be split into subsystems that are developed in parallel by separate Construction Teams (Chapter 12).

The Construction Team participates in the second JAD workshop in preparation for the Construction Phase.

In the second workshop, the results of the first workshop are reviewed and the design is completed. The second workshop should address the issue of security. The volumes of transactions should be estimated in preparation for physical design and configuration of the hardware.

The goal of the second workshop is to make a presentation to the Executive Owner and allow him to question the participants. He must feel comfortable with the design so that he can give the go-ahead for the Construction Phase.

## Expectation Management

A good JAD session generates excitement about the forthcoming system. End users often want the system *immediately*, especially if they are working with prototype versions of it. It is important to establish realistic expectations, explaining to them the nature of the development schedule. At the end of the final workshop, the timetable for delivering the system should be given.

In general, it is necessary to manage the expectations of the JAD participants. The technique is powerful but does not automatically produce solutions to difficult business problems.

## Varying the Procedure

Methodology Chart 8 shows a JAD procedure as part of a hyperdocument. The details of this are likely to vary from one JAD workshop to another. The person planning the events may start with the hyperdocument in Methodology Chart 8 and modify it to fit the specific situation. (See Methodology Chart 8.)

The modified hyperdocument, or portions of it, can be printed to form an agenda for the workshop participants. The agenda may be displayed on the projector screen and modified during the meeting if necessary.

## Summary

In summary, JAD works and has been highly successful because:

- It harnesses the know-how of the users.
- It cuts across organizational barriers.
- The group dynamics drive the design.
- It employs easy-to-understand diagrams.
- Screen generators, report generators and rough prototypes make the design tangible.
- It is an organized, controlled, structured process.
- A session leader facilitates discussion and drives the session to complete its agenda.
- It includes management direction.
- It anchors into the higher levels of the pyramid.
- The I-CASE tools enforce rigor.
- It utilizes I.S. advice and perspective.
- It creates, with I-CASE tools, designs that are implementable quickly and easy to maintain.
- It links directly to the RAD Construction Phase.

## Twelve Essentials for Success in JAD, the User Design Phase

To make the RAD User Design Phase work as effectively as possible, it is vital to do a number of things correctly. Everyone involved should heed the following twelve essentials for the User Design Phase.

### TWELVE ESSENTIALS FOR THE USER DESIGN PHASE

1. The User Design Phase must be conducted by an experienced, skilled, unbiased, full-time JAD professional.
2. A suitably high-level end user executive ("Executive Owner") must be committed to having the system and must be determined to move fast.
3. The right end users must attend the workshops.

4. The design must be done with the I-CASE tool that is used for the Construction Phase, and the results must be in the repository of this tool. The participants sign off on the design in the I-CASE repository.
5. Information from the repository should be used in the design (for example, the data model, Business Area Analysis and reusable constructs).
6. Participants attend the workshops full time.
7. The workshop room should have no telephone; there should be no interruptions; an off-site location works best. The sessions should start on time. The participants should be committed to work in the evening for the five days of the workshop.
8. During the workshop, all participants are treated as equals.
9. There should be thorough preparation prior to the workshop.
10. If appropriate, the JAD workshop should be preceded by a JRP workshop with participants skilled at higher-level planning.
11. All specifications prepared before the session by the RAD Workshop Leader should be treated as "proposed."
12. Technical jargon should be avoided.

# References

[ALBRECHT79] A. J. Albrecht, IBM Corp., "Measuring Application Development Productivity," *Proceedings*, SHARE/GUIDE/IBM Application Development Symposium, October 1979.

[ALI] The author has made a set of four videotapes to teach JAD, *JAD, Joint Application Design*, available from Applied Learning, Inc., Naperville, Illinois, 1989 (708–369–3000).

[RUSH85] Gary Rush, "The Fast Way to Define System Requirements," In Depth, *Computerworld*, October 7, 1985.

# CHAPTER 9

# Prototyping

## Introduction

Prototyping is a technique for building a quick and rough version of a desired system or parts of that system. The prototype illustrates the system to users and designers. It allows them to see flaws and invent ways to improve the system. It serves as a communications vehicle for allowing persons who require the system to review the proposed user interaction with the system. For this purpose, it is far more effective than reviewing paper specifications.

- A prototype is used where the functions and detailed design of a system are not yet fully understood.
- The prototype is used to explore and solidify the functions and design.

It has been said that if a picture is worth a thousand words, a prototype is worth ten thousand words. But a prototype is fundamentally different from a paper description. It is real and manipulatable. It can be adjusted and modified. The would-be users get a feel for what their system will be like. Its flaws are visible and tangible rather than buried in boring text. These advantages make a world of difference to system development. In addition, if the right tools are used, *prototypes can be created much more quickly than written specifications.*

Prototyping in a RAD lifecycle is fundamentally different from prototyping in some lifecycles in that the prototype must be part of the evolving system. Sometimes prototypes are built with a tool different from the final development tool and are eventually thrown away; in RAD lifecycles, they should be built *with* the final development tool so that they pass directly from the User Design Phase to the Construction Phase.

Without exception, prototyping ought to be used in the development of all interactive systems. When a prototype is reviewed seriously by end users, they almost always change something. This implies that, had they not reviewed the prototype, a system would have been built that was less than adequate. Prototyping does much to solve the problem of inadequate communication between designers and users.

The word **prototyping** suggests an analogy with engineering, where prototypes are used extensively. There are, however, fundamental differences between the prototyping of software and the prototyping of machines.

In engineering, a machine prototype usually takes longer to build and is much more expensive than the ultimate product. The ultimate product may come from a mass-production line, and the prototype is needed for testing the product before the production line is built.

In software, there is no manufacturing production line. Prototyping is practical only if the prototype can be built quickly and cheaply. Unlike production engineering, a software prototype is not a full-scale version of the eventual system; it is usually an incomplete or simplified version that has the essential functions of the working system but not the scale or performance. It lacks such features as security, auditability and recoverability.

There are many pitfalls in software prototyping; so, prototyping should be a component of an overall lifecycle where the lifecycle procedures help avoid the pitfalls.

Prototyping is employed in the User Design Phase of system building. During *User Design*, prototyping is used extensively in the design of screens, dialogs and reports. It is used to check that the functions of a system are what the users really want. Often, prototyping reveals the need to add or enhance functions. It is used in Joint Application Design sessions to help make the discussions more tangible.

It can also be used in the Requirements Planning Phase. During *Requirements Planning*, partial prototypes can help in checking the desirability of a system before committing funds. They can be used to stimulate user ideas or compare the attractiveness of alternative ideas. They can act as a catalyst to stimulate creative thinking about the system.

It should be part of the Construction Phase because an iterative lifecycle with a steadily evolving prototype should be used for construction. During *Construction*, a tool that permits the prototype to evolve into the final working system should be used. Some construction methodologies are based on prototyping/code-generation tools. This approach to construction is powerful, highly recommended and will probably become the predominant means of building systems.

With powerful code generators, it is difficult to distinguish between prototyping and construction. During the Construction Phase, a developer designs and generates the code for processing a transaction. The users examine the transaction and may suggest modifying it. The developer adjusts it until the users agree that it is what they want. The code that results is part of the final system. The developer then works on a different transaction. The final system is thus pieced together in a prototyping-like fashion.

## Uses of Prototyping

Prototyping is more valuable with some systems than with others. It is less valuable with batch processing than with interactive systems. Most batch systems, however, produce many reports, and these can be prototyped quickly with a report generator. On-line data entry may also be prototyped. Prototyping is of limited use in some logic-intensive systems although, in these cases, partial prototypes may check the human interaction. Users may check portions of the logic to see whether it behaves as they expect.

Prototyping is particularly valuable in the following situations:

- There is scope for user creativity to improve the system. (There usually is.)
- Users are unsure of exactly what they want.
- The system changes a basic business operation.
- An end-user dialog should be tried out with the users to see if it can be improved.

- The users do not understand all the impacts of the new system.
- The functions are subtle, and the users understand them better than the analysts.
- Screens and reports should be checked with management to see if they can be made more useful or easy to use.
- The users have difficulty expressing all the system requirements.
- The prototype may act as a catalyst to elicit alternative ideas.
- The relative merits of alternative solutions need to be explored.
- Experimentation may be done to achieve better business practices.

# Tools for Prototyping

Software prototyping became practical when fourth-generation languages and code generators emerged. With them, a working model of a system could be built quickly. As these tools improved, it became possible to build and change aspects of systems very quickly so that a designer skilled with a prototyping tool could react to users' suggestions and show them modifications, almost immediately in some cases.

Prototyping tools have screen painters, for example, with which a specimen screen can be created quickly. Screens can be linked to form dialogs. Reports can be generated on the fly. Database structures can be created and modified very quickly. Some tools give the ability to generate screens and reports on the fly during a meeting and display them with a large-screen monitor. This high-speed interaction encourages creative dialog with the intended users.

Expert system shells have been used for prototyping because of the ease with which changes to logic can be made. Since the rules specifying the logic are independent of each other, business functionality can easily evolve without concern for details such as process control logic. Also, these shells sometimes provide highly interactive development environments. This includes support for incremental rule compilation, which allows program changes to be made and retested, all within subsecond response times.

Fourth-generation languages and code generators are designed to create fully working systems rather than mere prototypes. Most of them, however, have facilities for creating prototypes quickly. When such tools are used, *the prototype can evolve into the final working system.* This is essential for RAD. Some tools sold as prototyping tools are far from having such capability.

Commitment to a fourth-generation language or code generator for full-scale development is a much broader decision than the choice of a tool for prototyping [JMPSa]. A major criterion is machine efficiency. Can the tool handle a large enough transaction volume, large enough databases and a large enough number of simultaneous users?

For RAD, the prototyping tool must be an integral part of an I-CASE toolset that designs, generates and optimizes the final code.

*From the prototyping point of view, the tool selection criteria relate mainly to how quick and easy the tool is to use and how easy the prototype is to modify and fine-tune.*

The objective of prototyping is to adapt the prototype to the requirements of the users as quickly and flexibly as possible.

---

### Box 9.1    Characteristics of the Prototyping Tool

*The tool should:*

- be an integrated part of the I-CASE toolset;
- use designs, templates and structures stored in the I-CASE repository;
- store the results of the prototyping in the I-CASE repository;
- be interactive;
- be easy to use;
- facilitate quick screen design and report design so that it can be used in a JAD session;
- make changes quick and easy;
- encourage stepwise refinement;
- facilitate quick building of prototypes that evolve into the final system;
- support desirable dialog structures, such as scroll bars, mouse operation, an action bar, drop-down menus, and so on;
- support appropriate database structures;
- support installation standards, such as IBM's Systems Application Architecture (SAA);
- provide facilities for testing;
- give good machine performance (with an optimizing compiler).

*So that the prototype can become the final system, the tool should have:*

- ability to achieve good machine performance;
- ability to support the database structure of the final system;
- appropriate networking access;
- ability to handle a suitably large number of users;
- ability to handle suitably large databases;
- ability to handle suitably high-traffic volumes;
- ability to link subroutines into the prototype;
- facilities for extracting data from files or databases and loading them into the prototype database—*or* on-line access to other files or databases.

*The system the tool generates should have:*

- features for recovery from failures;
- features for fallback;
- security features;
- features for auditability;
- features for ease of maintenance.

# Partial-System Prototyping

Some prototyping efforts create a version of a complete application. Some tackle only one facet of an application. Partial-system prototyping has proven particularly valuable on some systems. Sometimes project managers have not considered this approach because they assume that a complete system prototype is needed. Partial-system prototyping can be easier, and there is no excuse for not using it.

Partial prototypes are of a variety of different forms:

- *Dialog Prototype.* The prototype reveals the intended user interaction. This is probably the most common form of partial prototyping. It allows the users to see what they will be receiving, play with it, suggest omissions, improve ease of comprehension, generally react to the dialog and, finally, sign off on its design. Many software products have been used as dialog simulators.

  The design of the dialog greatly affects the usability and users' perception of the system. Many systems are partial failures because of poor user dialogs. Many analysts and programmers are not trained in what constitutes a psychologically effective dialog. They often create dialogs that are muddled, that are not clean and that lay traps for the unwary. It helps to build a prototype dialog that can be tested, criticized and improved before final implementation.

- *Data Entry.* One group of users may perform data entry. The data-entry subsystem may be prototyped and adjusted independently and may be linked to an existing system. Data-entry prototyping may be done to check the speed and accuracy of the data entry. Validity and integrity checks may be tested.

  Some systems have been split into a *front end* and a *back office.* The front end is interactive. The back office consists of multiple batch updating runs. The front end may be prototyped independently of the back office.

- *Reporting System.* The reports provided to users may be tried out on them before full system implementation. They may be either batch or on-line. Often, many adjustments are made in the reporting subsystem. Report generators may be used.

- *Data System.* A prototype database may be implemented with a small number of records. Users and analysts interact with it, generating reports or displaying information that might be useful to them. This interaction often results in requests for different types of data, new fields or different ways of organizing the data.

  With some prototyping tools, users or analysts have the ability to build their own files, manipulate them and display information from them. Such tools are used to explore how the users will employ information and what should be in the database.

- *Calculations and Logic.* Sometimes the logic or the calculations of an application are complex. Actuaries, engineers, investment analysts or other such users may use a language such as LOTUS 1–2-3, JAVELIN or FOCUS [JMPSb] to build examples of the computations they need. These may then be incorporated into larger systems and perhaps linked to other applications. The users may employ their calculation prototypes to check the accuracy of the results.

- *Application Package.* An application package may be tried out with a small group of users to determine whether it is satisfactory. The need for various modifications may become clear. These are tried out before the package is linked to other applications or put into volume use.

- *Concept.* Sometimes the concept of an application is in question. It needs testing and refining before too much money is spent on building the system. The testing may be done with a quick-to-implement data management system. Standard data-entry screens and standard report formats may be used so that the concepts may be tested and refined without too much work. Later, application-specific reports or screens may be built.

# From Business-Oriented Design to Working System

One of the most useful types of tool for rapid development is one that allows the developers to express a design in business-oriented terms, quickly create a prototype from it, check the prototype with the intended users and evolve the prototype until it becomes the final system. The developers can often create a core system quickly and then proceed to add successive layers of detail to it, like the layers of an onion.

Sometimes the basic 80 per cent of a system can be built in 20 per cent of the time. The remainder of the time is spent adding layers of refinement around the center, with the help of the users.

One tool designed for this approach is the Unisys system generator, LINC II [JMPSc]. Development rates of close to 200 function points per person-month are often achieved with LINC. LINC incorporates a design tool, screen painter, report generator, query facility and a powerful fourth-generation language with interactive logic editing, all linking into a data dictionary. Systems generated with LINC are compiled into COBOL 74 and give good machine performance. The tool creates on-line documentation.

With LINC, users and I.S. professionals can work together to create a logical representation of an organization in terms of **Components**, i.e., *objects* such as products, customers, suppliers, divisions, etc., and **Events**, such as payments, receipts, shipments and other business transactions. The business-oriented relationships between Components and Events are referred to as **profiles** residing in LINC's dictionary. An application using these profiles is created with procedural and nonprocedural facilities that employ the Unisys DMS II database management system and its resources (Figure 9.1).

Prototypes can be created quickly and then interactively developed into complex systems.

# Productivity with Prototype Evolution

In a study at the University of Auckland, Dr. Eberhard Rudolph set out to compare the productivity of the traditional COBOL and PL/I lifecycle with that of an iterative prototyping lifecycle using LINC [RUDOLPH84]. He measured development experi-

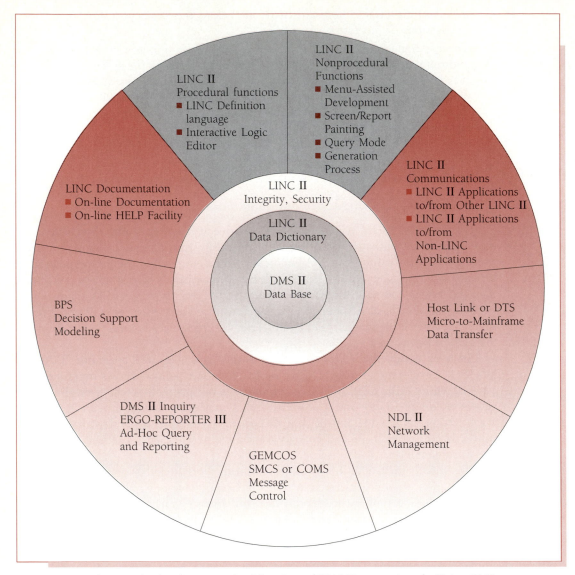

FIGURE 9.1  The procedural and nonprocedural functions of LINC II connect into the Unisys DMS II database management system and its facilities, using the LINC II integrated data dictionary. LINC II is designed so that prototypes can be created quickly and can then evolve into complex systems. Systems generated with LINC II compile into machine-efficient COBOL [JMPSc].

ence in using LINC in 11 systems in six corporations and compared this with COBOL and PL/I development of 21 systems in the same six corporations. Figures 9.2 and 9.3 show the result. The average productivity for the LINC development was 179 function points per person-month; that for the traditional lifecycle was about 7. For complex systems, the difference was greater than for simple systems.

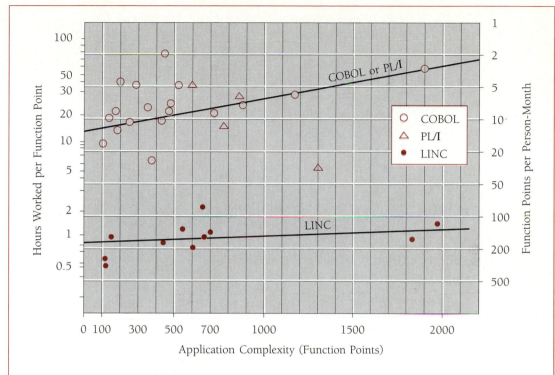

**FIGURE 9.2** Results of Comparison of LINC plus the Iterative Prototyping Lifecycle with That of the Traditional COBOL or PL/I Lifecycle

These measurements show variations in productivity between the traditional COBOL or PL/I lifecycle and an interactive prototyping lifecycle using the Unisys LINC system generator [RUDOLPH84].

**The 11 LINC applications were measured as follows:**

| Application | Work Needed to Develop the Application (Person-Hours) | Size of Application (Function Points) | Function Points per Person-Month |
|---|---|---|---|
| Meat processing | 495 | 601 | 195 |
| Share purchase | 148 | 149 | 160 |
| Corporate accounting | 2,535 | 1,986 | 125 |
| Job costing | 330 | 436 | 213 |
| Rates | 1,650 | 1,848 | 178 |
| Work in process | 660 | 549 | 133 |
| Purchased material | 75 | 110 | 235 |
| Retail parts | 660 | 675 | 165 |
| Wholesale distribution | 660 | 700 | 170 |
| Message switching | 62 | 117 | 302 |
| Teller system | 900 | 652 | 89 |
| | | Average | 179 |

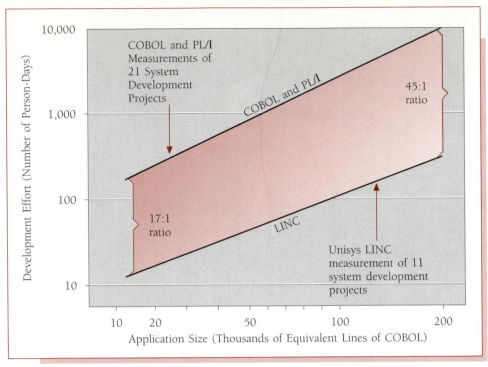

FIGURE 9.3 Total development effort in person-days is shown here for the traditional COBOL and PL/I lifecycle and the LINC protyping lifecycle of the systems in Figure 9.2 [RUDOLPH84].

# Overland Express, Inc.

Overland Express, Inc., is a U.S. nationwide trucking company. In 1985, following the deregulation of the transportation industry, Overland found itself in a fiercely competitive situation. It was deemed necessary to build a complex, high-performance system for running its production operations, which had to be operational within nine months. The system, when built, consisted of half a million lines of COBOL.

Normally, a system of this complexity would take three years to build. Overland started the project in November 1985, using LINC II with prototype evolution (Figure 9.4). One analyst from Overland and two from Unisys worked on the requirements definition, supervised by a Unisys project manager. Prototyping was started during the requirements definition stage. User concurrence on the requirements was gained by the end of December. Functional design was finished in January. This included completion of a working prototype with a demonstration database. The prototype was important in gaining key user acceptance.

Detailed design took another six weeks, during which the prototype was expanded into more detail. The system was then estimated to be 3400 function points. Construction started at the end of March and took three months. Five Overland analysts worked on data conversion and software interfaces to other systems. The system was cut over by July 4.

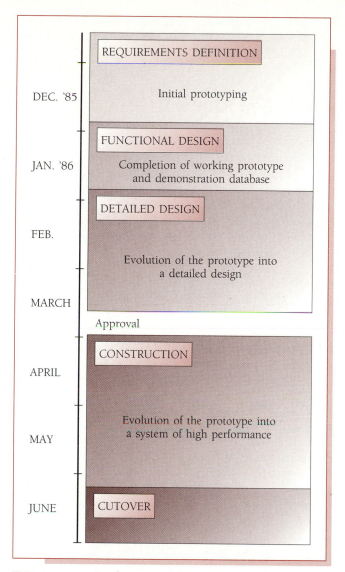

FIGURE 9.4 Development of "Discovery," a System of High Complexity (500,000 lines of COBOL)

This system was needed quickly by Overland Express for competitive reasons. A system of this size would normally take 3 years to develop with the traditional lifecycle—with a high probability of failure. It was the first use of Unisys LINC in Overland Express, Inc. Given more experience with LINC and RAD methodologies, the lifecycle could have been shortened further.

When this system was built, Overland had not used LINC II or any similar tools. LINC II, in fact, had not been generally released by Unisys. JRP and JAD workshops as described in Chapters 7 and 8 were not used. The cycle time could have been shortened if RAD techniques had been fully used by experienced developers. Nevertheless, Overland acquired its critical production system in less than eight months. It processed over 12,000 full-screen transactions per hour and proved reliable and easy to change.

## Who Will Build the Prototype?

Many prototypes are built by one person who is fast and competent with the prototyping tool. This person is often an I.S. professional but could be an end user. The prototype may be built by a two-person team, one end user and one I.S. professional. It is generally not appropriate to have large teams working on a prototype. Two people should be the maximum for most situations.

The prototype builder should be skilled and fast with the prototyping tools, able to modify the prototype quickly while interacting with the users.

Initial prototypes are often built while a JAD workshop is in progress.

## Building the Prototype

Good prototyping tools ought to *enforce* cleanly structured design—but many do not.

Prototyping should never be an excuse for casual work in which structured design is abandoned. Where this rule is not followed, a prototype that grows complex, written in languages like FOCUS, RAMIS, NOMAD, etc., can be a spaghetti-like mess that becomes difficult to modify or convert to a working system. The prototypers should first build something simple. This starts a debate early in the evolution that may flush out misconceptions. The initial prototype is successively enhanced. With complex systems it is desirable to build the functionality first and then polish the human factoring.

Prototyping should be a way to introduce end users' creativity into the design process. To achieve this, it is desirable to motivate the reviewers appropriately, to make them excited about their role in developing the system and encourage them to think inventively about how the system could improve their procedures. Brainstorming sessions may be used for discussing the potentials of the prototyped system.

## Who Will Review the Prototype?

As part of the planning process, the reviewers should be selected. The main reviewers are end users who will employ the eventual system. Some of the reviewers should be very knowledgeable about the application procedures.

A potential problem in prototyping occurs when reviewers do not spend the time or have the enthusiasm to do a thorough creative review. It is necessary to select reviewers with sufficient commitment who are determined that the system will meet the needs of their area as effectively as possible.

In its final stages, the prototype may also be reviewed by:

- technical staff who will build the final system;
- the human factoring expert, who may operate a usability laboratory (Chapter 17);
- management;
- the Executive Owner (Executive Sponsor);
- possibly external reviewers such as customers;
- possibly an external consultant.

# Step-by-Step or Continuous Evolution?

Prototypes can evolve either continuously or in a succession of discrete releases. The left side of Figure 9.5 shows discrete step-by-step evolution; the right side shows continuous evolution.

*Step-by-step evolution* progresses from one planned prototype to another. Each prototype is reviewed until the final system is achieved.

*Continuous evolution* progresses with a sequence of modifications, continuously adjusting the prototype until the target is reached. This requires intelligent, understanding end users working as a team, with the developer(s) reviewing the evolution. These reviewers should be available every day.

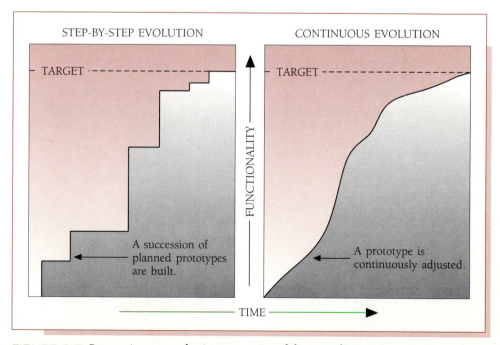

FIGURE 9.5 Prototyping can evolve in a succession of discrete releases, or continuous evolution can occur. The RAD lifecycle normally employs continuous evolution, which is faster and more satisfactory but requires the users who work with the prototype to be available at any time.

With step-by-step prototyping, for each prototype a list of desirable enhancements is created, and a target date is set for when the next version will be available for review. In one highly complex financial system, six prototypes were built over a period of six months. The prototypes steadily converged to the required system, and the last prototype became the working system.

With continuous evolution, the reviewers work regularly with the prototype builders, examining each enhancement when it is working. Continuous evolution tends to be used when there is a closely knit relationship between the builders and users. Sometimes in continuous evolution it is necessary to suspend the interaction while the builders step back, rethink and re-architect their system.

> Continuous evolution is generally the fastest form of iterative evolution and is recommended for the RAD lifecycle, but it needs to be well managed so that there is no inflation of requirements.

> When the feedback loop is too short, it may destabilize the project.

Selected users should be available whenever needed to validate or change the evolving prototype.

When demonstrating a prototype, the analyst may create small files of made-up data to illustrate what the system will do. In other cases, made-up data are not good enough. The users need to update real data or explore complex databases in order to experience what the proposed system will do for them. If real data are required, the users may be given prototypes connected to a *live* data system or may be given data that have been *extracted* from a live data system. The latter is generally safer and more flexible.

If the users do not update the data, they may be given report generators or other facilities that use data in a live database but that cannot modify the data. Often, however, the users want to manipulate or update the data. They should then be given extracted data to use, not live data.

When prototyping decision-support systems, the users ask for information relevant to the decisions. The analyst must find out where such data exist, capture them and reconstruct them in the data management system of the prototyping tool. Sometimes they exist on batch files, sometimes in corporate databases; sometimes they can be obtained from external sources.

# From Prototype to Working System

When the prototype is regarded as complete, there may still be much work to do in building the operational system. A list should be created of the system features that are missing from the prototype. These may include:

- features for recovery from failures;
- features for fallback;
- security features;
- features for auditability;

- features for ease of maintenance;
- machine efficiency;
- facilities for having multiple users;
- facilities for high-volume usage with adequate response times;
- larger database facilities;
- networking facilities;
- operation on a different machine;
- documentation.

In some cases, the prototype becomes the working system; in other cases, it needs rearchitecting before it is usable; in still other cases, an entirely different system is built in a different language.

> In the RAD lifecycle, it is important that the prototype evolve into a solid final system with a code generator that gives good machine performance.

## Expectation Management

A danger of prototyping is that the users, motivated to be excited about the prototype so that they make constructive suggestions, acquire expectations that cannot be fulfilled. They may expect a working system similar to the prototype to be available almost immediately and cannot understand why they have to wait so long. It is important to establish the expectations of the users correctly.

## Prototypes and Training

The prototype may be a useful training vehicle. People who will eventually use the system can work with the prototype for training and practice so that they are ready for the system when it eventually arrives.

## Pilots

The term **pilot** is also used for a system not yet fully operational.

> A **pilot system** is a preliminary system in which the functions and design are thought to be understood, but the system is cut over in a limited form so that experience can be gained with it before the full system is cut over.

A pilot system is a fully working system deployed at first with only a small number of users, a small number of terminals or a small database. When it is found to be satisfactory, the number of users may be increased and the database expanded. For example, if the final system is to have 500 terminals, a pilot system might be initially operated with 5. If the system is to be installed in 1000 dealerships, it might first be operated in 10. As a result of this pilot operation, modifications are usually made before the system is fully deployed.

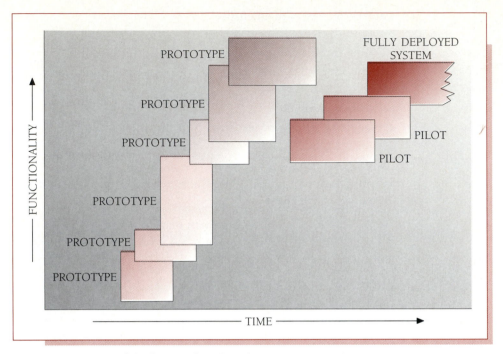

FIGURE 9.6 Some of the functionality of the final prototype may be cut back when the first pilot is installed.

A prototype is used where the functions and detailed design of a system are not yet fully understood. The prototype is used to explore and solidify the functions and design.

Sometimes a powerful prototyping tool enables its users to build a great deal of functionality into the prototypes as they progress through multiple iterations. The designers of the system may decide to cut down on some of the functions when the first pilot system is built. They may do this because some functions are deemed to be of limited value or may duplicate other functions or because some functions would worsen machine performance or increase implementation difficulty. Enthusiastic prototyping sometimes results in overengineering. It is desirable to avoid this in the expensive implementation phase.

Figure 9.6 shows a typical progression of a complex system for which the functions were only partially understood at the beginning. There are six prototypes of growing functionality. After the sixth prototype, the system is rearchitected and some functions are eliminated. The first pilot comes into use in a live environment. After a time, minor improvements are made to it. After the second pilot has proven itself, more improvements are made and the full system is deployed.

# Benefits and Dangers

Prototyping has many benefits and should be used for most systems. It also has some dangers if used casually. The dangers of prototyping are listed in Box 9.2a.

## Box 9.2a    The Dangers of Prototyping

- Quick, casual design may replace well-structured design.
- The prototype encourages the users to change their minds about requirements. They may continually invent requirements so that the prototype constantly changes and does not converge quickly to an implementable form.
- The users' expectation may become too high. They may think they can have the system immediately.
- There is a temptation to make the prototype the production system, without adequate consideration of security, auditability, fallback, recovery, maintainability, performance, networking or documentation.
- The user may take the prototype too literally, when the implemented system will be different.
- The user may be too casual about the prototype and not take the time to identify its potential flaws.

To avoid these dangers, prototyping should be part of a formal RAD methodology, which gives the developers guidance in the most effective techniques.

The dangers are easily countered by good management of the prototyping effort. To avoid the dangers, prototyping should be regarded as a component of an overall RAD methodology, where the methodology gives the developers guidance in the most effective techniques. The rest of the lifecycle enforces good design and implementation. Box 9.2b lists the benefits of prototyping.

## Box 9.2b    The Benefits of Prototyping

- Users understand and react to prototypes far better than to paper specifications. Often, they fail to understand or miss important points in paper specifications.
- With a good tool, it is quicker to build a prototype than to build paper specifications.
- Prototyping introduces early reality testing into a project. The users can see what is being built for them and critique it.
- Without prototyping, there is a substantial risk of building an inadequate system, wrong features or, at worst, a system that users will reject.
- It encourages users to contribute creative input into the design process.
- When using or reviewing a prototype, users tend to be unbiased by existing systems.
- Prototyping enables errors and weaknesses to be caught before expensive design and programming are done.

Box 9.2b    Continued

- Prototypes, or partial prototypes, are of great help in Joint Application Design (JAD or I.E./JAD) sessions.
- Prototypes can generate excitement and improve the morale of the users and developers.
- Prototypes are valuable for communicating what is required to programmers.
- Prototypes provide users with early experience with the system and may be used as training tools.
- Prototyping can give fast development by having the prototype evolve into the final system.

# Summary

Methodology Chart 9 gives a detailed procedure for prototyping. This may be modified to suit the circumstances and to fit it into the overall development lifecycle.

# References

[JMPSa] From *The James Martin Productivity Series*, Volume 1, *High-Productivity Technology*; Volume 5, *Application and Code Generators for I.S. Professionals*; Volume 6, *Computer-Aided Software Engineering*. The Martin Report, Inc., 22 Bessom Street, Marblehead, Massachusetts 01945 (617–639-1958).

[JMPSb] From *The James Martin Productivity Series*, Volume 4, *Application Generators for End Users*. The Martin Report, Inc., 22 Bessom Street, Marblehead, Massachusetts 01945 (617–639–1958).

[JMPSc] From *The James Martin Productivity Series*. A tutorial on LINC II is in Volume 5, *Application and Code Generators for I.S. Professionals*. The Martin Report, Inc., 22 Bessom Street, Marblehead, Massachusetts 01945 (617–639–1958).

[RUDOLPH84] E. E. Rudolph, *Productivity in Computer Application Development*, University of Auckland, Auckland, New Zealand, 1984.

# CHAPTER 10

# SWAT Teams

Particularly critical for fast development is the use of small teams of highly trained developers. It is desirable to put the best developers together with the best tools and train them thoroughly in the best techniques. The most powerful tools enable a team of two or three skilled developers to create a substantial system in two or three months.

*SWAT* stands for

- Skilled
- With
- Advanced
- Tools

A SWAT Team is a small team of highly trained developers who work together at high speed. They are highly skilled at using a toolset selected to facilitate the fastest possible iterative development.

Such a team normally consists of two, three or (often) four people. Each of the team members has a personal computer with an I-CASE toolset with which code can be generated and modified rapidly. The team members may work in the same room. Their personal computers may be networked together. The SWAT Team should start with the output of a JAD workshop and build the entire system (or sometimes a large subsystem).

The members of the SWAT Team should work together on multiple projects. Like members of a professional music quartet, they know each other's capabilities. Among them they have the complete set of capabilities to finish the system (or subsystem).

Some early SWAT Teams were found in small consulting companies doing contract system development. Such companies would adopt one fourth-generation language or code generator and build small teams that were highly skilled with that one tool. In bidding on a contract, they would decide whether their tool and technique were good for that system; if not, they would reject the contract. One such corporation was Fourth Generation Technology, Inc., in San Diego, which built systems rapidly with the fourth-generation language FOCUS (and only FOCUS). Some of these companies did well financially because they could develop systems much faster than organizations using traditional tools and techniques. As discussed in Chapter 3, the early fourth-generation languages were appropriate for systems with low throughput but not for heavy-duty computing. Later, the tools improved, and some code generators were capable of achieving high machine performance.

Increasingly, the more forward-thinking I.S. organizations began to create teams specialized in the use of advanced tools.

# Productivity

One of the characteristics of computing is that *skilled* professionals can achieve much more than the *average* professionals. *Good* programmers can write *three times as much* bug-free code as the *average* programmer. *Genius* programmers can write *ten times as much*.

A typical developer programming manually with a third-generation language might average 40 lines of code per day (taking into account the time spent on design, coding and testing). A brilliant programmer working hard often achieves 200 lines of code per day.

With CASE tools that generate code, more can be achieved. It is not uncommon to find bright developers producing more than 1000 equivalent-lines-of-COBOL per day. There is less need for genius. With the best I-CASE tools, many developers can train themselves to be high performers.

The goal of SWAT Team management is to group together high performers and make them highly skilled with the most powerful tools. Many examples exist of SWAT Teams averaging more than 1000 equivalent-lines-of-COBOL per day with I-CASE tools. An example is given later in this chapter. At the time of writing, there is a startling difference between the elapsed time for design and programming in the average I.S. shop and the equivalent in well-managed SWAT-Team development.

## The Effect of Large Teams

System development productivity is strongly affected by the number of people on the system development team. Large teams tend to give low development productivity. The reason is that the number of interactions between team members increases rapidly as team size increases. If there are $N$ people on a team, all interacting, the number of person-to-person interactions is $N(N - 1)/2$.

When people interact, there is miscommunication. The attempt to lessen miscommunication by documenting the interactions is time-consuming and often does not work well. The productivity-reducing effects are approximately proportional to the square of the number of interacting team members.

My young daughter knows only one piece of algebra: When $N$ people sit round a dinner table and all clink wine glasses, there should be $N(N - 1)/2$ clinks. At the start of dinner we say, "What is N?" and she works out $N(N - 1)/2$ to see whether algebra works. If there are 3 people, there are 3 clinks; if there are 10 people, there are 45 clinks; if there were 100 people and one second between each wine-glass clink, the clinking would go on for one hour and 22 minutes. In a team of 3 developers, the person-to-person interactions are manageable. With 10 developers, they are difficult to manage, and there will be many problems caused by miscommunication. A team of 100 developers all interacting with one another is virtually impossible to manage.

Statistics for conventional programming show much larger numbers of lines of code per person (averaged over the life of the project) for very small teams than for large teams. Application development projects with very large numbers of people are often disastrous. One-person projects exhibit the highest productivity. Figure 10.1 shows statistics for COBOL programming.

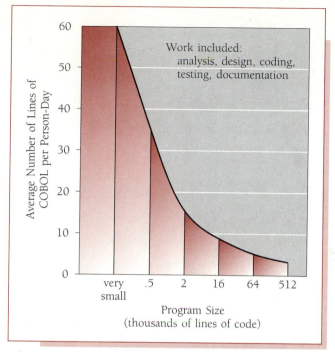

FIGURE 10.1 Statistics for COBOL Programmers with the Traditional Lifecycle (Source: COBOL statistics compiled by Capers Jones [JONES86].

There is a large variation in the average number of lines of COBOL per person-day, depending on the size of the program (and, hence, on the size of the team of programmers). The standard deviation in the number of lines of code per person-day is approximately equal to the mean. The numbers can be double this amount when COBOL productivity aids are used.

*Note:* Sometimes measurements of the number of lines of code per person-day relate only the coding and testing time, in which cases the numbers are substantially higher. It is appropriate to measure the total cycle time.

The average number of lines of code per person-year varies from 800 to 15,000, depending on the size of the program. To a large extent this reflects the effect of large teams. For example, 500-line programs are written by one person; 500,000-line programs are written by large teams. Figure 10.2 illustrates another variation in productivity [WILLET73].

A SWAT Team of three people in one room using the same toolset can operate rapidly with few communication problems.

## The Effect of Experience

Productivity of an individual improves with experience. He becomes more familiar with the toolset and with reusable structures. With the most user-friendly tools, de-

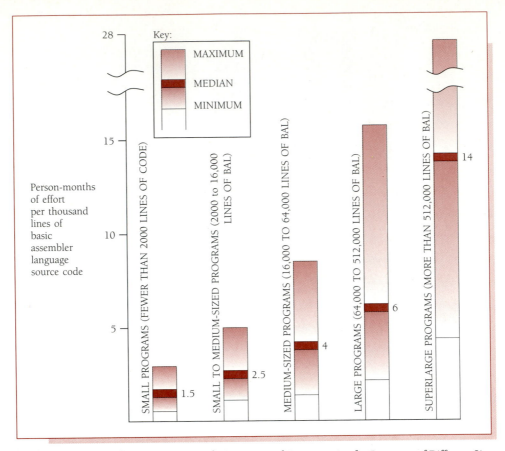

FIGURE 1O.2 Productivity Ranges with Conventional Programming for Programs of Different Sizes
Programmer productivity with large programs is one tenth of that achieved with small programs [WILLET73].

These statistics from AT&T in a TSO environment show a median of 3.4 lines of basic ASSEMBLER language code per day for programs over 512,000 lines of code. The minimum shown for such large programs is one line of code per day.

The key to high productivity is to split work into subsystems, each of which a small team can create with a powerful I-CASE toolset in three months or so, where the interfaces between the subsystems have consistency enforced by the computerized tools.

velopers climb the learning curve rapidly. It is common, however, that productivity on the second project is 25 per cent higher than on the first project tackled.

Figure 10.3 shows productivity improvements measured with developers using the Cortex Application Factory [PICARDI86].

In addition to growing experience with the toolset, SWAT Team members have a growing experience of working together. They often create their own reusable constructs and designs and have mutual understanding of these, which enables them to design and build systems more quickly. The SWAT Team improves with experience.

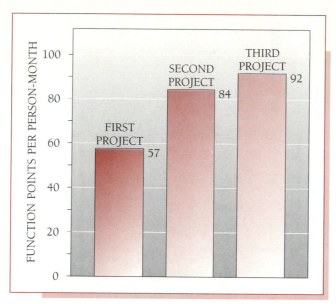

FIGURE 10.3 Measurement of the Effect of Experience
Developers become more *skilled* after their first, second, and subsequent projects. [PICARDI86].

# The Construction Process

In a recommended RAD lifecycle, the SWAT Team becomes involved after the first JAD workshop is held. (See Figure 10.4.)

Team members learn about the system as the design is being consolidated, and the users work with the prototypes. SWAT-Team members may help make improvements to the design. They should incorporate reusable components or designs that already exist so that the construction can proceed faster.

This SWAT Team involvement occurs before the Executive Owner gives the go-ahead for construction but when there is little reasonable doubt that the go-ahead will be given. In and before the second JAD workshop, SWAT-Team members establish a working relationship with the end users who will help them during the Construction Phase. The team members participate in the second JAD workshop, helping to consolidate the design.

An interactive system usually has many transaction-types. Each transaction-type may be assigned to one SWAT-Team member, who builds it, checks it with the users, modifies it as required and tests it. The first transactions may take many days to build. The later ones are built more rapidly because they are variations on transactions already built. Often, the team builds the core of the system relatively quickly (in, say, four or five weeks) and spends the rest of the remaining weeks refining it, adding new transactions and integrating the pieces as they are built.

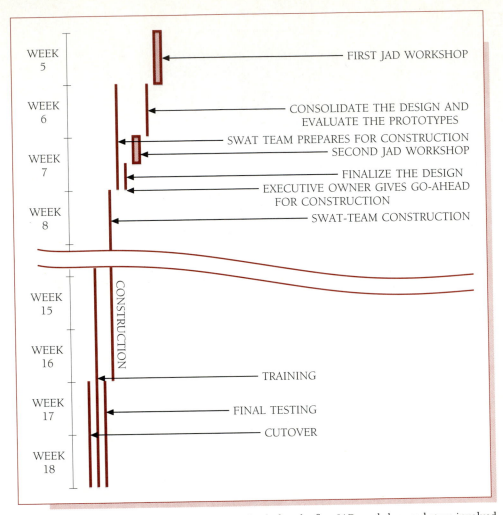

WEEK 5 ———————— FIRST JAD WORKSHOP

WEEK 6 ———————— CONSOLIDATE THE DESIGN AND
EVALUATE THE PROTOTYPES

———————— SWAT TEAM PREPARES FOR CONSTRUCTION
———————— SECOND JAD WORKSHOP

WEEK 7 ———————— FINALIZE THE DESIGN
———————— EXECUTIVE OWNER GIVES GO-AHEAD
FOR CONSTRUCTION

WEEK 8 ———————— SWAT-TEAM CONSTRUCTION

CONSTRUCTION

WEEK 15

WEEK 16 ———————— TRAINING

WEEK 17 ———————— FINAL TESTING
———————— CUTOVER

WEEK 18

FIGURE 10.4 The SWAT team becomes involved after the first JAD workshop and stays involved through cutover.

Most integration will occur when the components are designed; it will be done using the coordination software of the I-CASE toolset. Most testing will occur as the transactions are built. The final testing should be relatively quick, and the users should get exactly what they expect because they have checked out the program for each transaction as it was built.

As the transactions are built, they are used in the training program and by the staff who create the user documentation. On systems built this way, there should be no surprises for the end users when the system is cut over. A goal is to have zero requests for change in the few weeks after cutover and, if there are requests for change, to be able to accommodate them quickly.

# 60-Day Projects

SWAT Teams should work on systems or subsystems that can be completed in a reasonably short time. Three months (60 or so working days) is a reasonable target time. If the overall project is large and complex, it should be divided into subsystems, as described in Chapter 12, which can be built in parallel by separate teams.

A SWAT Team skilled with a powerful I-CASE toolset should be able to generate, on average, 600 lines of COBOL or equivalent per person-day. In 60 working days, three people may generate $60 \times 3 \times 600 = 108,000$ lines of COBOL. (In many cases, a skilled, well-established SWAT Team achieves substantially more than this.) Most data-processing applications contain fewer than 100,000 lines of COBOL or equivalent. These may be tackled by one SWAT Team. Projects of more than 1000 or 2000 function points might be split into subsystems that can be tackled by separate SWAT Teams. (The exact number will depend upon experience with the chosen toolset. Some SWAT Teams achieve over 2000 function points in 60 days.)

A SWAT Team may work very intensely for a 60-day period. It cannot keep up such intense work indefinitely. Periodically the team members need time off to relax and recharge their batteries. Confining the work to 60-day periods can help avoid the problem of individuals becoming burnt out.

# Case Study of SWAT-Team Development

Let us look at a detailed case example of SWAT-Team development [FAIRLEY89]. A personnel system called "Organization, Jobs and Control Plans" was built for Rank Xerox (UK) Ltd. It consisted of 42 types of on-line IMS DB transactions processed against a DB2 database of 25 tables (relations). The actual number of lines of COBOL generated was 350,000. However, in order to compare this with a traditional lifecycle approach, we should assume that a skeleton transaction program would have been used to reduce the number of written lines to about 275,000. Figure 10.5 gives numbers describing the complexity of the system.

The system was produced by 3.5 people in 14 working weeks. Traditional techniques, with hand coding of 275,000 lines of COBOL, would typically have taken more than 25 person-years and an elapsed time of two years or more. Function-point estimates give a similar indication of the difference between this project and traditional lifecycle development.

The system was built in an information-engineering environment (Chapter 21) in which a Business Area Analysis had been done for the Personnel business area. For that overall area, the following existed:

- entity-relationship model (but not a fully normalized data model);
- process decomposition diagram down to the elementary process level (and, in some cases, subelementary processes);

| | |
|---|---:|
| No. of entity types | 25 |
| No. of attributes | 142 |
| No. of entity-relationship memberships | 60 |
| No. of procedure steps | 42 |
| No. of procedure-step action diagrams | 42 |
| Total number of procedure action diagram statements | 9980 |
| No. of common action blocks | 92 |
| Average no. of statements per common action block | 40 |
| Average no. of lines of generated COBOL per procedure-step action diagram | 2346 |
| Average no. of lines of generated COBOL per common action block | 1438 |
| Average no. of lines of generated COBOL per dialog manager | 2899 |
| Total number of generated lines of COBOL (including data division) | 350000 |
| Number of person-days | 268 |
| Average lines of COBOL per person-day | 1306 |

FIGURE 10.5 Statistics for the Rank Xerox Case Example of a SWAT Team of 3.5 People Creating a Personnel System of 350,000 ines of COBOL in 14 Working Weeks [FAIRLEY89]

- equivalent process dependency diagram (which did not capture all the appropriate logic).
- matrix mapping processes against entities.

The Texas Instruments IEF toolset was used [IEF]. The models from the Business Area Analysis resided in the encyclopedia of this toolset, and the SWAT Team used the same toolset for detailed design and code generation.

The development of the system required a total of 268 person-days during the 14 working weeks. Figure 10.6 gives a breakdown of how the 14 weeks were utilized.

Different transactions were worked on by different team members. They averaged about 5 person-days per transaction to do the transaction design, screen and dialog design, detailed logic design, code generation and transaction testing. While this was the average, the actual time varied greatly. The first transaction took 25 person-days; subsequent ones took less time because they were similar; later, some transactions were completed in a few hours because they were minor variations on transactions already created.

A breakdown of the utilization of person-days of the SWAT Team developing the system described in Figure 10.5 is listed in Figure 10.7.

Prior to this activity, two weeks were taken up in familiarization and system structuring. After the transaction testing, the project completion took another two weeks.

---

## Project Startup

Familiarization and system structuring:                                    2 weeks

## Production

Transaction design, screen and dialog design detailed logic design,
code generation, transaction testing:                                      10 weeks

> The Construction Phase took about 5 person-days for each
> transaction. Different team members worked simultaneously
> on different transactions.

## Project Completion

System testing, user-acceptance testing, tidy-up, documentation,
hand-over:                                                                  2 weeks

                                                        TOTAL:  14 weeks

---

FIGURE 10.6 Breakdown of Elapsed Time on the Project Described in Figure 10.5 [FAIRLEY89]

The project report commented:

The one parameter which has the greatest influence on the total effort required is the number of transactions. It is felt that varying the number of entities, attributes or relationships has an effect significantly less than varying the number of transactions.

Project startup took two weeks, project completion took two weeks and the production phase in the middle took 5 man-days per transaction. This can probably be extrapolated to projects involving anything from 10 to 100 transactions, increasing the two week phases to three weeks in the latter case [FAIRLEY89].

On this, as with all other projects, there were some factors favorable to high-speed development and some unfavorable. It is always important to try to maximize the favorable factors and eliminate the unfavorable ones. Here the team listed the favorable and unfavorable factors as follows:

Favorable Factors

- a high-quality team;
- a strongly motivated team;
- a small team;
- a contractual wall around the project;
- an enthusiastic user department able to respond to questions fairly quickly;
- excellent DBA (database administration) support.

Unfavorable Factors

- lack of continuity in user involvement from the Business Area Analysis to system design;
- a Business Area Analysis model that did not capture all the business logic;
- poor mainframe response times;
- occasional nonavailability of mainframe resources.

| TOTAL EFFORT: | | 268 man-days |
|---|---|---|

TOTAL TIME:  16 elapsed weeks
Including Xmas and a part-time first week

—equivalent to 14 working weeks or 3 calendar months

| BREAKDOWN OF EFFORT | Man-Days | % of Total |
|---|---|---|
| Project management and team meetings | 24 | 9 % |
| User meetings and reviews | 14 | 5 % |
| Team Familiarization | 9 | 3 % |
| Encyclopedia maintenance and development coordination | 13 | 5 % |
| Detailed design of system structure | 11 | 4 % |
| Detailed design of screens, dialog and action diagrams | 66 | 25 % |
| Project database design, database transformation, generation and maintenance | 10 | 4 % |
| Code generation | 27 | 10 % |
| Mainframe upload/download time | 30 | 11 % |
| Time lost due to unavailability of mainframe resources | 10 | 4 % |
| TSO Testing | 32 | 12 % |
| IMS Testing | 5 | 2 % |
| User-acceptance testing support | 11 | 4 % |
| Tidy-up, documentation and hand-over | 6 | 2 % |
| Total | 268 | |

FIGURE 10.7 Breakdown of Utilization of Person-Days on the Project Described in Figure 10.5 [FAIRLEY89]

The team commented that the *five most important factors* in any implementation project are:

1. quality of the Business Area Analysis;
2. ability and experience of the development team;
3. size of the development team;
4. attitude and responsiveness of the user;
5. reliability and performance of the mainframe environment.

Based on the experience of this project, the team wrote a number of recommendations:

- *Project Team Size.* Keep it small. The team size of three to four people was ideal. A team size of about six people would probably give good results. Above this size, the productivity per man will decrease, and the effort required for encyclopedia (repository) maintenance and development coordination will increase.

- *Project Team Skills.* Avoid specialization. Each team member should be capable of analysis, design, action diagramming, code generation and TSO testing, and each should have TSO/ISPF experience. Database was the only area that was allocated to a single team member, who carried out maintenance of the entity-relationship diagram and data structure diagram, as well as database generation. This was done in order to apply strict controls to database changes.

- *Task Scheduling.* Be flexible. Avoid the traditional sequential approach, in which all the procedure logic design is done before any generation. Try things out as early as possible. Generate a database in the first week of the project. Generate and test transactions as soon as they are ready.

- *Encyclopedia (Repository) Management.* Think before you check out subsets from the encyclopedia (repository). Subsetting is very powerful and can help increase team efficiency. However, it can also have the opposite effect if not used properly. Subsets should be as small as possible. Full expansion is usually not needed. All subsets are temporary. No subset should remain checked out for long.

- *Mainframe Usage.* Grab as many lines as you can. In a perfect world, each team member would have an IEF workstation with mainframe communications *plus* an IBM terminal. An acceptable compromise is to have one workstation with communications per team member plus two shared terminals. Anything less will reduce productivity and, given the cost of a person-day, will easily outweigh the apparent cost savings on lines. The percentage of time spent on upload/download (Figure 10.7) will remain high if each team member can only use one workstation.

A considerable amount of time was taken up in interaction with the mainframe code generator and in mainframe upload and download, and 10 person-days were wasted due to unavailability of mainframe resources (Figure 10.7). There is much to be said for using a code generator that operates on the desktop machine, which the developers can interact with as fast as possible.

# Selection of Team Members

Building the most effective SWAT Teams is an art that needs careful observation of human personalities and interaction. The goal is to combine the most capable people with the most powerful toolset, but those people must enjoy working together so that the team is greater than the sum of its parts.

Each team member must be able to work fast and constructively, working well with the other team members. He should be able to work long hours when necessary. He must be fully familiar with the techniques that are used (for example, the CASE diagramming techniques) and must be as skilled as possible with the toolset and able to operate quickly with it.

Although many SWAT Teams are assembled quickly, it takes time to build the most effective team. Team members' personalities and skills must complement one another. Their work habits must be compatible. Their attitudes must be positive. They must be determined to make the team succeed.

## Criteria for Selection of SWAT-Team Members

*Each person:*

- will work fast and constructively;
- has an attitude geared to success;
- will cooperate well with the other team members;
- will work long hours when necessary;
- has good communications skills;
- is familiar with the basic techniques needed;
- is highly skilled with the I-CASE toolset and can operate fast with it.

*Some team members* may have certain specialized skills, such as database design or skill in writing good HELP screens.

*In combination,* the team has the complete set of skills required. A team that works well together should stay together for multiple projects.

Management should observe the team carefully during its first weeks to ensure that the personalities are working well together and make changes if they are not. The executive assembling the SWAT Teams should be a student of human personalities. As new projects come and go, some team members may have to be rotated from one team to another.

A period check should be made of the SWAT Team to see whether they are working effectively together and enjoying themselves. The quality of their work should be quietly audited.

In combination, the team should contain all the skills needed to create their subsystem. It is desirable for all members of the team to have all the basic skills. They are generalists, not specialists. Some more specialized skills may reside in one team member—for example, physical database design and optimization or skill in writing good HELP screens.

## Auditions

SWAT Teams may help recruit people for other SWAT Teams. Their experience tells them what is needed. A technique that is effective in the hiring process is **auditioning** [DEMARCO&LISTER87]. The candidate is asked to prepare a short presentation on some aspect of work relating to applications or their development or to management problems. A small audience, including SWAT-Team members, reacts to the presentation and asks the candidate questions. After the audition, each person present is asked to describe his reaction to the candidate. From this, judgments can be made about how the candidate would fit in.

When an established SWAT Team needs a new member, this person needs to be picked very carefully to ensure that he will fit in. An audition is appropriate. The SWAT Team should take the candidate out to dinner. Some of the previous work of the candidate should be inspected. SWAT-Team members might suggest their friends as candidates if a new member is needed. This may help ensure that the human chemistry is right. Auditions by a SWAT Team help preserve the team's own feeling that it is special. Failed auditions can boost morale in that the team feels it has the authority to preserve its own uniqueness.

# A New Breed of Professional

A member of a RAD SWAT Team uses a mix of skills different from that of the traditional systems analyst or traditional programmer. The SWAT-Team member is a generalist who must have the following skills:

- Analysis
- Design
- Code generation
- Testing
- Skill with the I-CASE tool
- Good interaction with the end users
- Ability to translate end-user statements into working prototypes
- Good interaction with other team members

I-CASE tools are powerful and easy to use; so, they make it practical to find this range of skills in one individual. SWAT-Team members enjoy using the powerful tools, but they must be good at human interaction as well as interaction with the toolset.

New graduates with the right personality tend to learn this skill set effectively. New graduates should be trained to do RAD development rather than traditional development. Some experienced I.S. staff who enjoy working with I-CASE tools become very effective SWAT Team members; however, some have a negative attitude toward this work. It is vital to select individuals with the right attitude who are determined to make SWAT development work as productively as possible. The SWAT-Team member is a new breed of computer professional.

The work is generally satisfying because the SWAT-Team members see results. They are involved with the lifecycle from JAD to cutover. Because it happens in three months, they do not lose sight of how their work affects the enterprise. They can participate in the sense of excitement about the new system. They feel personally accountable and responsible for building a good system.

# Staying Together

A team that works well together should stay together for many projects. They get to know each other's working style and capabilities. Whereas the JRP and JAD teams stay together for a week or for two week-long workshops, the SWAT Team should stay together for years if it works well. Team members may occasionally leave and be replaced, but the team retains its skill, reputation and character. Much more time can be taken in selecting the team members and making sure they really jell into the most effective team.

Rather than being assembled once, SWAT Teams are *grown* and cultivated. Careful attention must be paid to putting together individuals who respect each other and feel that, together, they can beat the world. The good manager of a RAD environment, responsible for many RAD projects, observes the SWAT Teams carefully, especially new ones, to make sure that they are jelling. If an individual is put on the team and does not fit in with the others after he and they have been given time to adapt, he should be replaced.

Some SWAT Teams stay together for years, respecting, trusting and enjoying each other's professionalism. An observer can see how well they know what is in each other's minds because they speak to each other in half-finished sentences. One person may start a sentence and another will add to it. They often talk in a team shorthand that an outsider cannot follow. They relate new situations to situations they have met in the past. They sometimes have a collective nickname, such as "The Three Amigos" or "The Genghis Khan Gang."

A long-established SWAT Team often has its own library of reusable designs. If its members use a repository-based toolset, they grow their own long-standing repository from which they can extract and modify design for many different projects. They sometimes volunteer to create a new system very rapidly because they know they can do so by adapting existing programs. The knowledge residing collectively in their heads and in their repository becomes formidable.

## Team Motivation

The I.S. management should engender a high level of pride in being a SWAT-Team member. The teams should be measured and their productivity published. There should be competition among the teams to achieve the best results. As in a football league, the teams should be ranked in order of performance, and an award should be given to the top-of-the-league team. An award dinner should be held with spouses present. The top team may be given a vacation, with spouses, in an exotic location.

A member of a well-motivated team has a very strong personal motivation to not let his teammates down. Management should determine the goals of the SWAT Team and motivate the team as strongly as possible to meet those goals. Each individual should be motivated personally and feel strong peer-group pressure to make the team achieve its targets and, if possible, do better than the targets. There should be cohesive striving for excellence.

## Common Goals

When a team jells, it does so because the team members have common goals and truly believe in these goals. The goals should be made crystal clear from the outset. The goals of the SWAT Team should be *high speed* and *high quality*. Together, these bring *low cost*; so, the three-ellipse RAD symbol might decorate the SWAT-Team room.

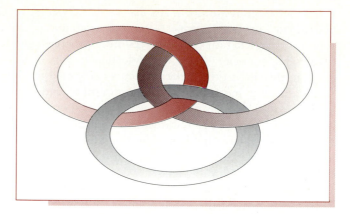

An emphasis on high quality is vital. A team of high-quality people is satisfied only if it produces high-quality work. Much of the pride of the team should come from its reputation for high quality. As we stressed earlier, an emphasis on high quality goes hand in hand with fast I-CASE development. If the developers work to a good JAD design, get it right the first time, satisfy the users with each transaction they build and use the coordinating and validation power of a good I-CASE tool, they will avoid the nasty surprises that often occur after programming with the traditional lifecycle.

## Metrics

Often the most important measurement of results is the simplest: *delivering the system on time*.

Other goals relate to team productivity, system quality and system usability. Measures can be devised for all of these:

- function-points (or equivalent-lines-of-COBOL) per person-day;
- number of bugs found in the delivered system;
- number of design defects in the delivered system;
- number of changes needed in the delivered system to aid usability.

(See Chapter 2.)

## Rewards

Motivation requires appropriate rewards. There should be rewards for the individual and rewards for the team as a whole.

*Some rewards are financial.* Salary raises should relate to achievement of the goals. A substantial portion of an individual's compensation should be a performance-related bonus. The bonus may apply to the team as a whole so that the team works together as strongly as possible to achieve the bonus. Not letting down one's colleagues can be a powerful motivation.

*Prestige-related rewards cost less and can be very effective.* High management should congratulate successful teams. A "victory celebration" should be planned for if the project is completed on time. The resulting programs should have "credit titles," as at the end of a movie, written in the documentation. Names of team members should appear in the credit titles if the project is completed on time.

In addition to motivating and rewarding the team as a whole, individuals should be rewarded. Individuals with repeated success should be promoted to a higher professional grade. They may be rewarded with prestige-oriented gifts such as lapel pins, tie pins, cufflinks, pens or binders, indicating their successful achievements. Management should write letters of congratulation to high achievers. Repeated success should be acknowledged at an awards dinner.

Organizations with many system developers should have a prestigious CASE Club, which meets periodically, holds lectures on advanced CASE techniques and has an annual conference in an exotic location.

Salesmen are motivated with commissions, awards, dinners, a high-performer club, a conference in the Caribbean and much hoopla. SWAT-Team members should have similar motivation.

# A Sense of Uniqueness

*Good SWAT Teams acquire personalities of their own.* The team members feel that they are part of something special. The team has a sense of identity. It has a name. It may have a special room of its own, decorated uniquely. It may have its place for dinner when it works late. It usually has insider jokes and catch phrases. The team sense of identity and uniqueness should be cultivated. It helps build team pride to ensure that team members do not let the team down, do not think of leaving and work hard to make the team's reputation even better.

*Good SWAT Teams tend to improve.* The surprising thing about some of the best SWAT Teams is not how good the team was at the beginning but how much it improved as time went by. One of the ways of improving is to build a well-understood repository of reusable constructs and transaction programs that can be quickly adopted to new applications (Chapters 15 and 22).

It tends to be in the teams that have a personality of their own that the cult of constant improvement occurs. The team members sense that some magic is happening; they feel unstoppable, capable of building transactions much faster than people ever have before.

*I.S. management has to trust the SWAT Teams.* A team must be free to do its own thing. It must be thoroughly trained and know its toolset and associated techniques. But its effectiveness will be lowered if an outside authority is telling it how to work. The team must operate with the users, letting them critique the transactions as they are built. Some managers worry about the team, are scared of its uniqueness or different behavior and worry about what will happen if the team fails. They may interfere defensively. Defensive management almost always lessens the effectiveness of a SWAT Team. Team members must feel that management trusts them. They must be free to charge ahead with their own special methods. They will sometimes make mistakes and learn from those mistakes. But the power of the team will be sapped if they are not free to do what they think will work fast.

*A SWAT Team is sometimes irritating to other developers or managers.* It can be exclusive and self-sufficient. But if it regularly achieves 200 function points per person-month, it is one of the most valuable resources an I.S. executive can have. However self-sufficient and aware of its own uniqueness it becomes, it must listen as carefully as possible to what its users need. The user interaction is an integral part of being effective in the RAD lifecycle.

The SWAT Team should not be allowed to become arrogant. It can *always* learn new things. Software development techniques and I-CASE tools are changing fast. One finds many stale software gurus who have not kept up with new technology and defensively deny that it is of value. Many once-great software corporations become arrogant and later find their share prices plunging catastrophically. Such arrogance is an enemy of success in technology. The SWAT Team, and the whole RAD organization, should be proud, have a sense of being special but, at the same time, have the humility to always look for ways to improve. Arrogance is the onset of decline.

# A Sense of Closure

A development team, like most of us, needs to feel that it is doing well. Periodically, its activities should result in a success that can be celebrated. This happens when the team works on the Construction Phase of the RAD lifecycle. After two or three months or so, the system is finished, and cutover has begun. At this time, there should be a victory celebration.

It should be called a "victory celebration," and a bottle of champagne should be cracked. Members of high management should be present. The SWAT-Team members should be made to feel as good about it as possible. They should be made to *feel* special if we expect them to *be* special.

On a shorter timescale, members of the team generate and test programs for processing individual transactions. These programs should be validated with end users as soon as they work and adjusted where necessary until the users (and the human-factors expert) agree that they are excellent. This provides satisfying mini-successes that encourage the team.

Humans need reassurance from time to time that they are appreciated and are doing well. This can occur naturally in the RAD lifecycle. It rarely happens in a three-year project. Psychologists call the reassurance from successfully completed acts *closures*. After a successful closure, an individual can clean up the remnants from the piece of work and move on happily to the next task. Management should understand the psychological effect of closures and make sure that the developers are congratulated so that they set forth on the next piece of work feeling good and with renewed energy.

> The worst situation for developers is the multiyear project where some people say, "It will never fly."

Large projects need to be split into pieces (Chapter 12), for which frequent closures can be experienced. Frequent closures make both management and developers feel good, especially when the stakes are high. End users are encouraged and made enthusiastic about helping the developers. End-user enthusiasm reinforces developers' enthusiasm. The project has a healthy, vibrant feel to it and is more likely to achieve an excellent result.

# Burnout

SWAT-Team members work very hard during the intensely motivated periods of system construction and testing. Most people who work with that intensity for too long become burned out. Therefore, the construction activity should not last longer than three or four months, and between such periods the developers should have enough time off to relax, spend more time with their families and generally recharge their batteries.

> Management should be constantly on the lookout for early-warning signs of burnout.

> SWAT-Team members, themselves, should be counseled to detect symptoms of burnout and take corrective action.

In practice, we have observed that most SWAT Teams thoroughly enjoy what they are doing, especially if they are working with elegant, powerful toolsets. The ability to see valuable results emerging within a 60-day period helps make the work enjoyable; it is very different from a two-year project.

> *People who are enjoying what they are doing usually do not suffer from burnout.*

The period of preparation prior to building a system takes several weeks. The SWAT-Team members may be involved with this at a relatively low activity level. They may participate in JAD sessions and usability design. Giving them this break from the intensity of SWAT-Team construction enables them to relax somewhat. The change in mental activity enables them to be ready to attack the next SWAT-Team effort with renewed vigor. They are often eager to be back doing what they do best.

During the JAD period, the end users should be intensely motivated; during the Construction Phase, the SWAT-Team members should be intensely motivated. Nobody should be in the pressure cooker all the time.

# Estimating

A SWAT Team must have a realistic target for project completion. If the target is hopelessly tight, the team is made tense and demoralized. Unachievable estimates sap the developers' energy. If management is pressing, regardless, for an unmeetable deadline, the team becomes cynical and loses much of its motivation. Capers Jones, the authority on estimating, comments, "When the schedule for a project is totally unreasonable and unrealistic, and no amount of overtime can allow it to be made, the project team becomes angry and frustrated . . . and morale drops to the bottom" [JONES86].

SWAT Teams that master modern tools achieve results that are very impressive compared with those of traditional programming, but if they are put into a no-win situation, their pride is wounded. At best, their productivity drops; at worst, the team may break up.

To achieve a realistic target, *the SWAT Team should do its own estimating* before the Construction Phase begins.

This estimate should be made at or before the final JAD workshop. It is listed as part of the JAD procedure in Methodology Chart 8.

An experienced SWAT Team knows what it can achieve. It examines the JAD design and uses its own estimating rules for determining how long the project will take and whether additional assistance is needed. It may allocate a certain period of time for start-up, a number of person-days for each transaction type, a period for integration testing and a period for handing over the project.

## System Scope

By the final JAD workshop, the number of function points has been estimated. The number of inputs, outputs, logical internal files, external files and queries has been estimated, and their complexity (high, medium or low) has been assessed. These are represented in a table, as shown in the function point calculation in Appendix I. They represent the *scope* of the system. Some I-CASE tools assist in the function point calculation.

The SWAT Team effectively "signs a contract" with management, agreeing to build a system of that scope by a certain date. If the *scope* changes during the Construction Phase, more development time may be needed. Any change in scope should be agreed upon with management during the Construction Phase.

# Project Study

Two researchers at the University of New South Wales studied projects in industry and measured programmer productivity [JEFFREY&LAWRENCE85].

- They found that productivity was higher when a programmer worked to his own estimate of the development effort rather than to his manager's estimate:

| ESTIMATE MADE: | AVERAGE PRODUCTIVITY IN FUNCTION POINTS |
|---|---|
| By programmer alone | 8.0 |
| By supervisor alone | 6.6 |
| Jointly by supervisor and programmer | 7.8 |

- The productivity was higher still when the estimates were made by a third party who was a systems analyst:

| ESTIMATE MADE: | AVERAGE PRODUCTIVITY IN FUNCTION POINTS |
|---|---|
| By programmer alone | 8.0 |
| By supervisor alone | 6.6 |
| Jointly by supervisor and programmer | 7.8 |
| By systems analyst | 9.5 |

The reason seems likely to be that *the better the estimate, the higher the productivity.*

If the estimate is unrealistically tight, morale slips. If the estimate allows too much time, the programmers tend to fill the time available. Typically, the systems analyst is more skilled at making estimates.

A SWAT Team should continually measure and record its own performance and analyze the measurements so that it becomes skilled at estimating and confident in the results it can achieve. In this way, good estimates and high team morale are likely to be achieved. A motivated SWAT Team will constantly try to improve the performance it can achieve.

# SWAT-Team Work Environment

The SWAT Team must have a work environment that allows them to be as productive as possible. Studies by Capers Jones [JONES86], and by others, have shown that developer productivity in a well-designed office is double that in a poorly designed one. I am appalled by the work environments of computer professionals I see in some organizations. My own productivity would be much lower if I had to work there.

The SWAT Team must have freedom from interruption. There should be private offices either for team individuals or for the team as a whole. Telephone calls should be divertible. Electronic mail or facsimile should replace the phone where appropriate. SWAT-Team members quickly learn when not to interrupt one another.

When I was at Oxford, every student room had an "oak," a sliding oak panel on the outside of the door that, if drawn, meant that the student could not be interrupted. The psychological security of having the oak drawn encouraged intense work. Today, it is unfashionable to have any indication on an office door that visitors are not welcome, but there should be some means of preventing interruptions while the team is striving to meet its target. Some executives are well protected by their secretaries. Similar protection is appropriate for the SWAT Team.

### SWAT-Team Rooms

The SWAT-Team members must be physically close together. They do not work well as a team if they are located on different floors. The SWAT Team also needs to be reasonably close to the users who form the Construction Assistance Team.

The SWAT Team may be in an office where each member has a personal computer connected to a local area network. They may share a laser printer. There may be an adjacent room for meetings that also has a personal computer, possibly with a large display for viewing by several people.

Developers may choose to work late at night or early in the morning. Their office and facilities should be available to them at all hours.

The office should be as pleasant as possible. Many creative people like to work near a window so that they have something pleasant to look at while they think. They can refocus their eyes on the distance periodically.

The SWAT Team should be allowed to design its own work environment, arrange its layout and decorate as it wishes. The team is more likely to stay together if it feels special. Having an office of its own design can help build the team uniqueness and loyalty.

## Avoidance of Interruptions

It usually makes sense to move the SWAT Teams away from the mass of corporate office space, especially open-plan space. There may be cheap but interesting space near the end users. Sometimes houses or apartments are converted. Developers off-site may suffer less from interruptions, noise and frustration. Unusual, idiosyncratic quarters can help the team form a group identity. Figure 10.8 shows an example of an environment for a SWAT Team.

To achieve rapid development, it is important that the developer work in an environment where he can think for long periods of time without interruption. The creative intellect-worker works very differently from a manager. A manager is a multiplexer, constantly switching his attention from one topic to another, rarely spending more than a few minutes on one topic, and is constantly being interrupted. A programmer,

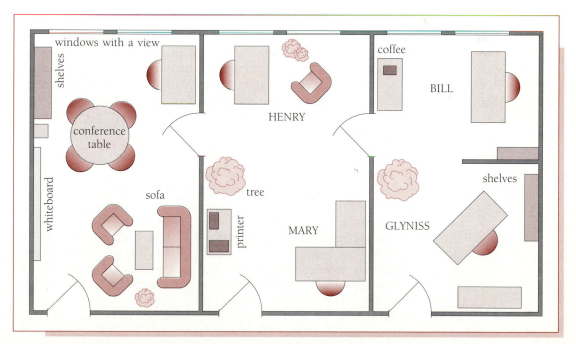

FIGURE 10.8 An Example of a SWAT-Team Working Environment
The SWAT Team should design its own furniture layout.

developer or writer, on the other hand, needs lengthy, continuous periods of mental activity. His brain manipulates a complex web of ideas, slowly organizing them and creating structures. Whenever he is interrupted, the links among the ideas are lost; the ideas might vaporize; it takes time to reestablish the threads. If the interruption is lengthy, he has to reinvent some of them.

## The Condition of "Flow"

Psychologists refer to the state when the brain is working with ideas, busily and efficiently manipulating them, as **flow** [BRADY86]. Flow is a condition of deep thought, euphoric if the ideas are flowing well. The person is barely aware of the passage of time. The genius programmer, composer or author sometimes sits up late into the night, uninterrupted, building with ideas. When an intellect-worker is excited about how ideas are flowing, he curses every telephone call. He wants peace and no interruptions. If there is a constant stream of interruptions, it is difficult or impossible to attain flow.

You cannot instantly switch on this state. It takes time to descend into the thought process, perhaps 10, perhaps 20 minutes of concentration before the ideas flow. Psychologists refer to this as the **immersion period**. During the immersion period, noise or distraction is particularly harmful.

To build systems fast, the RAD developers need to be in a *state of flow*, especially during the Construction Phase, for as much of the day as possible. Management, therefore, must protect them from interruptions. The developers need to have pleasant, quiet working conditions where they can remain immersed in their state of flow for long periods. Every time the phone rings or a visitor comes, the loss to creativity is greater than the interruption time.

The noise level should be low and of a nature that does not interrupt the mental flow. Individual SWAT-Team members meet with users regularly to review the transactions they are building. These meetings should not interrupt the other team members. If the team works in one room, there should be a separate room for user meetings, for general discussions and for team members to make phone calls.

## Having Enough Space

A pleasant office to work in has a greater effect on developer productivity than many people realize. According to Capers Jones, studies show that a developer who has 100 square feet of office space is twice as productive as a developer who is squeezed into 40 square feet [BRADY86]. Developers packed into tight quarters are easily distracted and have limited desk space. The desk in the office where I write has the same surface area as the floor space in some programmers' cubicles. Tom DeMarco and Timothy Lister studied programmer productivity over a period of 10 years or so, holding coding "war games" and measuring the results. Figure 10.9 shows effects of environmental factors on productivity [DEMARCO&LISTER87]. The first quartile in Figure 10.9 had an average performance 2.6 times better than the fourth quartile.

Office costs and developer salaries and benefits vary greatly, but the investment in a skilled developer is typically 20 times the cost of his workplace. So, if lessening the workspace halves the productivity, it is bad management to do so. Organizations that have analyzed such factors, such as IBM laboratories, give the developers good working

| Environments of the Best and Worst Performers in the Coding Research of DeMarco & Lister | | |
|---|---|---|
| Environmental Factor | Those Performing in 1st Quartile | Those Performing in 4th Quartile |
| 1. How much dedicated workspace do you have? | 78 sq. ft. | 46 sq. ft. |
| 2. Is it acceptably quiet? | 57 % yes | 29 % yes |
| 3. Is it acceptably private? | 62 % yes | 19 % yes |
| 4. Can you silence your phone? | 52 % yes | 10 % yes |
| 5. Can you divert your calls? | 76 % yes | 19 % yes |
| 6. Do people often interrupt you needlessly? | 38 % yes | 76 % yes |

FIGURE 10.9 Effect of Environmental Factors on Productivity

conditions. At the IBM Santa Teresa facility, researchers studied the work habits of software developers (and others) and concluded that there should be:

- 100 square feet of dedicated space per person;
- 30 square feet of surface per person;
- noise protection;
- enclosed one- or two-person offices for most developers.

Unfortunately, many organizations have ignored the fact that good working conditions for developers improve profits by improving productivity. Instead, they have put developers in poorly defined, open-plan offices, with less than 100 square feet of space and little noise protection. The environment suitable for order clerks or telemarketers is given to analysts and programmers. Interruptions are not controlled. Many developers comment that the only way they can get any work done is to stay later, after others have left. In their survey, DeMarco and Lister found that only 16 per cent of developers had 100 square feet of workspace or more, and only 11 per cent had enclosed offices or partitions of 6 feet or higher.

Box 10.1 lists characteristics of a work environment conducive to SWAT-Team productivity.

### Box 10.1   Characteristics of a SWAT-Team Work Environment

*Characteristics of the SWAT-Team Work Area:*

- SWAT-Team members should share a work office that affords both privacy and closeness.
- Adjacent to the work office, there should be a private room where team members can interact with users, hold discussions and make telephone calls without disturbing other team members.
- The SWAT-Team work area should be close to that of the end users and the Construction Assistance Team.

Box 10.1    Continued

- The SWAT Team should be able to work there at any hour it chooses.
- The SWAT Team must have privacy and freedom from interruptions.
  - A secretarial service should protect them from interruptions.
  - Telephone calls must be divertible.
  - Electronic mail should be used (to avoid interrupting work).
- The work environment should have no disruptive noise.
- The work environment should be as pleasant as possible. Team members should have a window with a view.
- The SWAT Team should design the layout and decoration of its own work area, to make it as productive and pleasant as possible and help give the team a feeling of uniqueness.

*Contents of the SWAT-Team Work Area:*

The work room should contain:
- 100 square feet of office space for each SWAT-Team member;
- 30 square feet of desk space for each SWAT-Team member;
- a shared printer;
- a computer and I-CASE toolset for each SWAT-Team member. The computers may be LAN-connected.

The discussion room should contain:
- a table for group discussions;
- a computer for demonstrating the application;
- a sofa and chairs;
- telephones;
- a white board;
- a flip-chart stand;
- a wall surface where paper can be pinned (or other means of wall-charting);
- coffee and refreshments.

# The E-Factor

Because developers need to work in a state of flow without interruptions, DeMarco and Lister defined a metric called the **Environmental Factor**, or **E-Factor** [DEMARCO&LISTER87]:

$$E\text{-}Factor = \frac{Number\ of\ Working\ Hours\ with\ No\ Interruption}{Number\ of\ Bodily\text{-}Present\ Working\ Hours}$$

If a person's work week is 40 hours, and during that week there are 10 hours when work can occur without interruption, the E-Factor is 0.25.

In some I.S. organizations, the E-Factor is zero. People laugh at the suggestion of having even an hour without interruption. DeMarco and Lister collected E-Factor data and found that they varied substantially, even within one organization. They refer to a government agency where, in spite of uniform office codes, the E-Factor varied from 0.10 to 0.38.

For RAD, especially during the Construction Phase, the developers' work environment should have an E-Factor as high as possible because it directly affects the time taken to get results. DeMarco and Lister point out that the existence of a metric causes people to work out methods to improve that measure. There are many steps that can be taken to heighten the E-Factor of the RAD developers' environment high.

# Capability of Repeated Success

When finding examples of very fast development, a question we asked was, "Is this an isolated example, or can it be repeated regularly on other projects?" The teams that completed the projects described in this chapter were confident that they could achieve similar speed of development on all commercial projects where the same toolset was used in a well-managed environment. Furthermore, they felt that there was no difficulty in training other teams to do the same.

The teams used their experience for estimating on other projects. It was commonly found that *other teams using the same methodology with the same toolset achieved similar development rates*.

## Essentials for Success

Box 10.2 gives the essentials for success in SWAT-Team management. These, combined with the essentials in Boxes 7.5 and 8.2, should help ensure that RAD happens effectively.

---

**Box 10.2    Essentials for Success in the Management of SWAT Teams**

- Select top-quality, capable team members who are determined to rise to the challenge.
- Choose team members who work well together as a team. Adjust the team if necessary to make it jell and become as powerful as possible.
- Allow the team to develop a feeling of uniqueness and team pride.
- Keep successful teams together for many projects, and engender a high level of team spirit.
- Use the most powerful toolset.
- Ensure that the team is motivated for high speed and high quality.

Box 10.2    Continued

- Use a methodology designed and tuned for high speed and high quality.
- Have the best possible training in the tools and methodology.
- Ensure full end-user participation.
- Structure the work so that each developer has a feeling of achieving something interesting and creative, with frequent closures.
- Establish clear goals and measurements, and rank the teams on how well they meet the goals.
- Ensure that the team keeps metrics of its performance and allow it to make its own estimates prior to the Construction Phase.
- Employ powerful motivation techniques.
- Provide good SWAT-Team working conditions (Box 10.1).
- Pay attention to avoidance of burnout.
- Make the development process as enjoyable as possible.
- Sweep away any bureaucracy or factors that could slow down the SWAT-Team development.
- Avoid defensive, interfering management; leave the team free to build the system its own way.

## Summary

Methodology Chart 10–1 is an extract relating to the management of SWAT Teams from the hyperdocument on RAD methodology. Methodology Chart 10–2 describes the Construction Phase using SWAT Teams.

## References

[BRADY86] J. Brady, "A Theory of Productivity in the Creative Process," *IEEE Computer Graphics and Applications*, May 1986, pp. 25–34.

[DEMARCO&LISTER87] T. DeMarco and T. Lister, *Peopleware, Productive Projects and Teams*, Dorset House, New York, 1987.

[FAIRLEY89] Details from Graeme Fairley, James Martin Associates, Ashford, Middlesex, U.K., in a detailed project report, March 1989.

[IEF] *IEF*, Information Engineering Facility I-CASE toolset covering all phases of information engineering, from Texas Instruments, Dallas, Texas. In the IEF, the repository is referred to as the encyclopedia.

[JEFFREY&LAWRENCE85] D. R. Jeffrey and M. J. Lawrence "Managing Programming Productivity," *Journal of Systems and Software*, January 1985, pp. quoted in

T. DeMarco and T. Lister, *Peopleware, Productive Projects and Teams*, Dorset House, New York, 1987.

[JONES86] Capers Jones, *Programming Productivity*, McGraw-Hill, New York, 1986.

[PICARDI86] A. Picardi, "Productivity Increases with the CORTEX Application Factory: Empirical Survey Results," *Proceedings,* DECUS Northeast Regional Conference, Boston, Massachusetts, June 5–6, 1986.

[WILLET73] G. W. Willet et al., *ISO Productivity Study*, ATT Long Lines, Kansas City, Missouri, April 1973.

# CHAPTER 11

# Timebox Development

## Deadlines

Creative people in many walks of life have a deadline. A magazine writer, television producer or seminar developer creates material for a certain date. Whatever else happens, he must not fail to meet the deadline.

To meet the deadline, he may allow the contents to slip. There may be items he wants to include but cannot do so in time. The producer of a television documentary or a seminar broadcast by satellite may say, "I wish I could have interviewed so-and-so" or "I wish we had better footage on this." However, there is no time to obtain the extra interview or footage. The deadline is absolute. The show must go on the air.

There is much similarity between television production and the building of information systems. Television production employs a planning phase, design and storyboarding, then construction. A difference is that most Information System (I.S.) development does not have a firm deadline. Sometimes developers claim for a year that the system is "95% complete."

## Timebox Methodologies— A Variant of RAD

Timebox methodologies apply a similar constraint to the building of I.S. applications. There is a deadline that is immovable, but the functionality of the system may slip. The system must work, carrying out its basic functions, but the fancier refinements may have to be postponed for a later release. (See Methodology Chart 11.)

The first 75% of a system's functionality can be created relatively quickly with a code generator, especially if reusable structures are employed as described in Chapters 15 and 22. The next 15% may take as long to create as the first 75%. The system may go through much refinement before the last 10% is completed.

Many of the features in the last 10% could be dropped or postponed for a subsequent release. If the refinements are added after the first version of the product has been in use, they will probably be different anyway, because when users work with a system, they change their minds about what they want its detailed functions to be.

In RAD methodologies, the core of a system is built quickly. Then the refinements are added to it. New transactions and new screens are added. The system grows like an onion, with successive layers of refinement being implemented. It is the onion-like refinement that makes practical the setting of a firm deadline. The timebox lifecycle allows refinements to be made until the deadline is close, and by then, a working system *must* be delivered.

# The Need for a 90-Day Lifecycle

The term **timebox** was first used at DuPont. In moving to a highly automated manufacturing environment in the Fibers Division, it was necessary to create complex application software quickly. If applications (of 100,000 equivalent-lines-of-COBOL or more) took two or three years to build, this would prevent the rapid evolution of an integrated manufacturing environment. DuPont decided that many of their applications, operating on a DEC VAX, should be built in 90 days. Later this became 120 days, largely because of the time needed to reorganize the end-user activities.

The move to the automated factory environment was a step into the unknown. There were bound to be mid-course corrections. There would probably be applications that did not work well. If it took two or three years to find out that an application was misconceived, that would be a disaster. If the problem were found in 90 days or so, then rapid evolution was possible. It is better to have a system of limited functionality working *quickly* than to wait two years for a comprehensive system.

If an application were built in 90 days and put into operation, the need would soon arise to have a second edition of that application. As with a second edition of a book, many things would be changed. Rather than making the first version rich in functionality, it is better to get a basic version of it working, learn from the experience of operating with it, and then design a second edition.

This implies two things:

The first version must be built quickly.

The application must be built so that it can be changed and added to quickly.

These constraints apply to most applications. The faster the rate of change and the greater the competitive pressures, the more important they are. In the DuPont Fibers Division, building applications fast was considered essential for competitive success.

A timebox methodology has been used with great success in DuPont [DUPONTa]. DuPont developers stress that the methodology works well for them and is highly practical. It has resulted in automation being introduced more rapidly and effectively. DuPont quotes large costs savings from the methodology. Variations of timebox techniques have since been used in many other corporations.

# Creeping Functionality

One of the dangers of prototyping methodologies or iterative development is that the functions of a system can grow in an uncontrolled fashion. Users or developers often keep adding functionality; so the design does not converge quickly into a usable system. This is sometimes referred to as **creeping functionality**. The more powerful the prototyping tools, the more the developers are encouraged to experiment, to add functions or to over-engineer the system. This can become expensive and can prevent a system from being delivered on time.

Perhaps the best way to combat creeping functionality is to place a rigid limit on the time permitted to produce a working system. Within a defined **timebox**, a working system must be built.

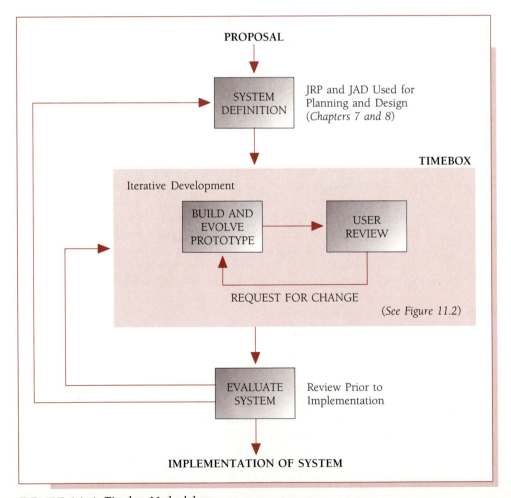

FIGURE 11.1  Timebox Methodology

# The Timebox

The timebox, in this methodology, applies to the Construction Phase. A Construction Team is given a timebox within which a system must be constructed. Before the timebox, the functions and design framework of the system are defined. After the timebox, the system is evaluated, and a quick decision is made whether to put it into production. Figure 11.1 illustrates this process.

The timebox is not extendable. A system must be produced within the time allocated. The functionality of the system may be trimmed back in order to complete it within the timebox. The system produced by the end of the timebox must be a system that is intended to be implemented.

Within the timebox, *continuous* iterative development is done, as shown in Figure 11.2, with end users and I.S. developers working closely together. This team is under pressure to produce a working system by the end of the timebox.

The timebox methodology, like RAD in general, depends upon having a powerful, easy-to-use development tool that generates executable code. It must be easy for developers to build and evolve prototypes with this tool. The tool must be capable of generating systems with good machine efficiency *so that the prototype evolves into the final working system.* The development techniques employed by the tool should be sufficiently user-friendly that users can easily participate in the development process.

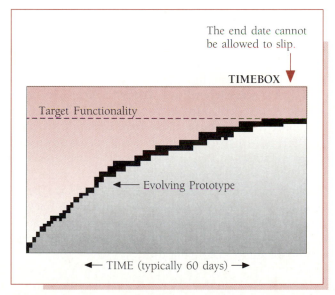

FIGURE 11.2 During the 60-day timebox, continuous evolution is used. Continuous evolution progresses with a sequence of modifications, continuously adjusting the prototype until the target is reached. This requires an intelligent, understanding team of end users working with the developers reviewing the evolution. The team must produce a fully working system before the end of the timebox.

It is desirable to have an I-CASE toolset to speed up the design process, check the design and generate code from the design.

A typical length for the timebox is 60 days. The team working within this period should not be large. Often it is a two-person team. From one to five people are appropriate. The timebox team is told that on Day 60, there will be a binary decision, success or failure: do they have a working system *or not?*

Much experience will be gained from implementing the first system, and the timebox can be re-entered to produce subsequent versions of the system with greater functionality. After users work with the system, the requirements for subsequent versions often are different from what they would otherwise have been.

# Quality: Not Limited with RAD

Limiting functionality in order to meet the deadline does *not* mean limiting quality. Pride in their work is essential for SWAT teams, and no self-respecting team would put out work of less than the highest quality.

The delivered system must be as bug-free as possible, excellently human-factored, and must provide a set of functions that will do useful work when the system is put into production. I-CASE tools make it much easier to achieve technical quality. Functionality can vary substantially without reducing the usability of the system.

The analogy with television production applies. A self-respecting team making a television program will not put out work of less than excellent technical quality. However, the amount of detail and polishing of the subject matter can vary over a wide range. The same applies to system development. One could go on adjusting and refining for months, but it is necessary to call a halt in order to meet the deadline.

The timebox approach uses tools that enable the core functionality to be built relatively quickly and then successively refined. The refinement goes on until a certain date, and then the system must be handed over to the Review Board.

Many software and electronic products today have excessive functionality, which bewilders the users. The return on development investment goes down when unwanted or marginal functions are added. I have a television-VHS-laserdisk system with no fewer than five hand-held controllers, each with 30 to 40 buttons. On most of the controllers, I use about 6 buttons; the other buttons are a nuisance because it is easy to press them incorrectly in the dark. On some of the controllers, I have put tape over the buttons that I do not use. A timebox approach to development helps control the technician's enthusiasm for adding functions that are of little value and which may make the product more difficult to learn and use.

# The SWAT Team Does the Estimating

A timebox approach, or team development in general, does not work well if there is pressure to meet an impossible deadline. The setting of the deadline, or the selection of functions to be accomplished in the timebox, should be done by the timebox team (or systems analyst) before the timebox starts. The team, where possible, should be familiar with the tools and techniques and confident about what it can accomplish with them.

When an enterprise is just starting to use the timebox approach, at least one member of the team should be experienced with the tools, and the others should be well trained and prepared to accept mentoring from their skilled colleagues.

The estimating and establishment of what is accomplishable in the timebox should be done *by the timebox SWAT Team* in the final JAD session, as described in the previous chapter.

## After the Timebox

After the timebox, implementation should proceed quickly, resulting in a full system, if it is small, or a pilot system, if it is large. New functions may be requested as implementation or usage proceeds. These may give rise to a further iteration of the entire lifecycle.

A brief summary report may be written after implementation, documenting experience that may help with subsequent implementations.

## Multiple Timeboxes

Some systems are too complex to finish in one timebox. These are split into subsystems, each of which performs a function in its own right, which can be demonstrated and which is small enough to be built in one timebox of 60 days by a small team. As experience builds up with the prototyping and code generation tool that makes the timebox methodology practical, it becomes easier to estimate what can be accomplished in the 60 days. This estimate should relate to function points (Appendix I).

The separate subsystems all use the same data model. The system should be split into subsystems using an I-CASE tool. The I-CASE tool, with its repository, coordinates the interfaces among the separately developed subsystems, as shown in Figure 11.3. This is discussed in more detail in Chapter 12.

## The Review Board

The development is controlled by a group called the **Review Board**. The Review Board signs off on the system design prior to entering the timebox. When the system is complete at the end of the timebox, it is evaluated by the Review Board. The Review Board (or individual members of that group) examine the prototype periodically as it evolves in the timebox. They should monitor progress to make sure that the prototype is on track, making helpful suggestions where they can. (See Appendix III.)

When evaluation is done after the timebox, it is hoped that the system can be approved for immediate implementation. In some cases, minor modifications may be needed. For unavoidable reasons, the requirements may have changed slightly. If the

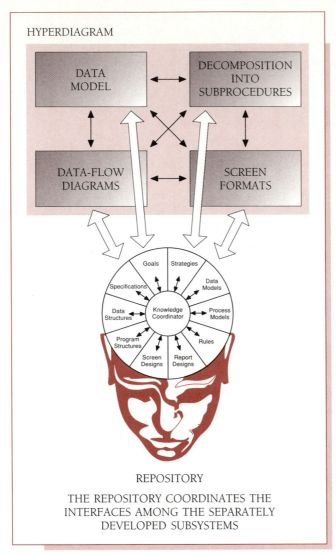

FIGURE 11.3 I-CASE tools allow a data model to be built and complex systems subdivided into pieces, which use the data model and which can each be built by a small team (or one person). The interfaces between the pieces are controlled on-line with comput-erized precision.

modifications can be made with another iteration of the development, the Review Board permits the timebox to be re-entered, setting a deadline for the change being completed. If the system proves to be unsuitable for implementation, another system definition workshop is held to determine what the problem is and how to modify the system definition. In DuPont's experience with the timebox methodology (at the time of this writing), this has never happened.

The Review Board should be relatively small. An end-user leader and an I.S. leader should be represented on it. Both of these individuals should be decision makers.

The Review Board *should* include:

- the Executive Owner or his representative—the person who provides the money and who has the final vote on resolving major end-user issues;
- a user who will be primarily responsible for the use of the system;
- an I.S. professional responsible for application quality—a professional who ensures that the system conforms to the data and process models in the repository.

The Review Board *may* include or call upon:

- other users;
- a technical support representative;
- an auditor, if the system is sensitive from the auditors' point of view (many are not).

In some cases, the Review Board is the same as the Requirements Planning Team that participated in the JRP workshop.

# The User Coordinator

The User Coordinator is the lead end user in the construction activity (Appendix III). He may be a member of the Construction Assistance Team. He also serves on the Review Board. He represents the end-user community and may involve other end users where appropriate to help review the prototypes and the evolving system.

He arranges for user documentation and training.

In some cases, the User Coordinator spends all of his time on the project. In other cases, he has another job to do and commits to spending a portion of his time on the project.

# Motivation

The term **Timebox Team** is sometimes used to refer to the combination of the SWAT Team, which builds the system, and the Construction Assistance Team of end users.

The Timebox Team should be strongly motivated to succeed. Management should create pressures for the Timebox Team to complete the system within the timebox. They are told that success or failure is judged by whether they create—by the deadline—a system that is, in fact, implemented. They are told that most timebox efforts do indeed succeed and that they must not distinguish themselves by being one of the rare failures. They should be assured that success will be rewarded and that their efforts are very visible to higher management. They should be told that if they succeed, a major victory celebration will be held.

Prior to building the system, the Timebox Team will help design it. After the timebox, they participate in implementing the system. They may participate in a new JAD to define a new edition of the system after the first has been put into operation.

# Experience at DuPont

Figure 11.4 shows examples of small timebox projects at DuPont, done by one or two developers [DUPONTa]. DuPont and its subsidiary, Information Engineering Associates, have completed several hundred timebox projects. Before a project begins, a careful check is made to determine whether it can be built with the available toolset and staff. No project is started by the timebox teams that does not fit within the scope of the methodology. Because of this, DuPont is able to claim that none of its timebox projects have been failures.

DuPont uses the Cortex toolset and originally built its methodology around the Cortex *Application Factory* [CORTEX] operating on a DEC VAX.

Figure 11.5 shows experience with a large project built in the Fibers Division of DuPont. This project was split into six main timebox developments (the black bars in Figure 11.5), each staffed with one, two or three developers. The dictionary-controlled code generator made possible this use of small teams working quickly. A one-month effort to design passive data preceded the timebox efforts, and three one-person efforts followed it, each making minor improvements or additions. Each bar in Figure 11.5 includes the planning and design of the subsystem as well as construction with a code generator. With traditional techniques, it would have taken about 20 person-years and an elapsed time of two years. Here it took 4½ person-years. The saving from this approach exceeded $1 million [DUPONTb].

| APPLICATION | STAFF | DATES START | DATES END | DEVELOPMENT COSTS ($ Thousands) Actual | DEVELOPMENT COSTS ($ Thousands) Estimated | DEVELOPMENT COSTS ($ Thousands) Savings | APPLICATION STATISTICS Screens | APPLICATION STATISTICS Reports | APPLICATION STATISTICS Files |
|---|---|---|---|---|---|---|---|---|---|
| KEVLAR BOX INVENTORY TRACKING | 1 | 07/01/85 | 09/01/85 | 5.0 | 30.0 | 25.0 | 41 | 7 | 17 |
| BCF STRETCH WRAP | 2 | 03/01/85 | 05/31/85 | 30.0 | 168.0 | 138.0 | 3 | 5 | 11 |
| SUGGESTION | 1 | 04/10/86 | 05/07/86 | 8.0 | 50.0 | 42.0 | 5 | 12 | 3 |
| SPINNING AREA MGT VERSION 1 | 1.5 | 01/16/86 | 04/30/86 | 25.0 | 50.0 | 25.0 | 16 | 4 | 12 |
| SPINNING AREA MGT VERSION 2 | 1 | 05/01/86 | 08/15/86 | 14.6 | 29.0 | 14.4 | 11 | 5 | 9 |
| PRODUCTION FEEDSTOCK | 1 | 05/01/86 | 06/15/86 | 7.5 | 45.1 | 37.6 | 12 | 4 | 11 |
| TRANSFER, PROGRESSION, REGRESSION | 2 | 07/01/85 | 09/01/85 | 20.0 | 125.0 | 105.0 | 12 | 11 | 12 |
| HAZARDOUS CHEMICALS | 1.5 | 06/01/86 | 08/01/86 | 8.4 | 10.8 | 2.4 | 9 | 3 | 2 |
| FINISHED PRODUCT SPECIFICATION | 2 | 01/15/86 | 04/15/86 | 20.0 | 45.0 | 25.0 | 38 | 16 | 24 |
| BADGE TRACK | 1 | 10/01/86 | 12/01/86 | 4.5 | 6.8 | 2.3 | 4 | 4 | 4 |
| | | | Totals: | 143 | 559.7 | 416.7 | | | |

FIGURE 11.4 Examples of Small Timebox Projects at DuPont [DUPONTa]
   Each of these was done in one Timebox with one or two developers. Figure 11.5 illustrates a large timebox project done with multiple timeboxes.

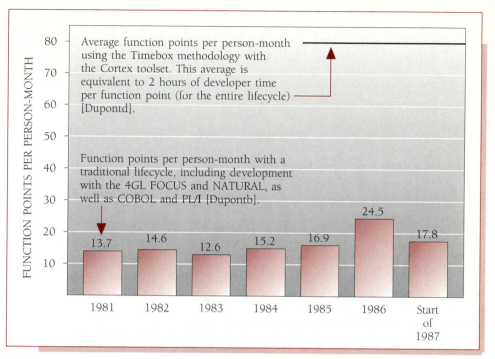

**FIGURE 11.5** An Example of a Project at DuPont of about 4000 Function Points Built with Six Main Timeboxes

Each bar in this chart includes planning and design of the subsystem, as well as construction with a code generator. With traditional techniques, it would have taken about 20 person-years and elapsed time of 2 years. Here, it took 4.5 person-years and 11 months. The savings from this approach was estimated to be $1.052 million [DUPONTb].

The total elapsed time in Figure 11.5 is 11 months. It could have been reduced to about six months if the six main timebox developments had started approximately simultaneously. Today's I-CASE toolsets (including Cortex's *CorVision*) are more powerful than the Cortex *Application Factory* and *Application Builder* [CORTEX] used for the projects in Figure 11.5. With today's tools, more complex systems can be created with parallel team efforts as described in Chapter 12, using a coordinating I-CASE model so that complex systems are subdivided into pieces that can each be built by a small team (or one person). The interfaces between the pieces are controlled on-line with computerized precision.

DuPont is achieving an average lifecycle productivity of about two hours per function point (80 function points per person-month) Figure 11.6 shows how this differs from the productivity achieved with traditional development at DuPont. (DuPont's productivity with traditional development was higher than that of most enterprises.)

Scott Shultz, who created the timebox methodology at DuPont, comments, "All applications were *completed* in less time than it would have taken just to write the specifications for COBOL or FORTRAN." He also comments, "All applications were completed at a lower cost than modifying an off-the-shelf package—assuming that one could be found."

| ACTIVITY | Number of developers | DATES | | COST ($ Thousands) | | | APPLICATION STATISTICS | | |
|---|---|---|---|---|---|---|---|---|---|
| | | START | END | Actual | Estimated | Savings | Screens | Reports | Files |
| 1  PASSIVE DATA | 3 | 09/01/85 | 10/01/85 | 15.0 | 52.6 | 37.6 | 108 | 41 | 49 |
| 2  PRODUCTION ORDERS | 2 | 10/01/85 | 03/01/86 | 90.2 | 315.6 | 225.5 | 52 | 10 | 45 |
| 3  PRODUCT SEPARATION | 3 | 11/01/85 | 03/01/86 | 75.2 | 263.0 | 187.9 | 23 | 2 | 32 |
| 4  TIME CARD | 2 | 12/01/85 | 02/01/86 | 30.1 | 105.2 | 75.2 | 14 | 3 | 16 |
| 5  CREATE PRODUCT | 1 | 01/01/86 | 05/01/86 | 60.1 | 210.4 | 150.3 | 31 | 3 | 55 |
| 6  OPERATIONAL CONDITION | 3 | 02/01/86 | 05/01/86 | 45.1 | 157.8 | 112.7 | 30 | 5 | 25 |
| 7  PROCESS TEST | 2 | 04/01/86 | 08/01/86 | 60.1 | 210.4 | 150.3 | 30 | 2 | 32 |
| 8  TRACKING | 1 | 07/01/86 | 08/01/86 | 15.0 | 52.6 | 37.6 | 25 | 4 | 32 |
| 9  SYSTEM IMPROVEMENTS | 1 | 07/01/86 | 08/01/86 | 15.0 | 52.6 | 37.6 | 10 | 4 | 8 |
| 10  JOB ASSIGNMENTS | 1 | 07/01/86 | 08/01/86 | 15.0 | 52.6 | 37.6 | 12 | 2 | 16 |
| | | | Totals: | 420.8 | 1473.2 | 1052.3 | | | |

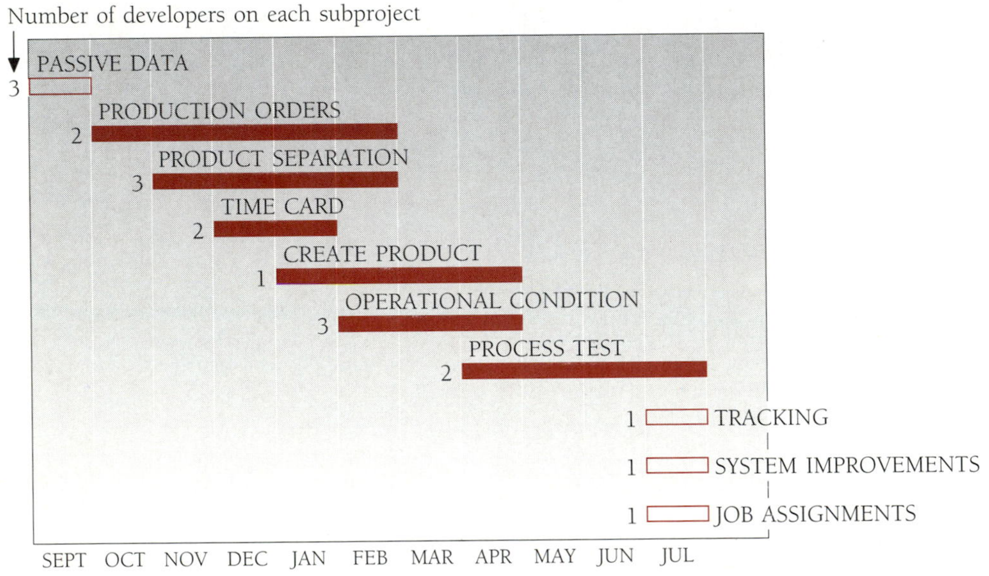

Number of developers on each subproject

FIGURE 11.6  The average development productivity achieved with the Timebox methodology compared with that attained with traditional methodologies (including the use of fourth-generation languages) in the I.S. organization of DuPont, Fibers Division [DUPONTb].

These comments are impressive; the cost savings are impressive; but the most valuable characteristic of the projects is that users obtained systems that really met their needs and that were built quickly.

# Details of the Procedure

Methodology Chart 11 shows details of the timebox procedure. Many variations are possible in the procedure, and different organizations are likely to adjust the methodology hyperdocument to their own requirements. (See Methodology Chart 11.)

Methodology Chart 25-1 shows a typical timescale for timebox development with a 13-week construction timebox. This would be appropriate for a system of 500 to 1500 function points, depending on the power of the toolset and the extent to which reusable constructs are employed (Chapter 15).

# References

[CORTEX] *CorVision*, product of Cortex, Inc., Waltham, Massachusetts.

[DUPONTa] Information from Scott Shultz, Manager, Information Engineering, E. I. DuPont de Nemours and Company, Inc., Wilmington, Delaware, 1989.

[DUPONTb] Information from W. Robert White, Information Engineering Associates, E. I. DuPont de Nemours and Company, Inc., Wilmington, Delaware, 1989.

# Parallel Development

The key to maximizing performance in supercomputers is to have multiple, high-speed processors operating in parallel. The key to developing *complex* applications quickly is to have multiple, high-speed SWAT Teams operating in parallel.

A complex system should be broken into subsystems that can be built by independent teams. The goal is for each subsystem to be built with high-speed development techniques and tested in its own right. The subdivision should be such that the teams can work independently.

## The Coordinating Model

Although the subsystems are built and tested independently, they must fit together with absolute precision. To achieve this, the interfaces among the subsystems must be designed with an I-CASE toolset that does complete consistency checking. These interfaces must be held constant while the independent teams develop their subsystems with the same I-CASE toolset. (See Methodology Chart 12.)

To help coordinate the work of the separate teams, a **coordinating model** is used. Separate subsystems plug into this model, as illustrated in Figure 12.1.

The **coordinating model** consists of a stable, normalized data model linked to a process model showing the dependencies among processes. It is built with the I-CASE tool and, during the modeling process, the system is divided into subsystems that are as autonomous as possible. These subsystems share the same coordinating model.

Where a subsystem uses data external to itself or passes data to another subsystem, these data are defined precisely in the coordinating model. The subsystem does not pass control information (other than defined data) to another subsystem. A goal is that, when the subsystem is being built, its developers should not change the external definitions of data. If, unfortunately, these definitions *have* to be changed, then an adjustment must be made to the coordinating model and the adjustment communicated to all subsystem teams. Each team uses the same I-CASE toolset as that used for creating the coordinating model, and the toolset checks to ensure that the subsystem fits the coordinating model exactly.

Almost any data processing project can be subdivided in this way. Organizations that have used this approach comment that *if you cannot subdivide a large data processing project, you do not yet understand it well enough,* and to proceed without such understanding is to ask for trouble.

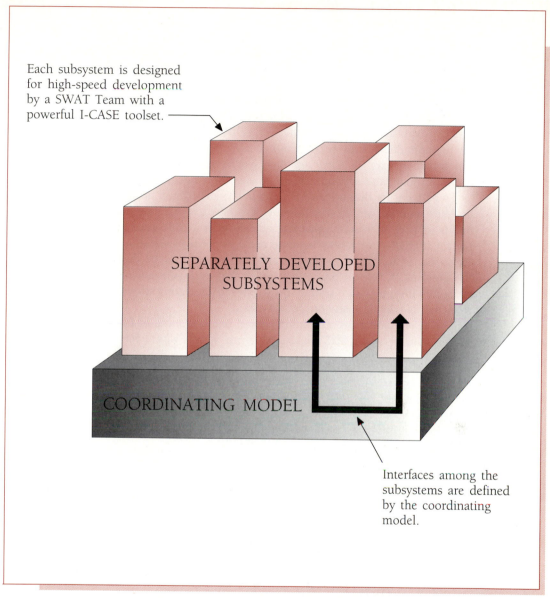

Each subsystem is designed for high-speed development by a SWAT Team with a powerful I-CASE toolset.

SEPARATELY DEVELOPED SUBSYSTEMS

COORDINATING MODEL

Interfaces among the subsystems are defined by the coordinating model.

FIGURE 12.1  The key to building complex systems quickly is to have multiple SWAT Teams operating simultaneously. These separate SWAT-Team projects must plug into a common coordinating model in an I-CASE repository. The I-CASE toolset must enforce rigorous interface control.

Each subsystem is designed for high-speed development by a SWAT Team with a powerful I-CASE toolset.

Interfaces among the subsystems are defined by the coordinating model.

# Parallel Lifecycle

The process of building complex systems progresses as shown in Figure 12.2. After initiation and Joint Requirements Planning, the coordinating model is built, as described in the next two chapters.

A rough version of the model is created prior to a Joint Application Design session. The JAD activity refines the coordinating model. Using the coordinating model, the system is split into subsystems that can be developed autonomously by SWAT Teams (or by individuals if the subsystem is simple enough). The subsystems are developed and tested in parallel. They are then linked together a stage at a time. Integration testing is done, and adjustments are made where necessary.

To help ensure that no SWAT Team delays the overall project, each subsystem may be built with the timebox techniques described in the previous chapter. Each team builds its core subsystem relatively quickly with a code generator. Eighty per cent of the functionality work may be done in 20 per cent of the time, and then refinements are made. Some of the less important refinements may be dropped in order to meet the deadline. A Review Board may check that each subsystem is complete enough to proceed with integration testing. If the integration testing is quickly successful, further refinements may be made to the subsystem.

The development process, taking about seven months in Figure 12.2, might apply to a system of about 5000 function points, which would have taken two or, more

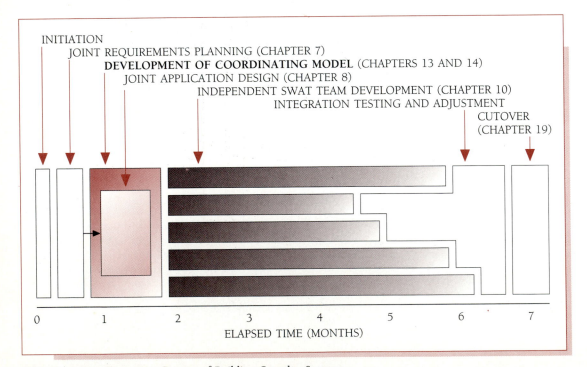

FIGURE 12.2 Progressive Process of Building Complex Systems

likely, three years to develop with the traditional lifecycle and manual coding. Figure 12.2 shows five SWAT developments in parallel. More complex systems should have a larger number of subsystems developed in parallel but not necessarily a much longer elapsed time.

## Metrics for Subdivision

If an application has a complexity assessed at fewer than 1000 function points, it may be tackled by one SWAT Team; if it has more than 1000 function points, it may be tackled by two or more SWAT Teams working in parallel. The function-point figure used to determine how many SWAT Teams are used will vary, depending on the toolset used and measurements of SWAT Teams using that toolset. If the teams employ a substantial quantity of reusable designs, one team can create a system of correspondingly greater complexity.

The subdivision will also depend on the nature of the application and how the application can be broken into autonomous subsystems. Most applications divide into natural subsystems, some of which may be much smaller than others. Some of the small subsystems may be done by one person.

For a powerful code generator, a rule of thumb might be:

< 200 function points: one person

200 to 1000 function points: one SWAT Team

> 1000 function points: 1000 function points (per SWAT Team)

For a powerful code generator and substantial employment of reusable structures (Chapter 15), the rule of thumb might be:

< 500 function points: one person

500 to 2000 function points: one SWAT Team

> 2000 function points: 2000 function points (per SWAT Team)

For a mature information-engineering environment with object-oriented analysis for maximum reusability and one which has had time to acquire much reusable design, the productivity may be higher:

< 1000 function points: one person

1000 to 4000 function points: one SWAT Team

> 4000 function points: 4000 function points (per SWAT Team)

The actual figures used for estimating should be based on the organization's experience with its toolset and RAD. The estimates are likely to be based on measures more precise than a function-point estimate. They may be based on numbers of transactions of different types or on a breakdown of time expenditure such as that in Figure 10.7.

## Applications Standards

Standards for application development should be established, and the separate teams should conform to these standards. In many cases, the standards can be enforced by the CASE tool. There should be a standard interface to the database (usually SQL), a standard network interface, standards for report layout (represented in the report generator) and standards for the screen dialog (represented in the dialog generator). Manufacturers have guidelines for screen dialogs, which should usually be adhered to. For example, an IBM manual gives guidelines for CUA (Common User Access) screen interaction [IBM89]; DEC gives guidelines for the use of DEC Windows [DEC88].

In addition to manufacturers' guidelines, an installation may have its own guidelines for dialog design, with recommended screen layouts, a common vocabulary, a common form of HELP facility error messages, and so on. The same guidelines may be used for all applications, so that creating the standards does not add to the development cycle time.

One person may be responsible for coordinating the user interface and for ensuring that usability testing is done (as described in Chapter 17). This person should visit all teams, check their prototypes and ensure that the screens and dialogs they are creating have maximum ease of use.

## Very Large Programs

The implementation of very large systems—for example, systems with more than 500,000 lines of code—has often been disastrous with traditional process-centered techniques. Statistics relating to COBOL indicate that projects of this size have large budgets and time estimates of two to three years but, even so, most projects overrun their cost and time estimates drastically and often fail to meet the user needs. About 25 per cent of such projects are canceled before completion [JONES].

A data-centered approach is more successful. Even with very large projects, it is relatively easy to create an entity-relationship model and normalize the data. The data on the input and output documents can be analyzed and then synthesized (with computer assistance) into a normalized data model. The large project can then be subdivided into pieces, each of which delivers a usable result in its own right. Interfacing between the pieces is provided by the data model.

The data model is built with an I-CASE toolset. The same toolset is used to decompose the system into subprocedures and to link the subprocedures with a data-flow diagram. The data-flow diagram, procedure decomposition diagram and data model are all fully integrated in the I-CASE repository with computerized coordination. Each subprocedure should be a subsystem that can be implemented in its own right. Any commonality between the subprocedures, such as common screen layouts, should be designed. A definition of the interface between the separately implemented pieces is created with computerized precision. As separate teams build the pieces, each will build to link to the interface definition that is in the repository. A quality I-CASE toolset ensures that all the pieces fit together with precision (Figure 12.1).

There can often be a high level of commonality among the subprocedures. There may be many transactions, for example, each of which conforms to a common structure. The system should be analyzed for reusable structures (Chapters 15 and 22). Standards should be established and templates created for screen layouts and dialog structures.

A goal should be to break large projects into pieces, each of which can be built and tested in three months or less. A well-managed SWAT Team can build a major subsystem in three months. Skilled individuals can build smaller subsystems in three months.

Many development projects have problems because developers leave, and their replacements take many months to become familiar with the system. This is less of a problem when the development is divided in three-month chunks.

Often, with traditional techniques, a project of 1 million lines of COBOL has required up to 200 analysts and programmers at its peak. Some have employed more than this. Such projects have often taken three years to implement. With traditional techniques it is nearly impossible to control the interfaces between 200 analysts and programmers. However, the data model for such a project can typically be created in a few weeks. The CASE decomposition into procedures can proceed in parallel with the data modeling; the procedure model and data model will be linked into an integrated I-CASE representation. The project may be subdivided into, say, ten pieces, each of which is implemented by a SWAT Team of three or so people, plus some smaller pieces, which are one-person projects.

The total elapsed time may be a quarter of that required for traditional development. The number of developers may be a fraction of that of traditional development. The total cost is much less. The saving in people and time justifies a major expenditure on I-CASE tools and training. Indeed, failure to use I-CASE tools, with methodologies something like those described in this book, is irresponsible management.

## Too Many Cooks

A dramatic example of a programming project going wrong was IBM's original development of the 360 operating system. The manager of the OS/360 architecture headed a team of ten people who, he said, could design the operating system in ten months. However, this would have been 90 days more than the timetable allowed; so the manager for the control program offered to put 150 men to work at once and complete the job on time. This was done, but the design slipped later than ever. Fred Brooks, the overall manager of the 360 software, commented that the flaws in this part of the operating system added a year to the debugging time in later stages of the project and resulted in a waste of millions of dollars [TIMELIFE89].

Fred Brooks made a comment that has been quoted ever since: "Adding manpower to a late software project makes it later" [BROOKS75].

OS/360 slipped into deeper and deeper trouble, eventually using ten times the number of programmers originally thought necessary. At the peak of activity, more than 2000 programmers worked on it. It consumed more than 5000 person-years.

Many of its promised functions were dropped. IBM, coining a new word, *decommitted* 31 operating system features promised in the announcement. Amazingly, OS/360 cost more than the Manhattan Project, which produced the first atomic bomb [TIMELIFE89]. It averaged less than half a line of code per person-day.

The effort to correct the problems, which would have sunk a lesser company, eventually paid off handsomely for IBM. The 360 had massive sales, and its architecture became the dominant mainframe architecture for decades.

Today's code generators could not be used for building an operating system, but CASE tools could help greatly in its design, enabling it to be split into separate projects with tightly controlled interfaces. We have far more ability to speed up the building of data processing applications than the building of intricate software such as operating systems.

# The Coordinating Model and Control of Parallel Efforts

The coordinating model, which facilitates control of parallel development efforts, should be built with the same I-CASE toolset that developers use. The coordinating model consists of a data model and a process model interlinked. The I-CASE toolset should be able to enforce consistency within the model and ensure that the separately evolving subsystems conform to the model exactly.

Some enterprises have a data administration function that has created an overall data model that describes data that are used by many different systems; some enterprises have done information engineering in which they have created a data model and process model for the entire business area (Chapter 21). In such circumstances, either part or all of the coordinating model may already reside in the repository of the CASE tool. Information engineering can speed up the development of systems in various ways (Chapter 21).

If no data model already exists, one can be created for the specific system. It is time-consuming to create a data model for an entire business area, but a data model for one system can be created quickly, as discussed in the following chapter. Some individuals are skilled at creating stable data models. They have done it before and know what to look for. It is helpful to have such an individual create the coordinating model for a project.

# Types of Diagrams

The coordinating model should use the following types of diagrams:

- *Data Model Diagram.* A normalized model is built of the data used in the business area. The structure of this model is drawn with an entity-relationship diagram. The detailed attributes are shown in windows of the CASE tool (Chapter 13).

- *Process Decomposition Diagram.* The functions of the system are decomposed into processes; high-level processes are decomposed into lower-level processes. A tree-structured decomposition is produced (Chapter 14).

- *Process Dependency Diagram.* Some processes are dependent upon other processes; they can be performed only after completion of the processes on which they are dependent. The dependency may exist because data used by a dependent process are created by another process. A process dependency diagram maps the dependencies (Chapter 14).

- *Data Flow Diagram.* A data flow diagram is a special case of a dependency diagram. It shows procedures that are dependent on one another because data flow from one procedure to another. It shows precisely what data flow (Chapter 14).

- *Process/Data Matrix.* A process/data matrix maps the processes against the normalized data, showing which processes create, read, update or delete the records. Creating this matrix helps ensure that the data and processes have all been discovered and that the process dependencies have been correctly assessed (Chapter 14).

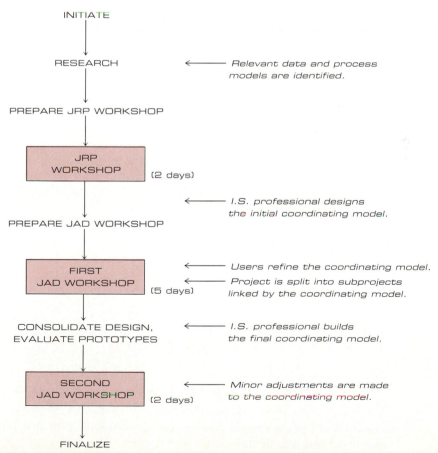

FIGURE 12.3 Stages in the Design of the Coordinating Model

I.S. professionals should create a rough coordinating model quickly as part of the preparation for the JAD session. Sometimes two I.S. professionals do this; one creates the data model and the other the process model. Information may be used from an existing data model maintained by the data administrator or from data and process models created in an overall Business Area Analysis.

The coordinating model will be examined and refined with end users during the JAD session. Users should try to ensure that all necessary entities and processes are represented in the model. All inputs to and outputs from the system should be identified and their contents analyzed and added to the data model.

During the JAD session, the system should be split into subsystems that can be built autonomously. The subsystem boundaries should be represented in the I-CASE toolset, and the data flowing between subsystems should be identified and designed with precision. The normalized model of data shared by the subsystems is also defined with precision. The SWAT Teams can then go to work independently on the subsystems.

After the first JAD workshop, the coordinating model should be refined by an I.S. modeling professional. The SWAT Team may contribute to the model, attempting to maximize the reusable structures. The second JAD workshop may review the refinements made to the coordinating model. Figure 12.3 shows the stages in the design of the coordinating model.

# Division into Subsystems

When the tree structure representing the decomposition of processes is built for an application, it should be divided into subtrees that represent subsystems that can be built largely independently of one another. There are usually natural subdivisions in a application. Each subsystem will be represented in the I-CASE tool with its own decomposition diagram, dependency or data flow diagram and its own subset of the data model. The I-CASE tool checks the integrity of this subsystem design and shows the data that flow between it and other subsystems.

A complex application can be subdivided in multiple ways. The choice of subdivision should be governed by the following rules:

Subsystems

- Each subsystem performs one or more discrete business processes.
- Each subsystem can be tested in its own right.
- Each subsystem executes a function that users can employ, where possible, and that can be tested in the usability lab (Chapter 17).

Data

- There is as little data flow as possible between one subsystem and another.
- The few data exchanged among subsystems are defined with precision.
- There should be no control flow among subsystems except that represented by clearly defined data items.

Design

- Reusable templates and constructs should be employed across all subsystems as much as possible.
- A design decision made in regard to one subsystem should have no effect on another subsystem (insofar as possible).
- Each subsystem is small enough to be built by one person or one SWAT Team in no more than three months.

Three basic diagrams of the coordinating model can be used to help in dividing the system into largely independent subsystems:

- *Process Decomposition Diagram.* The high-level blocks in the "composed-of" decomposition represent potential subsystems. Each block and its children may be a natural subsystem.
- *Process Dependency or Data-Flow Diagram.* The overall dependency diagram should be subdivided so that the dependencies between one subsystem and another are as few as possible. There should be a minimum amount of data flowing from one subsystem to another.
- *Entity/Process Matrix.* The entity/process matrix may be clustered on the basis of what processes *create* what entity-types. The clustering may be adjusted to minimize the interactions among systems.

As the I-CASE tool is used to help in the subdivision, it is used to create a process-and-data model for each subsystem. This submodel is the starting point for the SWAT Team, which will add more detail to the model, design the screens and logic, generate code and test the subsystem.

# Parallel Timebox Development

Figure 11.5 gave an illustration of a timebox development being used with great success on a complex system of about 3800 function points. The total development costs were estimated to be $1.052 million less than they would have been with traditional development. There were six major timeboxes, followed by three one-person activities to create additions and improvements. The total elapsed time could have been reduced by four months or so by initiating the six timebox projects together to give more simultaneous development. This is illustrated in Figure 12.4.

Parallel timebox development is one of the most effective approaches to building complex applications quickly. In order to start the timeboxes close together, as depicted in the bottom chart of Figure 12.4, a coordinating model is needed, built rigorously in an I-CASE environment. The separate timebox efforts plug into the model, and the toolset ensures precise consistency.

The timebox style of management helps prevent delay of the project by ensuring that no subsystem is late.

The parallel timebox development illustrated in Figure 11.5 was a successful example of building a complex system quickly.

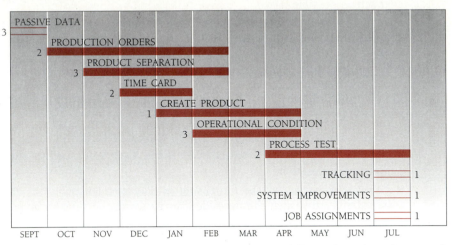

It could have been faster if the six main timeboxes had been more fully overlapped, as shown in the following diagram. To achieve this overlap, a coordinating model is built in an I-CASE toolset. The separate simultaneous developments conform to this coordinating model.

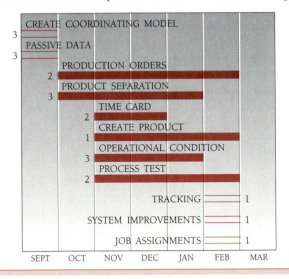

FIGURE 12.4  To achieve the shortest cycle time, the separate SWAT-Team projects should overlap as fully as possible.

# Avoiding Slippages

A major concern in the classical development lifecycle is that it is difficult to know whether a project is on time or slipping badly. Many large projects appear to be on time when, in fact, there are nasty and expensive surprises ahead. It is common to hear business executives complain, "It was supposed to be finished by June two years ago. When June arrived, *they* said they were 95 per cent complete. In October, they were still 95 per cent complete. Next June, it was still 95 per cent. We just don't seem to be able to manage *those people*." As we have commented, the average large system is more than a year late, and a high proportion of systems are canceled because of development difficulties after millions of dollars have been spent. If a mission-critical system is a year late (or canceled), this can have a serious impact on the corporation.

Dividing the development into building blocks, each of which is to be completed in three months or less, makes large projects more controllable. If any one building block is in trouble, the trouble will not remain hidden for long.

There is a danger that the building blocks may not work together. To avert this danger, careful attention must be paid to the coordinating model and the interfaces between systems that it defines. The I-CASE toolset must ensure that the subsystems being built fit exactly into the coordinating model. All developers have this model in the repository they use, and the knowledge coordinator tools ensure that their work integrates with the model correctly.

There is a danger that the integrated system may have inadequate machine performance. The subsystems, therefore, should be saturation-tested and benchmarked as they come into existence, and design calculations should be done to refine estimates of the overall performance.

Methodology Chart 12, relating to parallel development, is a window into the RAD lifecycle hyperdocument.

# References

[BROOKS75] Fred P. Brooks, Jr., *The Mythical Man-Month*, Addison-Wesley Publishing Co., Reading, Massachusetts, 1975.

[DEC88] *The XUI Style Guide*, Digital Equipment Corporation, Maynard, Massachusetts, 1988. The XUI (X-Windows User Interface) Toolkit makes it easy to write applications following the *XUI Style Guide*. The manual, provided for the OSF response, describes and defines the appearance, behavior and usage of the X User Interface (XUI) components.

[IBM89] 1. *CUA 1989 Evaluation*, December 1989, IBM Publication GG24–3456; 2. *Writing IMS SAA Applications, A Design Guide*, May 1989, IBM GG24–3324. These manuals on guidelines for the design of Common User Access are exceptionally helpful and might be made part of an installation standard.

[JONES] Statistics from Capers Jones.

[TIMELIFE89] *The Software Challenge*, Time-Life Books, Alexandria, Virginia, 1989.

# CHAPTER 13

# Data Modeling

A data model should be the foundation stone of application development.

The data should be designed first, followed by the procedures that use the data. A reason for this is that the data can be designed with formal techniques—entity-relationship modeling and normalization—and when this is done, the structure of the data model is stable, whereas the procedures that use these data are likely to change often.

## Data Modeling for the Business Area as a Whole

Data modeling is often done for the business area as a whole. This is the function of data administration, which is discussed in Chapter 20. If the enterprise has had good data administration, data models will exist prior to an application project. These data models can be used in the project, and this makes the development somewhat faster. There are other advantages in data administration, including the ability to streamline the business functions, have commonality of applications and reuse design.

If the enterprise has had no data administration or if no data models exist for the application area, then the developers should create a data model for the application, using the I-CASE toolset with which the application will be built.

## Rapid Data Modeling

While data modeling an entire business area takes time, a data model for one system can be built quickly. The goal should be to do this in a few days during the User Design Phase. The data model should be validated in the JAD workshops and improved if necessary.

Some I.S. professionals are experienced and skilled at data modeling. A person with this skill can create a data model for one application quickly. It is desirable to have such a person either as part of the project team or in a support role, supporting many projects.

Two approaches can be taken to data modeling: **top-down** and **bottom-up**. A skilled data modeler uses both approaches in combination (Figure 13.1) and builds the model in the I-CASE tool.

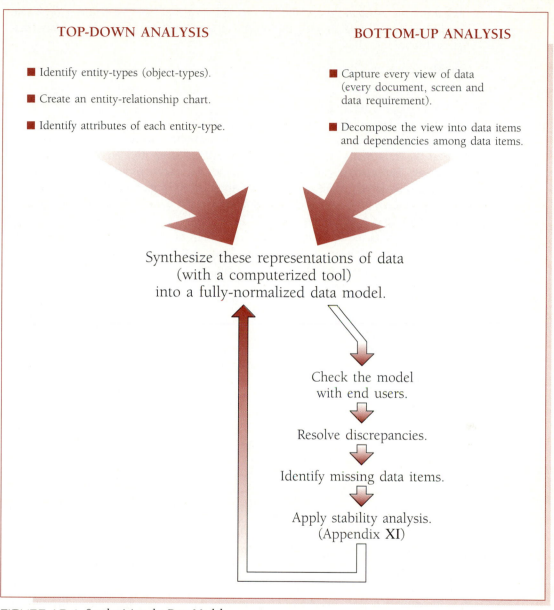

FIGURE 13.1 Synthesizing the Data Model

## Top-Down Design

With *top-down* design, the analyst asks:

- *What objects are involved in this application?* In database parlance, **objects** are referred to as **entities**.
- *What are the relationships among these objects?* The relationships are represented on an entity-relationship diagram.

• *What are the attributes that should be stored for each object-type (entity-type)?* The attributes are associated with the object in a correctly normalized fashion (discussed later).

(See Methodology Chart 13.)

### Bottom-Up Design

With *bottom-up* design, the analyst captures all the *views* of data associated with the application, decomposes each view and synthesizes them into the data model in such a way that the data items are correctly normalized. A computerized tool can help do the synthesis. The analyst captures all the paper or screen inputs and outputs. He captures the documents associated with the application (e.g., waybills, invoices, customs forms) and decomposes them into data items. The data items are integrated into the data model. (See Methodology Chart 13.)

The resulting data model is checked with the help of end users (in the JAD workshop). Any discrepancies in it are resolved. Any missing data are added. A formal procedure is used to make the data model as stable as possible. (See Appendix IX-1.)

As with all aspects of fast development, it is desirable to have a professional who knows exactly what he is doing use a powerful toolset to build the data model quickly. Some analysts have specialized in data modeling and can identify entities and normalize data quickly and accurately. Such persons do not take long to create the data model for an application and can ask users the right questions to refine the data model.

The remainder of this chapter describes the creation of a fully normalized data model. The chapter may be skipped by a reader already familiar with data modeling.

# Creation of a Fully Normalized Data Model

The data model must be correctly normalized. Normalization relates to the *logical structure* of data, *not the physical structure*. (See Methodology Chart 13.)

> The term **normalization of data** refers to the way data items are grouped together into record structures. Normalization is necessary for clear thinking about data.

It is possible that the physical implementation may deviate from normalized form in order to optimize machine performance. At the initial design stage, however, the data are normalized. If a data model exists for the business area as a whole, it is kept in a correctly normalized form. Fourth normal form is a grouping of data designed to avoid the anomalies and problems that can occur with data. The concept originated with the mathematics of E. F. Codd, given in Appendix VI. The steps in normalizing data are summarized in Figure 13.2.

When data are in fourth normal form, each data item in a record refers to a particular **key** that uniquely identifies it. The key itself may be composed of more than one data item. Each data item in the record is identified by the whole key, not just part of the

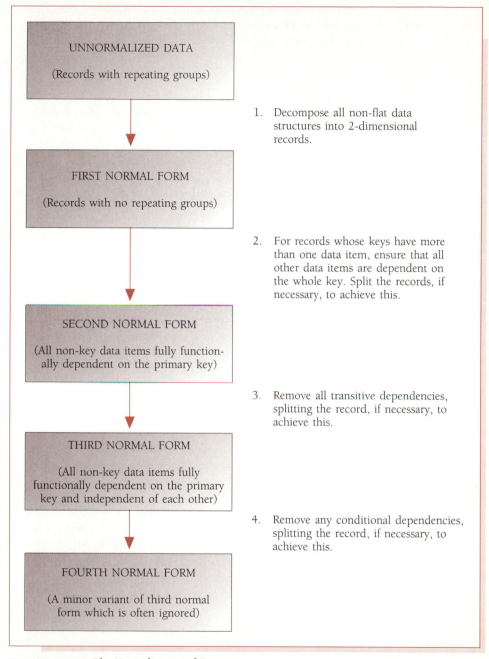

1.  Decompose all non-flat data structures into 2-dimensional records.

2.  For records whose keys have more than one data item, ensure that all other data items are dependent on the whole key. Split the records, if necessary, to achieve this.

3.  Remove all transitive dependencies, splitting the record, if necessary, to achieve this.

4.  Remove any conditional dependencies, splitting the record, if necessary, to achieve this.

FIGURE 13.2  The Normalization of Data

key. No data item in the record is identifiable by any other data item in the record that is not part of the key.

The nature of normalized data is described in the following slogan:

Every attribute is dependent on the key, the whole key, and nothing but the key.

The basic simplicity of fourth normal form makes the data records easy to understand and easier to change than when the data are organized in more convoluted ways. It formally groups the data items associated with each entity-type (and also those that are associated with more than one entity-type) and separates the data items that belong to different entity-types. Fourth normal form prevents anomalies that can otherwise occur. It permits rules to be established for controlling disintegrity of meaning in the use of database.

## Entities and Attributes

An **entity**, as we stated earlier, is something about which we store data. It may be a tangible object such as an employee, a part, a customer, a machine tool or an office. It may be a nontangible object such as a job title, a profit center, an association, a financial allowance, a purchase, an estimate or an insurance claim.

To model data, we study the entity-types of the enterprise. A typical corporation has several hundred entity-types. Its set of entity-types does not change much as time goes by unless it moves into a fundamentally different type of business. The entity-types are charted on an entity-relationship diagram, as discussed in Appendix IV.

An entity has various **attributes** that we wish to record, such as size, value, date, color, usage code, address, quality, performance code and so on. Often in data processing we are concerned with a collection of similar entities such as employees, and we wish to record information about the same attributes of each of them. A programmer commonly maintains a **record** about each entity, and a data item in each record relates to each attribute. Similar records are grouped into **files**. The result, shown in Figure 13.3, is a two-dimensional array.

Inside the box in Figure 13.4 is a set of data items. The value of each item is shown. Each row of data items relates to a particular entity. Each column contains a particular type of data item relating to a particular type of attribute. At the top of the diagram, outside the box, the names of the attributes are written. The leftmost column in the box contains the data items that identify the entity. The entity in this example is a person, an employee. The attribute, referred to as the **entity identifier**, in this case is EMPLOYEE NUMBER.

| | EMPLOYEE NUMBER | NAME | | SEX | GRADE | DATE OF BIRTH | DEPART-MENT | SKILL CODE | TITLE | | SALARY |
|---|---|---|---|---|---|---|---|---|---|---|---|

Record structure →

FIGURE 13.3 Two-Dimensional Array

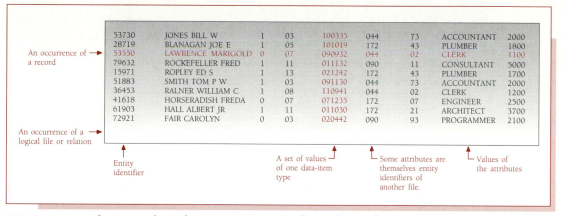

| | | | | | | | | |
|---|---|---|---|---|---|---|---|---|
| 53730 | JONES BILL W | 1 | 03 | 100335 | 044 | 73 | ACCOUNTANT | 2000 |
| 28719 | BLANAGAN JOE E | 1 | 05 | 101019 | 172 | 43 | PLUMBER | 1800 |
| 53550 | LAWRENCE MARIGOLD | 0 | 07 | 090932 | 044 | 02 | CLERK | 1100 |
| 79632 | ROCKEFELLER FRED | 1 | 11 | 011132 | 090 | 11 | CONSULTANT | 5000 |
| 15971 | ROPLEY ED S | 1 | 13 | 021242 | 172 | 43 | PLUMBER | 1700 |
| 51883 | SMITH TOM P W | 1 | 03 | 091130 | 044 | 73 | ACCOUNTANT | 2000 |
| 36453 | RALNER WILLIAM C | 1 | 08 | 110941 | 044 | 02 | CLERK | 1200 |
| 41618 | HORSERADISH FREDA | 0 | 07 | 071235 | 172 | 07 | ENGINEER | 2500 |
| 61903 | HALL ALBERT JR | 1 | 11 | 011030 | 172 | 21 | ARCHITECT | 3700 |
| 72921 | FAIR CAROLYN | 0 | 03 | 020442 | 090 | 93 | PROGRAMMER | 2100 |

An occurrence of → a record

An occurrence of a → logical file or relation

Entity identifier

A set of values of one data-item type

Some attributes are themselves entity identifiers of another file.

Values of the attributes

**FIGURE 13.4** The Terminology of Various Components of Records (See also Box 13.1.)

Such a two-dimensional array is sometimes referred to as a **flat file**. The use of flat files dates back to the earliest days of data processing, when the file or deck of cards such as that in Figure 13.5 might contain one record relating to one entity.

Certain card columns were allocated to each data-item type or attribute and were called a **field**. When magnetic tapes replaced decks of cards and disks replaced magnetic tapes, many programmers retained their view of data as being organized into flat files.

Box 13.1 gives the terminology used in discussing data.

## Entity Records

In examining the data that need to be stored for a system, we will initially think of a collection of flat files such as those in Figure 13.4 or 13.5.

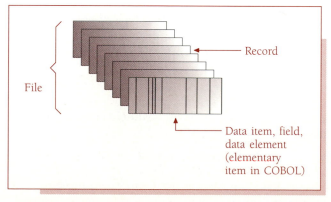

Record

File

Data item, field, data element (elementary item in COBOL)

**FIGURE 13.5** A Flat File; A Programmer's or User's View of the Data

---

## Box 13.1    Vocabulary Used in Discussing Data (Also see Figure 13.4.)

*The reader should distinguish clearly between the terms data type and data-item type.*

- DATA-TYPE refers to the data itself, i.e., data about data.
  Examples of data types are integer, rational number, Boolean and alphabetic string.

- ENTITY-TYPE refers to a given class of entities such as customer, part, account, employee, etc.

- ATTRIBUTE refers to a characteristic of an entity-type, for example, color, shape, shipment-date, type-of-account, dollar-value, etc.

*When we use the term data-item type, we are referring to either an entity-type or attribute.*

- DATA-ITEM expresses an attribute or entity identifier (a special type of attribute) in computable form, sometimes described as a field.

- DATA-ITEM TYPE refers to a given class of data items.
  Examples of data-item types are customer#, account#, address, dollar-value, color, etc.

*Entities and data items are instances of entity-types and data-item types. For example, DUPONT is an instance of the entity-type customer. RED is an instance of the attribute color. Data item 4789123 is an instance of the data-item type employee-number.*

*In discussion of data, we sometimes use a shorthand. We say "entity" when we mean "entity-type," "data item" when we mean "data-item type," and so on. "Data type" is never abbreviated.*

---

Each flat file contains information about one type of entity. A record in that file contains information about one occurrence of that entity. For example, a CUSTOMER record contains information about one CUSTOMER. We will refer to this as an **entity record**.

The entity record is a *logical view* of the data. The data may be stored in a different form *physically* in a database.

The entity record contains data about *one and only one* type of entity. It contains all of the attributes of that entity that are stored.

> Thus, when we use the term **entity record**, we are referring not to any collection of data items but to a rather special grouping of data. We refer to this as **normalized data** and use the term **fourth normal form**, which this chapter explains.

# Normalization of Data

Data on documents are not normalized. Data exist in real life as groups of data items. They exist on invoices, waybills, tax forms, driving licenses and so on. These groupings are not usually in normalized form. Not surprisingly, systems analysts have often created computer records of similar form which are also unnormalized. However, data that are not normalized can lead to various subtle problems.

Experience has shown that, when computer data are organized in fourth normal form, the resulting data structures are more stable and able to accommodate change. Each attribute relates to its own entity and is not mixed up with attributes relating to different entities. The actions that create and update data can then be applied with simple structured design to one normalized record at a time.

Some corporations have several years of experience in operating fourth-normal-form data structures. There is no question that they have greatly benefited from this type of design, especially when it is combined with other steps that are part of good data administration [MARTIN83].

Reacting to the perceived benefits, some corporations have incorporated into their database standards manuals the requirement that all database structures be *designed* in fourth normal form. Usually, normalized-form data are better in terms of *machine requirements* as well as in logical structuring, but this is not always the case. Sometimes the physical designer finds it desirable to deviate from fourth normal form. A compromise is then needed. Which is preferable: somewhat better machine performance or better protection from maintenance costs? Usually, potential maintenance costs are much more expensive.

The physical implementation may occasionally deviate from fourth normal form if the tradeoff is fully explored and documented. The basic ideas of this normalization of data are simple, but the ramifications are many and subtle, and they vary from one type of database usage to another. It is important to note that normalization describes the logical representation of data, not the physical one. There are multiple ways of implementing it physically.

# First Normal Form

**First normal form** refers to a collection of data organized into records that have no repeating groups of data items within a record. In other words, they are flat files—two-dimensional matrices of data items.

Such a flat file may be thought of as a simple two-dimensional table. It may, however, contain many thousands of records.

Most programming languages give programmers the ability to create and refer to records that are not flat, i.e., they contain repeating groups of data items within a record. In COBOL these are called **data tables**. There can be data tables within data tables—repeating groups within repeating groups.

This COBOL record contains two data groups, BIRTH and SKILLS:

```
RECORD NAME IS PERSON
01              EMPLOYEE # PICTURE "9(5)"
01              EMPNAME TYPE CHARACTER 20
01              SEX PICTURE "A"
01              EMPJCODE PICTURE "9999"
01              SALARY PICTURE "9(5)V99"
01              BIRTH
01      02          MONTH PICTURE "99"
        02          DAY
        02          YEAR PICTURE "99"
01              NOSKILLS TYPE BINARY
01              SKILLS OCCURS NOSKILLS TIMES
        02          SKILLCODE PICTURE "9999"
        02          SKILLYEARS PICTURE "99"
```

| PERSON | | | | | BIRTH | | | SKILLS | |
|---|---|---|---|---|---|---|---|---|---|
| EMPLOYEE# | EMPNAME | SEX | EMPCODE | SALARY | MONTH | DAY | YEAR | SKILL CODE | SKILL YEARS |

BIRTH causes no problems because it occurs only once in each record. SKILLS can occur several times in one record; so, it is a data table, and the record is not in first normal form. It is not a *flat*, two-dimensional record. To *normalize* it, the table SKILLS must be removed and put into a separate record.

Thus:

| PERSON | | | | | BIRTH | | |
|---|---|---|---|---|---|---|---|
| EMPLOYEE# | EMPNAME | SEX | EMPCODE | SALARY | MONTH | DAY | YEAR |

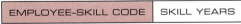

| SKILLS | |
|---|---|
| EMPLOYEE-SKILL CODE | SKILL YEARS |

The lower record has a concatenated key, EMPLOYEE# + SKILLCODE. We cannot know SKILLYEARS (the number of years of experience an employee has had with a given skill) unless we know EMPLOYEE# (the employee number to which this refers) and SKILLCODE (the skill in question).

In general, a nonflat record is normalized by converting it into two or more flat records.

If the preceding normalized records had been implemented in a CODASYL, DL/1 or other nonrelational database management system, we would not have to repeat the data item EMPLOYEE# in the lower record.

A linkage to the upper record would imply this key:

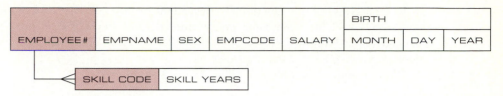

A relational database would employ a separate SKILLS record (relation) with a key EMPLOYEE + SKILLCODE; it thus avoids pointer mechanisms in the logical representation of data.

Here we are concerned not with *how* the physical implementation is done but with the *overall logical representation of data*. We need to analyze and chart an enterprise's information resources and how they are used. We draw the lower record with its complete concatenated key so that it can stand alone, and the key uniquely identifies the data in the record.

## Functional Dependency

In attempting to lay out the relationship between data items, the designer must concern himself with which data items are functionally dependent on which other data items. The phrase *functionally dependent* is defined as follows:

> Data item B of a record R is functionally dependent on data item A of R if, at every instant of time, each value in A has no more than one value in B associated with it in record R [CODD72].

Saying that B is functionally dependent on A is equivalent to saying that A *identifies* B. In other words, if we know the value of A, then we can find the value of B associated with it. For example, in an employee record, the SALARY data item is functionally dependent upon EMPLOYEE#. For one EMPLOYEE# there is one SALARY. To find the value of SALARY in a database, you would normally use EMPLOYEE#. The latter is a key that identifies the attribute SALARY.

We will draw a functional dependency with a line that has a small bar (like a 1) on it, thus:

EMPLOYEE# ———————+ SALARY

This indicates that one instance of SALARY is associated with each EMPLOYEE#. Consider the record for the entity EMPLOYEE:

| EMPLOYEE# | EMPLOYEE-NAME | SALARY | PROJECT# | COMPLETION-DATE |
|---|---|---|---|---|

The functional dependencies in this record are as follows:

| | |
|---|---|
| EMPLOYEE# | is dependent on EMPLOYEE-NAME |
| EMPLOYEE-NAME | is dependent on EMPLOYEE# |
| SALARY | is dependent on either EMPLOYEE-NAME or EMPLOYEE# |
| PROJECT# | is dependent on either EMPLOYEE-NAME or EMPLOYEE# |
| COMPLETION-DATE | is dependent on EMPLOYEE-NAME, EMPLOYEE# or PROJECT# |

EMPLOYEE# is not functionally dependent on SALARY because more than one employee could have the same salary. Similarly, EMPLOYEE# is not functionally dependent on PROJECT#, but COMPLETION-DATE is. No other data item is fully dependent on PROJECT#.

We can draw these functional dependencies as follows:

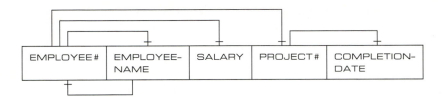

A data item can be functionally dependent on a group of data items rather than on a single data item. Consider, for example, the following record, which shows how programmers spent their time:

PROGRAMMER-ACTIVITY

| PROGRAMMER# | PACKAGE# | PROGRAMMER-NAME | PACKAGE-NAME | TOTAL-HOURS-WORKED |
|---|---|---|---|---|

The fields that constitute the primary key (unique identifier) are shaded. TOTAL-HOURS-WORKED is functionally dependent on the concatenated key (PROGRAMMER#, PACKAGE#).

The functional dependencies in this record can be drawn as follows:

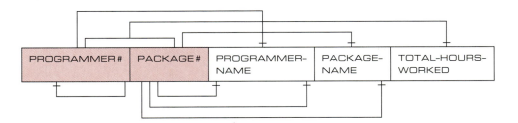

## Full Functional Dependency

A data item or a collection of data items, B of record R, can be said to be *fully functionally dependent* on another collection of data items, A of record R, if B is functionally dependent on the whole of A but not on any subset of A.

For example, in the preceding record, TOTAL-HOURS-WORKED is fully functionally dependent on the concatenated key (PROGRAMMER#, PACKAGE#) because it refers to how many hours a given programmer has worked on a given package. Neither PROGRAMMER# alone nor PACKAGE alone identifies TOTAL-HOURS-WORKED.

TOTAL-HOURS-WORKED, however, is the *only* data item that is fully functionally dependent on the concatenated key; PROGRAMMER-NAME is fully functionally dependent on PROGRAMMER# alone, and PACKAGE-NAME is fully functionally dependent on PACKAGE# alone. The lines with bars above make these dependencies clear.

# Second Normal Form

We are now in a position to define **second normal form**. Here, first, is a simple definition:

> A record is in second normal form if each attribute in the record is fully functionally dependent on the whole key of that record.

Where the key consists of more than one data item, the record may not be in second normal form. The record above, with the key PROGRAMMER# + PACKAGE#, is not in second normal form because TOTAL-HOURS-WORKED depends on the whole key, whereas PROGRAMMER-NAME and PACKAGE-NAME each depend on only one data item in the key.

A few problems can result from a record not being in second normal form. The following record is not in second normal form:

| PART# | SUPPLIER# | SUPPLIER-NAME | SUPPLIER-DETAILS | PRICE |
|-------|-----------|---------------|------------------|-------|

- We cannot enter details about a supplier until that supplier supplies a part. If the supplier does not supply a part, there is no key.
- If a supplier should temporarily cease to supply any part, then the deletion of the last record containing that SUPPLIER# will also delete the details of the supplier. It is normally desirable to preserve SUPPLIER-DETAILS.
- We have problems when we attempt to update the supplier details. We must search for every record that contains that supplier as part of the key. If a supplier supplies many parts, much redundant updating of supplier details will be needed.

Splitting the record removes these types of irregularities. This can be done by splitting the record into two records in second normal form, as shown in Figure 13.6. Only PRICE is fully functionally dependent on the concatenated key; so all other attributes are removed to the separate record on the left, which has SUPPLIER# only as its key.

Splitting to second normal form is the type of splitting that natural database growth tends to force, so it might as well be anticipated when the database is first set up. In general, every data item in a record should be dependent on the entire key; otherwise, it should be removed to a separate record. Figure 13.6 illustrates the splitting of the preceding record into second-normal-form records.

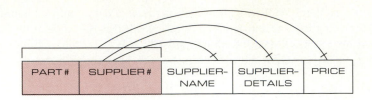

| PART# | SUPPLIER# | SUPPLIER-NAME | SUPPLIER-DETAILS | PRICE |
|---|---|---|---|---|

An instance of this record:

| PART# | SUPPLIER# | SUPPLIER-NAME | SUPPLIER-DETAILS | PRICE |
|---|---|---|---|---|
| 1 | 1000 | JONES | x | 20 |
| 1 | 1500 | ABC | x | 28 |
| 1 | 2050 | XYZ | y | 22 |
| 1 | 1900 | P-H | z | 30 |
| 2 | 3100 | ALLEN | z | 520 |
| 2 | 1000 | JONES | x | 500 |
| 2 | 2050 | XYZ | y | 590 |
| 3 | 2050 | XYZ | y | 1000 |
| 4 | 1000 | JONES | x | 80 |
| 4 | 3100 | ALLEN | z | 90 |
| 4 | 1900 | P-H | z | 95 |
| 5 | 1500 | ABC | x | 160 |
| 5 | 1000 | JONES | x | 140 |

To convert the above records into second normal form, we split it into
two records, thus:

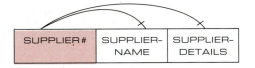

| SUPPLIER# | SUPPLIER-NAME | SUPPLIER-DETAILS |
|---|---|---|

| PART# | SUPPLIER# | PRICE |
|---|---|---|

An instance of the above pair of records:

| SUPPLIER# | SUPPLIER-NAME | SUPPLIER-DETAILS |
|---|---|---|
| 1000 | JONES | x |
| 1500 | ABC | x |
| 2050 | XYZ | y. |
| 1900 | P-H | z |
| 3100 | ALLEN | z |

| PART# | SUPPLIER# | PRICE |
|---|---|---|
| 1 | 1000 | 20 |
| 1 | 1500 | 28 |
| 1 | 2050 | 22 |
| 1 | 1900 | 30 |
| 2 | 3100 | 520 |
| 2 | 1000 | 500 |
| 2 | 2050 | 590 |
| 3 | 2050 | 1000 |
| 4 | 1000 | 80 |
| 4 | 3100 | 90 |
| 4 | 1900 | 95 |
| 5 | 1500 | 160 |
| 5 | 1000 | 140 |

FIGURE 13.6 Conversion to Second Normal Form

## Candidate Keys

The key of a normalized record must have the following properties:

- *Unique Identification.* For every record occurrence, the key must uniquely identify the record.
- *Nonredundancy.* No data item in the key can be discarded without destroying the property of unique identification.

It sometimes happens that more than one data item or set of data items can be the key of a record. Such alternative choices are referred to as **candidate keys.**

One candidate key must be designated the **primary key**. Thus, we will draw the functional dependencies for candidate keys that are not the primary key underneath the record:

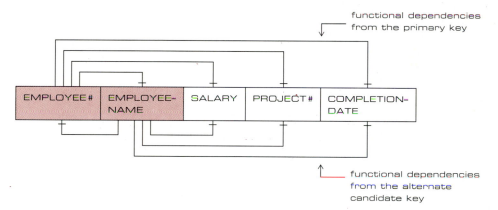

In this illustration, EMPLOYEE-NAME is regarded as a candidate key—an alternative to EMPLOYEE#. This is not generally done in practice because two employees might have the same name. Only EMPLOYEE# is truly unique.

The possible existence of candidate keys complicates the definitions of second and third normal form. A more comprehensive definition of second normal form is:

> A record R is in second normal form if it is in first normal form and every nonprime data item of R is fully functionally dependent on each candidate key of R [CODD72].

In the above EMPLOYEE record, the candidate keys have only one data item; hence, the record is always in second normal form because the nonprime data items must be fully dependent on the candidate keys. When the candidate keys consist of more than one data item, a first normal form may not be in second normal form.

# Third Normal Form

A record that is in second normal form can have another type of anomaly. It may have a data item that is not a key but that itself identifies other data items. This is referred to as a **transitive dependency**. Transitive dependencies can cause problems. The step of putting data into third normal form removes transitive dependencies.

Suppose that A, B and C are three data items or distinct collections of data items of a record R. If C is functionally dependent on B and B is functionally dependent on A, then C is functionally dependent on A. If the inverse mapping is nonsimple (i.e., if A is not functionally dependent on B or B is not functionally dependent on C), then C is said to be *transitively dependent* on A.

In a diagram, C is transitively dependent on A if:

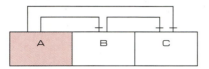

Conversion to third normal form removes this transitive dependence by splitting the record into two, thus:

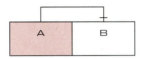   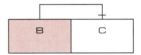

The following record is not in third normal form because COMPLETION-DATE is dependent on PROJECT#:

EMPLOYEE#

| EMPLOYEE# | EMPLOYEE-NAME | SALARY | PROJECT# | COMPLETION-DATE |
|-----------|---------------|--------|----------|-----------------|

Problems might result from the record not being in third normal form:

1. Before any employees are recruited for a project, the completion date of the project cannot be recorded because there is no EMPLOYEE record.
2. If all the employees should leave the project so that the project has no employees until others are recruited, all records containing the completion date would be deleted. This may be considered an unlikely occurrence, but on other types of files, a similar danger of loss of information can be less improbable.
3. If the completion date is changed, it will be necessary to search for all records containing that completion date and update them all.

A simple definition of **third normal form** is:

A record is in second normal form, and each attribute is functionally dependent on the key and *nothing but the key*.

A more formal definition, which incorporates candidate keys, is as follows:

A record R is in third normal form if it is in second normal form and every nonprime data item of R is nontransitively dependent on each candidate key of R [CODD72].

Figure 13.7 shows the conversion of the previous EMPLOYEE record to third normal form.

The conversion to third normal form produces a separate record for each entity—a normalized record. For example, Figure 13.7 produced a separate record for the entity PROJECT. Usually, this normalized record would be needed anyway. We need data separately stored for each entity.

# Conditional Dependencies

Usually, the normalization process stops at third normal form. There are two subtleties that could result in a further stage of normalization. First, if the primary key (unique identifier) extends three or more fields with multivalued dependencies within the key, a further stage of cleaning up may be needed. This is described in Chapter 13 of [MARTIN83]. Second, a record in third normal form might have a conditional dependency in it; this is removed by splitting the record again.

Consider this record with the primary key CUSTOMER-NUMBER:

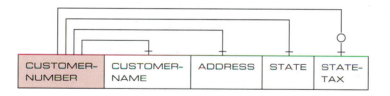

STATE-TAX exists only for customers in the state of the shipping company, e.g., Vermont. For most customers, there is no STATE-TAX because they are ordering from out of state. The existence of the field is conditional. The record may, therefore, be split so that STATE-TAX is in a separate, relatively small file:

CUSTOMERS

| CUSTOMER-NUMBER | CUSTOMER-NAME | ADDRESS | STATE-TAX |
|---|---|---|---|

VERMONT CUSTOMERS

| CUSTOMER-NUMBER | STATE-TAX |
|---|---|

The link from CUSTOMER-NUMBER to STATE-TAX is referred to as a **conditional dependency**. The removal of conditional dependencies is sometimes referred to as the **fourth stage of normalization**. It is shown as the bottom step in Figure 13.2.

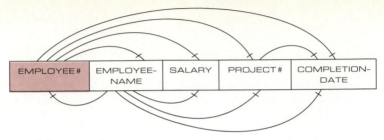

An instance of this record:

| EMPLOYEE # | EMPLOYEE-NAME | SALARY | PROJECT # | COMPLETION-DATE |
|---|---|---|---|---|
| 120 | JONES | 2000 | x | 17.7.84 |
| 121 | HARPO | 1700 | x | 17.7.84 |
| 270 | GARFUNKAL | 1800 | y | 12.1.87 |
| 273 | SELSI | 3600 | x | 17.7.84 |
| 274 | ABRAHMS | 3000 | z | 21.3.86 |
| 279 | HIGGINS | 2400 | y | 12.1.87 |
| 301 | FLANNEL | 1800 | z | 21.3.86 |
| 306 | MCGRAW | 2100 | x | 17.7.84 |
| 310 | ENSON | 3000 | z | 21.3.86 |
| 315 | GOLDSTEIN | 3100 | x | 17.7.84 |
| 317 | PUORRO | 2700 | y | 12.1.87 |
| 320 | MANSINI | 1700 | y | 12.1.87 |
| 321 | SPOTO | 2900 | x | 17.7.84 |
| 340 | SCHAFT | 3100 | x | 17.7.84 |
| 349 | GOLD | 1900 | z | 21.3.86 |

To convert the above records into third normal form, we split it into two records, thus:

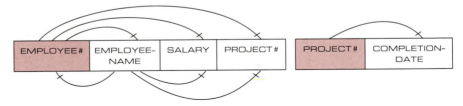

An instance of the above pair of records:

| EMPLOYEE # | EMPLOYEE-NAME | SALARY | PROJECT # |
|---|---|---|---|
| 120 | JONES | 2000 | x |
| 121 | HARPO | 1700 | x |
| 270 | GARFUNKAL | 1800 | y |
| 273 | SELSI | 3600 | x |
| 274 | ABRAHMS | 3000 | z |
| 279 | HIGGINS | 2400 | y |
| 301 | FLANNEL | 1800 | z |
| 306 | MCGRAW | 2100 | x |
| 310 | ENSON | 3000 | z |
| 315 | GOLDSTEIN | 3100 | x |
| 317 | PUORRO | 2700 | y |
| 320 | MANSINI | 1700 | y |
| 321 | SPOTO | 2900 | x |
| 340 | SCHAFT | 3100 | x |
| 349 | GOLD | 1900 | z |

| PROJECT # | COMPLETION-DATE |
|---|---|
| x | 17.7.84 |
| y | 12.1.87 |
| z | 21.3.86 |

FIGURE 13.7 Conversion to Third Normal Form

# Storage and Performance

*Conversion to third normal form almost always reduces the amount of storage used, often dramatically.* What about machine time and accesses? Often, these are reduced after normalization. Before normalization, many aspects of the data are tangled together and must all be read at once. After normalization, they are separated, so only a small record is read each time.

Also, because there is less value redundancy in third normal form, there is less duplication updating of the redundant values. Suppose, in the example in Figure 13.7, the completion date of project x slips (which it does every week!). In the record at the top of Figure 13.7, the completion date has to be changed seven times; in the third normal form version, it has to be changed only once. A similar argument applies to SUPPLIER-NAME and SUPPLIER-DETAILS in Figure 13.6. The argument would have more force if the examples had hundreds of employees, thousands of suppliers and many attributes that have to be updated.

There are, however, exceptions to this. On rare occasions, a designer may consciously design non-third-normal-form records for performance reasons.

Objections to normalization are occasionally heard on the grounds that it requires more storage or more machine time. A fourth-normal-form structure usually has more records after all the splitting described previously. Isn't that worse from the hardware point of view?

Not necessarily. In fact, although there are more records, they almost always take less storage. The reason is that non-fourth-normal-form records usually have much value redundancy.

Compare the records in Figure 13.6. Here records not in second normal form are converted to second normal form by splitting. It will be seen that the lower table of Figure 13.6 has fewer values of data than the upper table. There are fewer values of SUPPLIER-NAME and SUPPLIER-DETAILS. On such a small illustration, this shrinkage does not look very dramatic. If there had been thousands of suppliers and thousands of parts and many attributes of both, the total reduction would have been spectacular.

Again, compare the shaded parts of Figure 13.7. Here, a record is converted to third normal form by splitting. The number of values of data shrinks. There are fewer values of COMPLETION-DATE recorded after the split. Once more, if there had been many employees, many projects and many attributes of those projects, the shrinkage would have been dramatic.

# Semantic Disintegrity

A further reason for using normalized data is that certain database queries can run into problems when data are not clearly structured. A query, perhaps entered with a database query language, can appear to be valid but, in fact, have subtle illogical aspects—sometimes referred to as **semantic disintegrity**. When the data are in third normal form, rules can be devised for preventing semantic disintegrity or warning the user about his query.

# Clear Thinking about Data

Normalization is an aid to clear thinking about data. It is a formal method of separating the data items that relate to different entities.

A record of fourth normal form has the following clean, simple structures:

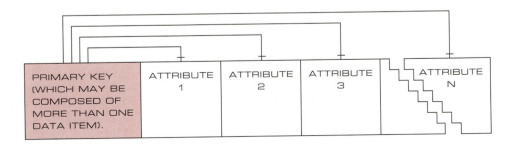

The functional dependency lines all come from the primary key. There are no hidden dependencies not relating to the key. If the key is concatenated, all data items are dependent on the entire key.

> Every data item in a record is dependent on the key, the whole key, and nothing but the key.

If a systems analyst remembers this definition (understanding that it is not rigorous, like those presented earlier in the chapter), he can quickly spot and modify records that are not in fourth normal form. He should be familiar enough with this so that alarm bells go off in his mind whenever he sees records that are not in third normal form.

This clean, simple, data grouping is easy to implement and to use. There are complications in store in the future if more complex record structures are used.

For the database administrator, normalization is an *aid to precision*. A normalized database can grow and evolve naturally. The updating rules are straightforward. A fourth-normal-form record type can have records added to it or can have records deleted without the problems that could occur with nonnormalization record types. Fourth-normal-form structuring gives a simple view of data to the programmers and users and makes them less likely to perform invalid operations.

Figure 13.8 gives a simplified illustration of the three main steps in achieving normalized data. Figure 13.9 illustrates the progression to fourth normal form.

# An Example of Normalization

Consider an ORDER record with the following unnormalized structure:

> ORDER (*Order #*, order date, customer number, customer name, customer address, export status, tax number, ((*Product #*, product name, quantity ordered, product price, product total)), order total)

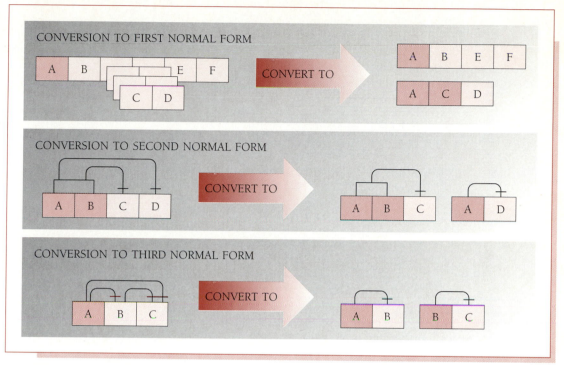

FIGURE 13.8 A Simplified Illustration of the Three Steps in Conversion of Data to Third Normal Form

Figure 13.9 gives an illustration with real data.

Apply the four normalization steps to this example. This is illustrated in Figure 13.9.

- Application of the **First Normal Form** rule (remove repeating groups) creates two records: ORDER and ORDER-PRODUCT. The primary key is made up of *Order#* and *Product#*.

- **Second Normal Form** removes the product name from the ORDER-PRODUCT record onto a new record, PRODUCT. PRODUCTNAME is wholly dependent on *Product#*; it is only partially dependent on the primary (combined or compound) key of ORDER-PRODUCT: *Order# + Product#*.

- **Third Normal Form** removes the customer details from the ORDER record to a separate CUSTOMER record. Customer name and address are wholly dependent on customer number; they are not dependent at all on the primary key of ORDER, i.e., *Order#*. (A customer will not change his name and address with each new order—unless he doesn't intend to pay for it!)

  The four resulting records—ORDER, CUSTOMER, ORDER-PRODUCT and PRODUCT in Figure 13.9— are in third normal form.

- The final step in Figure 13.9, removes the conditional dependency that causes there to be a tax number for domestic customers but not for foreign customers.

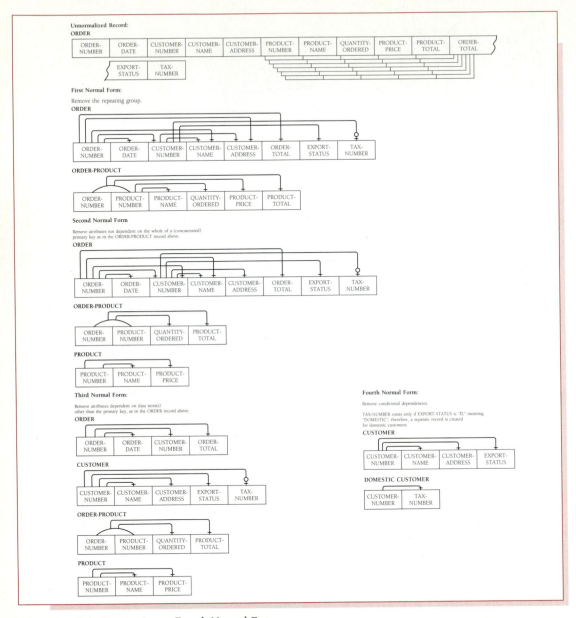

FIGURE 13.9 Progression to Fourth Normal Form

# JAD Review

Experience has shown that end users can almost always make valuable contributions when they are involved in the data modeling process [MARTIN83]. In fast application development, end-user validation of the data model should take place in the JAD workshop, as described in the previous chapter.

# References

[CODD72] E. F. Codd, "Further Normalization of the Data Base Relational Model," in *Data Base Systems*, Courant Computer Science Symposia, 6, edited by R. Rustin, Prentice-Hall, Inc., Englewood Cliffs, New Jersey, 1972 (201–592–2261) (reproduced in Appendix IV).

[MARTIN83] James Martin, *Managing the Data Base Environment*, Prentice-Hall, Inc., Englewood Cliffs, New Jersey, 1983 (201–592–2261).

CHAPTER 14

# Process Modeling

The data model is one half of the **coordinating model** discussed in Chapter 12. The other half is the **process model**. Data modeling and process modeling are done at the same time (unless a detailed data model already exists). The I-CASE tool must integrate the data model and process model.

When a business process is examined, the paper documents or computer records associated with it are analyzed with the synthesis techniques described in the previous chapter. The information that must pass between processes is similarly examined. When entities are described in data modeling, the question is asked, "What *processes* use these entities?"

## Process Decomposition

A **process** may be defined as a defined business activity, executions of which may be identified in terms of the input and output of specified types of data.

The entire application may be regarded as a process. This process is decomposed into subprocesses revealing greater detail. This is continued until elementary processes are identified.

An **elementary process** may be defined as the smallest unit of activity of meaning to the end user and which, when complete, leaves the data in a self-consistent state.

Process decomposition is drawn with a tree structure. The bottom nodes of the tree are elementary processes.

## "Composed-of" Diagrams

In process decomposition diagrams, a parent block is composed of its offspring blocks. It can be described as a "**composed-of**" diagram. The offspring together completely describe the parent. In some other tree structures this is not true. In some program structure diagrams, a parent block *invokes* its child blocks but may itself contain functions that are not in the child blocks; the child blocks are, in effect, subroutines.

In the first step of process modeling, we draw composed-of diagrams of processes until we reach elementary processes that cannot be decomposed further. Figures 14.1 and 14.2 are two examples of composed-of diagrams.

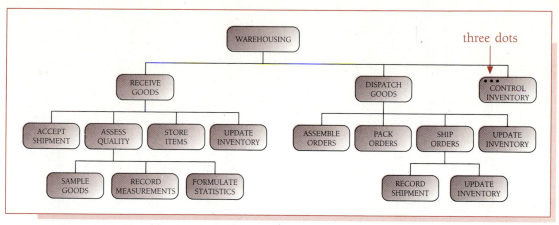

FIGURE 14.1 Example of a "Composed-of" Diagram

# Naming Conventions

As commented earlier, the names of *business functions* are usually nouns such as "marketing," "inventory control," "engineering," "financial planning" and so on. The names of *processes* should be constructed of an active verb and an object, for example:

- "allocate payment"
- "accept order"
- "determine gross receipts"
- "calculate interest"

Where possible, the object of an elementary process name should be an entity-type or an attribute that is in the data model, for example:

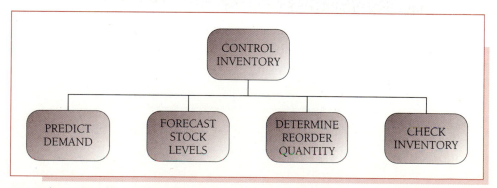

FIGURE 14.2 Additional Example of a "Composed-of" Diagram

- "create invoice"
  (Object of the clause is entity-type INVOICE.)
- "check customer credit"
  (Object of the clause is attribute CUSTOMERCREDIT)
- "issue material"
  (Object of the clause is entity-type PART.)

The names of processes should not reflect who, when or where but only *what* the process does.

# Use of a Diagramming Tool

The process decomposition diagram is built at the screen of an I-CASE workbench. If the preceding naming conventions are followed, it is usually unnecessary to enter explanatory details of a process. The workbench should provide a detail window for entering descriptive detail about a process if so desired.

The process decomposition diagram usually becomes too large to display on one screen. The workbench must use scrolling and zooming techniques for exploring a large diagram. A complex diagram may be nested into separate diagrams. Three dots are used, as on an action diagram (Appendix V), to show that the components of a process are hidden. Mouse-selecting the command "CONTRACT" causes the removal of a subtree and three dots to appear in its parent block. Mouse-selecting the command "EXPAND" can cause a contracted block to be expanded again. Figures 14.1 and 14.2 show illustrations of process decomposition diagrams printed from analysis workbench tools.

# Process Dependency Diagrams

Processes do not exist in isolation; they are dependent upon other processes. A process dependency diagram shows *how processes relate to one another*.

The following diagram notation shows that process B happens after process A. Process B cannot take place until process A has completed; so we say that process B is dependent upon process A:

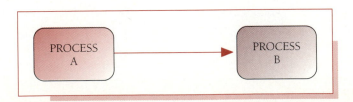

Sometimes there is a string of dependent processes:

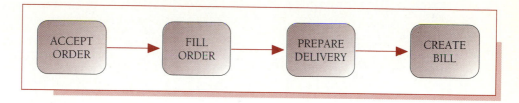

Sometimes one activity is dependent on multiple other activities. Lines from the preceding activity join boxes and enter the dependent activity box.

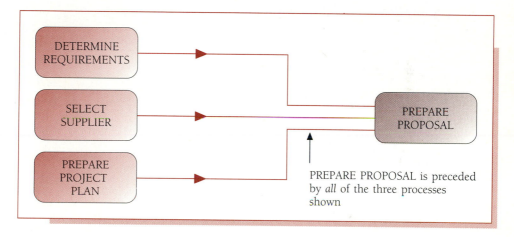

Conversely, one activity may give rise to many others:

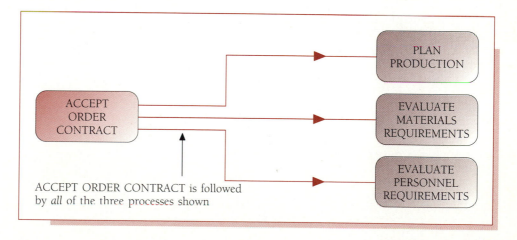

Complex diagrams should be broken into *layers*. Figure 14.3 shows a dependency diagram broken into three layers.

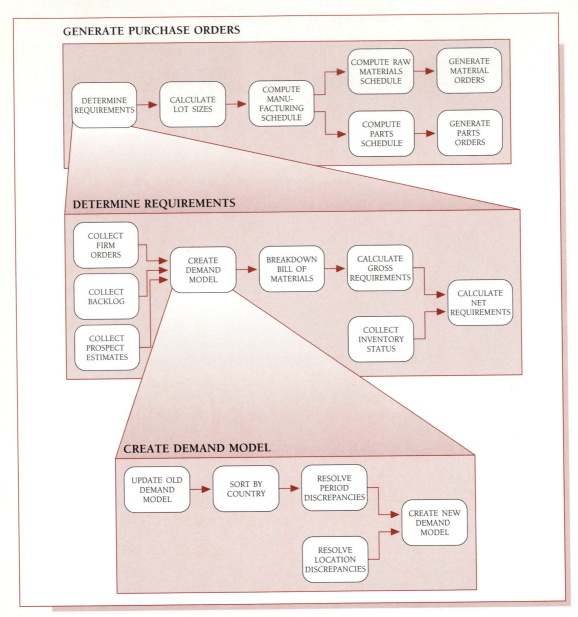

FIGURE 14.3 A Dependency Diagram Broken into Three Layers

# Cardinality

In the diagram in the text above, the dependent process is executed *once* after the preceding process. In some diagrams, we want to show that it may be executed multiple times:

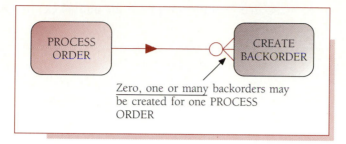

Zero, one or many backorders may
be created for one PROCESS
ORDER

Similarly, a dependent process may follow multiple executions of a preceding process:

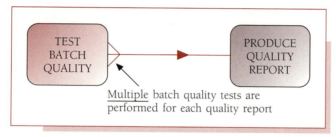

Multiple batch quality tests are
performed for each quality report

Less common is a one-to-many association at both ends of a link:

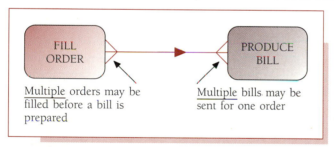

Multiple orders may be
filled before a bill is
prepared

Multiple bills may be
sent for one order

# Mutual Exclusivity

Sometimes one or the other of two activities must be performed but not both. Sometimes one of several activities must be performed. These *mutually exclusive* choices of activity are shown by a solid circle on a branching line—the "OR" circle used earlier:

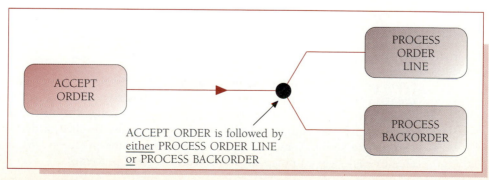

ACCEPT ORDER is followed by
either PROCESS ORDER LINE
or PROCESS BACKORDER

**Conditions** may be associated with the links from the mutual exclusivity circle:

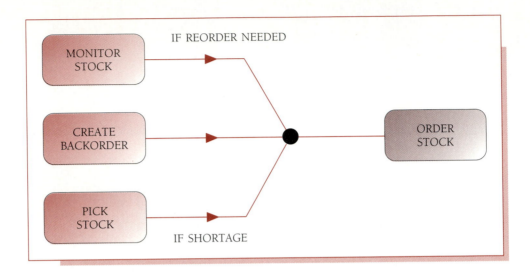

## Parallel Links

Occasionally, two or more links join the same two activity blocks. If these go in the same direction, this may indicate that the processes have been insufficiently or incorrectly decomposed. Links going in opposite directions between two processes occur in feedback loops or control mechanisms:

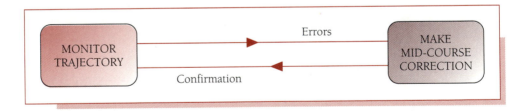

## Events

Some processes are triggered by other processes. Some processes are triggered by events. For example, the receipt of a payment may trigger a process. A process may be triggered by a customer telephoning to make a booking, a security alarm going off, the financial year ending, a bank's closing time being reached, a demand for information and so on. These are all events external to the processes. We may thus talk about *event-triggered* processes and *process-triggered* processes.

A large arrow on a diagram is used to show that an event occurs:

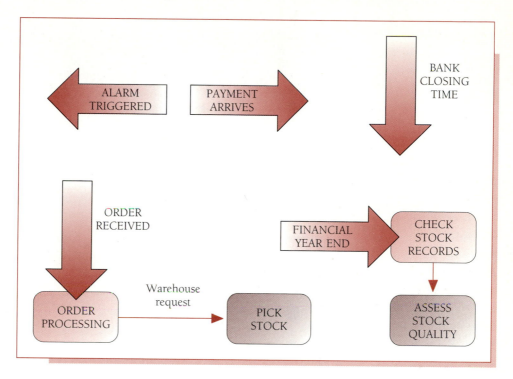

# Process Data-Flow Diagram

The process dependency diagram may now be expanded by adding data inputs and outputs to the process blocks. This makes it a **process data-flow diagram**.

A *process* data-flow diagram is different from a data-flow diagram used for *design*. It describes the *fundamental interactions* that are necessary among processes. It does not show what documents pass from one process to another. It avoids the specific design of procedures, leaving open the many options for this purpose. It does not show whether data pass from one process to another by direct transmittal or by one process updating an on-line database that the other process reads. It is concerned with *logical* interactions, not physical.

The left-hand side (a) of Figure 14.4 shows a process dependency diagram; the right-hand side (b) shows the same diagram with data added to form a data-flow diagram.

# The Entity/Process Matrix

When an analyst has decomposed an application into elementary processes and a data model has been built for that application, a matrix showing what data are used by each process should be created.

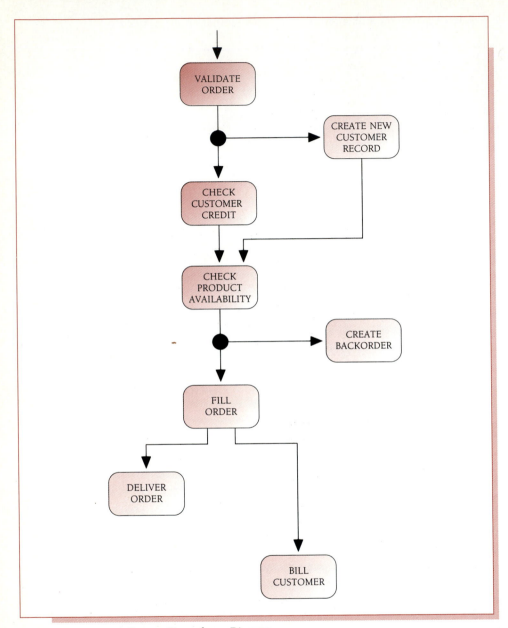

FIGURE 14.4(a) A Process Dependency Diagram

The empty matrix may be displayed automatically by the I-CASE tool. The analyst then fills in the matrix. The analyst may first indicate what process creates each entity record. He does this for *every* entity-type. Some entity records may not be created by any process in that application. In that case, he will indicate that it is an externally created entity record.

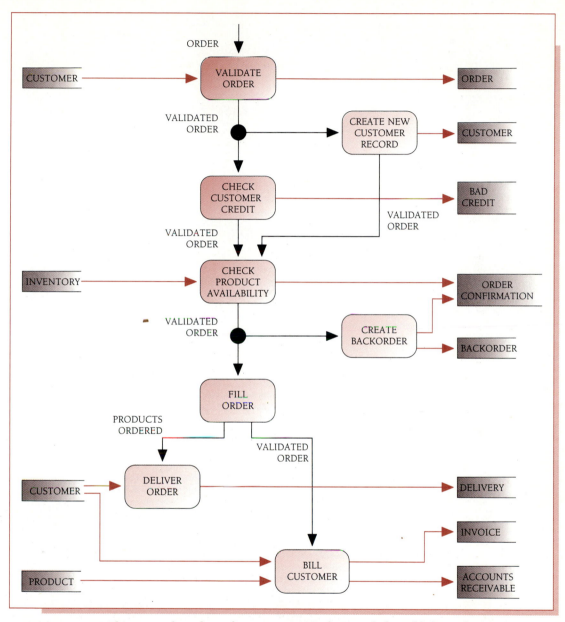

**FIGURE 14.4(b)** The process dependency diagram opposite is shown with data added to make it into a data-flow diagram.

When the analyst has a complete set of information about the *creation* of entity records, he may then indicate what processes *update* what entity records and then what processes *read* or *delete* what entity records.

Figure 14.5 shows a typical entity/process matrix. The whole matrix is too large to be seen all at one time on the workbench screen; thus, the analyst needs to be able to scroll the matrix both vertically and horizontally.

**ENTITIES**

- 16 Other Income
- 15 Customer Payments
- 14 Customer Purchase Order/ Invoice
- 13 Ledger Accounts
- 12 Accounting Regs, Practices
- 11 Financial Plans
- 10 Misc. Contacts/ VIPS
- 9 Boardmember
- 8 Stockholder
- 7 Job Requisition
- 6 MR Staffing Requirements and Plans
- 5 MR Benefits Regs and Plans
- 4 MR Compensation Regs, Plans, etc.
- 3 Applicant
- 2 Contract Employee
- 1 Employee

**PROCESSES**

| Process | 1+ | 2+ | 3+ | 4+ | 5+ | 6+ | 7+ | 8+ | 9+ | 10+ | 11+ | 12+ | 13+ | 14+ | 15+ | 16+ |
|---|---|---|---|---|---|---|---|---|---|---|---|---|---|---|---|---|
| 1 Evaluate Financial Proposals | | | | | | | | | | | | | | | | |
| 2 Estimate Near-Term Earnings | | | | | | | | | | | | | R | | | |
| 3 Budget Finances | R | R | | R | R | | | | | | CRUD | R | CRUD | | | |
| 4 Receive Funds | | | | | | | | | | | | R | | R | CRUD | CRUD |
| 5 Pay Funds | R | | | | | | | | | | | R | | | | |
| 6 Report Finances | R | | | | | | | | | | | R | RU | R | R | R |
| 7 Administer Taxes | | | | | | | | | | | | R | R | | R | R |
| 8 Maintain Financial Reg, Policies | | | | | | | | | | | R | CRUD | | | | |
| 9 Audit Finances | | | | | | | | | | | | R | R | | R | R |
| 10 Manage Financial Investments | | | | | | | | | CRUD | | | R | | | | |
| 11 Plan Human Resources | R | R | | | | CRUD | CRUD | | R | | R | | | | | |
| 12 Acquire Personnel | CRU | CRU | CRUD | | | R | R | | CRU | | | | | | | |
| 13 Position People in Jobs | | | R | | | R | RU | | R | | | | | | | |
| 14 Terminate/Retire People | RUD | RUD | | | | | | | RUD | | | | | | | |
| 15 Plan Career Paths | RU | | | R | R | R | | | | | | | | | | |
| 16 Develop Skills/Motivation | RU | RU | | | | R | R | | | | | | | | | |
| 17 Manage Individual Emp Relations | RU | RU | | | | R | | | | | | | | | | |
| 18 Manage Benefits Program | | | | | CRUD | | | | | | | | | | | |
| 19 Comply with Govt MR Regulations | R | | | R | | | | | | | | | | | | |
| 20 Maintain MR Regs, Policies | | | | CRUD | | CRUD | | | | | | | | | | |
| 21 Determine Production Requirements | | | | | | | | | | | | | R | | | |
| 22 Schedule Production | R | R | | | | | | | | | | | | | | |

FIGURE 14.5 A Matrix Mapping Entity-Types Against the Processes That Create or Use Those Entities

# Relations Among Diagrams

The diagrams used are strongly interrelated. The blocks on a process dependency diagram are the same blocks as some of those on the equivalent decomposition diagram. The inputs and outputs of process blocks on a data-flow diagram show data represented in the data model and data used in the corresponding action diagram. The

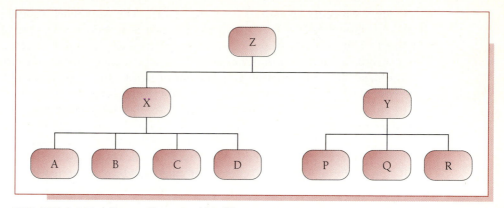

FIGURE 14.6 A Process Decomposition Diagram
The processes are examined further in the dependency diagrams of Figure 14.7.

data used by the processes are shown on the entity/matrix diagram, and these must correlate with the data-flow diagram.

We thus have a set of diagrams that are logically interrelated and form a **hyper-diagram**. Much computerized cross-checking should be done as the hyperdiagram is built and analyzed. The information on the different diagrams is validated and correlated by the workbench.

Figure 14.6 shows a process decomposition diagram. Figure 14.7 shows dependency diagrams with the same processes.

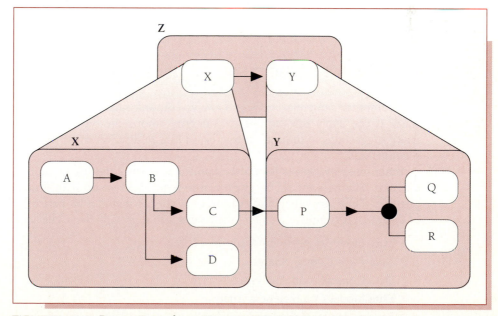

FIGURE 14.7 Process Dependency Diagrams Corresponding to the Decomposition Diagram of Figure 14.6

Figure 14.6 could be derived from Figure 14.7. The workbench should check that they correspond exactly. If another process block is added to one of the diagrams in Figure 14.7, it must *automatically* appear in Figure 14.6. If another block is added to the decomposition of process X in Figure 14.6, then a ghost of this block must appear on the dependency diagram of X on the left of Figure 14.7. The computer asks how this new block should be connected to the rest of the dependency diagram.

From the collection of entities and processes that the analyst has identified in a business area, the workbench can automatically produce an empty entity/process matrix. As the analyst fills this matrix, it can correlate this information with the data entering and leaving blocks on the data-flow diagram. The cross-correlation often leads to the discovery of other interactions that must be added to the model.

## Windows

We have stressed the importance of windows in using I-CASE tools. The user points to a block and displays details of it in a window. The window may display a different type of diagram, as shown in Figure 14.8.

The user asking to see details of a block may be given a choice. For example, if he points to a block on a data-flow diagram, he may be able to see details of lower-level processes on another data-flow diagram or a decomposition diagram, or he may see details of the data used in the block on an entity-relationship diagram. He may descend into further detail via a window that shows a listing of attributes from the data model.

The repository stores the details of the objects and relationships and can display them in different ways as requested, enabling the user to explore the relations among the different facets of the design.

## Cross-Checking and Analysis

The computer can cross-check and analyze the information given to it in a variety of ways. It can apply rules to enforce integrity among the types of information and to make suggestions to the analyst that cause him to discover other processes, entities or relationships.

Basic integrity checks should be applied whenever the user modifies or adds to a diagram. The user should be given real-time feedback of error information whenever possible. There are other types of integrity checks that can be performed when a set of diagrams is complete. Some of the analyses that provide these checks are as follows:

- Data Flow Connectivity Analysis;
- Data Flow Course Analysis;
- Data Conservation Analysis;
- Data Model Completeness Analysis;
- Process Model Completeness Check.

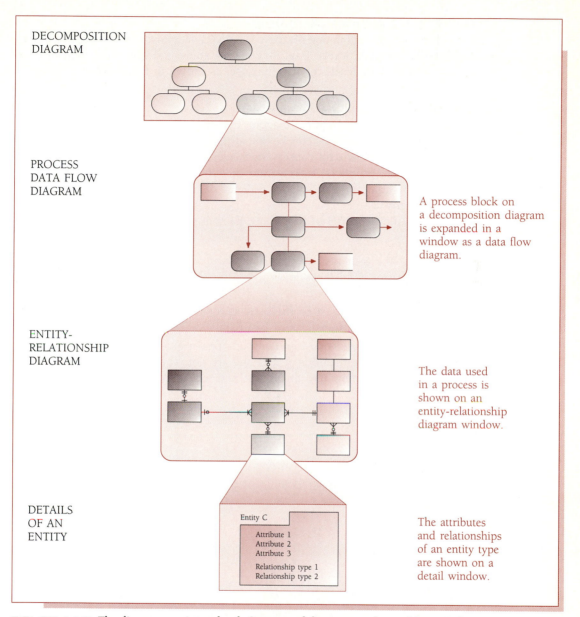

DECOMPOSITION
DIAGRAM

PROCESS
DATA FLOW
DIAGRAM

A process block on
a decomposition diagram
is expanded in a
window as a data flow
diagram.

ENTITY-
RELATIONSHIP
DIAGRAM

The data used
in a process is
shown on an
entity-relationship
diagram window.

DETAILS
OF AN
ENTITY

Entity C

Attribute 1
Attribute 2
Attribute 3

Relationship type 1
Relationship type 2

The attributes
and relationships
of an entity type
are shown on a
detail window.

FIGURE 14.8 The diagrams are interrelated. One type of diagram may be used in a window to
show details of another type of diagram. Courtesy of Knowledge Ware, Inc.

## Data Flow Connectivity Analysis

In a completed data-flow diagram, the connectivity of the diagram can be analyzed to
find any flows that are not continuous or not connected to valid sources or destinations.

## Data Flow Course Analysis

Only one level is displayed in one diagram. However, data flow through process blocks that may be on multiple levels. Data flow course analysis displays the path of data, regardless of how many levels the data traverse, as shown in Figure 14.9.

## Data Conservation Analysis

The different blocks on a data-flow diagram have different views of data represented in the data model. This analysis checks that all views are consistent with one another and that all blocks follow data conservation rules. When conservation is violated, it means that data are, in effect, leaking into or out of the system. Data conservation analysis finds the leaks. When they are corrected, it notifies the user that the data are conserved properly.

Data conservation consists of four rules. Each applies to a different kind of data-flow node.

- *Data Stores*. The contents of a data store must relate to the contents of the flows entering the store and flows leaving it. Data stores conserve data; they cannot generate, transform or lose data.
- *Junctions*. Total input must be the same as total output. Junctions transmit data; they cannot generate, transform or lose data.
- *External Agents*. There is no input/output rule for external agents. They are ultimate sources and destinations of data and are not required to conserve. External agents send certain flow into the system and receive certain flows from it.

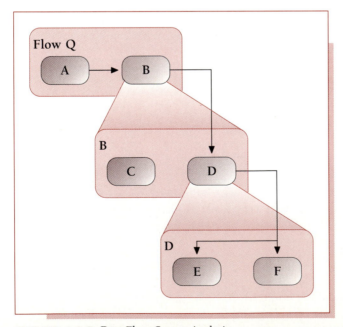

FIGURE 14.9 Data Flow Course Analysis

■ *Activities.* An activity's view of the entity model equals all of the data in all of the data flows that are visible in the activity's data-flow diagram. This includes flow entering the activity, flows leaving it and flows between its children—the activities, data stores and junctions that it immediately contains.

## Data Model Completeness Analysis

To create the normalized data model, many different views of data are synthesized. Each relates to a process. A check should be made to ensure that all processes have been considered in synthesizing the data models. There should be no processes without a data view and no entity-types that do not exist on a detailed data view.

A matrix mapping the views used in data synthesis against the processes may be generated automatically as an aid to the analyst to check that no views have been omitted.

## Process Model Completeness Check

The entity/process matrix can be checked automatically to confirm that there is a process to create and terminate every entity-type. One line on the matrix should be for *external* processes, as some entity records are created or deleted externally to the business area.

The computer should also notify the analyst of any entity-type that is not read or updated. There may be no reason to read or update an entity record after a process has created it, but this check sometimes causes the analyst to notice an omission in the process model.

In general, completeness checking and integrity checking are tedious to do by hand and are rarely done thoroughly. An automated workbench can apply rules that enforce completeness and integrity checks. A good workbench tool has a large number of rules, some of them interrelating multiple diagram types.

# Division into Separate Team Efforts

As we indicated in Chapter 12, the coordinating model will be subdivided to represent subsystems that can be developed by separate teams. The first cut at subdivision is usually done with the decomposition diagram. The decomposition tree is grouped into subtrees, each of which is appropriate in size for one SWAT Team to contract and test in three months or less. Some subtrees or process blocks may be appropriate for one individual to build.

The decomposition diagram relates to the dependency diagram that shows how each process is dependent on other processes. The subdivision may be adjusted when the dependency diagram is examined in order to minimize the dependencies among subsystems built by separate teams.

The dependency diagram is expanded into a data-flow diagram by adding details of the data stores and data flows, as in Figures 14.4a and 14.4b. The data on the data-flow diagram are represented in the data model. The mapping of processes to data is shown in the entity/process matrix. The subdivision into team efforts should be examined with these diagrams again to minimize the interaction among team efforts.

If the JAD activity is divided into two workshops, as recommended in Chapter 8, the subdivision of the coordinating model may be done toward the end of the first workshop. The separate subsystems should be examined by the teams assigned to build them, between the workshops. Questions will be raised and more detail added to the design. In the second JAD workshop, the design of the subsystems will be solidified so that construction can proceed.

## Summary

Methodology Chart 14-1 summarizes the procedures for creating the detailed process model. Methodology Chart 14-2 summarizes the procedure for creating the coordinating model for the system and validating it in the JAD workshops.

# CHAPTER 15

# Reusable Structures

The fastest application development generally occurs when applications are created from preexisting designs or building blocks. Perhaps the most important change in software development that I-CASE tools will bring is the building of systems from reusable parts.

There is a direct analogy with CAD/CAM systems used in engineering today. A design engineer creating a new product employs a graphics workstation that has access to a library of components and products. Wherever possible, he employs existing designs rather than create new parts. He often modifies an existing design to adapt it to his new needs. He is not building from scratch; he is building from existing parts wherever possible. In mature engineering, almost everything is built from existing parts. Would you fly today in a plane that was built from scratch?

## I-CASE for Reusability

The key to reusable design is having an I-CASE environment that makes relevant designs easy to find, easy to understand, easy to modify and easy to link to other components. The graphics capability of the I-CASE tools enables the designer to produce customized instances of the components. The reusable components need to be represented in the repository. The toolset should help the developer find the components that can help him. He can display these in various diagrammatic forms. The I-CASE tool makes the components easy to modify. Modified components can be linked together, and the I-CASE tool will check the integrity and consistency of the combination. It can detect incompatibilities and highlight them graphically, enabling designers to see what adjustments are needed in order to link those selected components. The tool generates code from the modified or synthesized design.

With quality I-CASE tools, it is generally quicker to modify an existing design, or to use existing building blocks, than to design the application from scratch. The tools, repository contents and methodology must make it *easier* to reuse components than to reinvent components.

Box 15.1 lists the benefits of reusability.

## Box 15.1   Benefits of Reusability

- *Speed of Development.* It is quicker to assemble applications from existing designs than to design them from scratch.
- *Low Cost.* Because it is quicker and easier, design from reusable components is likely to cost less.
- *Quality.* As reusable designs are thoroughly tested, perfected and comprehensive, the resulting product is less likely to have errors, instability, omissions and misunderstanding. It is more likely to incorporate the most elegant designs and well-thought-out ideas.
- *Reduction in Maintenance.* Reduction in maintenance work is linked to reduction in development effort. It is quick to create a variation of an existing design.
- *Increased Consistency.* Consistent design makes systems easier to use and components easier to assemble.
- *Shared Expertise.* The reusable design may have a high order of shared expertise built into it. The repository contains much of the company's business know-how or intellectual assets in reusable form.
- *Complexity.* Algorithms, structures or knowledge of great complexity may be built into the reusable modules, facilitating the use of powerful techniques. The user or analyst need not be aware of the underlying complexity.
- *Facilitates Learning of Good Design.* The reusable designs can employ the best techniques. Persons who work with them learn these techniques.
- *One-Person Teams.* Development from reusable components can be done by one person or by a small team.
- *Documentation.* Reusable components are well documented.
- *Ease of Change.* Reusable components are designed so that they are as easy to change as possible with an I-CASE tool that checks that complete integrity and consistency are maintained.
- *Standards.* Reusable designs help enforce standards. Evolving standards such as those for EDI (electronic data interchange) should be made available to developers in the repository.
- *Integration.* Reusable data models, process models and design help achieve integration of systems *vertically* in the enterprise and *horizontally* across the value chain.
- *Business Benefits.* Major business benefits are derived from the standards, integration and ease of change. An I.S. organization is better positioned to adapt its systems quickly to help the enterprise seize new opportunities quickly.

# Quality

Reusable components should be thought out carefully. Some reusable components may be highly complex. Because they are used many times, they should be adjusted and perfected on the basis of field experience. When this is done, reusable components have a high level of quality. It may be difficult for an individual development team to achieve this level of quality.

Reusability, then, helps achieve quality systems (as well as fast development). It can be a major contributor to the RAD goal of achieving high speed, low cost *and* quality.

# Resistance to Standard Formats

On the other hand, reusability imposes certain constraints on the design. There is less choice. It is like buying off-the-shelf clothes as opposed to custom-tailored clothes. The users may have to accept a particular style of screen dialog. The developers may have to accept a certain type of database access. Like persons who want tailored clothes, some users or developers want types of design different from the reusable ones. They need to be aware that their customized structure would be expensive compared with the off-the-shelf structure, and it may delay the project.

Usually, it is better to employ proven off-the-shelf designs rather than specially crafted designs that might have problems. Good management may be needed to direct the users' and developers' choice appropriately. Users must be made aware of the costs and timing. They usually prefer to obtain a reliable system quickly rather than an uncertain system that takes longer and costs more.

# Types of Reusable Components

There are several aspects of design that can be reused, leading to a diversity of forms of reusability:

- *Applications.* An entire application may be stored in the repository. It may be modified to fit the user's requirements. The stored application may be thoroughly thought out, comprehensive, tested and refined from extensive field experience.
- *Application Shells.* A generic application shell may be stored, which can be adapted to a variety of specific applications. The shell may be complex, with comprehensively designed security, auditability, checkpoint-restart, protection from failures, human factoring, cooperative processing and so on—all built with the best techniques. The developer uses the shell and fills in details such as the items on the screen, the items in a relational database and the requisite calculations. He can work with the users as he fills in the shell, customizing it to their needs. The resulting product is less likely to have errors, instability, omissions and misunderstandings.
- *Templates.* Rather than an entire application shell, templates may be stored.

Templates include specimen screens, dialogs or transactions. Employing the template saves design work and helps give consistency to the resulting user interface.

- *Building Blocks.* Applications may be created by assembling building blocks. Algorithms, structures or knowledge of great complexity may be built into reusable building blocks, facilitating the use of powerful techniques.

- *Data Models.* A generic data model may be stored. The data model for one airline is remarkably similar to the data model for another airline. They have essentially the same entity-types and attributes. The data model for one factory in a corporation may be similar to that for the other factories. The same is true for other business areas that exist in multiple locations. Generic industry data models may be used. Generic data models will be reviewed by I.S. professionals and users, who will adapt them to local variations.

- *Data Structures.* A record structure or portion of a database may be reusable. Data are shared among many applications and many locations. The correct normalization of data helps in achieving reusable data structures.

- *Objects.* An object-oriented approach may be taken to analysis and design. Object-types (entity-types) are identified across the enterprise. Their properties and behavior are defined. The same object-type is used in many applications. The data and routines associated with the object may be the same or similar wherever it appears.

- *Documents.* Standard forms of documents may be defined and used throughout an enterprise, their design being stored in the repository. This is especially important now that we are moving into the era of EDI (electronic data interchange). Documents interchanged electronically among separate corporations should be in the repository. The format of many such documents is defined by the ANSI X.12 and ISO (United Nations) EDIFACT standards. Many document formats are agreed upon by an enterprise and its trading partners.

- *Documentation.* Just as the system is designed for reusability, its documentation should be designed this way. User documentation, for example, should have reusable templates and text in an electronic publishing system. The amount of new writing needed to document a system or to create training materials should be minimized.

# A Repository: Essential for Reusable Design

A central repository is essential for reusable design. The repository needs an indexing system that makes it easy to find components that can be reused. Many of these components will need modification; so, the repository may be the encyclopedia of an I-CASE tool, which makes modification easy.

Sometimes the dictionary of a fourth-generation-language environment is used. For example, the administration of Washington State University has achieved an impressive degree of reusable code employing the fourth-generation language NATURAL 2, the

ADABAS database management system and the integrated dictionary of Software AG [ALI].

# Learning by Example

A major advantage of reusable designs is that designers can learn from the designs that are used. There is much to be said for learning by example. The reusable designs ought to employ the best design techniques. Working with them and modifying them is a good way to learn and gain experience with the technique. New graduates in their initial training classes should study the reusable formats and constructs.

Learning by example in this way is particularly useful for naive or inexperienced designers. However, it is also valuable for many seasoned professionals because the techniques, such as data modeling, action diagrams, critical success factor hierarchies, etc., are often better than the methods they have been using.

Some systems analysts have many years of experience but do sloppy work with poor techniques. The gap between the best software engineering practice and the average practice is very wide—probably wider than in any other engineering discipline. When RAD techniques are introduced, the goal of upgrading the quality of work of all analysts and implementors should be established.

# Standards

Hardware and software vendors are evolving standards for application design that extend the practicality of reusable design. IBM, for example, has SAA (Systems Application Architecture), which provides a common form of user dialog designed to be user-friendly, as well as common access to networks, relational databases and an application development environment. DEC, similarly, is evolving its Application Integration Architecture (AIA). A family of Open standards is evolving for the UNIX environment. Standards for the electronic representation of documents interchanged among corporations are evolving from the ANSI X.12 and the ISO EDIFACT committees.

An I.S. organization should have its own standards based upon the standards of its chosen vendors. Designs using these standards should reside in an I-CASE repository. The repository, for example, should contain standard templates for dialogs and documents.

# A Structure for On-Line Applications

Most on-line applications in an organization can fit into a common structure that enables the user to sign on, invoke the program he needs, enter data, recover from errors, terminate the application and so on. Figures 15.1 to 15.7 show such a structure

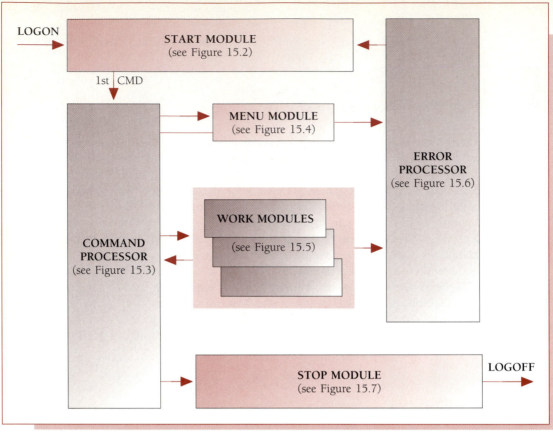

FIGURE 15.1 On-line applications may fit into a reusable frame, such as that shown here. Figures 15.2 through 15.7 give more details of this frame. The framework design is stored in the repository of an I-CASE toolset or code generator. This framework is used in the Administrative Computing Services Department of Washington State University [WSU89].

FIGURE 15.2 The START module of the reusable application framework in Figure 15.1 provides a clean, consistent entry to applications. It hides the technical environment from the user [WSU89].

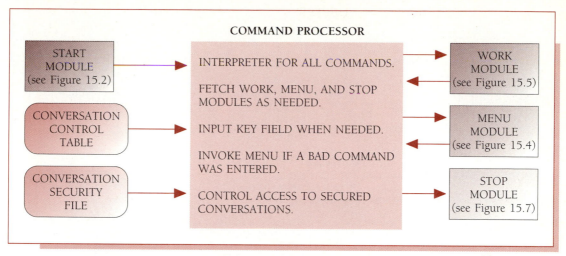

FIGURE 15.3 The COMMAND PROCESSOR of the reusable application framework in Figure 15.1 provides a consistent user interface across applications. Experienced users interact with the application via commands; novice users employ a menu dialog with the MENU module of Figure 15.4. The COMMAND PROCESSOR employs consistent PF key standards and a common command syntax for all on-line applications [WSU89].

as used by the Administrative Computing Services Department of Washington State University [WSU89].

This structure was built with the Software AG toolset and resides in a mainframe corporate dictionary. Many reusable work modules can be invoked by the application developer. The developer uses the fourth-generation language NATURAL and, using NATURAL Connection, can download NATURAL source code into his personal computer and modify it with the K-edit tool.

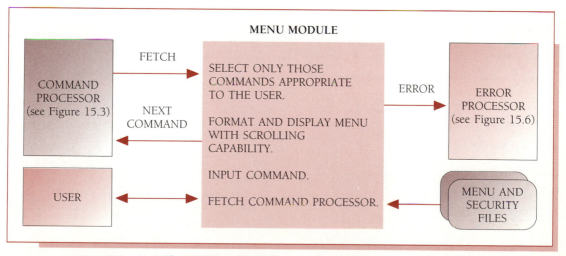

FIGURE 15.4 The MENU module of the reusable application framework in Figure 15.1 is a single program reusable in many applications. It provides a menu for the users. It displays an error screen if a bad command is entered [WSU89].

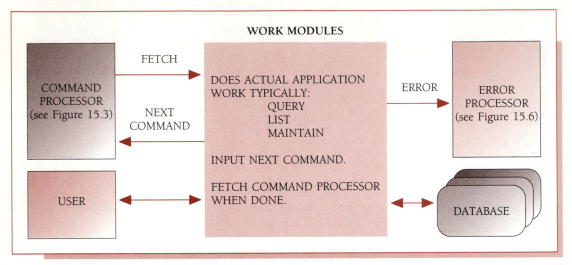

**FIGURE 15.5** The WORK modules of Figure 15.1 may consist of one program or a series of programs. The first program is invoked by the COMMAND PROCESSOR (Figure 15.3). The last program invokes the COMMAND PROCESSOR. The programs in the WORK module are task-specific. Many of them are common from one application to another, for example, a module for data entry [WSU89].

The personal computer environment hastens the development and testing, but the central dictionary helps maximize the employment of reusable work modules. The framework shown in Figures 15.1 to 15.7 makes all applications appear similar and consistent to the user. Furthermore, it isolates the user from the technology. The hardware, software or networking can be changed while preserving the same user interface.

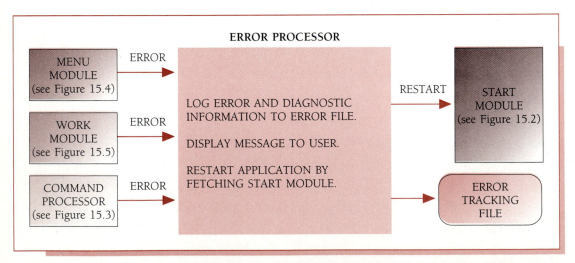

**FIGURE 15.6** The ERROR PROCESSOR of the reusable application framework in Figure 15.1 logs all errors consistently and displays a message to the user. It restarts the application by fetching the START module [WSU89].

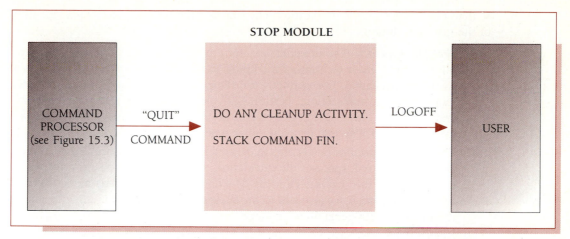

FIGURE 15.7 The STOP module of the reusable application framework in Figure 15.1 provides a clean, consistent exit from the applications. Like the other modules, it hides the technical environment from the user so that the user is not required to relearn when the technical environment changes [WSU89].

As part of their training course, new developers learn the framework of Figures 15.1 to 15.7 and learn some of the reusable work modules. They start, therefore, with consistent training about the architecture of applications.

All possible application-dependent blocks, like those in Figures 15.1 to 15.7, should be identified and made easy for developers to use.

# Code Generators

Code generators are sometimes designed to generate frameworks such as those in Figures 15.1 through 15.7. They may generate the skeleton of an on-line application and make it easy for the developer to fill in application-specific details and select reusable work modules.

# Different Procedures

There are several different techniques for the creation of systems from reusable design. The first major distinction is between starting with a whole design and adapting it in some way, as opposed to starting with building blocks that become linked together. We shall refer to these approaches as "*Start-with-the-Whole*" and "*Start with the Parts.*"

## Start-with-the-Whole

The Start-with-the-Whole approach is found in a number of application generators. A generic application may be provided, which is intended to be modified in some way so that it becomes a specific application. There are a variety of techniques for adaptation of the generic solution:

1. *Skeleton Approach.* The designer may be provided with the skeleton of an application and given techniques for filling in the skeleton so that it becomes a working application. For example, the skeleton may be that of an on-line system that accepts transactions, performs calculations, updates a database and generates reports. This skeleton can be converted into a purchase-order system, an inventory-control system or many other types of system.

   The designer specifies the records to be used in the database, specifies the screen designs to be used, specifies the calculations to be done and specifies the report formats. All of this may directly employ a data dictionary or data model. Where necessary, the designer may add to the skeleton, using a programming language (perhaps a fourth-generation language).

2. *Kitchen Sink Approach.* Rather than being given a skeleton to which he has to add, the designer may be given a facility richly endowed with optional features. One might say that the facility has "everything but the kitchen sink." Instead of adding to a skeleton, the designer prunes the features that are not wanted. It is easier, especially for an unskilled designer, to delete unwanted features than to add new ones..

3. *Parameter Approach.* The reusable software may have a set of parameters for varying its behavior. The designer may select parameters or features from menus. He may have a mouse-driven facility on a workstation for adapting the behavior of the software.

4. *Stepwise Refinement.* The designer may use the approach of refining the behavior of the software in a succession of small steps, testing at each step to ensure that he has not introduced erratic behavior. The software may provide the testing tools for this purpose and may be linked to design automation tools that make the software easy to modify.

## Start-with-the-Parts

In the Start-with-the-Parts approach, the designer is provided with building blocks. He may want to modify the building blocks, and this could be done with any of the preceding techniques:

- the Skeleton Approach;
- the Kitchen Sink Approach;
- the Parameter Approach;
- Stepwise Refinement.

The building blocks, or modifications of them, may be linked using different approaches:

1. *Ad-Hoc Linking.* The designer may create linkages between the building blocks in any way he wishes.

2. *Linking Employing a Data Model.* The only linkage between the building blocks may be data items or records that are defined in a formally designed data model. The data items or record pass between the building blocks.

3. *Linking Employing Formal Rules.* The building blocks may be objects represented in the repository, which can be linked with the help of an I-CASE tool that rigidly enforces the interface rules.

4. *Formal Decomposition.* The system may be represented by a decomposition tree (a "composed-of" hierarchy). The block at the top of the tree represents the entire system. It is decomposed into sub-blocks, and so on, to the bottom of the tree. The decomposition may be done with formal rules controlling the data items passed among the blocks. The building blocks may be subtrees of the formal decomposition.

## Combinations of These Methods

A mature workbench for building systems from predesigned parts might provide **start-with-the-whole components** and **building block components**. It might, for example, provide a skeleton application and building blocks that can be linked into the skeleton. For given business areas, it might provide reusable data models that can be pruned or added to as necessary.

A major disadvantage of the start-with-the-whole approach is that it is not highly generalized. The "whole" relates to a specific form or class of application. A major advantage is that the "whole" can be designed very thoroughly. It can include checkpoint/restart procedures, security procedures, facilities for auditing, and so on, that an average systems analyst might leave out or do badly. It can also be designed to be machine-efficient.

# Application-Independent Structures?

There are two basic approaches to reusability. One is to build from structures that are generic and contain no knowledge of the specific application. The other is to employ structures that contain application knowledge. The structures in Figures 15.1 through 15.7 are of the generic type. They can be applied to most on-line applications.

To maximize the benefits of reusability, both generic structures and application-specific structures should be employed.

# Purchase or Develop?

Reusable design or code can either be purchased or be developed in-house. Both purchased and developed components can be either generic or application-specific. This gives four approaches to reusability, as summarized in Figure 15.8. To maximize the effectiveness of rapid development, all four should be used, where appropriate, in appropriate combinations.

Some of the most spectacular examples of rapid development based on reusability have occurred in enterprises where wide-scale analysis for reusability has been done.

|  | PURCHASED | DEVELOPED IN-HOUSE |
|---|---|---|
| GENERIC | • Code generators<br>• Various application architectures (e.g., IBM's SAA)<br>• Purchasable generic framework<br>• Purchasable building blocks | • Installation standards<br>• Reusable application framework (as in Figures 15.1-15.7)<br>• Reusable building blocks<br>• Templates for dialogs and reports |
| APPLICATION-SPECIFIC | • Application packages<br>• Customizable designs for applications<br>• Designs in CASE format for specific industries<br>• Subroutine library | • Analysis for reusability across the enterprise (Chapter 22) |

FIGURE 15.8 Approaches to Reusability

I.S. architects look across the enterprise using a methodology to identify the opportunities for reusability.

Enterprisewide analysis for reusability takes time and substantial organization. In some corporations, it has resulted in major improvements in I.S. capability to help make its enterprise competitive.

It is appropriate to divide RAD techniques into those that can be applied quickly on a small scale and those that work within a planned infrastructure, which takes time to create (Chapter 20). Enterprisewide analysis for reusability falls into the latter category. It is extremely valuable but cannot happen overnight. A relatively small number of enterprises have done it effectively. Those that have find that their repository of reusable designs grows steadily, leading to greater capability to generate new applications quickly. This methodology for reusability is discussed in Chapter 22.

# Evolving Complexity

The future of computing is a battle with complexity. Computers give us the capability to operate software of immense complexity if we can succeed in creating it. To create very complex software, we have to employ reusable building blocks.

It is more appropriate to talk about *building* than *writing* a complex program. The construction of software has analogies with other building processes. We use scaffolding; we assemble components. However, *unlike* the design of buildings, it is often not practical to specify a complex design and build to the specification. The systems we create today tend to grow a piece at a time.

We need the tools and formalism to fit separate pieces together, in a system where many of the pieces are predesigned and/or precoded. The tools must ensure that the interface between the pieces is correct. As the systems grow, more precoded pieces go into their library. Small units are linked into larger units. A designer must employ the work of previous designers.

Isaac Newton wrote toward the end of his life that, insofar as he had achieved anything worthwhile, he had done so by standing on the shoulders of giants. Programmers do not tend to stand on each other's shoulders; they stand on each other's feet.

It is desirable that I-CASE tools be used to create ever-growing, ever-more-powerful libraries of components. Each new generation of components should employ the components of the previous generation, so that software becomes steadily more powerful. The I-CASE tool should be able to check fully the interfaces among the components to ensure complete consistency.

This elimination of *interface* errors is one of the reasons it is vital to use I-CASE tools with powerful rule-based consistency checking. It is desirable to be able to find out what exists in the library and to understand it and use it. Most large computing installations reinvent the same routines over and over again because this capability is missing.

Even relatively simple programs should be built up in blocks. These blocks need to be stored and made accessible for linking to other blocks. The I-CASE repository should serve this short-term need as well as the long-term need of providing a library of reusable components. Many components added to the library, then, are defined in terms of *other components* already in it.

Rigorous interfacing rules throughout the library and the systems that use it should allow the library to grow in an orderly fashion and should allow modules and systems to be interchanged among libraries. As the library builds up, the developers will have less to develop, and there will be less to verify. All modules in the library are *already* thoroughly tested, and the interface to them should be validated by the I-CASE toolset.

# Problems with Reusable Code

Today's low usage of reusable code stems from a number of fundamental problems, which include:

- difficulty in agreeing on what constitutes a reusable component;
- difficulty in understanding what a component does and how to use it;
- difficulty in understanding how to interface reusable components to the rest of a design;
- difficulty in combining flexibility with execution efficiency;
- difficulty in designing reusable components so that they are easy to modify;
- difficulty in organizing a library so that programmers know what is in it and can find and use what they need;
- difficulty in modifying generic structures without forcing retrofits;
- programming-language dependence.

To overcome these problems, *we need a formalism for representing reusable components.*

The formalism needs to make the components easy to understand and easy to modify. Particularly important, it needs to make the interfaces with the outside world rigorous. To make formalism practical and standardized among many reusable components, workbench tools are needed.

The big problem with today's subroutine libraries and application packages is that this formalism is absent or is not visible. It is often too difficult to modify packaged applications. To make them easy to modify and link to other applications, they should be represented with data models and diagrams of their design in I-CASE format, where the I-CASE tool makes them easy to find, easy to modify and easy to link to other components with comprehensive, computerized, interface checking. Probably one day, many applications design and building blocks will be sold in I-CASE format, designed to reside in an I-CASE repository and drive a code generator.

Box 15.2 lists the desirable properties of reusable components.

## Box 15.2 Desirable Properties of Reusable Components

- *Formal Semantic Basis.* A formalism that describes the component with precision should be used.
- *Expressiveness.* The formalism should be capable of expressing as many different kinds of components as possible.
- *Easy to Understand.*
- *Easy to Customize in an Unplanned Way.* It must be easier to customize the components than to rewrite them from scratch.
- *Easy to Add or Delete Details.*
- *Designed for Graphics Workbench.* In order to satisfy the previous three properties, the design should be represented with the graphics capability of an I-CASE toolset that integrates multiple diagrammatic representations.
- *Uses the Best Structured Techniques.* Normalized data and fully structured procedures should be represented graphically.
- *Clear, Simple, Precise Interfaces.* The formalism should define the interfaces between components with precision.
- *Self-Contained.* The components should be self-contained and have predictable behavior. There should be data passed between modules but, where possible, no control flow between modules.
- *Self-Organizing.* The components should know which other components they need so that the programmer does not have to remember or search for them.
- *Verifiable.* Techniques for verifying the behavior of components should be used where practical.
- *Flexible without Compromising Efficiency.* It should be possible to use standard components without suffering performance problems.
- *Programming-Language Independence.* The formalism should not be a specific programming language. It should be representable in multiple programming languages.
- *Application Standards.* Standards should be used as fully as possible for the interface to networks, interface to database, interface to operating systems,

Box 15.2    Continued

end-user dialog, cooperative processing, interface to programmer tools and code generator. IBM's SAA (Systems Application Architecture) is the leading example of this.

- *Document Standards.* Standards for electronically represented documents should be used, for example, the ANSI X.12/ISO, EDIFACT EDI standards.

# Design Using Software Chips

In hardware engineering, the change from transistor-by-transistor design to chip-by-chip design gave orders of magnitude improvements in productivity. It also made design by a much wider range of people practical. The change from line-at-a-time programming to design using software chips will be similarly effective.

# Self-Contained Modules

It is highly desirable that reusable modules be self-contained. They might be thought of as black boxes. Certain data go into the black box; it takes certain actions and produces certain output data.

Some program modules are written to handle multiple transactions simultaneously. The module may, for example, be waiting for a database action on one transaction while it continues processing another transaction. Such programs must be designed so that the separate transactions do not interfere with one another. One transaction, for example, must not modify switches in such a way that, when control passes to a second transaction, that transaction can change the switches and invalidate the ongoing processing of the first transaction. Programs that can be entered by multiple transactions without interference are referred to as **reentrant programs**. Reusable code modules need these types of safety features.

Often, diagrams are drawn of program modules showing data and control information passing among the modules. The data types in such a situation can be precisely defined and should employ data from a formally designed data model. The passing of control information causes more of a problem and can generally be avoided. The modules should communicate with one another using *only* the data in the data model. Each module is then self-contained, with clearly defined inputs and outputs.

# Analogy with House Design

If you go to an architect and ask him to build a house for you, he will not usually design the house from scratch. He may start with a preexisting design and modify it. He may assemble a design from separate, preexisting drawings. He has reusable plans,

| A House Builder Uses: | A Software Builder Should Use: |
|---|---|
| • Reusable plans, configurable in many ways | • Reusable plans, configurable in many ways |
| • Standard, well-proven designs and components | • Standard, well-proven designs and components |
| • Off-the-shelf units | • Off-the-shelf units that are easy to modify |
| • Catalogs of many components | • Catalogs of many components |
| • Good knowledge of what components are available | • Good knowledge of what components are available |
| • Standard plugs and sockets | • Standard interfaces |

FIGURE 15.9 Comparison of a House Builder and a Software Builder. The software builder ought to use many of the techniques of the house builder.

configurable in many ways. When he works on the details, he employs a large number of standard components—doors, windows, plumbing, fittings, electrical components, heating units, lights and so on. In his office are numerous catalogs of off-the-shelf components that he uses. Most components have standard plugs, sockets or measurements so that they fit together.

The building of data-processing applications may one day be similar (Figure 15.9). The designer may start with preexisting plans, reconfigurable in many ways. He may use a repository of designs and components, along with tools for adapting these to the system in question. There may be catalogs of many software components that can be purchased and loaded into the repository.

The designer may employ an expert system to help him find the component most useful to him. The house architect works with standard designs and components in order to minimize the amount of custom work. This reduces the time and cost of the project. Similarly, if the components were accessible, the system designer can minimize the amount of custom work for the same reason.

It seems likely that, in the future, a major sector of the software industry will grow up that sells reusable designs and programs built with workbench tools so that they can be easily found, understood, modified and interlinked. A vast range of value-added components and services can be built on top of the automated information-engineering tools.

# Actions to Achieve Generic Reusability

Actions are needed at many times and in many places to achieve generic reusability:

*For the I.S. Organization as a Whole*
- Establish general application standards.
- Establish a library of templates and reusable constructs in the I-CASE repository.
- Educate developers about the standards, templates and reusable constructs.

*Early in the Design Phase*

- While preparing for the first JAD workshop, identify all relevant standards, templates and reusable designs.
- Employ the reusable standards, templates and designs during the first JAD workshop.

*When Preparing for Construction*

- The SWAT Team reviewing the output of the first JAD workshop should adjust the design to speed up the construction process, if possible, by better employment of reusability.
- The adjustments from the SWAT Team should be reviewed in the second JAD workshop.

*When Preparing for Cutover*

- User documentation should be built from reusable templates and text in an electronic publishing system.
- Training materials should be created from reusable charts, slides and text.

# Summary

Methodology Chart 15 is a window relating to reusability in the RAD methodology hyperdocument [JMA].

# References

[ALI] Interview with Dave Wells of Washington State University in the James Martin videotape tutorial, *RAD, Rapid Application Development*, from Applied Learning, Inc., Naperville, Illinois (708-369–3000).

[JMA] *RAD Expert*, a methodology in hyperdocument form adaptable to different toolsets, available from James Martin Associates, Reston, Virginia (703–620–9504).

[WSU89] Courtesy of Washington State University, Administrative Computing Services Dept., State of Washington, 1989.

[WATERS85] R. C. Waters, "The Programmer's Apprentice: A Session with KBEmacs," *IEEE Transactions on Software Engineering*, November 1985.

# CHAPTER 16

# Bassett Frame Technology

Paul G. Bassett, while a professor at York University in Toronto, invented a new reusability paradigm. Bassett Frame Technology [BASS87] is a language-independent reusability technique that promises to change the way we think about software [BASS84]. It has been implemented in the NETRON/CAP code generator [NETRON] and has achieved some impressive results.*

Fundamental to all mature engineering disciplines is the notion of reuse. No civil engineer would dream of designing a bridge from scratch (and few would cross it if it were). Reuse is so basic to conventional engineering that the idea is not even part of the jargon; it is completely taken for granted. Design and construction are always based on standard, proven models. If such models are not available, the work is not considered engineering; it's called research!

## Software Chips

There is a massive amount of electronic devices being designed today for all manner of uses. Many household gadgets have hundreds of thousands of transistors in them. There is no way that such an array of hardware could be designed transistor by transistor. Instead, the designers use off-the-shelf chips, each containing many thousands of transistors. The chip has well-defined properties that are well documented and well understood. Its behavior may be variable over a wide range, with parameterization, read-only memory and random-access memory.

*The building of software systems in the future needs to be similar.*

Off-the-shelf software building blocks with well-defined properties have been referred to as **software chips** [WATERS85]. In Bassett's view, "software chips" is an inappropriate term because it fails to take into account how "softness" sets software apart from all other things. Unlike cars and TV sets, software has unlimited potential to be altered in response to changing circumstances. Payroll systems, for example, must quickly accommodate unpredictable tax law changes. Proliferating systems utilities, devices and database schemas constantly whipsaw software systems. Unfortunately, like metal fatigue, constant ad-hoc changes turn software into brittleware. The failure to engineer software to *avoid rigidity* has defeated most attempts to make it reusable.

*This chapter uses material written by Paul Bassett.

# Bassett Frames

In Bassett's technology, software is specified and automatically assembled from **frames**. Bassett's frames, unlike most hardware chips, are designed to be highly adaptable. A set of commands is employed for adapting each frame to the application in which it is used.

Because Bassett's frames are so adaptable, one frame library (developed by Netron, Inc.) has been used for a great diversity of *applications*, from insurance and banking to manufacturing and retailing, to government, utilities and aerospace, and for *platforms,* from micros to mainframes.

Among these, software can be cross-targeted, i.e., developed on one platform for production on another. (See Chapter 22 for details on how Westpac Banking Corporation is using frame technology.)

# Frame Technology in Action

Noma Industries is a successful, diversified North American manufacturer that grew rapidly during the 1980s from less than $0.1 billion to over $0.6 billion in annual revenues. Many know them as the Christmas-light people. Box 16.1 shows an extract from a software audit. In 1986, Noma's 14 operating divisions had about 20 million lines of COBOL in production, comprising 5125 programs in scores of applications.

As of 1986, Noma was developing or replacing systems at the rate of 4 million lines per year with 16 people (i.e., 1000 lines per person-day) organized into a half-dozen SWAT Teams. Noma's entire budget for systems, including hardware, software and operations, is well under one per cent of sales. Noma's senior management states that their growth and success are due significantly to the quality of the systems and the responsiveness of the I.S. staff to changing needs. Bob Ernst, Comptroller at Noma Outdoor Products (the world's largest maker of snow throwers) notes, "In the eight

## Box 16.1  Noma Industries Ltd., 1986 Systems Audit Aggregate Statistics

| | |
|---|---|
| Number of Divisions Using Frame Technology | 14 |
| Total Number of Programs (SPC frames) in Production | 5125 |
| Total Installed SLOC (Source Lines of Code) | 20.5 Million |
| COBOL SLOC Added or Replaced in 1986 | 3.9 Million |
| Total Staff | 16 |
| COBOL SLOC Added or Replaced per Person-Day | Approx. 1000 |
| I.S. Costs (Hardware, Software, Operations) | 0.6% of Sales |

years I have been here, I have seen our Brampton plant increase its business five-fold, within the same floor space, and decrease its front office staff by ten per cent.''

Equally remarkable are Noma's reuse statistics (Box 16.2). They use the NETRON/ CAP CASE toolset, which includes screen and report frame generators and a library of 35 frames, each of which handles an application-independent task such as I/O to various devices and database schemas. Noma developed an additional 33 proprietary frames to implement its standard systems and applications architecture. About 96 per cent of the 20 million lines of COBOL was derived from those 68 frames together with frame generators and data definition frames (defining over 10,000 data fields). The other 4 per cent, specifying the unique features of each program, was also derived from frames called **specification frames** or **SPCs**.

It is not necessary to develop a large, corporate frame library before reusability pays off. Developers typically achieve 80–90 per cent reuse levels using only the frames included with the tools.

To achieve statistics like Noma's requires embedding the technology and tools in a reuse culture. That culture depends on:

- the skills of the SWAT Team members;
- the RAD methodology;
- frame technology;
- a management shift to a frame perspective.

---

### Box 16.2   Noma Industries Ltd., 1986 Systems Audit Reuse Statistics

| | |
|---|---:|
| Number of Noma File Definitions | 1,970 |
| Number of Noma Data Fields | >10,000 |
| Number of NETRON/CAP Frames | 35 |
| Number of Noma Proprietary Frames | 33 |
| Per Cent of Custom SLOC (in SPC Frames) | 3.8% |

---

# Why Is Software So Difficult to Reuse?

Over the past four decades since software was invented, many tools and techniques have been developed in an effort to harness reusability. It is instructive to analyze the successes and frustrations of some of them.

## Cut and Paste

Even without automated tools, all good programmers reuse software. When assigned to write a new program, the usual approach is to dig up an already written program that somehow resembles the new assignment. Through cut-and-paste editing—searching, renaming, adding, deleting and rearranging—the new program is born.

The technique works because many pieces carry forward with little change. Considering the time required to debug the subtleties in those pieces, much effort can be avoided. People naturally prefer to reuse things that work than to start from scratch. Studies show that the most productive programmers are the ones with the best filing systems.

While cutting and pasting is a step in the right direction, its full potential is far from being realized because of the following:

1.  It is ad hoc. There is no systematic way of finding potentially reusable components. Many opportunities are missed.

2.  Because programs are not engineered for reuse, it often takes more work to find, extract and recustomize reusable parts than to write programs from scratch.

3.  Cutting and pasting involves time-consuming, error-prone, manual editing, done one character at a time, while being fastidious about grammar and punctuation. This is mostly low-level drudgery and forces programmers to interact with their machines rather than with their users.

4.  By far the largest opportunity cost is the loss of intellectual control over all the fragments of information that distinguish each program. They are scattered into the nooks and crannies of the source. Even though two programs may be 95% the same, they must be maintained as if they have nothing in common. This, more than any other reason, accounts for the alarming fact that 80% of all software effort is dedicated to keeping old systems alive.

## Skeleton Programs

Some shops, recognizing the tremendous potential of reusability, have developed libraries of skeleton programs—programs with *holes*. The programmer copies the skeleton and *fleshes out* the holes with the specifics of the needed program. This is a second step in the right direction. It overcomes the problems of points (1) and (2) mentioned in the preceding list but does nothing for (3) or (4).

## External Subroutines

Other shops have adopted external subroutine libraries as a reuse strategy. While there are many good reasons for using subroutines, reuse is not among them. Subroutines are flexible within the limits of their formal parameters. When these limits must be exceeded, such as when a date conversion routine must be changed to accommodate yet another date format, serious problems arise:

5.  If a routine is modified to accommodate new programs, it may well become incompatible with old ones, forcing expensive and error-prone retrofits. People hate running hard just to stay in the same place.

6. If yet another version of the routine is put into the library, knowing which version to use, if any, becomes the problem. Each routine is 95% the same as its siblings, and the differences are buried, making them difficult to find and understand. People drown in a sea of look-alikes.

The fundamental problem with subroutines, as far as reusability is concerned, is their *black-box* nature. They are meant to be used *as is*, linked into the program after it has been compiled. Software reuse demands flexibility at construction time, so that the functionality can be molded to the needs of each program.

## Object-Oriented Programming

Still other shops are trying object-oriented programming (OOP) [COX86] [GUTHERY89]. The goal of information-hiding through inheritance and polymorphism (packaging data with process) is commendable. In practice, however, OOP is a subroutine library in new clothes. In order to avoid the incompatibility of point (5), the class hierarchies of OOP result in large numbers of tiny objects, each dynamically linked to other objects. This not only leads to the difficulties of point (6) but suffers from further problems:

7. Highly generalized routines result in poor performance, especially when used intensively or in combination. It almost seems to be a no-win situation—as if efficiency and flexibility are mutually incompatible.

8. Incompatibilities that are very hard to debug develop among objects from different hierarchies.

9. There is no way to delete those inherited methods or data structures that are inappropriate to the needs of the child class. To quote Scott Guthery [GUTHERY89, p. 82], "You get the whole gorilla even if you just wanted a banana." Multiple inheritance only compounds this problem.

# Wish List

Software, unlike hardware, exists to be changed. Driven by unpredictably changing circumstances, *software is always in a process of "becoming"* and must be engineered accordingly.

The following wish list is clearly at the heart of an effective reusability schema:

1. *Stop reinventing similar wheels.* There is a surprisingly high degree of similarity among problems in a given domain. Typical I.S. programs are 90–99% similar across a shop.

2. *Express differences as well as similarities.* One man's exceptions are another man's rules. That is, the exceptions to the current rules can become the norm. Similarities and differences are two sides of the same coin, and an effective schema must handle both.

3. *Make software easy to reuse and change.* If less than 10% of a typical program is essentially unique, why not localize those fragments away from the common parts? Then the common parts can be reused without the usual isolation process

each time, and the localized custom fragments can be grasped and changed, without the usual search for needles in haystacks.

4. *Enhance quality.* A one-shot program seldom has the spit and polish inherent in a program that is made from parts that are used again and again.

5. *Foster flexible standards.* The foot should never be forced to fit the shoe. A standard (reusable) component should never be so rigid that it cannot be made to satisfy the requirements. We also need to avoid dumping 500-page standards manuals on people's desks, where they can hardly keep up with the insertion pages, let alone be faithful to the standard. Given that computers are the best rule followers ever invented, why not formalize standards so that they become the path of least resistance to getting the job done?

6. *Never force retrofits.* Let sleeping dogs lie. Any reusable component must be able to evolve in unpredictable ways, including a complete rewrite, without victimizing users of a previous version. The time to retrofit is when there is a business case for the changes.

7. *Never sacrifice performance.* Performance should never be sacrificed on the altar of flexibility; software should remain easy to modify and efficient to run. Time is a nonrenewable resource. Sweeping performance problems under a hardware rug is irresponsible. There are simple problems that can bring even the fastest machine to a virtual halt (e.g., add $\frac{1}{1} + \frac{1}{2} + \frac{1}{3} + \ldots$ until the sum exceeds 20).

8. *Automate system construction.* Contrary to the old adage, "Easier said than done," simply specifying what is new or different about a system should be enough to enable an effective schema to automate the *how*. This wish is critical to CASE.

Note that wishes (5) and (7) require the schema to have an *Open* architecture, and wish (8) requires the schema to "know" or find whichever components it needs. The list seems long and daunting; yet frame technology cuts through it in a single stroke.

# What Are Frames?

The frame concept has been introduced in many ways. Marvin Minsky was one of the earliest to see its potential [MINSKY75]. While intuitively related to frames like picture frames and car frames, the general concept is much more powerful:

Frames are formal metaphors.

A metaphor captures what is the *same* in things that are *different*. For example, the metaphor "an airplane is *like a bird*" points clearly to a "framework" of properties common to many different flying things. On the other hand, to adapt a bird into a plane requires that some properties be altered: replace the feathers, prohibit wing flapping, add an engine, and so on.

What alters the properties of a frame? Other frames! A bird frame, describing a prototypical bird, could have its properties extended and modified by duck frames, plane frames or even griffin frames. This adaptability is crucial: the power of metaphors is their applicability to novel situations, such as griffins. Figure 16.1 illustrates how a griffin frame could tailor bird and beast frames.

FIGURE 16.1 A Bassett Frame, unlike a software subroutine, is designed so that it can be adapted into something different. Bassett Frame Technology provides commands for this adaptation.

# Software-Engineering Frames

What do metaphors have to do with software? **Software metaphors** express things that are *similar* about programs that are *different*. The word *metaphor* may not be part of software jargon, but **entity-types** and **function-types** are well-known kinds of software metaphors. Familiar entity-types include employee, customer, order and supplier; function-types include screen I/O, batch updates, credit checks and interest calculations. Such types are common to many programs.

Programmers implicitly use "same-as, except" metaphors: "This program is the *same as* that one, *except* for this and *except* for that." A Bassett frame is a same-as, except combination of one or more entity-/function-*types*. A program (or any software module) is a same-as, except combination of one or more frames.

Object-Oriented Programming (OOP) uses a weaker "same-as, plus" form of inheritance and thus has difficulty binding object-types from different hierarchies. Frame technology provides the multiple inheritance of OOP combined with the ability not only to add new features but to *modify and delete at any level of detail*. One program, for example, may do data entry, update customer orders and calculate interest on deposits. One frame hierarchy will be able to assemble this program from a same-as, except combination of quite different frame *types*, each with a disparate subhierarchy.

**Bassett Frame Technology** formalizes the specification and composition of frames. A Bassett frame contains two things: a *standard definition of its data and functions,* which expresses the similarities that are available to all instances of use, and *engineering change commands,* which express the differences that are peculiar to each instance of use.

Data entry, for example, does not refer to a specific program; it refers to an infinite class of programs that share a standard set of properties: buffers and protocols for screen and error handling. Such properties comprise a standard definition in a reusable data-entry frame. On the other hand, each program requires a specific layout and specific actions associated with the screen entries. Such specifics can also be specified in frames that adapt the data-entry frame. Given specific and reusable frames, the computer can generate code.

Frames adapt frames through engineering change commands, also called **frame commands**. Each command can assign or reference **frame parameters** (properties). If an adapt*or* frame does not assign a value to a parameter, the adapt*ee* frame's default standard value is used. In other words, only the *differences* are expressed; differences peculiar to each adaptor frame are expressed as part of the adapt*or* frame.

## Hierarchies of Frames

Frames are organized into levels, as shown in Figure 16.2.

At the top of Figure 16.2 is a specification frame (called the SPC). This specifies a program or software module. SPCs are special frames because they are the only frames that application developers may create or modify. *All of the other frames are read-only.*

The lower we go in Figure 16.2, the more general is the frame type and the more often reused is the frame.

Each frame can be the root or "boss" of its own hierarchy of frames. Being the boss means that it has the final say about how any frame in its hierarchy is to be adapted to its purposes. The boss prevails in adapting the behavior of all subordinate frames. The boss, however, like the Mafia, may itself have bosses.

The boss of an entire hierarchy is the SPC. Its hierarchy is adapted to give tailored results. Any software system can be constructed from frames. Most of the complexity can be hidden in reusable frames. The technique makes complex systems easier to design and, particularly important, easier to adapt to changing needs.

Frame technology is a major improvement in our ability to employ software reusability. The breakthrough stems from being able to handle differences as well as similarities in what is reused. It has been employed with multiple programming languages, as well as in the production of manuals.

A frame's **ancestors** are any frames above that frame (as illustrated in Figure 16.2). A frame's **parent** is a frame immediately above it. A frame's **descendants** are any frames below that frame (as shown in Figure 16.2). A **child** is a frame immediately below it.

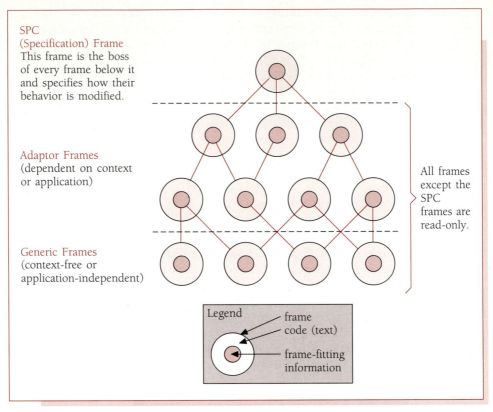

SPC
(Specification) Frame
This frame is the boss
of every frame below it
and specifies how their
behavior is modified.

Adaptor Frames
(dependent on context
or application)

All frames
except the
SPC
frames are
read-only.

Generic Frames
(context-free or
application-independent)

Legend

frame
code (text)

frame-fitting
information

FIGURE 16.2 Levels of Frame
    The lower we go in this picture, the more general is the frame type and the more reused is the frame.

A frame can have its behavior adapted by its ancestors. A frame can occur multiple times in the same hierarchy. It can have its behavior modified by multiple ancestors.

## Frame Commands

Each frame is designed so that, when necessary, its behavior can be modified by its ancestors. The frame contains information, in the form of **frame commands**, for adapting other frames (Figure 16.3).

A frame contains *code* or *text*, represented by the outer circle in Figures 16.2 and 16.3, and frame commands, represented by the inner circle. The commands are used to modify the code (text). The code could be in any programming language or in the language of a code generator.

There are several frame commands, such as:

- BREAK
- COPY
- INSERT

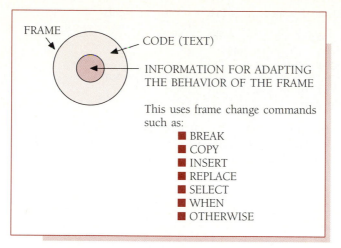

FRAME

CODE (TEXT)

INFORMATION FOR ADAPTING
THE BEHAVIOR OF THE FRAME

This uses frame change commands
such as:
- BREAK
- COPY
- INSERT
- REPLACE
- SELECT
- WHEN
- OTHERWISE

FIGURE 16.3 Structure of the Frames in Figure 16.2
   The information in the inner circle is used to automate the cut-
and-paste editing that, otherwise, a skilled programmer must do by
hand.

- REPLACE
- SELECT
- WHEN
- OTHERWISE

These commands can be thought of as being used to automate the cut-and-paste
editing that programmers used to do by hand.
   The frame processor uses the commands to adapt the frames and generate code.
The frame processor begins with an SPC (the top frame in Figure 16.2) and works its
way down in a depth-first, left-to-right fashion.
   The following are examples of how the frame commands are used.

- *BREAK* names and defines a default within a frame. The default may be overridden
   or extended by ancestor frames. If it is not, then the default is used.

In the following example, the default is called ''Egg'':

```
This is a Humpty-Dumpty problem type.
.BREAK Egg
  Humpty Dumpty sat on a wall.
  Humpty Dumpty had a great fall.
.END-BREAK Egg
  Poor Humpty died.
```

- *COPY* invokes descendant frames and can be used to insert frame-text into them:

```
.COPY Humpty-Dumpty
.INSERT-AFTER Egg
  All the king's horses and all the king's men
  Could not put Humpty together again.
.END-COPY
```

Putting together this and the previous example yields:

```
This is a Humpty-Dumpty problem type.
Humpty Dumpty sat on a wall.
Humpty Dumpty had a great fall.
All the king's horses and all the king's men
Could not put Humpty together again.
Poor Humpty died.
```

.COPY suspends processing of the current frame until the named frame has been fully processed. Each .INSERT can insert information into any descendant frame. Information can be inserted before or after the named default or can override the default, as illustrated by the third .INSERT below:

```
.COPY frame-name
.INSERT-BEFORE break-name-1
   frame-text
.INSERT-AFTER break-name-1
   frame-text
.INSERT break-name-2
   frame-text

   .

   .

   .

.END-COPY
```

The override may be null, in which case the effect is to delete the default frame-text. The net effect of this command is to treat a frame tree as a single frame whose details can be added, modified and/or deleted.

It is very important that a frame be able to tailor any descendant frames, not just its immediate children. As the root of a (sub-)tree, a frame is responsible for resolving conflicts among descendant frames that are not visible at lower, more general levels. Conversely, a frame should be unaware of how it is used. This context independence helps maximize reuse and is why inserts are not "daisy-chained" down the tree.

- *REPLACE...BY* is used to replace a named variable with another variable or with an expression, for example, an arithmetic expression. The expression is evaluated and the value assigned to the frame-variable. However, if an ancestor frame has already assigned a value to this frame-variable, then this .REPLACE is ignored because the ancestor's assignment takes precedence.

A frame-variable (when prefixed by a ";") can occur at any character position in the frame-text. (Various symbols such as space and hyphen act as suffixes.) Each occurrence is replaced by the current value of the frame-variable, including null.

We could have written ".REPLACE king BY queen" at the top of the second Humpty-Dumpty example. Then, if both text occurrences of "king" had been prefixed with ";" the output would have been:

```
All the queen's horses and all the queen's men ...
```

A frame-variable can have local effects in multiple locations throughout the tree rooted in the frame containing the assignment. They act as the glue that binds disparate parts of a frame tree together.

- *SELECT* chooses from a list of cases.

```
.SELECT frame-variable
. WHEN Boolean-expression-1
    frame-text
. WHEN Boolean-expression-2
    frame-text

    .

    .

. OTHERWISE
frame-text
.END-SELECT
```

Each choice is processed if the corresponding Boolean expression, combined with the frame-variable, is true. The .OTHERWISE choice is processed if no other case has been processed. Any choice may be null.

In the following example, if ";king" has the value "queen", the Humpty-Dumpty frame is processed. (Otherwise, the construct has no effect.)

```
.SELECT ;king
. WHEN queen
.   COPY Humpty-Dumpty
.   INSERT Egg
      The ;king sat on the throne.
      The ;king got hit by a stone.
.   END-COPY
. OTHERWISE
.END-INSERT
```

This example compounds .COPY with .SELECT. The effect is to replace the default for "Egg" if ";king" has the value "queen".

```
This is a Humpty-Dumpty problem type.
The queen sat on a throne.
The queen got hit by a stone.
Poor Humpty died.
```

.SELECT can be used to provide frames with automatic version control. Each time a reusable frame is upgraded in some way, the old parts are not deleted. The parts that change are put into .SELECTs along with the replacement parts, parameterized on a version symbol. Existing ancestors are blind to the new version and continue to use the version current at the time they were defined. New ancestors will automatically use the new version. The entire frame can be rewritten with the obsolete-but-still-used version placed in a .SELECT and filed in an archive library, so that new users see only the rewritten version.

- *WHILE* iterates the processing of its contents until one of the frame-variables on the .WHILE line becomes undefined. Consider the following example:

```
.REPLACE num BY 1
.WHILE ;(face;num)
  The ;(face;num) of hearts will make Humpty better.
.REPLACE num BY (;num+1)
.END-WHILE
```

Assuming that frame-variables ";face1", ";face2" and ";face3" have the values "king", "queen" and "jack", respectively, the result will be:

```
The king of hearts will make Humpty better.
The queen of hearts will make Humpty better.
The jack of hearts will make Humpty better.
```

This command is intended to emit a variable number of (different) instances. For example, a reusable screen-handling frame has a standard way to display, prompt, read and test any screen variable. But the the number and details of the screen variables obviously depend on the particular screen. An ancestor frame would specify that information in the frame-variables, and the screen-handling frame would iterate accordingly.

Taken together, these frame change commands not only provide the means to specify and build software from reusable parts, but they constitute a precise vocabulary with which to discuss subtle engineering issues.

# Information-Hiding

The concept of **information-hiding** often drives the design of frames. When a reusable solution is developed that involves a nontrivial combination of various frames, it is packaged into a frame called a **wrapper frame**. It is so called because it hides or "wraps up" the solution into a form that makes it easy to reuse. On the other hand, the developer can still inspect the solution and override any of the parameters set by the wrapper should the context require subtle changes. Information-hiding is a double-edged sword. It should be possible to treat things as black boxes whenever possible and as not-quite-black ones whenever necessary.

Well-designed frames localize in one place all the expertise needed for some *type* of problem. This includes the knowledge of how to use specific frames. One hallmark of well-engineered frame libraries is their largely self-organized nature. Developers are never bewildered because, at each abstraction level, there are only a few independent choices.

# The SWAT Team's View

The purpose of having frames is to make life easy for developers (Figure 16.4). To develop a "new" program, the developer fills in a prototype SPC frame called a **template**. A dozen templates will span virtually all the *types* of programs a company uses. These templates, also in the frame library, contain references to the needed frames and a list of all the parameters needed to customize them.

The developer is systematically reminded, by the information in the template, of all the things he may need to specify in designing a program. He is unaware of the two-dimensional frame hierarchy; the template simply presents a linear "checkoff list" commented and defaulted to guide his choices.

Should a parameter subtlety need to be resolved that is not documented in the

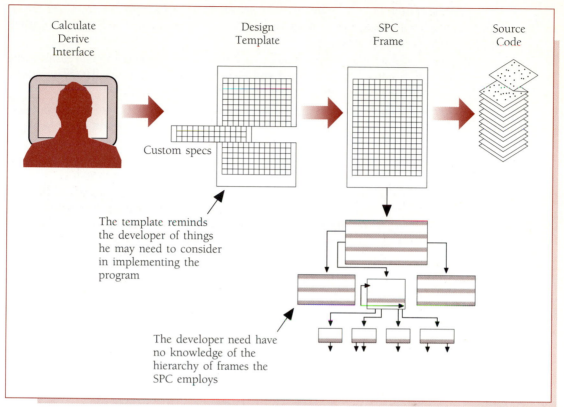

Calculate
Derive
Interface

Design
Template

SPC
Frame

Source
Code

Custom specs

The template reminds
the developer of things
he may need to consider
in implementing the
program

The developer need have
no knowledge of the
hierarchy of frames the
SPC employs

FIGURE 16.4 The Bassett Frame Development Process

template, the editor will take the developer to the relevant frame(s) and show him precisely the run-time behavior at the location(s) where the parameter has an effect. In other words, *black-box information-hiding is the norm*, but for subtle problems, the developer can delve into the black box and change it.

The filled-in template is now a custom SPC, a formal blueprint for assembling a program. It is typically five to fifteen per cent of the size of the program but, throughout the life of that program, is the only document for which the developer is responsible. It contains all and only what is unique about that program, that which cannot be specified in any other way. Any screen and report "paints" are converted into frames by frame generators. The SPC and its hierarchy of frames are processed by CASE tools to produce an executable program.

Further changes are always made to the specifications, the SPC and the screen and report specs, never to the source program.

# Revisiting the Wish List

1. *Stop reinventing similar wheels.* Frames exist precisely to avoid this problem.
2. *Express differences as well as similarities.* Frame commands exist precisely to highlight differences in use of each reusable frame. Because the differences can

be localized in frames that are themselves reused, one frame's exceptions can be another frame's norms. That is, if A is a wrapper frame for B, then A's users treat A as the norm.

3. *Make software easy to reuse and change.* Frames are designed to be reusable; the customizations can be grasped and changed without any needles-in-haystacks search because they are localized in the customizing frame.

4. *Enhance quality.* There is a natural motivation to put quality into frames because the frame is used many times. Even if a frame takes ten times more work to create than corresponding one-shot code, there is a positive return on investment after being reused 11 times, and after 100 times, the investment looks trivial, especially in light of the increased quality and robustness achieved.

5. *Foster flexible standards.* A frame is synonymous with a flexible standard. Because of the open architecture, organizations can create their own "textbook" solutions. Even better, the textbook can be automatically adapted to each situation. Standards can be formalized so that they become the path of least resistance to getting the job done. The foot is never forced to fit the shoe.

6. *Never force retrofits.* By means of the .SELECT and .REPLACE commands, any reusable frame can be modified or even completely rewritten in a manner invisible to all existing users. Given that an SPC represents only about 10% of the program, modest user requests for changes could result in a rewrite of the SPC, in which case the retrofit can be included without extra cost.

7. *Never sacrifice performance.* Frame technology enables flexibility at construction time to be independent of performance at execution time. If a more efficient algorithm can be applied to certain cases, it can coexist with the standard algorithm by using .SELECTs or .INSERTs. Because of the open architecture, frames can be as efficient as the best solutions that people can devise.

8. *Automate system construction.* Frame technology automates the construction of programs from custom specifications. NETRON/CAP is an example of a CASE toolset built on top of the technology to provide an efficient code generator.

# Frame-Based Business Engineering

There is a debate in the software industry over whether to centralize or decentralize I.S. development. Centralizers argue that corporate standards can be enforced and that there is more control and economy of scale. Decentralizers counterargue that developers should not be isolated from users, that large bureaucratic shops are inefficient and that more autonomy is needed to cope with the diversity of user needs. An optimal arrangement is to have the strengths of both while using each to offset the other's weaknesses.

There is a need for a centralized standards-setting and -enforcing group. It provides the common systems architecture, both data and process, through a repository of proprietary frames (including the very generic frames supplied by a software vendor). A common toolset and methodology are vital to maximize productivity and quality and to avoid fragmentation of skills and software compatibility. This should be a small group, responsible for the development, testing, documentation, distribution and support of corporate-proprietary frames.

## Growing a Frame Library

To make development with reusable frames as productive as possible, it is desirable to have a substantial library of frames. The more complete the library, the faster or more capable is the development process. To build a comprehensive library of frames, it is desirable to analyze the systems needed on an enterprisewide basis. An enterprise model reveals what commonalities can exist.

This implies that RAD should not simply be done on a project-by-project basis as the need arises, but rather that a systematic approach should be taken to analyzing the enterprise. Enterprise data models and process models should be built up in the repository and frames developed that achieve a high degree of reusability. Development of a new system can then happen very quickly because most of the components of that system already exist. Development proceeds by assembling and modifying existing building blocks.

Later chapters discuss enterprisewide analysis. Chapter 22 discusses reusability within an information-engineering environment, in which commonality of entity-types and process-types has been identified throughout a large part of an enterprise. Corporations that have used frame-based reusability within an infrastructure of information engineering have achieved very fast development of new systems.

In addition to the need for a centralized standards-setting and -enforcing group, there is an equal need to have small SWAT Teams immersed in the environments where the end users are located. Back-office systems are just another end-user environment, not part of the centralized standards group. These decentralized groups are responsible for the applications of a given line area, but they share the same tools, RAD methodology, and system infrastructure standards. The SWAT Team may also develop reusable frames. While originally intended only for the team's environment or project, such frames may also become grist for the centralized frame engineering mill.

A major benefit of this arrangement is that people can be easily shifted from area to area to balance demand. In particular, individuals from the centralized group can be seconded to various SWAT Teams for periods of time to ensure that they remain in touch with the realities of the development environments and to test things being developed as system standards.

Given the diversity facing organizations and the unpredictability of changing circumstances, the changeability of frames is vital. Often, much of the apparent diversity can be supported with a small number of frames that are common to one industry (e.g., retail banking), and the frames can be supplied to such organizations from an industry vendor.

With industry-standard frames as a base, each organization should add its own proprietary frames to the library. Some will be obvious from an understanding of existing corporate system standards for interfacing, security checking, and the like. Others will be discovered after the fact. A rule of thumb might be to write a reusable frame when the same *type* of problem is being seen for the third time.

An organization's proprietary frames capture its competitive edge. Being able to distill such intellectual assets into an objective, automated, yet flexible and easily redeployable form provides a powerful strategic weapon.

## Avoid Designing from Scratch

People in mature fields of engineering do not design structures down to every last nut, bolt and washer. They start with proven models. Such standard design models already embody hundreds, if not thousands, of lower-level details. This enables the designer to focus on the requirements that need unique design work, rather than being distracted by details that can and should be taken for granted. Adapting standard models to given requirements is a conservative, common-sense strategy that combines top-down and bottom-up techniques.

Given an effective reusability technology, software engineers can and should design the same way. A frame can be a proven design model, the parameters of which express the design options and the contents of which express the myriad lower-level details that can and should be taken for granted. The design task is reduced to extending and fitting existing, proven models together in novel ways.

# Iterative Design Refinement

Building a system with frames is usually a process of iteratively refining a design. Frames may exist such that a rough backbone of the system can be assembled quickly. A succession of refinements are then made to the backbone, each one being tested and checked out by the end users. Testing is spread throughout the development cycle. The benefits of refinements can be examined in the light of what is already implemented. The system grows quickly from a rough, partial prototype to one whose completeness and quality are suitable for cutover. A timebox approach may be used, as described in Chapter 11.

1. Iterative design refinement has attractive advantages:

   - *Each prerelease is real,* not a throwaway or shell prototype. It just happens that the first few may not be sufficient to cut over.
   - *Credibility and enthusiasm build,* due to frequent, visible progress.
   - *User requests are accommodated* in the next prerelease while holding firm the plans and schedule of the current one.
   - *Users may take less* in the first release (confident that I.S. is able to deliver) in order to start getting benefits sooner.
   - *Risk is limited;* management can dole out money in much smaller amounts; misconceived systems can be aborted early, based on hard evidence.

2. It avoids many problems inherent in traditional development:

   - *Analysis paralysis.*

- *Much wasted work* when subtle design errors are detected late.
- *Destabilization* when massive testing gets into trouble.
- *Gilding the system* with features whose benefits turn out to be not worth their cost.

Organizations that have adopted this form of reusability have become very enthusiastic about it.

# Maintenance

Frame technology changes the nature of maintenance. Maintenance of systems built with a powerful frame library becomes an ongoing extension of the iterative design refinement. The strategy of iterative design refinement is to break large projects into prereleases. An iteratively developed series of prereleases refines a design into a system released to production. In the postproduction stage, the strategy is the same: the design is further refined into a postrelease version that is rereleased to production. Postreleases are developed with the same methodology as prereleases. In other words, maintenance disappears as a distinct mindset and methodology. The single mindset and methodology of iterative design refinement span the entire life of a software system.

A separate maintenance department is then unnecessary and counterproductive. The SWAT Teams that develop prereleases can use the same tools and methodology to develop postreleases. Developers and users should have long-term responsibility for their systems' evolving needs.

# References

[BASS84] Paul G. Bassett, "Design Principles for Software Manufacturing Tools," *Proceedings*, ACM Conference on "Fifth-Generation Challenge," ACM, New York, 1984.

[BASS87] Paul G. Bassett, "Frame-Based Software Engineering," *IEEE Software*, July 1987, pp. 9–16.

[COX86] Brad J. Cox, *Object Oriented Programming*, Addison-Wesley Publishing Co., Reading, Massachusetts, 1986.

[GUTHERY89] Scott Guthery, "Are the Emperor's New Clothes Object Oriented?" *Dr. Dobb's Journal*, December 1989, pp. 80–86.

[MINSKY75] Marvin Minsky, "A Framework for Representing Knowledge," in *Psychology of Computer Vision*, Pat Winston, Ed., McGraw-Hill Book Co., New York, 1975, pp. 211–277.

[NETRON] *NETRON/CAP*, CASE toolset that produces COBOL systems from reusable Bassett Frames, product of Netron, Inc. (owned by NOMA), 99 St. Regis Crescent North, Downsview, Ontario M3J 1Y9, Canada (416-636–8333; fax: -4847)

[WATERS85] R. C. Waters, "The Programmer's Apprentice: A Session with KBEmacs," *IEEE Transactions on Software Engineering*, November 1985.

# CHAPTER 17

# Usability Testing

It is desirable to create applications that are as easy to use as they can possibly be. Many developers have created applications that are poorly human-factored, and this has proven to be very expensive. There are difficulties in gaining user acceptance. Training is expensive. Some users make mistakes with the system, and some resist using it. Difficulties with usability *slow down the deployment of the system*.

The race to develop applications quickly should never be done at the expense of good human-factoring. To ensure that systems are easy to use, usability testing should be done with end users. The I.S. organization should have a **human-factoring specialist**, who helps ensure that development teams are creating products with the most friendly user interface [LLOYDS].

## Objectives of Usability Testing

Usability testing should be done at the prototyping stages, when teams test subsystems, and when the final system is tested (Figure 17.1). It is built into the development lifecycles described in other chapters.

Figure 17.2 lists the usability objectives.

### Objectives of Usability Design and Testing

- *Intuitive Software*. It should be intuitively clear how to use the application. Characteristics of intuitive software are summarized in Box 17.1.
- *No Hidden Points of Confusion*. Users often take actions with software that result in their becoming confused. The software may put them in a situation where they do not know what to do next. Such sources of confusion should be detected and removed. What will cause user problems is often not clear to the developers until they see their application being tried out by end users.
- *Minimal Learning Time*. Users should be able to learn the application quickly so that cutover can proceed as quickly as possible. Often, serious delays are caused by difficulties in training the users.
- *User Self-Sufficiency*. Users, or user departments, should be self-sufficient and able to expand their own knowledge of the software and its use.
- *Little or No Classroom Training*. Users should be able to become skilled in using the application without classroom training.

Programmers sometimes think they are skilled at human-factoring when, in fact, the opposite is true. It can be a sobering experience for them to see videotapes of end

314

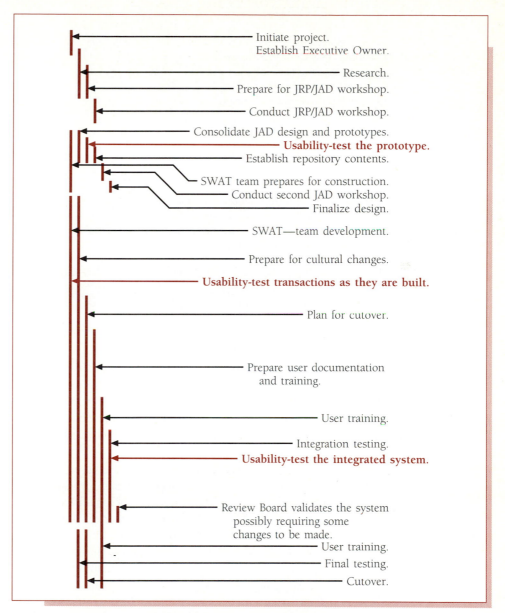

FIGURE 17.1 Times at Which Usability Testing Should Occur

users unable to cope with an application that the programmers deluded themselves into thinking was user-friendly. In some cases, developers have watched tapes showing their "user-friendly" application reducing end users to tears. This is a sobering experience for the developer; it makes the developer resolve to do a better job of human-factoring in the future.

Even the most skilled developer has the experience of writing instructions for end users, only to find that they misinterpret the instructions and take action that plunges

## USABILITY OBJECTIVES

- Intuitive Software
- No Hidden Points of Confusion
- Minimal Learning TIme
- User Self-Sufficiency
- Little or No Classroom Training
- Positive User Attitude

Think twice if you have to explain how it works.

FIGURE 17.2 Objectives of Usability Testing

## Box 17.1 Summary of the Characteristics of Intuitive Software

- *No Alien Syntax.* The user does not need to learn mnemonics, commands, special punctuation or formats.
- *Self-Explanatory.* The software explains clearly what the user has to do.
- *Obvious.* It is obvious how to operate the software and what the results mean. If you have to explain how it works, redesign the human interface.
- *Consistent.* The mechanisms of user interaction are the same for each type of transaction. Screen layouts are as similar as possible. Wording is as consistent as possible.
- *Standard.* The user interface conforms to *de-facto* standards, such as IBM's CUA (Common User Access), wherever possible. An installation may have its own dialog standards. The standards may include the wording to be used. Standards and consistency help make the software as *familiar* as possible to the user when he confronts a new application.
- *In-Context HELP.* The software has well-written, on-line HELP screens that relate to the screen at which the user requires help.
- *No Need for Manuals.* The software is easy to use without reference to a paper manual. (Paper documentation may exist so that the user has something to read when he is not using the machine.)
- *No Need for Classes.* The user can learn the software at the screen without having to go to classes.
- *No Hidden Points of Confusion.* The software does not create situations in which the user is confused and does not know what to do.
- *No Cryptic Error Messages.* All error messages are easy to read, easy to understand and tell the user what actions to take.
- *User Self-sufficiency.* The software encourages the user to be self-sufficient and to build upon his existing knowledge.

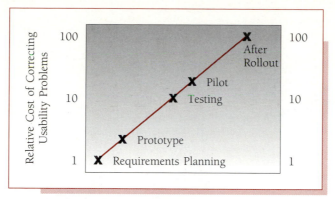

FIGURE 17.3 The earlier usability problems are detected. the lower the cost.

the software down a path that causes bewilderment. The developer needs to see this happen as early as possible in the development cycle and take corrective action.

The sooner problems in the usability of an application are detected, the lower the cost. Figure 17.3 illustrates this.

If the problem is pointed out during the planning stage, it does not add significantly to the cost or time of system development. If it is caught in a JAD workshop, it is not expensive. It may be discovered when prototypes are employed with end users. If a problem is caught during testing after the application is developed, it is usually more expensive to correct and may delay the cutover if it requires a major change.

Often, usability problems are not caught or corrected until the system is in use. They are then much more expensive, especially if the system has been fanned out to many locations. There is often resistance to making the desirable changes at this stage.

# Usability Laboratory

To help the developers understand usability problems, it is desirable to record what gets users into trouble. End users are selected to try out the system. Their problems may be recorded by talking into a sound recorder. Usually, it is better to videotape the problem. To do this, some I.S. departments have established a room equipped with inexpensive video cameras to study usability. This is sometimes referred to as a **usability laboratory**. Figure 17.4 shows a usability laboratory.

The user is given tasks to accomplish at the screen of the system, and his activity is recorded. He is encouraged to verbalize whatever concerns or uncertainties he has. Sometimes users mutter or swear at the system. One video camera may record his keyboard actions, while another records the system screen. The screen contents may be recorded directly on a VCR tape, with a board for this purpose inserted into the personal computer. The equipment in the usability lab need not be expensive.

In the setup in Figure 17.4, the user's actions are being watched and listened to by observers in a soundproof booth behind a one-way mirror. The user should be unaware of the actions or conversation of these observers. The videotapes being made may be roughly edited in this booth. The observers may add comments to the tape.

To make the test environment as close to the true work environment as possible, a sound tape may be played with the sounds of the work environment.

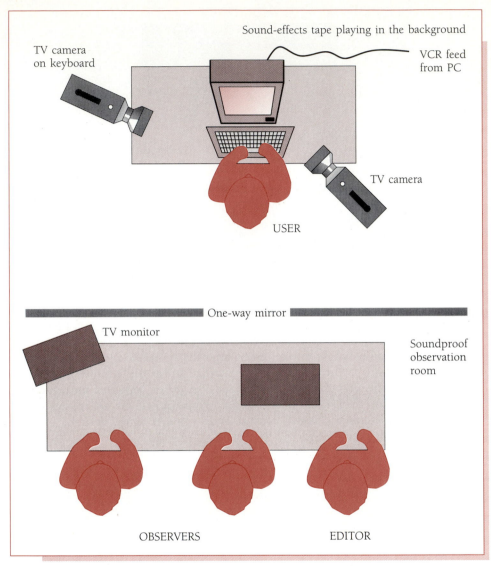

Sound-effects tape playing in the background

TV camera
on keyboard

VCR feed
from PC

TV camera

USER

One-way mirror

TV monitor

Soundproof
observation
room

OBSERVERS                    EDITOR

FIGURE 17.4 Layout of a Usability Laboratory
The usability laboratory need not be expensive.

An I.S. person briefs the user before the test and debriefs him afterwards. The user may refer to paper documentation and may ask for help from the person who briefs him if necessary. The debriefer adds comments to the recorded tape. The briefer/ debriefer may be the **human-factoring specialist** of the I.S. organization. He operates the usability lab, ensuring that the equipment works.

## The Evaluators

Real end users should evaluate the system. It is desirable to have a mix of users representative of the people who will encounter the system in operation. Some will be trained in the application, some not. Some may be experienced with personal computers, some not. It is often desirable to use a mixture of age groups in the testing. Some older users have far more problems with personal computers than young people.

The evaluators should be put under pressure to complete the assigned tasks with the system. They should not be allowed to give up easily. They must persevere when they have difficulties. Enforced perseverance enables more information to be recorded about what needs to be improved in the human-factoring, HELP functions and documentation.

In some usability labs, users are deliberately given the impression that it is *they* who are being tested, not the software. They then take the test seriously, often becoming upset when they cannot make the application work well. The developer sees a more emphatic user reaction to bad human-factoring.

## Measurements

Various measurements can be made of a usability test, including:

- whether the task was completed;
- length of time needed to learn the task;
- number of times the user had problems;
- number of HELP references;
- length of HELP references;
- number of times the user had to look something up in the documentation;
- number of times the user had to ask for human help.

Often, the subjective evaluation of a human-factoring specialist is more valuable than numerical evaluation.

## Test Report

A report may be made of the test, indicating changes needed in:

- screen wording;
- screen layout;
- screen interaction;
- use of the keyboard or mouse;
- dialog flow;
- error messages;
- recovery from errors;
- on-line HELP;
- on-line documentation;
- off-line documentation.

The report may indicate segments of videotape that show the users having difficulties. These segments should be keyed to requested changes.

Most problems in human-factoring (especially when using a standard form of dialog like IBM's CUA or UNIX MOTIF) can be corrected without programming. They are often caused by confusing wording on the screen, which is inexpensive to fix if the problem is recognized. A problem that requires changes in one transaction type may indicate that similar changes are needed in other transaction types.

# The Three "C"s of Usability

To create good user interfaces, attention must focus on:

- clarity,
- comprehension,
- consistency.

*Clarity needs good screen design and good phraseology.* The screen layout needs to be clear and uncluttered. The wording should be chosen carefully.

*Comprehension also needs well-chosen wording.* To do good human-factoring, a developer needs the talent to be literate, write clear English and avoid jargon. Some people are skilled in application design or programming and not skilled with English. The work should be polished by a person who is skilled with English and can write well. This may be one of the skills in a SWAT Team.

Pictures are extremely helpful in documentation, on-line HELP and tutorial explanation. They should be used where appropriate to make applications easy to learn and use. Hyperdocuments are an appropriate form of on-line documentation [MARTIN90]. Hyperdocuments are an extension of hypertext. Text or images on a screen have **buttons**. When the user *activates* a button, for example, by pointing to it with a mouse, a window or new screen is displayed with different text, images or program execution. The user can follow threads of ideas and open and close envelopes of documentation. There can be envelopes within envelopes within envelopes. A hyperdocument may have built-in expert systems or other software. The user can navigate through very complex documents easily and quickly in order to solve a problem. Some persons are highly skilled at using hyperdocument authoring software [MS].

*Consistency is important in making systems user-friendly.* A new application should look and feel as familiar as possible to the users. There should be consistent use of screen layouts, function keys, pull-down menus, multiple-choice mechanisms and so on. The choice of words and colors should be consistent.

The same word should always be used for the same item. Do not say *screen* on one occasion, *monitor* on another, *panel* on another and *display* on another to mean the same thing. To achieve consistency of wording, a glossary may be used by all developers. Naming conventions should be employed.

Vendors' standards, such as IBM's SAA (Systems Application Architecture), CUA (Common User Access) [IBM89] and DEC's DECWindows [DEC89], have guidelines associated with them for dialog design. These should be incorporated into installation standards. If all applications incorporate such standards, it is easier for users to learn a new application.

I-CASE generators employ screen and dialog design aids. Standard screen templates can be created for the corporation to help make different applications look and feel the same. This speeds up development as well as helping to achieve consistency and user-friendliness.

# Novice Mode and Expert Mode

Some dialogs need both a **novice mode** and an **expert mode**. When in *novice* mode, the dialog explains everything to the users. When in *expert* mode, it omits the explanation and permits the user to employ faster techniques, such as function keys rather than menu selection. The user employing expert mode can immediately switch back to novice mode if necessary.

# Human-Factoring Specialist

As we have commented, an installation should employ an I.S. professional who is an expert on human-factoring. He should examine prototypes and screens as they are created and give the developers help in achieving *clarity, comprehension* and *consistency*. The human-factoring should be made as excellent as possible before usability testing occurs.

The human-factoring specialist should brief and debrief the users who perform the usability testing. In doing this and observing user difficulties, this specialist makes himself more skilled on how to avoid usage problems.

The human-factoring specialist may operate the usability laboratory. After testing a number of applications with end users, he acquires the ability to spot many of the human-factoring problems without actually doing the testing. This skill is valuable to the Construction Teams.

# References

[DEC89] *DecWindows User's Guide*, Digital Equipment Corporation, Software Documentation Division, Nashua, New Hampshire, 1989.

[IBM89] 1. *CUA 1989 Evaluation*, December 1989, IBM Publication GG24–3456; 2. *Writing IMS SAA Applications, A Design Guide*, May 1989, IBM Publication GG24–3324. These manuals on guidelines for the design of Common User Access are exceptionally helpful and might be made part of an installation standard.

[LLOYDS] One of the best examples the author has found of usability testing in a usability laboratory is is Lloyds Bank, in London. Here, usability testing has helped speed up substantially the rate of deployment of systems to many bank branches.

[MARTIN90] James Martin, *Hyperdocuments and How to Create Them*, Prentice-Hall, Inc., Englewood Cliffs, New Jersey, 1990 (201–592–2261).

[MS] An example is *MediaScribe* from MediaBrain, Inc., Framingham, Massachusetts (508–875–6553).

# CHAPTER 18

# Planning for Cutover

When application development is done fast, it is necessary to plan cutover early. In most systems in the past, construction took a long time and was the main cause of delay in putting a new system to work. However, in installations with fast development, the cutover phase has sometimes been the main cause of delay. It takes time to train the users, modify their procedures and make the system operate smoothly. Because of this, preparation for cutover *needs to be done in parallel with the Construction Phase* and needs to be well planned so that it does not delay the cutover.

This chapter and the next describe the four phases of cutover:

1. Prepare for cultural changes.
2. Design for cutover.
3. Prepare for cutover.
4. Perform cutover.

## New Systems Can Cause Dramatic Cultural Changes in an Organization

A major reorganization may be desirable in order to take maximum advantage of the new system. Jobs may be displaced, or new types of talent may be necessary. The staffing levels often need to change. There may be changes in business policies as well as in procedures. It is desirable to ask, "Where is the optimum place that each business decision should be made, given flexible databases, a ubiquitous network and abundant computing power on any individual's desk?"

These cultural factors need to be addressed as early in the development lifecycle as possible. It may take substantial time to accomplish the necessary changes and, if not addressed well, they could cause the system to fail. Where possible, they should be addressed in the overall Business Area Analysis (Chapter 21). They should be examined carefully when a specific system is being planned and should be a major topic of the Joint Requirements Planning workshop. The JRP workshop may conclude that certain reorganizations have to be accomplished or cultural changes made before it is sensible to move into the User Design Phase.

# Prepare for Cultural Changes

Cultural changes include changes in:

- organizational structure;
- policies;
- business procedures;
- job content;
- skill requirements.

Preparation for cultural changes can be broken into the following activities:

- Identify any cultural changes.
- Design the organizational changes.
- Identify responsibilities for organizational changes.
- Schedule the organizational changes.

See Methodology Chart 18–1, "Preparation for Cultural Changes."

The first step of planning for cultural changes should be to list all changes of the preceding types that may be brought about by the new system. The organizational units that are affected should be listed. Some organizational units may be affected in a minor way. In others, the change may be drastic; for example, a department might be eliminated from the new system. The list of such changes should be reviewed with top management.

In some cases, new organizational units or new job positions are created. A mission statement should be written for the new jobs. These should be reviewed with high-level end-user management. It is often the case that some end-user managers are opposed to the desirable changes. The benefits of the changes *must* be understood by a level of management high enough to put the changes into effect.

It is necessary at an early stage to assign the responsibility for bringing about the organizational changes. It should be decided whether any specialized help is needed from human resource consultants or specialists in organizational change. The role of the Information Systems staff in bringing about the changes should be defined.

A plan should be created for an orderly transition to the new organization. The actions required to accomplish the transition should be listed, along with the name of the individual responsible for each action. The necessary resources should be listed. The sequence and timing of the actions should be charted. This set of actions should be meshed with the overall development and cutover schedules.

Approval should be obtained from the managers who are affected by the changes. It is necessary to obtain sign-offs on these approvals early in the development cycle; otherwise, a timely cutover might be jeopardized.

# Design for Cutover

Design for cutover can be broken into two types of activities:

- those that affect the end users;
- those that require I.S. professional design without strong user involvement.

Actions that affect the end users should be identified in the User Design Phase. They should be a major topic of the JAD (Joint Application Design) workshop. They include the following:

- Design whatever changes are needed in user procedures.
- Design changes in paperwork.
- Plan for changes in staffing.
- Plan for changed management requirements.
- Plan how the new system will be phased in.
- Plan whatever user training is needed.
- Design the user-training program.
- Determine who will conduct user training.
- Design the users' participation in the usability testing (Chapter 17).
- Determine who creates the user documentation.

Some design for cutover is more technical in nature and can be done by I.S. professionals without necessarily affecting the end users.

Technical design for cutover includes the following:

- Establish the implementation standards.
- Design the technical conversion procedures.
- Design the production procedures.
- Plan the hardware installation.
- Determine the testing strategy.
- Plan the testing environment.
- Create the technical documentation.
- Create the user documentation.
- Create the technical training program.

Methodology Chart 18-2 shows these two sets of cutover design activities in more detail.

Most organizations have standards that they use when planning the implementation of a system. There are installation standards, standards for setting up code libraries, job control and documentation libraries, testing procedures, documentation standards and so on. The standards may need to be changed when new software approaches are introduced. Naming conventions and dictionary use may be changed when a code generator comes into use. Standards may be changed to take better advantage of IBM's System Application Architecture (SAA) and the facilities associated with it or of other vendors' standards. When the system is being planned, the standards for implementation should be reviewed and adjusted if necessary.

An important part of planning for cutover is the creation of end-user documentation. Documentation used to consist of paperwork manuals. Today, it is desirable to avoid paperwork manuals where possible and put user documentation into the product itself, accessible from the user workstation. Users, like computer professionals, typically do not read the paper documentation.

Standards, if they do not already exist, should be established for on-line documentation. IBM's Common User Access [IBM89] provides software and guidelines for creating multiple levels of HELP screens that can guide the end user and replace much paperwork. Standards should be adopted for the building of HELP screens, and it is necessary to decide in the implementation cycle who will build them.

# Conversion Procedures

A major part of the planning for cutover is the design of the conversion procedures. The sequence of steps that are necessary for conversion should be determined. Some may be concerned with conversion from manual procedures, others with conversion of computer systems. Particularly important are the steps needed to convert or capture the data, load the database and verify that it is correct.

When the steps necessary for conversion have been listed, they should be reviewed with end-user management and refined as necessary. The resources required for conversion should be determined and a plan drawn up for obtaining them at the appropriate time. Individuals should be assigned to steps for which end users are responsible.

The sequence of steps necessary for conversion should be charted and meshed with the overall development schedule.

The design of the data conversion procedures should begin with examination of the data structure used in the new system. Every data element should be examined and a determination made of whether it will be entered manually or obtained automatically from an existing system. Both the manual data entry procedures and automatic conversion procedures need to be designed. Before designing them in detail, the list of data elements and their proposed conversion procedures should be reviewed with appropriate end users to determine whether anything has been overlooked.

To design the manual procedures, the documents that contain the data should be examined. Data entry screens must be built for the manual entry. These screens, created quickly with a screen painter, should be prototyped with those end users who will do the data entry. Dry runs of the manual data entry should be done to ensure that it will go well when cutover occurs, and an estimate should be made of how long it will take.

The software for automated data conversion should be designed, built quickly with an automated tool and tested to ensure that it works well. There should be a determination of how data errors and missing data will be dealt with.

It should be decided how both the manual and automatic data conversion will be checked for accuracy. Batch runs for balancing control totals may be used, along with other means for checking accuracy. The sequence of tests and acceptance criteria that will be used to verify a successful conversion should be designed and reviewed with end-user management. End users sometimes have much subtle knowledge about sources of errors and how to avoid errors in data. The procedures for data conversion may be modified to meet the test criteria. The test criteria should be documented.

# Production Procedures

The procedures for operation of the system need to be designed. These include computer center operations, end-user procedures for personal computers or terminals and the manual and paperwork procedures that must accompany the new system. The procedures should be planned and reviewed with end-user management at an early stage in the development lifecycle. Substantial preparation may have to be done by user departments, and this may delay cutover when a high-speed lifecycle is used if it is not planned well in advance.

As well as planning for normal system operation, it is vital to plan what will be done when things go wrong. Fallback procedures describing how to function when the system fails must be designed. Procedures must be designed for restart and recovery. These procedures need to be reviewed with end-user management.

Security procedures should be carefully thought out, along with how the system will be audited. If the system is sensitive from the security point of view, a decision should be made on whether to employ a security specialist.

The installation of the hardware needs to be planned. It should be decided whether the hardware will be phased in a stage at a time (e.g., one location at a time). If so, a staged installation plan should be designed. Vendors should be contacted to arrange for the installation to meet the project schedule.

# Planning for Testing

A thorough plan must be drawn up for how the system will be tested. For each type of activity, a detailed test plan should be created. All the cases that need testing should be listed and a detailed test script created. The tests may be performed in groups. For each group, the transaction types and the characteristics of each test case should be listed. This testing plan should be reviewed with end-user management to ensure that nothing has been forgotten.

- *Various types of tests need to be planned.*
  - *Program/Transaction Test.* For each transaction type, verify that the program handles all its transactions correctly, perform a transaction crash test and verify that the program handles the transaction in all cases without crashing.
  - *System Integration Test.* Plan the sequence in which separately developed subsystems will be tested in combination. Plan how to verify that subsystems developed in parallel work together.
  - *Intersystem Integration Test.* Plan the integration tests needed to verify that the system accepts input from and provides output to other systems with which it interfaces. Plan how to test that the systems work together fully.

- *Volume Test.* Plan how large volumes of transactions are to be tested (simulation or actual data tests).
- *Regression Test for Maintenance Changes.* Plan the procedures for verifying that the system still works as maintenance changes are made.
- *Acceptance Test.* Plan how verification will be obtained from end users that the system is acceptable for production.

- *The sequence of testing should be planned.* If the system is to be phased in, one subsystem at a time, the test sequence should reflect this. Ensure that systems that produce data for other systems are tested first. The construction sequence and the testing sequence should be meshed.
- *A test generator should be used to generate the test cases.* Examples include the DATAMACS Test Data Generator from Computer Associates. Where such a product cannot generate the test cases completely, it should be planned how the test data will be created.
- *There may be other types of software needed for testing.* It should be determined whether testing tools not already available need to be purchased. Some custom software may be needed for testing. If so, this should be determined and the software designed and built in plenty of time.
- *The libraries necessary for testing need to be planned.* These include libraries of source code and object code, job control code and data. The library software and conventions need to be planned if these are not already an installation standard.

# Documentation

Documentation is necessary both for cutover and for subsequent operation and maintenance. Two categories of documentation are needed: **technical documentation** and **documentation for end users**. Both of these have changed since the traditional development lifecycle was used.

*Technical* documentation should reside in the I-CASE repository. Much of it is now formal and computable and is created as part of the analysis and design process. A code generator should be used that automatically generates complete technical documentation in the form of a development workbook. Comments, which are intended for humans rather than computers, are added to the formal models and design representations and appear in the printed workbook. A major purpose of the comments is to facilitate the maintenance task. Building this type of documentation as data modeling, process modeling and design are being done is part of good management practice.

*User* documentation has changed with modern tools because, as far as possible, it should be on-line. There should be little or no external paperwork documentation. Most users do not read detailed user manuals. They may read relatively small paper documents that help them get started. They need help at the screen when they get into trouble.

IBM's SAA (Systems Application Architecture) defines six categories of HELP which can be created for each application [IBM89]:

1. *HELP*, which provides help about the field on which the cursor is positioned.
2. *Extended HELP*, which tells users about the task they are performing in the application panel.
3. *Keys HELP*, which produces a list of all keys this application uses and their functions.
4. *HELP Index*, which produces an alphabetical index of all the HELP information for the application.
5. *HELP Contents*, which produces a table of contents of HELP information, organized by topic.
6. *Tutorial HELP*, which provides access to a tutorial related to the panel on which the user is working.

Most documentation for computer applications should be on-line so that it is immediately available on the screen when users need it.

As commented earlier, a particularly effective way of creating on-line documentation is with hyperdocument software [MARTIN90]. With hypertext, a user may point at highlighted words in text, and the software skips to other text. The user can open and close **envelopes** of text—envelopes within envelopes within envelopes—and can explore large bodies of text at high speed to find what is useful at a particular moment. Hyperdocuments link hypertext to charts and scanned images, to computing capability (sometimes with artificial intelligence), to other software and, possibly, to recorded speech or video.

## Reusable Document Structures

The concepts of reusability should be applied to user documentation, whether it is on paper or on line. With paper documentation, electronic publishing software may be used. Reusable templates should be employed, which are adjusted or filled in for each specific application. The table of contents should be as similar as possible for each application. Where reusable structures are employed in the software design, such as those in Figures 15.1 to 15.7, reusable documentation structures may be employed in conjunction with them. Similarly, for on-line documentation, reusable structures should be employed. Reusable software structures and reusable documentation become easier to use. Hyperdocument software makes this easy.

Standard reusable document structures and templates speed up the creation of documentation, but they have another important advantage—user familiarity. The user becomes accustomed to the look and feel of the documentation, and the documentation becomes easier to use.

## Skill Needed

The type of skill needed to create good documentation is different from the skill of the average programmer. It requires a sense of literacy, writing style and teaching skills. Most programmers are poor at creating user documentation. Some individuals who specialize in it can do it fast and competently, especially when reusable document structures are employed. It is desirable to assign such a person and estimate the time needed. The creation of user documentation should begin immediately after the go-ahead for the Construction Phase and should proceed in parallel with construction.

The effectiveness of the documentation should be tested. HELP screens and hyper-documents should be tested with end users and adjusted to make them as effective as possible. It is often desirable to do this in a usability-lab environment, where the reaction of users can be videotaped for later study. (See Chapter 17.)

## Planning for Documentation

- Determine what user documentation should be on-line.
- Determine what external paper documentation is needed. (Minimize external documentation.)
- Determine what software (such as hyperdocument software) will be used for on-line documentation.
- Determine what reusable templates, layouts and contents will be employed.
- Determine who will do the documentation.
- Design the structure and contents of the HELP screens.
- Design the structure and contents of other on-line documentation.
- Design the structure and contents of paper documentation.
- Determine the timetable for creation of documentation.

# User Training

Good user training is essential for achieving success with a new system. The training needs careful preparation, and the time available for this is much less when development is done with a high-speed, automated lifecycle. Development of the training should proceed in parallel with development of the system. Development of the training should progress through the following stages:

- Determine who needs training and what the objectives are.
- Outline the curriculum.
- Plan the development of training materials.
- Develop the training schedule.
- Produce the training materials.

These stages are outlined in more detail in Methodology Chart 18-2.

The first step is to identify which skills and methods will change and consequently cause a need for training. The objectives of the training should be written down, and a determination should be made of who has to be trained. This should all be reviewed with end-user management.

An outline of the curriculum must then be created. The author should do this with an action-diagram editor or hyperdocument editor [MS] because this makes it easy to build and continuously change the hierarchical structures that represent the curriculum. It also allows the author to make the best use of reusable structures and text. The I-CASE tool itself may be used for curriculum design.

It should be decided who will conduct the training and what media will be used. It may be necessary to develop a teach-the-teachers program if a large number of users have to be trained. Often, the most appropriate form of training is to make a selected user in each department a specialist who will train and help the other users in his department. The question of who will do the training relates to the question of what media will be used. The following types of teaching should be considered:

- lectures with slides;
- classroom training with overhead projector foils;
- personal assistance in the user's department;
- use of prototypes;
- use of extended HELP screens;
- use of hyperdocuments;
- computer-based training;
- videotape.

It is desirable to make the system self-teaching to the extent that this is practical and economic. Good use of HELP screens and on-line documentation is desirable for this. Sometimes computer-based training may be appropriate, though this is often too expensive. For some systems it is appropriate to make a videotape for mass introduction to the system. It should also be determined whether training purchased from an outside source would be available.

To help in both creating the training and as a training aid itself, prototypes of the system should be used early in the development lifecycle.

A schedule should be drawn up for creating the training materials, preparing the trainers and delivering the training. The schedule should indicate when prototypes will be available. The training schedule should be meshed with the system development schedule.

Specific steps are recommended for creating the training.

- Test the prototypes that will be used for training.
- Design, write and implement the HELP screens.
- Design the structure of lectures or courses.
- Design the projection foils and other materials.
- Review the training materials with users.
- Adjust the training materials based on user feedback.
- Package the training materials with an overall training curriculum and plan.
- If necessary, develop an instructor's guide.

# References

[IBM89] 1. *Systems Application Architecture Common User Access*, December 1989, IBM Publication SC26-4583; 2. *SAA: Systems Application Architecture Common User Access Advanced Interface*, July 1989, IBM Publication SC26–4582.

[MARTIN90] James Martin, *Hyperdocuments and How to Create Them*, Prentice-Hall, Inc., Englewood Cliffs, New Jersey, 1990 (201–592–2261).

[MS] An example is *MediaScribe* from MediaBrain, Inc., Framingham, Massachusetts (508–875–6553).

# CHAPTER 19

# Cutover

This chapter describes the process of putting the system into operation—**cutover**. It assumes that design for cutover has been done, as described in the previous chapter. (See Methodology Chart 19, "Cutover Phase.")

Prior to cutting over the system, specific activities need to be done:

- Develop the conversion system.
- Finalize the development product.
- Prepare for final testing.
- Carry out the final testing.
- Plan and conduct the training program.

(See Methodology Chart 18-1, "Preparation for Cultural Changes.")

In some RAD installations, a goal is to get a version of the system into operation quickly, learn from the experience of the system and then, if necessary, produce a modified version of the system. A succession of improved versions may be built so that the business procedures become as streamlined and strategic as possible.

## Conversion

As described earlier, systems are needed for automatic conversion of data and for manual entry of those data that cannot be converted automatically. These systems should be built as quickly as possible, with automated tools. They should be carefully tested and reviewed with end-user management. Tests need to be designed to ensure that the converted data work well with the new application programs.

The new system may have to work in conjunction with old systems. Data must be converted so that they can pass from the old systems to the new one and, possibly, from the new system to the old ones so that the old ones can remain in use. The interface between the old and the new systems needs to be designed, built and tested well in advance.

It may be necessary to develop an interface to application packages. This also requires data conversion, which should be designed, built and tested in advance.

Prior to cutover, all the necessary files should be converted and the necessary data entered.

# Finalizing the Development Product

There should be a quality audit of the development product prior to cutover to ensure that it is well structured, is well documented and conforms to the installation standards. This audit may examine the machine performance of the system and recommend areas where improvement is necessary. The quality audit will be quicker and easier if a good application generator is used.

Any defects or inefficiencies revealed by the quality audit should be corrected. It may be necessary to use a code optimizer to improve code performance. Most generators generate fully structured code, but this does not run quite as efficiently as code that has been carefully optimized. To correct this, an automatic code optimizer may be used, such as the COBOL optimizer from Computer Associates.

There may be differences between the development environment and the production environment that may require modification of the development product (e.g., the Job Control Language may require changes). The necessary changes should be identified and made.

# Final Testing

To prepare for final testing, the software must be installed, the test libraries built and the test data generated. If possible, test data generator software should be used. The testing must be coordinated with the development team.

Testing may progress through a number of stages.

- *Program/Transaction Test.* For each transaction type, verify that the program handles all its transactions correctly, perform a transaction crash test and verify that the program handles the transaction in all cases without crashing.
- *System Integration Test.* Verify that subsystems developed in parallel work together.
- *Intersystem Integration Test.* Verify that the system accepts input from and provides output to other systems with which it interfaces. Verify that the systems work together fully.
- *Volume Test.* Verify that the system can process the volume of transactions expected.
- *Regression Test for Maintenance Changes.* Verify that the system still works as maintenance changes are made.
- *Acceptance Test.* Obtain verification from the users that the system is acceptable for production.

Statistics should be collected on these tests for project management purposes, and the test results should be documented.

# Conduct Training

Training of the users must take place prior to cutover, Where possible, cutover should be a phased operation, with experience from the initial installation being used to make the subsequent installation operate as smoothly as possible. It should be determined which end users will be trained initially. This training should be done and its success evaluated. The training materials and techniques should be improved on the basis of this experience. This may require changes in the software HELP screens and error messages.

A plan should exist for the spread of training, corresponding to the deployment of the system.

# Perform Cutover

The actual cutover process can be broken into the following activities:

- Set up the production procedures.
- Install the production system environment.
- Perform data conversion.
- Implement the new system in production.
- Review the system installation.

(See Methodology Chart 18-2, "Performing Cutover.")

# The Production Procedures

A variety of procedures is needed to operate the system. Manual and administration procedures have to accompany the computerized procedures. These should have been designed, documented and verified well before cutover. The procedures are often designed so that the new system can operate in parallel with the old system until confidence is built up in the new system.

The following production procedures need to be set up:

- the procedures for normal system operation;
- any manual or paperwork procedures that must accompany the new installation;
- the procedures for restart and recovery;
- the fallback procedures;
- the procedures for security;
- the audit procedures;
- the procedures for phasing out the old system when the new system is running satisfactorily.

Review these procedures with both the data center personnel and the end users to ensure their understanding.

The new system may be installed in one location. It may then be adjusted until it is working smoothly and then fanned out to many locations. A timetable for this fan-out is necessary so that the procedures can be set up appropriately in all locations.

The hardware needs to be installed. It should be installed with a schedule that relates to the planned fan-out. The ongoing installation of the hardware at other sites needs to be coordinated with the vendors. There needs to be a complete test of the hardware and its software. The systems programming administrators must schedule the time needed to install and test the software.

# Installation

When the software is installed, the data are loaded into the system's database. The data conversion programs are executed, and the manually prepared data are entered. The resulting database is tested to verify the data quality, and the results are then reviewed to ensure that the acceptance test criteria are met.

The new system is moved into production mode, following the migration plan, possibly running in parallel with the old system. The new software components are locked into the development and test library. The old system is phased out as confidence is developed in the new system.

## Installation Review

When experience is gained with the new system, the system should be reviewed, with the intent of improving its performance where necessary, ensuring the best user acceptance and optimizing the system functionality.

The following steps are taken:

- Evaluate system performance.
- Determine what system tuning is needed.
- Evaluate user acceptance of the system.
- Determine what improvements are needed in user training.
- Schedule the improvements in training.
- Determine what system modifications are needed.
- Schedule the system modifications.

# CHAPTER 20

# RAD within a Planned Architecture

## The Need for Integration

Rapid application development will become increasingly essential for business survival. However, there is a danger inherent in rapid development. Systems that meet their users' needs become institutionalized. If many such systems are built to solve isolated problems, the result becomes a large, undisciplined mass of institutionalized applications that do not work together. The lack of interoperability is harmful.

Value is created in a corporation by a chain of activities. Marketing leads to sales; sales lead to production; production needs inventory planning, which requires purchasing; produced goods must be delivered; customers must be billed and the money collected; this incoming cash pays for more selling, purchasing and production. This is referred to as the **value chain**. The value chain activities are interrelated, and their information processing must be interrelated.

In many corporations, manufacturing systems and marketing systems were built by different groups. Each group designed its own data, created its own networks and made its own choice of computer vendor. In the mid-1980s, it became clear that much information needed to pass from marketing to manufacturing and from manufacturing to marketing. The moves toward computer-integrated manufacturing (CIM) and electronic data interchange (EDI) became of strategic importance. It became desirable to automate production scheduling in order to improve production efficiency, but this required access to inventory and order information that was on incompatible systems.

In a report on I.S. strategy, DuPont commented, "This functional mind-set, worsened by vendor-aligned computing cultures within our I.S. and user organizations, resulted in data and program designs that were not supportive of computer-integrated business. It is absolutely essential that we remove these technological, functional and cultural barriers if we are to move toward value-chain integration [DUPONT]."

Computer-aided design needs to link to computer-aided manufacturing; production control systems need to link to production scheduling; production scheduling needs to link to inventory and purchasing systems, which need to link to marketing. Marketing systems need to link to order processing systems; customer order systems need to link to sales and service. It is rather like the old spiritual song, "The knee bone's connected to the shin bone, the shin bone's connected to the ankle bone, the ankle bone's connected to the foot bone..." Nature's creatures are organisms that cannot work unless their foot bones are connected to their ankle bones.

A corporation is also an organism that needs its computerized components to work smoothly together. RAD enables us to build components quickly, but unless those components are designed to fit into a planned infrastructure, the result will not be an electronic organism but a rapidly growing mass of disconnected fragments. Many corporations could sing, "The foot bone's not connected to the ankle bone..."

# Growing Inflexibility

As computing systems grow, they become more and more complex. Complex systems are difficult to change unless they have been created with a skillfully designed architecture that allows one piece to be changed without changing the other pieces.

In most corporations, until recently, there was no design of an overall I.S. architecture. As the installed base of applications grew, the flexibility decreased, as shown in Figure 20.1. The consequent cost of maintenance grew, often to 70% or 80% of the I.S. budget. The core systems on which the business depended were built before good design disciplines were practiced. These systems are complex and often fragile in the sense that an attempt to change them triggers an avalanche of programming problems. The task of replacing them is overwhelming.

Because these systems are also difficult to change, they tend to put the business in a straitjacket. It cannot change its procedures quickly. CEOs and business strategists are repeatedly frustrated because, when they perceive a need for change, the I.S. department says that it cannot be done or cannot be done quickly. As noted in Chapter 1, a DuPont business strategist stated that his top criterion for I.S. was that information systems should never interfere with the business' ability to seize an opportunity. This

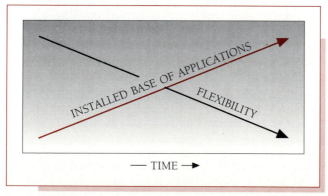

FIGURE 20.1  As the installed base of applications grows and becomes more complex, flexibility decreases. I.S. productivity also decreases because the constant effort to modify existing systems becomes a task of growing difficulty. To combat this problem, RAD techniques must be used within an infrastructure designed for rapid evolution of integrated systems.

criterion can be met only with RAD techniques, and the separately developed systems need to work together.

The solution to these problems is to use RAD techniques within a carefully planned architecture. The design of the architecture is a matter of top strategic importance in I.S. Indeed, it is of top strategic importance to the enterprise as a whole because it directly affects the capability to seize new business opportunities.

# Architecture

The framework within which RAD takes place requires two essential and separate parts, the *technical* architecture and the *information* architecture.

## Technical Architecture

Most large enterprises have installed computers from multiple vendors  These computers have been generally incompatible and have often had incompatible operating systems, database management systems and network architectures. Because of the incompatibilities, applications developed for one machine have not been easily portable to a different machine. Data used on one system cannot be used without conversion by another system. One computer cannot access data on a different computer, and separately developed systems cannot be integrated in ways that are important to the business.

Users cannot access many of the information resources that would help them make better decisions, and the procedures of the enterprise cannot be streamlined in ways that would save money. Flexibility is lost. The systems do interfere with the business' ability to seize important opportunities.

The enterprise of the immediate future is going to need much more integration of its computer systems. There will be powerful workstations or personal computers on every knowledgeworker's desk. Many blue-collar workers will interact with computers.

All of these user systems need to access a diversity of servers and databases. Large enterprises will have many thousands of computers linked by networks—personal computers, departmental computers, mainframe installations and, sometimes, super-computers. Many databases will exist, and much data will be distributed. If there is not smooth connectivity among these systems, the enterprise will be harmed financially.

There are basically two ways to achieve smooth connectivity:

1. Standardize on a proprietary architecture such as that of IBM or DEC.
2. Standardize on Open systems, following international standards where possible.

IBM's Systems Application Architecture (SAA) is designed to achieve connectivity and a common user interface among IBM's major product lines. DEC's Decnet and Application Integration Architecture (AIA) are designed to achieve similar objectives in DEC's world.

All vendors are creating software and hardware for Open systems following the standards listed in Box 20.1. DEC offers a choice of its proprietary architecture or Open systems. IBM also offers a choice, but its main development efforts and sales recommendations are for SAA.

## Box 20.1   Major Open Systems Standards

Operating Systems and Associated Tools

- *UNIX*, an ATT proprietary operating system that has become the basis for Open operating systems from both OSF and UI. (See following items.)
- *OSF, Open Software Foundation*, a consortium of computer vendors, chip suppliers and software developers, with the purpose of specifying a standard UNIX-based operating system, related application environments and user interface standards. (Major members are IBM, Digital, Hewlett-Packard, Hitachi, Nixdorf, Siemens, Phillips and Group Bull.) OSF is a rival to UI.
- *UI, Unix International*, an international nonprofit association of computer vendors, chip suppliers and software developers, with the purpose of establishing UNIX and related standards and directing the development and licensing of UNIX products. (Major members are ATT, Sun, Texas Instruments, Unisys, NCR, Amdahl, Fujitsu and Hewlett-Packard.) UI is a rival to OSF.
- *IEEE 1003.1 POSIX, Portable Operating System Interface for Computer Environments*, specifies basic UNIX services in support of portable applications.
- *X.OPEN*, an international association of I.S. vendors and a user advisory council committed to creating an environment that permits the sharing of portable UNIX-based applications.
- *CAE, Common Application Environment*, a set of actual and de facto standards that X.OPEN has tied together to enable vendors to create portable applications.

User Interface and Graphics

- *X.Windows*, a network-transparent window system that has become the set of graphics primitives behind the user interface provided by OSF and UI.
- *MOTIF*, OSF's user interface specification and implementation—also known as UEC (User Environment Component) (analogous to OpenLook from UI).
- *OpenLook*, UI's user interface specification and implementation (analogous to UEC from OSF).
- *GKS, Graphic Kernel System*, definition of a device-independent set of graphics capabilities that can be called by a program to produce geometric graphics.
- *PHIGS, Programmers' Hierarchical Graphics Standard*, a three-dimensional CAD (Computer-Aided Design) standardized protocol for loading graphics into a workstation, displaying them and manipulating them.

Networking

- ISO's *OSI, Open Systems Interconnection*, a network architecture with international standards and rules for implementing those standards.

Box 20.1    Continued

- *ISDN, Integrated Digital Services Network*, a set of international standards and implementations of a switched digital network over which voice, data and any digitized signal may be sent.
- *IEEE 802*, a family of standards for implementing LANs (Local Area Networks), including Ethernet, Token Bus and Token Ring LANs.
- *FDDI, Fiber Distributed Data Interface*, an IEEE standard for optical-fiber LANs transmitting 100 megabytes per second (Mb/s).
- *TCP/IP Transmission Control Protocol/Interface Protocol*, a family of vendor-independent standards for implementing computer networks.

Messaging and Directory Services

- *CCITT X.400*: a CCITT family of standards for message handling and electronic mail.

- *CCITT X.500*: CCITT standards for directory services.

Documents

- *ODA/ODIF, Office Document Architecture/Office Document Interchange Format*: a set of vendor-independent standards to handle compound documents that might include text, graphics, spreadsheets, photographs and, possibly, audio, video or animation.

Electronic Data Interchange (EDI)
EDI uses the X.400 message-handling standards.

- *ANSI X.12*: recommended standards for business documents in electronic form (so that invoices, purchase orders, etc. can be sent electronically from one computer to another).
- *ISO EDIFACT*: recommended standards for EDI, analogous to the ANSI X.12 standards.

Database Access

- *SQL, Structured Query Language*: an ANSI language for accessing and manipulating data in a relational database.

Many corporations have tried to straddle two architectures that are basically incompatible. This has been better than no architecture but has resulted in problems. DuPont, for example, formulated a strategy in 1979 of having two "preferred vendors"—IBM and DEC. The manufacturing environment used DEC. The general business and sales environment used IBM. The strategy was of value to DuPont, but by 1989 it became clear that the manufacturing systems needed to be integrated with the general business, inventory and order-processing systems. To have a fence separating them, with DEC on one side and IBM on the other, prevented the smooth evolution of systems for optimized production scheduling and for providing customers with the best service. This and other integration problems led DuPont to drive toward an Open Systems Architecture [DUPONT].

An ideal open systems environment would allow components from different vendors to be plugged together like the components of stereo systems. One could then buy interesting new components from any vendor with assurance that they would work with existing systems. In the future, it is likely that there will be many powerful and innovative tools, applications and machines from a variety of vendors. If these follow the standards of Open systems, they can work together.

The computer industry today has been compared to the car industry eighty years ago, when there were no standard controls for driving a car, few traffic laws and no standard road signs. Computing tomorrow needs networks, like our worldwide road systems, and standards so that machines and systems from all vendors can intercommunicate. The standards are complex and difficult to implement. Until they are pervasive and efficient, I.S. executives must set their own rules for connectivity.

## Information Architecture

The components of the technical architecture come from the computer industry vendors; the components of the information architecture are designed inside the enterprise. The methodology primarily used for designing the information architecture is information engineering, described in the following chapter.

**Information engineering** is a top-down approach to information planning and system implementation. It identifies the objects (entities) in an enterprise about which information is stored. It decomposes the functions of the enterprise in processes and builds data models and process models for each business area. These models are stored in a repository with rule-based processing (sometimes referred to as an **encyclopedia**) that checks the integrity of the models, enforcing consistency in their design, as with the coordinating model described in Chapters 12, 13 and 14. The I-CASE tools for design and construction use the same repository. Different systems, designed by different people at different times in different places, all use the same overall data models and process models, and the I-CASE tools ensure that they are consistent. The RAD lifecycle functions within this environment. Separately developed systems can be created rapidly but are consistent with one another.

RAD in an information-engineering environment proceeds somewhat faster than the same development in a non-information-engineering environment because the data model already exists. This is illustrated in Figure 20.2.

FIGURE 20.2  Architectural Framework within Which RAD Takes Place
     To be as effective as possible, Rapid Application Development (RAD) techniques need to fit into a hardware and software architecture designed for connectivity and portability and into an information-engineering framework designed to integrate systems with shared data and reusable designs.

## Integration of Data

When different applications share the same database, the flow of information in an enterprise can be simplified and streamlined. Traditionally, each functional area in an organization has developed its own files and procedures. There has been much redundancy in data. A medium-sized firm might have many departments, each doing its own purchasing, for example. Before computerization, this redundancy did not matter; it was probably the best way to operate. After computerization, however, it did matter.

There might be a dozen sets of incompatible purchasing files. The incompatibility prevented overall management information from being pulled together.

Earlier, data processing installations implemented applications independently of one another. (Many still do.) Integrating the different applications seemed too difficult. Integration grew slowly within departments or functional areas. To achieve integration among functional areas would have required new types of management.

Each functional area had its own procedures, which it understood very well. It did not understand the procedures of other areas. Each kept its own files. The structure of these files was unique to the responsibilities of that area. Unfortunately, data had to pass among the areas, and management data had to be extracted from multiple areas. These data were usually incompatible. Worse, individual areas frequently found the need to change their data structures, and often did so without appreciating the chain reaction of problems caused by the change. Figure 20.3 shows the environment of this data processing style.

When each functional area has its own files and procedures, there is a complex flow of paperwork between the areas to reflect changes in all versions of the data. When this is computerized with separate files, the system is complex and inflexible. Data for different areas are separately designed and not equivalent. Accuracy is lost. Items slip through the cracks in the paperwork processes. Maintenance and change are difficult to accomplish; so the procedures become rigid. Management information spanning the areas cannot be extracted.

In this nonintegrated environment, most communication of changes is done by paperwork, which is error-prone, time-consuming and highly labor-intensive. Suppose, for example, that Engineering prepares an engineering change report and makes multiple copies: one for Production Control, one for Inventory Control, one for Accounting and so on. Production Control concludes that the engineering change requires changes to the product file. It requires a new request for materials to be sent to Inventory Control. Inventory Control must determine the effects of the change on purchasing operations. These affect the costs of raw materials and parts. Inventory Control communicates these to Accounting. Accounting concludes that a change in sales price is necessary to retain profitability and communicates this need to Marketing, and so on.

A much better solution is to have a database shared by the different applications, as shown in Figure 20.4. The different departments are on-line to the same database. The complex flows of paperwork disappear.

When data are consolidated in database systems, data modeling is the key to success. The data structures become more complex, but the data flows are greatly simplified. The data are consistent and accurate. New forms of management information can be extracted quickly with end-user languages. Changes in procedures can be made rapidly with these languages. Paperwork is greatly lessened. The administrative procedures of the organization need to be completely rethought. Fundamentally different analysis and design techniques are needed.

In one factory, more than $1 million worth of work-in-progress was unaccounted for on the shop floor due to items slipping through the cracks in the paperwork process. This unaccountability was a major motivation for the end-user management to create an integrated on-line system, which totally changed the administrative procedures of the factory.

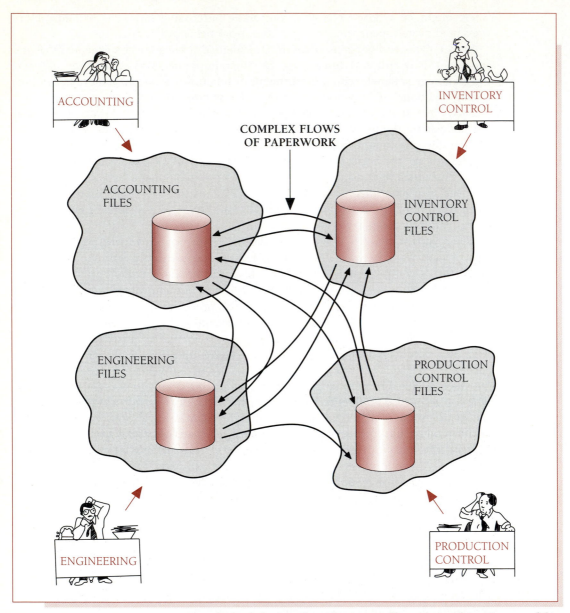

FIGURE 20.3 Traditionally, each functional area has its own files and procedures. Because of this, there is a complex flow of paperwork among the areas to reflect changes in all versions of the data. When this is computerized with separate files, the system is complex and inflexible. Data are separately designed and not equivalent for different areas. Accuracy is lost. Items "slip through the cracks" in the paperwork processes. Maintenance and change are difficult to accomplish; so the procedures become rigid. Management information spanning the areas cannot be extracted.

FIGURE 20.4 When data are consolidated into an integrated database, data modeling is the key to success. The data structures become more complex, but the data flows are greatly simplified. The data are consistent and accurate. New forms of management information can be extracted quickly with fourth-generation languages, and changes in procedures can be made rapidly with these languages. Paperwork is greatly lessened. The administrative procedures of the organization need to be rethought completely. Fundamentally different techniques are needed for analysis and design.

## Data Administration

In the 1970s, the practice of data administration grew up. Some enterprises learned how to do it effectively. They appointed a data administrator at a high level in the I.S. organization. The data administrator's job was to:

- identify the types of data used in an enterprise;
- obtain agreement about their names and definitions;

- design an entity-relationship model with fully normalized data for all (or most) of the data in the enterprise;
- represent the data model in a data dictionary;
- ensure that system builders conform to the data models as far as possible;
- resolve conflicts about incompatible representations of data;
- advise in the selection of database management systems, a goal being to achieve data independence in programs;
- advise in the design of databases that used the data model;
- advise in the selection of database languages, including end-user languages.

By the 1980s, there was much experience with data administration. Books were written on how to succeed in doing it as effectively as possible [MARTIN83]. The practice of data administration steadily broadened into the discipline of information engineering, discussed in the following chapter.

# Reusable Design

One of the biggest payoffs from information engineering can be that it leads to a high level of reusability. Both data and procedure design are reused. Sometimes, procedures are designed in a generic fashion so that they can be adjusted for use in many different systems. Code is generated from the reusable designs.

The fastest application development we have found is that utilizing reusable components. Once the management framework is established, the family of reusable components steadily grows in an enterprise until a comprehensive collection of components exists in the repository. The I-CASE toolset helps the developer find the components for a given system and adjust them as needed. Chapter 22 discusses application-dependent reusability.

# Optimizing the Whole

Individual computer users or system developers do not generally have a high-level view of the needs of the enterprise. They have local problems that have to be solved. RAD techniques are appealing to users who need a computer application quickly. Left to their own devices, they will build a system optimized to their local situation.

Optimizing systems for the enterprise as a whole requires different actions from optimizing systems for individual departments. A system optimized for one department may be suboptimal for the enterprise as a whole.

To achieve global optimization, there needs to be a global architecture. This takes time to create. Once it is created, systems for local use may be more effective and will probably be built faster. A high-level principle of I.S., then, should be to optimize the whole rather than the parts.

Given the specialization necessary in I.S., there is a natural tendency to optimize the parts. Individuals or departments want to select their own personal computer, LAN, fourth-generation language, database system and so on. They want to design their own data structures. Even if they select the best components and do excellent design, the result will not yield the best whole if it is done in isolation. The whole needs seamless interfaces among components built by many different groups. Fortunately, today's I-CASE environment provides tools that help achieve this. The best I-CASE tools were designed for a progression from top-level information strategy planning to detailed business-area modeling to RAD lifecycles for quickly creating systems that fit into the planned framework.

# Quality of Integration

Quality measurements are usually applied to individual systems. A broad quality assessment should be applied to the overall information technology in a corporation:

> *How well can the corporation merge and synthesize information through the management layers of the enterprise and along the value chain of the business?*

A fundamental objective of the I.S. architecture of an enterprise must be to make integration of separately developed systems as easy as possible and, within that integrated environment, to create new systems rapidly. Without this capability, time-critical competitive opportunities will be lost.

# References

[DUPONT] "A New Strategy for the Selection, Assimilation and Utilization of Information Technology for Fibers," Fibers Department, E. I. duPont de Nemours and Company, Inc., Wilmington, Delaware, 1989. This document was given to selected computer vendors and industry leaders to encourage evolution of Open standards and software.

[MARTIN83] James Martin, *Managing the Data Base Environment*, Prentice-Hall, Inc., Englewood Cliffs, New Jersey, 1983 (201–592–2261).

# CHAPTER 21

# Information Engineering

## Introduction

Information Engineering (I.E.) is defined as:

the application of an interlocking set of formal techniques for the planning, analysis, design and construction of information systems on an enterprise-wide basis or across a major sector of the enterprise.

Software engineering applies structured techniques to one project. Information engineering applies structured techniques to the enterprise as a whole or to a large sector of the enterprise. The techniques of information engineering encompass those of software engineering in a modified form [MARTIN90a].

Because an enterprise is very complex, planning, analysis, design and construction cannot be achieved on an enterprisewide basis without automated tools. Information engineering (I.E.) has been defined with reference to automated techniques as follows:

an interlocking set of automated techniques in which enterprise models, data models and process models are built up in a repository and are used to create and maintain data-processing systems.

The Repository of the IBM AD Cycle was designed for this purpose. It was derived from its predecessor, the Encyclopedia of the *IEW* of IBM's business partner, KnowledgeWare [IEW]. This was derived from the same set of ideas, at the same time, as Texas Instruments' *IEF* Encyclopedia [IEF], designed by James Martin Associates.

Information engineering has sometimes been described as an organizationwide set of automated disciplines for getting the *right information* to the *right people* at the *right time*.

Just as software engineering is practiced slightly differently in different organizations, so are there variations on the theme of information engineering. It should not be regarded as one rigid methodology but, rather, like software engineering, as a generic class of methodologies. These variants have in common the characteristics listed in Box 21.1. The methodology must be formal, computerized and accepted throughout that part of the enterprise that practices information engineering.

In traditional data processing, separate systems were built independently. Systems were usually incompatible with one another, had incompatible data and could be linked together only with difficulty. Some enterprises have hundreds of incompatible computer applications, all difficult and expensive to maintain. These systems are often

## Box 21.1 Characteristics of Information Engineering

- I.E. applies structured techniques on an enterprisewide basis, or to a larger sector of an enterprise, rather than on a projectwide basis.
- I.E. progresses in a top-down fashion through the following stages:

  - Enterprise Strategic Systems Planning
  - Enterprise Information Planning
  - Business Area Analysis
  - Individual System Planning
  - System Design
  - Construction
  - Cutover

- As it progresses through these stages, I.E. builds a steadily evolving repository (encyclopedia) of knowledge about the enterprise, its data models, process models and system designs.
- I.E. creates a framework for developing a computerized enterprise. Separately developed systems fit into this framework. Within the framework, systems can be built and modified quickly using RAD.
- The enterprisewide approach makes it possible to achieve coordination among separately built systems and facilitates the maximum use of reusable design and reusable code.
- I.E. involves end users strongly at each of the stages just mentioned.
- I.E. facilitates the long-term *evolution* of systems.
- I.E. identifies how computing can best aid the strategic goals of the enterprise.

unnecessarily redundant and expensive, and the information needed for overall management control cannot be extracted from them.

With information engineering, high-level plans and models are created, and separately built systems link into these plans and models. Particularly important are the data models of business areas. Associated with this is a model of the processes in each area. These models constitute a framework that is represented in a computer. Separately developed systems fit into this framework. Figure 21.1 illustrates the framework.

Strategic planning is applied to the enterprise as a whole. More detailed analysis is applied to separate business areas within the enterprise. RAD techniques are applied to individual systems.

The same I-CASE toolset and repository are used for all of the I.E. stages. Detailed information is stored in the repository about the enterprise strategy and the Business Area Analysis. The latter uses detailed data models and process models. Different teams of system developers, in different places and at different times, will build systems that link into the computerized framework. Their personal computers and I-CASE tools will be on-line to the shared repository, sometimes via telephone lines.

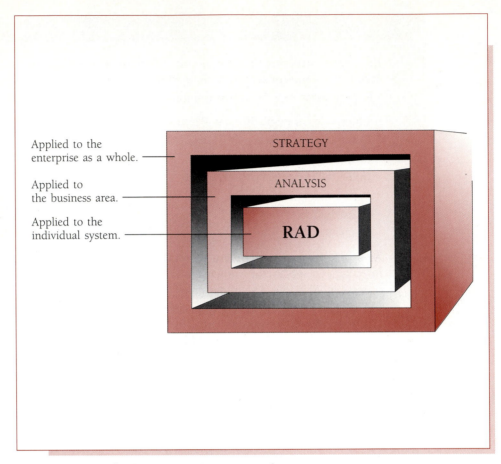

Applied to the
enterprise as a whole.

Applied to
the business area.

Applied to the
individual system.

STRATEGY

ANALYSIS

**RAD**

FIGURE 21.1  Information Engineering Framework

# The I.E. Pyramid

A pyramid, like that presented in Chapter 3, is employed to represent information engineering (Figure 21.2).

## Four Layers

The *top layer* is Information Strategy Planning. The strategic planning of I.S. (Information Systems) should relate strongly to the strategic planning of the business.

At the top there must be awareness of what strategic opportunities exist for making the enterprise more competitive. There must be a strategy relating to future technology and how it could affect the business, its products or services, or its goals and critical success factors. This is important because technology is changing so fast. No enterprise is untouched by the growing power of technology; some organizations and industries will be changed drastically by it.

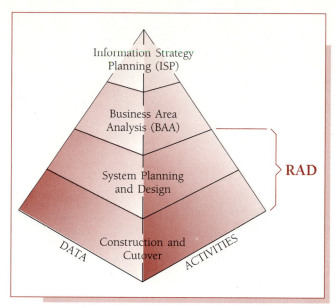

FIGURE 21.2 The Information Engineering Pyramid
The four layers correspond to the three parts of Figure 21.1.

The top-level planning needs to guide and prioritize the expenditures on computing so that the Information Systems (I.S.) department can contribute to the corporate objectives as effectively as possible.

The *second level* relates to a business area. Whereas the top level relates to the enterprise as a whole (or to a major portion of the enterprise), the second level relates to a business area. A model is built of the fundamental data and processes needed to operate the business area, and the need for new or better systems is assessed.

The *third layer* narrows the focus further to a specific system. It employs the RAD Requirements Planning and User Design Phases. Here, a coordinating model may be built, as described in Chapters 12 through 14. This is similar to the model for the business area. If a good business model exists, the coordinating model for the system can be quickly extracted from it and possibly enhanced for the specific system (Figure 21.3).

The *bottom layer* consists of the RAD Construction and Cutover Phases.

## Data and Activities

On the left side of the pyramid are **data**; on the right are **activities**. Both the data and activities progress from a high-level, management-oriented view at the top to a fully detailed implementation at the bottom.

Information engineering itself needs to fit into a higher-level framework, which involves the strategic planning for technology, networks and how they could affect the business (Figure 20.2).

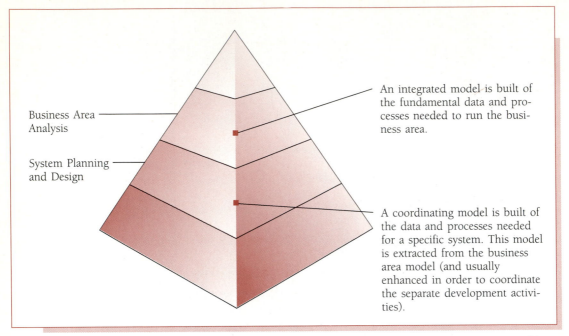

Business Area
Analysis

System Planning
and Design

An integrated model is built of
the fundamental data and processes needed to run the business area.

A coordinating model is built of
the data and processes needed
for a specific system. This model
is extracted from the business
area model (and usually
enhanced in order to coordinate
the separate development activities).

FIGURE 21.3 The combined data-and-process model built during the Business Area Analysis is
similar to the coordinating model of the RAD lifecycle. If the BAA has been done well, the coordinating
model can be extracted from it quickly.

Information engineering applies an engineering-like discipline to all facets and levels
of the pyramid, resulting in timely implementation of high-quality systems grounded
in the business plans of the enterprise. An engineering-like discipline needs formal
techniques. These are implemented with computerized tools, which guide and help
the planners, analysts and implementors. While the tools impose formality on all stages,
they should be designed to maximize the speed with which systems can be built and
the ease with which they can be modified.

The RAD toolset and the I.E. toolset are the same.

## Importance of Automated Tools

The disciplines of information engineering are not practical without automated tools.

A large amount of knowledge about the enterprise and its systems is collected over
an extended period and is constantly updated. This requires a computerized repository
with extensive capability for cross-checking and coordinating the knowledge.

It is important that there be a seamless interface between the tools used for each
part of the pyramid. The information collected at the higher stages should be used
automatically as the analysts and implementors progress to the more detailed stages.
The repository and knowledge coordinator of the I-CASE toolset coordinate the activities at all levels of the pyramid (Figure 21.4).

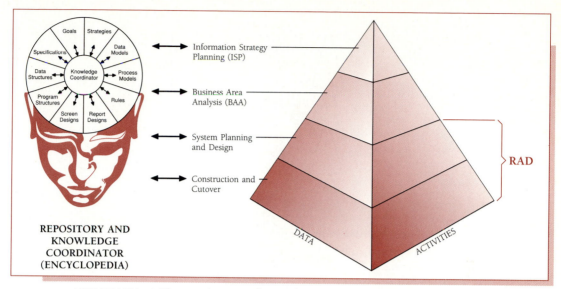

FIGURE 21.4 The repository coordinates the activities at all levels of the pyramid.

# Divide and Conquer

Rebuilding all of the data-processing resources that an enterprise requires is an excessively complex undertaking. An objective of information engineering is to make the separate systems relate to one another in an adequate fashion. This does not happen when there is no coordination of the separate development activities. Information engineering, therefore, starts with a top management view of the enterprise and progresses downward into greater detail (Figure 21.5).

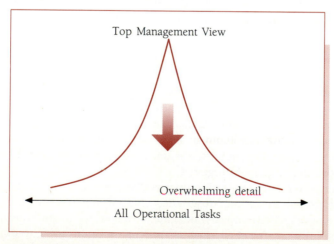

FIGURE 21.5 Top-Down System Design

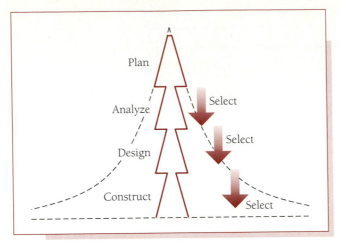

FIGURE 21.6 Divide-and-Conquer Approach to Manageable System Development

As the progression into detail occurs, selections must be made concerning which business areas should be analyzed and which systems should be designed. A divide-and-conquer approach is used (Figure 21.6).

Information engineering begins at the top of an enterprise by conducting an Information Strategy Plan. From this plan, a business area is selected for analysis. A portion of the business area is selected for detailed system design.

If the system is complex, it is divided into subsystems, each of which can be built by one SWAT Team. Figure 21.7 shows these four levels.

## Top Management

It is the job of every top executive today to build a computerized enterprise, and a computerized enterprise cannot be created effectively without information engineering.

To succeed fully, information engineering needs the commitment of top management; it is a corporatewide activity that needs firm direction from the top. The methodology relates to top management planning.

It would be unthinkable to build a space shuttle without an overall plan. Once the overall plan exists, however, separate teams can go to work on the components. Corporate information systems development is not much less complex than building a space shuttle; yet, in most corporations, it is done without an overall plan of sufficient detail to make the components fit together.

The overall architect of the shuttle cannot conceivably specify the detailed design of the rockets, electronics or other subsystems. These details have to be developed by different teams working autonomously. Imagine, however, what would happen if these teams enthusiastically created their own subsystems without any coordination from the top. The data-processing world is full of inspired subsystem builders who want to

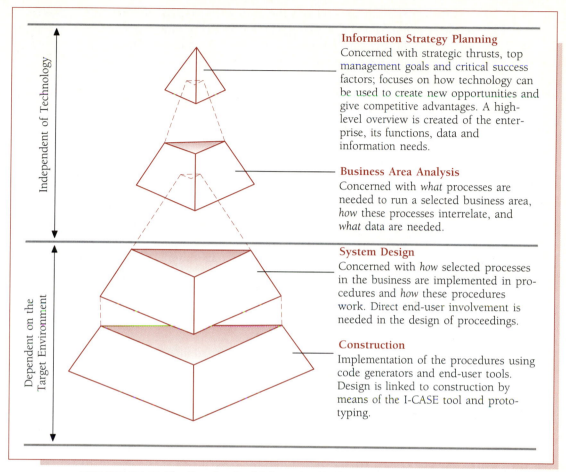

FIGURE 21.7 The Four Levels of Information Engineering

**Information Strategy Planning**
Concerned with strategic thrusts, top management goals and critical success factors; focuses on how technology can be used to create new opportunities and give competitive advantages. A high-level overview is created of the enterprise, its functions, data and information needs.

**Business Area Analysis**
Concerned with *what* processes are needed to run a selected business area, *how* these processes interrelate, and *what* data are needed.

**System Design**
Concerned with *how* selected processes in the business are implemented in procedures and *how* these procedures work. Direct end-user involvement is needed in the design of proceedings.

**Construction**
Implementation of the procedures using code generators and end-user tools. Design is linked to construction by means of the I-CASE tool and prototyping.

*Independent of Technology*

*Dependent on the Target Environment*

be left alone. Their numbers are rapidly increasing as small computers proliferate and end users learn to acquire their own facilities. There is all the difference in the world between a corporation with computing that fits into an overall architecture and a corporation with incompatible systems.

Systems must be integrated throughout the value chain in an enterprise.

# Three Phases

As shown in Figure 21.1, information engineering has three distinct phases:

1. *Strategy—applied to the enterprise as a whole.*

The *strategy* level takes a corporatewide viewpoint. It is concerned with how systems will be integrated.

How will they be integrated along the value chain so that information can pass from the sales planning and order entry systems to the production planning and control systems; to the inventory control and purchasing systems; to the delivery and billing systems; and to the financial control systems?

How will systems be integrated vertically so that information passes from the low-level, operational systems up to the tactical planning systems and up to the executive information systems?

The *strategy* level is concerned with creating a systems architecture so that changes in procedures can be designed and implemented quickly while preserving the integration along the value chain. It is concerned with the ability to seize new business opportunities quickly, even though they need massive computing support. It is concerned with how to use computing to make the enterprise more competitive.

The *strategy* level should be of direct interest to top management and needs top-management involvement. An ISP (Information Strategy Planning) study will have been conducted. This has taken from three to nine months in most enterprises. It is accomplished by a small team that studies the enterprise and interviews its management. Information Strategy Planning requires commitment from top management. The results are interesting and stimulating to top management because they are concerned with how technology can be used as a weapon against competition. Diagrammed representations of the enterprise are created, which challenge management to think about its structure, its goals, the information needed and the factors for success. The Information Strategy Planning process often results in identification of organizational and operational problems and solutions.

2. *Analysis—applied to the business area.*

The *analysis* level examines a business area. It is done separately for each business area, but the results are integrated into the overall repository, which has knowledge of the ISP and of the analysis done for other business areas. The knowledge coordinator of the I-CASE toolset helps integrate the models created for separate business areas.

A BAA (Business Area Analysis) study is conducted separately for each business area. A typical Business Area Analysis takes about six months, depending on the breadth of the area selected. Several such studies for different business areas may be done by different teams simultaneously.

Business Area Analysis does not attempt to design systems; it merely attempts to understand and model the processes and data required to run the business area. It is concerned with what processes are needed to run the business area, how these processes interrelate and what data are needed. A fully normalized data model is built. The process model is mapped against the data model.

The BAA model is similar to the coordinating model for system implementation but is broader in scope. If it is well designed, the core of the coordinating model for implementation is extracted from it.

3. *RAD—applied to the individual system.*

All three phases of I.E. should use the same integrated toolset.

# System Creation

Systems are created within the framework of the Information Strategy Planning (ISP) and the Business Area Analysis (BAA), using the information that they store in the repository, according to the RAD lifecycle described in this book. Systems can be implemented without a BAA, and a BAA can be done without an ISP; however, this results in incompatible systems. The enterprise needs integration of systems across its value chain.

It takes time to perform the ISP and the set of BAAs that an enterprise needs. However, if they have been done well, the lifecycle for system creation is shorter and less costly, especially if the ISP and BAA concentrated on reusable design. More important, the separately developed systems will work together.

Information engineering steadily builds a formal body of knowledge about the enterprise, its data, processes and systems. This knowledge resides in the repository and becomes a steadily more valuable resource for planning and building the computer systems of the enterprise.

# Stage 1: Information Strategy Planning (ISP)

An enterprise normally begins the information engineering process by developing an **information strategy plan**. This plan is concerned with the goals and targets of the business and with how technology can be used to create new opportunities or competitive advantages. Technological opportunities are identified. Critical success factors for the enterprise are decomposed into critical success factors for the divisions and then related to the motivations of executives.

The information strategy plan maps the basic functions of the enterprise and produces a high-level model of the enterprise, its departments, its functions and its data. It creates an overview entity-relationship diagram and maps the entity-types to the functions of the enterprise.

## Two Types of Studies at the Top
## of the I.E. Pyramid

At the top of the information engineering pyramid, two types of studies are carried out (Figure 21.8):

The first of these is an analysis of *how the enterprise functions*:

> A determination of the strategic opportunities, goals, critical success factors and information needs of different parts of the enterprise; a determination of how new technologies might be used to meet the goals better and create new business opportunities.

The second is a management-oriented study—*how technology might help*. This is a management-oriented study of how, with the help of technology, the enterprise might be made to function better:

> The creation of an overview model of the enterprise and the splitting of this into areas appropriate for Business Area Analysis.

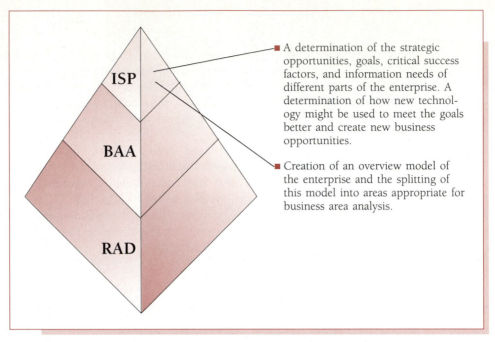

A determination of the strategic opportunities, goals, critical success factors, and information needs of different parts of the enterprise. A determination of how new technology might be used to meet the goals better and create new business opportunities.

Creation of an overview model of the enterprise and the splitting of this model into areas appropriate for business area analysis.

FIGURE 21.8  At the top of the pyramid, two types of studies are carried out.

## Box 21.2    Objectives of Information Strategy Planning

This set of objectives is normally of great interest to top management.

- Investigate how better use of technology can enable an enterprise to gain a competitive advantage.
- Establish goals and critical success factors for the enterprise.
- Use critical success factor analysis for steering the enterprise to enable it to better achieve its goals.
- Determine what information can enable management to perform its work better.
- Prioritize the building of information systems in terms of their overall effect on the bottom line.
- Create an overview model of the enterprise, its processes and information.
- Subdivide the overview model into business areas ready for Business Area Analysis (level 2 of the pyramid).
- Determine which business areas to analyze first.
- Enable top management to view its enterprise in terms of goals, functions, information, critical success factors and organizational structure.

These studies can be thought of independently, although they are often done by the same team at the same time. Doing them concurrently enables information for both to be gathered in the same management interviews, thereby minimizing the management time involved. The studies are strongly related. As the overview of the enterprise and its goals emerge, ways of restructuring the enterprise that enable it to meet its goals better may become apparent.

It is important that Information Strategy Planning be understandable to both top management and end users. It should be reviewed and updated continually as part of the business planning cycle. The results should be recorded and maintained continually in the repository.

The upper part of Box 21.3 contains the steps that relate to business strategy; the lower part relates to the technical I.E. infrastructure. Different enterprises use somewhat different steps; so, flexibility is needed in the software tools used for Information Strategy Planning.

Information Strategy Planning has proven to be a valuable technique even when the other phases of information engineering have not been completed. With Information Strategy Planning, top management's attention is focused on technological opportunities and on what is happening within the enterprise. In fact, it has often resulted in organizational restructuring.

Most businesses have a business plan that is updated periodically and is concerned with setting targets, goals and strategies. The planning process may analyze the trends in the industry, technology and competition. Top management planning sessions

---

### Box 21.3    Steps in Information Strategy Planning

*Business-Oriented*

- Computerize the organization chart of the enterprise.
- Identify the organization's goals, targets and strategies.
- Examine technological trends and how they might be used by the enterprise to create new opportunities or competitive advantages.
- Determine critical success factors for the enterprise and break these down into critical success factors throughout the organization chart.
- Interview key executives to determine problems, opportunities and information needs.
- Record all of this information in the repository of the I-CASE tool.

*Technology-Oriented*

- Develop an enterprise model showing the basic functions of the enterprise on a function decomposition diagram.
- Develop an overview entity-relationship model.
- Analyze the functions and entities with a matrix tool and determine business areas (ready for level 2 of the pyramid: Business Area Analysis).
- Set priorities for information system development.

should use the information in the repository and encourage regular review of the goals and critical success factors. The hierarchy of critical success factors should be related to the motivation of employees via management by objectives, thereby establishing a mechanism for steering the entire organization toward the achievement of its goals.

Business strategy planning, then, forms a basic input to the top level of the pyramid. Figure 21.9 shows some of the computerized charts used in Information Strategy Planning (ISP).

The time taken to do an ISP has typically ranged from 3 to 12 months. In one large oil company of great complexity, it took 9 months and involved nine high-level executives on a part-time basis. If an ISP takes longer than 12 months to do, something is wrong. Six months is a reasonable target in a medium-sized enterprise. It happens faster when the person responsible for it knows exactly what to do or has professional consulting help. He needs computerized tools and needs to solicit the help of key top executives. This is likely to happen only if the top executive is committed to the project and understands its potential benefits.

An ISP is not frozen when it is finished. It produces a collection of knowledge that is valuable in running the enterprise, setting its goals and determining how to meet those goals. Information from this part of the repository is valuable at top-level planning sessions. Some corporations review critical success factors at Board meetings. The section of the repository storing the ISP should be made accessible and updatable on an ongoing basis. Like the rest of the repository, it is a valuable corporate asset.

# Stage 2: Business Area Analysis (BAA)

Top top-level planning determines which business areas should be the first targets for Business Area Analysis. The overall objective of this second stage of information engineering is to understand what processes and data are necessary to make the enterprise work and to determine how these processes and data interrelate.

As the system is developed, the functions identified in the first stage are decomposed into processes; a process dependency diagram is drawn, showing how the processes interrelate; and a matrix is built to show what data entities are used, updated and created through what processes. Figure 21.10 shows the types of diagrams used.

Again, the information represented in diagrams on the workstation screen is stored and updated in the repository. The repository is designed to help in the collection of data and in the application of integrity controls. When Stage 2 is complete, a structured graphic description, designed with an interlocking mesh of cross-checks, exists for the enterprise and its organization, goals, data and processes.

A typical Business Area Analysis takes three to six months. The procedure is made practical by dividing the business into areas sufficiently small that they can be analyzed in this time. Earlier attempts to do normalized data models of entire enterprises have sometimes failed because of the magnitude of the task. It is better to do one area at a time, choosing the more important areas first.

Business Area Analysis should be independent of the technology the enterprise might use. Technology is changing fast. This level of the pyramid is concerned with the fundamental data needed and the fundamental processes that the enterprise must carry out. The data will still be needed and the processes must still be performed even if great technological change occurs. Level 2 of the pyramid is concerned with what is needed, and level 3 is concerned with how systems are implemented.

Business Area Analysis should also be independent of current systems. The old systems in use in an enterprise often constrain it to use inefficient procedures with batch processing, dumb terminals, unnecessary keypunching, redundancy, too much paperwork and the bureaucracy that goes with paperwork. Entirely different procedures may be designed if there can be a personal computer on every knowledgeworker's desk, on line to databases anywhere in the enterprise. Fundamental analysis of what processes are needed often causes a fundamental rethinking of what is the best way to implement them.

Business Area Analysis (BAA) has particular characteristics:

- It is conducted separately for each business area.
- It creates a detailed data model for the business area.
- It creates a detailed process model and links it to the data model.
- The results are recorded and maintained in the repository.
- It requires intensive user involvement.
- It remains independent of technology.
- It remains independent of current systems and procedures.
- It often causes a rethinking of systems and procedures.
- It identifies areas for system design.

The information collected in the repository in the two top stages of information engineering gives an overview that can be analyzed and cross-checked in many ways. A variety of rules are applied by the knowledge coordinator of the I-CASE toolset, as they are in the RAD process. The information can be collected at different times and can be assembled in different ways. Steadily, the computerized knowledge of the enterprise becomes more complete.

# Joint Requirements Planning (JRP)

JAD-like workshops with users and executives, prepared and moderated by a RAD Workshop Leader, are appropriate at all levels of I.S. development. At the highest level, top management participation is needed in Information Strategy Planning. At the Business Area Analysis level, data modeling and process modeling need to be done jointly with the users. At the third level, Joint Application Design (JAD) can greatly improve the design process. At the bottom layer, end users may employ report generators or user-oriented fourth-generation languages. On the other hand, construction may be done entirely by I.S. professionals—but in an iterative fashion in which the users interact with the system as it evolves.

Sometimes a rough Business Area Analysis (BAA) has been done. The JAD session reveals its imprecision, and so the data models and process models are adjusted as the JAD progresses. This is more likely to happen to the process models than to a fully normalized data model. Often, the flow of work among processes is redesigned during the JRP or JAD sessions. Sometimes the flow of work between departments should be changed. Today's networks make databases accessible from every desk, and this often changes the places where decisions ought to be made, sometimes causing middle-management functions to be bypassed or whole business areas to be restructured. If

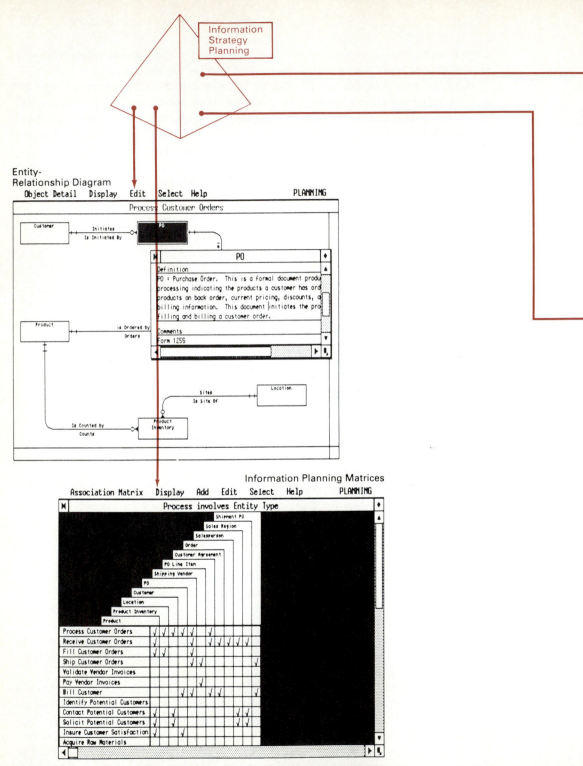

FIGURE 21.9 Some of the Computerized Charts Used in Strategy Planning

Organization Chart

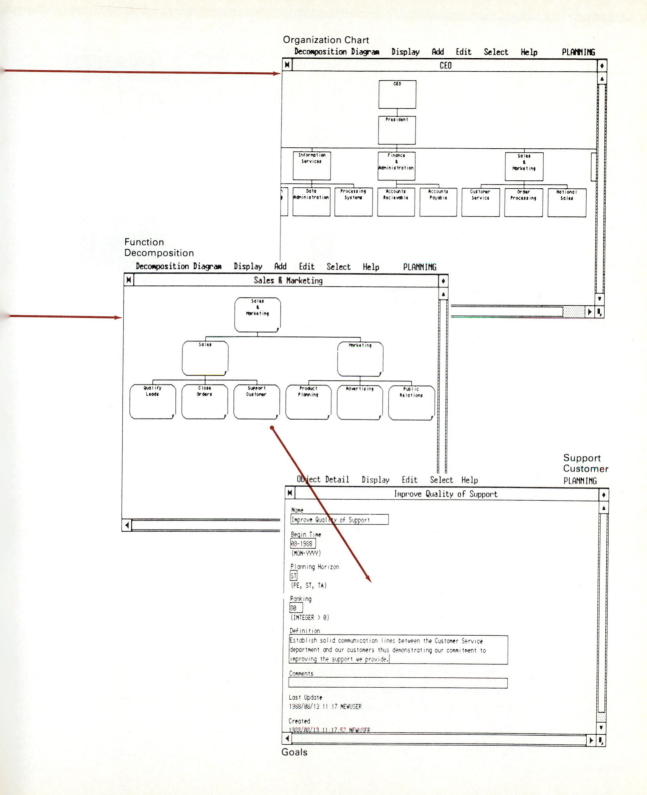

Function
Decomposition

Support
Customer

Goals

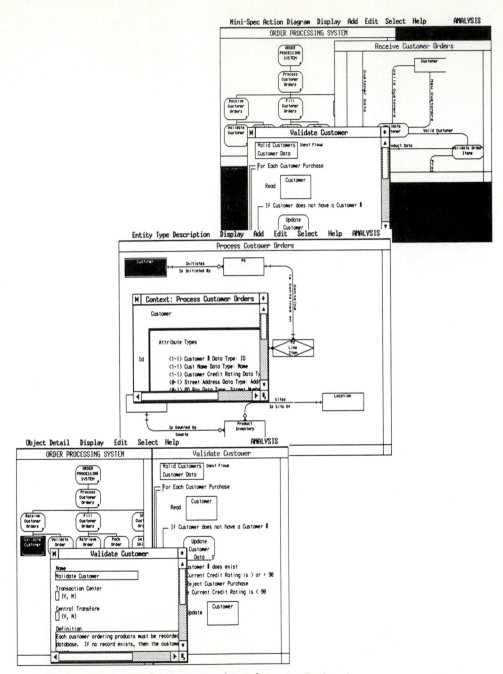

FIGURE 21.10 Types of Diagrams Used in Information Engineering

redesign on this scale is needed, it is necessary that the managers who can put such changes into effect be present at the session.

Such workshops may, thus, cut across the organization from high-level managers to clerks. It can be very constructive to have this range of players present in a workshop, using precise design diagrams and having the goal of achieving consensus on new procedures.

Where high-level restructuring is under discussion, the joint session may remain entirely at the Business Area Analysis level and not drop down to design issues. Screen design and detailed data flow may be saved for a later JAD session. The diagrams representing the restructuring are stored in the repository.

JAD-like sessions can, thus, take different forms and operate at different levels. Many such sessions have been used only for requirements definition and external design. Some companies have also used such workshops for strategic planning and some for internal design. With a repository-based I-CASE tool, workshops at higher levels may feed workshops at lower levels.

JRP (Joint Requirements Planning) has also been used for application package selection and review, package modification and maintenance planning. With systems that cover many locations, the JRP or JAD documentation developed at one location has then been used at other locations. Distant locations may extract the information from the repository, via a network, for local use.

## I. E.  Methodology

Doing an ISP and a BAA well is a complex procedure. As with RAD, the procedure should have a computerized representation of the methodology. The RAD methodology should be integrated with the information engineering methodology, and the whole family of procedures should be represented in a hyperdocument that can be customized to the toolset used and to the circumstances in question.

See Methodology Charts 21–1 and 21–2, extracts from such a hyperdocument.

To practice the upper layers of information engineering, much more detail is needed than is given in this book. The reader is referred to the author's trilogy on information engineering [MARTIN90a] and to its associated methodology [JMA].

## Long-Term Investment

Before information engineering is established, project managers or analysts may regard the planning and modeling phases as being too time-consuming. It typically takes six months to do an ISP study and six months to do a Business Area Analysis. Multiple BAAs are needed for the different business areas, and two or three years may elapse before a complete set of data models and process models exists for the enterprise.

In an organization with no data administration, an appealing dream is that the development of new systems could be put on hold while corporate data models and process models are established. In reality, this is entirely impractical. New systems are being developed while the data models are evolving. Models for the new systems can be created quickly as part of their development, but they may become incompatible with the eventual corporate data models.

To lessen this problem, the data for the new systems should be fully normalized so that they can be converted easily to new, fully normalized data models when necessary. Before cutover, the new systems should be made as compatible as possible with the emerging corporate data models and process models.

The planning and modeling stages of the I.E. pyramid are a long-term investment, but this should not delay the achievement of benefits from I.E. Systems should be built with RAD techniques using a coordinating model, with the intent that this model should eventually be integrated into the overall I.E. modeling. If the data are correctly normalized, this integration is made easier. The RAD toolset should be the same as the I.E. toolset, and the systems should be designed so that they can be retrofitted to the I.E. data models and process models as they evolve.

# Financial Justification

It is usually easy to justify the benefits of rapid development. The benefits from the slower process of building the I.E. infrastructure are less obvious. If thought out carefully, they can be very large. Box 21.4 summarizes the benefits of I.E.

Many of the benefits of information engineering are long-term. It takes years before

---

**Box 21.4    The Payoff from Information Engineering**

*Short-Term Payoff*

- Management's needs for information are identified and fulfilled rapidly where possible, for example, with executive information systems or spreadsheet software.
- Attention is focused in an organized fashion on goals, problems and critical success factors. Some immediate actions can be taken relating to these. Critical success factor measures are monitored. That which is monitored tends to improve.
- Certain information systems can be built quickly, using RAD techniques.

*Long-Term Payoff*

- Strategic uses of technology are identified, leading to the building of strategic information systems. This may have a very high payoff.
- Management's understanding of the enterprise is improved, often leading to enterprise reorganization. This is also important but impossible to quantify in advance.
- The same data are represented in the same way in different systems, leading to integration among systems where needed. Without this integration, some important information needs cannot be met. I.E. avoids a Tower of Babel in computerized data.
- Common usage of database systems leads to simpler, less expensive data flows (Figures 20.3 and 20.4).

- Analysis of reusable objects and processes across the enterprise leads to faster, lower-cost development.
- Business Area Analysis leads to faster development and better-thought-out systems.
- The costs of maintenance are lowered dramatically.
- An evolutionary growth of systems is made practical. Systems can steadily grow in comprehensiveness, becoming uniquely valuable to the enterprise.

the full effects are obtained from data modeling, process modeling and the analysis of reusable objects. Eventually these activities enable an enterprise to have better information, better-integrated systems, faster development and much lower maintenance costs. Often the most important benefit is that claimed by Westpac [HORBATIUK]:

*"We can seize new business opportunities faster than our competition."*

An investment program is needed to fund information engineering because it is not part of any one user area. Enterprisewide data modeling, process modeling and identification of reusable objects and processes take time and money.

To convince high management to spend money on long-term benefits, it is desirable to create a business plan, much as an entrepreneurial company creates a business plan in order to obtain an investment from venture capitalists. Venture capitalists do not expect immediate payback from their investments, but they do expect that the long-term net return will be higher than that of other investments to justify the risks involved. The justification of information engineering needs estimates of the long-term net return on investment.

I.E. provides some benefits that affect the I.S. operations and another class of benefits from the effects on business operations. It is desirable to identify all achievable benefits when establishing the justification for I.E. The costs and benefits should be estimated over a five-year period because of the long-term payoff.

Figure 21.11 gives an example of this for a corporation with a gross revenue of $1 billion. This corporation has communications and office automation expenditures. Its development backlog is three years and it has a large invisible backlog. The total I.S. staff is 270 people, of whom 170 work on maintenance and enhancement of existing systems. Figure 21.11 shows the current expenditures, the estimated expenditures on I.E. Some of the benefits would have been achieved by RAD techniques without I.E.

It is assumed that all software and workbench computers are purchased. Most of the expenditure for tools therefore occurs in years 1 and 2. There are also training and consulting costs in years 1 and 2. To offset the startup costs, there is an emphasis on obtaining benefits *quickly* by identifying important management information needs and responding to them, and by using automated design and coding extensively before the corporate data modeling and process modeling are completed. There are business benefits from better information and faster development in the first year.

The reduction in system development costs due to data models and reusable design and code is substantial but takes some time to achieve. The reduction in maintenance costs is larger and takes even longer to achieve.

It is important that Information Strategy Planning be understandable to both top management and end users. It should be reviewed and updated continually as part of

## Current Revenue and I.S. Costs

| | |
|---|---|
| Gross revenue | 1,000,000 |
| Total I.S. expenditure (including telecommunications and office automation) | 50,000 |
| Total I.S. staff and support: 260 people | 20,000 |
| Total I.S. staff working on maintenance and enhancement: 170 people | 12,000 |
| Current mainframe backlog: 3 years (not including large invisible backlog) | |

## Estimated Cost of Information Engineering

| | Year 1 | Year 2 | Year 3 | Year 4 | Year 5 |
|---|---|---|---|---|---|
| Staff doing ISP | 300 | 50 | 50 | 50 | 50 |
| Staff doing BAA | 300 | 600 | 600 | 200 | 150 |
| Tools for ISP and BAA | 200 | 50 | 50 | 50 | 50 |
| Tools for design and coding | 800 | 800 | 600 | 400 | 400 |
| Training costs | 120 | 200 | 100 | 50 | 50 |
| Consulting costs | 200 | 100 | — | — | — |
| | 1920 | 1800 | 1400 | 750 | 700 |

## I.S. Benefits from Information Engineering

| | | | | | |
|---|---|---|---|---|---|
| Increased productivity in system design and construction | | | | | |
|   i. Due to automated tools | 500 | 2000 | 3000 | 3000 | 3000 |
|   ii. Due to existence of data models | | 500 | 1000 | 1000 | |
|   iii. Due to reusable design and code | | | 2000 | 3000 | 3000 |
| Reduction in maintenance costs | | | 2000 | 4000 | 6000 |
| | 500 | 2500 | 8000 | 11000 | 13000 |

## Business Benefits from Information Engineering

| | Year 1 | Year 2 | Year 3 | Year 4 | Year 5 |
|---|---|---|---|---|---|
| Administrative savings from better-integrated systems | | | 500 | 1000 | 2000 |
| Business benefits from better-quality systems | | | 500 | 1000 | 1000 |
| Business benefits from better information to end users | 200 | 1000 | 2000 | 3000 | 4000 |
| Business benefits from faster development of procedures | 200 | 500 | 1000 | 2000 | 2000 |
| Benefits from strategic business opportunities (which might be much higher) | | 500 | 2000 | 4000 | 4000 |
| | 400 | 2000 | 6000 | 11000 | 13000 |
| **Net benefits (loss)** | (1020) | 2700 | 12600 | 21250 | 25300 |
| **Percent of current gross revenue** | (0.1%) | 0.3% | 1.3% | 2.1% | 2.5% |

FIGURE 21.11: Example of the Benefits of RAD in an I.E. Environment

the business planning cycle. The results should be recorded and maintained continually in the repository.

Substantial re-engineering of old systems has been done to achieve this. An evolutionary lifecycle is emphasized in which systems can be modified and added to quickly and easily by changing design screens and regenerating code.

The corporation steadily acquires better-quality systems and better-integrated systems. The benefits of this start to build up in year 3. One of the benefits is simpler administration procedures with fewer staff.

A major effect of information engineering is faster development and modification of procedures. In some organizations the business effect of this has been substantial. It becomes larger in the fourth and fifth years because the data models are complete and some of the old systems have been re-engineered by then. It is difficult to estimate the business benefits quantitatively.

Still more difficult to estimate are the benefits from identifying and building strategic or mission-critical systems. The best examples of such systems have had a major impact on corporate growth and profits. The estimate in Figure 21.11 is 0.4 percent of gross revenue, and it may be possible to do much better than this.

There is much uncertainty in estimates of business effects such as those in Figure 21.11, as indeed there are in most business plans requesting venture capital. A venture capitalist monitors his investment to try to make the estimated benefits achievable. Similarly, the progress of information engineering should be monitored from the business point of view to try to maximize its benefits. Where benefits a fraction of those in Figure 21.11 can be achieved, no enterprise of any size can afford not to do information engineering.

The example in Figure 21.11 is discussed in more detail in the author's trilogy on information engineering [MARTIN90b].

# References

[HORBATIUK] Peter Horbatiuk, Chief of Research and Development, Westpac Banking Corp., Sydney, Australia, 1989.

[IEF] *IEF*, Information Engineering Facility, I-CASE toolset covering all phases of information engineering, from Texas Instruments, Plano, Texas. In the *IEF*, the repository is referred to as the encyclopedia.

[IEW] *IEW*, Information Engineering Workbench, repository-based I-CASE toolset covering all phases of the lifecycle, from KnowledgeWare, Inc., Atlanta, Georgia.

[JMA] *IE Expert*, (Information Engineering Expert) a detailed methodology in computerized form, available from James Martin Associates, Reston, Virginia (703–620–9504), and London.

[MARTIN90a] James Martin, *Information Engineering* (a trilogy), Prentice-Hall, Inc., Englewood Cliffs, New Jersey, 1990 (201–592–2261).

[MARTIN90b] James Martin, *Information Engineering*, Book I: *Introduction*, Ch. 7, "How Do You Justify the Expenditure on Information Engineering?" Prentice-Hall, Inc., Englewood Cliffs, New Jersey, 1990 (201–592–2261).

# CHAPTER 22

# Analysis for Reusability

We have emphasized that one of the most powerful RAD techniques is the construction of systems from components that already exist. A system may be constructed from reusable building blocks, or an existing design may be modified to create a new application. Chapter 15 described different patterns of reusability.

To maximize the value of reusability, large-scale planning is needed. Reusable design should be a major goal of information engineering. In most large enterprises, many systems exist that do almost the same functions. There are multiple order entry systems, multiple inventory control systems, and so on. These systems have been separately designed and separately coded. They have to be separately maintained, which is expensive.

Analysis for reusability establishes the common procedures and subprocedures that are needed across an enterprise. An attempt is made to create these from a single set of basic designs rather than from multiple sets of designs. The basic designs are kept in an I-CASE repository and can be easily adapted to the needs of separate systems.

## Object-Oriented Analysis

Analysis for reusability starts with data modeling. The objects (entities) about which data are stored are identified. An entity-relationship diagram is created. The data associated with the object-type are identified and represented in a normalized data model.

Certain behavior is associated with an object-type. That behavior needs to be programmed regardless of the department in which the object-type is being used or in what application it is participating. There is certain information associated with a bank customer, for example, and certain validations that are applied, whether the application is a loan application, savings, checking, mortgage, credit card, investment or whatever. Validity checks, editing, user dialog, security checks, backup, accuracy checks, auditing and so on can be designed once and used repeatedly.

Object-oriented analysis identifies the object-types in an enterprise, as well as their properties. Object-subtypes *inherit* the properties of their parents. Behavior is associated with the object-types where the object will exhibit that behavior regardless of the specific application.

Some processing routines are associated not with one object-type but with an association between two or more object-types (e.g., when a CUSTOMER places an ORDER, when a PASSENGER makes or changes a RESERVATION or when a WAREHOUSE ships a DELIVERY). Certain reports must be printed, certain information must be filed or a given user dialog must occur; certain validation checks must be applied, and an audit trail must be maintained, regardless of the location, department, type of warehouse or type of application. Procedures should be designed and programmed that are reusable across the enterprise (rather than being designed and programmed uniquely for each project).

> An objective of information engineering is to identify commonality in both data and processes and, consequently, to minimize redundant system development work.

Data modeling makes it clear that the same object-types are used in numerous applications. Whenever they are used, there may be certain routines that will be invoked, such as computing derived attributes, applying integrity checks or creating summary data. A corporation may have many factories that, to a large extent, have the same object-types.

Many of the data-processing procedures can be the same from one factory to another; some will be entirely different. The accounting and reporting should be the same in each factory so that higher-level management can make comparisons. Dialogs programmed for data entry, updating, reporting and so on should be common across applications and locations. HELP panels should be common. When process decomposition is done and processes are mapped against object-types, commonality among processes can be discovered. Certain screen designs, user dialogs, validation routines and so on may be needed whenever an object-type is employed.

Often, the processing done on an object or the dialog used is not identical from one process to another but is sufficiently close that the same code or dialog can be used after minor modifications. The end user would like the different applications to look similar and have a common dialog style in order to increase familiarity and minimize the training needs. It is desirable to identify *similar* processes as well as *identical* processes in order to minimize the subsequent design, coding and training requirements. The repository should be able to indicate blocks that are similar.

Data modeling and process modeling should be applied to one business area at a time; otherwise, they become unwieldy, and the team bogs down. Nevertheless, there will be object-types that are used outside that business area, and associated with these will be processes that are usable outside that business area. The *enterprisewide* object-types are discovered (at a summary level) during the ISP study and are recorded in the repository. During Business Area Analysis, the object-types and processes that appear to have applicability beyond that business area should be marked in the repository. When other business areas are analyzed, the common object-types and processes will be identified in detail so that procedures can be designed to span business areas.

When a reusable process block or procedure is decomposed, it should be decomposed only once, as shown in Figure 22.1.

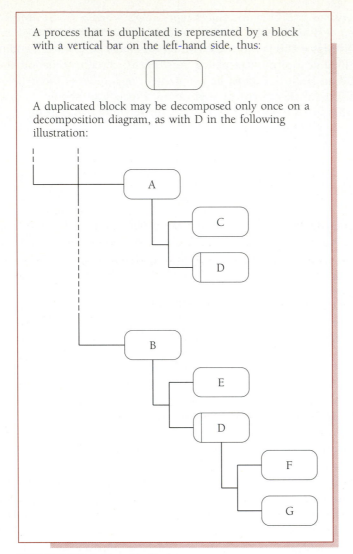

A process that is duplicated is represented by a block with a vertical bar on the left-hand side, thus:

A duplicated block may be decomposed only once on a decomposition diagram, as with D in the following illustration:

FIGURE 22. 1  Reusable Design
   Block D is decomposed only once.

# Standards for Application Design

As noted in Chapter 15, *standards* for application design extend the practicality of reusable design. These include standards established in the I.S. organization for access to networks, access to databases, standard document formats such as those defined in EDI standards, standard user dialogs, IBM's SAA (Systems Application Architecture) and so on. There should be standard templates, dialog structures, sign-on procedures, and so on. Common use of such standards throughout an I.S. organization give an increase in development productivity.

# Westpac

The most spectacular examples of reusable design and code are generally found in corporations that have done information engineering with a repository-based I-CASE toolset. Westpac, a large multinational bank based in Sydney, Australia, set out to rebuild its entire collection of core I.S. systems. It spent about $100 million over a five-year period doing this. The result is referred to as Core Systems 1990 (CS90). CS90 is designed to maximize reusability [TRUEBLUE88].

Westpac's business goals were to:

- Create an environment that enabled the bank to create new services or respond to new business opportunities significantly faster than its competition. This became particularly important when Australia deregulated its financial activities.
- Undercut its competition by being able to build new services at a lower cost.
- Streamline the bank's operations, making them less expensive.
- Provide better service to customers by, for example, giving customized loans as opposed to off-the-shelf packages.

Peter Street, the executive implementing the project, commented to the press: "If you are building a product from reusable components that have already been tested, it can be done very quickly. It's just a matter of producing a variation on a theme.... Westpac will be able to deliver financial products much faster and cheaper than its competition" [STREET].

Peter Horbatiuk, Chief of Research and Development for Westpac, commented that Westpac was able to rebuild all of its core systems with 55 programs, whereas with conventional systems analysis, 1780 programs would have been needed—an extraordinary example of reusability [HORBATIUK]. The 55 programs were in the form of designs that were input to a code generator; minor variations on each design enabled multiple transaction types to be generated.

Westpac used object-oriented design and proceeded through a number of steps:

- The analysts identified all of the object-types (entity-types) involved in the banking process. They found that there were 19 high-level object-types, with many subtypes of each (a total of 130 subtypes). A typical high-level object-type is an ACCOUNT. All ACCOUNTs have certain properties. Subtypes of this object-type are specific types of account.
- They normalized the data associated with each object-type and subtype (the subtype inheriting the properties of its parent).
- For each object-type and subtype, the analysts identified processes that would be applicable, regardless of the application in which the object-type was used (again, the subtypes inheriting the behavior of their parents).
- For each object-type, they identified the possible transitions in its data and pre- and postconditions for the transition.

All of this information was carefully validated with the users and stored in the repository of the KnowledgeWare *IEW* toolset. The same toolset was used for detailed design of the procedures [ALI].

# Software Factory

The reader might imagine a furniture factory evolving through three generations. In the first generation, there are craftsmen with chisels and planes making the furniture by hand. This is like programmers writing code. The craftsmen insist that making furniture is an art (or, at least, a craft), not an engineering discipline.

The next generation acquires power tools. This is like the acquisition of I-CASE tools, which generate code from computer-aided design. When the new skills have been learned, productivity increases substantially.

The third generation reorganizes the factory so that furniture can be made from standard parts. One machine makes table legs, another makes tabletops of different sizes, and so on. Customer orders are fulfilled by assembling prebuilt components. Some customization, such as the use of different stains and finishes, is done for each customer. The factory can now respond to large orders quickly and profitably. This is like a development organization building applications with many transaction types out of reusable designs. Some customization is done, but the application can be delivered quickly. The development organization building systems from reusable components might be referred to as a **software factory**.

I.S. systems are much more complex than furniture. There are many object-types, and they exhibit complex behavior. Computerized help is needed in finding the reusable components and making sure they fit into the overall design with no interface problems.

Nevertheless, it seems likely that we will have three generations of application building:

- Build each application by hand (line-by-line programming).
- Build each application with power tools.
- Assemble applications from components that can be easily modified to fit the users' needs.

# Customized Applications

The concept of reusable design had been criticized because it might impose too much conformity on I.S. products. In practice, reusability—employed appropriately—has had the opposite effect. It enables applications to be customized quickly out of components that can be adapted to individual needs.

Alan Hohne, Westpac's General Manager of Information Systems, has drawn an analogy using a historic comment by Henry Ford. Hohne commented, "CS90 will allow us to respond much more quickly to market segments or individuals. The *previous* systems are like saying you can have a Model-T any color you like *as long as it's black*" [HOHNE89]. With CS90, a customer applying for a loan, for example, can have a package specially tailored to his needs. Bank managers "will build their own products with the aid of computerized advice" [HOHNE89]. They assemble the components that enable them to adapt the application to the customer needs. Alan Hohne comments, "In a deregulated market, you must have a much wider variety of products in order to satisfy the needs of customers. That normally spells death to a large generalist. . . . We have set out to have the flexibility and responsiveness of the small niche player while being a large generalist" [HOHNE89].

*This achievement of flexibility and responsiveness within a large-scale framework should be one of the key goals of I.S. organizations.* It is one of the next megatrends.

## Human Coordination

As reusability becomes a way of life in an enterprise, the more it spreads, the more applications can be built from reusable components. A system designer requiring a program component must first find out whether a similar component exists that he can adapt. If so, he uses it; if not, he writes a component in such a way that it might be reused in the future by some other analyst. *All* development, thus, relates either to reuse of an existing component or creation of a component with future reuse potential.

After this pattern of development has been in place for some years, a high level of reusability is achieved. One of the characteristics of reusability is that the facilities for reusability take time to build up, but they eventually enable an enterprise to create most applications rapidly. NETRON/CAP supplies a library of about 50 frames that handle most of the generic I/O associated with screens, reports and databases [BASSETT].

Human coordination of the reusable components stored in the repository is necessary. A development team might create a new component or might improve upon an existing component. The reusability coordinator must decide whether to make the new component generally available in the repository. It is important that the central repository of reusable components does not become a mess. The components should be carefully cataloged, most of them relating to object-types. A knowledgeable human decision is needed regarding when to store a new version of a component and whether the old version must be retained.

## All Levels of the Pyramid

Reusable design is valuable at all levels of the information-engineering pyramid [MARTIN90].

At all levels of the information-engineering pyramid, there should be a search for commonality. Commonality of entity-types is usually obvious in the building of the entity-relationship model. There should be identification of common functions at the *planning* level, common processes at the *analysis* level and common procedures, screens, dialogs and subroutines at the *design* level. The commonality of design modules will lead to commonality of code modules.

The data models and process models result not only in great commonality of design and code but also in much better management information because all the relevant information about a customer or financial situation can be identified and retrieved. The uniformity of reporting across a complex organization improves the capability of taking effective management action.

In order to find commonality, a central repository is essential.

Analysts in different places use a shared repository that steadily accumulates knowledge of the enterprise. When an analyst is planning a procedure that uses an entity-type, the repository will inform him what other procedures use that entity-type so that he can employ common modules where possible. Usually, a central group reporting to a Chief Information Engineer (or equivalent) helps ensure that common modules are used where possible.

Where a code generator is driven from a design workbench, the primary reusability emphasis may be on reusable design. Design modules that are reusable are stored in the repository and modified if necessary before code is generated.

Methodology Chart 22 summarizes a procedure for identifying reusable modules. This needs to be part of both the BAA (Business Area Analysis) and system design procedures.

# Reusable Data Models

At the second level of the pyramid, industry data models and process models could be the starting point. A large amount of experience has now been gained in creating data models. Consultants who have done data modeling in different corporations of the same type usually comment that data models for the same area are remarkably similar. If the rules of full normalization are followed, the data model for one airline is very similar to the data model for another airline; the data model for one electric utility is very similar to that of another electric utility. It *usually* takes the data modeling team months to create an overall entity model or a detailed model for a given business area. If, instead of working from scratch, the developers started with a graphically displayed industry model that is easy to modify, the time taken to build the required model would be much less, and often there would be fewer items omitted or misunderstood. The quality of the resulting model is likely to be higher.

A large corporation often has many factories or local operations. A data model created for one of them can be transferred to the others. At each site, local variations may be made in the model. Starting from the same data model at each site gives a higher degree of uniformity of data and object-oriented (entity-oriented) procedures among the sites. This makes it easier to transfer procedure designs and programs later from one site to others. In some corporations, a policy exists for achieving standardization of data among sites. The ability of the I-CASE toolset to compare separate data models and display the differences with highlighting or color makes it easy to examine incompatibilities and see whether they can be corrected.

It is desirable, where possible, to have the same data formats in different companies for such systems as invoices, payments, receipts, orders and acknowledgments. If this compatibility exists, a computer generating these documents in one company can transmit them electronically to the computer of another company, thus avoiding the need for printing, mailing and keypunching (with its attendant errors).

Standards bodies have created standards for certain electronic documents (the ANSI X.12 and the ISO EDIFACT Recommendations for EDI—Electronic Data Interchange). Various industries such as banking, trucking and airlines have their own standard formats for intercorporate computer communications. The U.S. Department of Defense has recommended certain standard formats to its suppliers. Standards exist for CAD

(Computer-Aided Design) descriptions of parts, and these descriptions are sent from one company to another. All of these standards need to be represented with I-CASE techniques and should reside in the repositories of I-CASE tools.

## Process Models

While data models are very similar among similar corporations, process models have more differences. It is often the differences in processes or procedures that give corporations their uniqueness, sales arguments and competitive advantages. Whereas data models can be designed to be stable, processes and procedures in a vigorous, healthy corporation tend to be dynamic and changing.

Having said that, we must note that the similarities are still striking. There are several types of invoicing procedures, mail order procedures, accounting procedures and so on. Where one particular type is used, it is similar in most enterprises. The easy way to design it is to start with a graphic representation of a system or subsystem that has already been built, used and debugged, and then to adjust it as appropriate.

Taking an object-oriented approach to process modeling results in many processes being associated with an entity-type or entity-relationship that is independent of a specific application or department. These entity-related processes (and procedures) are transferable from one enterprise to another where the entity-type itself is transferable.

## Procedures

At the second level of the pyramid, a **data model** is a valuable reusable component in its own right. A **process model** is useful in its own right when linked to a data model.

As we drop down to the third level of the pyramid, we are concerned with representing procedures in sufficient detail that code can be generated. The I-CASE tool makes the multiple aspects of the procedure visible: its data flow diagram, its decomposition diagram, its data model, its action diagram and, possibly, other more detailed or precise representations. These different views are linked together in an I-CASE representation, which also links them to the models of Business Area Analysis. The toolset applies rules for validation and coordination. The designer has multiple windows that can display the different types of detail.

## Reusable Code

At the bottom level of the pyramid, we are concerned with reusable code.

Since the beginning of computing, attempts have been made to employ reusable code. Long ago, there were macroinstructions, subroutines and application packages. Libraries of these were established. Control mechanisms were made standard and usable by most programs—input/output control systems, file and database management systems, teleprocessing control programs, operating systems, and so on. Later, application generators of various types were used—first, simple ones such as report generators and screen painters, then more complex ones for generating complete applications.

Subroutines were the first labor-saving device invented by programmers. A subroutine for computing Sin $x$ was written in 1944 for the Mark I calculator. Most installations have a large library of useful subroutines, and this facilitates the programming of standard applications. When a subroutine is written to handle a general case, it employs parameters—values that can be changed from one subroutine call to another.

The use of subroutines (and reusable code in general) is a good idea, and there has been a long-standing desire in computer science to build and use libraries of standard software components. Unfortunately, there has been only limited success in doing this. Most programmers still hand-code procedures that could, in principle, come from a library.

Although most programmers make limited use of reusable code, it is interesting to study how the very best professional programmers do their work. The best programmers produce more than ten times the work of average programmers. A few genius programmers who specialize in specific areas such as compiler writing achieve astonishingly high productivity. They do so by having their own private, often informal, library of structures and code they can quickly adapt to a new set of requirements. They can quickly find the designs or code they need from what, to other people, might seem to be a large, disorganized mass of knowledge. They use their own computerized library of structures and subroutines but also have in their heads many professional heuristics, which enable them to find what they need from their libraries, modify it and use memorized structures and techniques for building the components.

The challenge of reusable code is to find out how the techniques of the one-person genius can be made usable with automated assistance by all programmers.

## Incompatible Data

It is likely that more and more application packages will be used in corporations. The growth of the software-package industry will be helped by I-CASE tools that make packages easier to change.

A new application package is likely to have data that are incompatible with the data models that already exist in a corporation. The package itself may have (certainly should have) a data model. The I-CASE tool should enable an analyst to compare data models and identify where they differ. It is often necessary for incompatible data models and their applications to exist together. There may be automatic conversion of data items or normalized data records as data pass from one compatibility zone to another.

## References

[ALI] Interview with Steve Alworth, Westpac Banking Corp., Sydney, Australia, in the James Martin videotape tutorial on Rapid Application Development from Applied Learning, Inc., Naperville, Illinois (708–369–3000).

[BASSETT] Communication from Paul Bassett, Vice President, Netron, Inc., (owned by NOMA), 99 St. Regis Crescent North, Downsview, Ontario M3J 1Y9, Canada (416–636–8333; fax: -4847).

[HOHNE89] Alan Hohne, quoted in "Technology," *Triple A*, Sydney, Australia, March 1989.

[HORBATIUK] Peter Horbatiuk, Chief of Research and Development, Westpac Banking Corp., Sydney, Australia, 1989.

[MARTIN90] James Martin, *Information Engineering* (a trilogy), Prentice-Hall, Inc., Englewood Cliffs, New Jersey, 1990 (201–592–2261).

[STREET] Peter Street, Westpac Banking Corp., Sydney, Australia, describing the impact of Westpac's redesign of its core systems (CS 90).

[TRUEBLUE88] "Case Study—Westpac," *True Blue Magazine*, Australia, December 1988.

# CHAPTER 23

# Rapid Maintenance and Evolution

## I-CASE Maintenance

We want not only rapid development of systems; we want rapid evolution. In systems developed by traditional manual techniques, maintenance is a major problem. Systems are often difficult and time-consuming to change. After being modified multiple times, they often become fragile, and even minor changes result in bugs and breakdowns.

A goal of RAD methodologies should be to produce systems that are quick and easy to change and that can evolve continuously. Maintenance should not be done by digging around in spaghetti code but by modification of the design on the screen of an I-CASE tool, followed by regeneration of code. In this way, changes can be made simply and quickly.

Traditional maintenance is often made more difficult by inadequate documentation. When maintenance programmers make changes, they often neglect to make corresponding changes to the documentation. The documentation then no longer reflects the program. With I-CASE tools, the contents of the repository are the documentation. Paper documentation can be generated from the repository when required. When changes are made to the design, the repository is automatically updated.

The use of I-CASE tools prevents a spaghetti-code mess like that of the past and produces clearly structured engineering with relatively fast and easy techniques for maintenance. The documentation automatically reflects any modifications in code.

## Cost Reductions

Once applications are built or rebuilt in I-CASE form, they are relatively inexpensive to maintain. Some organizations have succeeded in cutting their maintenance budget drastically by the use of I-CASE tools. In development done at DuPont using the techniques described in Chapter 11, the maintenance costs have been reduced by 75% to 90% [DUPONTa]. Barclays Bank in London plans to cut its maintenance from 70% of its I.S. budget to 20%, using the T.I. Information Engineering Facility (IEF). Texas Instruments has commented that its own systems built with the IEF have a maintenance lifecycle one fifth the elapsed time of that for systems built with traditional techniques [WHITE89].

Reducing the costs of maintenance is vitally important. Most systems cost more money in maintenance than in their original development. Old systems tend to become increasingly expensive to maintain. New systems are often more complex (Figure 1.7), and increasing complexity, unless carefully controlled, brings increasing maintenance cost.

One of America's best telephone switches ran into so many software maintenance difficulties that its cost of maintenance exceeded $1 million *per day*. The switch would never have been built if that figure could have be forecast [WILLET73].

A study by the U.S. Air Force [LT88] estimated that, if maintenance productivity cannot be changed, by the year 2000 one quarter of the draft-age population of the U.S. will be required to maintain its software!

A staggering amount of money is being spent on the maintenance of old software. It is estimated that the worldwide salary and overhead expenses for programmers and analysts working on maintenance are over $100 billion [IBM85].

As high as the potential cost savings are, the most important reason for RAD-style maintenance is that systems can be modified quickly so that they can be adapted rapidly as the business needs change.

# Rebuilding Old Systems

The existing systems in most enterprises have large quantities of old code, most of which was hand-built in an unstructured fashion. Their data have usually not been modeled, and little or no attempt has been made to achieve data compatibility between different systems. As well as *file systems*, there are often old *database systems* that were designed before today's principles of good database design were understood. The data are unnormalized and unrelated to the data administration process. Many of these old systems are fragile and expensive to maintain.

Traditional maintenance of programs is an unsatisfactory and expensive process. It has been likened to attempting to repair a wooden boat while it is at sea. New planks can be replaced only by using existing planks for support. The process must be done in small steps; otherwise, the boat will sink. After much maintenance of this type has been done, the boat becomes fragile. Attempts to change its design at sea are frustrated because no plans accurately reflect its current design. Sooner or later, the boat must be brought to a shipyard and rebuilt.

Old systems need to be rebuilt using I-CASE tools and information-engineering principles. They cannot all be rebuilt quickly because this would involve too much work. The best that can be hoped for is a steady, one-at-a-time *migration* of the old systems into the cleanly engineered form.

Virtually all large enterprises today have old systems that seriously inhibit flexibility. These systems were built before modern design and development techniques were understood. Ongoing attempts to adapt them to urgent needs have resulted in patches and quick fixes, which make the systems even more undisciplined and difficult to maintain. The task of replacing these systems is so overwhelming that many corporations avoid the issue. But, sooner or later, they will *have* to be replaced. The question is not *if* they will be replaced but *when* and *how*.

# A Technology for Maintenance

The basic technology that underlies expert systems is uniquely suited to address the maintenance issue. This basic technology, *object-oriented* programming and *rule-based* programming, has two key characteristics. First, it provides a very expressive language for representing business functionality. This means that each business policy can be represented in a single, executable software statement. Second, each policy or software statement is independently a true statement.

These two factors combine to provide a significant maintainability benefit: *When a business policy changes, the software statement that represents that policy can be easily identified and modified.* There is no need to be concerned with how the change impacts the rest of the program since there is no complex flow of control structure that inter-relates the various software statements.

At Ford Motor Company, expert systems technology has been applied to address the maintenance issue [BUNNEY90]. An existing COBOL application was reimplemented in an expert systems shell, *ART-IM* from Inference, strictly for its maintenance benefits. This application audits warranty claims submitted by Ford dealerships throughout the world. It is a typical high-volume business application—not the kind of application usually associated with expert systems.

From conception to production, the conversion from COBOL to *ART-IM* took less than six months. The conversion process simply involved replacing most of the Procedure Division of the COBOL program with *ART-IM* rules. The expert system is embedded in a COBOL program in a standard MVS jobstream and runs daily on an IBM mainframe computer.

Another benefit Ford has seen is the ability to get end users more directly involved in maintenance of the application. Because of the simplicity of the rule language, they can read and understand the logic driving the processing—something not achievable with COBOL.

The ability to make application changes ten-fold faster—and more reliably—has prompted Ford to begin applying the technology to other applications, both new and existing.

# Fundamental Retooling

The core applications in most large enterprises need not minor modifications but fundamental retooling. They are clumsy, obsolete, out of phase with modern technology and do not meet the information needs of the business.

As we commented in Chapter 1, sometimes an industry needs fundamental retooling because its factories are obsolete. Failure to retool eventually puts corporations out of business. Today, the information factory in most corporations needs fundamental retooling. There is a formidable list of reasons why old systems need to be rebuilt. Box 23.1 lists them.

Some corporations have bitten the bullet and set out to rebuild their core applications entirely. This is expensive but is done in order to achieve major competitive

## Box 23.1    Reasons Old Systems Need to Be Rebuilt

*Restructuring the Applications*

- Evolution from batch to on-line processing.
- Use of a shared data (database) environment to streamline the flow of information, reduce redundancy and minimize the human processing steps.
- Use of systems with distributed processing and distributed data.
- Use of personal computers.
- Use of workgroup or departmental computing.
- Evolution to cooperative processing, in which an application uses software on the desktop machine as well as software that is in a mainframe or server machine, for example, IBM's SAA (Systems Application Architecture).
- Evolution to EDI (Electronic Data Interchange).
- Evolution of on-line links to trading partners.
- Integration of separate systems so that information can be passed up and down the management hierarchy and from one system to another in the value chain.

*Upgrading the Code and Tools*

- Evolution to structured design of all applications in an I-CASE environment.
- Evolution to well-designed, normalized data structures.
- Evolution to a repository-based information-engineering environment.
- Evolution to a RAD environment.
- Evolution to reusable design (and code generation), based on object-oriented analysis and an I-CASE repository.
- Evolution to end-user database access with fourth-generation languages.
- Evolution to application standards for screen design and usability.
- Evolution to user dialogs that employ modern, easy-to-use human factoring (such as that of the Macintosh, IBM's CUA—*Common User Access*, Unix International's *OpenLook* and the Open Software Foundation's *User Environment Component*).
- Evolution to application architectures such as IBM's SAA (Systems Application Architecture) or DEC's AIA (Application Integration Architecture).
- Evolution to software following international standards for connectivity, interoperability and user interfaces.
- The rebuilding of the core systems so that they have low maintenance costs and can be quickly adapted to changing business needs.
- The rebuilding of systems so that they can *evolve* to a high level of complexity, where appropriate, in a highly structured fashion.

Box 23. 1    Continued

*Upgrading Technology*

- Evolution from dumb terminals to personal computers.
- Evolution from mainframe-terminal environments to workstation-server environments.
- Evolution of LAN environments (Local Area Networking), including new-generation LANs.
- Evolution of Open networking, giving across-the-board interconnectivity.
- Evolution of wideband networks (including T1, T3 and ISDN).
- Evolution of intercorporate networks.
- Use of relational databases rather than pointer-structured databases such as IMS or IDMS. In some cases, relational database machines are used, giving high performance with large databases, large throughputs or multiway (e.g., 10-way) JOINS.
- Use of SQL for accessing data, and distributed data.
  (ISO 9075 and ANSI X.3.135 standards)
- Evolution of distributed database management.
- Evolution to an integrated office environment.
- Evolution of image processing.
- Evolution toward Open architectures (e.g., UNIX environments).

*Adaptation of the Enterprise*

- Education and positioning of knowledgeworkers to take advantage of powerful workstation environments.
- Education and restructuring of management to take full advantage of innovative systems.
- Positioning the enterprise to take maximum advantage of rapid technological change.
- Restructuring of departments and restructuring of the enterprise to take advantage of networks, relational databases, distributed data, EDI, decision-support environments, expert systems, integrated office facilities, powerful desktop machines, LAN environments, wideband networking and intercorporate networks.

advantages. One such corporation is Westpac, whose drive to rebuild its core systems (CS90) was described in Chapter 21.

An effort to achieve the types of restructuring listed in Box 23.1 needs major top-level strategic planning. It is a vital issue for top management. As with any long-term plan, the expected costs and benefits need to be estimated.

The benefits of restructuring include:

- long-term cost savings in I.S. development;
- long-term cost savings in maintenance;
- extended business life of new systems;
- improved knowledgeworker productivity;
- reduced knowledgeworker headcount;
- improved decision-making;
- business advantages from being able to build mission-critical systems quickly;
- business advantages from globalization and value chain integration;
- business advantages from quick responses to competitive situations.

The Fibers Department of DuPont put together a strategy for doing some of the restructuring indicated in Box 23.1 and projected that, although the restructuring costs were high, the projected saving in the 1990s would exceed $1 billion [DUPONTb].

# Evolutionary Growth of Systems

The most impressive of complex systems are not created with a single design and implementation. They evolve, being improved in many steps at different times and places.

A system designer looks at the works of nature with awe. A cheetah watching for prey at dawn suddenly races through scrub at 70 miles per hour with astonishing grace to kill a leaping antelope. A hummingbird, which engineers once "proved" was an aerodynamic impossibility, flits from flower to flower and then migrates to South America. The human brain, full of diabolical schemes and wonderful poetry, has proved to be far beyond our most ambitious artificial-intelligence techniques. These are not systems for which God wrote specifications; they are systems that *evolved* over millions of years.

The future will bring impressive software and corporate computer systems, and these will also be *grown* over many years, with many people and organizations adding to them. It is difficult or impossible to *grow* software that is a mess. To achieve long-term evolution of software, we need structured models of data and structured models of processes. Designs too complex for one human to know in detail must be represented in an orderly fashion in a repository so that many people in many places can add to the design. The design needs standards and reusable components and an architecture that facilitates the incremental addition of new functions. So that executives can control the behavior of computers that automatically place orders, select suppliers, make trades and so on, the behavior should be expressible in rules and diagrams that executives understand.

When development tools are designed to enable systems to evolve easily, the development lifecycle truly becomes a cycle, as shown in Figure 23.1.

With repository-based I-CASE tools, maintenance in the future will probably consist mainly of adding features to systems or changing them in an evolutionary fashion.

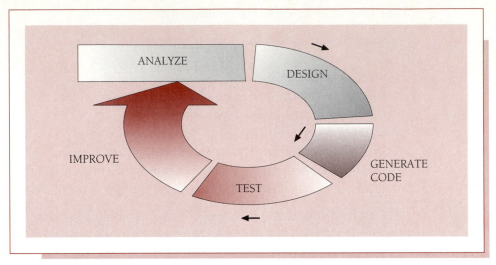

FIGURE 23.1  Evolutionary Lifecycle

Applications will grow and grow, their details represented in the repository—until, in some cases, they become uniquely valuable corporate resources that competitors could not replicate quickly.

In order to achieve long-term evolutionary growth, various facilities are desirable, as listed in Box 23.2.

## Box 23.2   Facilities Needed for the Evolutionary Growth of Systems

- An application architecture designed to facilitate change over a long period.
- Representation of the architecture and design in an I-CASE repository that facilitates input by different people in different places at different times.
- An I-CASE environment that enforces fully structured design and uses a comprehensive rule-based facility to ensure complete coordination of different parts of the design, guaranteeing overall design integrity among inputs from different developers.
- Code generated directly from the I-CASE design. A toolset that gives the fastest possible cycle of *design*, *code generation*, *testing* and *modification*.
- An information-engineering environment with:
     -an entity-relationship data model;
     -normalized data;
     -a detailed process model;
     -object-oriented design showing reusable processes;
     -full integration of the data model and process model.
- An I-CASE toolset that permits easy modification of the system within the information-engineering framework.

- Standards and templates for user-dialog design.
- Application standards such as IBM's SAA (Systems Application Architecture), DEC's AIA (Application Integration Architecture) or others.
- Reusable modules in an I-CASE repository in an object-oriented information-engineering environment.
- Design that is expressible in diagrams (and possibly rules) that business executives and end users understand.
- Design that is logically independent of the technology environment so that it remains valid when the technology (hardware or software) changes and, hence, can be used to generate code for environments of different technology.

# References

[BUNNEY90] W. Bunney, S. Curson, J. Lemmer, J. Scollard, J. DeSantis and R. Smith, "Ford Motor Company's Expert System for Claims Authorization and Processing: ESCAPE," *Proceedings*, Second Annual Conference on Innovative Applications of Artificial Intelligence, May 1990.

[DUPONTa] Information from Mr. Scott Shultz, Manager, Information Engineering, E. I. DuPont de Nemours and Company, Inc., Wilmington, Delaware.

[DUPONTb] "A New Strategy for the Selection, Assimilation and Utilization of Information Technology for Fibers," Fibers Department, E. I. DuPont de Nemours and Company, Inc., Wilmington, Delaware, 1989. This document was given to selected computer vendors and industry leaders to encourage evolution of Open standards and software.

[IBM85] In 1985, IBM estimated that the worldwide salary and overhead expenses for programmers and analysts was $139 billion. Since then, this expenditure has been rising at about 10% per year. More than half of this is spent on maintenance, including enhancements to existing code.

[LT88] From a paper by Eric Bush, "A Case for Existing Systems," Language Technology, Inc., Salem, Massachusetts, 1988.

[WHITE89] Information from John White, Vice-President of I.S., Texas Instruments, Dallas, Texas, 1989.

[WILLET73] G. W. Willet et al., *ISO Productivity Study*, ATT Long Lines, Kansas City, Missouri, April 1973.

# CHAPTER 24

# Migration and Reverse Engineering

## Introduction

The eventual goal of information engineering is that all systems are built with an I.E. toolset and have the following properties:

- All data are represented in normalized data models in the repository.
- All procedures are mapped in the repository.
- All programs are generated or built in a fully structured fashion using the repository's contents.
- Procedures can be built quickly with RAD techniques.
- Applications can be modified quickly and easily using the repository-based design workbench and code generator.

The enterprise then has clean engineering of its computer applications and can evolve its procedures rapidly to meet changing needs.

Some information engineers dream of working in a new corporation that does not yet have any data processing. Its data and procedures could be modeled correctly and cleanly from the start. Top-down plans could be implemented without problems caused by existing systems. Unfortunately, most information engineers have to live with the sins of the past.

Old systems need to be rebuilt, for all the reasons discussed in the previous chapter, using I-CASE tools with a repository and information-engineering principles. They cannot all be rebuilt quickly because this would involve too much work. The best that can be hoped for is a steady, one-at-a-time *migration* of the old systems into the cleanly engineered form.

In corporations that have successfully implemented I-CASE methodologies, there are two development worlds. The I-CASE world has the ability to evolve systems, constantly improving their design and regenerating code. They may evolve within an I.E. framework with stable data models. The systems are cleanly engineered and easy to change. However, there is also an underworld of old systems, badly structured with manual code and manual design and no data models. In many corporations, more programmers work in this underworld, maintaining bad-quality code, than work in the I-CASE world (the upper half of Figure 24.1).

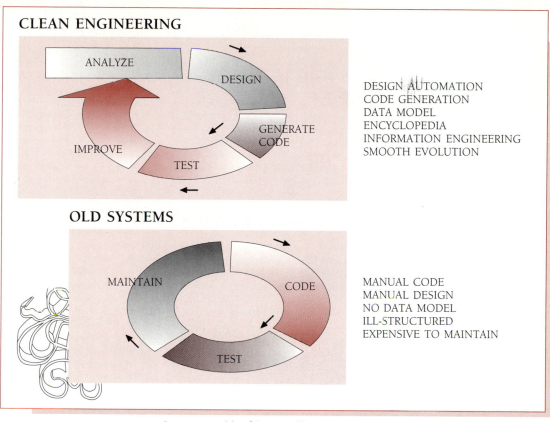

FIGURE 24.1 The Two Worlds of Systems Development

The problem is rather like the slum-clearance problem in a city. A city might have a new center, elegant architecture, a well-thought-out street plan with pedestrian malls and parks, but still have large, abominable areas of slums and old, decrepit buildings. There is no easy solution to the slum clearance problem. The best that can be hoped for is a steady migration from the slums and their replacement with well-planned facilities.

Many corporations have attempted a major conversion from a file system to a database system and have failed, abandoning the attempt before it was completed. Often, the reason for this is that it takes much more manpower than is anticipated; so much has to be reprogrammed. Often the attempt to convert is killed by the persons who control the I.S. finances. The conversion process itself creates no new applications. I.S. user management perceives a large amount of effort and expense with nothing to show for it. There is a long and serious application backlog. Management says, "Why are you spending all of this time on conversion when we desperately need you to be creating new application systems? Get on with something more useful!" In one organization after another, the attempt to make a major conversion has failed. This has been true in some of the most prestigious data-processing organizations.

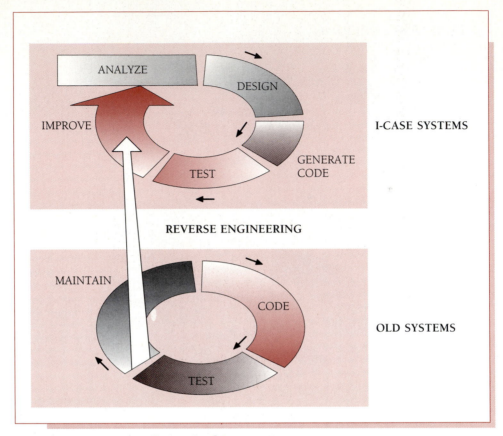

FIGURE 24.2  A Reverse-Engineering Step

Fortunately, new toolsets are becoming available to facilitate the complex process of rebuilding systems. The old system is *reverse-engineered* into a cleanly structured form, using tools that automate the tedious parts of this process. The new structure is adapted so that it uses the I.E. data models. The programs are captured and represented in an I-CASE format so that they can then be modified as required using I-CASE tools.

Figure 24.2 shows a reverse-engineering step. The code of the old system is restructured with an automated tool and entered into an I-CASE tool so that it can be analyzed and redesigned to become part of the I-CASE evolutionary lifecycle.

In connection with this, three terms are used:

- **Restructuring:** conversion (with an automated tool) of unstructured code into fully structured code.
- **Reverse Engineering:** conversion of unstructured code into structured code and entry of this (automatically if possible) into an I-CASE tool with which it can be improved or redesigned.
- **Re-Engineering:** modification of the design of a system, adding functionality where required, and (automated) production of code for the improved system.

If reverse engineering is done as shown in Figure 24.2, old systems can be rebuilt as evolutionary systems, as shown in the upper part of the diagram. Eventually, the messy underworld of Figure 24.2 should disappear.

# Four Approaches

There are basically four approaches to the I.S. slum clearance problem:

1. *Do not convert.* Allow applications to continue their existence unconverted but, when necessary, *build a bridge* to the systems that use the I.E. data models and process models.
2. *Restructure.* Restructure the messy applications quickly (preferably with automated tools), but do not rebuild them to conform to the I.E. world. The slum areas are improved but not rebuilt to be part of the new planning. In many cases, it is necessary to *build a bridge* to the I.E. world.
3. *Rebuild.* Reverse-engineer the old applications to conform to the I.E. data models and process models. This is like redesigning and rebuilding areas of the city.
4. *Scrap them and start afresh.* It is sometimes cheaper to re-create new sets of applications and scrap the old ones, like bulldozing away the city slums.

In large I.E. installations, a mix of these approaches will probably be used.

An old system exists; how should you decide whether to convert it?

There are two questions that should be asked.

- First, *does it work?* If it works well, then there is a strong argument for leaving it alone. If it works inadequately, then it should be revamped anyway and may be cut over to the I.E. environment.
- Second, *does it incur high maintenance costs?* If so, then it is a candidate for restructuring or rebuilding with automated tools.

It may be deemed appropriate to automatically restructure an old system and modify it by programming rather than to rebuild it with reverse engineering and I-CASE tools. If an application system works adequately and needs little maintenance, then its conversion should probably be postponed. Spend the effort on something else; there are so many other applications needed. If the decision is made that an old application should live on without being rebuilt, it is often necessary to build a bridge between it and the I.E. environment.

In planning data resources, it is often unwise to assume that old systems will be converted easily to the I.E. form. A realistic appraisal is needed of the costs and difficulties of conversion. The dismal history of uncompleted conversions should be weighed. Often system designers in their initial enthusiasm for information engineering assume that the old systems will be converted. It is discovered too late that they will not. It is safer instead to assume that many old systems will survive and to plan a bridge that links them to the new world.

# Steps in Re-Engineering

The term **reverse engineering** usually implies that automated tools will be used. Today no tool will convert old programs *automatically* so that they conform to I.E. models. Several tools help in doing this task, and it should be regarded as a computer-assisted human task.

Several tasks need to be done to re-engineer an application. They are:

1. *Structuring the code.* The application may be written with spaghetti code. It needs to be converted to structured programming. Several tools exists for automatically restructuring COBOL programs. The product RECODER from Language Technology Inc., for example, converts COBOL programs that are messy, unstructured and badly coded into fully structured COBOL. It is completely automatic, leaving no part of the structuring task to be done manually. Its vendor claims that it can structure any COBOL program, no matter how patched or complex [LT88]. The resulting program is functionally identical to the original.

   Any logic errors in the original program will be automatically transferred to the restructured program, but they will probably be easier to identify and correct. The restructuring tools automatically identify dead branches in the code and produce reports on these. The restructured code is usually more bulky than the original and may execute somewhat more slowly. After the following re-engineering stages, the new code may be fed through a code optimizer to automatically make it more efficient.

   The restructured code may be tested, perhaps with the original test data, to ensure that it is functionally equivalent to the original.

2. *Entering the restructured code into an I-CASE tool.* In order to work further on the program, it should be entered into an I-CASE tool. After the program has been converted to a fully structured form, it should be converted into an action diagram in an I-CASE tool that can display this diagram in other forms (decomposition diagram, structure chart) and link it to data models, screen designs and so on.

3. *Converting the data elements.* The data elements (fields) in the old program are probably incompatible with the data elements in the I.E. data dictionary. Each data element from the old program should be associated with a data element in the I.E. dictionary. If no corresponding data element can be found, a new one should be entered into the I.E. data model. The data elements in the old program should then be converted automatically. When the data elements have been converted, the restructured programs may again be tested to ensure that they work well before more complex redesign is started.

   Some data dictionaries collect data definitions (with varying degrees of automation) from existing files, COBOL data divisions and directories of database management systems. This variety of definitions can be gathered into a data dictionary. Definitions and data element formats that are more uniform can be substituted a step at a time.

   If data definitions from many applications are loaded into the dictionary, the mess revealed may be so great as to discourage any attempt to clean it up. It is generally desirable to tackle a small area at a time.

4. *Normalizing data structures to conform to I.E. models.* The data in the old program are likely to be unnormalized. Even when the data elements are made the same as those in the I.E. data model, they are not necessarily grouped into records that conform to the data model. The data structures need to be converted.

   Conversion of the record structures may proceed in stages. *First,* the data structures from the existing programs are captured automatically and displayed. *Second,* the data elements are converted as previously described. *Third,* the data are normalized and the normalized structure made to conform to the I.E. data model. The normalization should be done at the screen of an I-CASE tool, with automated assistance.

5. *Generating modified data structures.* From the data model new data structures will be created for the database management system in question. This work is essentially the same as the design stage of creating a new application and needs the same I-CASE tools that help convert data model diagrams in data structure diagrams.

   Creating the new data structures often needs modifications of the way in which the programs access the data. It therefore needs to be done in conjunction with program design (as it would be when a new application is being built). It needs hyperdiagrams that link data design and program design.

6. *Generating data description code.* From the new data structure diagrams, data description code for the programs should be generated automatically (again, done by I-CASE tools). Thus, as shown in Figure 24.3, conversion of data is

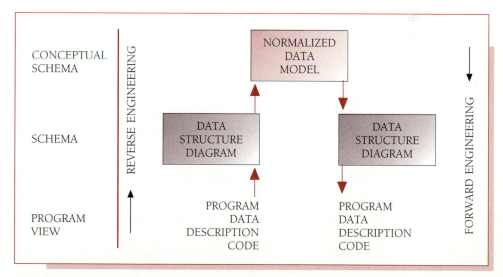

FIGURE 24.3 Reverse engineering captures the data description code, creates a data structure diagram and modifies this to conform to (and possibly add to) the normalized data model (conceptual schema). Design of the data in new systems progresses with I-CASE tools from data model to data structure diagram to database code (the right side of this diagram).

done at three levels: the **physical data level** represented in the program, the **schema description** and the **data model** (or conceptual schema). These are the three levels of the classic ANSI SPARC description of database technology [ANSI75].

7. *Converting the file or database management system*. The application may be modified to use a different database management system. It may be converted from file management to database management. It may be converted from a hierarchical DBMS (like *IMS*) or a CODASYL DBMS (like *IDMS*) to a relational DBMS (like *DB2, ORACLE, INGRES,* etc.). Database design tools and a database generator may be used to help accomplish this.

8. *Converting or enhancing reports*. It is usually desirable to improve the reports produced by the old program. New reports may be designed with the I-CASE report generator.

9. *Redesigning the human interface*. The user/screen dialog of the old program may need improving. It may be the strategy of the I.S. organization to adopt IBM's Systems Application Architecture, for example, to achieve uniformity of style for all user interactions so that systems become familiar to users and easy to use. The I-CASE screen painter may be employed to redesign the screens.

10. *Modifying the application to conform to new process models*. The basic procedure is often redesigned when applications are modified. New process models that are part of I.E. design may be used. New modules may be linked into the old ones.

11. *Adopting new standards*. The installation strategy may be to adapt standards (e.g., IBM's Systems Application Architecture or the Department of Defense's 2167 Standard) when applications are rebuilt. An I-CASE toolset may be used that relates to these standards.

12. *Converting system interfaces*. The application may be modified to use a different telecommunications monitor or operating system. Again, it may be adapted to IBM's Systems Application Architecture, for example. A code generator may be used to help in this conversion.

13. *Converting to a code generator*. The program may be rebuilt using a code generator in order to make future modification quick and easy to accomplish. The decision to use a code generator affects steps 3 to 13.

14. *Generating documentation*. The I-CASE tools or code generator should generate documentation to help with subsequent maintenance. This documentation should conform to the installation's standards.

15. *Using a code optimizer*. Because structured code is sometimes less machine-efficient than nonstructured code, a code optimizer may be used to improve its efficiency.

Methodology Chart 24 summarizes the 15 steps of reverse engineering.

Steps 4 to 15 are done with I-CASE tools, which were intended for the design of new systems rather than for reverse engineering. Tools also exist that automatically restructure code and aid in the conversion of data elements. These tools need to be integrated with the I-CASE tools to give a complete toolset for reverse engineering.

# Tools for Reverse-Engineering the Data

Figure 24.4 illustrates the tools needed for reverse-engineering the data. At the bottom left is a tool that captures the physical descriptions of data from the programs. An I-CASE data structure diagramming tool may be used. The data captured may be in file form or in the form of a database structure such as *IMS* or *IDMS*. The diagramming tool may represent this structure. An analyst may clean up the data at this stage, removing redundancies and adjusting data types and definitions to make them conform to those in a data administrator's dictionary.

The data descriptions are then taken into a data analysis tool with which they can be represented as an entity-relationship model and the data fully normalized. The central repository of data models is used so that maximum conformity can be achieved with the data models for that business area.

The data in the normalized data models are then redesigned as a data structure diagram for the database management system in question (as they would be when new systems are being designed). At the bottom right of Figure 24.4, the redesigned data structures are converted into database code that will be used by the redesigned program.

Human intelligence is likely to be needed at both the data modeling and the data structure stages of Figure 24.4. The analyst needs an I-CASE tool that allows him to adjust the models and structures on the screen. He may be given guidance in both the data modeling and data structuring stages by an expert system. As with other tools using the repository, rule-based processing should ensure that full consistency and correct design are achieved.

# Tools for Reverse-Engineering the Code

Figure 24.5 illustrates the tools needed for reverse-engineering the program code. At the bottom left, spaghetti code is taken into a restructuring engine. The restructured code is represented with diagrams that can be displayed and manipulated on the screen of an I-CASE tool. The best way of representing and manipulating structured code is with an action diagram.

The screens, dialog and reports produced by the programs will usually be redesigned. The I-CASE design tool needs a powerful screen painter and report generator. The new screens, dialog and reports will be built into the action-diagram structure.

At the top of Figure 24.5 are I-CASE tool representations of process models and new requirements. These may be used to aid the redesign of the programs. Again,

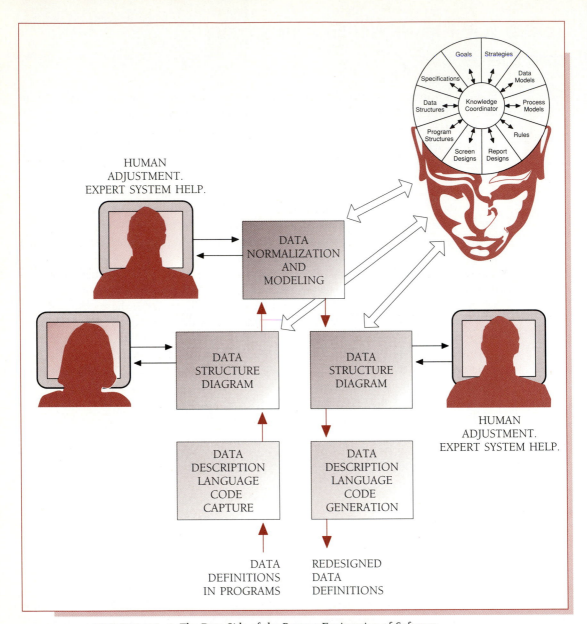

FIGURE 24.4  The Data Side of the Reverse Engineering of Software

an expert system may be used to guide the designer, and rule-based processing used in conjunction with the repository should ensure complete consistency and good design.

When the program is redesigned, the design tool should drive a code generator that produces machine-efficient code. The design tools and code generator may conform

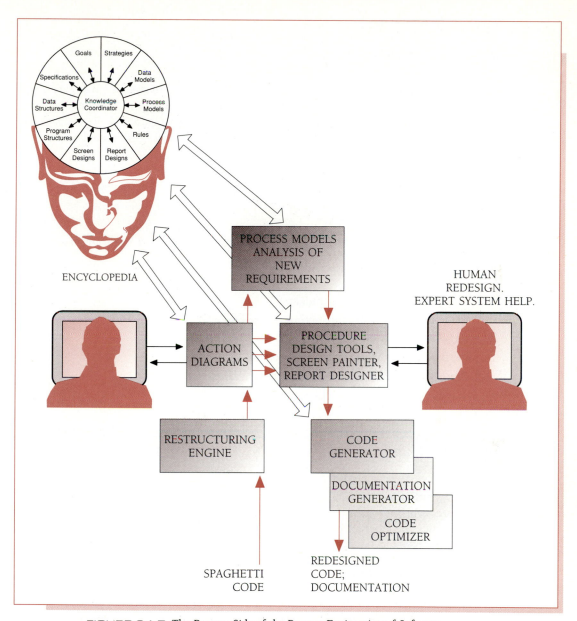

Goals
Strategies
Specifications
Data Models
Data Structures
Knowledge Coordinator
Process Models
Program Structures
Rules
Screen Designs
Report Designs

ENCYCLOPEDIA

PROCESS MODELS
ANALYSIS OF
NEW
REQUIREMENTS

HUMAN
REDESIGN.
EXPERT SYSTEM HELP.

ACTION
DIAGRAMS

PROCEDURE
DESIGN TOOLS,
SCREEN PAINTER,
REPORT DESIGNER

RESTRUCTURING
ENGINE

CODE
GENERATOR

DOCUMENTATION
GENERATOR

CODE
OPTIMIZER

SPAGHETTI
CODE

REDESIGNED
CODE;
DOCUMENTATION

**FIGURE 24.5** The Process Side of the Reverse Engineering of Software

to standards for application design. These may be standards of the installation in question or they may be industry or vendor standards such as IBM's SAA (Systems Application Architecture). They may employ reusable designs or building blocks that reside in the corporation's repository.

# Integrating Code and Data Redesign

The reverse engineering of data (in Figure 24.4) and program design (in Figure 24.5) need to be combined. The data models, data structure diagrams, action diagrams, procedure design diagrams, screen designs and report designs are all logically interrelated and need to be linked, using a common repository with integrated knowledge coordination, as described earlier.

# Six Categories of Program

For the purpose of migration, all programs should be classified into one of six categories:

- those that are static;
- those requiring minor maintenance;
- those requiring restructuring but not re-engineering;
- those requiring re-engineering;
- those requiring re-engineering to an I.E. environment;
- those for which complete redevelopment is needed.

These are further discussed in Box 24.1.

---

**Box 24. 1**
**Categorization of Programs for Migration Purposes**

For migration purposes, all applications should be categorized into the following six categories:

1. *Static.* The program operates satisfactorily and does not need to be changed. (No change is required.)
2. *Minor maintenance.* Changes of a minor nature are needed and can be made without rebuilding the program. (The most economical solution is to maintain the program in its present form.)
3. *Restructure but do not re-engineer.* The changes are not great enough to necessitate re-engineering. The program may be automatically restructured and modified without I-CASE re-engineering to conform to the I.E. models. (The most economical solution is to restructure the program automatically and maintain it in that form without re-engineering it.)
4. *Re-engineer but not to the I.E. environment.*
   (The most economical solution is to reverse-engineer the program into an I-CASE tool and use that tool to maintain it but not convert it fully to the I.E. environment.)
5. *Re-engineer to the I.E. environment.* The program is automatically restructured, reverse-engineered into a CASE tool and re-engineered to

conform to the I.E. models. New code is generated. (The most economical solution for the long term is to reverse-engineer the program into the I.E. environment, designing it for low-cost maintenance in that environment.)

6. *Scrap and rebuild.* A major redesign of procedures needs a complete redevelopment of the program. (The most economical solution is to scrap the program and create a new one.)

A study of maintenance costs at IBM showed that, if 12% or more of the code is to be changed, it is cheaper to scrap the program and redevelop it. This breakeven percentage is lower when I-CASE tools are used to generate the program.

There is often a strong argument for re-engineering or redeveloping programs so that they conform to the I.E. models and then fit into an evolutionary lifecycle in which they can be constantly improved with I-CASE tools. In other words, there is a strong argument for moving them from the underworld of Figure 24.1 to the upper, cleanly engineered world.

The decision about which of the above six categories a program falls into is largely a financial one. Re-engineering or reconstructing with a code generator may be less expensive than maintaining the old code for several years. Often, there is a major intangible benefit associated with shifting the system to the upper plane of Figure 24.1.

# Building a Bridge

With Categories 1, 2 and 3, the old programs continue to exist, with their old structures of data, which are probably incompatible with the I.E. data models. It will therefore be necessary to build a bridge such that, whenever data are passed from the old systems to the new ones, or vice versa, the data are converted. Figure 24.6 shows a typical bridge.

At the center of Figure 24.6 is the I.E. environment, with well-modeled data. At the top is the output file from an existing application program. The data in it must update the I.E. databases, and a simple utility program is written for this. The old file records become a "user view" or subschema that must be represented in the databases. To accomplish this, some of the field formats may have to be adjusted by the utility program. There may be items in the file that would not have appeared in the databases had they been designed by themselves, but they must now be there for compatibility reasons.

The databases are updated by new programs and, from the updated version, the old files are derived. The bottom part of Figure 24.6 shows this being done by another utility program. This conversion program is needed every time the old application programs are used. It may be, in effect, a high-speed dump that creates batch files to be run once a week or so. It may create on-line files for terminal usage. This bridge must be one of the first database programs to be tested to ensure that the old application programs continue to run. In many cases, an input to a database system must also be used to create input to a separate file system, possibly on a different machine. Such

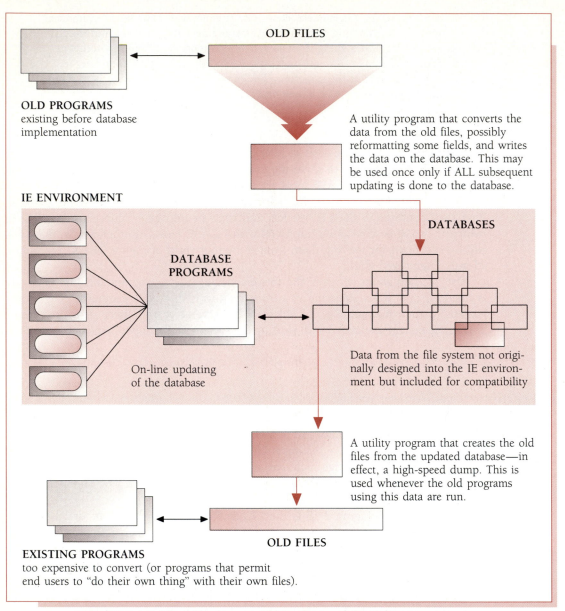

**OLD FILES**

**OLD PROGRAMS**
existing before database
implementation

A utility program that converts the
data from the old files, possibly
reformatting some fields, and writes
the data on the database. This may
be used once only if ALL subsequent
updating is done to the database.

**IE ENVIRONMENT**

**DATABASE PROGRAMS**

**DATABASES**

On-line updating
of the database

Data from the file system not originally designed into the IE environment but included for compatibility

A utility program that creates the old
files from the updated database—in
effect, a high-speed dump. This is
used whenever the old programs
using this data are run.

**OLD FILES**

**EXISTING PROGRAMS**
too expensive to convert (or programs that permit
end users to "do their own thing" with their own files).

FIGURE 24.6  The Bridge between Old Programs and the I.E. Environment

input should be entered into the system only once. A necessary function of the database
system is to create the required input for other operations.

A similar bridge may be used for creating files that end users manipulate in their
own way. This use of separate **extract files** keeps end users out of production databases.
Disjoint end-user databases are created for report-generation or decision-support
purposes.

# Conversion Modeling

Whether old systems are *converted* or *a bridge is built*, the process needs to be taken into consideration in the *data modeling operation*. If conversion is done, the user views employed by the old systems should be an input to the data modeling process. If a bridge is used, the design of the bridge should be an input to the data modeling and procedure modeling. The resulting model will often contain data items that would not have been included had the bridge to the old world been unnecessary. They are put into the new databases to permit coexistence with the old systems. This is a messy but necessary compromise for which the data administrator must plan.

Such planning and modeling are an essential part of evolving from the old systems to an information-engineering environment. The conversion programs—one might think of them as utility programs—are not difficult to write, but they have to be planned well in advance. They should be almost the first database programs to be tested because the old systems must keep going.

# Gradual Conversion

In long-established installations, conversion to an I.E. environment usually has to be a gradual process. There are too many files and programs for quick conversion, and the investment in them is high. It becomes a long-term strategic goal to eventually have all applications use the data and process models and be built with the repository-based tools. Once rebuilt (especially if rebuilt with an application generator), applications become much cheaper to maintain. In a typical corporation's portfolio of applications, *most* will be rebuilt at some time in the next eight years. The portfolio is slowly adapted to conform to the I.E. environment; then, the information resource of the corporation is under control.

What types of systems should be converted first?

The applications that fall into categories 4 and 5 should be rebuilt with information engineering.

In general, applications with the *largest financial payoff* are likely to be tackled first.

In some installations, different areas of activities have been tackled one at a time. Insurance companies refer to their different types of insurance as **lines of business**. One insurance company approached the conversion problem by bringing one line of business at a time into database operation with integrated data models.

Some installations have implemented all of the on-line applications of a given database with an integrated data model and have left the off-line (batch) systems in an unconverted form for the time being, using a bridge similar to that in Figure 24.5. All on-line systems or end-user systems have conformed to the I.E. environment.

# Making Future Conversion Easy

It is desirable to build systems that will be easy to change in the future. A major objective of clean engineering is to make systems easy to change.

The slum clearance problem is difficult and expensive to cope with. A major goal in enterprises today should be to stop building slums. Applications being built today should be fully structured and based on normalized data models in an I-CASE repository. It is irresponsible to build applications today without clean engineering.

A major reason for moving to database systems is to make application conversion easier. Different reports and query processing can be generated quickly. The ease of modifying major applications depends on whether the database management system has field sensitivity and other features that aid maintenance. It also depends on whether the data are correctly normalized. Good database installations have achieved much greater conversion flexibility.

There are, however, ways in which database systems have made conversion more difficult. The attempt to change to a different DBMS can be difficult—*extremely* difficult if that DBMS is differently structured, for example, the change from a CODASYL to a hierarchical database. Using a code generator can make conversion much easier if the generator can generate code for both types of databases. The generator that generates database code for multiple database management systems can insulate the program from DBMS conversion problems.

To achieve ease of conversion in the future, applications should be developed with the characteristics listed in Box 24.2.

---

**Box 24.2   Creating Applications to Meet Future Business Needs**

How to create applications that can be modified quickly to meet future business needs and that have lower maintenance costs:

- *Standardize on an I-CASE repository across the enterprise.*
- Do planning, modeling, design and code generation with an I-CASE tool that employs the chosen repository.
- Establish diagramming standards where the diagrams are supported by the I-CASE toolset. Train all people involved with implementation how to use the diagrams.
- Use technical documentation generated by the I-CASE toolset.
- Adhere to the principles and practice of information engineering.
- Create data and process models for the business area that are independent of specific procedures (BAA, as described in Chapter 20).
- Create procedure designs that are independent of technology.
- Employ a code generator that can translate the designs into implementations with different technology (e.g., one that can generate code and data descriptions for different database environments).

- Use *relational* database management systems.
- Use a database management system with field independence and features that enable changes to be made without rewriting existing programs.
- Design fully normalized data models. (Sometimes, implementation may deviate from fully normalized data for performance reasons.)
- Use fully structured code built with an action diagram editor (which is part of the I-CASE environment).
- Use application standards such as IBM's Systems Application Architecture (SAA), DEC's Application Integration Architecture (AIA) or evolving Open architectures.
- Avoid unusual hardware, operating systems or facilities that could make future migration difficult.
- Plan to do future maintenance by regeneration.
- Make upper-level management aware of the business reasons for achieving clean engineering and automation in application development.

# References

[ANSI75] *ANSI X.3 SPARC/DBMS*, Study Group report published by the American National Standards Institute, Washington, D.C., 1975.

[LT88] Literature on RECODER from Language Technology, Inc., Salem, Massachusetts, 1988.

# CHAPTER 25

# Essential Factors for Success

This chapter, combined with its relevant Methodology Charts, is a summary of factors that are important if RAD is to succeed as fully as possible. These lists of essential factors are built into the methodology hyperdocument and may be adjusted to reflect the experience in specific I.S. organizations.

Methodology Charts 25–1 through 25–3 show timetables for 13-week, 21-week and 26-week RAD lifecycles. Most RAD projects fit within this range. Such timetables are likely to be adjusted when the project is initiated, during the Requirements Planning Phase, during the second JAD workshop and, possibly, when the Review Board examines the system at the end of the Construction Phase. The user of the computerized methodology may point to any of the items on the timetable and link to the guidelines for accomplishing it.

See Methodology Charts 25–1, 25–2, and 25–3.

Methodology Chart 25–4 lists the essentials for success at the various lifecycle stages.

# CHAPTER 26

# The Future

## Inhuman Use of Human Beings

Norbert Wiener, the great pioneer of computers, wrote a book the title of which will be long remembered: *The Inhuman Use of Human Beings* [WIENER79]. His view was that jobs that are inhuman because of drudgery should be done by machines, not people. Among these jobs, he did not include that of the COBOL programmer.

In a sense, the programmer's job is inhuman because we require him to write a large amount of complex code without errors. In order to meet the needs of business, we want him to produce 100 function points per person-month or more. We want complex new procedures programmed in three months. This is beyond the capability of COBOL programmers.

## Meat Machines

The human brain is good at some tasks and bad at others. The computer is good at certain tasks that the brain does badly. The challenge of computing is to forge a creative partnership, using the best of both.

The electronic machine is fast and absolutely precise. It executes its instructions unerringly. Our meat machine of a brain is slow and, usually, imprecise. It cannot do long, meticulous logic operations without making mistakes. Fortunately, it has some remarkable properties. It can invent, conceptualize, demand improvements, create visions. The human can write music, start wars, build cities, create art, fall in love and dream of colonizing the solar system, but he cannot write COBOL that is guaranteed to be bug-free.

Many of the tasks that I.S. professionals do are tasks that are unsuited to our meat-machine brain. They need the precision of an electronic machine. Humans create program specifications that are full of inconsistencies and vagueness. A computer should help the human create specifications and check them at each step for consistency. It should not be a human job to write programs from the specifications because humans cannot do that well. A computer should generate the code needed. When the human wants to make changes, and he does frequently, he has real problems if he attempts to change the code. A seemingly innocent change has ramifications that he does not perceive and causes a chain reaction of errors.

If the programs needed are large, we are in even worse trouble because many people need to work together on them. When humans try to interact at the level of meticulous detail needed, all manner of communication errors occur. When one human makes a change, it affects the work of the others but, often, the subtle interconnection is not perceived. Meat machines do not communicate with precision.

The end user perceives the meat machines in the I.S. department to be a problem but does not know what to do about it. A major part of the problem is that humans are so slow; they often take two years to produce results, and they do not start for a long time because of the backlog. It is rather like communicating with a development team in another solar system, where the signals take years to get there and back.

Error-free coding is not natural for our animal-like brains. We cannot handle the meticulous detail and the vast numbers of combinatorial paths. Furthermore, if thousands of lines of code must be produced per day, then the job is even more inhuman. It is a job for machines, not people. Only recently have we come to understand how to make machines do it.

We are only at the primitive beginning of the era of code generators, specification tools and software design automation. We are just at the beginning of the era of artificial intelligence, with which machines can reason automatically using large numbers of rules. As these capabilities mature, they will become vastly more powerful than they are today.

## Chain Reaction

> The automation of software development is the beginning of a chain reaction.

As developers build software out of building blocks, they can create more complex building blocks. High-level constructs can be built out of primitive constructs. Still higher-level ones can be built out of these, and so on. Highly powerful constructs will evolve for different system types and application areas.

Essential to this is the rigor of the mechanism that enforces correct interfacing among the modules. This rigor allows pyramiding so that modules can be built out of other modules. The rigor is achieved by using rules and rule-based processing to enforce integrity in the designs and ensure consistency when separate components are linked. As designers of rule-based I-CASE tools have discovered, a large number of rules are needed to enforce consistency and integrity.

Also essential to the chain reaction is an intelligent repository that stores a large quantity of reusable designs from which procedures can be built. Large mainframe repositories, which many developers use, will be used, as well as desktop repositories.

As the software pyramids grow, it will be necessary to make the software as easy to use as possible. The complexity of software will become formidable but will be hidden from the users—just as the complexity of the telephone network is hidden from telephone users.

Higher-level semantics will be needed for instructing computers to do complex tasks. High-level design languages will allow fast, very complex design. Decision-support dialogs will aid very complex decision-making. Each category of professional will employ a computer dialog appropriate for his profession. Click-and-point, object-oriented dialogs using icons will be employed. Speech input and output will evolve.

The pyramiding of complex software will evolve along with the human-interface tools for making the software easy to use.

Libraries of constructs need to be built for different classes of applications. Some examples of application classes that need their own libraries of operations and control structures are:

- commercial procedures;
- financial applications;
- design of operating systems;
- automatic database navigation;
- query languages;
- design of circuits with NOR, NAND gates, and so on;
- control of robots;
- cryptanalysis;
- missile control;
- building architecture;
- design graphics;
- network design;
- avionics;
- CAD/CAM, computer-aided design and manufacturing;
- production control;
- project management;
- decision-support graphics.

The list is endless.

## Optical Disks

Developers in the future will have optical disks containing a vast amount of software. One CD-ROM today can hold object code that would take more than 10,000 person-years to create. Future developers will have CD-ROMs containing many applications and building blocks built for reusability, in I-CASE format so that their design can be displayed on the screen, modified and linked to other system components. The tools will need search mechanisms and expert systems to help the developers find the reusable components most appropriate to their needs. Computer users will also have CD-ROMs full of software. More than 100 million lines of code can reside on one CD-ROM. Disks will be sold with many applications and tools integrated together.

## A Way to Think about Systems

I-CASE tools represent a way to think about systems that leads to higher-precision specification and design. As such, the subject ought to be taught in business schools and management training courses, as well as in computer science schools and systems analysts' courses. At its different levels, it can be understood by both business people and computer professionals. It provides a vital way to bridge the gap between these two cultures.

Business schools, in teaching how businesses work, should use flow charts, decomposition diagrams, matrices, entity-relationship charts, and the logic of action diagrams. New types of charts will probably be devised to help human communication. If they are to become a basis for system specification, they should be designed so that they have the precision that enables rule-based tools to check their integrity and consistency with other diagrams.

# Next-Generation CASE

The next step for I-CASE is the incorporation of the technology from the expert systems industry. This will lead to a more intelligent environment for building applications, as well as to significantly improved support for more complex or mission-critical applications. It will provide the basis for direct execution of specifications from the business planning stage all the way to the cutover stage.

# Code Generation from the Enterprise Model

Executable program code should be generated from the highest-level specification possible. A major evolution in I-CASE tools will be to push the code generation higher in the process. If the enterprise model contains rules expressing how the enterprise functions, code can be generated directly from the enterprise model. The enterprise model should be understood by the business managers. It should be an aid to clear thinking about how they want the enterprise to operate. A precise expression of how the enterprise operates should reside in the repository and should be discussed in workshop sessions. Code should be generatable directly from this. A change in business procedures should then be directly translatable into the code for implementing the procedures.

The term **Code Generation from the Enterprise Model (CGEM)** has been used to describe this higher-level code generation. The RAD lifecycle may become faster as the tools become more powerful, libraries of reusable constructs become mature and enterprise models evolve so that they represent the business rules more comprehensively. There is still likely to be a stage in the lifecycle in which the code generated is successively refined. The tools may become powerful enough so that it is possible to complete an application by the end of the second JAD workshop.

Much development will consist of the successive refinement of existing applications rather than the creation of entirely new applications.

# Standards and Open Systems

The world of the future will be one of Open systems and standards. Single-vendor, proprietary, "vanity" architectures will give way to architectures designed for open connectivity, portability and worldwide access to databases. Vast networks of optical fibers will be woven around the earth. The farthest computer will be 68 milliseconds away. Mankind will have a billion interconnectable computers.

Large enterprises will have hundreds of thousands of computers, with millions of MIPS worldwide. Managements that fail to build an efficiently functioning organism with this power will not survive. The efficient corporate organism will have repositories that store a large amount of knowledge about the enterprise, its data, functions, objects and procedure designs. The objects and procedures will be designed for reusability across the enterprise. Commercial paperwork will be replaced by electronic documents in the format of international standards because computers everywhere will exchange such documents with other computers. Millions of electronic transactions will pass between corporations worldwide every second. Standards will evolve for the representation of the objects used in commerce—customers, accounts, orders, parts, locations and so on. Standardization and reusability techniques go hand-in-hand.

# Open Repository

The repository for I-CASE tools stores information about the object-types that are used in system development. The structure of this repository is very complex, especially when it is designed for information engineering and reusability. The structure is intimately coupled to the rules that check the integrity of the knowledge in the repository.

The *IBM AD Cycle* provides a framework for application development into which the tools of many vendors can fit (Figure 3.1). Essential to this is the AD Platform, which incorporates the:

- *Repository* with a well defined information model (metamodel);
- *Repository Services* for checking the consistency and integrity of information stored in the Repository;
- *Tool Services* for ensuring that tools produce valid information, with integrity, for storing in the Repository;
- *Common User Access (CUA)*, a standard user interface to make tools look and feel similar to the user and easy to use;
- *Workstation Services* for enabling personal computers to interact with the centrally stored Repository and Services.

This set of facilities provides an *"open" de facto* standard in IBM's SAA world. What is also needed is a similar set of standards that is a vendor-independent, industry standard, which would connect to the other computer industry Open standards.

Development tools will evolve and change. A diversity of such tools will be built by many corporations, often small, inventive corporations. The repositories ought to be usable with all of these tools. Corporate repositories are already growing to a formidable size and are becoming a vital strategic resource, in some cases helping the corporation stay ahead of its competition. Repositories of reusable components will also contain a large quantity of knowledge—sometimes sold as CD-ROMs. If these repositories are of a standard format, they will be usable with many different design tools. If there is not an Open standard for the repository and its tool interfaces, it would be like having no standard for music CDs. Sony CDs would not play on Philips equipment, and so on. An Open standard for the I-CASE repository and its interfaces is as important to software development as the CD standard is to the music industry.

# Packaged Software

Open standards, or proprietary standards, for the I-CASE repository will have a major impact on the packaged-software industry. A problem with mainframe application packages is that I.S. organizations that buy them often have to modify the package to adapt it to their needs. The packages are difficult and expensive to modify. One survey by EDS showed that modification and maintenance of mainframe package software averaged six times the original cost of the software.

To overcome this problem, packaged software should be sold in I-CASE form so that it can be adapted and modified easily with I-CASE tools. Having an Open standard for the I-CASE repository will facilitate this greatly. The potential value of reusable designs is immense. As described in Figure 15.9, applications may one day be built with off-the-shelf designs and components that can be assembled and modified very quickly. This opportunity presents a great challenge to the packaged-software industry.

Conversion of the software industry to I-CASE design will not happen overnight. The investment tied up in existing software is large, and the resistance of major software companies to new methods is high. It may be that relatively small or new corporations sell reusable I-CASE designs first.

# Parallelism

Processor chips of the future will be mass-produced in vast quantities. When many millions of one processor chip are made, that processor can be very low in cost. Japan has plans to flood the world with low-cost processor chips. In the future, it will be highly desirable for powerful computers to be built out of many small computers that yield to the economics of mass production. Examples of highly parallel machines have existed for some time. The problem with them is that it has been extremely difficult to design software for applications that run efficiently on them.

The search for ways to introduce a high degree of parallelism into computing is an important one. A million-dollar computer should not be doing one thing at a time; it should be doing ten thousand things at a time. The *Connection Machine*, from Thinking Machines, Inc., has 65,536 small processors operating in parallel. Such machines will be built from mass-produced wafers, each of which has many chips.

Software for highly-parallel machines will necessarily be intricate and tricky. Analysts do not think naturally in terms of parallel processes. The culture of computing an algorithm theory relates to sequential operations, not parallel ones. To bridge the gap between how analysts think and how parallel computers should be used, we need design tools and nonprocedural languages (e.g., *SQL* and *PROLOG*), which can be translated by generators into parallel processing. Some types of formal decomposition indicate clearly what steps in complex procedures can take place in parallel

[HAMILTON76]. Higher levels of CASE tools, reusable constructs, higher-level semantics and code generators will make the mass use of parallel machines practical.

The challenge of the computer industry today is to evolve automated software development techniques that make it practical to use complex microelectronic wafers, each containing large numbers of advanced RISC processors.

As commented earlier, the complexity of living things built by nature is awesome to a computer professional. The brain is so intricate that it cannot be mapped, imitated or understood in detail; it is rich in diversity; yet, it is self-protecting and self-renewing. The things of nature are complex because they are grown, not specified and built. As we continue to grow the components of software and information systems, they will become complex (though not compared with the brain). We need disciplines and tools that facilitate and enable us to manage such growth.

*The designers of the future must stand on the shoulders of the designers of the present.*

As the pyramids of complexity build up, we will reach very-high-level constructs, and there will be vast libraries of such constructs, often designed for parallel RISC engines. Sophisticated tools and languages will enable developers to employ the constructs they need. Many millions of computers on worldwide data networks will exchange constructs from these libraries. Knowledge-based systems will acquire ever more knowledge and become self-feeding. Intelligent network directories will allow machines and users to find the resources they need.

The hand-COBOL programmer with his ad-hoc designs will become a romantic part of computer history, like the weavers in their cottages when the industrial revolution began.

# References

[HAMILTON76] For example, that in M. Hamilton and S. Zeldin, "Higher Order Software—A Methodology for Defining Software," *IEEE Transactions on Software Engineering*, March 1976, pp. 25–32.

[WIENER79] Norbert Wiener, *Inhuman Uses of Human Beings*, M.I.T. Press, Boston, Massachusetts 1979.

# METHODOLOGY
# CHARTS

---

Methodology Chart 7:   REQUIREMENTS PLANNING PHASE

> The procedure given below may be modified with MediaScribe
> to meet the needs of the particular situation.

## Joint Requirements Planning (JRP)

Joint Requirements Planning, JRP, is a technique for harnessing
business executives and end users in the examination of requirements
of a proposed system. It is a highly successful technique when used
correctly and should be employed for most systems.

Key executives and users are selected to participate in workshops in
which a requirements document is created. The workshop progresses
through a planned set of steps under the guidance of a skilled RAD
Workshop Leader, who is usually the RAD Workshop Leader who will
conduct a follow-on Joint Application Design session. The JRP session
is similar to the JAD session.

At the start of the workshop, the users are encouraged to do most of
the talking. I.S. professionals relate the end users' statements to
the knowledge in the repository and attempt to create a pragmatic
representation of system functions that will make the system as
valuable as possible.

## Before the Project Begins
### Select the tools.

It is desirable to select one toolset and perfect its use. The
methodology is highly dependent on a toolset that enables fast
and easy design, and a rapid cycle of modify-generate-test. The
methodology is built around the toolset and adapted to it.
Selecting the right toolset is highly critical.

The I-CASE environment should be well established with I.S.
professionals well trained in the use of the toolset.

### Characteristics of the I-CASE Toolset   (Capabilities)

> I-CASE Toolset:   an integrated-CASE toolset with an
>                   intelligent central repository (encyclopedia).

THE TOOLSET SHOULD INCLUDE THE FOLLOWING:

- A complete data-modeling capability, with entity-relationship
  diagrams and the ability to represent normalized data.

- A complete process-modeling capability with decomposition
  diagrams, dependency diagrams and data-flow diagrams.

- The ability to display and cluster matrices and map processes
  against entities, showing how the processes use the entities.

- A versatile screen painter (which can be used very quickly in
  JAD sessions).

- Ability to link screens and responses into a dialog.

- A versatile report generator (which can be used very quickly
  in JAD sessions).

- The ability to draw the logic of processes with action (hyper)
  diagrams.

- The capability of fully checking the consistency and integrity of all of the above representations of information.

- The capability of converting the design directly into code that is machine-efficient.

> THE TOOLSET SHOULD:
>
> - be interactive;
> - be quick and easy to use;
> - give the most automated capability for design;
> - convert the design directly into code;
> - enable code to be generated and tested as quickly as possible;
> - give the fastest possible cycle of generate-test-modify, generate-test-modify...

Establish the methodology.

Adapt the methodology to the toolset.
The methodology should be adapted to fit the toolset.

Use and tune the methodology.
The methodology should be applied to many projects and tuned on the basis of experience.

Select and train the practitioners.
See Chapters 5 and 10.

ESSENTIALS FOR SUCCESS IN THE MANAGEMENT OF SWAT TEAMS
See Methodology Chart 10-1.

RAD WORKSHOP LEADER

> A specialist who organizes and conducts the workshops for Joint Requirements Planning (Chapter 7) and Joint Application Design (Chapter 8).

HUMAN-FACTORS EXPERT

> Specialist in human factoring who is responsible for usability testing (Chapter 17).

DATA MODELING EXPERT (PROFESSIONAL)

> A specialist with experience in data modeling who can create data models rapidly and competently (Chapter 13).

Some professionals have experience in data modeling, are highly skilled at it, and can create correct models quickly. The Data Modeling Expert may be a data administrator or part of the data administration staff.

Initiate the project.

Determine the need for the system.

*continued on next page*

Write, in one page, the functions of the system.
Establish an Executive Sponsor.

Obtain commitment of the Executive Owner.

> Development should not proceed unless a suitably high-level
> end-user executive is FULLY COMMITTED to having the system
> built and taking the necessary steps to make end-user
> managers move rapidly and commit the time needed for
> development and cutover.

Establish the I.S. team.
From the I.S. Community:

PROJECT MANAGER

> The person responsible for the overall development effort.

In a project with one Construction Team, this person may be the
team leader.

CONSTRUCTION TEAM

> A small team of implementors, highly skilled with the toolset,
> who build the system -- typically two, three or four people
> (Chapter 10).

For large projects, there will be multiple Construction Teams
(Chapter 12).

°° RAD WORKSHOP LEADER    (See separate entry above.)
°° HUMAN-FACTORS EXPERT   (See separate entry above.)
°° DATA MODELING EXPERT (PROFESSIONAL)   (See separate entry above.)
REPOSITORY MANAGER

> Executive responsible for I-CASE repository and its integrity.

He may control what reusable constructs are in the repository.
The Repository Manager is particularly important in an environment
of Information Engineering (Chapter 21) reusable design
(Chapters 15 and 22).

Customize the methodology for this system.
Select the appropriate variants of the methodology.

Major Variants of RAD

Toolset Variants

> The technical details are customized to the toolset used
> because different toolsets have somewhat different capabilities.

Timebox

> The timebox variant sets a firm deadline on the Construction
> Phase. Refinements can be slipped, but the deadline can not
> (Chapter 11).

Combination of the Requirements Planning and User Design Phases

> If the requirements are well known, obvious or simple, it is
> not necessary to have a separate JRP workshop. The JAD workshop
> should include the JRP activity.

If the user participants in the JRP and JAD workshops are to be the same, the workshops should be combined. (Usually, however, the JRP participants are of a higher level than the JAD participants.)

Parallel Development

Complex systems of, say, more than a thousand function points, are split into subsystems on which separate SWAT Teams work independently, with a coordinating model (Chapter 12).

Reusability

Reusable constructs are used to the maximum extent. The lifecycle is managed so that where it creates new constructs they are designed to be reusable if possible (Chapter 15).

Data Administration

The lifecycle employs existing data models (Chapter 20).

Information Engineering

The lifecycle is an integral part of an information engineering methodology (Chapter 21).

Object-Oriented Reusability

An object-oriented approach to information engineering is used to achieve the maximum application-dependent reusability (Chapter 2

These variants can be used in combination.

Adjust the lifecycle hyperdiagram to show the variants selected.

Requirements Planning Phase

°°°Suggested Timetable:  See Methodology Chart 25-2.

Preliminaries
Establish the need for a system.

Determine which executives to talk to in establishing the need for the system.

Determine the scope of the system.

- Examine strategic business opportunities that may be relevant to this system.
- Establish management's objectives for the project.
- Determine which locations are involved.
- Determine which departments are involved.
- Examine relevant goals, problems and critical success factors.
- Determine what business assumptions are to be made by the planning group.
- Determine which business processes are involved.

Determine the key user executives.

- Determine which end users feel strongly about the need for the system.

- Determine which user executives will be involved with the system.

*continued on next page*

- Determine what end users are particularly knowledgeable about the subject areas of the system.

- Determine who will participate in the JRP workshop.

Establish the I.S. team.

- PROJECT MANAGER
- CONSTRUCTION TEAM
- RAD WORKSHOP LEADER
- HUMAN-FACTORS EXPERT
- DATA MODELING EXPERT

Establish the RAD Workshop Leader.

The RAD Workshop Leader should be a full-time JAD professional skilled because of experience in conducting other JRP and JAD sessions.

Characteristics of a Good RAD Workshop Leader

- Excellent human communication skills.

- Impartial, unbiased, neutral.

- Good negotiating skills; sensitive to corporate politics; diplomatic.

- Good at conducting a meeting; has meeting leadership qualities like a good Board Chairman; makes the meeting move quickly to conclusion and avoid tangents; can turn a floundering meeting into a productive session; can summarize what has been said.

- Understands group dynamics and can excite the participants, getting them to work hard on items that need detailing.

- Something of a "ham" in front of an audience.

- Capable of organizing the research, documents and people.

- Not an expert on the applications but capable of researching and learning quickly.

- Fully familiar with the diagramming techniques used in the workshop; familiar with data modeling and process modeling.

- Fully familiar with the RAD lifecycle; familiar but not necessarily skilled with the tools used.

- A professional who has become skilled at the job by practice in other JRP and JAD sessions.

Customize the methodology for this system.

Select the appropriate variants of the methodology.

°° Major Variants of RAD        (See separate entry above.)

Adjust the lifecycle hyperdiagram to show the variants selected.

Research

Identify overall objectives of the system.

- List strategic business opportunities that may be relevant to this system.

- List relevant goals and problems.

- List relevant critical success factors.

Become familiar with the current system (if any).

- Learn enough about the application to become familiar with the terminology and buzzwords.

- Examine the system input and output.

- Take a user-guided tour through the working environment.

- Examine all documentation that relates to the current system.

- Extract documentation that is relevant to the new system.

- Put relevant documentation into the I-CASE tool.

Explore what changes are needed in the current system.

Do the users like it?
Is it easy to use?
What changes would the users like made?
What new functions should be added?

Find what relevant information exists in the I-CASE repository.

Explore the ISP study or similar planning (if it exists).

- Extract the relevant information from the repository.

- Print matrices from the repository mapping goals, problems, critical success factors, and so on, with corporate functions, locations, executives, and so on.

- Add detailed comments to the above matrices where necessary.

See [MARTIN90c].

Explore the BAA study or similar planning (if it exists).

- Extract the relevant information from the repository.

- Extract the relevant process decomposition diagram.

- Extract the relevant entity-relationship diagram.

- Extract or create the relevant process flow diagram, showing how the processes are dependent on one another.

- Add comments to the above diagrams where necessary.

See [MARTIN90c].

Explore what structures or designs might be reusable.
See Chapter 15.

Identify reusable screen templates.
Identify reusable structures.

*continued on next page*

Identify reusable objects and processes.
Investigate what existing applications might be modified.
Explore any other relevant information in the repository.

Research similar systems that might offer guidance or ideas.

Research similar systems (if any) inside the enterprise.
Examine similar systems elsewhere, if possible.
Research literature on other systems.

Create a tentative overview of the new system in the I-CASE repository.

Create a tentative process decomposition diagram.
Create a tentative process flow diagram.
Create relevant planning matrices.

Prepare the workshop.

Select the workshop participants.

Full-Time Participants

In general, the participants should be full-time.

```
┌─────────────────────────────────────────────┐
│        THE WORKSHOP SHOULD NOT BE HELD        │
│   UNTIL THE KEY PARTICIPANTS ARE AVAILABLE.   │
└─────────────────────────────────────────────┘
```

End-User Participants

End users selected should

- be intelligent,
- be creative,
- have good human communication skills,
- want to understand information-system techniques,
- be highly knowledgeable about their own business areas.

These will include:

key end users who want the system
user executives who will be involved with the system

Some of the executives who were present at the JRP workshop
should be present at the follow-on JAD workshop.

I.S. Participants

- Session Leader
- Scribe
- I.S. Professionals

The I.S. professionals present should be fully familiar with
the I-CASE tool and techniques.

One or more members of the SWAT Team that will construct
the system should attend the second workshop.

Visiting Participants
Insiders

Persons from within the corporation may be invited to present specialized knowledge.

Outsiders
If the system serves individuals in other corporations such as suppliers, distributors, buyers or customers, their attendance should be considered.

Prepare the materials.

To illustrate the business activities, consider using:
• slides
• videotape
• overhead transparencies.

Prepare relevant diagrams and listings in the repository.

Print relevant diagrams and listings from the repository for the participants to review.

Create a binder of material for the participants.

Make overhead transparencies, where appropriate, of the information in the repository.

Customize the JRP agenda.

Duplicate and modify this document where it can usefully form part of the agenda.

List the processes involved.

Prepare an agenda, if necessary, for each process involved.

Hold the kick-off meeting.

The kick-off meeting should be held several days before the workshop so that the participants have time to prepare.

• Have the Executive Owner (Executive Owner) make the opening speech, making the objectives clear to the participants.

• Explain the RAD lifecycle.

• Show the participants the JRP timetable.

• Give participants literature on the JRP procedure (Chapter 7), including the "Ten Essentials of the Requirements-Planning Phase."

TEN ESSENTIALS FOR SUCCESS IN THE REQUIREMENTS-PLANNING PHASE

> These apply to nontrivial requirements planning. Where the requirements are fairly obvious or simple, JRP should be combined with JAD.

1. A suitably high-level end-user executive ("Executive Owner") must be committed to having the system and must be determined to move fast.

2. The Requirements Planning Phase must be conducted by an experienced, skilled, unbiased, full-time JAD professional who organizes a JRP workshop (sometimes combined with the JAD workshop).

*continued on next page*

3. The workshop must be attended by suitably high-level user executives who can brainstorm the potential functions of the system and its deployment across the enterprise.

4. The participants attend the workshop full time.

5. There should be thorough preparation prior to the workshop to identify the potential benefits and negatives of the proposed system. All such material should be treated as a proposed basis for brainstorming.

6. During the workshop, all participants are treated as equals.

7. The possible functions of the system should be prioritized, understanding that not all of them can be implemented in the first version of the system.

8. Any cultural changes, or changes in people's jobs, must be identified and planned for.

9. The workshop room should have no telephone; there should be no interruptions; an off-site location works best. The sessions should start on time. The participants should be committed to work in the evening for the duration of the workshop.

10. Technical jargon should be avoided.

- Give them the JRP agenda.

- Give participants the preparatory material for them to study. Inform them that they must understand it well before the workshop.

- Present a brief overview of the preparatory material.

- Answer any questions the participants may have.

- Instruct the participants to contact the RAD Workshop Leader when questions arise after they review the material.

Prepare the room.
Facilities Required in the JRP/JAD Room

- Large white board with colored pens.

- Flip-chart board, colored pens and space to display multiple flip charts.

- Overhead projector and screen, with pre-prepared and blank transparencies; colored pens.

- Possibly, a magnetic or felt board with a kit for building diagrams.

- PC with the prototyping and I-CASE toolset.

- Large-screen monitor or projector so that all participants can see and discuss what is on the screen of the prototyping and I-CASE toolset.

- Printer so that I-CASE designs can be printed for the participants.

- Portable copier so that all participants can be

given copies of information created.

- Polaroid camera to record white-board drawings or wall charts.

- Slide projector if the RAD Workshop Leader has prepared slides.

- Videotape player and television monitor if the RAD Workshop Leader has planned to use videotapes.

- Coffee and refreshments.

- Name cards and stationery for participants.

- No telephone!

Conduct the workshop.
Opening Speech

The Executive Owner should make the opening speech, motivating the participants to do an excellent job.

Initial Review

Review with participants the purpose and objectives.
Review the agenda.
Describe any strategic business opportunities from the system.
Review relevant goals, problems, and critical success factors.
Review the business assumptions that are to be made.

For the system as a whole, determine its functions.

- List the system objectives.

- Brainstorm the possible functions of the system.

- List those functions that seem valuable.

- Relate the functions to the goals, problems, critical success factors and strategic business opportunities.

- Evaluate return on investment of the functions.

- List intangible benefits of the functions.

- Prioritize the functions. Determine what functions should be implemented in the next version of the system, eliminating those that are of questionable value or that are difficult to build at this stage. Adjust the decomposition diagram to reflect the functions selected.

- Create an overview process decomposition diagram.

- Create an overview process flow diagram.

- Address unresolved issues.

List unresolved issues.
Determine responsibility and deadline for unresolved issues.

Details of Issue
- Issue:

*continued on next page*

- • Person assigned to resolve the issue:
- • Assign date:
- • Date to be resolved by:
- • Resolution:

Examine each process.

- • List its objectives.
- • Brainstorm ways to streamline the system, lessen overhead and lessen human work.
- • Describe how the process will operate.
- • Adjust the function list if necessary.
- • Specify audit and security requirements.
- • Address unresolved issues.  (See separate entry above.)
- • List questions and suggestions ready for the JAD workshop.

Determine what cultural changes will be caused by the system.

List the types of cultural changes that the new system might bring about.

They may include:

- • changes in organizational structure.
- • changes in policies.
- • changes in business procedures.
- • changes in staffing levels.
- • changes in job content.
- • changes in skill requirements.

Review this list with appropriately senior end-user management.

Summarize the benefits and risks.
Assess the benefits.

They may include:
- • financial savings;
- • opportunity costs;
- • better quality;
- • improved competitive position;
- • other tangible benefits;
- • intangible benefits.

Determine how to maximize the benefits.

Look for business ways to obtain leverage from the system.

Determine which potential functions of the system have the most effect on profits or business objectives.

Assess the risks.
There may be:
- • inadequate user motivation;
- • lack of user acceptance of changed way of working;
- • user difficulties learning or adapting to the system;
- • possible misconceptions in the system concept;
- • possible development cost overruns;
- • possible technical problems.

Determine how to minimize the risks.

The risks should be examined in detail.

An Executive Sponsor at a suitably high level must be totally

committed to the project. He should address his attention to
user motivation.

- Use of JAD substantially reduces the risks of user
  nonacceptance and business misconceptions.

- A prototyping methodology substantially reduces the risks
  as misconceptions and technical difficulties are more likely
  to be discovered early.

- The development risks are likely to be much lower
  if the project fits comfortably into the chosen methodology
  and can be developed with the tools in question.

Create the JRP documentation.
The documentation should be in the repository of the I-CASE tool.
The documentation differs somewhat from one JRP to another.

TYPICAL JRP DOCUMENTATION INCLUDES THE FOLLOWING:

List of departments and locations served by the system.
List of system objectives.
Details of possible system functions.

- List of possible system functions.

- List of benefits of each function (tangible and intangible).

- Rough estimate of the return on investment of the function
  (possibly indicated as HIGH, MEDIUM, LOW and ZERO).

- Prioritization of the functions.
  (Three categories of priority might be used, possibly more).

  - Which functions MUST be present in the first version
    of the system.

  - Which functions MIGHT be present in the first version
    of the system if they can be built quickly.

  - Which functions OUGHT TO BE SAVED for a subsequent version
    of the system.

A process decomposition diagram of the system.
A process flow diagram of the system.
Flow diagram showing interfaces with other systems.
Listing of unresolved issues.
- Issue:
- Person assigned to resolve the issue:
- Assign date:
- Date to be resolved by:
- Resolution:

Implementation target dates.
What happens next.

Determine who participates in follow-on phases.

Appoint the User Coordinator.

A user appointed by the Executive Owner to oversee the project
from the users' viewpoint.

(Sometimes this individual is the Executive Owner or a person
appointed by the Executive Owner.)

*continued on next page*

- is the leading spokesperson of the end users who need the system.

- involves other users where appropriate to help review the evolving prototypes, or to help in system building.

- arranges for user documentation and training.

- is responsible for cutover planning.

- is the lead user developer on the time-box team(s).

- involves other users where appropriate to help review the evolving prototypes.

- serves on the Prototype Review Board.

Establish the Review Board.

> The team of users who review the system after construction and decide whether any modifications are needed before cutover.

Prior to the timebox, the Review Board reviews the requirements; at the end of the timebox it reviews the results.

The Review Board reports to the Executive Owner.  It includes:
- leading spokespeople of the end users who need the system;
- the Executive Owner (Executive Sponsor);
- an I.S. executive;
- possibly an external consultant.

The Review Board may be the same as the Requirements Planning Team involved in the Requirements Planning Phase.

The Review Board ensures that sufficient commitment exists for a thorough review job to be done.

Establish the User Design Team.

> The team of users who participate in the design workshop.

This is the set of users and user executives who participate in the JAD workshops.

A final selection will be made by the RAD Workshop Leader when doing the JAD preparation.

Some of these may be members of the requirements-planning team. Others should be able to participate in more detailed design (Chapter 8).

Establish the Cutover Team.

> The team of people responsible for planning and executing the activities that are necessary for cutover.

Establish appropriate user expectations.

Show the participants a timetable for the RAD lifecycle.

Explain their participation in the lifecycle.

Ensure that the users have realistic expectations

of when the completed system could become available.

Finalize.
Complete the documentation.

Complete the documentation in the I-CASE tool.
Print the documentation from the I-CASE tool.

Make cost and time estimates.

Estimate roughly the complexity of the system in function points.
See Appendix I and Chapter 2.

Estimate roughly the overall development time. (See Chapter 10.)
Estimate roughly the overall development cost.

Present the results to the Executive Owner of the system.

The Executive Owner may need the results refined until he feels
comfortable in giving a go-ahead for the next stage.

Obtain a go-ahead decision from the Executive Owner.

The Executive Owner should make a quick decision whether to
give the go-ahead for the User Design Stage and release the
funds for it.

If the project is to go ahead:

- Obtain a commitment of the necessary funds.

- Obtain a commitment to go ahead with the preparation for cutover.

- Obtain a commitment of the time required from end users.

- Obtain a commitment to move fast, avoiding political or
  bureaucratic delays, with the planning for handling the
  necessary organizational changes.

The Executive Owner should make a closing speech.

Reference
[MARTIN90c]  James Martin, Information Engineering (a trilogy)
Book II: Planning and Analysis,
Prentice-Hall, Inc., Englewood Cliffs, New Jersey, 1990 (201-592-2261).

Methodology Chart 8:  THE USER DESIGN PHASE

> The procedure given below may be modified with MediaScribe
> to meet the needs of the particular situation.

## Joint Application Design (JAD)

Joint Application Design, JAD, is a technique for harnessing end users
into the requirements analysis, specification and design of systems.
It is a highly successful technique when used correctly, resulting in
high-quality design being created rapidly. Key end users are selected
to participate in workshops in which the preliminary design of the
system is created. The workshops progress through a planned set of
steps.

At the start of the workshop, the users are encouraged to do most of
the talking. I.S. staff in the session translate what the users want
into structured specifications and design, in such a way that the
users can understand and discuss the design. Along with the
specifications are created the relevant data model, the screen
designs, report designs and, possibly, rough prototypes. Particularly
important in the RAD lifecycle, the design is created in the
repository of an I-CASE tool that coordinates the design with other
information in the repository, and with which the design can used
directly in the Construction Phase.

Sometimes the JRP and JAD procedures are combined. If the requirements
are simple or well known it is not necessary to have a separate JRP
workshop. The JAD workshop should include the JRP activity.

If the user participants in the JRP and JAD workshops are the same,
the workshops should be combined. Usually the JRP participants are of
higher level than the JAD participants, so the workshops are separate.

This document describes a stand-alone JAD with the assumption that a
JRP workshop has been completed, as described in Chapter 7, Box 7.5.

## The User Design Phase

°°°Suggested Timetable:  See Methodology Chart 25-2.

### Before the Design Phase Begins

The results of the JRP workshop are in the repository of the
I-CASE tool. The end users present have signed off on the results.
The Executive Owner has released the funds to proceed with the User
Design Phase.

### Prepare for JAD workshop.
#### Select the workshop participants.
##### Full-Time Participants

In general, the participants should be full-time.

> THE WORKSHOP SHOULD NOT BE HELD
> UNTIL THE KEY PARTICIPANTS ARE AVAILABLE.

##### I.S. Participants

- Session Leader
- Scribe
- I.S. Professionals

The I.S. professionals present should be fully familiar with the I-CASE tool and techniques.

One or more members of the SWAT Team that will construct the system should attend the second workshop.

## End-User Participants

End users selected should

- be intelligent,
- be creative,
- have good human communication skills,
- want to understand information-system techniques,
- be highly knowledgeable about their own business areas.

These will include:

key end users who want the system
user executives who will be involved with the system

Some of the executives who were present at the JRP workshop should be present at the follow-on JAD workshop.

## Visiting Participants
### Insiders

Persons from within the corporation may be invited to present specialized knowledge.

### Outsiders

If the system serves individuals in other corporations such as suppliers, distributors, buyers or customers, their attendance should be considered.

## Prepare the materials.
Prepare binders containing the JRP results for the participants.
Extract other relevant information from the repository (if any).

If a BAA study has been done:

- Extract the relevant subset of the process decomposition diagram.

- Extract the relevant subset of the entity-relationship diagram.

- Extract the relevant subset of the process flow (dependency) diagram, showing how the processes are dependent on one another.

- Add detailed comments to the above diagrams where necessary. See Chapter 21 and [MARTIN90c].

Explore what structures or designs might be reusable.
See Chapter 15.

Identify reusable screen templates.
Identify reusable structures.
Identify reusable objects and processes.
Investigate what existing applications might be modified.
Explore any other relevant information in the repository.

*continued on next page*

Print relevant diagrams and listings from the repository for the participants to review.

Make overhead transparencies, where appropriate, of the information in the repository.

Establish standards, templates and reusable constructs.
See Chapter 15.

An I.S. professional, possibly the JAD Scribe, should understand the capabilities of the code generator, and be familiar with the reusable designs in the repository, so that reusability can be employed to the maximum extent.

Customize the JAD agenda.

Determine number and duration of JAD sessions if different from that below.

Duplicate and modify this document where it can usefully form part of the agenda.

List the processes involved.

°° Prepare an agenda for each process.

Prepare the participants.

Give participants literature on the JAD procedure (Chapter 8).

The participants should be made familiar with the "Twelve Essentials for JAD in a RAD Lifecycle."

TWELVE ESSENTIALS FOR SUCCESS IN THE USER DESIGN PHASE

To make the RAD User Design Phase work as effectively as possible, it is vital to do a number of things correctly. Everyone involved should heed the twelve essentials listed for the User Design Phase.

---

### TWELVE ESSENTIALS FOR THE USER DESIGN PHASE

1. The User Design Phase must be conducted by an experienced, skilled, unbiased, full-time JAD professional.

2. A suitably high-level end user executive ("Executive Owner") must be committed to having the system and must be determined to move fast.

3. The right end users must attend the workshops.

4. The design must be done with the I-CASE tool that is used for the Construction Phase, and the results must be in the repository of this tool. The participants sign off on the design in the I-CASE repository.

5. Information from the repository should be used in the design (for example, the data model, Business Area Analysis and reusable constructs).

6. Participants attend the workshop full time.

7.  The workshop room should have no telephone; there should be no interruptions; an off-site location works best. The sessions should start on time. The participants should be committed to work in the evening for the five days of the workshop.

8.  During the workshop, all participants are treated as equals.

9.  There should be thorough preparation prior to the workshop.

10. If appropriate, the JAD workshop should be preceded by a JRP workshop with participants skilled at higher-level planning.

11. All specifications prepared before the session by the RAD Workshop Leader should be treated as "proposed."

12. Technical jargon should be avoided.

Train the participants in the diagramming techniques where necessary. The participants should be able to read and understand:

- entity-relationship diagrams;
- process decomposition diagrams;
- process dependency (or data-flow) diagrams;
- action diagrams.

Give the participants the JAD agenda.

Hold kickoff meeting.

The kickoff meeting should be held some days before the JAD workshop so that the participants have time to prepare.

- Have the Executive Owner (Executive Owner) make the opening speech, making the objectives clear to the participants.

- Review the timetable for the workshop.

- Review the agenda.

- Give participants the preparatory material for them to study. Inform them that they must understand it well before the first workshop.

- Review the initial data models and process models with the participants.

- Review relevant goals, problems and critical success factors.

- Review the business assumptions that are to be made.

Prepare the room.
Facilities Required in the JRP/JAD Room

- Large white board with colored pens.

- Flip-chart board, colored pens and space to display multiple flip charts.

*continued on next page*

- Overhead projector and screen, with pre-prepared and blank transparencies; colored pens.

- Possibly, a magnetic or felt board with a kit for building diagrams.

- PC with the prototyping and I-CASE toolset.

- Large-screen monitor or projector so that all participants can see and discuss what is on the screen of the prototyping and I-CASE toolset.

- Printer so that I-CASE designs can be printed for the participants.

- Portable copier so that all participants can be given copies of information created.

- Polaroid camera to record white-board drawings or wall charts.

- Slide projector if the RAD Workshop Leader has prepared slides.

- Videotape player and television monitor if the RAD Workshop Leader has planned to use videotapes.

- Coffee and refreshments.

- Name cards and stationery for participants.

- No telephone!

Conduct the first design workshop.

The Executive Owner should visit the workshop periodically to lend support.

- Review the output from the JRP workshop.
- Clarify the scope of the JAD workshop.

Carry out the design.

The following techniques are used to create the design.

The design is represented in four main types of diagrams, integrated by the I-CASE tool:

- entity-relationship diagrams;
- process decomposition diagrams (Chapter 14);
- process dependency (or data-flow) diagrams (Chapter 14);
- action diagrams.

Screens are designed and discussed with the end users.

A prototype dialog is discussed with the end users.

Reports are designed and discussed with the end users.

Determine what data the system uses.

Examine the entity-relationship diagram (if any), adjusting it as necessary.

Build a data model for the system.

Add detailed comments to the model where necessary.

Determine what processes the system uses.

Examine any process decomposition diagrams,
adjusting them as necessary.

Complete the process decomposition diagram for the system.

Examine any process-flow (data-flow) diagrams,
adjusting them as necessary.

Complete the data-flow diagrams for the system.

Examine each process in detail.

Determine the steps in the procedure to be used.
The steps may be examined within the following framework:

°° 1: PLANNING
°° 2: RECEIVING
°° 3: PROCESSING RECEIPTS
°° 4: MONITORING
°° 5: ASSIGNING
°° 6: PROCESSING
°° 7: RECORDING
°° 8: SENDING
°° 9: EVALUATING

Build an initial data flow diagram for each process.

Enter the procedure steps into the data flow diagram on the
screen of the I-CASE tool. (The initial diagram is an approximate
diagram. The knowledge coordinator or comprehensive checking
capabilities of the I-CASE tool are switched off at this time.
They will be used later to solidify the design.)

Examine each procedure step in more detail.

Describe its purpose.
Determine its input data.
Determine its output data.
Determine what processing occurs and represent it with an
   action diagram.
Adjust the data flow diagram if necessary.
Design and paint the screens.
Design and create the reports.

For each procedure step, create a partial prototype.

Create a prototype of the screens, dialog and reports used.
Develop and enhance more complete prototypes as appropriate.

Address security.

Determine security requirements.
Design authorization scheme.
Determine how security will be handled.

Address unresolved issues.

List unresolved issues.
Determine responsibility and deadline for unresolved issues.

*continued on next page*

Details of Issue
- Issue:
- Person assigned to resolve the issue:
- Assign date:
- Date to be resolved by:
- Resolution:

Determine the user training needs.

- what user training is needed.
- who will be responsible for user training.

Determine the user documentation needs.

- what user documentation will be needed.
- who will be responsible for user documentation.

Plan for conversion.

Determine the sequence of steps required for conversion.

Define the sequence of steps that will be used to load the database and verify that it is correct.

Review the conversion procedure with end-user management.

Determine the resources required for conversion.

Determine when these resources will be required.

Assign individuals to steps for which end users are responsible.

Document the conversion sequence and responsibilities.

Develop a schedule for the cutover to the new system in production mode.

Plan the production procedures.

Establish the procedures for normal system operation.

Plan any manual or paperwork procedures that must accompany the new installation. Determine who will design these.

Plan the procedures for restart and recovery.
Plan the fallback procedures.

Establish the security requirements. Plan the audit procedures.

Establish the User Construction Team.

Establish which users will work with the Construction Team (on a part-time basis), reviewing the transaction-processing modules as they evolve. These users may be mainly those present in the JAD workshop.

Determine whether the users themselves will build components, employing report generators, forth-generation languages, or other user tools.

Plan the second JAD workshop.

Determine what has to be accomplished before the second workshop.
Establish who will accomplish it.
Determine how long it should take.
Establish date and time of the second workshop.

Complete the output from the first workshop.

The Scribe cleans up and polishes the design, possibly with the help of other I.S. professionals who were in the first JAD workshop.

The following steps are taken:

Solidify the design from the first workshop.

Formally analyze the specifications and design, and improve them where necessary.

Use the knowledge coordinator of the I-CASE tool to ensure that the design is internally consistent, and consistent with other knowledge in the repository.

Create or enhance the prototypes.

Complete the documentation from the first workshop.

Give the documentation to the end users for study prior to the second workshop.

End users should list questions and suggestions ready for the second workshop.

Establish the Construction Teams.

Establish the SWAT Team.  See Chapter 10.

Determine which SWAT Team will build the system and who will be members of the team.

Establish the Construction Assistance Team.

Users in the JAD workshop may constitute the Construction Assistance Team.

Involve the SWAT Team.

Familiarize members of the SWAT Team with first JAD workshop output.

Establish a friendly relationship between the SWAT Team and the Construction Assistance Team and ensure that they will work well together.

The SWAT Team studies the output of the first JAD workshop, examines the prototypes and I-CASE design.

Motivate the SWAT Team.  See Chapter 10.

Review and refine the design.

Various end users work with the prototypes and comment on them. Modifications may be made as appropriate.

The SWAT Team participates in the refinement of the prototypes.

The prototypes are adjusted, if necessary, to employ reusable

*continued on next page*

constructs.

The SWAT Team helps polish the design, especially with a view to
employing reusable constructs.

The SWAT Team makes modifications that can speed up the
Construction Phase. Issues that remained unresolved from the
first workshop are dealt with.

Usability-test the prototypes.   See Chapter 17.

Establish the project repository contents.

The Scribe establishes the subset of the repository that is to be
used for this project, ensuring that the design from the first
workshop is fully represented in it.

The SWAT Team examines the repository output of the first JAD
workshop and refines it if necessary.

The SWAT Team determines what reusable constructs can be
employed in the project and establishes those in the repository.

Conduct the second design workshop.

The SWAT Team participates in the second JAD workshop.

One or more members of the SWAT Team that will construct the
system should attend the second workshop.

The SWAT Team helps refine the final design, data model, process
model, prototypes, and dialog templates.

The SWAT Team establishes a good, friendly working relationship
with the end users.

The SWAT Team ensures that the output of the User Design Phase is
such that they can move quickly to achieve the targets of the
Construction Phase.

The SWAT Team should make the estimates for the Construction
Phase, based on recorded metrics of its own past experience and
that of similar teams.   See Chapter 10, "Estimating..."

The SWAT Team's estimates should be agreed upon with the project
management.

The following actions take place:

Review experience in using the prototypes.
Review the end users' questions and suggestions.
Discuss enhancements that are necessary.

Each procedure step must be examined.

Ensure that reusable constructs can be used as fully as appropriate.
Review the inputs and outputs.
Review the screens and dialog used.
Review any reports generated.
Review and enhance more complete prototypes as appropriate.
Review the overall data flow diagram.
Review the information in the database.

Review the overall design and update as necessary.
Specify security requirements.
Estimate volumes.

Address unresolved issues.   (See separate entry above.)

Estimate the required effort and cost.

> The estimating method must relate to experience with the
> I-CASE toolset. Manpower statistics for COBOL/PLI/FORTRAN
> have almost no relevance.

Obtain manpower statistics of experience with the I-CASE toolset,
preferably from the SWAT Team that will build the system.

Estimate the number of function points of the system.

The SWAT Team should make the estimates.

The SWAT Team's estimates should be agreed upon
with the project management.

Split the project into multiple SWAT-Team efforts, if necessary.
See Chapter 12 (Parallel Swat-Team Development).

Estimate what application functions can be built with one
SWAT-Team effort of two or three months.

If the project is too large for one SWAT-Team effort of, say,
three months, divide it into separate subsystems
that can be built simultaneously by separate SWAT Teams.

Use the workbench tools to do the subdivision into separate
SWAT-Team efforts (process decomposition diagram and process
dependency diagram or data-flow diagram).

Ensure that the interfaces between the separate SWAT-Team efforts
are defined with precision with the I-CASE tool.

Review the actions necessary for cutover.
See Methodology Charts 19-1, 18-1 and 18-2.

Establish appropriate user expectations.

Show the participants a timetable for the RAD lifecycle.

Explain their participation in the Construction Phase.

Ensure that the users' expectations of when the completed system
could become available are realistic.

Finalize design.

Further enhance the design if necessary.

The SWAT Team ensures that the output of the User Design Phase is
such that they can move quickly to achieve the targets of the
Construction Phase.

Formally analyze the specifications and design and improve them
where necessary.

Use the knowledge coordinator of the design tool to ensure that

*continued on next page*

the design is internally consistent, and consistent with other knowledge in the encyclopedia.

Resolve any remaining unresolved issues.

Ensure that the design is complete enough to proceed with the Construction Phase.

Complete the documentation.

Complete the documentation in the I-CASE tool.
Print the documentation from the I-CASE tool.

Obtain sign-off of the User Design Team.

The users involved should sign off on the design as represented in the repository of the I-CASE tool, ready to move quickly into the Construction Phase.

Present the results to the Executive Owner of the system.

The Executive Owner may need the results refined until he feels comfortable in giving a go-ahead for the Construction Phase.

Obtain a go-ahead decision from the Executive Owner.

The Executive Owner should make a quick decision whether to give the go-ahead for the Construction Phase, and release funds for it.

If the Project Is to Go Ahead

- Obtain a commitment of the necessary funds.

- Obtain a commitment to go ahead with the preparation for cutover.

- Obtain a commitment of the time required from end users.

- Obtain a commitment to move fast, avoiding political or bureaucratic delays, with the planning for handling the necessary organizational changes.

The Executive Owner should make a closing speech.

Reference

[MARTIN90c]  James Martin, Information Engineering (a trilogy), Book II: Planning and Analysis, Prentice Hall, Inc., Englewood Cliffs, New Jersey, 1990 (201-592-2261).

Methodology Chart 9:    PROTOTYPING

Prototyping

Prototyping is a technique for building a quick and rough version of a desired system or parts of that system. The prototype illustrates the system to users and designers. It allows them to see flaws and invent ways to improve the system. It serves as a communications vehicle for allowing persons who require the system to review the proposed user interaction with the system. For this purpose, it is far more effective than reviewing paper specifications.

- A prototype is used where the functions and detailed design of a system are not yet fully understood.

- The prototype is used to explore and solidify the functions and design.

> The procedure given below may be modified with MediaScribe to meet the needs of the particular situation.

Determine who will review the prototype.

The main reviewers are end users who need the system.

> Ensure that sufficient commitment exists that a thorough review job will be done.

In its final stages, the prototype may also be reviewed by:

- technical staff who will build the final system;.
- the human factoring expert, who may operate a usability laboratory (Chapter 17);
- management;
- the Executive Owner (Executive Sponsor);
- possibly external reviewers such as customers;
- possibly an external consultant.

Determine who will build the prototype.

- the Scribe at a JAD session;
- an I.S. professional;
- an end user;
- an end user working with an I.S. professional; or
- a SWAT Team.

Characteristics of the Prototyping Tool

THE TOOL SHOULD:

- be an integrated part of the I-CASE toolset;

- use designs, templates and structures stored in the I-CASE repository;

- store the results of the prototyping in the I-CASE repository;

- be interactive;

- be easy to use;

- facilitate quick screen design and report design so that it can be used in a JAD session;

*continued on next page*

- make changes quick and easy;

- encourage step-wise refinement;

- facilitate quick building of prototypes that evolve into the
  final system;

- support desirable dialog structures, such as scroll bars, mouse
  operation, an action bar, drop-down menus, etc;

- support appropriate database structures;

- support installation standards, such as IBM's SAA (Systems
  Application Architecture);

- provide facilities for testing;

- give good machine performance (with an optimizing compiler).

So the prototype can become the final system, the tool should have:

- ability to achieve good machine performance.
- ability to support the data-base structure of the final system.
- appropriate networking access.
- ability to handle a suitably large number of users.
- ability to handle suitably large databases.
- ability to handle suitably high traffic volumes.
- ability to link subroutines into the prototype.
- facilities for extracting data from files or databases
  and loading them into the prototype database --
  OR on-line access to other files or databases.

The system the tool generates should have:

- features for recovery from failures.
- features for fallback.
- security features.
- features for auditability.
- features for ease of maintenance.

Build detailed prototype.

Put the data into the prototyping tool.

Obtain the source data.
Determine whether the source data will need converting.
Convert the source data if necessary.
Extract the data into the prototyping tool.

Evolve the prototype with the end users.

Refine the prototype continuously, working with the end user(s),
until an acceptable system is achieved.

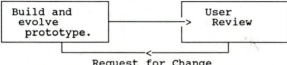

```
┌─────────────┐                    ┌─────────────┐
│ Build and   │                    │   User      │
│  evolve     │───────────────────>│   Review    │
│ prototype.  │                    │             │
└─────────────┘                    └─────────────┘
       │           <─────────────────────┘
       └── Request for Change
```

°° Step-by-Step or Continuous Evolution?  See Chapter 9.

Determine final system needs that are missing from the prototype.

Typical examples are:

- features for recovery from failures.
- features for fallback.
- security features.
- features for auditability.
- features for ease of maintenance.
- machine efficiency.
- facilities for having multiple users.
- ability to handle the anticipated transaction volumes with adequate performance and response times.
- suitably large database facilities.
- networking facilities.
- operation on a different machine.
- documentation.

Determine whether the prototype will be used for training.

Prototypes can be effective for training future users of the application, and the training manager may want minor modifications making to them for this purpose.

Establish appropriate user expectations.

Ensure that the users know what has to be done before the system is cut over and do not have false expectations about getting the prototype immediately.

Ensure that the users know when the system is to be cut over.

Ensure that the users and management have realistic expectations about what the system will be like and when it will be available.

Methodology Chart 10-1:   THE MANAGEMENT OF SWAT TEAMS

SWAT TEAM

> A SMALL group of HIGH QUALITY developers, HIGHLY SKILLED
> with the MOST POWERFUL tools, who WORK WELL TOGETHER as a
> team and have the COMPLETE SET OF SKILLS needed for FAST,
> ITERATIVE development with the end users.

> The procedure given below may be modified with MediaScribe
> to meet the needs of the particular situation.

ESSENTIALS FOR SUCCESS IN THE MANAGEMENT OF SWAT TEAMS

- Select top-quality, capable team members who are
  determined to rise to the challenge.

- Choose team members who work well together as a team.
  Adjust the team if necessary to make it "jell" and
  be as powerful as possible.

- Allow the team to develop a feeling of uniqueness and team pride.

- Keep successful teams together for many projects,
  and engender a high level of team spirit.

- Use the most powerful toolset.

- Ensure that the team is motivated for high speed and high quality.

- Use a methodology designed and tuned for high speed and
  high quality.

- Have the best possible training in the tools and methodology.

- Ensure full end-user participation.

- Structure the work so that each developer has a feeling of
  achieving something interesting and creative, with frequent
  "closures."

- Establish clear goals and measurements, and rank the teams on
  how well they meet the goals.

- Ensure that the team keeps metrics of its performance and allow
  it to make its own estimates prior to the Construction Phase.

- Employ powerful motivational techniques.

- Provide good SWAT-Team working conditions (Box 10.1).

- Pay attention to avoidance of burn-out.

- Make the development process as enjoyable as possible.

- Sweep away any bureaucracy or factors that could slow down
  the SWAT-Team development.

- Avoid defensive, interfering management; leave the team free
  to build the system its own way.

Criteria for Selection of SWAT-Team Members

EACH PERSON
- will work fast and constructively.
- has an attitude geared to success.
- will cooperate well with the other team members.
- will work long hours when necessary.
- has good communications skills.
- is familiar with the basic techniques needed.
- is highly skilled with the I-CASE toolset and can operate fast with it.

SOME TEAM MEMBERS may have certain, more specialized skills, such as database design or skill in writing good HELP screens.

IN COMBINATION, the team has the complete set of the skills required. A team that works well together should stay together for multiple projects.

## Physical Work Environment

### Characteristics of the SWAT-Team Work Area

SWAT-Team members should share a work office that affords both privacy and closeness.

Adjacent to the work office, there should be a private room where team members can interact with users, hold discussions and make telephone calls without disturbing other team members.

The SWAT-Team work area should be close to that of the end users and the Construction Assistance Team.

The SWAT Team should be able to work there at any hour they choose.

The SWAT Team must have privacy and freedom from interruptions.

- A secretarial service should protect them from interruptions.
- Telephone calls must be divertable.
- Electronic mail should be used (to avoid interrupting work).

The work environment should have no disruptive noise.

The work environment should be as pleasant as possible.

Team members should have a window with a view.

The SWAT Team should design the layout and decoration of its own work area, to make it as productive and pleasant as possible and help give the team a feeling of uniqueness.

### Contents of the SWAT-Team Work Area

The work room should contain:
- 100 square feet of office space for each SWAT-Team member.
- 30 square feet of desk space for each SWAT-Team member.
- a computer and I-CASE toolset for each SWAT-Team member. The computers may be LAN-connected.
- a shared printer.

The discussion room should contain:
- a table for group discussions;
- a computer for demonstrating the application;
- a sofa and chairs;

*continued on next page*

- telephones;
- a white board;
- a flip-chart stand;
- a wall surface where paper can be pinned
  (or other means of wall-charting);
- coffee and refreshments.

## Goals and Metrics

### Establish the system goals.

- Determine the date by which the system must be completed.
- Establish a target for system productivity.
- Establish a target for system quality.
- Determine whether the team must create user documentation.

### Establish how the team will be measured.

- function points per person-month;
- on-time delivery of the system;
- number of bugs in the delivered system;
- number of design defects in the delivered system;
- number of changes needed in the delivered system to aid usability
  (Chapter 17).

### Establish measurement expertise.  See Chapters 10 and 2.

The team should become skilled at measuring its own performance
so that it can confidently make estimates of the time needed to
for construction.

The team should maintain a file of metrics for this purpose.

## Motivation
See Chapter 6.

### Establish the financial rewards.

Relate salary raises to achievement of goals.

Create a bonus scheme that is a substantial part of the financial
compensation.

Establish a bonus for individuals that is related to achievement of
goals.

Establish a bonus for the team as a whole so that individuals are
motivated to succeed in order that they do not let their colleagues
down.

### Establish nonfinancial rewards.

Engender a substantial sense of pride in excellent development.

Have high management congratulate successful teams.

Plan a victory celebration if the system is completed on time.

Put team-member names in the software "credit titles" if the project
is completed on time.

Promote team members with repeated success to a higher professional
grade.

Make team members with repeated success members of a highly prestigious RAD club, which meets monthly and holds an annual conference in an exotic location.

Acknowledge repeated success with gifts such as pins, pens, cufflinks and binders.

Acknowledge repeated success at a rewards dinner.

Engender team spirit.

Engender a substantial sense of pride in being a member of the team.

Reward the team as a group so that individuals are motivated to succeed in order that they do not let their team down.

Measure and publish the team productivity and quality metrics.

Encourage competition among separate teams.

Rank the teams in order of performance, and give an award to the top-of-the-league team, possibly a short vacation with spouses in an exotic location.

Hold an annual awards dinner with spouses present.

Avoidance of Burnout

Divide large projects into subsystems that can be developed and tested autonomously, such that each subsystem can be completed in 1 to 4 months.

No single SWAT Team project should last longer than 4 months.

Allow the team members enough time off between projects to relax and recharge their batteries.

Be alert to symptoms of individuals becoming burnt out.

Be sure that the individuals are capable of achieving what is asked of them.

Structure the development so that each individual has a feeling of achieving something interesting and creative.

Make the development process as enjoyable as possible; the developers should be having fun.

Procedure

Familiarize.

Involve the SWAT Team. Familiarize members of the SWAT Team with first JAD workshop output.

Establish a friendly relationship between the SWAT Team and the Construction Assistance Team and ensure that they will work well together.

The SWAT Team studies the output of the first JAD workshop, examines the prototypes and I-CASE design.

Establish the project repository contents.

*continued on next page*

The SWAT Team examines the repository output of the first JAD workshop and refines it if necessary.

The SWAT Team determines what reusable constructs can be employed in the project and establishes those in the repository.

Refine the output of the first JAD workshop.

The SWAT Team participates in the refinement of the prototypes.

The prototypes are adjusted, if necessary, to employ reusable constructs.

The SWAT Team helps polish the design, especially with a view to employing reusable constructs.

The SWAT Team makes modifications that can speed up the Construction Phase. Issues that remained unresolved from the first workshop are dealt with.

The SWAT Team participates in the second JAD workshop.

One or more members of the SWAT Team that will construct the system should attend the second workshop.

The SWAT Team helps refine the final design, data model, process model, prototypes, and dialog templates.

The SWAT Team establishes a good, friendly working relationship with the end users.

The SWAT Team ensures that the output of the User Design Phase is such that they can move quickly to achieve the targets of the Construction Phase.

The SWAT Team should make the estimates for the Construction Phase, based on recorded metrics of its own past experience and that of similar teams.  See Chapter 10, "Estimating..."

The SWAT Team's estimates should be agreed upon with the project management.

Methodology Chart 10-2:  CONSTRUCTION PHASE

> The procedure given below may be modified with MediaScribe
> to meet the needs of the particular situation.

Before the Construction Phase Begins

Obtain sign-off of the User Design Team.

The users involved should sign off on the design as represented in
the repository of the I-CASE tool, ready to move quickly into the
Construction Phase.

Present the results to the Executive Owner of the system.

The Executive Owner may need the results refined until he feels
comfortable in giving a go-ahead for the Construction Phase.

Obtain a go-ahead decision from the Executive Owner.

The Executive Owner should make a quick decision whether to give the
go-ahead for the Construction Phase, and release the funds for it.

The Executive Owner must be FULLY COMMITTED to having the system
built and taking the necessary steps to make end-user managers move
rapidly and commit the time needed for development and cutover.

Select and prepare the SWAT Team.

The SWAT Team should have become familiar with the system between
the JAD workshops and should have participated in the final
workshop.

The SWAT Team should have adapted the design to its own techniques,
particularly to reusable constructs.

Construction Phase

Do detailed design of the system structure.

Extend the JAD design as necessary.
Employ reusable constructs to the maximum extent.
Do detailed database design.

Build transactions.

The system is built one transaction at a time.
Each transaction is built with reusable templates.

BENEFITS  OF  REUSABILITY
See Chapter 15.

- SPEED OF DEVELOPMENT
- LOW COST
- QUALITY
- REDUCTION IN MAINTENANCE
- SHARED EXPERTISE
- COMPLEXITY
- FACILITATES LEARNING OF GOOD DESIGN
- ONE-PERSON TEAMS
- DOCUMENTATION
- EASE OF CHANGE
- STANDARDS
- INTEGRATION

*continued on next page*

°° BUSINESS BENEFITS

A small group of core transactions are built and tested. These are
then refined and modified to form other transactions.

Each transaction is quickly designed with the I-CASE tool, and code
is generated and tested. The system generator should go from design
to runnable code in minutes.

Design logic errors should be quickly resolved, with a visually-oriented
symbolic debugging tool.

The resulting transaction is shown to the end-user Construction
Assistance Team for validation, and modified as required.

Perform usability tests.

Groups of transactions should be checked in the Usability Lab to
discover any modifications that should be made to improve usability.
This should done early enough so that when changes are made they do
not impact the schedule.

> How to use the application should be intuitively clear.

Summary of Characteristics of Intuitive Software
See Chapter 17.

°° NO ALIEN SYNTAX
°° SELF-EXPLANATORY
°° OBVIOUS
°° CONSISTENT
°° STANDARD
°° IN-CONTEXT HELP
°° NO NEED FOR MANUALS
°° NO NEED FOR CLASSES
°° NO HIDDEN POINTS OF CONFUSION
°° NO CRYPTIC ERROR MESSAGES
°° USER SELF-SUFFICIENCY

Perform ongoing integration.

When a transaction has been designed, coordinate the design with the
rest of the system using the knowledge coordinator of the I-CASE
toolset, so that integration of the design proceeds continuously.

Generate complete load modules (e.g., for CICS or MVS).

When a transaction has been built and validated, test its
integration with the rest of the system so that integration testing
proceeds continuously.

°° Prepare for cultural changes.  See Methodology Chart 18-1.
Design and prepare for cutover.

Design and preparation for cutover should be done while the system
is being built because the time available for cutover is short.

A team operating in parallel with the SWAT Teams should be designing
the facilities for cutover.

Cutover needs careful planning and execution.
See Methodology Chart 18-1 and Chapter 19.

Integration Testing

After the separate subsystems have been fully debugged and approved, they will be linked as appropriate and tested working in combination. This stage should be relatively short as ongoing integration testing has been done throughout the construction.

Create physical design.

Determine whether data will be distributed. See Appendices IX-1, IX-2 and IX-3.

Determine traffic volumes.
°° Perform data use analysis.  See Appendix IX-1.
°° Do physical database design.  See Appendix IX-2.
Determine hardware requirements.
Examine how to optimize performance.
Complete documentation of the final design.

Have the Review Board examine the system.

The Review Board determines whether the system contains an appropriate set of functions to be taken into production.

If not, it identifies with the SWAT Team what enhancements should be made and how long it should take to make these enhancements.

Obtain a decision whether to go ahead with installation.

After reviewing the results of integration testing, usability testing, and design for cutover a final decision should made by the Executive Owner whether the project goes into the installation stage.

If the Project Is to Go Ahead

• Obtain a commitment of the necessary funds.

• Obtain a commitment to go ahead with the preparation for cutover.

• Obtain a commitment of the time required from end users.

• Obtain a commitment to move fast, avoiding political or bureaucratic delays, with the planning for handling the necessary organizational changes.

Methodology Chart 11:   TIMEBOX DEVELOPMENT

Timebox Methodology

The timebox methodology is a highly successful variant of the RAD
lifecycle. It sets a firm deadline for the end of the Construction
Phase. Refinements can be slipped, but the deadline can not.

The core system is built quickly, using the code generator and
reusable constructs where possible. The functionality of the core
system is then successively polished and added to. This enhancement
must stop so that the deadline can be met. The refinements are thus
restricted in order to meet the deadline.

The Review Board decides whether to put the system into production or
to make minor changes before cutover.

> The procedure given below may be modified with MediaScribe
> to meet the needs of the particular situation.

Suggested Timetable Using a 17-Week Timebox

In this specimen timetable, the Requirements Planning and User Design
Phases are combined.

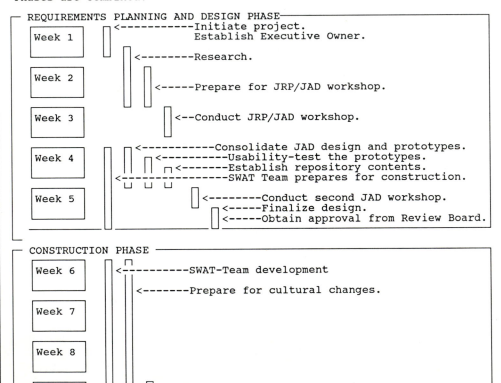

REQUIREMENTS PLANNING AND DESIGN PHASE

Week 1    <----------Initiate project.
                     Establish Executive Owner.

          <--------Research.

          <------Prepare for JRP/JAD workshop.

Week 2

Week 3    <--Conduct JRP/JAD workshop.

Week 4    <----------Consolidate JAD design and prototypes.
          <----------Usability-test the prototypes.
          <------Establish repository contents.
          <---------------SWAT Team prepares for construction.

Week 5    <--------Conduct second JAD workshop.
          <-----Finalize design.
          <-----Obtain approval from Review Board.

CONSTRUCTION PHASE

Week 6    <----------SWAT-Team development

          <-------Prepare for cultural changes.

Week 7

Week 8

Week 9    <------Plan for cutover.

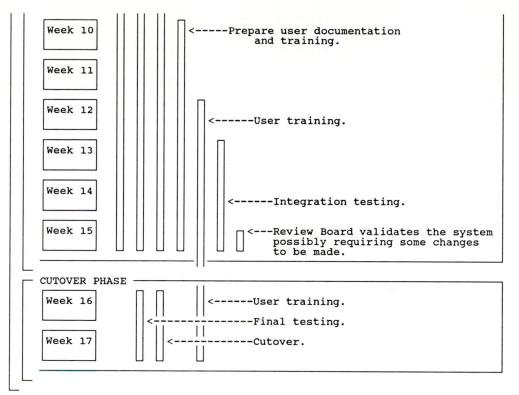

```
     ┌─ Week 10     <-----Prepare user documentation
     │                         and training.

        Week 11

        Week 12       <------User training.

        Week 13

        Week 14       <------Integration testing.

        Week 15       <---Review Board validates the system
                            possibly requiring some changes
                            to be made.

  ┌─ CUTOVER PHASE ──────────────────────────────────────────
  │   Week 16            <------User training.
                   <---------------Final testing.
      Week 17      <-----------Cutover.
```

Before the Project Begins

Select the tools.  See Chapter 3.

It is desirable to select one toolset and perfect its use. The
methodology is highly dependent on a toolset that enables fast and
easy design, and a rapid cycle of modify-generate-test. The
methodology is built around the toolset and adapted to it. Selecting
the right toolset is highly critical.

The I-CASE environment should be well established with I.S.
professionals well trained in the use of the toolset.

Characteristics of the I-CASE Toolset   (Capabilities)

| I-CASE Toolset:   an integrated-CASE toolset with an intelligent central repository (encyclopedia). |
| --- |

THE TOOLSET SHOULD INCLUDE THE FOLLOWING:

• A complete data-modeling capability, with entity-relationship
  diagrams and the ability to represent normalized data.

• A complete process-modeling capability with decomposition
  diagrams, dependency diagrams and data-flow diagrams.

*continued on next page*

- The ability to display and cluster matrices and map processes against entities, showing how the processes use the entities.

- A versatile screen painter (which can be used very quickly in JAD sessions).

- Ability to link screens and responses into a dialog.

- A versatile report generator (which can be used very quickly in JAD sessions).

- The ability to draw the logic of processes with action (hyper) diagrams.

- The capability of fully checking the consistency and integrity of all of the above representations of information.

- The capability of converting the design directly into code that is machine-efficient.

```
THE TOOLSET SHOULD:

 ·   be interactive.
 ·   be quick and easy to use.
 ·   give the most automated capability for design.
 ·   convert the design directly into code.
 ·   enable code to be generated and tested as quickly as possible.
 ·   give the fastest possible cycle of generate-test-modify,
     generate-test-modify...
```

Establish the methodology.

Adapt the methodology to the toolset.

The methodology should be adapted to fit the toolset.
See Chapter 4, "RAD Methodology..."

Use and tune the methodology.

The methodology should be applied to many projects and tuned on the basis of experience.
See Chapter 4, "Best Combinations..."

Select and train the practitioners.  See Chapter 10.

ESSENTIALS FOR SUCCESS IN THE MANAGEMENT OF SWAT TEAMS

- Select top-quality, capable team members who are determined to rise to the challenge.

- Choose team members who work well together as a team. Adjust the team if necessary to make it "jell" and be as powerful as possible.

- Allow the team to develop a feeling of uniqueness and team pride.

- Keep successful teams together for many projects, and engender a high level of team spirit.

- Use the most powerful toolset.

- Ensure that the team is motivated for high speed and high quality.

- Use a methodology designed and tuned for high speed and high quality.

- Have the best possible training in the tools and methodology.

- Ensure full end-user participation.

- Structure the work so that each developer has a feeling of achieving something interesting and creative, with frequent "closures."

- Establish clear goals and measurements, and rank the teams on how well they meet the goals.

- Ensure that the team keeps metrics of its performance and allow it to make its own estimates prior to the Construction Phase.

- Employ powerful motivational techniques.

- Provide good SWAT-Team working conditions (Box 10.1).

- Pay attention to avoidance of burn-out.

- Make the development process as enjoyable as possible.

- Sweep away any bureaucracy or factors that could slow down the SWAT-Team development.

- Avoid defensive, interfering management; leave the team free to build the system its own way.

Initiate the project.

Determine the need for the system.
Write, in one page, the functions of the system.
Establish an Executive Owner.

Obtain commitment of the Executive Owner.

Development should not proceed unless a suitably high-level end-user executive is FULLY COMMITTED to having the system built and taking the necessary steps to make end-user managers move rapidly and commit the time needed for development and cutover.

Establish the I.S. team.

- PROJECT MANAGER
- CONSTRUCTION TEAM
- RAD WORKSHOP LEADER
- HUMAN-FACTORS EXPERT
- DATA MODELING EXPERT

Requirements Planning Phase
See Chapter 7

Establish the Review Board.

the team of users who review the system after construction and decide whether any modifications are needed before cutover.

Prior to the timebox, the Review Board reviews the requirements; at

*continued on next page*

the end of the timebox it reviews the results.

The Review Board reports to the Executive Owner.  It includes:

- leading spokespeople of the end users who need the system;
- the Executive Owner (Executive Sponsor);
- an I.S. executive;
- possibly an external consultant.

The Review Board may be the same as the Requirements Planning Team involved in the Requirements Planning Phase.

The Review Board ensures that sufficient commitment exists that a thorough review job will be done.

## User Design Phase

### Estimate the required effort and cost.

> The estimating method must relate to experience with the prototyping/code-generator tool. Manpower statistics for COBOL/PLI/FORTRAN have almost no relevance.

- Obtain manpower statistics of experience with the prototyping/generator tool.

- Estimate the number of screens.

- Estimate the number of reports.

- Estimate the number of logical files.

- Estimate the proportion of the system that can be generated nonprocedurally, and the proportion that needs procedural (fourth-generation) coding.

- Estimate the number of lines of procedural code.

- Estimate the manpower effort for procedural code.

### Split the project into multiple timeboxes, if necessary.

Estimate what application functions can be built during the 60-day timebox with a small (2- or 3-person) team.

If the project is too large for one timebox, divide it into multiple timeboxes that can proceed simultaneously.

Use the workbench tools to do the subdivision into separate timebox efforts (process decomposition diagram and process dependency diagram or data-flow diagram).

Ensure that the interfaces between the separate timebox efforts are defined with precision with the I-CASE tool.

### Select the timebox team(s).
See Chapter 10 and Methodology Chart 10-1.

#### Criteria for Selection of SWAT-Team Members

EACH PERSON  · will work fast and constructively.
· has an attitude geared to success.
· will cooperate well with the other team members.

- will work long hours when necessary.
- has good communications skills.
- is familiar with the basic techniques needed.
- is highly skilled with the I-CASE toolset and can operate fast with it.

SOME TEAM MEMBERS may have certain, more specialized skills, such as database design or skill in writing good HELP screens.

IN COMBINATION, the team has the complete set of the skills required. A team that works well together should stay together for multiple projects.

Motivate the Timebox Team(s).

Ensure that the team knows that success or failure is determined by whether they build an implementable system by the end of the timebox. They cannot extend the timebox deadline.

Ensure them that success will be rewarded.

Tell them that a victory celebration will be held when the system is judged successful.

Tell them that failures are rare and that they must not distinguish themselves by creating a failure.

Ensure them that their activities are very visible to higher management.

Ensure that the Review Board agrees to the design.

Construction Phase
See Methodology Chart 10-2.

The core system is built quickly using the code generator and reusable constructs where possible. The functionality of the core system is then successively polished and added to. This enhancement must stop so that the deadline can be met. The refinements are thus restricted in order to meet the deadline.

Cutover Phase
See Methodology Chart 19.

Methodology Chart 12:   PARALLEL DEVELOPMENT

Parallel SWAT-Team Development

This variant of RAD is intended for high-speed development of large
applications, having a level of complexity of greater than, say, a
thousand function points.

It requires an I-CASE environment with a powerful code generator,
integrated with full data modeling, process modeling, and procedure
design capabilities, an intelligent repository (encyclopedia), and the
capability to coordinate all such information, ensuring complete
integrity.

It requires SWAT Teams highly trained in high-speed use of the I-CASE
toolset.

The costs and risks of new system development are minimized by
emphasizing JRP, JAD, prototyping, and development of subsystems each
with a low cycle-time, within the framework of a rigorous data model
and process model.

Care is taken not to change the data model or interfaces to other
subsystems, unless absolutely necessary. If such a change is made,it
must be agreed to by the overall system coordinator, who will discuss
it with the other teams. The change will be entered into the
encyclopedia used by all teams, and the I-CASE tool will check that
their work integrates with the change precisely.

> The procedure given below may be modified with MediaScribe
> to meet the needs of the particular situation.

Create the coordinating model. See Chapter 12.

The Coordinating Model is an integrated data and process model in the
I-CASE repository, which is used for coordinating the work of
different developers or SWAT Teams.

The preliminary version of the coordinating model is created by I.S.
professionals. The model is reviewed in a JAD workshop, where it will
be validated, adjusted and expanded.

The building of the preliminary coordinating model should proceed in
parallel with preparation for the JAD workshop.

°° Prepare.
°° Hold kickoff meeting.
Create a preliminary data model.

   • Extract the entity-relationship model for this business area
     from the repository.

   • Determine what events occur in this business area.

   • Associate the events with entity-types (a behavior model).

   • Draw the lifecycle of each entity.

   • Enter initial attributes of each entity.

Create a preliminary process model.

   • Extract the business-function decomposition model for this
     business area from the repository.

- Decompose the functions into processes.

- Successively refine the information in the following stages until a complete representation of the data and processes is achieved.

  - Create a detailed data model.

    See Methodology Chart 13 and Chapter 13.

    Data modeling can be done with a bottom-up approach or a top-down approach. To do it thoroughly, both should be used, with a computerized tool to synthesize the results.

  - Create a detailed process model.

    See Methodology Chart 14-2 and Chapter 14.

    - Create a process decomposition diagram.
      - Decompose processes eventually into elementary processes.

        An elementary process is one that cannot be decomposed further without making design decisions that say HOW a procedure operates rather than WHAT a process does.

        An elementary process may be defined as:

        the smallest unit of activity of meaning to the end user, which when complete, leaves the data in a self-consistent state.

        When events occur, these cannot trigger a sub-elementary process.

        Decompose until elementary processes are derived. Check that each lowest-level is elementary; if not, decompose it further.

        Do not waste time perfecting the intermediate structure of the decomposition; the elementary processes are what matter.

        Record a definition of each elementary process.

    - Create a process dependency diagram.

      Correlate this with the process decomposition diagram. Consider what information flows from one process to another.

      - Draw process dependency diagrams.

        Develop a set of process dependency diagrams that show, among them, all the elementary processes.

        Dependency diagrams will be created for higher-level process blocks, and these will be nested to lower levels, using the encyclopedia-based tool and its knowledge coordinator.

        It is likely that errors will be found in the decomposition diagram while drawing the dependency diagrams; these should be corrected.

        Do not waste time perfecting the intermediate structure of the dependency diagrams; it is the elementary processes that matter.

  - Generate an entity-type/process matrix.

*continued on next page*

Build a matrix mapping elementary processes and entity types.
Indicate what process CREATES each entity record.
Indicate what processes UPDATE, READ or DELETE each entity record.

Develop the process/entity matrix.

Create (automatically) a matrix mapping the elementary processes and entity-types.

Fill in the matrix with CREATE, READ, UPDATE and DELETE codes (CRUDs).

Build matrices.

Associate entity-types, processes and events with organizational units and locations.

Associate entity-types, processes and events with goals and problems.

Analyze and correlate (automatically) the above information.

Use a workbench tool that analyzes and correlates the above information with a knowledge coordinator.

Use the knowledge coordinator of the design tool to ensure that the model is internally consistent, and consistent with other knowledge in the repository.

In the JAD workshop, check the Coordinating Model.

Review the data dictionary listing to ensure that all end users agree about the definitions of the data-items.

Review the data model to ensure that their data requirements can be derived from it.

Add to the data model as appropriate.

Add to the process model as appropriate.

Review the process model to determine whether any processes have been omitted.

Brainstorm the possible future uses of the data. For any uses that the model does not serve, create new input to the data model.

Brainstorm possible additions that might be needed in the process model. After any changes are made, use fast computerized redesign to maintain the interest of the end users.

Divide the Coordinating Model into subsystems for SWAT-Team development.

Rules for Subdivision of Systems (for Parallel SWAT-Team Development)

Systems should be subdivided in a way that:

• Each subsystem performs one or more discreet business processes.

• Each subsystem can be tested in its own right.

- Each subsystem executes a function that users can employ, where possible, and that can be tested in the usability laboratory (Chapter 17).

- There is as little data flow as possible between one subsystem and another.

- The data exchanged among subsystems are defined with precision.

- As far as possible, a design decision made in one subsystem should have no effect on another subsystem.

- Each subsystem is small enough to be built by one person or one SWAT Team in not more than three months.

The rules for subdivision should be based on experience with toolset and methodology. Typical rules of thumb might be as follows:

For a powerful code generator:

```
        < 200 function points:    1 person.
 200 to 1000 function points:    1 SWAT Team.
      > 1000 function points:    1000 function points
                                    per SWAT Team.
```

For a powerful code generator and substantial employment of reusable structures:

```
        < 500 function points:    1 person.
 500 to 2000 function points:    1 SWAT Team.
      > 2000 function points:    2000 function points
                                    per SWAT Team.
```

For a mature information-engineering environment with object-oriented analysis for maximum reusability, which has had time to acquire much reusable design:

```
        < 1000 function points:    1 person.
 1000 to 4000 function points:    1 SWAT Team.
      > 4000 function points:     4000 function points
                                    per SWAT Team.
```

Determine how many SWAT Teams will work in parallel.

Estimate the complexity of the system in function points. See Appendix I.

Use the function-point estimate to determine how many 3-month SWAT-Team efforts are needed.

Use the basic diagrams to help divide the model into subsystems that can be developed by separate teams.

Use the process decomposition diagram to help show natural systems. High-level blocks and their children may be natural clusters.

Use the process dependency diagram to help show natural systems.

Identify what data must flow from one system to another.

Subdivide the dependency diagram so that there is as little flow of data from one subdivision to another.

*continued on next page*

Refine the dependency diagram to agree with the clustered matrix.

Use the process/entity matrix to help show natural systems.

The matrix may be clustered on the basis of what processes CREATE what entity-types.

The matrix tool may have a clustering algorithm that can be used.

Refine the clusterings to minimize the interaction among systems.

Parallel SWAT-Team Procedure

STAGE 1.  PLAN
·· Initiate the project.
·· Obtain commitment of the Executive Sponsor.
·· Appoint a professional to lead the activity.
·· Conduct a Joint Requirements Planning (JRP) workshop.
·· Make cost and time estimates.
·· Obtain a decision whether to go ahead with design.

STAGE 2.  DESIGN
·· Appoint the End-User Coordinator.
·· Determine application standards.
·· Create a preliminary version of the coordinating model.
·· Prepare for a JAD workshop.
·· In the JAD workshop, review and refine the coordinating model.
·· Divide coordinating model into submodels for SWAT-Team development.
·· In the JAD workshop, design the procedures.
·· Create and review prototypes.
·· Conduct the second JAD workshop.
·· Obtain a decision whether to go ahead with construction.

STAGE 3.  CONSTRUCT
·· Design and Preparation for Cutover
·· Parallel SWAT-Team Development
·· Prepare for cultural changes.
·· Usability Testing
·· Integration Testing
·· Create physical design.
·· Prepare for cutover.
·· Obtain a decision whether to go ahead with installation.

STAGE 4.  INSTALL
·· Install and adjust pilot system.
·· Expand pilot to full system.

Methodology Chart 13:   DATA MODELING

> The procedure given below may be modified with MediaScribe
> to meet the needs of the particular situation.

## Data Modeling

Data modeling is part of the basic Information Resource Management
process. It should be done independently of the development of any
particular application. It is managed by the Data Administrator.

Whether or not an enterprise has a Data Administration function, a
data model should be created for a RAD project. A person skilled in
data modeling can do this quickly for any one application.

Comprehensive checks on the modeling process are described below that
are sometimes referred to as STABILITY ANALYSIS. The objective is to
make the data model as stable as possible so that it can support major
changes in corporate procedures. Stable data models have had the
effect of drastically reducing program maintenance costs.

## Detailed Data Modeling

Detailed data modeling is tackled in one business area at a time.
Although described here as a self-contained activity it needs to
be an integral part of the Business Area Analysis procedure.

See Chapter 21, Methodology Chart 21-2 and Appendix XI.

## Preparation for Data Modeling

Appoint a data-modeling professional to lead the activity.

If a skilled data-modeling professional exists in-house,
make him responsible for completion of the model on time.

Else
   Employ a consultant skilled in data-modeling.

   Make him responsible for completion of the model on time,
   and for training in-house data-modeling professionals.

   Appoint one or more in-house professionals to become
   data-modeling experts.

   Appoint an in-house professional to take over the work from the
   consultant and be responsible for the model.

Ensure that the necessary tools are installed and working.

   Install a data modeling tool that synthesizes and normalizes
   multiple views of data.

   Use the installation's I-CASE toolset to form the data-model
   repository and coordination tool. The tool that does synthesis and
   normalization should preferably be part of the I-CASE tool.

Form an end-user committee to review the data model.

   Select end-user participants.

   End users selected should

         • be intelligent,

*continued on next page*

- be creative,
- have good human communication skills,
- want to understand information-system techniques,
- be highly knowledgeable about their own business areas.

Give the participants a brief course in the basic principles of data modeling.  See [MARTIN83].

∘∘ Document a naming convention for the data items.

Data Modeling Techniques

Data modeling can be done with a bottom-up approach or a top-down approach. To do it thoroughly, both should be used, with a computerized tool to synthesize the results.

Top-Down Data Modeling Steps

- Determine the entity-types for this project.

- Enter the primary keys for these entity-types.

- Add intersection entity-types where appropriate (with automated assistance).

- Add whatever attributes can be identified.

- Ensure that the attribute groupings are in Fourth Normal Form.

- Enhance this data model with the synthesis and user-checking techniques described elsewhere.

Bottom-Up Data Modeling Steps

Bottom-up data modeling identifies all possible views of the data (all paperwork, screens, reports and so on), analyzes these data and synthesizes them with a computerized tool into a fourth-normal-form data model (Chapter 13).

Data Synthesis
Do the following steps iteratively until the model is complete.

IDENTIFY ALL POSSIBLE USER-VIEWS OF DATA.

- Capture all documents that will be derived from the system.

- Capture all documents that will be input to the system.

- Determine by discussion with the end users what types of data they want to obtain from the systems now and in the future.

- Determine from the systems analysts whether any new record or document requirements are emerging.

- Examine existing files, databases or dictionaries that relate to these data.

Will existing files or databases coexist with the new systems or be converted?

- If they will coexist, plan what data are needed in the new systems to form a bridge with the old systems.

Will application package files or databases coexist with the new systems?

- If so, plan what data are needed in the new systems
  to form a bridge with the packages.

ANALYZE EACH USER-VIEW.

Break each user view into its data elements, and
identify the functional dependency of each data element.

Enter this information into the synthesis tool.

CHECK EACH USER VIEW.

For all of the above user views, do the following:

- Inspect each input.

- Employ the naming convention.

- Inspect each input to see whether it can be simplified.

- Check whether any of the input data-items already exist
  in the model under a different name or in a slightly
  different form. If so, ensure that this redundancy is removed.

- For each data-item, check that no different data-item
  in the model has the same name.

- Be sure that concatenated keys are correctly represented
  in the input to the synthesis process.

- Be sure that all attributes entered are dependent on
  the WHOLE of the key that identifies them.

- Be sure that all attributes entered as input contain
  no transitive dependencies (no hidden keys).

- Question the validity of all links that represent business
  rules, as opposed to the natural properties of the data.
  Could these rules be changed in the future?

- Question any link with a "1" cardinality to ask
  whether it could become a "many" cardinality in the future.

CHECK THE SYNTHESIZED MODEL.

With the user committee:

- Review the data dictionary listing to ensure that
  all end users agree on the definitions of the data-items.

- Review the data model to ensure that
  their data requirements can be derived from it.

- Brainstorm the possible future uses of the data.
  For any uses that the model does not serve,
  create new input to the synthesis process.

Examine every attribute field in the model to see whether it
could become a primary key in the future.

Complete the reverse mapping of any links between keys to
identify any possible MANY-TO-MANY links. Create an extra
concatenated key to take care of any possible future
intersection data.

*continued on next page*

If candidate keys exist in the data model, ensure that they are, in fact, likely to remain candidate keys in the future.

Use fast computerized redesign after any changes are made, to maintain the interest of the end users.

Reference
[MARTIN83] James Martin, Managing the Data Base Environment, Prentice Hall, Inc., Englewood Cliffs, New Jersey, 1983 (201-592-2261).

Methodology Chart 14-1:   PROCEDURE FOR CREATING A PROCESS MODEL

> The procedure given below may be modified with MediaScribe to meet the needs of the particular situation.

Create a preliminary data model.

- Extract the entity-relationship model for this business area from the repository.

- Determine what events occur in this business area.

- Associate the events with entity-types (a behavior model).

- Draw the lifecycle of each entity.

- Enter initial attributes of each entity.

Create a preliminary process model.

- Extract the business-function decomposition model for this business area from the repository.

- Decompose the functions into processes.

Successively refine the information in the following stages until a complete representation of the data and processes is achieved.

Create a detailed data model.

See Methodology Chart 13 and Chapter 13.

Data modeling can be done with a bottom-up approach or a top-down approach. To do it thoroughly, both should be used, with a computerized tool to synthesize the results.

Create a detailed process model.

See Methodology Chart 14-2 and Chapter 14.

Create a process decomposition diagram.
Decompose processes eventually into elementary processes.

When events occur, these cannot trigger a sub-elementary process.

Decompose until elementary processes are derived. Check that each lowest-level is elementary; if not, decompose it further.

Do not waste time perfecting the intermediate structure of the decomposition; the elementary processes are what matter.

Record a definition of each elementary process.

Create a process dependency diagram.

Correlate this with the process decomposition diagram. Consider what information flows from one process to another.

Draw process dependency diagrams.

Develop a set of process dependency diagrams that show, among them, all the elementary processes.

Dependency diagrams will be created for higher-level process

*continued on next page*

blocks, and these will be nested to lower levels, using the encyclopedia-based tool and its knowledge coordinator.

It is likely that errors will be found in the decomposition diagram while drawing the dependency diagrams; these should be corrected.

Do not waste time perfecting the intermediate structure of the dependency diagrams; it is the elementary processes that matter.

Generate an entity-type/process matrix.

Build a matrix mapping elementary processes and entity types.
Indicate what process CREATES each entity record.
Indicate what processes UPDATE, READ or DELETE each entity record.

Develop the process/entity matrix.

Create (automatically) a matrix mapping the elementary processes and entity-types.

Fill in the matrix with CREATE, READ, UPDATE and DELETE codes (CRUDs).

Build matrices.

Associate entity-types, processes and events with organizational units and locations.

Associate entity-types, processes and events with goals and problems.

Analyze and correlate (automatically) the above information.

Use a workbench tool that analyzes and correlates the above information with a knowledge coordinator.

Use the knowledge coordinator of the design tool to ensure that the model is internally consistent, and consistent with other knowledge in the repository.

Methodology Chart 14-2:    CREATION OF THE COORDINATING MODEL

Coordinating Model

The Coordinating Model is an integrated data and process model in the I-CASE repository, which is used for coordinating the work of different developers or SWAT Teams.

The preliminary version of the coordinating model is created by I.S. professionals. The model is reviewed in a JAD workshop, where it will be validated, adjusted and expanded.

The building of the preliminary coordinating model should proceed in parallel with preparation for the JAD workshop.

> The procedure given below may be modified with MediaScribe to meet the needs of the particular situation.

Steps in Creating the Coordinating Model

Create the preliminary Coordinating Model.

Appoint a modeling professional.

The person who leads the data modeling activity will usually be responsible for the process model as well -- the two being developed together, using an I-CASE tool that integrates them.

Create the initial version of the Coordinating Model.

Extract from the repository the entity-relationship model for this business area (if one exists).

Create an initial entity-relationship model for the system.

Extract from the repository the process decomposition model for this business area (if one exists).

Create an initial process decomposition for the system.

Determine what events occur in this system that create or change data.

Associate the events with entity-types (a behavior model).

Consider the lifecycle of each entity (and possibly draw it).

Enter the attributes of each entity.

In the JAD workshop, check the Coordinating Model.

Review the data dictionary listing to ensure that all end users agree about the definitions of the data-items.

Review the data model to ensure that their data requirements can be derived from it.

Add to the data model as appropriate.

Add to the process model as appropriate.

Review the process model to determine whether any processes have been omitted.

*continued on next page*

Brainstorm the possible future uses of the data. For any uses that the model does not serve, create new input to the data model.

Brainstorm possible additions that might be needed in the process model. After any changes are made, use fast computerized redesign to maintain the interest of the end users.

Successively refine the Coordinating Model.

The Coordinating Model should be successively refined in the JAD workshop, and off-line by the data modeling professional, until a complete representation of the data and processes is achieved.

The information is refined in the following stages:

Create a detailed data model.
See Methodology Chart 13.

Validate the data model in the JAD workshop, adding anything that might have been forgotten.

Create a detailed process model.
See Methodology Chart 14-1.

Validate the process model in the JAD workshop, adding anything that might have been forgotten.

Build matrices.

Generate an entity-type/process matrix.

Build a matrix mapping elementary processes and entity-types.

Indicate what process CREATES each entity record.

Indicate what processes UPDATE, READ or DELETE each entity record.

Validate the matrix in the JAD workshop, adding anything that might have been forgotten.

Associate entity-types, processes and events with organizational units and locations.

Analyze and correlate (automatically) the above information.

Use an I-CASE tool that analyzes and correlates the above information with a knowledge coordinator.

Use the knowledge coordinator of the design tool to ensure that the model is internally consistent and consistent with other knowledge in the repository.

Divide the system into subsystems for SWAT-Team development.

Rules for Subdivision of Systems (for Parallel SWAT-Team Development)

Systems should be subdivided in a way that:

• Each subsystem performs one or more discreet business processes.

• Each subsystem can be tested in its own right.

• Each subsystem executes a function that users can employ, where possible, and that can be tested in the usability laboratory (Chapter 17).

- There is as little data flow as possible between one subsystem and another.

- The data exchanged among subsystems are defined with precision.

- As far as possible, a design decision made in one subsystem should have no effect on another subsystem.

- Each subsystem is small enough to be built by one person or one SWAT Team in not more than three months.

The rules for subdivision should be based on experience with toolset and methodology. Typical rules of thumb might be as follows:

For a powerful code generator:

```
          < 200 function points:    1 person.
200 to 1000 function points:    1 SWAT Team.
          > 1000 function points:   1000 function points
                                      per SWAT Team.
```

For a powerful code generator and substantial employment of reusable structures:

```
          < 500 function points:    1 person.
500 to 2000 function points:    1 SWAT Team.
          > 2000 function points:   2000 function points
                                      per SWAT Team.
```

For a mature information-engineering environment with object-oriented analysis for maximum reusability, which has had time to acquire much reusable design:

```
           < 1000 function points:   1 person.
1000 to 4000 function points:   1 SWAT Team.
           > 4000 function points:   4000 function points
                                       per SWAT Team.
```

Determine how many SWAT Teams will work in parallel.

Estimate the complexity of the system in function points.

Use the function-point estimate to determine how many 3-month SWAT-Team efforts are needed.

Use the basic diagrams to help divide the model into subsystems that can be developed by separate teams.

Use the process decomposition diagram to help show natural systems. High-level blocks and their children may be natural clusters.

Use the process dependency diagram to help show natural systems.

Identify what data must flow from one system to another.

Subdivide the dependency diagram so that there is as little flow of data from one subdivision to another.

Refine the dependency diagram to agree with the clustered matrix.

*continued on next page*

Use the process/entity matrix to help show natural systems.

The matrix may be clustered on the basis of what processes CREATE what entity-types.

The matrix tool may have a clustering algorithm that can be used.

Refine the clusterings to minimize the interaction among systems.

Methodology Chart 15:   ACTIONS TAKEN TO ACHIEVE GENERIC REUSABILITY

> The procedure given below may be modified with MediaScribe to meet the needs of the particular situation.

Actions Taken for the I.S. Organization as a Whole
- Establish general application standards.
  - Reasons for Standards

    Application standards are selected to make the system as easy to use as possible, allowing users to become familiar with how to interact with the system.

    Application standards are selected to allow the maximum degree of reusable design, thereby speeding up design and construction.

  - Design Standards List

    - database access standards;
    - network access standards;
    - screen layout standards;
    - dialog standards  (e.g., an installation-specific version of IBM's CUA -- Common User Access);
    - keyboard standards (e.g., common function keys);
    - a common sign-on procedure;
    - a common English vocabulary employed in user interfaces;
    - guidelines for HELP screens;
    - and so on.

  - Methodology Standards

    - Diagramming Standards
      See Appendix IV.

    °° other

- Establish templates and reusable constructs.

  An I.S. professional, possibly the JAD Scribe, should understand the capabilities of the code generator, and be familiar with the reusable designs in the repository, so that reusability can be employed to the maximum extent.

  - Templates

    - for dialog, action bar, pull-down menus, pop-on windows and so on;
    - for transaction processing dialog;
    - for data entry screens;
    - for other screens;
    - for HELP screens;
    - for error messages and so on.

  - Reusable Constructs
    - Generic Reusable Constructs
      - Examples of Reusable Building Blocks

        °° START MODULE
        °° COMMAND PROCESSOR
        °° MENU MODULE
        °° SECURITY MODULE
        °° WORK MODULES
        °° TRANSACTION PROCESSOR
        °° QUERY MODULE
        °° USER DIALOG MODULE

*continued on next page*

```
              °° ERROR PROCESSOR
              °° STOP MODULE

       °° Application-Specific Reusable Constructs
```

Establish standards and reusable modules for documentation.

   Technical Documentation Standards

   Technical documentation should be printed from the repository.
   The I.S. organization should have established:

- diagramming standards;
- standard formats for documentation;
- a standard Table of Contents for the development workbook.

   User Documentation Standards
   The I.S. organization should have established:

- standard formats for user documentation;
- a reusable template and text for the "Getting Started" manual;
- a standard Table of Contents for the user guidebook;
- reusable templates and text in an electronic publishing system
  for all user documentation.

Educate the developers about the standards.
Make the standards part of the training courses for new developers.

Actions Taken during the Lifecycle of a Project

```
   <-----------Initiate project.
               Establish Executive Owner.

     <--------Research.

       <------Prepare for JRP workshop.

         <--Conduct JRP workshop.
           <--Finalize requirements plan.            \ | /

   <---------Prepare for JAD workshop.————————·Identify all relevant
                                               standards, templates and
                                               reusable designs.

     <------Conduct first JAD workshop.————————·Review reusable standards,
                                                templates and designs with
                                                the users.

     <----Consolidate JAD design.
       <---Design coordinating model.————————·SWAT Team may adjust the
         <--Usability-test the prototypes.|   initial design to speed up
           <-Establish project repository  the construction process,
   <----SWAT Team prepares for construction.|  if possible, by better
                                               employment of reusability.
             <-Conduct 2nd JAD workshop.——·Review any adjustments in
           <--Finalize design and            the second workshop.
               project repository.————————·Establish the reusable
                                            items in the project
   <----------Prepare for cultural changes. | repository.
```

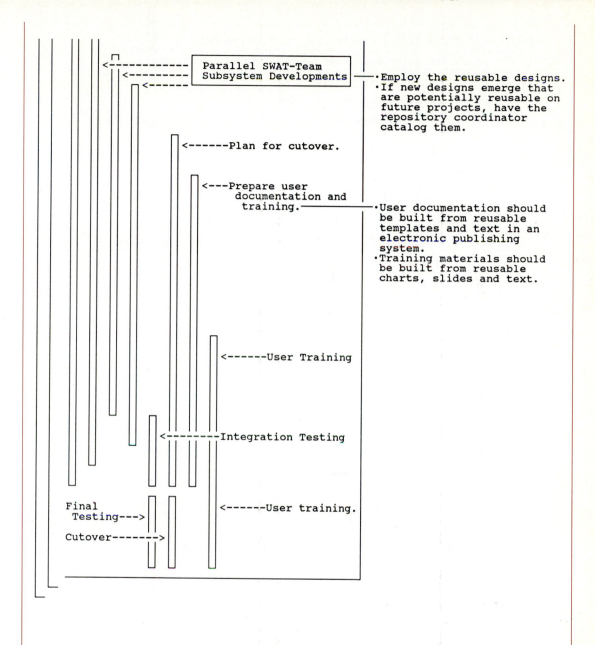

Parallel SWAT-Team
Subsystem Developments

<------ •Employ the reusable designs.
•If new designs emerge that
are potentially reusable on
future projects, have the
repository coordinator
catalog them.

<------Plan for cutover.

<---Prepare user
      documentation and
      training.——————— •User documentation should
be built from reusable
templates and text in an
electronic publishing
system.
•Training materials should
be built from reusable
charts, slides and text.

<------User Training

<--------Integration Testing

Final
Testing--->

Cutover------->           <------User training.

Methodology Chart 18-1:   PREPARE FOR CULTURAL CHANGES.

> The procedure given below may be modified with MediaScribe
> to meet the needs of the particular situation.

Identify any possible cultural changes.

List the types of cultural changes that the new system might bring
about.

They may include:

- changes in organizational structure;
- changes in policies;
- changes in business procedures;
- changes in staffing levels;
- changes in job content;
- changes in skill requirements.

Review this list with appropriately senior end-user management.

Design the organizational changes.

- Determine what change in existing organizational units is
  necessary to gain optimal benefits from the new system.

- Determine organizational units that will no longer be needed.

- Determine organizational units whose functions will change.

- Design an organizational structure that provides the
  appropriate skills and appropriate numbers of people
  at the required locations.

- Create a mission statement for any new or changed
  organizational units.

- Where required, create new position descriptions or revise
  existing ones.

- Review the user dislocation and organizational disruption
  with top management.

Identify responsibilities for organizational changes.

Ensure that top management understand the cultural changes
implied by the system.

Identify which high-level end-user management should be
responsible for preparing for the cultural changes.

Determine whether human resource specialists or organizational
design specialists are needed to assist in making the changes.

Determine the role of the Information Systems staff in making
the changes.

Schedule the organizational changes.

- Create a plan for an orderly transition to the new organization.

- List the actions required to accomplish this transition.

- Determine the individual responsible for each item on the list.

- List what resources must be acquired, replaced or eliminated.

- Chart the sequence and timing of the necessary actions.

- Mesh the transition schedule with the development and cutover schedules.

- Obtain approval and sign-offs from appropriate levels of management for the transition schedule. (It is vital to obtain these sign-offs early enough; otherwise, timely cutover to the new system could be jeopardized.)

Methodology Chart 18-2:   PERFORM CUTOVER

Set up the production procedures.

SET UP:
 • the procedures for normal system operation;
 • any manual or paperwork procedures that must accompany
     the new installation;
 • the procedures for restart and recovery;
 • the fallback procedures;
 • the procedures for security;
 • the audit procedures;
 • the procedures for phasing out the old system when the
     new system is running satisfactorily.

Review the above procedures with the data center personnel to
ensure their understanding. Review the above procedures with the
end users to ensure their understanding.

Install the production system environment.

 • Install the initial production hardware.

 • Confirm that a complete test of the hardware
   has been successfully completed.

 • Coordinate with systems programming administration
   to schedule the installation.

 • Install the software on the production system.

 • Test that the software is correctly installed.

 • Coordinate with vendors for the ongoing
   hardware installation at other sites.

Perform data conversion.

 Execute the data conversion programs.
 Load existing data into the system's database.
 Load manually-prepared data, if needed.
 Test the data loading and conversion to verify data quality.
 Review the results to ensure that acceptance test criteria are met.

Implement the new system in production.

 • Move the new system to production mode, following the migration
   plan, possibly running in parallel with the old system.

 • Lock the new software components into the development and test
   library.

 • Phase out the old system as confidence is developed in the new
   system.

Review the system installation.

     Evaluate the system performance.
     Determine what system tuning is needed.
     Evaluate user acceptance of the system.
     Determine what improvements are needed in user training.
     Schedule the improvements in training.
     Determine what system modifications are needed.
     Schedule the system modifications.

```
┌─ If no modifications needed, exit.
┌─ Else

    Document adjustments needed.
    Determine date for installation of next version.
    Make adjustments.
```

Methodology Chart 19:   CUTOVER PHASE

> The procedure given below may be modified with MediaScribe
> to meet the needs of the particular situation.

Prepare for cutover.

Develop the conversion system.

- Determine what is needed for conversion.
- Generate subsystems needed to convert existing data.
- Generate systems needed for the entry of new data.
- Develop an interface to old systems that will remain in existence.
- Develop an interface to application packages, if necessary.
- Design tests to ensure that conversion facilities work correctly.

Finalize the development product.

Perform quality audit.

Ensure that
- the I-CASE toolset has been used in the approved manner;
- it conforms to the development standards that have been followed;
- the user documentation is good enough.

Refine the development product.

If necessary use a code optimizer to improve code performance (for example, the COBOL optimizer from Computer Associates).

Identify any differences between the development environment and the production environment that may require modification to the development product (for example, the Job Control Language may require changes). Make the necessary changes.

Prepare for final testing.

Install the software to be used for final testing.

Install test data generator.
Install test utilities.
Install network debugging utilities.

Build the test libraries.

Coordinate the testing with the development team.

Carry out the final testing.

Testing may progress though a number of stages.

Program/Transaction Test
For each transaction type:

Verify that the program handles all its transactions correctly.

Perform transaction crash test.

Verify that the program handles the transaction in all cases without crashing.

System Integration Test

Verify that subsystems developed in parallel work together.

Intersystem Integration Test

Verify that the system accepts input from and provides output to other systems with which it interfaces.

Verify that the systems work together fully.

Volume Test

Verify that the system can process the volume of transactions expected.

Regression Test for Maintenance Changes

Verify that the system still works as maintenance changes are made.

Acceptance Test

Obtain verification from the users that the system is acceptable for production.

Collect statistics for project management.
Document the test results.

Plan and conduct the training program.

Develop the training plan.

- Determine who will create the training materials.
- Determine who will conduct the training.
- Determine which users will be trained initially.
- Determine the time and location of training.

Conduct training.

Conduct the first training session.

Evaluate the success of the training to determine if the user understanding of the system meets the requirements.

Refine the training materials and HELP screens on the basis of experience.

Conduct further training courses.
Refine training materials and HELP screens as appropriate.

Perform cutover.
See Methodology Chart 18-2.

Methodology Chart 21-1:    I.E. PROCEDURE FOR INFORMATION STRATEGY PLANNING
                           (ISP)

Information Engineering Pyramid

```
┌─────────────────────────────────────────────────────────┐
│ ISP is the top layer of Information Engineering.         │
└─────────────────────────────────────────────────────────┘


                                      /|\
      INFORMATION STRATEGY PLANNING/   |   \
                                  /   -|- ------\
      BUSINESS AREA ANALYSIS /    /----- ------\    \
                            /     |              \
                      /------------- ------------\
      RAD            /   Requirements Planning Phase \
                 /      User Design Phase              \
              /         Construction                     \
           /            Cutover                            \
        /_____|_____\
```

```
┌─────────────────────────────────────────────────────────┐
│ The procedure given below may be modified with MediaScribe│
│ to meet the needs of the particular situation.            │
└─────────────────────────────────────────────────────────┘
```

ISP Procedure
See [MARTIN90c].

Initiate.

Understand the benefits of an ISP study.
See Chapter 21  ("Financial Justification ...," Box 21.4).

Determine the scope of the ISP.

        Will the whole enterprise be studied ?
        If not, what parts of it are included ?

Ensure that the prerequisites exist.

        •    A champion for the project is committed to it.
        •    Appropriately skilled individuals are available.
        •    The scope of the plan is identified.
        •    A charter for the plan has been established.
        •    A strategic business plan exists.
        •    A data administration function exists.

    Select the senior management participants.

Obtain top-management commitment.

The ISP project should not proceed until the top executive of the
organization understands the need for it and is fully committed to
helping make the project succeed.

Conduct a brief top-management-oriented seminar on the needs for
information engineering.

Distribute brief top-management-oriented reading matter on the needs
for information engineering.

Obtain top-management agreement to go ahead with an ISP study.

Prepare.

Determine which locations are involved.
Determine which ORGANIZATIONS locations are involved.
Establish the ISP team for this project.
If an outside consultant is to be employed,
Select the consultant.

Appoint the in-house ISP project leader who will work with the consultant.

Ensure that the in-house project leader is well trained.

He should have general business savvy and be a person likely to be highly respected by top management.

He should be trained in the following:
- communication skills;
- negotiation;
- Information Engineering;
- the diagramming techniques;
- the automated tools used.

Establish the in-house team that will work with the consultant.

A small team should be used. Two or three people are often appropriate. There may be an end user on the team.

Select future in-house BAA project leaders who will be trained during this study.

Else
Appoint the in-house ISP project leader.

Ensure that the in-house project leader is well trained.

He should have general business savvy and be a person likely to be highly respected by top management.

He should be trained in the following:
- communication skills;
- negotiation;
- Information Engineering;
- the diagramming techniques;
- the automated tools used.

Establish the in-house ISP team.

A small team should be used. Two or three people are often appropriate. There may be an end user on the team.

Select future in-house BAA project leaders who will be trained during this study.

Ensure that the appropriate tools are installed and working.

A repository-based I-CASE toolset is needed, which will be used for Business Area Analysis also, and for the follow-on stages of the RAD lifecycle.

The toolset must have the full information-engineering capability.

Ensure that the ISP team is adequately trained.

They should be trained in the following:

*continued on next page*

- communication skills;
- Information Engineering;
- the diagramming techniques;
- the automated tools used.

Collect and evaluate existing strategic plans:

- the strategic business plan;
- existing ISP plans (if any);
- strategic information technology plans (if any);
- existing critical success factor studies (if any);
- top management goals and objectives;
- existing data models (if any);
- other relevant plans or system architecture documents.

Define a plan for successfully completing this ISP project.
Modify this action diagram as required.

Determine the target date for completing the study.

Hold kickoff meeting.

> All the senior management participants should attend.

- Have the chief executive of the enterprise make the opening speech.

- Review with the participants the purpose and objectives.

- Review the business assumptions that are to be made.

- Review the agenda.

- Give participants the preparatory material for them to study.

Create an overview model of the enterprise.

Enter the following information into the encyclopedia:

- An organizational chart showing all organizational units.

- The persons who manage the organizational units.

- Identify the major business functions.

- Decompose into lower-level functions with a function decomposition diagram.

- Add detailed comments to the above diagrams where necessary.

Create a matrix mapping executives against business functions.

The involvement of the executive may be recorded with the following codes:
R: direct management RESPONSIBILITY
A: executive or policy-making AUTHORITY
I: INVOLVED in the function
E: technical EXPERTISE
W: actual execution of the WORK

Create a matrix mapping functions against organizational units.
Create a matrix mapping functions against executives.

Print relevant versions of the above diagrams from the encyclopedia for the participants to review.

Conduct business-oriented strategic analyses.

The following four types of analyses may be carried on in parallel with, or independently of the other ISP analyses.

Conduct Analysis of Goals and Problems.

Conduct Critical Success Factor Analysis.

Conduct Technology Impact Analysis.

Conduct Strategic Information Systems Study.

Create a top-level analysis of corporate data.

- Identify the data subjects.

- Decompose into entity types.

- Create an initial entity-relationship diagram.

- Create a matrix mapping functions against entity types.

- Create a matrix mapping organizational units against entity types.

- Print relevant versions of the above diagrams from the encyclopedia for the participants to review.

Refine the enterprise model and entity-relationship diagram.

- Conduct meetings with end users and management to critique the enterprise model.

- Make any improvements to the enterprise model as a result of the presentations to end users and management.

- Refine the entity-relationship diagram.

- Refine the matrix of entity types and business functions.

- Refine the matrix of entity types and organizational units.

- Obtain approval for the enterprise model.

Group the enterprise model into natural clusters.

Cluster the function/entity matrix to show natural systems.

Use the clustering algorithm of the strategic planning tool.
Cluster on the basis of what functions CREATE what entity types.
Assign all remaining functions and entity types to clusters.
Refine the groupings manually to identify natural systems.
Identify what data must flow from one system to another.
Refine the clusterings to minimize the interaction among systems.

Cluster the function/entity matrix to show natural business areas.

Adjust the clustered function/entity matrix to form BAA boundaries.
Assign all functions to a business area.
Determine the locations of that business area.
Build a matrix of business areas and locations.
Build a matrix of business areas and departments.

*continued on next page*

Refine the business areas as necessary.

Refine BAA project boundaries.
Consider:
- time to implement BAA;
- effort required to implement BAA;
- how the proposed BAA fits with the current organization;
- risk assessment;
- user acceptance/participation;
- user sophistication/readiness;
- technical complexity.

Analyze current systems to determine what changes are needed.

Build matrices, mapping I.S. systems against organizational units;
" executives;
" business functions;
" entity types.

Cluster the above matrices into business areas.

Identify which systems are -> in need of replacement or redesign.
-> expensive in maintenance costs.

Prepare follow-on from Strategic Information Planning.

Comment

When the ISP results are presented to top management, a detailed action plan should accompany them saying what happens next. It is desirable that the ISP study be immediately followed by vigorous action that leads to implementing better systems.

Prioritize the business areas for Business Area Analysis.

There are multiple factors that affect the prioritization of which business area to work on first.

Rank each of the factors below on a scale of 1 to 7.
Potential Benefits
Return on Investment
(may be difficult to calculate and requires value judgments)
- tangibles;
- intangibles.

- achievement of critical success factors;
- achievement of goals;
- solution to serious problems.

Demand

- pressure of demand from senior end users for new or improved systems;

- assessed need;

- political overtones.

Organizational Impact

- number of organizations and people affected;
- whether the organizations are geographically dispersed;
- qualitative effect.

Existing Systems

- adequacy or value of existing systems;

- relationship with existing systems;

- estimated future costs of maintenance.
  (Systems that are fragile or have high maintenance costs
  should be replaced.)

Likely Success

- Complexity. (Relatively simple areas should be
  the first to be tackled until experience is gained.)

- Degree of business acceptance.

- Length of project.

- Prerequisites.

- Risks.

Resources Required

- whether existing data or process models exist;
- whether a suitable toolkit is installed;
- quality of available analysts;
- funds required.

Concurrent Implementation

- Whether multiple Business Area Analysis projects can proceed
  concurrently.

- Whether one project will train people who can quickly move to
  other projects.

- Whether an existing data administration function has already
  done good data modeling.

Initiate Business Area Analysis.
See Chapter 21 ("Three Phases ...,"  2. Analysis).

Determine what systems should be built immediately.

The ISP generates certain urgent needs for systems for senior
management. These should be satisfied as quickly as possible with
relatively simple techniques such as spreadsheet tools,
decision-support software, or executive-information-system software.

Initiate actions to keep the ISP up-to-date.

Appoint technology-minded person to keep the Technology
Impact Analysis up-to-date.

Plan that Critical Success Factors shall be reviewed
periodically at business strategy planning meetings.

Plan that Critical Success Factors shall be presented at
Board meetings for review.

Plan that the Goal-and-Problem analysis shall be updated

*continued on next page*

when management appraisal interviews are conducted as part
of the Management-by-Objectives procedure.

Ensure that the business-function decomposition diagrams and
entity-relationship diagrams are updated in the encyclopedia
when Business Area Analysis is done.

Ensure that the ISP is re-examined when major changes occur
in the enterprise (such as a takeover).

Make top-management presentation.
Obtain agreement to follow-on actions.


Reference
[MARTIN90c]
James Martin, Information Engineering (a trilogy),
Book II: Planning and Analysis,
Prentice Hall, Inc., Englewood Cliffs, New Jersey, 1990 (201-592-2261).

Methodology Chart 21-2:   I.E. PROCEDURE FOR BUSINESS AREA ANALYSIS (BAA)

> The procedure given below may be modified with MediaScribe
> to meet the needs of the particular situation.

The Information Engineering Pyramid

BAA is the second layer of Information Engineering

```
                                    /|\
        INFORMATION STRATEGY PLANNING/ | \
                          /    |    \
                       /-------|------\
        BUSINESS AREA ANALYSIS /      |       \
                     /---------|---------\
        RAD          /  Requirements Planning Phase \
                  /   User Design Phase         \
                /     Construction               \
              /       Cutover                     \
            /_____|_____\
```

Business Area Analysis

For details see [MARTIN90c].

Initiate.

Obtain commitment of Executive Sponsor.

The BAA project should not proceed unless a suitably high
level executive is fully committed to helping make the
project succeed.

Ensure that the appropriate tools are installed and working.

A repository-based I-CASE toolset is needed, which should
have been used for the Information Strategy Planning, and
which will be used for the follow-on stages of the RAD
lifecycle. The toolset must have the full information-
engineering capability.

Select the business area.

Dividing the enterprise into business areas and determining
which to analyze first was the final stage of Information
Strategy Planning.

Determine the scope of the business area.

Determine which entities are involved.
Determine which business functions are involved.
Determine which locations are involved.
Determine which departments are involved.

Examine relevant goals, problems, and critical success
factors (from the encyclopedia).

Develop BAA project plan.

Edit this methodology chart as appropriate to form the
project procedure.

Establish the BAA team for this project.

*continued on next page*

If an outside consultant is to be employed, select the consultant.

Appoint the in-house BAA project leader who will work with the consultant.

Ensure that the in-house project leader is well trained.

A BAA project leader should have this as his job for a year or more. BAA leaders become skilled with experience.

Establish the in-house team that will work with the consultant.

A small team should be used. Two or three people are often appropriate. There may be an end user on the team.

Select future in-house BAA project leaders, who will be trained during this study.

Else appoint the in-house BAA project leader.

Ensure that the in-house project leader is well trained.

Establish the in-house BAA team.

A small team should be used. Two or three people are often appropriate. There may be an end user on the team.

Select future in-house BAA project leaders, who will be trained during this study.

Ensure that the BAA team is adequately trained.

They should be trained in the following:
- Information Engineering;
- Analysis and Design;
- Data Modeling;
- Diagramming Techniques;
- Use of Automated Tools;
- Communication Skills.

Prepare.

Create initial documentation.

Extract the relevant functional decomposition diagram from the encyclopedia.

Extract the relevant entity-relationship diagram from the encyclopedia.

Add detailed comments to the above diagrams where necessary.

Print relevant versions of the above diagrams from the encyclopedia for the participants to review.

Select the user participants.

Prepare the user participants.

Give user participants literature on the BAA procedure.

Give them the initial printouts from the encyclopedia.

Conduct training class for the user participants.
- Introduce user participants to the BAA technique.
- Train user participants in the diagramming techniques.
- Review the initial printouts from the encyclopedia.

Determine the target date for completing the study.

Hold kickoff meeting.

Have the Executive Sponsor make the opening speech.

Review with participants the purpose and objectives.

Review the agenda.

Give participants the preparatory material for them to study.

Inform them that they must understand it well before the first workshop.

Review the initial data models and process models with the participants.

Review relevant goals, problems, and critical success factors.

Review the business assumptions that are to be made.

Create a preliminary data model.

- Extract the entity-relationship model for this business area from the repository.

- Determine what events occur in this business area.

- Associate the events with entity-types (a behavior model).

- Draw the life-cycle of each entity.

- Enter initial attributes of each entity.

Create a preliminary process model.

- Extract the business-function decomposition model for this business area from the repository.

- Decompose the functions into processes.

Successively refine the information in the following stages until a complete representation of the data and processes is achieved.

Create a detailed data model.

See Chapter 13 and Methodology Chart 13.

Create a detailed process model.

See Chapter 14, Methodology Chart 14-1 and Methodology Chart 14-2.

Create a process decomposition diagram.

Decompose processes eventually into elementary processes.

When events occur, these cannot trigger a sub-elementary process.

*continued on next page*

Decompose until elementary processes are derived. Check that each lowest-level is elementary; if not, decompose it further.

Do not waste time perfecting the intermediate structure of the decomposition; the elementary processes are what matter.

Record a definition of each elementary process.

Create a process dependency diagram.

Correlate this with the process decomposition diagram.
Consider what information flows from one process to another.

Draw process dependency diagrams.

Develop a set of process dependency diagrams that show, among them, all the elementary processes.

Dependency diagrams will be created for higher-level process blocks, and these will be nested to lower levels, using the encyclopedia-based tool and its knowledge coordinator.

It is likely that errors will be found in the decomposition diagram while drawing the dependency diagrams; these should be corrected.

Do not waste time perfecting the intermediate structure of the dependency diagrams; it is the elementary processes that matter.

Generate an entity-type/process matrix.

Build a matrix mapping elementary processes and entity types.
Indicate what process CREATES each entity record.
Indicate what processes UPDATE, READ or DELETE each entity record.

Develop the process/entity matrix.

Create (automatically) a matrix mapping the elementary processes and entity-types.

Fill in the matrix with CREATE, READ, UPDATE and DELETE codes (CRUDs).

Build matrices.

Associate entity-types, processes and events with organizational units and locations.

Associate entity-types, processes and events with goals and problems.

Generate an entity-type/process matrix.
Build a matrix mapping elementary processes and entity-types
Indicate what process CREATES each entity record.
Indicate what processes UPDATE, READ or DELETE each entity record.

Analyze and correlate (automatically) the above information.

Use a workbench tool that analyzes and correlates the above information with a knowledge coordinator.

Use the knowledge coordinator of the design tool to ensure that the model is internally consistent, and consistent with other knowledge in the repository.

Prepare for system design.

Review the analysis of current systems created during the ISP study.

Identify system design projects.

Refine system design project boundaries.

Prioritize the system-building projects.

There are multiple factors that affect the prioritization of system building.

Rank each of the factors below on a scale of 1 to 7:

- return on investment;
- achievement of critical success factor;
- achievement of goal;
- solution to serious problem;
- adequacy of current system;
- maintenance cost of current system;
- speed of implementation;
- manpower or resource availability;
- risk.

Other business areas are likely to be competing for the same development resources; so, the decision of what to build first may be taken at a higher level than the business area.

Schedule the system-building projects.
Obtain approval for system projects.

Present the results to the Executive Sponsor.

Methodology Chart 22:   IDENTIFYING REUSABLE MODULES

> The procedure given below may be modified with MediaScribe to meet the needs of the particular situation.

Identify reusable processes wherever possible.
  Determine where application packages will be used.

  For each application package:

  Create a process model of the package.

  Create a model of the data stored by the package. Determine whether this will cause equivalent entity-types to be stored redundantly.

  Identify processes that can be reusable WITHIN the business area.

  - Associate processes with entity-types (using the process-/entity-type matrix).

  - Identify processes that are associated with an entity-type and that are used whenever an entity is created, read, updated, or deleted, for example validity checks, editing, user dialog, security checks, backup, accuracy checks, audit trail, etc.

  - Identify processes that are associated with a relationship between entity-types (on the entity-relationship diagram) and that are invoked each time that relationship is used, for example updating accounts whenever an order is associated with a customer. Again, validity checks, editing, user dialog, security checks, backup, accuracy checks, audit trail, etc. may be identified.

  - Identify processes that are not identical but are similar enough that common design can be used.

  Identify processes that may be reusable BETWEEN business areas.

  - Examine processes marked in previous BAA studies as potentially reusable across different business areas.

  - Establish the extent to which common design can be used.

  - Examine those entity-types that are used in other business areas as well as the one being analyzed. Determine what processes can be associated with those entity-types or their entity relationships.

  - Mark processes from this BAA study that are potentially reusable across different business areas.

Mark, in the encyclopedia, all processes that are fully or partially reusable.

Design bridges necessary to employ reusable packages and modules.

  - Design interfaces to reusable systems from other locations if necessary.

  - Design interfaces to application packages if necessary.

- Design interfaces to old systems that will remain in existence.

- Design tests to ensure that these bridge facilities work correctly.

Reference

[MARTIN90c]
James Martin, Information Engineering (a trilogy),
Book II: Planning and Analysis,
Prentice Hall, Inc., Englewood Cliffs, New Jersey, 1990 (201-592-2261).

Methodology Chart 23:   RAPID MAINTENANCE

> The procedure given below may be modified with MediaScribe
> to meet the needs of the particular situation.

* Create the preliminary data model.

  - Extract the entity-relationship model for this business area
    from the repository.

  - Determine what events occur in this business area.

  - Associate the events with entity-types (a behavior model).

  - Draw the life-cycle of each entity.

  - Enter initial attributes of each entity.

Create the preliminary process model.

  - Extract the business-function decomposition model for this
    business area from the repository.

  - Decompose the functions into processes.

Successively refine the information in the following stages
until a complete representation of the data and processes is achieved.

  Create a detailed data model.
  See Chapter 13 and Methodology Chart 13.

  Create a detailed process model.
  See Chapter 14 and Methodology Chart 14-1.

  Build matrices.

    Associate entity-types, processes and events
    with organizational units and locations.

    Associate entity-types, processes and events
    with goals and problems.

    Generate an entity-type/process matrix.
    Build a matrix mapping elementary processes and entity-types
    Indicate what process CREATES each entity record.
    Indicate what processes UPDATE, READ or DELETE each entity record.

  Identify reusable processes wherever possible.
  See Chapters 15 and 22.

    Identify processes that can be reusable WITHIN the business area.

    - Associate processes with entity-types
      (using the process-/entity-type matrix).

    - Identify processes that are associated with an entity-type and
      that are used whenever an entity is created, read, updated, or
      deleted, for example validity checks, editing, user dialog,
      security checks, backup, accuracy checks, audit trail, etc.

    - Identify processes that are associated with a relationship
      between entity-types (on the entity-relationship diagram) and
      that are invoked each time that relationship is used, for
      example updating accounts whenever an order is associated with a

customer. Again, validity checks, editing, user dialog, security checks, backup, accuracy checks, audit trail, etc. may be identified.

- Identify processes that are not identical but are similar enough that common design can be used.

Identify processes that may be reusable BETWEEN business areas.

- Examine processes marked in previous BAA studies as potentially reusable across different business areas.

- Establish the extent to which common design can be used.

- Examine those entity-types that are used in other business areas as well as the one being analyzed. Determine what processes can be associated with those entity-types or their entity relationships.

- Mark processes from this BAA study that are potentially reusable across different business areas.

Mark, in the encyclopedia, all processes that are fully or partially reusable.

Design bridges for reusable packages and modules.

- Design interfaces to reusable systems from other locations if necessary.

- Design interfaces to application packages if necessary.

- Design interfaces to old systems that will remain in existence.

- Design tests to ensure that these bridge facilities work correctly.

Analyze and correlate (automatically) the above information.

Use a workbench tool that analyzes and correlates the above information with a knowledge coordinator.

Use the knowledge coordinator of the design tool to ensure that the BAA is internally consistent, and consistent with other knowledge in the encyclopedia.

Methodology Chart 24:   MIGRATION AND REVERSE ENGINEERING

> The procedure given below may be modified with MediaScribe
> to meet the needs of the particular situation.

## 15 Steps of Reverse Engineering

Reverse engineering may proceed in 15 possible steps. The following
steps are done with I-CASE tools for building new systems:

1. Structure the code (automatically).

   Use software for automatically converting the old program into a
   fully structured program, if possible, (for example, RECODER
   from Language Technology, Inc.).

2. Enter the restructured code into the I.E. CASE tool.

   The restructured code should be in action diagram format so that
   it can be displayed and manipulated on the screen of the CASE
   tool. It is desirable that conversion to action diagram format
   should be done automatically. If the tools do not do this it
   must be done manually.

3. Capture the data of the old system (automatically).

   The data division of COBOL, or its equivalent in other
   languages, should be read automatically into the CASE tool.

   The CASE tool should display the data structures graphically.

4. Convert the data elements.

   Data elements should be converted one at a time to conform to
   the data element representation in the I.E. dictionary.

   This should be done with computer assistance so that no
   instances of the data element are omitted.

   Any data elements that do not have equivalents in the I.E.
   dictionary should be added to it.

5. Normalize the data to conform to the I.E. model.

   The old data structures and the I.E. data structures should be
   shown graphically on the screen so that they can be compared.

   With the aid of the CASE tool the old data structures should be
   converted into normalized structures.

   It should be determined what conversion must be to take the old
   data structures into the I.E. environment.

6. Consider adoption of a new DBMS.

   If the old system used file management, as opposed to database
   management, or used a nonrelational DBMS, it may be converted
   to use a relational database.

   The system may be redesigned to use a distributed database.
   (See Chapter 16.)

7. Adapt the application to the I.E. process model.

   Determine what changes are needed in the programs to make them conform to the I.E. process model.

Adapt the design to make maximum use of reusable modules.

Adapt the design to make use of object-oriented (entity-oriented) procedures where desirable.

8. Adapt the application design to new standards if necessary.

The application may be redesigned to conform to IBM's SAA, or equivalent.

The application may be redesigned to conform to application standards of the installation.

9. Adapt the application design to new system interfaces if needed.

The application may be redesigned to use new networking standards.

The application may be redesigned to use cooperative processing or personal computers.

The application may be redesigned as a distributed system.

The application may be adapted to new hardware.

10. Generate modified data structures from the I.E. model.

The normalized I.E. model is adjusted so that it can encompass the old system.

Data structures for the DBMS in question are created with the CASE tool, as they would be for a new system.

11. Generate the data description code.

The code generator of the I.E. tool should be used to generate the data description code.

12. Redesign the reports.

Create the reports needed quickly, using a report generator, which is preferably part of the I.E. CASE toolset.

Review the reports with the end users.

The new reports may be designed and reviewed in a JAD session.

Adjust the reports as required.

13. Redesign the human interface.

The human interface should conform to modern standards such as IBM's CUA (the Common User Access of SAA, Systems Application Architecture).

Create the new screens quickly, using a screen painter, which is preferably part of the I.E. CASE toolset.

Link the screens into a dialog.

Review the screens and dialog with the end users.

The new dialog may be designed and reviewed in a JAD session.

*continued on next page*

Adjust the dialog as required.

Create on-line HELP facilities.

14. Generate new program code, database code and documentation.

The I.E. generator should generate the new system. Every means should be taken to make it easy to modify in the future.

15. Use a code optimizer, if necessary, to improve performance.

Fully structured code, while good for maintenance, does not have optimal run-time performance. Its performance can be improved with a code optimizer such as Computer Associates' COBOL optimizer.

Maintenance should not be done on the optimized code but on the structured code, represented on the CASE screen. This code will be reoptimized after modification.

## 6 Categories of Applications (for Migration Purposes)

For migration purposes, all applications should be categorized into the following 6 migration categories:

1. STATIC

The program operates satisfactorily and does not need to be changed.

*No change is required.

2. MINOR MAINTENANCE

Changes of a minor nature are needed and can be done without rebuilding the program.

*The most economic solution is to maintain the program in its present form.

3. RESTRUCTURE BUT DO NOT RE-ENGINEER

The changes are not great enough to necessitate re-engineering. The program may be automatically restructured and modified without I-CASE re-engineering to conform to the I.E. models.

*The most economic solution is to restructure the program (automatically) and maintain it in that form without re-engineering it.

4. RE-ENGINEER BUT NOT TO THE I.E. ENVIRONMENT

*The most economic solution is to reverse-engineer the program into an I-CASE tool and use that to maintain it but not convert it fully to the I.E. environment.

5. RE-ENGINEER TO THE I.E. ENVIRONMENT

The program is automatically restructured, reverse-engineered into a CASE tool and re-engineered to conform to the I.E. models. New code is generated.

*The most economic solution (for the long term) is to reverse-engineer the program into the I.E. environment, designing it for low-cost maintenance in that environment.

6.   SCRAP AND REBUILD

A major redesign of procedures needs a complete redevelopment of the program.

*The most economic solution is to scrap the program and create a new one.

Procedure for Reverse Engineering

Schedule the system-building projects.

- Decide what new systems will be built.
- Obtain approval for specific system projects.
- Determine the resources needed.
- Present the results to the executive sponsor.
- Schedule the development activity.

Develop a reverse-engineering strategy.

Reverse engineering may proceed in 15 possible steps. (See separate entry above.)

Categorize applications by migration requirement.

Use the list of all application programs. Record an estimate of the cost of maintaining the program in its current form for each of the next five years.

Categorize all applications into migration categories. (See separate entry above.)

Design a data conversion bridge for non-I.E. programs.

Note

When data from non-I.E. programs pass to programs in the I.E. environment, or vice versa, the data will have to be converted. This is the case when application packages are used, as well as with in-house non-I.E. programs.

Determine what data conversions are necessary.

Chart on a data flow diagram the links needing data conversion.

Design the data conversion.

Determine whether the data conversion program can be created automatically.

Schedule the building and testing of the data conversion bridge.

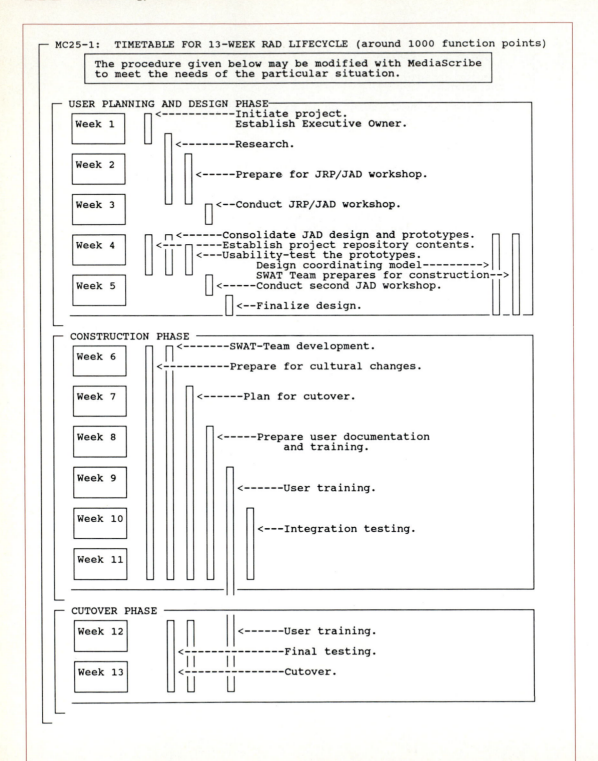

MC25-1: TIMETABLE FOR 13-WEEK RAD LIFECYCLE (around 1000 function points)

The procedure given below may be modified with MediaScribe to meet the needs of the particular situation.

USER PLANNING AND DESIGN PHASE

Week 1    <-----------Initiate project.
                Establish Executive Owner.

     <--------Research.

Week 2

     <-----Prepare for JRP/JAD workshop.

Week 3    <--Conduct JRP/JAD workshop.

     <------Consolidate JAD design and prototypes.
Week 4    <---- ----Establish project repository contents.
     <---Usability-test the prototypes.
            Design coordinating model--------->
            SWAT Team prepares for construction-->
Week 5    <------Conduct second JAD workshop.

     <--Finalize design.

CONSTRUCTION PHASE

Week 6    <-------SWAT-Team development.
     <----------Prepare for cultural changes.

Week 7    <------Plan for cutover.

Week 8    <-----Prepare user documentation
           and training.

Week 9    <------User training.

Week 10    <---Integration testing.

Week 11

CUTOVER PHASE

Week 12    <------User training.
     <--------------Final testing.
Week 13    <--------------Cutover.

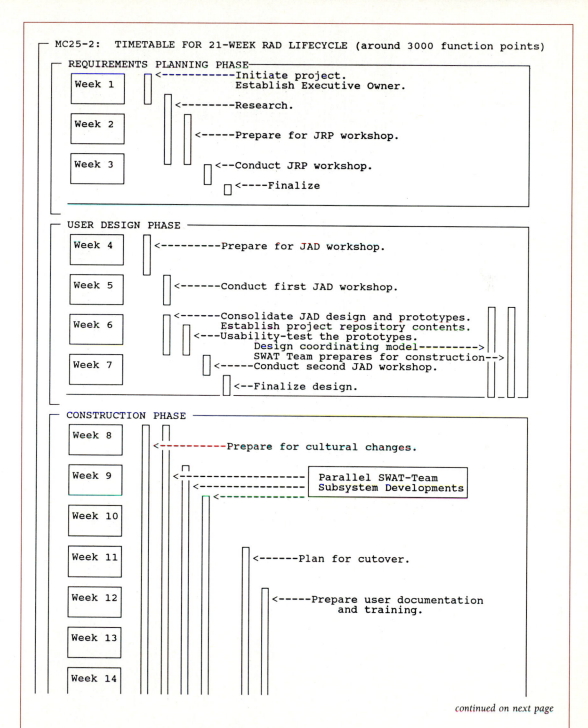

MC25-2:   TIMETABLE FOR 21-WEEK RAD LIFECYCLE (around 3000 function points)

REQUIREMENTS PLANNING PHASE

Week 1        <-----------Initiate project.
                         Establish Executive Owner.

              <--------Research.

Week 2

              <------Prepare for JRP workshop.

Week 3        <--Conduct JRP workshop.

                  <----Finalize

USER DESIGN PHASE

Week 4        <---------Prepare for JAD workshop.

Week 5        <------Conduct first JAD workshop.

              <------Consolidate JAD design and prototypes.
Week 6          Establish project repository contents.
              <---Usability-test the prototypes.
                  Design coordinating model--------->
                  SWAT Team prepares for construction-->
Week 7        <-----Conduct second JAD workshop.

              <--Finalize design.

CONSTRUCTION PHASE

Week 8        <----------Prepare for cultural changes.

Week 9        <------------------- Parallel SWAT-Team
              <------------------- Subsystem Developments
              <------------

Week 10

Week 11       <------Plan for cutover.

Week 12       <-----Prepare user documentation
                    and training.

Week 13

Week 14

*continued on next page*

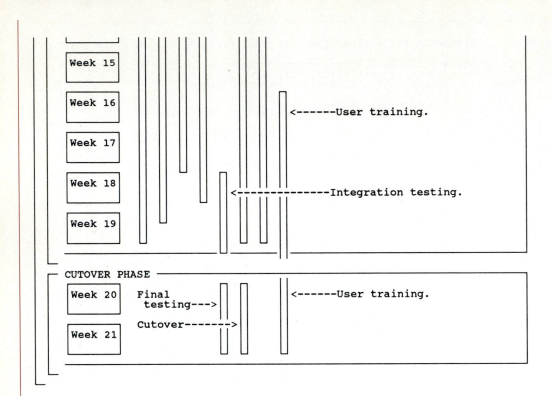

Week 15

Week 16    <------User training.

Week 17

Week 18    <--------------Integration testing.

Week 19

CUTOVER PHASE

Week 20    Final
             testing--->        <------User training.

           Cutover------->
Week 21

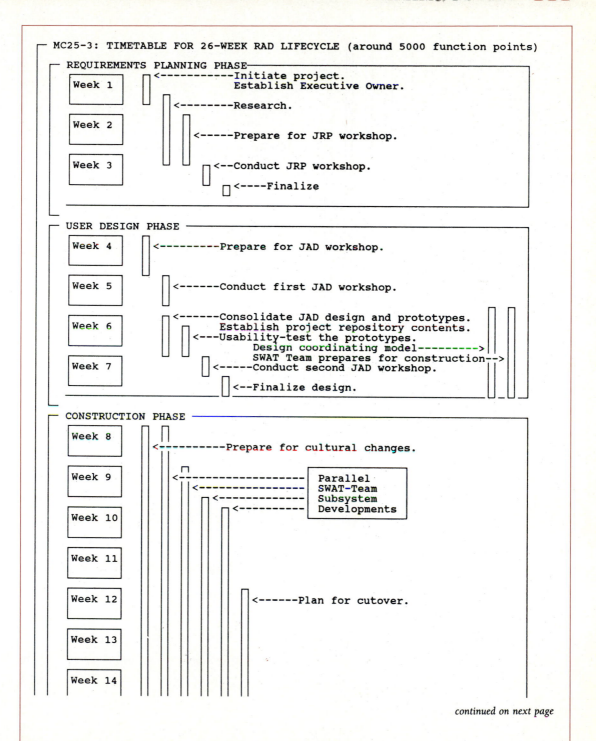

```
MC25-3: TIMETABLE FOR 26-WEEK RAD LIFECYCLE (around 5000 function points)
  REQUIREMENTS PLANNING PHASE
   ┌──────────┐   <───────────Initiate project.
   │ Week 1   │                Establish Executive Owner.
   └──────────┘
                   <────────Research.
   ┌──────────┐
   │ Week 2   │
   └──────────┘   <─────Prepare for JRP workshop.

   ┌──────────┐        <──Conduct JRP workshop.
   │ Week 3   │
   └──────────┘            <─────Finalize

  USER DESIGN PHASE
   ┌──────────┐   <─────────Prepare for JAD workshop.
   │ Week 4   │
   └──────────┘

   ┌──────────┐    <──────Conduct first JAD workshop.
   │ Week 5   │
   └──────────┘

   ┌──────────┐    <──────Consolidate JAD design and prototypes.
   │ Week 6   │              Establish project repository contents.
   └──────────┘   <───Usability-test the prototypes.
                           Design coordinating model─────────>
   ┌──────────┐            SWAT Team prepares for construction-->
   │ Week 7   │   <──────Conduct second JAD workshop.
   └──────────┘       <──Finalize design.

  CONSTRUCTION PHASE
   ┌──────────┐   <──────────Prepare for cultural changes.
   │ Week 8   │
   └──────────┘
                     <───────────────────┐
   ┌──────────┐      <───────────────    Parallel
   │ Week 9   │        <─────────────    SWAT-Team
   └──────────┘          <──────────     Subsystem
                                         Developments
   ┌──────────┐
   │ Week 10  │
   └──────────┘

   ┌──────────┐
   │ Week 11  │
   └──────────┘

   ┌──────────┐       <──────Plan for cutover.
   │ Week 12  │
   └──────────┘

   ┌──────────┐
   │ Week 13  │
   └──────────┘

   ┌──────────┐
   │ Week 14  │
   └──────────┘
```

*continued on next page*

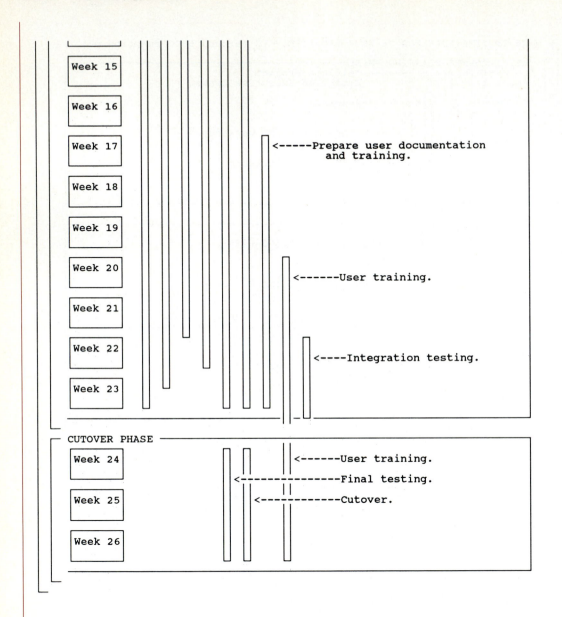

Week 15

Week 16

Week 17          <-----Prepare user documentation
                        and training.

Week 18

Week 19

Week 20          <------User training.

Week 21

Week 22          <----Integration testing.

Week 23

CUTOVER PHASE

Week 24          <------User training.
                 <----------------Final testing.
Week 25          <------------Cutover.

Week 26

Methodology Chart 25-4:   ESSENTIALS FOR MAXIMUM SUCCESS

> The procedure given below may be modified with MediaScribe
> to meet the needs of the particular situation.

## ESSENTIALS FOR SUCCESS BEFORE THE PROJECT BEGINS

1. The Project Manager must fully understand and be committed to a
   RAD methodology. (The project leader may manage more than one
   project).

2. A suitably high-level end-user executive ("Executive Owner")
   must be committed to having the system and paying for it, and
   must be determined to move fast.

3. The methodology should be clearly written, preferably in
   hyperdocument form, as in this document.

4. A suitable, fully integrated I-CASE toolset must be used, with
   a repository and the characteristics listed in Chapter 3.

5. The methodology should be customized to take maximum advantage
   of the toolset used.

6. A trained, experienced RAD Workshop Leader must be available,
   possibly from a consulting firm.

7. A trained, experienced SWAT Team must be available, possibly
   from a consulting firm.

## ESSENTIALS FOR SUCCESS IN THE REQUIREMENTS-PLANNING PHASE

> These apply to nontrivial requirements planning.
> Where the requirements are fairly obvious or simple,
> JRP should be combined with JAD.

1. A suitably high-level end-user executive ("Executive Owner")
   must be committed to having the system and must be determined
   to move fast.

2. The Requirements Planning Phase must be conducted by an
   experienced, skilled, unbiased, full-time professional
   (RAD Workshop Leader) who organizes a JRP workshop
   (sometimes combined with the JAD workshop).

3. The workshop must be attended by suitably high-level user
   executives who can brainstorm the potential functions of the
   system and its deployment across the enterprise.

4. The participants attend the workshop full time.

5. There should be thorough preparation prior to the workshop
   to identify the potential benefits and negatives of the
   proposed system. All such material should be treated as a
   proposed basis for brainstorming.

6. During the workshop, all participants are treated as equals.

7. The possible functions of the system should be prioritized,
   understanding that not all of them can be implemented in
   the first version of the system.

*continued on next page*

8. Any cultural changes, or changes in people's jobs, must be identified and planned for.

9. The workshop room should have no telephone; there should be no interruptions; an off-site location works best. The sessions should start on time. The participants should be committed to work in the evening for the duration of the workshop.

10. Technical jargon should be avoided.

## ESSENTIALS FOR SUCCESS IN THE USER DESIGN PHASE

To make the RAD User Design Phase work as effectively as possible, it is vital to do a number of things correctly. Everyone involved should heed the twelve essentials listed for the User Design Phase.

### TWELVE ESSENTIALS FOR THE USER DESIGN PHASE

1. The User Design Phase must be conducted by an experienced, skilled, unbiased, full-time, professional RAD Workshop Leader.

2. A suitably high-level end user executive ("Executive Owner") must be committed to having the system and must be determined to move fast.

3. The right end users must attend the workshops.

4. The design must be done with the I-CASE tool that is used for the Construction Phase, and the results must be in the repository of this tool. The participants sign off on the design in the I-CASE repository.

5. Information from the repository should be used in the design (for example, the data model, Business Area Analysis and reusable constructs).

6. Participants attend the workshop full time.

7. The workshop room should have no telephone; there should be no interruptions; an off-site location works best. The sessions should start on time. The participants should be committed to work in the evening for the five days of the workshop.

8. During the workshop, all participants are treated as equals.

9. There should be thorough preparation prior to the workshop.

10. If appropriate, the JAD workshop should be preceded by a JRP workshop with participants skilled at higher-level planning.

11. All specifications prepared before the session by the RAD Workshop Leader should be treated as "proposed."

12. Technical jargon should be avoided.

ESSENTIALS FOR SUCCESS IN THE CONSTRUCTION PHASE

1. A SWAT Team, trained and experienced with the tools and methodology, should be employed (possibly from a consulting firm). The SWAT Team should have the characteristics listed in Chapter 10.

2. A team of end users should be assigned to work with the developers, validating the transactions as they are built.

3. Prior to construction, transaction templates, standards and reusable constructs should be established and should be in the construction repository.

4. A coordinating model should exist, with the characteristics described in Chapter 12, and should be in the construction repository.

5. Each transaction should be designed, built and tested quickly, validated with the end users and adjusted until they are fully satisfied with it.

6. The pieces should be integrated, with the aid of the I-CASE tool, as they are built.

ESSENTIALS FOR SUCCESS IN THE CUTOVER PHASE

1. Be sure that cutover is planned early enough in the lifecycle.

2. In the JRP workshop, identify all cultural changes, determine what actions about them are needed, establish a timetable for those actions, and allocate responsibility.

3. In the first JAD workshop, identify all user training needs, determine what actions about them are needed, establish a timetable for those actions, and allocate responsibility.

4. In the first JAD workshop, identify all user documentation needs, determine what actions about them are needed, establish a timetable for those actions, and allocate responsibility.

# APPENDIXES

# How to Calculate Function Points

Appendix I:  How to Calculate Function Points

> The complexity of a data-processing application may be expressed
> as a number of function points. The function-point estimate is
> used for various metrics of development productivity (Chapter 2).

STEP 1:   Determine the boundary of the application or development
          effort to which the function-point calculation will be applied.

STEP 2:   Count and classify five user function types.

1. External Input Types

Count the unique user input types.  These include:

- transactions from the user;
- transactions from other applications;
- data and control input types.

They do not include input files or the input part of queries.

An input type is considered unique if it has a different format from
or requires different processing logic than the other input types.

Classify the complexity of each input type as LOW, AVERAGE or HIGH.

> LOW:     Few data-element types.
>          Few internal-file types are referenced.
>          Human factoring is not a major concern in the design
>           of the input type.
>
> HIGH:    Many data-element types.
>          Many internal file-types are referenced.
>          Human-factoring considerations significantly affect
>           the design of the input type.
>
> MEDIUM:  Between HIGH and LOW.

Calculate an aggregate complexity factor for input.

Aggregate complexity factor for input =
          Number of LOW-complexity input types     x  3
        + Number of MEDIUM-complexity input types  x  4
        + Number of HIGH-complexity input types    x  6.

2. External Output Types

Count the unique user output types.  These include:

- transactions to the user;
- transactions to other applications;
- data and control output types.

They do not include output files or output response to queries.

An output type is considered unique if it has a different format from
or requires different processing logic than the other output types.

*continued on next page*

Classify the complexity of each output type as LOW, AVERAGE or HIGH.

```
LOW:      Few data-element types.
          Few internal-file types are referenced.
          Human factoring is not a major concern in the design
           of the output type.

HIGH:     Many data-element types.
          Many internal file-types are referenced.
          Human-factoring considerations significantly affect
           the design of the output type.

MEDIUM:   Between HIGH and LOW.
```

For reports the following definitions should be used:

```
LOW:      One or two columns.
          Simple data transformations.

MEDIUM:   Multiple columns with subtotals.
          Multiple data-element transformations.

HIGH:     Multiple and intricate data-element transformations.
          Multiple and complex file references.
```

Calculate an aggregate complexity factor for output.

```
Aggregate complexity factor for output =
        Number of LOW-complexity output types      x   4
    +   Number of MEDIUM-complexity output types    x   5
    +   Number of HIGH-complexity output types      x   7.
```

## 3. Logical Internal File Types

Count the logical internal file types.
Count logical files, not physical files.  These include:

- each logical file within a database;
- each logical group of data from the viewpoint of the user.

They do not include logical internal files that are not accessible
to the user through external input, output or queries.

Classify the complexity of each logical file as LOW, AVERAGE or HIGH

```
LOW:      Few record types.
          Few data-element types.
          No significant performance or recovery considerations.

HIGH:     Many record types.
          Many data-element types.
          Performance and recovery are significant considerations.

MEDIUM:   Between HIGH and LOW.
```

Calculate an aggregate complexity factor.

```
Aggregate complexity factor for logical internal file types =
        Number of LOW-complexity input types      x   7
    +   Number of MEDIUM-complexity input types    x  10
    +   Number of HIGH-complexity input types      x  15.
```

4. External File Types

Count the external file types with which the application interfaces.
These include:

- each input file type.
- each output file type.
- data and control information.

Files passed between or shared by applications should be counted
as external file types for EACH application.

Files used by the application and also shared with other applications
should be counted as BOTH logical internal files and external files.

Classify the complexity of each file type as LOW, AVERAGE or HIGH.

| | |
|---|---|
| LOW: | Few record types.<br>Few data-element types.<br>No significant performance or recovery considerations. |
| HIGH: | Many record types.<br>Many data-element types.<br>Performance and recovery are significant considerations. |
| MEDIUM: | Between HIGH and LOW. |

Calculate an aggregate complexity factor.

Aggregate complexity factor for logical internal file types =
```
          Number of LOW-complexity input types    x   5
        + Number of MEDIUM-complexity input types  x   7
        + Number of HIGH-complexity input types    x  10.
```

5. Query Types

Count the unique query types (input/output combination). They include:

- queries from the user.
- queries from other applications.

They do not include transactions that update a file.

A query type is considered unique if it has a different format from
or requires different processing logic than the other query types.

Classify the complexity of each query as LOW, AVERAGE or HIGH.

| | |
|---|---|
| LOW: | Few data-element types.<br>Few internal-file types are referenced.<br>Human factoring is not a major concern. |
| HIGH: | Many data-element types.<br>Many internal file-types are referenced.<br>Human-factoring considerations significantly affect<br>  the design of the query. |
| MEDIUM: | Between HIGH and LOW. |

*continued on next page*

For reports the following definitions should be used:

```
LOW:       One or two columns.
           Simple data transformations.

MEDIUM:    Multiple columns with subtotals.
           Multiple data-element transformations.

HIGH:      Multiple and intricate data-element transformations.
           Multiple and complex file references.
```

Calculate an aggregate complexity factor for output.

```
Aggregate complexity factor for output =
          Number of LOW-complexity output types     x  3
      +   Number of MEDIUM-complexity output types   x  4
      +   Number of HIGH-complexity output types     x  6.
```

STEP 3:   Sum the complexity factors of the five user function types.
Add each of the five aggregate complexity factors, as in the table below:

FUNCTION COUNT:

| Description | Function Complexity | | | Total |
|---|---|---|---|---|
| | LOW | MEDIUM | HIGH | |
| External Input | ..x 3 = .. | ..x  4= .. | ..x  6 = .. | .. |
| External Output | ..x 4 = .. | ..x  5= .. | ..x  7 = .. | .. |
| Logical Internal File | ..x 7 = .. | ..x 10= .. | ..x 15 = .. | .. |
| External File | ..x 5 = .. | ..x  7= .. | ..x 10 = .. | .. |
| Query | ..x 3 = .. | ..x  4= .. | ..x  6 = .. | .. |
| TOTAL UNADJUSTED FUNCTION POINTS | | | | .. |

STEP 4:   Apply an adjustment for 14 general application characteristics.

Estimate a DEGREE-OF-INFLUENCE factor for each of the characteristics.

The degree-of-influence factors are estimated according to the following:

```
factor not present:            0
insignificant influence:       1
moderate influence:            2
average influence:             3
significant influence:         4
strong influence throughout:   5
```

Estimate this factor for each of the following general application
characteristics:

Data Communications
Data or control information is sent via data communications links.

**Distributed Functions**
The application has distributed data or distributed processing.

**Performance**
Performance objectives, such as low response time, influence the design, development, installation and support of the application.

**Heavily Used Configuration**
The application will run on heavily used existing equipment, and this requires special design considerations.

**Transaction Rate**
A high transaction rate influences the design, development, installation and support of the application.

**On-Line Data Entry**
The application has on-line data entry or control functions.

**End-User Efficiency**
The functions provided emphasize design for end-user efficiency.

**On-Line Update Capability**
There is on-line updating of internal files.

**Complex Processing**
The application has complex processing, such as:
- complex logic;
- extensive mathematical processing;
- much exception processing;
- control processing;
- sensitive security requirements.

**Reusability**
The design or code is to be used in other applications.

**Installation Ease**
Installation ease or ease of conversion adds to the complexity. Conversion must be tested during the system test phase.

**Operational Ease**
Operational requirements such as the following add to the complexity:
- recovery procedures;
- backup procedures;
- startup procedures;
- minimization of manual activities, such as volume or paper handling or operator intervention.

**Multiple Sites**
The application will be installed at multiple sites.

**Facility for Change**
The application is designed to facilitate change and has, for example,
- flexible query capability;
- tables maintainable by the user.

*continued on next page*

Sum the 14 DEGREE-OF-INFLUENCE factors.  The following table may be used:

| General Application Characteristics | DEGREE-OF-INFLUENCE Factors |
|---|---|
| 1. Data Communications | .. |
| 2. Distributed Functions | .. |
| 3. Performance | .. |
| 4. Heavily Used Configuration | .. |
| 5. Transaction Rate | .. |
| 6. On-Line Data Entry | .. |
| 7. End-User Efficiency | .. |
| 8. On-Line Updating | .. |
| 9. Complex Processing | .. |
| 10. Reusability | .. |
| 11. Installation Ease | .. |
| 12. Operational Ease | .. |
| 13. Multiple Sites | .. |
| 14. Facilitate Change | .. |
| Sum of DEGREE-OF-INFLUENCE Factors | .. |

key:

| factor not present: | 0 |
|---|---|
| insignificant influence: | 1 |
| moderate influence: | 2 |
| average influence: | 3 |
| significant influence: | 4 |
| strong influence throughout: | 5 |

Calculate the General Characteristics Adjustment (GCA).

GCA = 0.65 + (0.01 x sum of Degree-of-Influence factors)

The sum of the 14 degree-of-influence factors can range from 0 to 35. The General Characteristics Adjustment (GCA) thus ranges from −35% to +35%.

Multiply the unadjusted function points by GCA.

Final Function Points = Total Unadjusted Function Points  x  GCA.

Summary
Function point calculation may be done with the following table:

FUNCTION COUNT:

| Description | Function Complexity | | | Total |
|---|---|---|---|---|
| | LOW | MEDIUM | HIGH | |
| External Input | ..x 3 = .. | ..x 4 = .. | ..x 6 = .. | .. |
| External Output | ..x 4 = .. | ..x 5 = .. | ..x 7 = .. | .. |
| Logical Internal File | ..x 7 = .. | ..x 10 = .. | ..x 15 = .. | .. |
| External File | ..x 5 = .. | ..x 7 = .. | ..x 10 = .. | .. |
| Query | ..x 3 = .. | ..x 4 = .. | ..x 6 = .. | .. |
| TOTAL UNADJUSTED FUNCTION POINTS | | | | .. |

See previous table of General Application Characteristics for
calculation of degree-of-influence factors.

> Final Function Points = Total Unadjusted Function Points  x
>     0.65 + (0.01 x sum of Degree-of-Influence factors)

Reference

Function-point calculation, as described here, originated at IBM,
where it is extensively used. The original guidelines for function-point
calculation are in:

"AD/M Productivity Measurement and Estimate Validation," Document Number
 CIS & A Guideline 313, November 1st, 1984, GUIDE I/P Improvement Program.

   IBM Corporate Information Systems and Administration
   2000 Purchase Street, Purchase, New York 10577

# Guide. AD/M Productivity Measurement and Estimate Validation

Document Number—CIS and A Guideline 313
November 1st, 1984
The original guidelines on Function Points

I/P Improvement Program

IBM Corporate Information Systems and Administration
2000 Purchase Street
Purchase, NY, 10577

ABSTRACT

The overall objectives of application development and maintenance
(AD/M) productivity measurement and estimate validation are stated.
The fundamental concepts of work-product (output), work-effort
(input), and attributes (factors affecting productivity) are defined.
The relationships among measurement, quality, management,
flexibility, non-technical user, and estimate validation are
described.

A work-product measure called Function Points is defined. The
components of the Function Points measure are defined, namely: the
information processing function associated with the input, output,
file, interface file, and inquiry types; the adjustment for general
information processing function; and the Function Points calculation.
The work-hours and work-months measure of work-effort are defined,
and a way of describing the attributes is established.

The current recommended practices for determining the defined
measures, and implementing function point measurements at an AD/M
site, are described.[1] Work-sheets are provided to guide a measurement
process based on the definitions and current practices. The current
recommended practices are expected to be kept current by periodic
update as practices change.

---

[1]Throughout the guideline the left margin bar marks the lines that have changed from the
draft dated April 2, 1984.

CONTENTS

1.0 Introduction                                                        522
1.1 Objectives                                                          522
1.2 Considerations                                                      522
    1.2.1 Non-Technical User                                            523
    1.2.2 Flexibility                                                   523
    1.2.3 Quality                                                       523
    1.2.4 Estimating                                                    524
1.3 Concept                                                             524
    1.3.1 Work-Product                                                  524
    1.3.2 Work-Effort                                                   525
    1.3.3 Attributes                                                    527

2.0 Function Points Definitions                                         528
2.1 General                                                             528
    2.1.1 Development Work-Product and Support Work-Product Measures 528
    2.1.2 Measurement Timing                                            529
    2.1.3 Common Application Development                                529
    2.1.4 Application Boundaries                                        529
    2.1.5 Brought-In Application Code                                   530
    2.1.6 Consider All Users                                            531
2.2 Function Points Measure                                             531
    2.2.1 External Input Type                                           532
    2.2.2 External Output Type                                          532
    2.2.3 Logical Internal File Type                                    533
    2.2.4 External Interface File Type                                  534
    2.2.5 External Inquiry Type                                         534
    2.2.6 General Information Processing Function                       535
    2.2.7 Function Points Calculation                                   537
2.3 Work-Effort                                                         539
    2.3.1 Effort Reporting                                              539
    2.3.2 Work-Effort Definitions                                       540
    2.3.3 Work-Effort Measure                                           540
2.4 Attributes                                                          541
    2.4.1 Attribute Selection                                           541
    2.4.2 Attribute Recording                                           542
    2.4.3 Validating Estimates                                          543

3.0 Function Points Current Practices                                   545
3.1 General                                                             545
3.2 Function Points Measure                                             545
    3.2.1 External Input Type                                           546
    3.2.2 External Output Type                                          548
    3.2.3 Logical Internal File Type                                    550
    3.2.4 External Interface File Type                                  552
    3.2.5 External Inquiry Type                                         554
    3.2.6 General Information Processing Function                       556
3.3 Function Points Implementation                                      560

4.0 Function Points Worksheets                                          562
4.1 Function Points Calculation                                         562
4.2 IN., OUT., INQ., Function Type and Level of Info. Proc.
    Func. Record                                                        563
4.3 FILES, INTERFACES, Function Type and Level of Info. Proc.
    Func. Record                                                        564

## LIST OF ILLUSTRATIONS

## 1.0 INTRODUCTION

This guideline covers the measurement of the productivity results and trends in the application development and maintenance (AD/M) activities at an AD/M site.

The purpose of the guideline is to provide each AD/M site a consistent way to measure, portray, and demonstrate the productivity of their AD/M activities. It is also intended to help distinguish good AD/M actions and characteristics from bad, and to help improve the estimating process. It should, consistently and fairly, promote helpful exchange and use of data among activities at a site, and among sites, divisions, country organizations, and groups.

## 1.1 OBJECTIVES

A successful AD/M activity or project, in terms of AD/M responsibilities, is one that satisfies the agreed-to user's requirements, on schedule, and within budget. However, since it is based on estimates and agreements, the record of successful activities or projects can be misleading. Without a trend of their measured productivity, or a profile of measured productivity from other sites, it is difficult for a site to determine that the estimates are competitive (that is, among the most effective alternatives). Site management may not know how much more efficiently the activity or project might have been done.

An effective AD/M productivity measure should accomplish several objectives:

1. Consistently determine the productivity and productivity trends of AD/M development, enhancement, installation, or support activities, or projects, relative to other similar activities at the site, and other AD/M sites.

2. Promote actions or decisions that can improve the output of the AD/M site.

3. Demonstrate the results of the actions taken to improve the output of the AD/M site.

4. Support the estimating process at the AD/M site.

5. Support the management process at the AD/M site.

## 1.2 CONSIDERATIONS

Two basic measures must be established for any productivity measure. One measure must define work-product output, and the other must define work-effort input, or cost. Work-product divided by work-effort is called "productivity." Its trend should be up. Work-effort divided by work-product is called "unit cost." Its trend should be down. Either measure can be used, depending on the emphasis wanted (more product or less cost?). In this guideline, both will be considered to be productivity measures.

The productivity measure or unit cost measure places an AD/M activity, project, or site on a relative scale. The attributes of the application, activity, project, or site determine the reasons for that relative placement. Attributes are factors that influence productivity, such as: application size; user maturity; development environment; team maturity; percent new, modified, or used as-is; management processes; development processes; tools; and techniques. Attributes are the things one must analyze, understand, and change to move the productivity or cost trends in the right direction. Understanding the effect of the attributes on productivity is also essential to rational estimate validation. Therefore, attributes must be identified and recorded as diligently as the work-product and work-effort measures, and the work-product measure must be independent of the attributes.

## 1.2.1 Non-Technical User

It is desirable that the work-product measure be meaningful to the non-technical user. The user can then review, and agree with, the work-product measure applied to an activity or project. This can help ensure that a high quality activity or project is being measured. (That is, one that meets the user's requirements). It can also help the user understand the estimates on future activities or projects, and promote more informed discussions about changes.

## 1.2.2 Flexibility

To encourage a number of options for improving productivity, the work-product measure should facilitate analysis to allow choices among technologies. The measure should accommodate new approaches, such as higher level languages, code generators, and shared applications, without a change in the output measure. If the objective of the AD/M site is to deliver information processing function to the user, then the work-product measure should be based on the information processing function from the user's view.

## 1.2.3 Quality

The activities and tasks in AD/M are interdependent. The quality and completeness of early design tasks can affect the productivity of later development tasks. More significantly, an incomplete or low quality development project, can make the support activity very unproductive. The management and review processes, for each activity, task, phase, or project, must ensure that each work-product meets the quality required of the activity. No provision should be made to measure and include an unacceptable work-product. Low quality work-products identified by the management and review processes, or by poor results in the subsequent activities, should be assessed, and the weaknesses found should be used to improve the AD/M process.

## 1.2.4 Estimating

Three activities must be accomplished to estimate an AD/M activity or project effectively:

1. The tasks must be identified, listed, and sized.

2. Based on the tasks, an estimate must be developed.

3. The estimate must be validated, using other methods.

These estimating activities should be accomplished in the early phases of the activity or project. Therefore, if the work-product measure is to be helpful in validating estimates, it should be formed of elements that can be determined consistently in the early phases of a project.

## 1.3 CONCEPT

## 1.3.1 Work-Product

Function Points is an AD/M work-product measure based on user information processing function. It is evolving into the primary measure of AD/M work-product in IBM. Function Points measures an application by quantifying the information processing function associated with major external data or control input, output, or file types. This specific information processing is then adjusted for general information processing function by applying an adjustment based on general application characteristics, such as: communications, performance, transaction rate, and ease of installation. The result is Function Points.[2] An overview of Function Points is shown in Figure 1 on page 526.

---

[2]A complete definition of Function Points is given in Section 2.0. The current counting practices for Function Points are shown in Section 3.0.

Function Points are evaluated for an application by:

1. Considering an external boundary around the application software.

2. Listing each of the following major data or control user function types as viewed by the user.

3. Classifying each of the user function types to one of three levels of information processing function as shown.

4. Counting the occurrences of each of the 15 possible combinations of user function type and level of information processing function:

| User Function Types: | Level of Information Processing Function: |
|---|---|
| ▪ External Input | ▪ Low |
| ▪ External Output | ▪ Average |
| ▪ Logical Internal File | ▪ High |
| ▪ External Interface File | |
| ▪ External Inquiry | |

5. Weighting each of the combinations by a factor, and summing to measure the level of information processing function provided by the data or control types.

6. Adjusting the resulting sum to account for general information processing function by applying a factor based on the following:

General Application Characteristics:

| 1. Data communication | 8. On-line update |
|---|---|
| 2. Distributed function | 9. Complex processing |
| 3. Performance | 10. Usable in other applications |
| 4. Heavily used configuration | |
| 5. Transaction rates | 11. Installation ease |
| 6. Online data entry | 12. Operational ease |
| 7. Design for end user efficiency | 13. Multiple sites |
| | 14. Facilitate change |

1.3.2 Work-Effort

To complete a productivity measurement, measures of work-effort are needed. The measures must record the amount of work-effort, and the tasks, activities, and phases included. Two definitions should be understood:

1. The net work-hour, work-month, or work-year, which assumes that all recorded time is spent working. None of the recorded time is used for holiday, vacation, general education, or other personal absence.

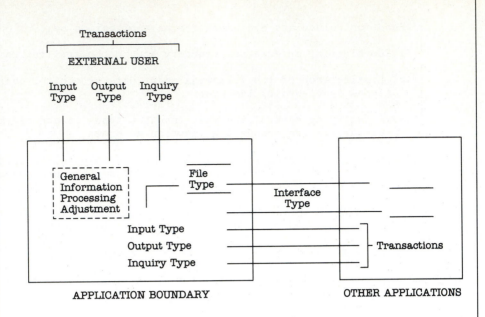

Transactions

EXTERNAL USER

Input          Output          Inquiry
Type           Type            Type

General
Information                    File
Processing                     Type
Adjustment                                    Interface
                                              Type

                Input Type
                Output Type                                 Transactions
                Inquiry Type

APPLICATION BOUNDARY                          OTHER APPLICATIONS

Figure 1. Function Points Overview.

The Funcation Points measure has been chosen for the following
reasons:

1. The measure isolates the work-product measure from the attributes,
   facilitating the analysis and identification of attributes that
   improve productivity.

2. The measure is based on the users external view of the
   application. It is not a technology dependent measure. This will
   allow choice in the technology used internally, without changing
   the measure.

3. The counts, classifications, and general characteristics can all
   be determined early in the development cycle, as soon as the
   external design has been completed. This will enable Function
   Points to be used in the estimating process.

4. Function Points can be understood and evaluated by a non-technical
   user who knows the application. This will enable the informed user
   to review and agree with the AD/M work-product measure.

5. Function Points have been shown to be an effective measure of AD/M
   work-product.

   Function Points have been used by 26 IBM AD/M Sites to measure the
   work-product of application development projects. The measurements
   have encompassed 289,500 function points of work-product, and 1854
   gross work-years of application development work-effort. From
   another viewpoint the work-products included about 19 million
   source lines of code. The resulting productivity trend lines and
   profiles appear to be useful.

2. The gross work-hour, work-month, or work-year, which assumes that the recorded time accounts for the time spent working, and the personal absence, as described above.

The work content of a gross work-hour, work-month, or work-year is generally about 75% of the work content of a net work-hour, work-month, or work-year in most organizations. (For example, the same work-effort on a project could be reported as 100 net work-months or 133 gross work-months.)

Conceptually, these measures are straightforward and have been used for many years, but differences in work practices at the various AD/M sites can cause the measures to differ. Therefore, the conversion factor between net and gross work-effort should be determined and stated by each organization with their productivity measures.

All the work-effort used to accomplish the tasks, activities, and phases of the pertinent AD/M process should be included, without regard for organization lines. For example, if a user works on design tasks for an application development project, the user's time should be included in the work-effort for the project. The work-effort measures should include the work-hours, work-months, or work-years that were used to accomplish the following phases of the AD/M process:[3]

- Design—Study, Requirements, External Design, Internal Design, and Development Planning.
- Development—Design, Code, Unit Test, Integration, System Test, Documentation, Installation Planning, and Support Planning.
- Installation—Education, Data Conversion, and Installation.
- Support[4]—Installed Application Support, Fixing, and Retrospective Analysis.


## 1.3.3 Attributes

When selecting the attributes of an AD/M activity, project, or site, to be identified and recorded, one must balance the desire to record only a few attributes against the need to avoid overlooking those really influencing productivity. Generally the selection proceeds as follows:

1. A series of productivity measurements are made and recorded. These measurements are arranged in order of productivity to highlight deviations from "average."

2. The known characteristics of the activities, projects, or site are then systematically examined to see which characteristics, or attributes, are most often associated with higher productivity, and/or least often associated with lower productivity.

---

[3]The work-effort measures and activities, phases, and tasks recommended to be measured and recorded are defined more completely in Sections 2.0 and 4.0.
[4]Function changes or enhancements are expected to be reported as projects under the design, development, and installation phases.

3. Those attributes that seem to be most important are then analyzed more completely to determine their effect on productivity, and how completely they explain the deviations from "average."

4. These results are then used to:

   - Identify the attributes to be measured and recorded systematically for all activities and projects.
   - Pursuade those responsible to change the attributes of sites, projects, and activities as indicated, thus inducing a productivity increase.
   - Estimate and validate the resources planned for future activities and projects.

The concept of this guideline will be to measure and record the most important attributes thought to affect productivity significantly, with provision for identifying and recording new attributes as they become more important.[5]

## 2.0 FUNCTION POINTS DEFINITIONS

This section provides the basic definitions supporting the measurement, recording, and analysis of Function Points, Work-effort, and Attributes.

### 2.1 GENERAL

The following considerations are generally applicable to the specific definitions of Function Points, Work-effort, and Attributes in later paragraphs in this section.

### 2.1.1 Development Work-Product and Support Work-Product Measures

Development productivity should be measured by counting the Function Points added[6] or changed by the development or enhancement project. Therefore:

- Development Work-Product—The absolute value sum of all Function Points added, changed, or deleted by the development or enhancement project.

Support productivity should be measured by counting the total Function Points supported by the support project during the support period. Therefore:

- Support Work-Product—The original Function Points of the application, adjusted for any changes introduced by subsequent

---

[5]The attributes recommended to be measured and recorded for AD/M activities, projects, and sites will be listed and described more completely in Section 2.0 and Section 4.0.
[6]Added Function Points include reused code if that code was selected, modified, integrated, tested, or installed by the development team. (See section 2.1.5).

development or enhancement projects. These changes are: (1) Plus or minus changes in level of information processing function (i.e., low, average, or high) in the original Function Points, (2) plus added Function Points, and/or (3) minus deleted Function Points.

## 2.1.2 Measurement Timing

To provide the work-product, work-effort, and attributes records needed for each development project, enhancement project, and support project to be analyzed, the indicated measures should be recorded at the following times in the application life cycle:

- The estimated development work-product, estimated work-effort, and planned attributes should be determined at the completion of the External Design Phase for each development and enhancement project. (When the complete user external view of the application has been documented).
- The development work-product, actual work-effort, and attributes should be determined at the completion of the Installation Phase, for each development and enhancement project. (When the application is ready for use).
- The support work-product, actual support work-effort, and attributes should be determined at the end of each calendar year of support and use, for each support project.

## 2.1.3 Common Application Development

To provide a consistent base for planning and measuring the installation, support, and enhancement of common applications, development centers responsible for common applications should provide the following data, when announcing (end of Phase 2), and when shipping (end of Phase 4), applications:

1. The Function Point measures of the common application.

   a. The development measure of the changes so local modification and installation effort can be planned.

   b. The support measure so maintenance effort can be planned.

2. Counting data for the application, equivalent in detail to the worksheets in this guideline.

## 2.1.4 Application Boundaries

Normally, as shown in Figure 1 on page 526, a single continuous external boundary is considered when counting Function Points. However, there are two general situations where counting an application in parts, is necessary:

1. It is agreed and specified with the user that the application be developed in multiple functional stages, and it is intended that the user specify or approve the characteristics of the data exchanges among the multiple stages.

   These multiple functional stages should be counted, estimated, and measured as separate applications, including all inputs, outputs, interfaces, and inquiries crossing all boundaries, because it is intended to be managed as multiple projects.

2. The application is planned to be developed as a single application using one development project, but it is so large that it is necessary to divide it into sub-applications for counting Function Points.

   The internal boundaries are arbitrary and are for counting purposes only. The sub-applications should be counted separately, but none of the inputs, outputs, interfaces, and inquiries, crossing the arbitrary internal boundaries to the other sub-applications, should be counted. The Function Points of the sub-applications should then be summed to give the total Function Points of the application for estimation and measurement, because it is intended to be managed as a single project.

## 2.1.5 Brought-In Application Code

Count the Function Points provided by brought-in application code (reused code), such as: an IBM IUP, PP, or FDP; an internal shared application; or a purchased application if that code was selected, modified, integrated, tested, or installed by the project team. However, do not count the Function Points provided by the brought-in code that provided user function beyond that stated in the approved requirements.

Some examples are:

1. Do count the Function Points provided by an application obtained from another IBM site, or project, and installed by the project team.

2. Do count the Function Points provided by a screen compiler, if that software was made available as a part of the application by the project team.

3. Do not count ADF updates of all files if the user only required updates of three files, even though the capability may be automatically provided.

4. Do not recount the Function Points provided by IMS if IMS had already been installed at the site.

## 2.1.6 Consider All Users

Consider all users of the application, since each application may have provision for many specified user functions, such as:

- End user functions. (enter data, inquire, etc.).
- Conversion and installation user functions. (file scan, file compare discrepancy list, etc.).
- Operations user functions. (recovery, control totals, etc.).

If the user functions are specified to be provided by the development team, they are user functions that should be included in measuring the development work-product.

If the user functions are specified to be maintained by the support team, they should be included in measuring the support work-product. (It is possible that some conversion and installation user functions may not be specified to be maintained and should not be included in the support work-product).

## 2.2 FUNCTION POINTS MEASURE

After the general considerations described in the preceding paragraphs have been decided, the Function Points measure is accomplished in three general steps:

1. Classify and count the five user function types

2. Adjust for general information processing function

3. Make the Function Points calculation

The paragraphs in this section define and describe each of these steps. The first step is accomplished as follows:

Classify, to three levels of information processing function, the following user functions that were made available to the user through the design, development, testing, or support efforts of the development, enhancement, or support project team:

1. External input types

2. External output types

3. Logical internal file types

4. External interface file types

5. External inquiry types

Then list and count these user functions. The counts should be recorded for use in the Function Points calculation, on an appropriate work-sheet. Examples of useful Function Points work-sheets are provided in Section 4.0, Function Points Work-sheets.

The definitions of each of the user functions to be counted, and the levels of information processing function, are provided in the following sections.

## 2.2.1 External Input Type

Count each unique user data or user control input type that enters the external boundary of the application being measured, and adds or changes data in a logical internal file type. An external input type should be considered unique if it has a different format, or if the external design requires a processing logic different from other external input types of the same format. As illustrated in Figure 1 on page 526, include external input types that enter directly as transactions from the user, and those that enter as transactions from other applications, such as input files of transactions.

Each external input type should be classified to one of three levels of information processing function, as follows:

- Low—Few data element types are entered, or are made available from logical internal files, by the external input type, and few logical internal file types are referenced by the external input type. User human factors considerations are not significant in the design of the external input type.
- Average—The level of information processing function of the external input type is not clearly either low or high.
- High—Many data element types are entered, or are made available from logical internal files, by the external input type, and many logical internal file types are referenced by the external input type. User human factors considerations significantly affect the design of the external input type.[7]

Do not include input files of records as external input types, because these are counted as external interface file types.

Do not include the input part of the external inquiry types as external input types, because these are counted as external inquiry types.

## 2.2.2 External Output Type

Count each unique user data or control output type that leaves the external boundary of the application being measured. An external output type should be considered unique if it has a different format, or if the external design requires a processing logic different from other external output types of the same format. As illustrated in Figure 1 on page 526, include external output types that leave directly as reports and messages to the user, and those that leave as reports and messages to other applications, such as output files of reports and messages.

Each external output type should be classified to one of three levels of information processing function, using definitions similar to those for the external input types:

- Low—Few data element types are included in the external output type, and few logical internal file types are referenced by the external output type. User human factors considerations are not significant in the design of the external output type.
- Average—The level of information processing function of the external output type is not clearly either low or high.
- High—Many data element types are included in the external output type, and many logical internal file types are referenced by the external output type. User human factors considerations significantly affect the design of the external output type.[7]

For reports, the following additional definitions should be used:

- Low—One or two columns. Simple data element transformations.
- Average—Multiple columns with sub-totals. Multiple data element transformations.
- High—Multiple and intricate data element transformations. Multiple and complex file references to be correlated. Significant performance considerations.[7]

Do not include output files of records as external output types, because these are counted as external interface file types.

Do not include the output response of external inquiry types as external output types, because these are counted as external inquiry types.


## 2.2.3 Logical Internal File Type

Count each major logical group of user data or control information in the application as a logical internal file type. Include each logical file, or within a data base, each logical group of data from the viewpoint of the user, that is generated, used, and maintained by the application. Count logical files as described in the external design, not physical files.

The logical internal file types should be classified to one of three levels of information processing function, as follows:

- Low—Few record types. Few data element types. No significant performance or recovery considerations.
- Average—The level of information processing function of the logical internal file type is not clearly either low or high.
- High—Many record types. Many data element types. Performance and recovery are significant considerations.[7]

---

[7]More specific practices for determining the level of information processing function are described in the Current Practices Section 3.0.

Do not include logical internal files that are not accessible to the user through external input, output, or inquiry types.


## 2.2.4 External Interface File Type

Files passed or shared between applications should be counted as external interface file types within each application. Count each major logical group of user data or control information that enters or leaves the application as an external interface file type.

External interface file types should be classified to one of three levels of information processing function, using definitions similar to those for logical internal file types:

- Low—Few record types. Few data element types. No significant performance or recovery considerations.
- Average—The level of information processing function of the logical external interface file type is not clearly either low or high.
- High—Many record types. Many data element types. Performance and recovery are significant considerations.[7]

File types that are used by the application and are also shared with other applications should be counted as both Logical Internal File Types and External Interface File Types.


## 2.2.5 External Inquiry Type

Count each unique input/output combination, where an input causes and generates an immediate output, as an external inquiry type. An external inquiry type should be considered unique if it has a format different from other external inquiry types in either its input or output parts, or if the external design requires a processing logic different from other external inquiry types of the same format. As illustrated in Figure 1 on page 526, include external inquiry types that enter directly from the user, and those that enter from other applications.

The external inquiry types should be classified to one of three levels of information processing function, as follows:

1. Classify the input part of the external inquiry type using definitions similar to the external input type. (paragraph 2.2.1).

2. Classify the output part of the external inquiry type using definitions similar to the external output type. (paragraph 2.2.2).

3. The level of information processing function of the external inquiry type is the greater of the two classifications.

To help distinguish external inquiry types from external input types, consider that the input data of an external inquiry type is entered only to direct the search, and no update of logical internal file types occurs.

Do not confuse a query facility with an external inquiry type. An external inquiry type is a direct search for specific data, usually using only a single key. A query facility, such as QBE or SQL, provides an organized structure of external input, output, and inquiry types to compose many possible inquiries using many keys and operations. These external input, output, and inquiry types should all be counted to measure a query facility.

## 2.2.6 General Information Processing Function

The previous sections define the external input, external output, internal file, external interface file, and external inquiry types to be listed, classified, and counted. The Function Points Calculation (paragraph 2.2.7) describes how to use these counts to measure the level of information processing function associated with those user functions. This paragraph describes how to apply an adjustment based on the general application characteristics that affect the information processing delivered to the user.

The adjustment for general information processing function should be accomplished in three steps, as follows:

1. The degree of influence, on the application, of each of the 14 general characteristics, should be estimated from the user's view of the application.

2. The 14 degrees of influence should be summed, and the total should be used to develop an adjustment factor ranging from 0.65 to 1.35. (This gives an adjustment of +/- 35%).

3. The level of information processing function measure should be multiplied by the adjustment factor to develop the work-product measure called Function Points.

The first step is accomplished as follows: Estimate the degree of influence, on the application, of each of the 14 general characteristics that follow. Use the degree of influence measures in the following list, and record the estimates on a work-sheet similar to Figure 7 on page 562.

Degree of Influence Measures:

- Not present, or no influence if present                    = 0
- Insignificant influence                                     = 1
- Moderate influence                                          = 2
- Average influence                                           = 3
- Significant influence                                       = 4
- Strong influence, throughout                                = 5

General Application Characteristics

1. The data and control information used in the application are sent or received over communication facilities. Terminals connected locally to the control unit are considered to use communication facilities.
2. Distributed data or processing functions are a characteristic of the application.
3. Application performance objectives, stated or approved by the user, in either response or throughput, influenced the design, development, installation, and support of the application.
4. A heavily used operational configuration, requiring special design considerations, is a characteristic of the application. (e.g., the user wants to run the application on existing or committed equipment that will be heavily used).
5. The transaction rate is high and it influenced the design, development, installation, and support of the application.
6. On-line data entry and control functions are provided in the application.
7. The on-line functions provided emphasize a design for end user efficiency.
8. The application provides on-line update for the logical internal files.
9. Complex processing is a characteristic of the application. Examples are:

   - Sensitive control and/or security processing.
   - Extensive logical and mathematical processing.
   - Much exception processing resulting in incomplete transactions that must be processed again.

10. The application, and the code in the application, has been specifically designed, developed, and supported to be usable in other applications.
11. Conversion and installation ease are characteristics of the application. A conversion and installation plan and/or conversion tools were provided and were tested during the system test phase.
12. Operational ease is a characteristic of the application. Effective start-up, back-up, and recovery procedures were provided, and they were tested during the system test phase. The application minimizes the need for manual activities, such as tape mounts, paper handling, and direct on-location manual intervention.
13. The application has been specifically designed, developed, and supported to be installed at multiple sites for multiple organizations.
14. The application has been specifically designed, developed, and supported to facilitate change. Examples are:

   - Flexible query capability is provided.
   - Business control data is grouped in tables maintainable by the user.

## 2.2.7 Function Points Calculation

The previous sections describe how the function types are listed, classified, and counted, and how the general information processing function adjustment is determined. This paragraph describes how to make the calculations that develop the Function Points measures.

Using the definitions in Paragraph 2.1.1, two equations have been developed to more specifically define the development work-product measure and the support work-product[8] measure:

Development Work-Product FP Measure = $(\text{Add} + \text{ChgA})\text{GCA2} + (\text{Del})\text{GCA1}$ = _____ .

Support Work-Product FP Measure = $\text{Orig FP} + (\text{Add} + \text{ChgA})\text{GCA2} - (\text{Del} + \text{ChgB})\text{GCA1}$ = _____ .

Orig FP = adjusted FP of the application, evaluated as they were before the project started.

Add = unadjusted FP added to the application, evaluated as they are expected to be at the completion of the project.

ChgA = unadjusted FP changed in the application, evaluated as they are expected to be at the completion of the project.

Del = unadjusted FP deleted from the application, evaluated as they were before the project started.

ChgB = unadjusted FP changed in the application, evaluated as they were before the project started.

GCA1 = the general information processing function adjustment pertaining to the application before the project started.

GCA2 = the general information processing function adjustment pertaining to the application after the project completion.

---

[8]The Support Work-product measure may be determined by the equation or by recounting the whole application when changes occur.

43

44
45
46

The lists of the function types developed, using Figure 8 on page 40 and Figure 9 on page 564 as work-sheets, provide the information for calculating the unadjusted FP. A portion of the filled-in form might look like this:

| In., Out., Inq., Function List | | | | Level of Info. Proc. Func. Record | | | | | | | |
| --- | --- | --- | --- | --- | --- | --- | --- | --- | --- | --- | --- |
| | | | | Before | | | | After | | | |
| Type | ID | Ref | Description | DET | FTR | Del | Chg | DET | FTR | Add | Chg |
| IT | TS01 | 001 | Sign-on screen | 4 | 1 | L | ___ | ___ | | | ___ |
| IT | PSCC | 001 | Cost center transaction | ___ | | ___ | | 29 | 2 | H | ___ |
| IT | PSDC | 001 | Department change transaction | 5 | 1 | ___ | L | 12 | 2 | | A |

Type = the function type.

ID, Ref, and Description = the specific function type.

Before = the level of information processing function record of the specific function type as it was before the project was started.

After = the level of information processing function record of the specific function type as it was expected to be after the project was completed.

DET = number of data element types in the function type.

FTR = number of file types referenced by the function type.

Del = the level of information processing function of the deleted function type before deletion.

Chg = the level of information processing function of the changed function type before and after the change.

Add = the level of information processing function of the added function type.

If the application consists of only new or added function types, the development work-product FP measure equals the support work-product FP measure. The form shown in Figure 7 on page 562 can be used to calculate both measures as follows:

1.  Using the lists discussed above, each function type at each level of information processing function is counted and entered in the function count matrix.

2.  The weights shown on the form are applied and the results are summed to give the unadjusted function points.

3.  The general information processing function adjustment pertaining to the application at the completion of the project is developed using the general application characteristics described in Paragraph 2.2.6.

4. The general information processing function adjustment is applied to the unadjusted function points to give the Function Points measure.

If the application is an enhancement project consisting of added, deleted, and/or changed function types, the development work-product FP measure does not equal the support work-product FP measure. The appropriate forms are shown in Figure 10 on page 565 for the development work-product, and Figure 11 on page 566 for the support work-product. They are used as follows:

1. The function types are counted and entered into the appropriate added, deleted, or changed matrices.

2. The added, deleted, or changed unadjusted function points are determined on each form.

3. The general information processing function adjustments pertaining to the beginning or the end of the project are applied to each form to give the Function Points measures.

These measures of work-product can then be used with the measures of work-effort (section 2.3), and the attributes of applications and projects (section 2.4), to accomplish the following analyses:

1. Identify and promote the attributes associated with higher productivity.

2. Identify and avoid the attributes associated with lower productivity.

3. Develop and use estimating processes based on measurements.

4. Portray productivity trends.

## 2.3 WORK-EFFORT

### 2.3.1 Effort Reporting

The record of estimated and actual work effort is needed for each project that is to be used in productivity measurement and analysis or estimate validation. The following work-effort information should be known:

1. The original estimate.

2. The estimate of approved changes.

3. The actual results.

To record the actual results most reliably, a systematic method of accounting for work-effort should be used. Effort Reporting should result in an objective and accurate record of past work-effort so that past projects can be analyzed objectively and accurately, and reliable estimates can be made for future projects.

Effort reporting should be used to establish three measures:

1. The net work-effort on the project.

2. The time away from the project on authorized absence.

3. The gross work-effort on the project.

Effort reporting can also be used to establish the average conversion factors for an organization to apply to the net and gross work-effort definitions in the following section.

## 2.3.2 Work-Effort Definitions

- Net Work-Hour—One hour of work by one person.
- Gross Work-Year—About 1565 net work-hours, or 2080 gross work-hours.
- Gross Work-Month—About 130 net work-hours, or 173 gross work-hours.
- The Net work-effort number, in IBM, normally equals about 0.75 the Gross work-effort number

## 2.3.3 Work-Effort Measure

Since the work-effort definitions are all stated in terms of the net work-hour, they can be consistently interpreted if the conversion factor between net and gross work-effort is stated for each organization. This can be most conveniently recorded and remembered as the net work-hours per gross work-month. (It should be about 130 net work-hours).

Two work-effort measures are called for in this guideline. Namely, work-months for the development productivity measure, and work-hours for the support productivity measure. For consistency and a more direct relationship to head-count, these measures should be stated in gross work-months and gross work-hours. Work-sheets are shown in Figure 12 on page 567 and Figure 13 on page 568.

The gross work-months or gross work-hours can generally be determined in two possible ways:

1. The gross work-months or gross work-hours are recorded directly from the project work-effort record.

2. The net work-months or work-hours are recorded directly from the project work-effort record, and are then converted to gross measures by a conversion factor derived from the work-effort record of the site.

Method number two is recommended because the first method can give incorrect productivity results on short projects. Since vacations are usually concentrated in the summer months, the work content of a gross work-month in the summer can be significantly less than the work content of a gross work-month in the winter. The recommended approach avoids this problem by measuring the work content specifically in net work-effort.

## 2.4 ATTRIBUTES

### 2.4.1 Attribute Selection

Each characteristic or attribute of a project that might be measured and recorded for future analysis should be considered as follows:

1. How important is it?

   In the context of this guideline, how significant is its expected effect on productivity?[9]

2. Can it be changed?

   Can the attribute be changed at the site, or is it only interesting information that cannot be used to effect improvement? The answers to this question depend heavily on level of management involved, and time available to make the change. A factor, such as development environment, that is not changeable by a first line manager may well be changeable by a site director of I/S. A factor, such as development team maturity, that cannot be changed for a project already underway, may certainly be changed given hiring or training objectives, time, and resources. Generally, if an issue is important and the facts are available, change can be accomplished.

3. Is it a variable at the site?

   A characteristic or attribute that is unvarying across all the activities and projects at a site cannot be used to explain deviations among the projects at the site. However, it may be needed to analyze the productivity differences between two sites. An attribute should not be excluded from the record only because it is a part of every activity and project at the site.

---

[9]It is interesting to note how quickly these expectations can change. For example, who would have seen the need three years ago, to differentiate between subsecond response time and one or two second response time, in productivity analysis?

The key issue is clearly the importance of the attribute to productivity. Therefore, all attributes that are thought to affect productivity significantly should be measured and recorded.

### 2.4.2 Attribute Recording

The initial approach to recording the attributes of a project or activity is almost always overly simplistic. Then, the inadequacies of a simple checklist are discovered. Yes and No do not describe the degree to which a tool or technique applies to the project.

For example, it is realized that far different results should be expected from the following extremes:

1. A mature tool, that the team has used before successfully, that can influence 100% of the work-effort on the project.

2. A newly released tool, being used by the team for the first time, that is potentially applicable to only 10% of the work-effort.

A technique for recording these levels of applicability is needed. Therefore, the following information should be recorded for each attribute recorded for analysis:

- Maturity of the tool or technique?

  - Low - Tool or technique is new. No people experienced in its use are available for consultation.

  - Moderate - Tool or technique has been in use long enough that people experienced in its use are available for consultation.

  - High - Tool or technique has been in use long enough that experience has been incorporated in improvements to the tool or technique.

- Maturity of the project team in regard to the tool or technique?

  - Low - Project team has not used the tool or technique before.

  - Moderate - Project team has used the tool or technique once before.

  - High - Project team has used the tool or technique more than once before.

- Applicability of the tool or technique to the work-effort on the project?

  - Low - Tool or technique is potentially applicable to less than 1/3 of the work-effort on the project.

— Moderate - Tool or technique is potentially applicable to between 1/3 and 2/3 of the work-effort on the project.

— High - Tool or technique is potentially applicable to over 2/3 of the work-effort on the project.

A form for recording these attributes is shown in Figure 14 on page 569. This record will provide the information to more accurately weight the contribution to productivity expected from the tool or technique.

## 2.4.3 Validating Estimates

An estimate for an application development project should consist of the following:

1. An estimate of the resources required - work-effort.

2. A task plan - tasks, dependencies, durations, work-effort.

3. A schedule - start and end dates.

Each estimate should be validated by using two or more estimating methods and looking for reasonable consistency among the estimates. The Function Points work-product measure provides a way to get one of the validating estimates. The following procedure is an effective way to validate estimates using Function Points:

1. Gather data on a number of completed projects:

   • Function Points — the work-product delivered.
   • Work-months — the work-effort used.
   • Attributes — the characteristics expected to influence productivity.

2. Sort projects into related groups:

   • Application areas. (e.g., process control, business control, accounting).
   • Project type. (e.g., new development, modification, package installation).

3. Analyze related groups separately:

   • Independent variable — Function Points delivered.
   • Dependent variable — Gross Work-months used.
   • Inspect data and fit appropriate model(s).
   • Power curve model is recommended — WM = a (FP) exp(b).

This model can be used directly to validate estimates if the attributes are acceptably consistent among the projects, if the correlation factor between the model and data is acceptable, and if the project to be validated is similar to those used to form the model.

4. For each project, determine the deviation from the model.

   - Amount above or below expected productivity.
   - Arrange projects in order of relative productivity.

5. Determine the degree to which attributes apply to each project:

   - Attribute maturity.
   - Team maturity with the attribute.
   - Attribute applicability to the work-effort (%).

6. Record the attributes on the ordered project list:

   - Look for patterns.
   - Most often associated with higher productivity.
   - Least often associated with lower productivity.
   - Identify the most important attributes for further analysis.

7. Analyze to determine the productivity effect of the attribute:

   - Multiple linear regression is effective with enough data, and/or fewer attributes.
   - Determine effect of each attribute.
   - Back out the effect of the attributes used on each project — lower-bound model.
   - Include the effect of the attributes not used on each project — upper-bound model.

8. Develop an estimate validator by interpolating the effects of the attributes to the extent they are planned to be used on the projects to be validated.

   This model may be used to validate estimates for projects that do not have similar attributes.

## 3.0 FUNCTION POINTS CURRENT PRACTICES

### 3.1 GENERAL

### 3.2 FUNCTION POINTS MEASURE

The following numbered sections provide the current recommended practices in IBM I/S for classifying the level of information processing function and counting the five major data or control types, adjusting for general information processing function, and calculating Function Points:

1. External Input

2. External Output

3. Logical Internal File

4. External Interface File

5. External Inquiry

6. General Information Processing Function

7. Function Points Calculation

These current practices are based on the definitions in Section 2.2 and are intended to provide more objective consistency among individuals and sites in measuring work-products with Function Points. Where current practices are provided, each of the numbered sections will follow a similar format:

1. Objective definitions of the level of information processing function classifications.

2. A checklist of potential data or control types.

3. Specific counting recommendations for particular described data or control types.

Since the current practices are interpretations based on the definitions in Section 2.2, any issues not covered in the current practices must be resolved by use of the definitions.

### 3.2.1 External Input Type

| | 1 to 4 DET | 5 to 15 DET | 16 or more DET |
|---|---|---|---|
| 0 or 1 FTR | L | L | A |
| 2 FTR | L | A | H |
| 3 or more FTR | A | H | H |

DET = data element types

FTR = file types referenced

RET = record types

L = low

A = average

H = high

Additional factors:

Consider the following factors, relative to average, to adjust the result up or down not more than one level:

- Automatic cursor movement

- Other human factors

- Data conversion

- Application performance

Figure 2.  External Input Type - Level of Information Processing Function.

Potential Input Types:

- keyed Document
- OCR Document
- Screen
- Tape Transaction
- Card
- Diskette Transaction
- Paper Tape Transaction
- Transaction From Another Application

- Switch
- Digital Sensor
- Analog Sensor
- Magnetic Stripe
- PF Key
- Light Pen
- User Application Control

Counting Recommendations:

The recommendation most closely describing each input type should be used in counting each input type.

| DESCRIPTIONS: | COUNT AS: |
|---|---|
| • Data screen input | 1 IT |
| • Multiple data screens entered, accumulated, and processed as one transaction, with no processing of individual screens | 1 IT |
| • Function screen input | 1 IT |
| • Function screen with multiple different functions | 1 IT/Function |
| • Automatic data or function transactions from other applications | 1 IT |
| • Inquiry followed by an update iput | 1 QT, 1 IT |
| • Alternate input with same processing logic as primary input | 0 IT |
| • PF Key duplicate of a screen already counted as an input | 0 IT |
| • Light pen duplicate of a screen already counted as an input | 0 IT |
| • Two input screens with the same format and processing logic | 1 IT |
| • Two screens with the same format and different processing logic | 2 IT |
| • Selection menu screen input with save capability | 1 IT |
| • ADF Target screen input | 1 IT |
| • Screen that is both input and output | 1 IT, 1 OT |
| • User maintained table or file | potentially 1 FT, 1 OT, 1 QT, 1 IT |
| • User application control input | 1 IT |
| • Repeat screen input | 0 IT |
| • Input forms (OCR) | 1 IT |

## 3.2.2 External Output Type

| | 1 to 5 DET | 6 to 19 DET | 20 or more DET |
|---|---|---|---|
| 0 or 1 FTR | L | L | A |
| 2 or 3 FTR | L | A | H |
| 4 or more FTR | A | H | H |

DET = data element types

FTR = file types referenced

RET = record types

L = low

A = average

H = high

Additional factors:

Consider the following factors, relative to average, to adjust the result up or down not more than one level:

- Layout or human factors

- Number of control breaks

- Data transformations

- Application performance

Figure 3.  External Output Type - Level of Information Processing Function.

Potential Output Types:

- Screen Report
- Terminal Report
- Batch Report
- Tape Transaction
- Card
- Diskette Transaction
- Paper Tape Transaction
- Screen Message
- Transaction to Another Application

- Digital Line
- Digital Actuator
- Analog Actuator
- User Application Control
- Magnetic Stripe
- Invoice
- Check
- Bill of Material

Counting Recommendations:

The recommendation most closely describing each output type should be used in counting each output type.

DESCRIPTIONS:                                                                    COUNT AS:

- Data screen output                                                             1 OT

- Automatic data or function transactions to other applications                 1 OT

- Operator message frame (format) from the application for
  multiple similar operator messages                                            1 OT
  (Level of information processing function is determined by
  treating different messages as different data element types)

- Message frame (format) for multiple error messages or
  confirmation messages associated with 1 IT                                    1 OT
  (Level of information processing function is determined by
  treating different messages as different data element types)

- Individual error message output within a message frame                        0 OT

- Individual confirmation message output within a message frame                 0 OT

- Batch printed report                                                          1 OT

- Batch run report                                                              1 OT

- Batch error report                                                            1 OT

- Terminal printed report                                                       1 OT

- Control total output                                                          1 OT

- Audit list or check list report                                              1 OT

- User maintained table or file        potentially 1 FT, 1 IT, 1 QT, 1 OT

- Selection menu screen output with save capability                            1 OT

- Repeat screen output                                                         0 OT

- Start screen output                                                          1 OT

- End screen output                                                            1 OT

3.2.3 Logical Internal File Type

| | 1 to 19 DET | 20 to 50 DET | 51 or more DET |
|---|---|---|---|
| 1 RET | L | L | A |
| 2 to 5 RET | L | A | H |
| 6 or more RET | A | H | H |

DET = data element types

FTR = file types referenced

RET = record types

L = low

A = average

H = high

Additional factors:

Consider the following factors, relative to average, to adjust the result up or down not more than one level:

- Application performance

- Search Criteria

- Recovery and backup

Figure 4.  Logical Internal File Type - Level of Information Processing Function.

Potential File Types:

- Logical Internal File

- Data Base

- User Table

- Message Table or FIle

- File for Control of Batch Sequential Processing

- File for User Query

Counting Recommendations:

The recommendation most closely describing each internal file type should be used in counting each internal file type.

DESCRIPTIONS:                                                    COUNT AS:

- Logical entity of data from user viewpoint                      1 FT

- Logical internal file generated or maintained by
  the application                                                 1 FT

- Files accessible to the user through keyword(s) or
  parameter(s)                                                    1 FT

- User maintained table or file      potentially 1 IT, 1 OT, 1 QT, 1 FT

- File used for data or control by sequential (batch) application 1 FT

- Each hierarchical path (leg) through a data base, derived
  from user requirements (include paths formed by secondary
  indices and logical relationships)                             1 FT

- Hierarchical paths not derived from user requirements           0 FT

- Intermediate or sort work file                                  0 FT

## 3.2.4 External Interface File Type

| | 1 to 19 DET | 20 to 50 DET | 51 or more DET |
|---|---|---|---|
| 1 RET | L | L | A |
| 2 to 5 RET | L | A | H |
| 6 or more RET | A | H | H |

DET = data element types

FTR = file types referenced

RET = record types

L = low

A = average

H = high

Additional factors:

Consider the following factors, relative to average, to adjust the result up or down not more than one level:

- Application performance

- Search Criteria

- Recovery and backup

- Multiple distribution

Figure 5.  External Interface File Type - Level of Information
          Processing Function.

Potential Interface File Types:

- Logical Internal File Accessible from Another Application

- Shared Data Base

- Logical Internal File Accessible to Another Application

Counting Recommendations:

The recommendation most closely describing each interface file type should be used in counting each interface file type.

DESCRIPTIONS:                                                    COUNT AS:

▪ File of records from another application                          1 EI

▪ File of records to another application, even though
  counted as 1 FT in this application                               1 EI

▪ File of records to multiple other applications (multiple
  distribution is a level of information processing function
  consideration)                                                    1 EI

▪ Data base shared to other application                             1 EI

▪ Data base shared from other applications                          1 EI

3.2.5 External Inquiry Type

Input Part:

| | 1 to 4 DET | 5 to 15 DET | 16 or more DET |
|---|---|---|---|
| 0 or 1 FTR | L | L | A |
| 2 FTR | L | A | H |
| 3 or more FTR | A | H | H |

DET = data element types

FTR = file types referenced

RET = record types

L = low

A = average

H = high

Output Part:

| | 1 to 5 DET | 6 to 19 DET | 20 or more DET |
|---|---|---|---|
| 0 or 1 FTR | L | L | A |
| 2 or 3 FTR | L | A | H |
| 4 or more FTR | A | H | H |

Additional factors:

Consider the following factors, relative to average, to adjust the result up or down not more than one level:

- Automatic cursor movement

- Layout or other human factor

- Application performance

- Number of subtotal types

- Data transformations

Figure 6.  External Inquiry Type - Level of Information Processing
            Function.

Potential Input Types:

- User Inquiry with NO File Update

- Help Message and Screen

- Selection Menu Screen

- ADF Menu

- ADF Key Selection Screen

- ADF Master Rules Screen

Counting Recommendations:

The recommendation most closely describing each inquiry type should be used in counting each inquiry type.

DESCRIPTIONS:                                                      COUNT AS:

- Online input and online output with no update of data in files    1 QT

- Inquiry followed by an update input                             1 QT, 1 IT

- Help screen input and output                                      1 QT

- Selection menu screen input and output                            1 QT

- User maintained table or file      potentially 1 FT, 1 IT, 1 OT, 1 QT

- ADF menu input and output                                         1 QT

- ADF Key Selection screen input and output                         1 QT

- ADF Master Rules screen input and output                          1 QT

- A major query facility or language should be decomposed into its hierarchical structure of IT(s), OT(s), and QT(s) using the existing definitions and current practices.

## 3.2.6 General Information Processing Function

1. The data and control information used in the application are sent
   or received over communication facilities. Terminals connected
   locally to the control unit are considered to use communication
   facilities.

   Score as:

   0     Application is pure batch processing.

   1-2   Remote printing and/or remote data entry.

   3-5   Interactive teleprocessing (TP).

   3     TP front end to a batch process.

   5     Application is dominantly interactive TP.

2. Distributed data or processing functions are a characteristic of
   the application.

   Score as:
   0     Application does not aid the transfer of data or processing
         function between components of the system.

   1     Application prepares data for end user processing on
         another component of the system.

   2-4   Data is prepared for transfer, is transferred, and is
         processed on another component of the system.

   5     Processing functions are dynamically performed on the most
         appropriate component of the system.

3. Application performance objectives, stated or approved by the
   user, in either response or throughput, influenced the design,
   development, installation, and support of the application.

   Score as:

   0-3   No special performance requirements are stated by the user.
         Performance analysis and design considerations are
         standard.

   4     Stated user performance requirements are stringent enough
         to require performance analysis tasks in the design phase.

   5     Stated user performance requirements are stringent enough
         to, in addition, require performance analysis tools to be
         used to the design, development, and/or installation
         phases.

4. A heavily used operational configuration, requiring special design considerations, is a characteristic of the application. (e.g., the user wants to run the application on existing or committed equipment that will be heavily used).

Score as:

0-3   Typical application run on standard production machine. No stated operation restrictions.

4     Stated operation restrictions require special constraints on the application in the central processor.

5     In addition, there are special constraints on the application in distributed components of the system.

5. The transaction rate is high and it influenced the design, development, installation, and support of the application.

Score as:

0-3   Transaction rates are such that performance analysis considerations are standard.

4     High transaction rates stated by the user in the application requirements or service level agreements are high enough to require performance analysis tasks in the design phase.

5     High transaction rates stated by the user in the application requirements or service level agreements are high enough to, in addition, require the use of performance analysis tools in the design, development, and/or installation phases.

6. On-line data entry and control functions are provided in the application.

Score as:

0-2   None - 15% of the transactions are interactive data entry.

3-4   15% - 30% of the transactions are interactive data entry.

5     30% - 50% of the transactions are interactive data entry.

7. The on-line functions provided emphasize a design for end user efficiency.

Score as:

0-3   No stated special user requirements concerning end-user efficiency.

4    Stated requirements for end-user efficiency are strong
     enough to require design tasks for human factors to be
     included.

5    Stated requirements for end-user efficiency are strong
     enough to require use of special tools such as
     "prototyping."

8. The application provides on-line update for the logical internal
   files.

   Score as:

   0    None.

   1-2  Online update of control files. Volume of updating is low
        and recovery is easy.

   3    Online update of major logical internal files.

   4    In addition, protection against data loss is essential.

   5    In addition, high volumes bring cost considerations into
        the recovery considerations.

9. Complex processing is a characteristic of the application.
   Examples are:

   ▪ Sensitive control and/or security processing.
   ▪ Extensive logical and mathematical processing.
   ▪ Much exception processing resulting in incomplete transactions
     that must be processed again.

   Which of the following characteristics apply to the application:

   ▪ Extensive logical and/or mathematical processing.
   ▪ Much exception processing, many incomplete transactions, and
     much reprocessing of transactions.
   ▪ Sensitive control and/or security processing.

   Score as:

   0    None of the above apply.

   1-3  Any one of the above applies.

   4    Any two of the above apply.

   5    All of the above apply.

10. The application, and the code in the application, has been
    specifically designed, developed, and supported to be usable in
    other applications.

Score as:

0-1    A local application addressing the needs of one user
       organization.

2-3    Application used or produced common modules that considered
       more than one user's needs.

4-5    In addition, the application was specifically packaged and/
       or documented to ease re-use.

11. Conversion and installation ease are characteristics of the
    application. A conversion and installation plan and/or conversion
    tools were provided and were tested during the system test phase.

    Score as:

    0-1    No special conversion and installation considerations were
           stated by the user.

    2-3    Conversion and installation requirements were stated by the
           user and conversion and installation guides were provided
           and tested.

    4-5    In addition, conversion and installation tools were
           provided and tested.

12. Operational ease is a characteristic of the application.
    Effective start-up, back-up, and recovery procedures were
    provided, and they were tested during the system test phase. The
    application minimizes the need for manual activities, such as
    tape mounts, paper handling, and direct on-location manual
    intervention.

    Score as:

    0      No special operational considerations were stated by the
           user.

    1-2    Effective startup, backup, and recovery processes were
           required, provided, and tested.

    3-4    In addition, the application minimizes the need for manual
           activities, such as tape mounts and paper handling.

    5      Application is designed for unattended operation.

13. The application has been specifically designed, developed, and
    supported to be installed at multiple sites for multiple
    organizations.

    Score as:

    0      No user requirement to consider the needs of more than one
           user site.

1-3    Needs of multiple sites were considered in the design.

4-5    Documentation and support plan are provided and tested to support the application at multiple sites.

14. The application has been specifically designed, developed, and supported to facilitate change. Examples are:

- Flexible query capability is provided.
- Business control data is grouped in tables maintainable by the user.

Score as:

0      No special user requirement to design the application to minimize or facilitate change

1-3    Flexible query capability is provided.

4-5    In addition, control data is kept in tables that are maintained by the user with online interactive processes.

## 3.3 FUNCTION POINTS IMPLEMENTATION

The following list is recommended as an implementation sequence to establish Function Points at a site:

1. Study this guideline thoroughly.

2. Plan to use persons with the most knowledge of each application to count the function points. Do not plan for a central counting group. It is easier to learn function points than to learn the applications.

3. Count function points on several applications installed at the site. This can build experience and confidence. It also can provide local function point data for use in the workshop.

4. Train people to count function points through the Function Point Workshop, offered on your site by the Dallas I/S Education Facility. The workshop can train 15 to 25 people and takes about 6 to 7 hours. A case study provides counting practice and experience.

5. Initiate the counting of function points on new development and/or enhancement projects. The function point measure should be produced at end of each of the following phases:

- External design.
- Installation and acceptance.

6. Establish the function point measure for the applications in the installed application base:

- Prepare an inventory listing the applications in the installed application base.
- Determine the function point measure of each of the applications in one of the following ways:
  - Recommended approach:

    Count the function points on each application in the inventory.

  - Approximation 1:

    Count the function points and source lines of code on a sample of the inventory and establish a model or models linking function points and source lines of code. Then determine the function points on each application by counting the source lines of code on each application and using the appropriate model to approximate the function points.

  - Approximation 2:

    Count the source lines of code on the new development and enhancement projects. Then use the function point and source lines of code measures to establish a model or models linking function points and source lines of code. Then determine the function points on each application by counting the source lines of code on each application and using the appropriate model to approximate the function points.

7. Maintain the application inventory function point record by incorporating the function point measures of each new development and enhancement as they are installed.

   If the approximations are used to establish the function point inventory, they should be converted to counted function points at the time of the next enhancement of each application.

8. Experience at three sites has produced the following estimates of function point counting work-effort:

   - New development or enhancement project with accurate and current external design document available - less than one work-hour per 100 function points.
   - Installed application with external design document available - more than one work-hour per 100 function points.
   - Installed application with external design document not available - more than three work-hours per 100 function points.

9. In addition to the people counting the function points on the applications, a full time coordinator for each average site, (about 200 developers), should review each function point measure for consistency, perform the analysis, and provide the feedback reports.

## 4.0 FUNCTION POINTS WORKSHEETS

## 4.1 FUNCTION POINTS CALCULATION

Application: _____.   Appl ID: _____.

Prepared by: _____ __/__/__. Reviewed by: _____ __/__/__.

Notes:

- Function Count:

| Type ID | Description | Level of Information Processing Function | | | Total |
|---------|-------------|------|---------|------|-------|
|         |             | Low  | Average | High |       |
| IT | External Input | ___ x 3 = ___ | ___ x 4 = ___ | ___ x 6 = ___ | ___ |
| OT | External Output | ___ x 4 = ___ | ___ x 5 = ___ | ___ x 7 = ___ | ___ |
| FT | Logical Internal File | ___ x 7 = ___ | ___ x10 = ___ | ___ x15 = ___ | ___ |
| EI | Ext Interface File | ___ x 5 = ___ | ___ x 7 = ___ | ___ x10 = ___ | ___ |
| QT | External Inquiry | ___ x 3 = ___ | ___ x 4 = ___ | ___ x 6 = ___ | ___ |
| FC | Function Count | Total Unadjusted Function Points | | | ___ |

- General Information Processing Function

| ID | Characteristic | DI | ID | Characteristic | DI |
|----|----------------|-----|-----|----------------|-----|
| C1 | Data Communications | ___ | C8 | Online Update | ___ |
| C2 | Distributed Functions | ___ | C9 | Complex Processing | ___ |
| C3 | Performance | ___ | C10 | Reuseability | ___ |
| C4 | Heavily Used Configuration | ___ | C11 | Installation Ease | ___ |
| C5 | Transaction Rate | ___ | C12 | Operational Ease | ___ |
| C6 | Online Data Entry | ___ | C13 | Multiple Sites | ___ |
| C7 | End User Efficiency | ___ | C14 | Facilitate Change | ___ |
| GC | General Characteristics | | Total Degree of Influence | | ___ |

- DI Values:

| | | |
|---|---|---|
| — Not present, or no influence = 0 | — Average influence | = 3 |
| — Insignificant influence   = 1 | — Significant influence | = 4 |
| — Moderate influence   = 2 | — Strong influence, throughout | = 5 |

GCA   General Characteristics Adjustment   $= 0.65 + (0.01 \times GC) =$ _____ .

FP    Function Points Measure   $= FC \times GCA2$   = _____ .

Figure 7. Function Points Calculation Worksheet

## 4.2 IN., OUT., INQ., FUNCTION TYPE AND LEVEL OF INFO. PROC. FUNC. RECORD

Application: _____. Appl ID: _____.

Prepared by: _____ __/__/__. Reviewed by: _____ __/__/__.

Notes:

| In., Out., Inq., Function List | | | | Level of Info. Proc. Func. Record | | | | | | | |
|------|----|-----|-------------|-----|-----|-----|-----|-----|-----|-----|-----|
| | | | | Before | | | | After | | | |
| Type | ID | Ref | Description | DET | FTR | Del | Chg | DET | FTR | Add | Chg |
| | | | | | | | | | | | |
| | | | | | | | | | | | |
| | | | | | | | | | | | |
| | | | | | | | | | | | |
| | | | | | | | | | | | |
| | | | | | | | | | | | |
| | | | | | | | | | | | |
| | | | | | | | | | | | |
| | | | | | | | | | | | |
| | | | | | | | | | | | |
| | | | | | | | | | | | |
| | | | | | | | | | | | |
| | | | | | | | | | | | |
| | | | | | | | | | | | |
| | | | | | | | | | | | |
| | | | | | | | | | | | |
| | | | | | | | | | | | |
| | | | | | | | | | | | |
| | | | | | | | | | | | |
| | | | | | | | | | | | |
| | | | | | | | | | | | |
| | | | | | | | | | | | |
| | | | | | | | | | | | |
| | | | | | | | | | | | |
| | | | | | | | | | | | |

DET = Number of Data Element Types in the In., Out., Inq.
FTR = Number of File Types Referenced by the In., Out., Inq.
Add., Del., Chg. = Level of Information Processing Function of the
                   In., Out., Inq. added, deleted, changed.

Figure 8. IN., OUT., INQ., Function Type and Level of Info. Proc.
          Func. Record Worksheet.

4.3 FILES, INTERFACES, FUNCTION TYPE AND LEVEL OF INFO. PROC. FUNC. RECORD

Application: _____.   Appl ID: _____.

Prepared by: _____ __/__/__.  Reviewed by: _____ __/__/__.

Notes:

| Files, Interfaces, Function List | | | | Level of Info. Proc. Func. Record | | | | | | | |
|---|---|---|---|---|---|---|---|---|---|---|---|
| | | | | Before | | | | After | | | |
| Type | ID | Ref | Description | DET | RET | Del | Chg | DET | RET | Add | Chg |
| ____ | ____ | ____ | _____ | ____ | ____ | ____ | ____ | ____ | ____ | ____ | ____ |
| ____ | ____ | ____ | _____ | ____ | ____ | ____ | ____ | ____ | ____ | ____ | ____ |
| ____ | ____ | ____ | _____ | ____ | ____ | ____ | ____ | ____ | ____ | ____ | ____ |
| ____ | ____ | ____ | _____ | ____ | ____ | ____ | ____ | ____ | ____ | ____ | ____ |
| ____ | ____ | ____ | _____ | ____ | ____ | ____ | ____ | ____ | ____ | ____ | ____ |
| ____ | ____ | ____ | _____ | ____ | ____ | ____ | ____ | ____ | ____ | ____ | ____ |
| ____ | ____ | ____ | _____ | ____ | ____ | ____ | ____ | ____ | ____ | ____ | ____ |
| ____ | ____ | ____ | _____ | ____ | ____ | ____ | ____ | ____ | ____ | ____ | ____ |
| ____ | ____ | ____ | _____ | ____ | ____ | ____ | ____ | ____ | ____ | ____ | ____ |
| ____ | ____ | ____ | _____ | ____ | ____ | ____ | ____ | ____ | ____ | ____ | ____ |
| ____ | ____ | ____ | _____ | ____ | ____ | ____ | ____ | ____ | ____ | ____ | ____ |
| ____ | ____ | ____ | _____ | ____ | ____ | ____ | ____ | ____ | ____ | ____ | ____ |
| ____ | ____ | ____ | _____ | ____ | ____ | ____ | ____ | ____ | ____ | ____ | ____ |
| ____ | ____ | ____ | _____ | ____ | ____ | ____ | ____ | ____ | ____ | ____ | ____ |
| ____ | ____ | ____ | _____ | ____ | ____ | ____ | ____ | ____ | ____ | ____ | ____ |
| ____ | ____ | ____ | _____ | ____ | ____ | ____ | ____ | ____ | ____ | ____ | ____ |
| ____ | ____ | ____ | _____ | ____ | ____ | ____ | ____ | ____ | ____ | ____ | ____ |
| ____ | ____ | ____ | _____ | ____ | ____ | ____ | ____ | ____ | ____ | ____ | ____ |
| ____ | ____ | ____ | _____ | ____ | ____ | ____ | ____ | ____ | ____ | ____ | ____ |
| ____ | ____ | ____ | _____ | ____ | ____ | ____ | ____ | ____ | ____ | ____ | ____ |
| ____ | ____ | ____ | _____ | ____ | ____ | ____ | ____ | ____ | ____ | ____ | ____ |
| ____ | ____ | ____ | _____ | ____ | ____ | ____ | ____ | ____ | ____ | ____ | ____ |

DET = Number of Data Element Types in the Files, Interfaces.
RET = Number of Record Types in the Files, Interfaces
Add., Del., Chg. = Level of Information Processing Function of the
                   Files, Interfaces, added, deleted, changed.


Figure 9.  FILES, INTERFACES, Function Type and Level of Info. Proc.
           Func. Record Worksheet.

## 4.4 DEVELOPMENT WORK-PRODUCT

Application: _____.    Appl ID: _____.

Prepared by: _____ __/__/__. Reviewed by: _____ __/__/__.

Notes:

- Added Function Count:

| Type ID | Description | Level of Information Processing Function | | | Total |
|---------|-------------|------|---------|------|-------|
| | | Low | Average | High | |
| IT | External Input | ___ x 3 = ___ | ___ x 4 = ___ | ___ x 6 = ___ | _____ |
| OT | External Output | ___ x 4 = ___ | ___ x 5 = ___ | ___ x 7 = ___ | _____ |
| FT | Logical Internal File | ___ x 7 = ___ | ___ x10 = ___ | ___ x15 = ___ | _____ |
| EI | Ext Interface File | ___ x 5 = ___ | ___ x 7 = ___ | ___ x10 = ___ | _____ |
| QT | External Inquiry | ___ x 3 = ___ | ___ x 4 = ___ | ___ x 6 = ___ | _____ |
| Add | Total New or Added Unadjusted Function Points | | | | _____ |

- Changed "Evaluated After" Function Count:

| Type ID | Description | Low | Average | High | Total |
|---------|-------------|-----|---------|------|-------|
| IT | External Input | ___ x 3 = ___ | ___ x 4 = ___ | ___ x 6 = ___ | _____ |
| OT | External Output | ___ x 4 = ___ | ___ x 5 = ___ | ___ x 7 = ___ | _____ |
| FT | Logical Internal File | ___ x 7 = ___ | ___ x10 = ___ | ___ x15 = ___ | _____ |
| EI | Ext Interface File | ___ x 5 = ___ | ___ x 7 = ___ | ___ x10 = ___ | _____ |
| QT | External Inquiry | ___ x 3 = ___ | ___ x 4 = ___ | ___ x 6 = ___ | _____ |
| ChgA | Total Changed "After" Unadjusted Function Points | | | | _____ |

- Deleted Function Count:

| Type ID | Description | Low | Average | High | Total |
|---------|-------------|-----|---------|------|-------|
| IT | External Input | ___ x 3 = ___ | ___ x 4 = ___ | ___ x 6 = ___ | _____ |
| OT | External Output | ___ x 4 = ___ | ___ x 5 = ___ | ___ x 7 = ___ | _____ |
| FT | Logical Internal File | ___ x 7 = ___ | ___ x10 = ___ | ___ x15 = ___ | _____ |
| EI | Ext Interface File | ___ x 5 = ___ | ___ x 7 = ___ | ___ x10 = ___ | _____ |
| QT | External Inquiry | ___ x 3 = ___ | ___ x 4 = ___ | ___ x 6 = ___ | _____ |
| Del | Total Deleted Unadjusted Function Points | | | | _____ |

Dev Development Work-Product FP Meas. = (Add + ChgA)GCA2 + (Del)GCA1 = _____

Figure 10. Development Work-Product Function Points Worksheet.

## 4.5 SUPPORT WORK-PRODUCT

Application: _____.   Appl ID: _____.

Prepared by: _____ __/__/__.  Reviewed by: _____ __/__/__.

▪ Added Function Count:

| Type ID | Description | Level of Information Processing Function | | | Total |
|---|---|---|---|---|---|
| | | Low | Average | High | |
| IT | External Input | ___ x 3 = ___ | ___ x 4 = ___ | ___ x 6 = ___ | _____ |
| OT | External Output | ___ x 4 = ___ | ___ x 5 = ___ | ___ x 7 = ___ | _____ |
| FT | Logical Internal File | ___ x 7 = ___ | ___ x10 = ___ | ___ x15 = ___ | _____ |
| EI | Ext Interface File | ___ x 5 = ___ | ___ x 7 = ___ | ___ x10 = ___ | _____ |
| QT | External Inquiry | ___ x 3 = ___ | ___ x 4 = ___ | ___ x 6 = ___ | _____ |
| Add | Total New or Added Unadjusted Function Points | | | | _____ |

▪ Changed "Evaluated After" Function Count:

| IT | External Input | ___ x 3 = ___ | ___ x 4 = ___ | ___ x 6 = ___ | _____ |
|---|---|---|---|---|---|
| OT | External Output | ___ x 4 = ___ | ___ x 5 = ___ | ___ x 7 = ___ | _____ |
| FT | Logical Internal File | ___ x 7 = ___ | ___ x10 = ___ | ___ x15 = ___ | _____ |
| EI | Ext Interface File | ___ x 5 = ___ | ___ x 7 = ___ | ___ x10 = ___ | _____ |
| QT | External Inquiry | ___ x 3 = ___ | ___ x 4 = ___ | ___ x 6 = ___ | _____ |
| ChgA | Total Changed "After" Unadjusted Function Points | | | | _____ |

▪ Deleted Function Count:

| IT | External Input | ___ x 3 = ___ | ___ x 4 = ___ | ___ x 6 = ___ | _____ |
|---|---|---|---|---|---|
| OT | External Output | ___ x 4 = ___ | ___ x 5 = ___ | ___ x 7 = ___ | _____ |
| FT | Logical Internal File | ___ x 7 = ___ | ___ x10 = ___ | ___ x15 = ___ | _____ |
| EI | Ext Interface File | ___ x 5 = ___ | ___ x 7 = ___ | ___ x10 = ___ | _____ |
| QT | External Inquiry | ___ x 3 = ___ | ___ x 4 = ___ | ___ x 6 = ___ | _____ |
| Del | Total Deleted Unadjusted Function Points | | | | _____ |

▪ Changed "Evaluated Before" Function Count:

| IT | External Input | ___ x 3 = ___ | ___ x 4 = ___ | ___ x 6 = ___ | _____ |
|---|---|---|---|---|---|
| OT | External Output | ___ x 4 = ___ | ___ x 5 = ___ | ___ x 7 = ___ | _____ |
| FT | Logical Internal File | ___ x 7 = ___ | ___ x10 = ___ | ___ x15 = ___ | _____ |
| EI | Ext Interface File | ___ x 5 = ___ | ___ x 7 = ___ | ___ x10 = ___ | _____ |
| QT | External Inquiry | ___ x 3 = ___ | ___ x 4 = ___ | ___ x 6 = ___ | _____ |
| ChgB | Total Changed "Before" Unadjusted Function Points | | | | _____ |

SPT Support Work-Product FP Measure = Orig FP + (Add + ChgA)GCA2
$$- (Del + ChgB)GCA1 = \text{_____} .$$

Figure 11.  Support Work-Product Function Points Worksheet.

## 4.6 DEVELOPMENT OR ENHANCEMENT WORK-EFFORT RECORD WORK-SHEET

Application: _____. Appl ID: _____.

Prepared by: _____ __/__/__. Reviewed by: _____ __/__/__.

| Development or Enhancement Standard Tasks: | Intitial Estimate gwm | Approved Changes gwm | Final Estimate gwm | | Final Actual gwm |
|---|---|---|---|---|---|
| Project Management | | | | | |
| Requirements | | | | | |
| System Design — External Design — Internal Design | | | | | |
| Program Development — Detail Design — Coding — Unit Test — Program Integration | | | | | |
| System Test | | | | | |
| User Documentation | | | | | |
| User Education | | | | | |
| File Conversion | | | | | |
| STANDARD TASK TOTAL | | | | | |
| Non-Standard Tasks: | | | | | |
| Studies | | | | | |
| Package Modification | | | | | |
| Other | | | | | |
| NON-ST'D TASK TOTAL | | | | | |
| DEVELOPMENT TOTAL | | | | | |
| Net Work-Hours per Gross Work-Month | | | | | _____ nwh |

Work-Effort Record in Gross Work-Months — gwm

Figure 12. Development or Enhancement Work-Effort Record Worksheet.

## 4.7 SUPPORT WORK-EFFORT RECORD WORK-SHEET

Application: _____. Appl ID: _____.

Prepared by: _____ __/__/__. Reviewed by: _____ __/__/__.

| Maintenance or Support Standard Tasks: | Annual Work-Effort Record in Gross Work-Months - gwh | | | | |
|---|---|---|---|---|---|
| | Intitial Estimate gwh | Approved Changes gwh | Final Estimate gwh | | Final Actual gwh |
| Application Support | _____ | _____ | _____ | | _____ |
| Problem Analysis | _____ | _____ | _____ | | _____ |
| Fixing | _____ | _____ | _____ | | _____ |
| SUPPORT TOTAL | _____ | _____ | _____ | | _____ |

| Application History: | Annual Support Record | | |
|---|---|---|---|
| | Total Annual Enhancement Activity FP | Year-End Support Work-Product FB | Annual Support Work-Effort gwh |
| End-of-Development | /////////// | _____ | /////////// |
| Yr 1 _____ | _____ | _____ | _____ |
| Yr 2 _____ | _____ | _____ | _____ |
| Yr 3 _____ | _____ | _____ | _____ |
| Yr 4 _____ | _____ | _____ | _____ |
| Yr 5 _____ | _____ | _____ | _____ |
| Yr 6 _____ | _____ | _____ | _____ |
| Yr 7 _____ | _____ | _____ | _____ |
| Yr 8 _____ | _____ | _____ | _____ |
| Net Work-Hours per Gross Work-Month | | | _____ nwh |

Figure 13. Support Work-Effort Record Worksheet.

## 4.8 ATTRIBUTES RECORD WORK-SHEET

Application: _____ .  Appl ID: _____ .

Prepared by: _____ __/__/__ .  Reviewed by: _____ __/__/__ .


Notes:

| Attribute Description | Applicability Level | | |
|---|---|---|---|
| | Attr Matu | Team Matu | Attr Appl |
| | | | |
| | | | |
| | | | |
| | | | |
| | | | |
| | | | |
| | | | |
| | | | |
| | | | |
| | | | |
| | | | |
| | | | |

Factors:(See Section 2.4.2).

Attr Matu = Maturity of the Attribute.
Team Matu = Maturity of the Team regarding the Attribute.
Attr Appl = Applicability of the Attribute to the Work-Effort.

Instructions:(See Section 2.4).

1. List the Attributes of the Project expected to have a significant effect on productivity.
2. Record the Applicability Level of each of the Factors using the definitions in Section 2.4.2.(Low, Mod, High, or NA).

Figure 14. Attributes Record Worksheet.


End of Document

# The Roles People Play

Appendix III:  The Roles People Play

## User Review Board

> The User Review Board is the team of users who review the system
> after construction and decide whether any modifications are needed
> before cutover.

Prior to the timebox, the Review Board reviews the requirements;
at the end of the timebox, it reviews the results.

The Review Board reports to the Executive Owner.  It includes:

- leading spokespeople for the end users who need the system;
- the Executive Owner (Executive Sponsor);
- an I.S. executive;
- possibly an external consultant.

The Review Board may be the same as the Requirements Planning
Team involved in the Requirements Planning Phase.

The Review Board ensures that sufficient commitment exists so
that a thorough review job will be done.

## User Coordinator

> The User Coordinator is a user appointed by the Executive Owner
> to oversee the project from the users' viewpoint.

(Sometimes this individual is the Executive Owner or a person
 appointed by the Executive Owner.)  This person:

- is the leading spokesperson for the end users who need the system;

- involves other users, where appropriate, to help review the
  evolving prototypes or to help build the system;

- arranges for user documentation and training;

- is responsible for cutover planning;

- is the lead user developer on the Timebox Team(s);

- involves other users, where appropriate, to help review
  the evolving prototypes;

- serves on the Prototype Review Board.

## Key Players in the RAD Lifecycle

### From the User Community

#### Executive Owner

> The Executive Owner is sometimes called the Executive Sponsor,
> a high-level user executive who funds the system and "owns" it.

This executive must be committed to achieving results quickly.

The Executive Owner is the user executive who is responsible for the system and whose budget is to be spent on it. This executive should be made familiar with the RAD lifecycle and should be determined to move fast.

Because this executive is financially committed, he is entitled to kill the system after the JRP if the planning does not indicate that the system will meet his needs with a suitably high return on investment.

- He is an end-user executive of high enough position to be responsible for the system.

- He is fully committed to having the system, meaning that funds are being made available from his budget.

- He will be a driving force in helping to make the design and cutover of the system successful.

- He will ensure that end-user managers commit the time needed to aid in planning, development and cutover.

- He is ready to move fast, eliminating political or bureaucratic delays.

°° User Coordinator   (See separate entry above.)
Requirements Planning Team

> The Requirements Planning Team is the team of high-level users who participate in the requirement planning workshop (Chapter 7).

User Design Team

> The User Design Team is made up of users who participate in the design workshop.

This is the set of users and user executives who participate in the JAD workshops.

A final selection will be made by the RAD Workshop Leader when doing the JAD preparation.

Some of these may be members of the Requirements Planning Team. Others should be able to participate in more detailed design (Chapter 8).

°° User Review Board   (See separate entry above.)
Training Manager

> A Training Manager is responsible for training users in how to use the system.

This person organizes the design and creation of training materials and plans the training process (Chapter 19).

(The training manager may be from the I.S. community.)

From the I.S. Community:

Project Manager

> A Project Manager is responsible for the overall development effort.

In a project with one Construction Team, this person may be the team leader.

Construction Team

> The Construction Team is a small team of implementors, highly skilled with the toolset, who build the system -- typically two, three or four people (Chapter 10).

For large projects, there will be multiple Construction Teams (Chapter 12).

RAD Workshop Leader

> The Workshop Leader is a specialist who organizes and conducts the workshops for JRP (Chapter 7) and JAD (Chapter 8).

Human-Factors Expert

> A Human-Factors Expert, a specialist in human factoring, is responsible for usability testing (Chapter 17).

Data Modeling Expert (Professional)

> The Data Modeling Expert is an experienced specialist who can create data models rapidly and competently (Chapter 13).

Some professionals have experience in data modeling, are highly skilled at it and can create correct models quickly. The Data Modeling Expert may be a data administrator or part of the data administration staff.

Repository Manager

> The Repository Manager is the executive responsible for the I-CASE repository and its integrity.

He may control what reusable constructs are in the repository. The Repository Manager is particularly important in an environment of information engineering (Chapter 21) and reusable design (Chapters 15 and 22).

# Diagramming

## Diagrams Used in Modeling and System Design

When analysts draw diagrams on paper, these are often casual diagrams. They can be drawn in any way that appeals to the analyst. With I-CASE development, the diagrams become a language of high precision. The computer must understand the exact meaning of the diagram, must link it to other diagrams and must apply a large number of rules to it to provide integrity checks and coordination. The computer must extract information from the diagrams to drive a code generator.

Today's system design and implementation are best done with I-CASE tools. These tools are graphically oriented; with them, the types of diagrams used to represent systems are critical. All people involved in the design of applications (users and I.S. professionals) should be fully familiar with the diagrams used.

To achieve this familiarity, precise diagramming standards are needed. The standards need to be understood by every user. They are a vehicle for person-to-person as well as person-to-machine communication. They need to be sufficiently easy to understand so that non-I.S. staff can employ them without difficulty.

An I.S. organization must create an environment for fast development. It must create its own set of diagramming standards. The standards relate to the choice of toolset and methodology. This appendix discusses the diagramming standards. They are discussed more fully in the author's book, [MARTIN86].

### Symbols Used

To make the various types of diagrams as easy to teach as possible, the minimum number of symbols should be used. The same types of symbols appear on different types of diagrams. Figure IV.1 shows a recommended family of symbols that are used in some of the leading I-CASE toolsets. A later section of this appendix, "Diagramming Techniques and Standards," illustrates how these symbols are used.

### Main Types of Diagrams

Figures IV.2, IV.3, and IV.4 show the main types of diagrams used in building systems.

## ENTITY-RELATIONSHIP DIAGRAM

Figure IV.2 shows an entity-relationship diagram. A block on this diagram is an entity-type (object-type); a line connecting blocks is a relationship between the blocks. When a CASE tool is used to draw an entity-relationship diagram, windows are used to show details of an entity or of a relationship. Figure IV.3 shows the screen of an I-CASE tool used for entity-relationship diagramming, as well as a window with details of a relationship on the diagram.

## DECOMPOSITION DIAGRAM

Figure IV.4 shows a decomposition diagram. The function POLICY SERVING is divided into four processes: SELL TO CUSTOMER, SERIVCE A POLICY, PROCESS A CLAIM and TERMINATE A POLICY. SERVICE A POLICY is subdivided into five subprocesses.

The function POLICY SERVICING is decomposed into processes and subprocesses. This diagram is redrawn with cardinality symbols in Figure IV.5 and is expanded into more detail in Figures IV.6 and IV.7.

These diagrams are used at a high level to describe the basic functions of the enterprise and at a lower level to decompose functions into processes and subprocesses.

A decomposition diagram can show cardinalities, conditions and mutually exclusive decompositions. These are illustrated in Figures IV.5 and IV.6.

The decomposition diagram of Figure IV.4 is drawn so that it spreads out horizontally; those of Figures IV.5 and IV.6 are drawn so that they spread out vertically. Any decomposition could be drawn in either way. The vertical spread is more convenient if long titles or descriptions of each block are used. Users can scroll down vertical-spread diagrams the same way they scroll down text.

*Action Diagram.*   Any decomposition can be represented as an action diagram. Figure IV.7 shows an action diagram equivalent to Figure IV.6. A block diagram, like Figure IV.4, may be more visually appealing than an action diagram, but an action diagram may contain more information, as each item can be long and can consist of multiple lines where necessary.

A decomposition diagram can be automatically converted into action-diagram format, and the action diagram can be developed into a program structure and then into executable code. Figure IV.8 shows two action diagrams of specifications.

## Three Dots

Three dots (ellipses) are used to indicate that more information exists than is shown on a diagram. The additional information can be displayed by pointing to the item in question and saying "expand." Similarly, by pointing to a high-level item and saying "contract," the items subordinate to that item can be hidden, and three dots will appear to show that they are hidden. Three dots appear in various places in Figures IV.5 through IV.8.

This ability to expand and contract is extremely useful in working with complex information. The analyst or designer will often contract within contract or expand within expand.

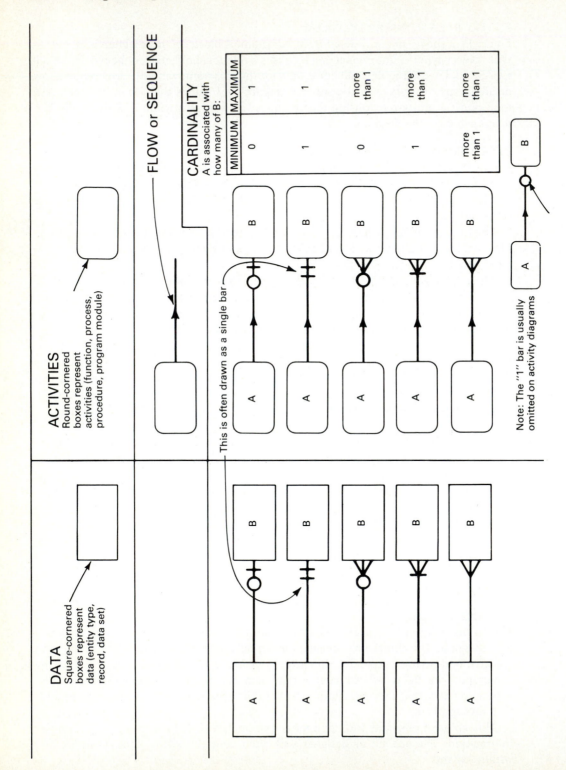

## DATA
Square-cornered boxes represent data (entity type, record, data set)

## ACTIVITIES
Round-cornered boxes represent activities (function, process, procedure, program module)

## FLOW or SEQUENCE

## CARDINALITY
A is associated with how many of B:

| MINIMUM | MAXIMUM |
|---------|---------|
| 0 | 1 |
| 1 | 1 |
| 0 | more than 1 |
| 1 | more than 1 |
| more than 1 | more than 1 |

This is often drawn as a single bar

Note: The "1" bar is usually omitted on activity diagrams

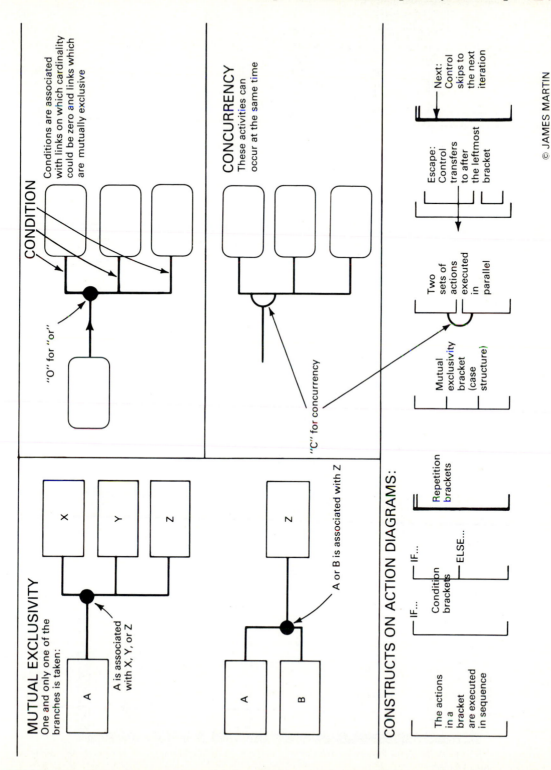

FIGURE IV.1  The symbols used on the various types of I.E. diagrams.

© JAMES MARTIN

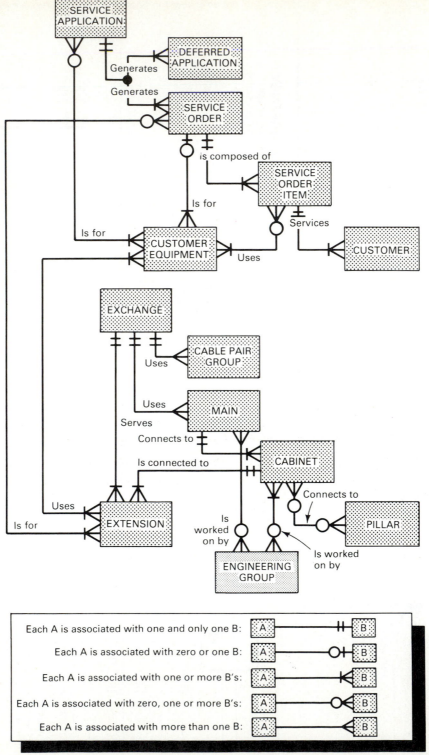

FIGURE IV.2 Part of an entity-relationship diagram for a telephone community with the relationships labeled.

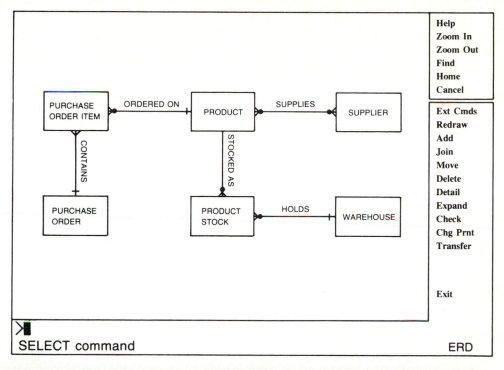

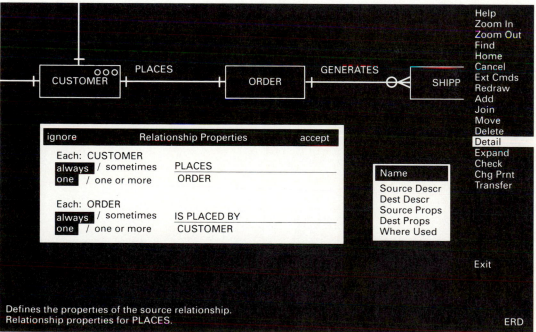

FIGURE IV.3 A screen of Texas Instruments' Information Engineering Facility™ showing an entity-relationship diagram and a window giving details of a relationship [IEF].

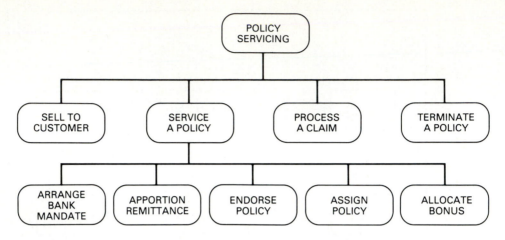

FIGURE IV.4 A decomposition diagram. The function POLICY SERVICING is decomposed into processes and subprocesses. This diagram is redrawn with cardinality symbols in Fig. IV.5 and is expanded into more detail in Figs. IV.6 and IV.7.

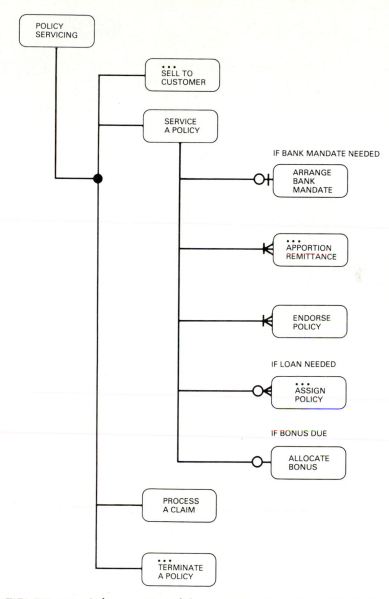

FIGURE IV.5 A decomposition of the processes performed in POLICY SER-
VICING. Three dots in several of the boxes indicate that parts of the diagram
have been contracted (on a workstation screen). Figure IV.6 shows the diagram
when these processes are reexpaneded.

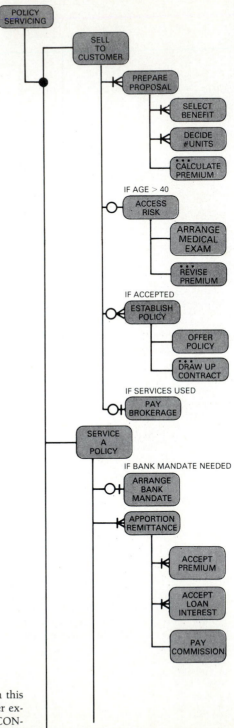

FIGURE IV.6 Three dots in some of the boxes in this decomposition indicate that the boxes can be further expanded on a workstation screen. The ability to use CONTRACT and EXPAND commands is very useful with large diagrams.

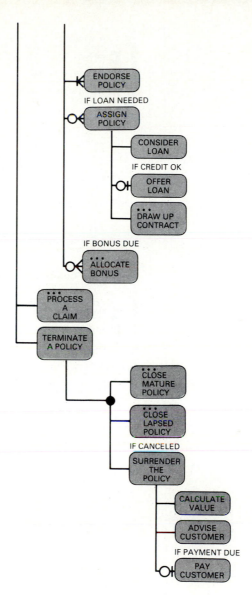

FIGURE IV.6  (*Continued*)

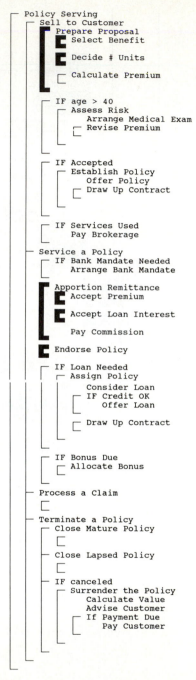

FIGURE IV.7 The same information as in Fig. IV.6 represented with an action diagram.

```
* Subscription system
    Do while there are subscription transactions
    Get valid transaction

        Read    ┌──────────────┐
                │  TRANSACTION │
                └──────────────┘

        Validate transaction
            Check general format
            If error
                o────────────────────o
                │ Process error │
                o────────────────────o

            If transaction type is new
                Check name and address
                Check for numeric ZIP
                Check for valid terms
                Check for payment
                If  errors
                    Set invalid indicator
                Else
                    Set valid indicator

            Else if transaction type is renewal
                Check for valid terms
                Check for payment
                If errors
                    Set invalid indicator
                Else
                    Set valid indicator

            Else if transaction type is cancellation
                Set cancellation flag

            If invalid indicator is set
                o────────────────────o
                │ Process Error │
                o────────────────────o


        Update   ┌──────────────┐
                 │  TRANSACTION │
                 └──────────────┘


    Process valid transaction
        If transaction type is new
            o────────────────────────────o
            │ Process New Subscription │
            o────────────────────────────o
        Else if transaction type is renewal
            o────────────────────o
            │ Process Renewal │
            o────────────────────o
        Else if transaction type is cancellation
            o────────────────────────o
            │ Process Cancellation │
            o────────────────────────o
        Else
            o────────────────────o
            │ Process Error │
            o────────────────────o
```

FIGURE IV.8  Two action diagrams used to represent specifications.

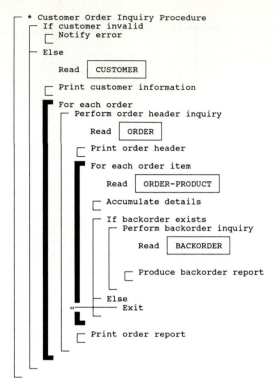

```
* Customer Order Inquiry Procedure
  If customer invalid
    Notify error

  Else

      Read   CUSTOMER

      Print customer information

      For each order
        Perform order header inquiry

            Read   ORDER

            Print order header

            For each order item

                Read   ORDER-PRODUCT

              Accumulate details

              If backorder exists
                Perform backorder inquiry

                    Read   BACKORDER

                  Produce backorder report

              Else
                Exit

          Print order report
```

FIGURE IV.8 *(Continued)*

## Dependency Diagram

A dependency diagram shows that certain processes or procedures are dependent on other processes or procedures. In other words, it is not possible to execute a process or procedure until one or more other processes (or procedures) have been completed. Figure IV.9 shows a simple dependency diagram.

Here FILL ORDER cannot be performed until ACCEPT ORDER has been done. CREATE BILL and PREPARE DELIVERY are not done until FILL ORDER is performed.

A decomposition diagram, such as the following, does not show this dependency:

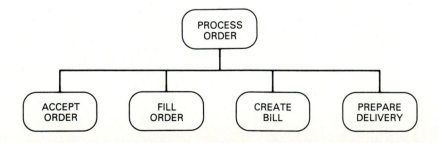

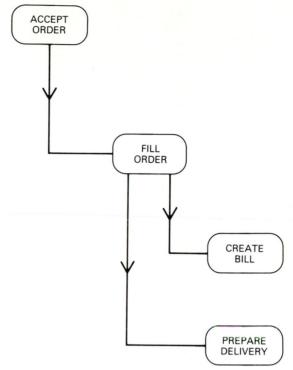

FIGURE IV.9 A process dependency diagram, sometimes called a *process flow diagram*. It shows how one process is dependent on another; that is, one process cannot be executed until a previous one has been executed. This diagram is expanded into a data flow diagram in Fig. IV.10 and further expanded in Fig. IV.11. The analyst's thought process evolved further in Fig. IV.12 with action diagram.

## Data-Flow Diagram

A data-flow diagram is a special form of dependency diagram. It is normally used with procedures (which show how something is done). In a data-flow diagram, one procedure is dependent on another procedure because data must pass between the procedures. A data-flow diagram shows what data pass, as well as the sources and destinations of data. Figure IV.10 shows a data-flow diagram that is an extension of Figure IV.9.

A designer, using a CASE tool, may start by drawing a dependency diagram, such as Figure IV.9, and then extend it into a data-flow diagram, such as Figure IV.10.

Data-flow diagrams and dependency diagrams are usually nested. One block may be shown in more detail on another such diagram. For example, the block ACCEPT ORDER in Figure IV.10 is expanded into another data-flow diagram in Figure IV.11.

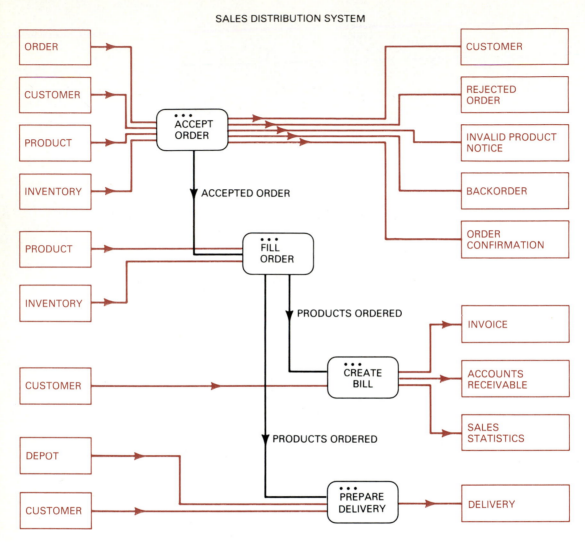

FIGURE IV. 10 A data-flow diagram for a sales distribution system. The black part shows procedures and data passing between procedures. The red part shows the data stores used by the procedures. The three dots at the start of a procedure label indicate that the procedure has been designed in more detail and that an expanded verison of the procedure may be displayed. Figure IV.11 shows the ACCEPT ORDER procedure in more detail.

In Figure IV.10, each of the procedure blocks has three dots, showing that each of them can be expanded into a more detailed data-flow diagram. The red parts of Figures IV.10 and IV.11 show the sources and destinations of data—in this case, records on the storage units.

## SQUARE-CORNERED AND ROUND-CORNERED BOXES
A recommended standard is that data be drawn as square-cornered boxes and activities as round-cornered boxes. In Figure IV.11, observe the use of square-cornered and

ACCEPT ORDER  PROCEDURE

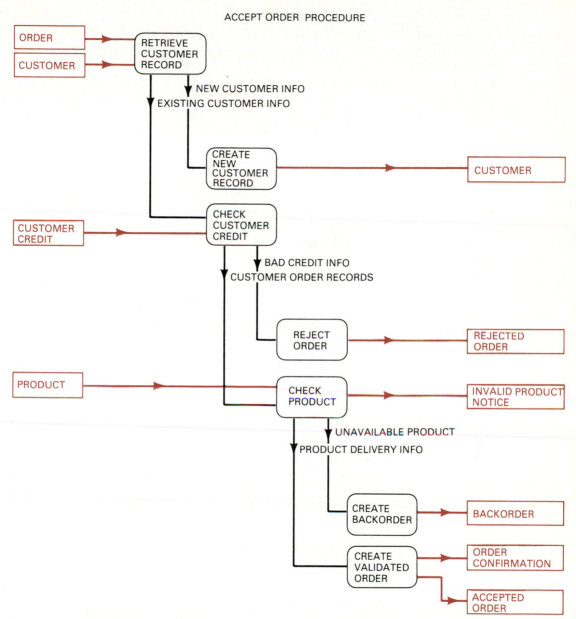

FIGURE IV.11  The top activity in Fig. IV.10 (ACCEPT ORDER) is expanded here into a more detailed data-flow diagram.

round-cornered boxes. Square-cornered boxes are used for entity-types, records, data stores, files, and so on. Round-cornered boxes are used for functions, processes, procedures and program modules. In rough hand-drawn sketches, activities are sometimes sketched with ellipses because these are easier to draw free-hand than neat round-cornered boxes.

## ADDING DETAIL TO DATA-FLOW DIAGRAMS

The procedure blocks on a data-flow diagram or dependency diagram need to be expanded to show detail. The detail may be shown with an action diagram. The user of an appropriate CASE tool may point to a procedure block and instruct it to display that block as an action diagram. The data-flow diagram and the corresponding action diagram may appear on the screen together, as shown in Figure IV.12.

The action diagram window on the right side of Figure IV.12 shows details of the procedure Validate Customer, which is the center block in the data-flow diagram on the left side of the figure. Most action diagrams are much more complex than this one and are scrolled up and down on the screen.

The boxes at the top and bottom of the action diagram contain the data input to and output from the action diagram. These must correspond exactly to the inputs to and outputs from the equivalent procedure on the data-flow diagram (as they do in Figure IV.12). The input and output boxes of the action diagram were probably generated from the data-flow diagram. The action diagram may be expanded into substantial detail and code generated from it.

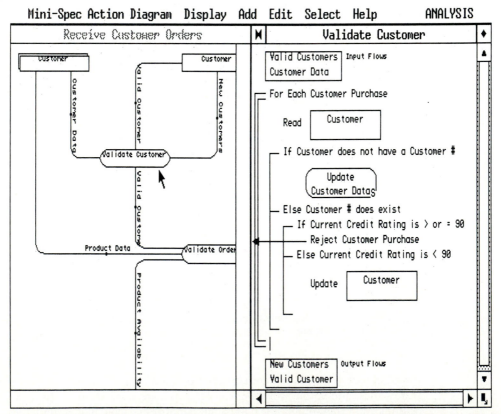

FIGURE IV.12 Action diagram window showing details of a block on a data flow diagram. The top and bottom of the action diagram indicate the input data and output data. These must correspond to the information on the data flow diagram (Courtesy of KnowledgeWare.)

A dependency diagram or data-flow diagram is useful for showing high-level dependencies, processes or procedures. It is less useful for showing the detail of one procedure. Figure IV.13 shows the same procedure as Figure IV.11 represented as an action diagram. The square-cornered boxes on the action diagram show data records read, updated or created. Figure IV.13 has more detail than the data-flow diagram of Figure IV.11 and is an appropriate representation for code generation.

## Decision Trees

Certain types of logic are best represented with decision trees or decision tables. Figure IV.14 shows a decision tree for computing the order discount percentage. Decision trees or tables can be converted automatically to action diagrams or code modules.

## Dialog Structures

Workstation dialogs often use hierarchical menus. Because action diagrams represent hierarchies, they are useful for designing dialog structures such as the one shown in Figure IV.15. Where dialogs are not hierarchical, a different type of diagram can show the possible dialog interactions. The diagram in Figure IV.16 uses horizontal lines to represent screens and vertical lines to represent possible jumps between screens as the user interacts with the system. The designer can point to any of the horizontal lines and display the screen layout. A screen-painter tool should be connected to a dialog design tool.

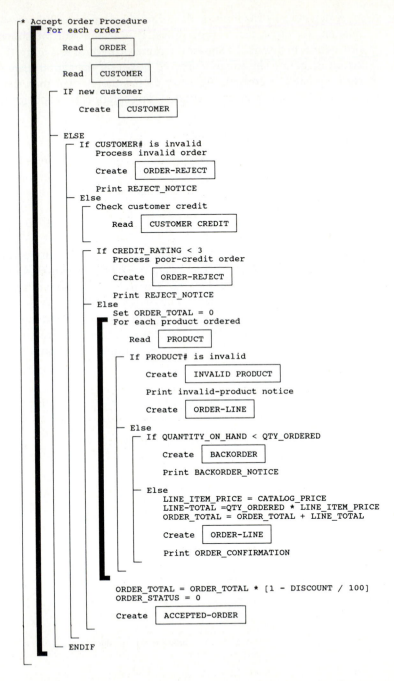

FIGURE IV.13 The designer who created the ACCEPT ORDER procedure in Fig. IV.11 takes it into more detail here with an action diagram.

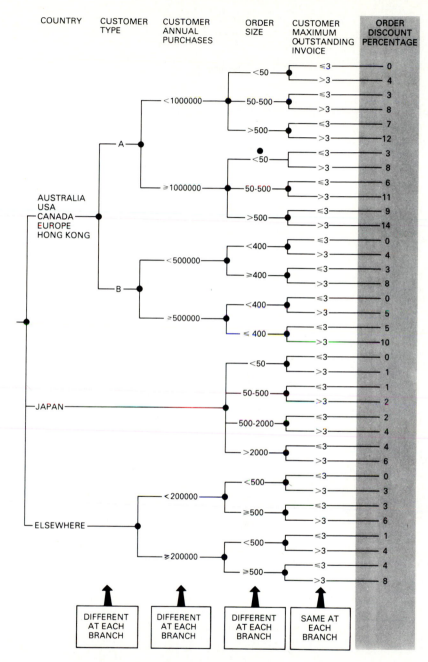

FIGURE IV.14  A decision tree in which branches are identical for some fields and different for others.

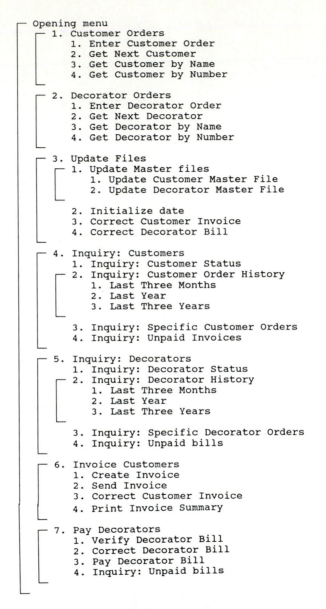

```
┌─ Opening menu
│  ┌─ 1. Customer Orders
│  │     1. Enter Customer Order
│  │     2. Get Next Customer
│  │     3. Get Customer by Name
│  └─    4. Get Customer by Number
│
│  ┌─ 2. Decorator Orders
│  │     1. Enter Decorator Order
│  │     2. Get Next Decorator
│  │     3. Get Decorator by Name
│  └─    4. Get Decorator by Number
│
│  ┌─ 3. Update Files
│  │  ┌─ 1. Update Master files
│  │  │     1. Update Customer Master File
│  │  └─    2. Update Decorator Master File
│  │
│  │     2. Initialize date
│  │     3. Correct Customer Invoice
│  └─    4. Correct Decorator Bill
│
│  ┌─ 4. Inquiry: Customers
│  │     1. Inquiry: Customer Status
│  │  ┌─ 2. Inquiry: Customer Order History
│  │  │     1. Last Three Months
│  │  │     2. Last Year
│  │  └─    3. Last Three Years
│  │
│  │     3. Inquiry: Specific Customer Orders
│  └─    4. Inquiry: Unpaid Invoices
│
│  ┌─ 5. Inquiry: Decorators
│  │     1. Inquiry: Decorator Status
│  │  ┌─ 2. Inquiry: Decorator History
│  │  │     1. Last Three Months
│  │  │     2. Last Year
│  │  └─    3. Last Three Years
│  │
│  │     3. Inquiry: Specific Decorator Orders
│  └─    4. Inquiry: Unpaid bills
│
│  ┌─ 6. Invoice Customers
│  │     1. Create Invoice
│  │     2. Send Invoice
│  │     3. Correct Customer Invoice
│  └─    4. Print Invoice Summary
│
│  ┌─ 7. Pay Decorators
│  │     1. Verify Decorator Bill
│  │     2. Correct Decorator Bill
│  │     3. Pay Decorator Bill
└─ └─    4. Inquiry: Unpaid bills
```

FIGURE IV. 15 A hierarchical dialog structure represented as an action diagram.

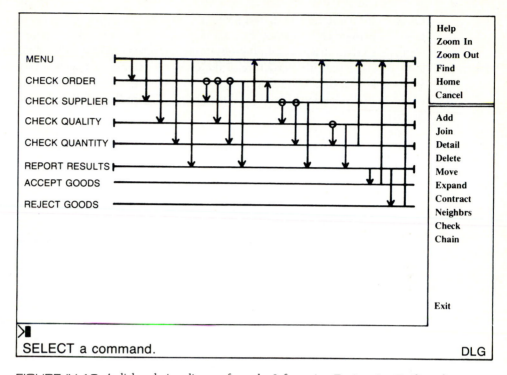

FIGURE IV.16  A dialog design diagram from the Information Engineering Facility of Texas Instruments. [IEF]

## Data Structure Diagram

During business area analysis, data are designed with entity-relationship diagrams and normalized data structures. In the system design phase, an extract from this data model is represented with the structure of the chosen database management system (i.e., in an IMS, IDMS, or relationship structure) or possibly a file structure (e.g., VSAM). A data structure diagram is used for this purpose. Figure IV.17 illustrates a data structure diagram.

The toolkit should be able to generate the database description directly from the diagrammatic representation (e.g., the Program Specification Blocks) and the Database Description code .

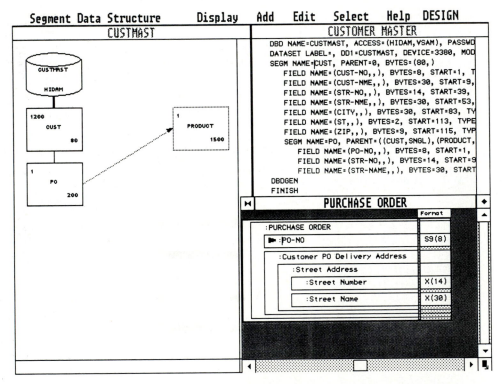

FIGURE IV.17 Data structure diagram for IMS. This is derived using the data model and is used to generate the database description code. (From the KnowlegeWare tool set [IEW].)

## Program Structure

A diagram showing program structure must be able to represent loops, conditions, multiway selection structures, escapes, database accesses, subroutine calls and nested routines. Action diagram editors were designed for this purpose. The brackets and text of the action diagram can be set to executable code. This code may be produced by a generator.

Figure IV.18 shows COBOL in action diagram format on an IEF screen.

Boxes IV.1 to IV.4 show executable code.

Using an action diagram editor for code ensures good structuring of code, makes the structure visible and makes all structures appear like those in the programmers' training courses.

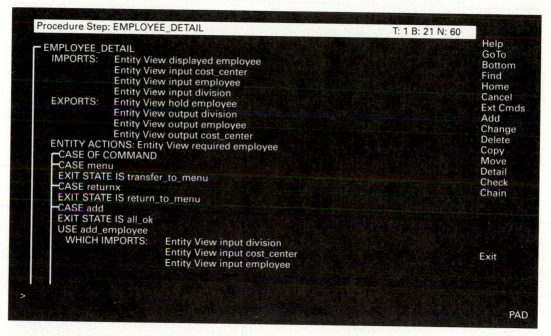

FIGURE IV.18 Action diagram of COBOL code from Texas Instruments [IEF].

## BOX IV. 1    Action Diagram of Executable Code Written in C.

```
*   /* Executable Section */
    switch (adtab[curline].action){

    case ACT_JUNK:
    case ACT_CASE:
    case ACT_EXIT:
        itfrst = curline;
        itnext = curline +1;
        break;

    case ACT_BEGL:
    case ACT_BEGB:
        adlevel = 1;
        itfrst = curline;
        for (itnext = curline+1; itnext <= numadtab & adlevel >0; it6next++){

            switch (adtab[itnext].action) {
            case ACT_BEGL:
            case ACT_BEGB:
                adlevel++;
                break;
            case ACT_END:
                adlevel--;
                }
            }
        if (adlevel > 0)
            aborts ("ad: ? no matching end ??");

        break;

    default:
        itfirst = numadtab;
        itnext = numadtab;
        beep();
        }
    itdel = itnext - itfirst;
    for (itab = itfirst; itab < numadtab; itab++) {
        adtab[itab].action = adtab[itab+itdel].action;
        adtab[itab].count  = adtab[itab+itdel].count;
        adtab[itab].text   = adtab[itab+itdel].text;
        }
    numadtab -= itdel;
    if (curline > numadtab)
        curline = numadtab;

    showbuffer ();
```

**BOX IV.2   Action Diagram of Executable Code in the Language PL/1.**

```
SUBSCRIPTION_SYSTEM: PROCEDURE OPTIONS (MAIN);
 * /*
       SUBSCRIPTION SYSTEM TRANSACTION PROCESSING
   */

 * /* Variable Declarations */

    %DECLARE YES              CHARACTER;   %YES      = '''1''B';
    %DECLARE NO               CHARACTER;   %NO       = '''0''B';
    %DECLARE ERROR            CHARACTER;   %ERROR    = '''1''B';
    %DECLARE NO_ERROR         CHARACTER;   %NO_ERROR = '''0''B';

    DECLARE
        DATA_FILE             FILE SEQUENTIAL RECORD,
        EOF_DATA_FILE         BIT(1) INITIAL (NO),
        RC                    BIT(1),
        RC1                   BIT(1),
        RC2                   BIT(1),
        RC3                   BIT(1),
        RC4                   BIT(1),
        01 TRANSACTION,
           02 TYPE            CHARACTER(15),
           02 STATUS          BIT(1),
           02 CANCELLATION    BIT(1),
           02 CUSTOMER,
              03 NAME         CHARACTER(30),
              03 ADDRESS,
                 04 STREET    CHARACTER(30),
                 04 CITY      CHARACTER(30),
                 04 STATE     CHARACTER(30),
                 04 ZIP_CODE  CHARACTER(9),

           02 TERMS (10)      CHARACTER(80),
           02 PAYMENT         CHARACTER(80);


 ON ENDFILE (DATA_FILE)
    EOF_DATA_FILE = YES;

 OPEN FILE (DATA_FILE);
 DO WHILE (^EOF_DATA_FILE);

    /* GET TRANSACTION */
    READ FILE (DATA_FILE) INTO (TRANSACTION);

    /* VALIDATE TRANSACTION */
    CALL CHECK_FORMAT (TRANSACTION, RC);
    IF RC = ERROR THEN
       CALL PROCESS_ERROR (TRANSACTION, RC, NO, NO, NO, NO);
```

## BOX IV.2 (Continued)

```
SELECT;
WHEN (TRANSACTION.TYPE = 'NEW') DO;
    CANCELLATION = NO;
    CALL CHECK_NAME_ADDRESS (CUSTOMER, RC1);
    CALL CHECK_ZIP_CODE (ZIP_CODE, RC2);
    CALL CHECK_TERMS (TERMS, RC3);
    CALL CHECK_PAYMENT (PAYMENT, RC4);
    IF (RC1 | RC2 | RC3 | RC4) = ERROR THEN
        STATUS = ERROR;
    ELSE
        STATUS = NO_ERROR;

    END;
WHEN (TRANSACTION.TYPE = 'RENEWAL') DO;
    CANCELLATION = NO;
    RC1 = NO_ERROR;
    RC2 = NO_ERROR;
    CALL CHECK_TERMS (TERMS,RC3);
    CALL CHECK_PAYMENT (PAYMENT, RC4);
    IF (RC3 | RC4) = ERROR THEN
        STATUS = ERROR;
    ELSE
        STATUS = NO_ERROR;

    END;
WHEN (TRANSACTION.TYPE = 'CANCELLATION') DO;
    STATUS = NO_ERROR;
    CANCELLATION = NO;
    END;
END;

/* PROCESS VALID TRANSACTION */
IF STATUS = NO_ERROR THEN
    SELECT;
    WHEN (TRANSACTION.TYPE = 'NEW')
        CALL NEW_SUBSCRIPTION (TRANSACTION);
    WHEN (TRANSACTION.TYPE = 'RENEWAL')
        CALL SUBSCRIPTION_RENEWAL (TRANSACTION);
    WHEN (TRANSACTION.TYPE = 'CANCELLATION')
        CALL SUBSCRIPTION_CANCELLATION (TRANSACTION);
    END;
ELSE
    IF STATUS = ERROR THEN
        CALL PROCESS_ERROR (TRANSACTION, NO, RC1, RC2, RC3, RC4);

    /* GET NEXT TRANSACTION */
    READ FILE (DATA_FILE) INTO (TRANSACTION);
    END;

END SUBSCRIPTION_SYSTEM;
```

**BOX IV.3   Action Diagram of Executable Code Written in the Fourth-Generation Language IDEAL, from ADR.**

```
  ┌ <<ORDER PROCESSING>> PROC
  │    EACH CUSTOMER
  │  ┌ IF CUSTOMER# INVALID
  │  │    PRINT REJECT NOTICE
  «──┤    END PROC
  │  └ END IF
  │  ┌ IF CREDIT_RATING > 3
  │  │    WRITE CUSTOMER ORDER
  │  │    SET ORDER_TOTAL = 0
  │  ┃    LOOP WHILE EACH PRODUCT
  │  ┃  ┌ IF PRODUCT# INVALID
  │  ┃  │    PRINT ERROR MESSAGE
  «──┃──┤    END PROC
  │  ┃  └ END IF
  │  ┃  ┌ IF QUANTITY_ON_HAND > 0
  │  ┃  │    SET LINE_ITEM_PRICE = CATALOG_PRICE
  │  ┃  │    SET LINE-TOTAL =QTY_ORDERED * LINE_ITEM_PRICE
  │  ┃  │    SET ORDER_TOTAL = ORDER_TOTAL + LINE_TOTAL
  │  ┃  │    WRITE ORDER_LINE
  │  ┃  │    EACH ORDER_RATE
  │  ┃  │    SET ACTUAL_USAGE = ACTUAL_USAGE + QTY_ORDERED
  │  ┃  │    WRITE ORDER_RATE
  │  ┃  ├ ELSE
  │  ┃  │    WRITE BACKORDER
  │  ┃  │    PRINT BACKORDER_NOTICE
  │  ┃  └ END IF
  │  ┃    END LOOP
  │  │    SET ORDER_TOTAL = ORDER_TOTAL * [1 - DISCOUNT / 100]
  │  │    SET ORDER_STATUS = 0
  │  │    WRITE CUSTOMER_ORDER
  │  ├ ELSE
  │  │    CALL POOR_CREDIT
  │  └ END IF
  └ END PROC
```

## Matrices

Matrices are used in I.E. to show the relationships among objects. They are used in planning, for example, to show which projects relate to goals, problems, critical success factors or strategic opportunities. They are used in business area analysis to show which entity-types are used by which processes. Figure IV.19 shows a matrix, which is scrollable on the workbench screen, that maps entity-types against business functions.

## The Meaning of the Diagrams

As stressed earlier, a CASE tool should store the meaning of the diagrams and be able to process that meaning to detect errors, inconsistencies and clues that something might be wrong. A good CASE tool does not store the pictures; it stores the meaning of the pictures. The tool should be an expert system that applies automated reasoning to the diagrammatic input, correlating the meaning of different types of diagrams. The meaning of the diagrams resides in an encyclopedia that applies automated reasoning to this knowledge (Figure IV.20).

Key: (Enter highest classification only)

- C = CREATE
- D = DELETE
- U = UPDATE
- R = READ ONLY

BUSINESS FUNCTIONS / ENTITY TYPES

| ENTITY TYPES | GOVERNMENT_CONTRACTS | PURHCASING | RECEIVING | WAREHOUSING | LEGAL_SERVICES | GENERAL_ACCOUNTING | COST_ACCOUNTING | ORDER_PROCESSING | SHIPPING | PACKING | MATERIAL_REQUIREMENTS | RELEASE_PLANNING | FINITE_CAPACITY_SCHEDU | FACTORY_MONITORING | METHODS_ENGINEERING | FACILITIES_MAINTENANC | BASIC_RESEARCH | PRODUCT_DESIGN | SCRAP_DISPOSAL | EMPLOYEE_RECORDS_MAIN | PAYROLL_AND_BENEFITS | EMPLOYEE_TRAINING | SECURITY | TRANSPORTATION_PLANNI | FLEET_MANAGEMENT | FLEET_ACQUISITION | FLEET_MAINTENANCE | VEHICLE_DISPOSAL |
|---|---|---|---|---|---|---|---|---|---|---|---|---|---|---|---|---|---|---|---|---|---|---|---|---|---|---|---|---|
| SALES ORDER | | | | | | R | R | C | U | U | R | R | R | | | | R | | | | | | | R | R | | | |
| CUSTOMER | | | | | | | U | R | R | | | | | | | | R | | | | | | | R | | | | |
| CONTRACT | C | | | | | | | | | | | | | | | | R | | | | | | | | | | | |
| SHIPMENT | | | C | | | | | | | | | | | | | | | | | | | | | R | | | | |
| SUPPLIER | R | R | U | | R | R | | | | | | | | | | | R | | | | | | | R | | | | |
| PURCHASE ORDER | | | | | | | R | R | | | R | R | R | | | | R | | | | | | R | | | | | |
| PRODUCT | | R | R | | | | R | | | | R | R | R | R | R | R | R | C | R | | | | | R | | | | |
| RAW_MATERIAL | | U | U | | | | | | | | U | | | | | | R | | | | | | | | | | | |
| CHEMICAL | | U | U | | | | | | | | U | | | | | | R | | | | | | | | | | | |
| SHOP_SUPPLY | | C | | | | | | | | | R | R | | | | | | | | | | | | | | | | |
| WORK_ORDER | | | | | | | | | | | R | C | U | R | | | | | | | | | | | | | | |
| WAREHOUSE | | R | C | | | | | | | | | | | | | U | | | | | | | | | | | | |
| BIN | | U | C | | | | | | | | R | | | | | U | | | | | | | | | | | | |
| SUPPLIER_INVOICE | U | C | | | R | U | | | | | | | | | | | | | | | | | | | | | | |
| LEDGER_ENTRY | | | | | | C | C | | | | | | | | | | | | | | | | | | | | | |
| PRODUCT_INVENTORY | | R | U | R | | | | | U | | U | | R | R | | | | | | | U | | | | | | | |

Border menu: Files, Save, Print, Mode, Horiz, Vert, Cells, Edit, Add, Move, Delete, Edit, Screen, Home, End, Find, Utilities, Cluster, Stats, Sort, Erase, Tools, Quit

> **Business Function/Entity    Type Usage**

**Select Mode from Border Menu**

FIGURE IV.19  A matrix mapping entity-types and business functions [IEF].

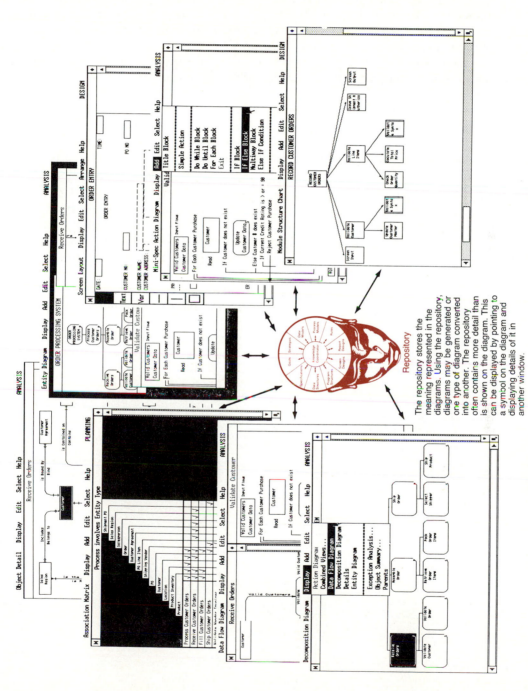

FIGURE IV.20 The meaning of the diagrams is stored in a repository. Using the repository, diagrams may be generated or one type of diagram may be converted into another. The repository often contains more detail than are displayed on a diagram. The additional detail may be displayed by pointing to an icon and requesting more detail.

## Integration of the Diagrams

An I-CASE toolset should have the ability to correlate the diagrammatic information across an entire set of diagrams, checking to ensure that their information is fully consistent. This coordination is not done in one large gulp but in small steps each time new information is added to the repository.

A major advantage of computerized tools is that the machine can coordinate the information on multiple diagrams across the entire design span; the human brain cannot do that with accuracy.

Good system design starts by identifying the entity-types, creating an entity-relationship diagram and normalizing the data. The data model is used in designing the procedures with data-flow diagrams, decision trees, screen and report designs, dialog-flow diagrams and action diagrams. Figure IV.21 indicates the progression of diagrams that are used for this purpose.

## Hyperdiagrams

As emphasized earlier, the diagrams are not isolated. There are many logical linkages among them. In combination, the diagrams of an I-CASE toolset form a hyperdiagram (Chapter 3). When something is changed on one diagram, the change must be automatically reflected in other diagrams.

Each diagram is one of many manifestations of a more complex set of information. When that information is changed and diagrams are displayed, many different diagrams may reflect the change.

Figure IV.22 shows a set of diagrams in windows of an I-CASE toolset, which comprise one analyst's work—one hyperview. The separate diagrams are all logically interlinked and hence consistent.

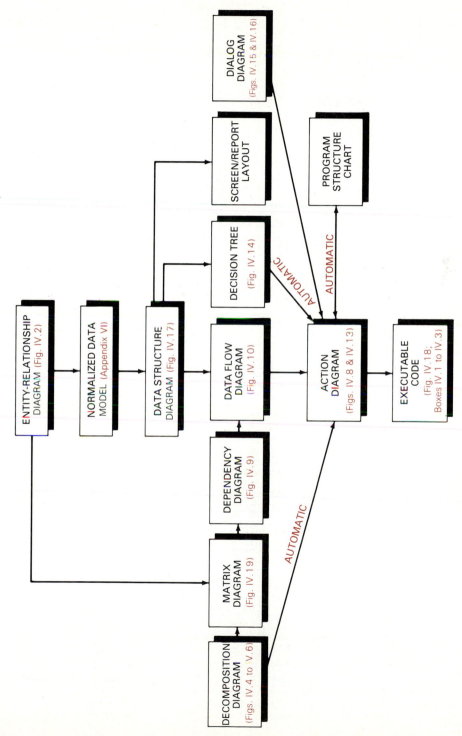

FIGURE IV.21  The progression of diagrams that are used for I.E. The meaning represented by these diagrams needs to be fully integrated in the repository. Details are entered in windows. The progression leads to code generation.

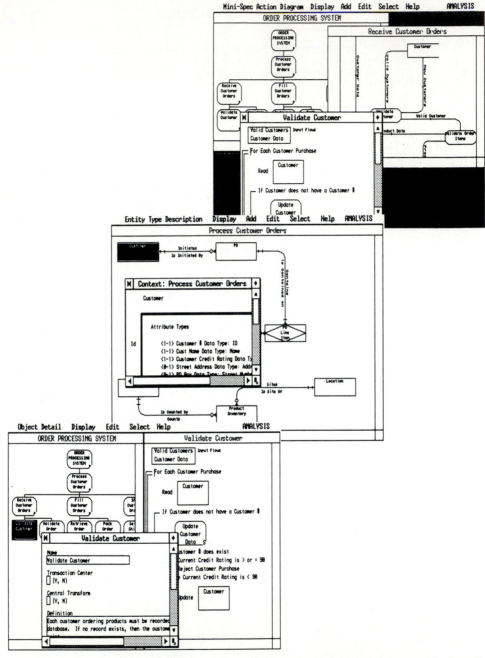

FIGURE IV.22 All of these diagrams are parts of one hyperdiagram. They are parts of a logically consistent whole. The analyst may examine more information about this hyperdiagram by selecting blocks (or links between blocks) and displaying them in detail windows. The windows can be scrolled or expanded to show more detail than here. The computer enforces consistency within the hyperdiagram and among hyperdiagrams.

# Diagramming Techniques and Standards

Because diagrams are the basis of computer-aided analysis and design, it is essential that good diagramming techniques be used. The first of the following boxes summarizes characteristics that are desirable in diagramming techniques.

We have stated that an I.S. organization committed to IE should adopt diagramming standards. The next box presents the principles of diagramming standards. The diagramming techniques should be a corporatewide standard, firmly adhered to.

---

## Summary of Good Diagramming Techniques

Good diagramming techniques should be all of the following:

- **An Aid to Clear Thinking**
  Good diagrams help people understand complex ideas. A diagramming notation should be designed to help thinking and communication and for computer-aided thinking. The diagrams should be an aid in teaching computer methods.

- **Easy to Understand**
  The diagrams should use constructs that are obvious in meaning and as familiar as possible. They should avoid mnemonics and symbols that are not explained on the diagram or with immediately available keys.

- **An Aid to End-User Communication**
  End users should be able to learn to read, critique and draw the diagrams quickly, so that the diagrams form a good basis for communication between users and data processing professionals.

- **Meaningful**
  It is the meaning, rather than the graphic image, that is valuable. The meaning should be encoded in an encyclopedia from which one or more types of diagrams can be generated. The encyclopedia will often store more information than is visible on the screen. It may be displayed by pointing to an icon and using the command SHOW.

- **A Basis for Program Code Generation**
  It should be possible to generate code from the diagrams, along with tools such as dictionaries, report formatters and screen pointers. To achieve this, the diagrams must be more complete and rigorous than the diagrams of the first generation of structured techniques.

- **Printable on Normal-Sized Paper**
  Wall charts of vast size are to be avoided because they inhibit change and portability. Diagrams should be subdividable into normal-sized pages. They may be designed to spread out vertically on fan-fold paper.

- Subsettable
  Complex diagrams should be subsettable so that they can be subdivided into easy-to-understand components. The user should be able to extract easy-to-use subsets at a computer screen.

- Navigable
  The user should be able to navigate easily around complex diagrams and changing their representation, if necessary, using techniques such as PAGE, SCROLL, ZOOM, ZOOC, NEXT, EXPAND and SHOW.

- Designed for Minimum Searching
  A user should be able to find information with as little searching as possible. Closely related information should be close together on the diagram to minimize page turning, interscreen navigation and the need to follow lengthy lines.

- Decomposable Into Detail
  A simple overview diagram should be decomposable into successively finer levels of detail. Where possible, the detail diagram should be of the same form as the higher-level diagram. The decomposition may proceed until appropriately diagrammed program code is reached.

- Designed for Screen Manipulation
  The diagrams should be designed to be manipulated easily and powerfully on a workstation screen (preferably a personal computer).

- Designed for Computer-Aided Thinking
  A computer can give a designer a great deal of help in stepping through the design, using data correctly, using library functions, design verification and so on. The computer-aided design technique should support the designer's thinking as much as possible.

- Easy to Draw by Hand
  Automation will not completely replace sheets of paper. The diagramming technique should facilitate quick sketching by hand with a template. Machine-drawn versions of the diagrams may improve on the hand-drawn versions by using color, shading, library techniques, motion and computer mainpulation.

- Drawable on Cheap Printers
  The diagrams should be drawable with desktop dot-matrix printers. A variant of the diagrams should be printable with the ASCII character set so that a mainframe line printer can print them. The ASCII variant may be relatively crude and may modify some of the conventions slightly. The need for ASCII printing should not prevent the use of well-human-factored icons and style on dot-matrix printers.

- Designed with a Minimum Number of Symbol Types
  The number of graphic symbols a user must understand should be minimized. Each underlying idea should be represented by a single symbol, not by different symbols in different places. (There may have to be variations of a symbol to suit different printers or display devices.)

- Assertive

  The presence of a graphic symbol should denote the presence of some knowledge; the absence of the symbol should denote the lack of that knowledge. For example, the absence of a mark on a line should not denote meaning about that line (such as a one-to-one association between the blocks linked by the line). Following this principle permits a type of subsetting, producing a diagram in which some symbols are omitted in order to highlight others, to avoid clutter or to produce an overview diagram.

- Based on Clear, Visual Logic

  There is a visual logic that makes some ways of depicting an idea better than others. Diagrams should make abstract ideas concrete by using images and spatial sense to capture ideas as logically as possible. For example, arrows should represent flow or sequence, as this is intuitively clear, but a different symbol should represent cardinality.

- Logical, Not Decorative

  The use of decoration that does not enhance visual logic should be avoided. The instinct to be artistic must be suppressed and replaced with an urge to maximize clarity.

- Readable Using English (Human-Language) Sentences

  The symbols on a link or bracket should translate as directly as possible into a clear human-language sentence.

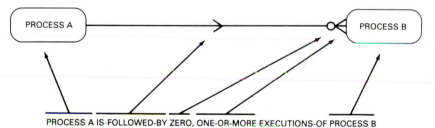

PROCESS A IS-FOLLOWED-BY ZERO, ONE-OR-MORE EXECUTIONS-OF PROCESS B

- Able to Support Different Ways of Thinking with Consistent Symbols

  Different styles of diagrams are appropriate for different aspects of system design. Decision trees are appropriate for certain situations, data flow diagrams for others, decomposition diagrams for others, and so on. A common family of symbols should support the different ways of thinking about systems, data and logic.

- Automatically Convertible

  It is sometimes useful to convert one style of representation (one view of the world) into another. For example, decision trees, dependency diagrams or data navigation diagrams can be converted to action diagrams. The diagramming technique should be designed so that the conversion can be done by computer. The user may employ windows on a workstation screen showing the alternate representations. Different types of representations often need to be linked to represent an overall system design.

- Methodologically Sound
Diagramming techniques are a visual representation of underlying methodologies. The methodologies need to be sound and need to represent the most useful concepts of data analysis, structured techniques and code generation.

## Principles of Diagramming Standards and Automation

1. Principles of Diagramming Standards
   - I.S. professionals and end users should be provided with a set of diagramming techniques that are aids to clear thinking about different aspects of planning analysis, design and programming.
   - The separate types of diagrams should use the minimum number of icons.
   - They should be as easy to learn as possible.
   - Conversion between diagrams should be automatic whenever possible.
   - The diagramming techniques should be a corporatewide standard, firmly adhered to.

2. Automation of Diagramming
   - The diagrams should be the basis of computer-aided planning, analysis, design and construction, using I-CASE tools.
   - Higher-level design diagrams should convert automatically to action diagrams where relevant. Action diagrams can be decomposed into executable code.
   - The family of diagrams should be a basis for code generation.
   - The diagrams should be easy to change the file at the computer screen.
   - The diagrams should relate to data models.
   - The diagrams convey meaning, which is stored in a system repository. The repository often stores more detail than is shown on any one screen.
   - The diagrams and associated text windows in the repository should be the system documentation.

# Reference

James Martin, *Recommended Diagramming Standards for Analysts and Programmers.* Prentice-Hall, Inc., Englewood Cliffs, New Jersey, 1985.

# Action Diagrams

## Overview Versus Detailed Logic Diagramming

Of the diagramming techniques that evolved in the 1970s and earlier, some are usable for the *overview* of program structure and some are usable for the *detailed* program logic. Structure charts, HIPO diagrams, Warnier-Orr diagrams, and Michael Jackson charts draw overall program structures but not the detailed tests, conditions and logic. Their advocates usually resort to structured English or pseudocode to represent the detail. Flowcharts and Nassi-Shneiderman charts show the detailed logic of a program, but not the structural overview.

There is no reason why the diagramming of the *overview* should be incompatible with the diagramming of the *detail*. Indeed, it is highly desirable that these two aspects of program design should employ the same type of diagram because complex systems are created by successively filling in detail (top-down design) and linking together blocks of low-level detail (bottom-up design). The design needs to move naturally between the high levels and low levels of design. The low level should be a natural extension of the high level. **Action diagrams** achieve this. They give a natural way to draw program overviews such as structure charts, HIPO or Warnier-Orr diagrams, *and* detailed logic such as flowcharts or Nassi-Shneiderman charts. They were originally designed to be as easy to teach to end users as possible and to assist end users in applying fourth-generation languages. Most of the leading CASE tools use action diagrams.

Glancing ahead, Figs. V.2 and V.3 show simple examples of action diagrams. Figure V.8 shows an extension of Fig. V.2. They are useful for showing, and modifying, human agendas and procedures, and are used in the procedure boxes throughout this trilogy. They are particularly useful because of the ease with which they can be expanded, contracted and edited on the screen of a personal computer.

# Brackets

A program module is drawn as a bracket:

Brackets are the basic building blocks of action diagrams. The bracket can be of any length; so there is space in it for as much text or detail as is needed.

Inside the bracket is a sequence of operations. A simple control rule applies to the bracket. You enter it at the top, do the things in it in a top-to-bottom sequence and exit at the bottom.

Inside the bracket there may be other brackets. Many brackets may be nested. The nesting shows the hierarchical structure of a program. Figure V.1 shows the representation of a hierarchical structure with brackets.

Some brackets are *repetition* brackets. The items in the bracket are executed many times. The repetition bracket has a double line at its top:

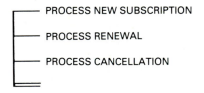

When one of several processes is to be used (mutually exclusive selection), a bracket with multiple divisions is used:

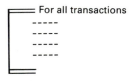

This is the programmer's multiple-option structures, called a "case structure." One, and only one, of the divisions in the bracket above is executed.

# Ultimate Decomposition

Figure V.2 illustrates an action diagram overview of a program structure. It can be extended to show conditions, case structures and loops of different types—it can show detailed program logic. Figure V.3 expands the process in Fig. V.2 called VALIDATE SUB ITEM. Figures V.2 and V.3 could be merged into one chart.

Decomposition Diagram, Structure Chart, HIPO Chart, etc.

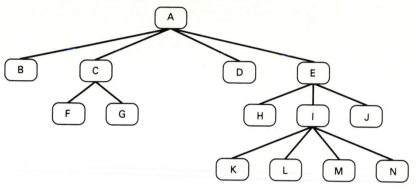

Action Diagram

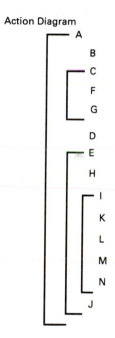

FIGURE V. 1  A hierarchical block structure and the equivalent action diagram.

Glancing ahead, Fig. V.7 shows *executable* program code written in a fourth-generation language. This diagramming technique can thus be extended all the way from the highest-level overview to working code in a fourth-generation language. When it is used on a computer screen, the developers can edit and adjust the diagram and successively fill in detail until they have working code that can be tested interpretively. We refer to this as **ultimate decomposition**.

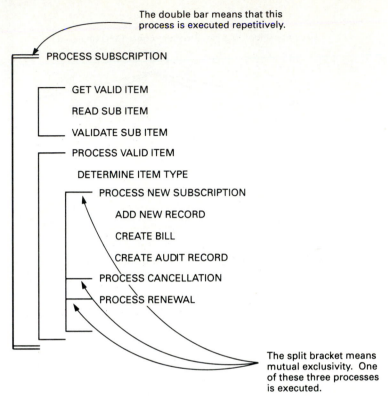

FIGURE V.2 A high-level action diagram. This action diagram can now be expanded into a chart showing the detailed program logic. VALIDATE SUBITEM from this chart is expanded into detailed logic in Fig. V.3.

# Conditions

Often a program module or subroutine is executed only IF a certain condition applies. In this case the condition is written at the head of a bracket:

A condition bracket should normally have an "ELSE" partition:

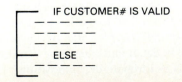

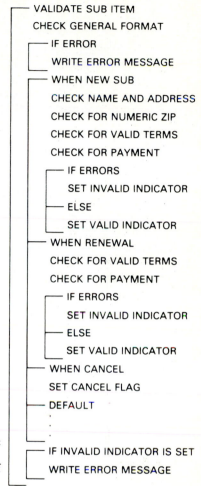

```
      ┌─── VALIDATE SUB ITEM
      │    CHECK GENERAL FORMAT
      │    ┌─── IF ERROR
      │    └    WRITE ERROR MESSAGE
      │    ┌─── WHEN NEW SUB
      │    │    CHECK NAME AND ADDRESS
      │    │    CHECK FOR NUMERIC ZIP
      │    │    CHECK FOR VALID TERMS
      │    │    CHECK FOR PAYMENT
      │    │    ┌─── IF ERRORS
      │    │    │    SET INVALID INDICATOR
      │    │    ├─── ELSE
      │    │    └    SET VALID INDICATOR
      │    ├─── WHEN RENEWAL
      │    │    CHECK FOR VALID TERMS
      │    │    CHECK FOR PAYMENT
      │    │    ┌─── IF ERRORS
      │    │    │    SET INVALID INDICATOR
      │    │    ├─── ELSE
      │    │    └    SET VALID INDICATOR
      │    ├─── WHEN CANCEL
      │    │    SET CANCEL FLAG
      │    ├─── DEFAULT
      │    │     .
      │    └     .
      │    ┌─── IF INVALID INDICATOR IS SET
      └    └    WRITE ERROR MESSAGE
```

FIGURE V.3 An action diagram showing the detailed logic inside the process VALIDATE SUBITEM. This diagram showing detailed logic is an extension of the overview diagram of Fig. V.2.

This has only two mutually exclusive conditions, an IF and an ELSE. Sometimes there are many mutual-exclusive conditions, as follows:

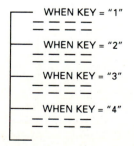

```
  ┌──── WHEN KEY = "1"
  │     ─ ─ ─ ─
  │     ─ ─ ─ ─
  ├──── WHEN KEY = "2"
  │     ─ ─ ─ ─
  │     ─ ─ ─ ─
  ├──── WHEN KEY = "3"
  │     ─ ─ ─ ─
  │     ─ ─ ─ ─
  ├──── WHEN KEY = "4"
  │     ─ ─ ─ ─
  └     ─ ─ ─ ─
```

# Loops

A loop is represented with a repetition bracket with the double line at its top. When many people first start to program, they make mistakes with the point at which they test a loop. Sometimes the test should be made *before* the actions of the loop are performed, and sometimes the test should be made *after*. This difference can be made clear on brackets by drawing the test at either the top or bottom of the bracket:

If the test is at the head of the loop as with a WHILE loop, the actions in the loop may never be executed if the WHILE condition is not satisfied. If the test is at the bottom of the loop, as with an UNTIL loop, the actions in the loop are executed at least once. They will be executed more than once if the condition is fulfilled.

# Sets of Data

Sometimes a procedure needs to be executed on all of the items in a set of items. It might be applied to all transactions or all records in a file, for example:

Action diagrams are used with fourth-generation languages such as NOMAD, MANTIS, FOCUS, RAMIS and IDEAL. They are a good tool for teaching end users to work with these languages. Some such languages have a FOR construct with a WHERE clause to qualify the FOR. For example:

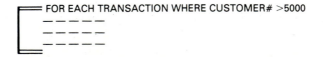

# Subprocedures

Sometimes a user needs to add an item to an action diagram, which is itself a procedure that may contain actions. This subprocedure, or subroutine, is drawn with a round-cornered box. A subprocedure might be used in several procedures. It will be exploded into detail, in another chart, showing the actions it contains.

BACKORDER
PROCEDURE

## Subprocedures Not Yet Designed

In some cases the procedure designer has sections of a procedure that are not yet thought out in detail. He can represent this as a box with rounded corners and a right edge made of question marks:

ERROR       ?
PROCEDURE   ?
            ?

## Common Procedures

Some procedures appear more than once in an action diagram because they are called (or invoked) from more than one place in the logic. These procedures are called **common procedures**. They are indicated by drawing a vertical line down the left-hand side of the procedure box:

ERROR
PROCEDURE

The use of procedure boxes enables an action diagrammer to concentrate on those parts of a procedure with which he is familiar. Another person may, perhaps, fill in the details in the boxes. This enables an elusive or complex procedure formation problem to be worked out a stage at a time.

The use of these boxes makes action diagrams a powerful tool for designing procedures at many levels of abstraction. As with other structured techniques, top-down design can be done by first creating a gross structure with such boxes, while remaining vague about the contents of each box. The gross structure can then be broken down into successive levels of detail. Each explosion of a box adds another degree of detail, which might itself contain actions and boxes. Similarly, bottom-up design can be done by specifying small procedures as action diagrams whose names appear as boxes in higher-level action diagrams.

## Terminations

Certain conditions may cause a procedure to be terminated. They may cause the termination of the bracket in which the condition occurs, or they may cause the termination of multiple brackets. Terminations are drawn with an arrow to the left though one or more brackets, as follows:

It is important to note than an escape structure allows only a forward skip to the exit point of a bracket. This restriction keeps the structure simple and does not allow action diagrams to degenerate into unstructured "spaghetti" logic.

An escape is different from a GO TO instruction. It represents an orderly close-down of the brackets escaped from. Some fourth-generation languages have an escape construct and no GO TO instruction. The escape command has names such as EXIT, QUIT and BREAK.

# Go To

When a language has a well-implemented *escape*, there is no need for GO TO instructions. However, some languages have GO TO instructions and no escape. Using good structured design, the GO TO would be employed to emulate an escape. Any attempt to branch to a distant part of the program should be avoided.

It has, nevertheless, been suggested that a GO TO should be included in the action diagram vocabulary. This can be done by using a dashed arrow to replace the solid escape arrow, thus:

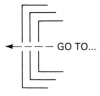

In the interests of structured design we have not included this construct in our recommended list of action diagram features.

# Next Iteration

In a repetition bracket a *next-iteration* construct is useful. With this, control skips the remaining instructions in a repetition bracket and goes to the next iteration of the loop. A next-iteration construct (abbreviated "NEXT") is drawn as follows:

The arrow does not break through the bracket as with an escape construct.

## Fourth-Generation Languages

When fourth-generation languages are used, the wording on the action diagram may be the wording that is used in coding programs with the language. Examples of this are as follows:

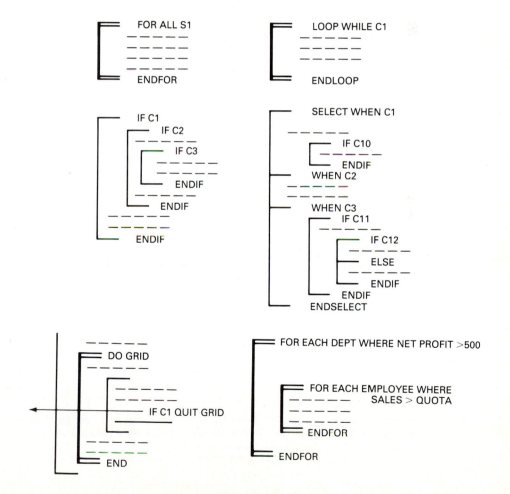

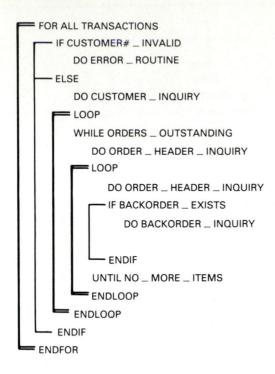

```
FOR ALL TRANSACTIONS
    IF CUSTOMER# _ INVALID
        DO ERROR _ ROUTINE
    ELSE
        DO CUSTOMER _ INQUIRY
        LOOP
        WHILE ORDERS _ OUTSTANDING
            DO ORDER _ HEADER _ INQUIRY
            LOOP
                DO ORDER _ HEADER _ INQUIRY
                IF BACKORDER _ EXISTS
                    DO BACKORDER _ INQUIRY

                ENDIF
            UNTIL NO _ MORE _ ITEMS
            ENDLOOP
        ENDLOOP
    ENDIF
ENDFOR
```

FIGURE V.4 Action diagrams can be labeled with the control statement of forth-generation language and form an excellent way to teach such languages. This example uses statements from the language IDEAL from ADR.

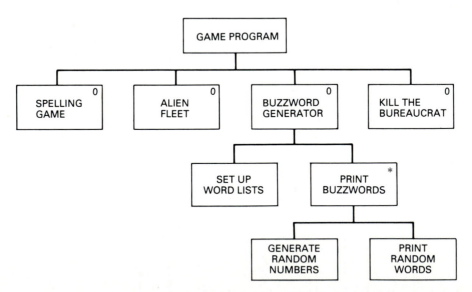

FIGURE V.5 The "o" and "*" in the top right-hand corner of blocks on charts such as this do not have obvious meaning. The form of the diagram should be selected to make the meaning as obvious as possible to relatively uninitiated readers.

```
┌─ GAME PROGRAM
│  ┌─ SPELLING GAME
│  ├─ ALIEN FLEET
│  ├─ BUZZWORD GENERATOR
│     SET UP THREE WORD LISTS
│    ┌═ PRINT BUZZWORDS
│    │    GENERATE THREE RANDOM NUMBERS FROM 1 TO 10
│    │    PRINT RANDOM WORD FROM EACH FOR THE
│    └       THREE LISTS
│  ├─ KILL THE BUREAUCRAT
└
```

FIGURE V.6  An action diagram equivalent to the Jackson diagram of Fig. V.5.

Figure V.4 shows an action diagram for a procedure using control statements from the language IDEAL for ADR [MARTIN&MCCLURE89].

# Decomposition to Program Code

Figure V.5 shows a Jackson diagram of a game program. With action diagrams we can decompose this until we have program code. Figure V.6 shows an action diagram equivalent to Figure V.5. The action diagram gives more room for explanation. Instead of saying "PRINT RANDOM WORDS" it says "PRINT RANDOM WORD FROM EACH OF THE THREE LISTS."

```
┌─✱ BUZZWORD GENERATOR
│  PRINT INSTRUCTION TO OPERATOR
│  SET UP ADJECTIVE1 LIST
│  SET UP ADJECTIVE2 LIST
│  SET UP NOUN LIST
│   ┌─ UNTIL OPERATOR PRESSES "ESC"
│   │    COUNT = 1
│   │   ┌═ UNTIL COUNT = 22
│   │   │    GENERATE 3 RANDOM NUMBERS FROM 1 TO 10
│   │   │    PRINT ADJECTIVE1, ADJECTIVE2, NOUN
│   │   └    ADD 1 TO COUNT
│   └    WAIT
└
```

FIGURE V.7  An expansion of the buzzword generator portion of Fig. V.6.

Figure V.7 decomposes the part of the diagram labeled BUZZWORD GENERATOR. The inner bracket is a repetition bracket that executes 22 times. This is inside a bracket that is terminated by the operator pressing the ESC (escape) key. The last statement in this bracket is WAIT, indicating that the system will wait after executing the remainder of the bracket until the operator presses the ESC key. This gives the operator as much time as he wants to read the printout.

Figure V.8 decomposes the diagram further into an executable program. This program is written in the fourth-generation language MANTIS, from CINCOM, Inc.†

# Titles Versus Code Structure

At the higher levels of the design process, action diagram brackets represent the *names* of processes and subprocesses. As the designer descends into program-level detail, the brackets become *program constructs:* IF brackets, CASE brackets, LOOP brackets, and so on. To show the difference, different colors may be used. The *name* brackets may be red and the *program-construct* brackets black. If a black-and-white copier or terminal is used, the *name* brackets may be dotted or gray and the *program-construct* brackets black. The program-construct brackets may be labeled with appropriate control words. These may be the control words of a particular programming language, or they may be language-independent words.

A bracket that shows a title rather than an action to be implemented, or a program instruction, may be drawn as a dotted or dashed line. It may have a character preceding the title, such as an *, &, or C, to indicate that the title line should be treated as a comment by the compiler. Different compilers use different characters for this purpose.

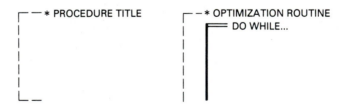

Title brackets may be single "if else," case structure, or repetition brackets.

The designer may use a mix of title brackets and program brackets such that by displaying the title brackets only (with action diagramming software), an overview structure of the program is seen. He may also use comments to clarify his design. The comment line starts with an asterisk. The software may be instructed to display or to hide the comments.

---

†The example in Figs. V.7 and V.8 is adapted from a program in the *MANTIS User's Guide*, Cincom Systems Inc., Cincinnati, Ohio, 1982.

```
┌─ ENTER BUZZWORD GENERATOR
│
│      CLEAR
│      SHOW "I WILL GENERATE A SCREEN FULL OF 'BUZZ PHRASES' EVERY "
│      "'TIME YOU HIT 'ENTER'. WHEN YOU WANT TO STOP, HIT 'ESC'.
│
│      TEXT ADJECTIVE1 (10,16), ADJECTIVE2 (10,16), NOUN (10,16)
│
│      ADJECTIVE1 (1) = "INTEGRATED", "TOTAL", "SYSTEMATIZED", "PARALLEL",
│          "'FUNCTIONAL", "RESPONSIVE", "OPTIONAL", "SYNCHRONIXED",
│          "'COMPATIBLE", BALANCED"
│
│      ADJECTIVE2 (1) = "MANAGEMENT", "ORGANIZATIONAL", "MONITORED",
│          "'RECIPROCAL", "DIGITAL", "LOGISTICAL", "TRANSITIONAL",
│          "'INCREMENTAL", "THIRD GENERATION", "POLICY"
│
│      NOUN(1) = "OPTION", "FLEXIBILITY", "CAPABILITY", "MOBILITY",
│          "'PROGRAMMING", "CONCEPT", "TIME PHASE","PROJECTION",
│          "'HARDWARE", "CONTINGENCY"
│
│      SEED
│
├─ UNTIL KEY = "ESC"
┤   COUNT = 1
│
│   ┌─ UNTIL COUNT = 22
│   │   A = INT(RND(10) + 1)
│   ┤   B = INT(RND(10) + 1)
│   │   C = INT(RND(10) + 1)
│   │
│   │   SHOW ADJECTIVE1(A) + " " + ADJECTIVE2(B) + " " + NOUN(C)
│   │
│   │   COUNT = COUNT + 1
│   └─ END
│
│       WAIT
└─ END
│
│      CHAIN "GAMES_MENU"
└─     EXIT
```

FIGURE V.8 An expansion of the action diagram of Fig. V.7 into program code. This is an executable program in the foruth-generation language, MANTIS. Successive decomposition of a diagram until it becomes executable code is called **ultimate decomposition.**


Figure V.9 shows the program constructs with language-independent control words. Figure V.10 shows the same constructs with the words of the fourth-generation language IDEAL. It is desirable that any fourth-generation language should have a set of clear words equivalent to Figure. V.9, and it would help if standard words for this existed in the computer industry. In these two illustrations, the control words are shown in bold print. The other statements are in normal print.

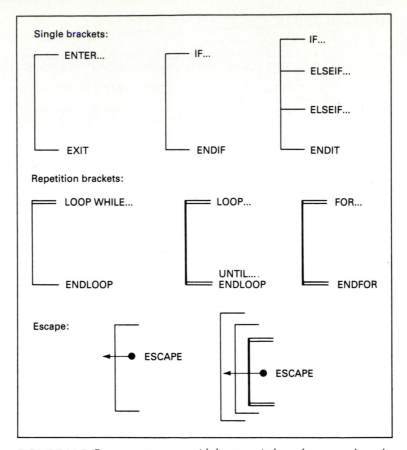

FIGURE V.9  Program constructs with language-independent control words.

# Concurrency

Where brackets may be executed concurrently, they are to be joined with a semicircular link:

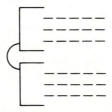

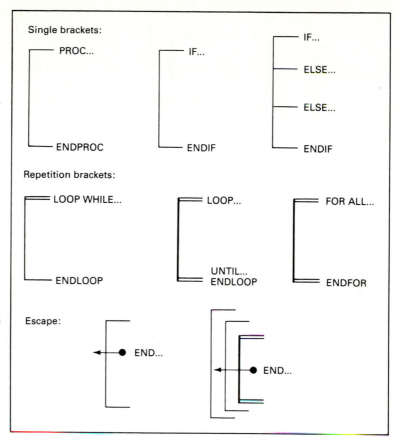

FIGURE V. 10 Program constructs with the control words of the fourth-generation language IDEAL.

# Input and Output Data

The brackets of the action diagram are quick and easy to draw. If the user wants to show the data that enter and leave a process, the bracket is expanded into a rectangle as shown in Fig. V.11. The data entering the process are written at the top right corner of the block. The data leaving are written at the bottom right corner.

This type of functional decomposition is designed for computerized checking to ensure that all the inputs and outputs balance. Figure V.12 shows nested blocks and the arrows represent checks that inputs are used and the outputs come from somewhere. Some CASE tools show the inputs to a bracket at its top and the outputs at its bottom.

A diagramming technique, today, should be designed for both quick manual manipulation and for computerized manipulation. Users and analysts will want to draw

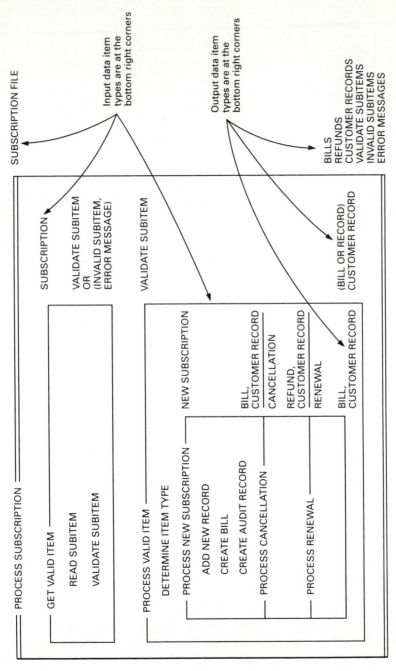

FIGURE V.11  The bracket format of Fig. V.2 is here expanded into the rectangular format used to show the data item types that are input and output to each process. In some CASE tools the inputs are shown at the top and the outputs at the bottom of an action diagram bracket. The computer should perform the checking illustrated in Figure V.12.

rough sketches on paper or argue at a blackboard using the technique. They will also want to build complex diagrams at a computer screen, using the computer to validate, edit and maintain the diagrams, possibly linking them to a dictionary, database model, and so on. The tool acts rather like a word processor for diagramming, making it easy for users to modify their diagram. Unlike a word processor, it can perform complex validation and cross-checking on the diagram. In the design of complex specifications, the automated correlation of inputs and outputs among program modules is essential if mistakes are to be avoided.

In showing input and output data, Fig. V.11 contains the information on a data flow diagram. It can be converted into a layered data flow diagram as in Fig. V.13. Unlike a data flow diagram, it can be directly extended to show the program structure, including conditions, case constructs and loop control.

It is highly desirable that a programmer should sketch the structure of programs with action diagram brackets. Often the coder has made a logic error in the use of loops, END statements, CASE structures, EXITs, and so on. When he is taught to draw action diagram brackets and fit the code to them, these structure errors become apparent. Control statements can be automatically placed on brackets by a CASE tool. The CASE tool should do all the cross-checking that is possible.

## Sample Database Actions

Most of the action diagrams drawn for commercial data-processing systems relate to databases or on-line files. A common action of these diagrams is the database or file operation. It is desirable that these operations relate to the dictionary and data model employed.

We will distinguish between simple and compound database actions. A simple database action is an operation applied to *one instance of one record type*. There are four types of simple actions:

- CREATE
- READ
- UPDATE
- DELETE

The memorable acronym CRUD is sometimes used to refer to these and to help remember them.

On an action diagram, a simple database action is represented by a rectangular box. The name of the record is written inside the box; the type of action is written on the left side of the box:

READ | SUBSCRIBER

Figure V.14 shows an action diagram with several database actions.

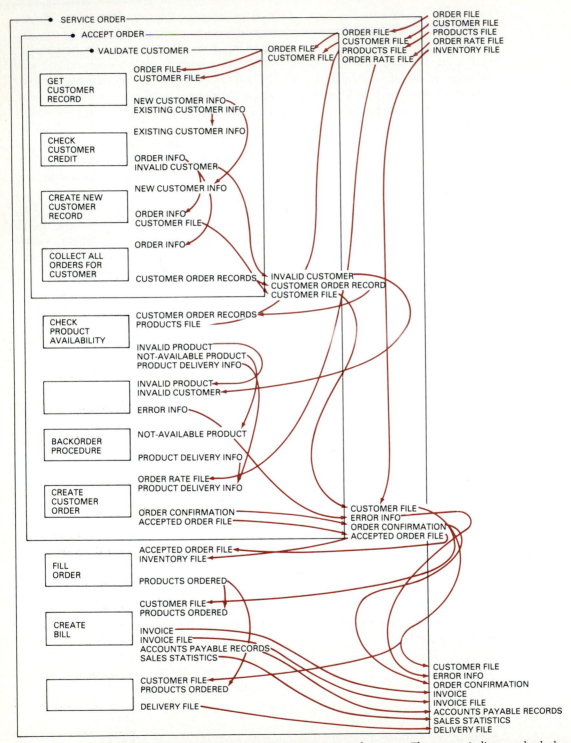

FIGURE V.12 An action diagram showing inputs and outputs. The arrows indicate a check that the graphics tool should make on the usage of inputs and outputs.

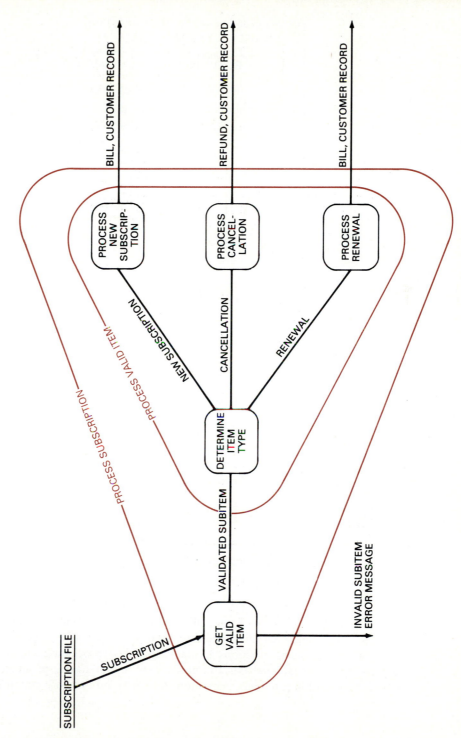

FIGURE V.13 A data flow diagram corresponding to Fig. V.11.

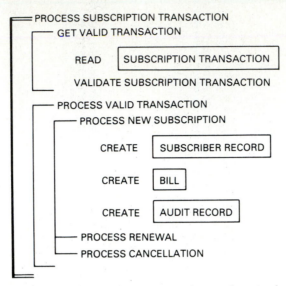

FIGURE V.14 An action diagram showing four simple database actions.

# Compound Database Actions

A *compound database action* also takes a single action against a database, but the action may use multiple records of the same type and sometimes of more than one type. It may search or sort a logical file. It may be a relational operation that uses an entire relation. It may be a relational operation requiring a join on two or more relations. Fourth-generation languages have instructions for a variety of compound database actions. Examples of such instructions are:

- SEARCH
- SORT
- SELECT certain records from a relation or a file
- JOIN two or more relations or files
- PROJECT a relation or file to obtain a subset of it
- DUPLICATE

CREATE, READ, UPDATE, and DELETE may also be used for compound-database actions. For example, DELETE could be used to delete a whole file.

Most of the database actions in traditional data processing are simple database actions. As relational databases and nonprocedural languages spread, *compound* database actions will become more common. A compound database action is represented as a double rectangular box. The name of the record is written inside the box; the database action is written on the left-hand side of the box:

Often a compound database action needs a qualifying statement associated with it to describe how it is performed. For example:

## Automatic Navigation

A compound database action may require automatic navigation by the database management system. Relational databases and a few nonrelational ones have this capability. For a database without automatic navigation, a compiler of a fourth-generation may generate the required sequence of data accesses. With a compound database action, search parameters or conditions are often an integral part of the action itself. They are written inside a bracket containing the access box.

## Simple Versus Compound Database Accesses

There are many procedures that can be done with either simple database accesses or compound accesses. If a traditional DBMS is used, the programmer navigates through the database with simple accesses. If the DBMS or language compiler has automatic navigation, higher-level statements using compound database accesses may be employed.

Suppose, for example, that we want to give a $1000 bonus to all employees who are salespeople in the Southeast region. In IBM's database language SQL, we would write:

```
UPDATE EMPLOYEE
SET SALARY = SALARY + 1000
WHERE JOB = 'SALESMAN'
AND REGION = 'SOUTHEAST'
```

We can diagram this with a compound database action as follows:

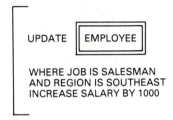

With simple actions (no automatic navigation), we can diagram the same procedure as follows:

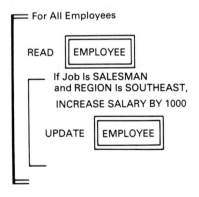

# Relational Joins

A relational join merges two relations (logical files or tables) on the basis of a common data item. For example, the EMPLOYEE relation and the REGION relation for a company may look like this:

REGION

| REGION-ID | LOCATION | REGION-STATUS | SALES-YTD | |
|---|---|---|---|---|
| 001 | NEW YORK | 1 | 198,725 | |
| 004 | CHICAGO | 7 | 92,615 | |
| 006 | LA | 3 | 156,230 | |

EMPLOYEE

| SSN | NAME | SALARY | JOBCODE | LOCATION |
|---|---|---|---|---|
| 337-48-2713 | SMITH | 42000 | 07 | CHICAGO |
| 341-25-3340 | JOHNSON | 39000 | 15 | LA |
| 391-62-1167 | STRATTON | 27000 | 05 | LA |

These relations are combined in such a way that the LOCATION data item of the EMPLOYEE relation becomes the same as the LOCATION data item of the REGION relation. We can express this with the statement

```
REGION.LOCATION = EMPLOYEE.LOCATION
```

The result is a combined record as follows:

| SSN | NAME | SALARY | JOB-CODE | LOCATION | REGION-ID | REGION-STATUS | SALES-YTD |
|---|---|---|---|---|---|---|---|
| 337-48-2713 | SMITH | 42000 | 07 | CHICAGO | 004 | 7 | 92,615 |
| 341-25-3340 | JOHNSON | 39000 | 15 | LA | 006 | 3 | 156,230 |
| 391-62-1167 | STRATTON | 27000 | 05 | LA | 006 | 3 | 156,230 |

The database system may not combine them in reality but may join the appropriate data in response to the request. A join is shown on an action diagram by linking the boxes with an access operation applying to the combination:

READ    REGION — EMPLOYEE    REGION.LOCATION = EMPLOYEE.LOCATION

A statement may follow the joined records showing how they are joined. Often this is not necessary because the joined records contain one common data item, which is the basis for the join. For example, the EMPLOYEE record probably contains the data item LOCATION, in which case we can simply show:

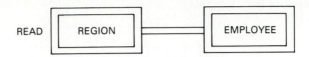

We might, for example, constrain the join operation by asking for employees whose job code is 15, whose salary exceeds $35,000 and whose region status is 3. The result would then be

| SSN | NAME | SALARY | |
|-----|------|--------|--|
| 341-25-3340 | JOHNSON | 39000 | |

From the join of EMPLOYEE and REGION, we might say SELECT SSN, NAME, REGION-STATUS, LOCATION. With the database language SQL from IBM, and others, this operation would be expressed as follows:

```
SELECT SSN, NAME, REGION-STATUS, LOCATION
FROM REGION, EMPLOYEE
WHERE REGION.LOCATION = EMPLOYEE.LOCATION
AND JOB-CODE = 15
AND SALARY > 35000
```

This can be written on an action diagram as follows:

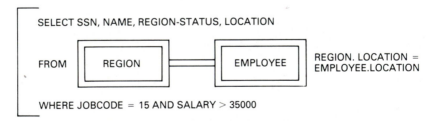

From the join of EMPLOYEE and REGION, we might say SELECT SSN, NAME, REGION-STATUS, LOCATION. With the database language SQL from IBM, and others, this operation would be expressed as follows:

Similarly, a relational join can be represented with either a sequence of single actions or one compound action, as shown in Fig V.15. In this example, there are multiple projects in an EMPLOYEE PROJECT record showing how employees were rated for their work on each project to which they were assigned. They were given a salary raise if their average rating exceeded 6.

*Data used in this example:*

EMPLOYEE

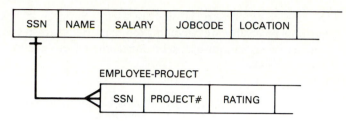

*A procedure for giving employees an increase in salary,
using simple database action:*

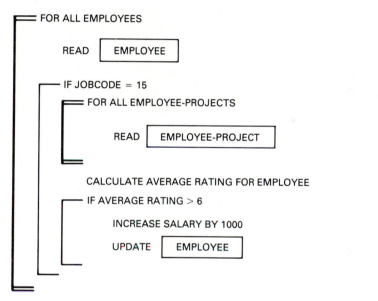

*The same procedure using a compound database action:*

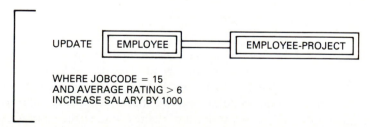

FIGURE V. 15  Illustration of a procedure that may be done with either three
simple database access commands or one compound access command.

# Three-Way Joins

In some cases, three-way joins are useful. Suppose an accountant is concerned that accounts receivable are becoming too high. He wants to telephone any branch manager who has a six-month-old debt outstanding from a customer. The following record structures exist:

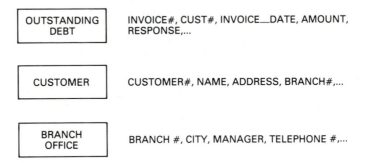

He enters the following query:

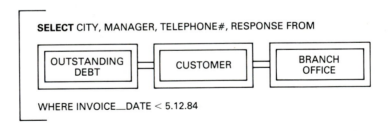

The three-way join is shown in a similar fashion to two-way joins.

# Contract and Expand

A very useful feature of an action diagram editor is the ability to *contract* large action diagrams, hiding much of the detail. The user selects a bracket and says "CON-TRACT." The bracket shrinks so that only its top is seen. Any nested brackets within the contracted bracket disappear. To show the user that information has been hidden, three dots are inserted in front of the text line of the contracted bracket.

In Fig. V.16 the user sets the cursor on a portion of a case structure and says "CONTRACT." The resulting contracted code contains a line beginning with three dots. In Fig. V.17 the user selects this line and say "EXPAND."

"CONTRACT" may be used multiple times to create hierarchies of contraction. "EXPAND" then reveals lines which themselves can be expanded. Contracting and expanding permit large programs to be manipulated with ease.

# Action Diagram Editors
# and Case Tools

Action diagram editors exist for personal computers and are also part of most of the good quality CASE tools. The control words of diverse programming languages can be added to the action diagrams by the computer.

The brackets used can be selected from a menu and can be stretched, edited, cut and pasted, and duplicated. The computer can apply a variety of integrity checks. Large programs can be displayed in overview form. Code can be contracted to hide the details and then reexpanded at will.

Experience with action diagram editors has shown that end users can employ them to sketch the systems and procedures they need. When this occurs, action diagrams form a useful communication vehicle between users and systems analysts. The design so created has successively greater detail added to it until it becomes executable code.

# Automatic Derivation
# of Action Diagrams

Action diagrams can be derived automatically from correctly drawn decomposition diagrams, dependency diagrams, decision trees, or state transition diagrams. If a computer algorithm is used for doing this, it needs to check the completeness or integrity of the dependency diagram or navigation diagram. This helps validate or improve the analyst's design.

# Conversion of Action Diagrams
# to Code

Different computer languages have different commands relating to the constructs drawn on action diagrams. If the action diagram is being edited on a computer screen, a menu of commands can be provided for any particular language. Using the language IDEAL, for example, the designer might select the word LOOP for the top of a repetition bracket, and the software automatically puts ENDLOOP at the bottom of the bracket and asks the designer for the loop control statement. The designer might select IF, and the software creates the following bracket:

The user is asked to specify the IF condition.

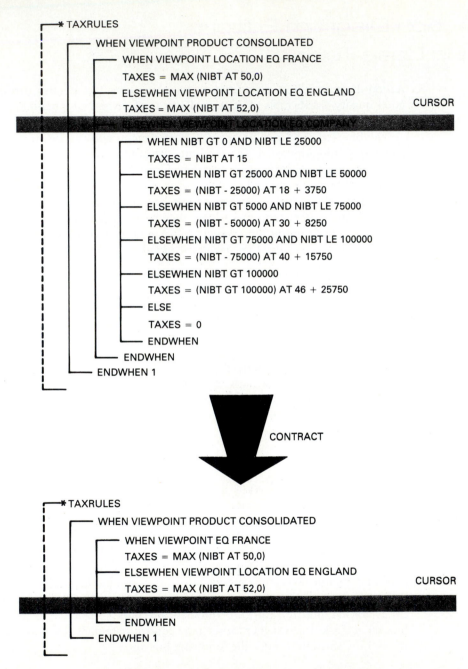

```
*─ TAXRULES
   ├──── WHEN VIEWPOINT PRODUCT CONSOLIDATED
   │     ├──── WHEN VIEWPOINT LOCATION EQ FRANCE
   │     │     TAXES = MAX (NIBT AT 50,0)
   │     ├──── ELSEWHEN VIEWPOINT LOCATION EQ ENGLAND
   │     │     TAXES = MAX (NIBT AT 52,0)                          CURSOR
   │     ▇▇▇▇▇ ELSEWHEN VIEWPOINT LOCATION EQ COMPANY ▇▇▇▇▇▇▇▇▇▇▇▇▇▇▇
   │           ├──── WHEN NIBT GT 0 AND NIBT LE 25000
   │           │     TAXES = NIBT AT 15
   │           ├──── ELSEWHEN NIBT GT 25000 AND NIBT LE 50000
   │           │     TAXES = (NIBT - 25000) AT 18 + 3750
   │           ├──── ELSEWHEN NIBT GT 5000 AND NIBT LE 75000
   │           │     TAXES = (NIBT - 50000) AT 30 + 8250
   │           ├──── ELSEWHEN NIBT GT 75000 AND NIBT LE 100000
   │           │     TAXES = (NIBT - 75000) AT 40 + 15750
   │           ├──── ELSEWHEN NIBT GT 100000
   │           │     TAXES = (NIBT GT 100000) AT 46 + 25750
   │           ├──── ELSE
   │           │     TAXES = 0
   │           └──── ENDWHEN
   │     └──── ENDWHEN
   └──── ENDWHEN 1
```

**CONTRACT**

```
*─ TAXRULES
   ├──── WHEN VIEWPOINT PRODUCT CONSOLIDATED
   │     ├──── WHEN VIEWPOINT EQ FRANCE
   │     │     TAXES = MAX (NIBT AT 50,0)
   │     ├──── ELSEWHEN VIEWPOINT LOCATION EQ ENGLAND
   │     │     TAXES = MAX (NIBT AT 52,0)                          CURSOR
   │     ▇▇▇▇▇▇▇▇▇▇▇▇▇▇▇▇▇▇▇▇▇▇▇▇▇▇▇▇▇▇▇▇▇▇▇▇▇▇▇▇▇▇▇▇▇▇▇▇▇▇▇▇▇▇▇▇▇▇
   │     └──── ENDWHEN
   └──── ENDWHEN 1
```

FIGURE V. 16 The CONTRACT command that hides the contents of a bracket. To show that there is hidden information, three dots are placed at the start of the contracted line.

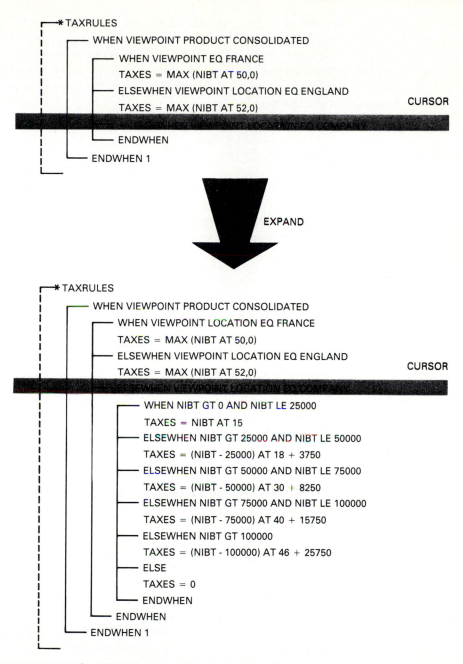

```
 ┌─*TAXRULES
 │ ┌── WHEN VIEWPOINT PRODUCT CONSOLIDATED
 │ │    ┌── WHEN VIEWPOINT EQ FRANCE
 │ │    │   TAXES = MAX (NIBT AT 50,0)
 │ │    ├── ELSEWHEN VIEWPOINT LOCATION EQ ENGLAND
 │ │    │   TAXES = MAX (NIBT AT 52,0)                    CURSOR
 ══════════════════ WHEN VIEWPOINT LOCATION EQ COMPANY ══════════
 │ │    └── ENDWHEN
 │ └── ENDWHEN
 └── ENDWHEN 1
```

EXPAND

```
 ┌─*TAXRULES
 │ ┌── WHEN VIEWPOINT PRODUCT CONSOLIDATED
 │ │    ┌── WHEN VIEWPOINT LOCATION EQ FRANCE
 │ │    │   TAXES = MAX (NIBT AT 50,0)
 │ │    ├── ELSEWHEN VIEWPOINT LOCATION EQ ENGLAND
 │ │    │   TAXES = MAX (NIBT AT 52,0)                    CURSOR
 ══════════════ ELSEWHEN VIEWPOINT LOCATION EQ COMPANY ══════════
 │ │    │    ┌── WHEN NIBT GT 0 AND NIBT LE 25000
 │ │    │    │   TAXES = NIBT AT 15
 │ │    │    ├── ELSEWHEN NIBT GT 25000 AND NIBT LE 50000
 │ │    │    │   TAXES = (NIBT - 25000) AT 18 + 3750
 │ │    │    ├── ELSEWHEN NIBT GT 50000 AND NIBT LE 75000
 │ │    │    │   TAXES = (NIBT - 50000) AT 30 + 8250
 │ │    │    ├── ELSEWHEN NIBT GT 75000 AND NIBT LE 100000
 │ │    │    │   TAXES = (NIBT - 75000) AT 40 + 15750
 │ │    │    ├── ELSEWHEN NIBT GT 100000
 │ │    │    │   TAXES = (NIBT - 100000) AT 46 + 25750
 │ │    │    ├── ELSE
 │ │    │    │   TAXES = 0
 │ │    │    └── ENDWHEN
 │ │    └── ENDWHEN
 │ └── ENDWHEN 1
 └
```

FIGURE V. 17 The EXPAND command can be applied to lines beginning with three dots. It reveals their hidden contents. This and Fig. V.16 show the use of CONTRACT and EXPAND. With these commands, large designs can be reduced to summary form. These commands are very useful in practice.

Such structures with the commands for a given language may be generated automatically from a dependency diagram or data navigation diagram. The objective is to speed up as much as possible the task of creating error-free code.

With different menus of commands for different languages, a designer may switch from one language to another if necessary. This facilitates the adoption of different languages in the future.

# Action Diagrams for Management Procedures

Like any other procedure, a management procedure can be represented with an action diagram. It is convenient to represent fourth-generation computer methodologies with action diagrams because such methodologies are likely to be customized to fit the circumstances in question. A fourth-generation development lifecycle is not a fixed unchangeable lifecycle.

Throughout this book action diagrams are used to represent the methodologies of information engineering. These methodology action diagrams are found in boxes in the chapters that describe the methodology in question. Such procedures can quickly be adjusted with an action diagram editor to fit the circumstances in question.

# Advantages

Action diagrams were designed to solve some of the concerns with other diagramming techniques. They were designed to have the following properties:

1. They are quick and easy to draw and to change.
2. They are good for manual sketching and for computerized editing.
3. A single technique extends from the highest overview down to coding-level detail (ultimate decomposition).
4. They draw all the constructs of traditional structured programming and are more graphic than pseudocode.
5. They are easy to teach to end users; they encourage end users to extend their capability into examination or design of detailed process logic. They are thus designed as an information center tool.
6. They can be printed on normal-width paper rather than wall charts, making them appropriate for design with personal computers.
7. Various types of diagrams, if drawn with precision, can be converted *automatically* into action diagrams.
8. Action diagrams are designed to link to a data model.

BOX V.1   Summary of Notation Used in Action
Diagrams

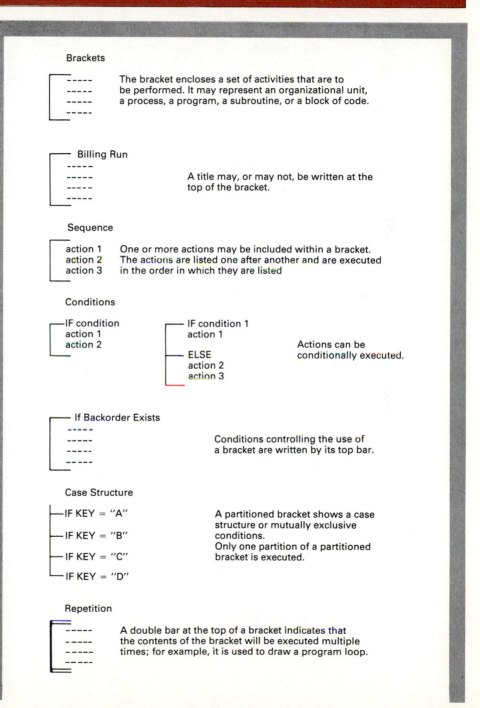

Brackets

The bracket encloses a set of activities that are to
be performed. It may represent an organizational unit,
a process, a program, a subroutine, or a block of code.

Billing Run

A title may, or may not, be written at the
top of the bracket.

Sequence

action 1
action 2
action 3

One or more actions may be included within a bracket.
The actions are listed one after another and are executed
in the order in which they are listed

Conditions

IF condition
action 1
action 2

IF condition 1
action 1

ELSE
action 2
action 3

Actions can be
conditionally executed.

If Backorder Exists

Conditions controlling the use of
a bracket are written by its top bar.

Case Structure

IF KEY = "A"

IF KEY = "B"

IF KEY = "C"

IF KEY = "D"

A partitioned bracket shows a case
structure or mutually exclusive
conditions.
Only one partition of a partitioned
bracket is executed.

Repetition

A double bar at the top of a bracket indicates that
the contents of the bracket will be executed multiple
times; for example, it is used to draw a program loop.

*(Continued)*

BOX V. 1    (Continued)

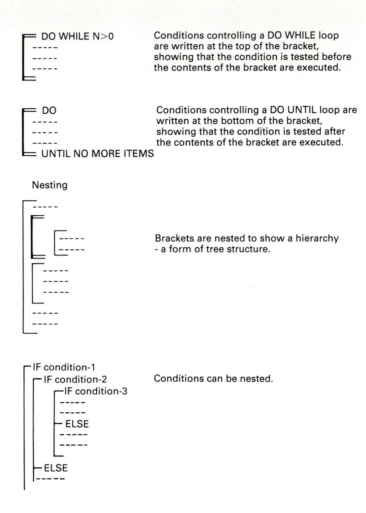

DO WHILE N>0    Conditions controlling a DO WHILE loop
                are written at the top of the bracket,
                showing that the condition is tested before
                the contents of the bracket are executed.

DO              Conditions controlling a DO UNTIL loop are
                written at the bottom of the bracket,
                showing that the condition is tested after
                the contents of the bracket are executed.
UNTIL NO MORE ITEMS

Nesting

                Brackets are nested to show a hierarchy
                - a form of tree structure.

IF condition-1
IF condition-2    Conditions can be nested.
IF condition-3

ELSE

ELSE

BOX V.1    (Continued)

Exits

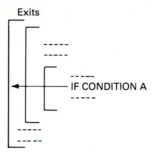

An arrow to the left through
one or more brackets indicates
that the brackets it passes
through are terminated, if the
condition written by the arrow
is satisfied.

Subprocedures

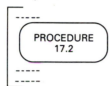

A round-cornered box within a
bracket indicates a procedure
diagrammed elsewhere.

A round-cornered box with a
broken edge indicates a
procedure not yet thought
out in more detail.

Common Procedures

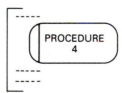

A procedure box with a vertical
line drawn through the left
side indicates a common procedure
(i.e., a procedure that appears
multiple times in the action
diagram).

Concurrency

Where brackets may be executed
concurrently, they are joined by
a semicircular link.

(Continued)

## BOX V. 1    (Continued)

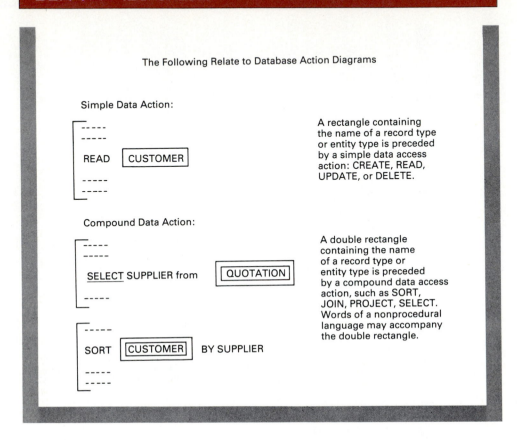

The Following Relate to Database Action Diagrams

Simple Data Action:

READ    CUSTOMER

A rectangle containing the name of a record type or entity type is preceded by a simple data access action: CREATE, READ, UPDATE, or DELETE.

Compound Data Action:

SELECT SUPPLIER from    QUOTATION

SORT    CUSTOMER    BY SUPPLIER

A double rectangle containing the name of a record type or entity type is preceded by a compound data access action, such as SORT, JOIN, PROJECT, SELECT. Words of a nonprocedural language may accompany the double rectangle.

9. They work well with fourth-generation languages and can be tailored to a specific language dialect.

10. They are designed for computerized cross-checking of data usage on complex *specifications*.

Box V.1 summarizes the diagramming conventions of action diagrams.

# Reference

[MARTIN&MCCLURE89]James Martin and Carma McClure, *Action Diagrams: Clearly Structured Specifications, Programs, and Procedures, Second Edition*. Englewood Cliffs, N.J.: Prentice-Hall, 1989.

# Normalization of Data

E. F. Codd
IBM Research Laboratory
San Jose, California

This definitive paper on third normal form, published by Ted Codd in 1972, is included here for the convenience of the reader. The full reference is E. F. Codd, "Further Normalization of the Data Base Relational Model," in *Data Base Systems*, Randall Rustin, ed. © 1972, pp. 65–98. Reprinted by permission of Prentice-Hall, Inc., Englewood Cliffs, N.J.

In an earlier paper, the author proposed a relational model of data as a basis for protecting users of formatted data systems from the potentially disruptive changes in data representation caused by growth in the database and changes in traffic. A first normal form for the time-varying collection of relations was introduced. In this paper, second and third normal forms are defined with the objective of making the collection of relations easier to understand and control, simpler to operate upon, and more informative to the casual user. The question, "Can application programs be kept in a viable state when database relations are restructured?" is discussed briefly, and it is conjectured that third normal form will significantly extend the life expectancy of application programs.

## 1. Introduction

### 1.1 Objectives of Normalization

In an earlier paper [1] the author proposed a relational model of data as a basis for protecting users of formatted data systems from the potentially disruptive changes in data representation caused by growth in the variety of data types in the database and by statistical changes in the transaction or request traffic. Using this model, both the application programmer and the interactive user view the database as a time-varying collection of normalized relations of assorted degrees. Definitions of these terms and of the basic relational operations of projection and natural join are given in Appendix A1 of this section.

The possibility of further normalization of the database relational model was mentioned in [1]. The objectives of this further normalization are:

1. to free the collection of relations from undersirable insertion, update and deletion dependencies;

2. to reduce the need for restructuring the collection of relations as new types of data are introduced, and thus increase the life span of application programs;

3. to make the relational model more informative to users;

4. to make the collection of relations neutral to the query statistics, where these statistics are liable to change as time goes by.

The rules or conventions upon which the second and third normal forms are based can be interpreted as guidelines for the database designer. They are also of concern in the design of general purpose, relational database systems.

## 1.2  Functional Dependence

When setting up a relational database, the designer is contronted with many possibilities in selecting the relational schema itself, let alone its representation in storage. A fundamental consideration is that of identifying which attributes are functionally dependent on others (see Appendix A1 for definition of "attribute"). Attribute B of relation R is *functionally dependent* on attribute A of R if, at every instant of time, each value in A has no more than one value in B associated with it under R. In other words, the projection $\Pi_{A,B}(R)$ is at every instant of time a function from $\Pi_A(R)$ to $\Pi_B(R)$ (this function can be, and usually will be, time-varying). We write R.A $\rightarrow$ R.B if B is functionally dependent on A in R, and R.A $\nrightarrow$ R.B if B is not functionally dependent on A in R. If both R.A. $\rightarrow$ R.B and R.B. $\rightarrow$ R.A hold, then at all times R.A and R.B are in one-to-one correspondence, and we write R.A $\longleftrightarrow$ R.B.

The definition given above can be extended to collections of attributes. Thus, if D,E are distinct collections of attributes of R, E is functionally dependent on D if, at every instant of time, each D-value has no more than one E-value associated with it under R. The notation $\rightarrow$, $\nrightarrow$ introduced for individual attributes is applied similarly to collections of attributes. A functional dependence of the form R.D. $\rightarrow$ R.E where E is a subset of D will be called a *trivial dependence*.

As an example to illustrate functional dependence (both trivial and nontrivial), consider the relation

$$U(E\#,D\#,V\#)$$

where E# = employee serial number; D# = serial number of department to which employee belongs; and V# = serial number of division to which employee belongs.

Suppose that an employee never belongs to more than one department, that a department never belongs to more than one division, and an employee belongs to the division to which his department belongs. Then, we observe that

$$U.E\# \rightarrow U.D\# \tag{1}$$

$$U.D\# \rightarrow U.V\# \tag{2}$$

$$U.E\# \rightarrow U.V\# \tag{3}$$

$$U.(E\#,D\#) \rightarrow U.V\# \tag{4}$$

where (4) is a consequence of (3) and (3) is a consequence of (1) and (2) together.

Suppose we are also given the following additional facts: normally, there are many employees belonging to a given department and many departments belonging to a given division. Then, we may observe that

$$U.D\# \not\rightarrow U.E\#$$

and

$$U.V\# \not\rightarrow U.D\#$$

An example of a trivial dependence is:

$$U.(E\#,D\#) \rightarrow U.E\#$$

since E# is included in (E#,D#).

## 1.3 Candidate Keys

Each *candidate key* K of relation R is, by definition, a combination of attributes (possibly a single attribute) of R with properties $P_1$ and $P_2$:

$P_1$: (*Unique Identification*) In each tuple of R the value of K uniquely identifies that tuple; i.e., $R.K \rightarrow R.\Omega$ where $\Omega$ denotes the collection of all attributes of the specified relation;

$P_2$: (*Non-redundancy*) No attribute in K can be discarded without destroying property $P_1$.

Obviously, there always exists at least one candidate key, because the combination of *all* attributes of R possesses property $P_1$. It is then a matter of looking for a subset with property $P_2$.

Two properties of candidate keys can be deduced from $P_1$ and $P_2$:

$P_3$: Each attribute of R is functionally dependent on each candidate key of R;

$P_4$: The collection of attributes of R in a candidate key K is a maximal functionally independent set (i.e., every proper subset of the attributes of K is functionally independent of every other proper subset of attributes of K, and no other attributes of R can be added without destroying this functional independence).

It is left to the reader to show that

1. $P_1$ is logically equivalent to $P_3$.
2. $P_1 \wedge P_2$ implies $P_4$.
3. A maximal functionally independent set of attributes is not necessarily a candidate key.

For each relation R in a database, one of its candidate keys is arbitrarily designated as the *primary key* of R. The usual operational distinction between the primary key and other candidate keys (if any) is that no tuple is allowed to have an undefined value for any of the primary key components, whereas any other components may have an undefined value. This restriction is imposed because of the vital role played by primary keys in search algorithms. The statement "B functionally depends on A in R" may be expressed in the alternative form "A identifies B in R" since in this case A satisfies condition $P_1$ for $\Pi_{A,B}(R)$.

# 2.   Second Normal Form

## 2. 1   Introductory Example

The basic ideas underlying the second and third normal forms are simple, but they have many subtle ramifications. The author has found that numerous examples are needed to explain and motivate the precise definitions of these normal forms. Accordingly, we begin with the simplest case of a relation in first normal form but not in second (i.e., a relation of degree 3):

$$T(\underline{S\#,P\#},SC)$$

where S# = supplier number, P# = part number, SC = supplier city.

A triple (x,y,z) belongs to T if the supplier with serial number x supplies the part with serial number y, and supplier x has his base of operations in city z. A given part may be supplied by many suppliers, and a given supplier may supply many parts. Thus, the following time-independent conditions hold:

$$T.S\# \not\to T.P\#$$

$$T.P\# \not\to T.S.\#$$

In other words, although the attributes S#, P# are related under T, they are functionally independent of one another under T. Now, each supplier has (in this example) only one base of operations and therefore only one city. Thus,

$$T.S\# \to T.SC$$

Intuitively, we can see that the only choice for the primary key of T is the attribute combination (S#,P#).

Looking at a sample instantaneous tabulation of T (Fig. VI.1), the undesirable properties of the T schema become immediately apparent. We observe for example that, if supplier u relocates his base of operations from Poole to Tolpuddle, more than one tuple has to be updated. Worse still, the number of tuples to be updated can, and usually will, change with time. It just happens to be three tuples at this instant.

Now suppose supplier v ceases to supply parts 1 and 3, but may in the near future supply some other parts. Accordingly, we wish to retain the information that supplier v is located in Feistritz. Deletion of one of the two tuples does not cause the complete disappearance of the association of v with Feistritz, but deletion of both tuples does. This is an example of a deletion dependency which is a consequence of the relational schema itself. It is left to the reader to illustrate a corresponding insertion dependency using this example.

Conversion of T to second normal form consists of replacing T by two of its projections:

$$T_1 = II_{S\#,P\#}(T)$$

$$T_2 = II_{S\#,SC}(T)$$

We thus obtain the relations tabulated in Fig. VI.2.

Note how the undesirable insertion, update and deletion dependencies have disappeared. No essential information has been lost, since at any time the original relation T may be recovered by taking the natural join (see Section A.3) of $T_1$ and $T_2$ on S#.

T(S#,P#,SC)

| u | 1 | 'POOLE' |
| u | 2 | 'POOLE' |
| u | 3 | 'POOLE' |
| v | 1 | 'FEISTRITZ' |
| v | 3 | 'FEISTRITZ' |

FIGURE VI.1  A relation not in second normal form.

| $T_1$(S#,P#) | | $T_2$(S#,SC) | |
|---|---|---|---|
| u | 1 | u | 'POOLE' |
| u | 2 | v | 'FEISTRITZ' |
| u | 3 | | |
| v | 1 | | |
| v | 3 | | |

FIGURE VI.2  Relations in second normal form.

## 2.2  More Probing Examples

Unfortunately, the simple example above does not illustrate all of the complexities which can arise. For expository purposes we now consider five possible relations in a data base concerning suppliers, parts, and projects. In a crude sense these relations represent five alternative possibilities—it is not intended that they coexist in a single database. Note, however, that some contain more information (in the form of additional attributes) than others. In each case the primary key is underlined.

$$R_1(\underline{S\#,P\#,J\#})$$

$$R_2(\underline{X\#},S\#,P\#,J\#)$$

$$R_3(\underline{X\#},S\#,P\#,J\#,Q)$$

$$R_4(\underline{X\#},S\#,P\#,J\#,Q,SC)$$

$$R_5(\underline{S\#,P\#,J\#},Q,SC)$$

where S# = supplier number, P# = part number, J# = project number, X# = serial number, Q = quantity supplied, SC = supplier city.

A triple (x,y,z) belongs to $R_1$ if supplier x supplies part y to project z. The same interpretation holds for $II_{S\#,P\#,J\#}(R_i)$ for i = 2,3,4,5. In each of the five relations, a given combination of supplier and part may be associated with more than one project, a given combination of part and project may be associated with more than one supplier, and a given combination of project and supplier may be associated with more than one part. Thus, for all i

$$R_i \cdot (S\#,P\#) \not\rightarrow R_i \cdot (J\#)$$

$$R_i \cdot (P\#,J\#) \not\rightarrow R_i \cdot (S\#)$$

$$R_i \cdot (J\#,S\#) \not\rightarrow R_i \cdot (P\#)$$

In each of the relations that have the attribute Q, there is only one value of Q for a given value of the attribute combination (S#,P#,J#). Thus,

$$R_i \cdot (S\#,P\#,J\#) \rightarrow R_i \cdot Q \text{ for } i = 3,4,5.$$

However, the value of Q is not uniquely determined by any proper subset of these attributes. Thus, for i = 3,4,5

$$R_i \cdot (S\#,P\#) \not\rightarrow R_i \cdot Q$$

$$R_i \cdot (P\#,J\#) \not\rightarrow R_i \cdot Q$$

$$R_i \cdot (J\#,S\#) \not\rightarrow R_i \cdot Q$$

In each of the relations that have the attribute SC, there is only one value of SC for a given value of S#. Thus, for i = 4,5

$$R_i \cdot S\# \rightarrow R_i \cdot SC$$

In three of the relations a serial number key X# has been introduced and selected as the primary key, even though there is already an attribute combination (S#,P#,J#) capable of acting as the primary key. Thus, for i = 2,3,4

$$R_i \cdot X\# \leftrightarrow R_i \cdot (S\#,P\#,J\#).$$

This is not at all unusual in practice (consider a purchase order number, for instance).

In what follows, we shall suppose that in the given relations there are no functional dependencies other than those itemized above together with those that can be formally deduced from them. Figure VI.3 summarizes the non-trivial dependencies (but not the non-dependencies) in a parent relation R from which $R_1,R_2,R_3,R_4,R_5$ can be derived by projection.

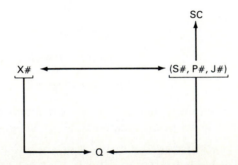

FIGURE VI.3 Attribute dependencies in R.

In all five sample relations above, (S#,P#,J#) is a candidate key. In $R_1$ and $R_5$ it is the primary key also. X# is both a candidate key and the primary key in relations $R_2$, $R_3$, $R_4$.

## 2.3 Prime Attributes

We have observed that in a given relation there may be several distinct candidate keys (although distinct, they need not be disjoint) and, in this case, one is arbitrarily designated as the primary key. Let us call any attribute of R which participates in at least one candidate key of R a *prime attribute* of R. All other attributes of R are called *non-prime*. In sample relations $R_1$,$R_2$ all attributes are prime. In $R_3$ the only non-prime attribute is Q, while in $R_4$,$R_5$ both Q and SC are non-prime.

## 2.4 Full Functional Dependence

Suppose D,E are two distinct subcollections of the attributes of a relation R and

$$R.D \rightarrow R.E$$

If, in addition, E is not functionally dependent on any subset of D (other than D itself) then E is said to be *fully dependent* on D in R. Intuitively, E is functionally dependent on the whole of D, but not on any part of it. An example of full dependence is:

$$R_3 \cdot (S\#,P\#,J\#) \rightarrow R_3 \cdot Q$$

## 2.5 Definition of Second Normal Form

A relation R is in *second normal form* if it is in first normal form and every non-prime attribute of R is fully dependent on each candidate key of R. Although each prime attribute is dependent on each candidate key *of which it is a component*, it is possible for a prime attribute to be non-fully dependent on a candidate key of which it is not a component. Thus, this definition is changed in meaning if the term "non-prime" is dropped. An example which illustrates this distinction is R(A,B,C,D,E,F) where

$$R.(A,B,C) \leftrightarrow R.(D,E) \rightarrow R.F$$

$$R.(A,B) \rightarrow R.D$$

$$R.E \rightarrow R.C$$

Prime attribute C is not fully dependent on candidate key (D,E); neither is D on (A,B,C). This definition rules out both kinds of undesirable dependence of the attribute SC in the example above:

1. the obvious functional dependence of SC in $R_5$ on a portion S# of the primary key;
2. the less obvious functional dependence of SC in $R_4$ on a portion S# of a candidate key that is not the primary key.

Thus, $R_4$ and $R_5$ are not in second normal form.

Two special cases of the definition are worth noting. Suppose R is in first normal form and one or both of the following conditions hold:

C1: R has no non-prime attribute;

C2: Every candidate key of R consists of just a single attribute.

Then, without further investigation, we can say that R is in second normal form. Observe that both $R_1$ and $R_2$ are in second normal form because special case C1 applies. Relation $R_3$ is an example of a relation in second normal form but not as a result of the special conditions C1,C2 above.

## 2.6  Optimal Second Normal Form

In Section 1, a simple example of conversion from first to second normal form was discussed. The operation of projection, employed twice in that example, is adequate for the general case. However, to keep the user from being confused by unnecessary relation names (and to keep the system catalog from getting clogged by such names), projection should be applied sparingly when normalizing. Consider the relation

$$T(\underline{S\#,P\#},SN,SC)$$

where

$$S\# \rightarrow SN \text{ (supplier name)}$$

$$S\# \rightarrow SC \text{ (supplier city)}$$

If we apply projection sparingly in converting to second normal form, we obtain collection $C_1$, say:

$$\Pi_{S\#,P\#}(T), \Pi_{S\#,SN,SC}(T)$$

On the other hand, we could apply projection liberally and obtain collection $C_2$ say:

$$\Pi_{S\#,P\#}(T), \Pi_{S\#,SN}(T), \Pi_{S\#,SC}(T).$$

Both $C_1$ and $C_2$ are in second normal form and both retain all the essential information in the original relation T. However, collection $C_1$ contains the fewest possible relations, and is accordingly said to be in *optimal second normal form*. $C_2$ is in non-optimal second normal form.

# 3.  Third Normal Form

## 3.1  Transitive Dependence

Suppose that A,B,C are three distinct collections of attributes of a relation R (hence R is of degree 3 or more). Suppose that all three of the following time-independent conditions hold:

$$R.A \rightarrow R.B, \qquad R.B \nrightarrow R.A,$$

$$R.B \rightarrow R.C$$

From this we may conclude that two other conditions must hold:

$$R.A \rightarrow R.C \qquad R.C \not\rightarrow R.A$$

and we may represent the entire set of conditions on A,B,C as shown in Fig. VI.4. Note that R.C → R.B is neither prohibited nor required.

In such a case we say that C is *transitively dependent* on A under R. In the special case where R.C → R.B also, both B and C are transitively dependent on A under R.

To illustrate transitive dependence, consider a relation W concerning employees and their departments:

$$W(\underline{E\#},JC,D\#,M\#,CT)$$

where E# = employee serial number, JC = employee jobcode, D# = department number of employee, M# = serial number of department manager, CT = contract type (government or non-government).

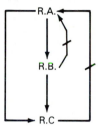

FIGURE VI.4 Transitive dependence of *C* on *A* under *R*.

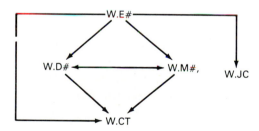

FIGURE VI.5 Example of several transitive dependencies.

Suppose that each employee is given only one jobcode and is assigned to only one department. Each department has its own manager and is involved in work on either government or non-government contracts, not both. The nontrivial functional dependencies in W are as shown in Fig. VI.5 (the non-dependencies are implied). If M# were not present, the only transitive dependence would be that of CT on E#. With M# present, there are two additional transitive dependencies: both D# and M# are transitively dependent on E#. Note, however, that CT is not transitively dependent on either D# or M#.

Looking at a sample instantaneous tabulation of W (Fig. VI.6), the undesirable properties of the W schema become immediately apparent. We observe, for example, that, if the manager of department y should change, more than one tuple has to be updated. The actual number of tuples to be updated can, and usually will, change with time. A similar remark applies if department x is switched from government work (contract type g) to non-government work (contract type n).

Deletion of the tuple for an employee has two possible consequences: deletion of the corresponding department information if his tuple is the sole one remaining just prior to deletion, and non-deletion of the department information otherwise. If the database system does not permit any primary key to have an undefined value, then D# and CT information for a new department cannot be established in relation W before people are assigned to that department. If, on the other hand, the primary key E# could have an undefined value, and if a tuple were introduced with such a value for E# together with defined values for D# (a new department) and CT, then insertion of E# and JC values for the first employee in that department involves no new tuple, whereas each subsequent assignment of an employee to that department does require a new tuple to be inserted.

| W(E#, | JC, | D#, | M#, | CT) |
|---|---|---|---|---|
| 1 | a | x | 11 | g |
| 2 | c | x | 11 | g |
| 3 | a | y | 12 | n |
| 4 | b | x | 11 | g |
| 5 | b | y | 12 | n |
| 6 | c | y | 12 | n |
| 7 | a | z | 13 | n |
| 8 | c | z | 13 | n |

FIGURE VI.6  A relation not in third normal form.

| W₁(E#, | JC, | D#) | W₂(D#, | M# | CT) |
|---|---|---|---|---|---|
| 1 | a | x | x | 11 | g |
| 2 | c | x | y | 12 | n |
| 3 | a | y | z | 13 | n |
| 4 | b | x | | | |
| 5 | b | y | | | |
| 6 | c | y | | | |
| 7 | a | z | | | |
| 8 | c | z | | | |

FIGURE VI.7  Relations in third normal form.

Conversion of W to third normal form consists of replacing W by two of its projections:

$$W_1 = \Pi_{E\#,JC,D\#}(W)$$

$$W_2 = \Pi_{D\#,M\#,CT}(W)$$

We thus obtain the relations tabulated in Fig. VI.7.

Note how the undesirable insertion, update and deletion dependencies have disappeared with the removal of the transitive dependencies. No essential information has been lost, since at any time the original relation W may be recovered by taking the natural join of $W_1$ and $W_2$ on D#.

## 3.2 Keybreaking Transitive Dependence

It is not always possible to remove all transitive dependencies without breaking a key or losing information. This is illustrated by a relation R(A,B,C) in which

$$R.(A,B) \rightarrow R.C, \ R.C \nrightarrow R.(A,B)$$

$$R.C \rightarrow R.B$$

Thus, B is transitively dependent on the primary key (A,B).

## 3.3 Definition of Third Normal Form

A relation R is in *third normal form* if it is in second normal form and every non-prime attribute of R is non-transitively dependent on each candidate key of R. Relations $T_1, T_2, R_1, R_2, R_3$ of Section 2.1 are in third normal form. Relations $R_4, R_5$ are not in third normal form, because they are not even in second. Relation U of section 1.2 is in second normal form but not in third, because of the transitive dependence of V# on E#.

Any relation R in third normal form has the following property:

> **$P_5$: 'Every non-prime attribute of R is both fully dependent and non-transitively dependent on each candidate key of R.**

This property is an immediate consequence of the definition given above. Note that the definition has been so formulated that it does not prohibit transitive dependence of a prime attribute on a candidate key of R, as in Section 3.2.

## 3.4 Optimal Third Normal Form

Suppose $C_2$ is a collection of relations in optimal second normal form and projection is applied to convert to third normal form. The resulting collection of relations $C_3$ is in optimal third normal form relative to $C_2$ if both of the following conditions hold:

1. $C_3$ must contain the fewest possible relations (as in the case of the optimal second normal form), each in third normal form;
2. Each relation in $C_3$ must not have any pair of attributes such that one member of the pair is strictly transitively dependent on the other in some relation of $C_2$. (This condition forces attributes which are "remotely related" to be separated from one another in the normalized collection of relations.)

    (*Note*: Attribute C is *strictly transitively dependent* on attribute A under R if there is an attribute B such that

$$R.A \rightarrow R.B, \qquad R.B \nrightarrow R.A$$

$$R.B \rightarrow R.C, \qquad R.C \nrightarrow R,B$$

This is a special case of transitive dependence.)

Application of these conditions is illustrated in Figs. VI.8(a) and VI.8(b) using the relation W of Section 3.1. Figure VI.8(a) treats the normalization of $W_0$ (obtained from W by dropping manager number M#). Figure VI.8(b) treats the normalizition of W itself, and shows how one-to-one correspondences are forced to occur between candidate keys of the projections (instead of between non-prime attributes). Note also the non-uniqueness of the optimal third normal form in Fig. VI.8(b).

$$W_0(\underline{E\#}, \quad JC, \quad D\#, \quad CT)$$

| Collection of Projections of $W_0$ | | | TNF | Optimal | Violates |
|---|---|---|---|---|---|
| E# → JC | E# → D# | E# → CT | Yes | No | 1, 2 |
| E# → JC, D# | E# → CT | | Yes | No | 2 |
| E# → JC, D# | D# → CT | | Yes | Yes | NIL |

FIGURE VI.8(a) Conversion of $W_0$ to third normal form.

$$W(\underline{E\#}, \quad JC, \quad D\#, \quad M\#, \quad CT)$$

| Collection of, Projections of W | | | TNF | Optimal | Comments |
|---|---|---|---|---|---|
| E# → JC, D#, M# | E# → CT  OR  M# → CT  OR  D# → CT | | No | — | D# and M# are transitively dependent on E# |
| E# → JC | E# → D# | D# ↕ M# → CT | Yes | No | Violates 1 |
| E# → JC, D# | D# ↕ M# → CT | | Yes | Yes | Violates NIL |
| E# → JC, M# | D# ↕ M# → CT | | Yes | Yes | Violates NIL |

FIGURE VI.8(b) Conversion of W to third normal form.

# 4. Admissible States

When converting a time-varying database from first normal form to second or from second to third, certain new insertion and deletion possibilities are introduced. Let us look at the example in Section 2.1 again.

In first normal form, the database $B_1$ consists of the single time-varying relation denoted by the schema

$$T(S\#,P\#,SC)$$

In second normal form, the corresponding database $B_2$ consists of two relations denoted by the schema

$$T_1(\underline{S\#,P\#}) \qquad T_2(\underline{S\#},SC)$$

where, for any time

1. $T_1 = \Pi_{S\#,P\#}(T)$
2. $T_2 = \Pi_{S\#,SC}(T)$

As usual, the primary keys are underlined.

A database state (i.e., instantaneous snapshot) is *admissible* relative to a given schema if

1. each relation named in the schema has tuples whose components belong to the specified domains;
2. all tuples of a relation named in the schema are distinct;
3. no tuple has an undefined value for its primary key (and thus no *component* of the primary key may have an undefined value).

The last condition makes an operational distinction between that candidate key selected to act as the primary key of a relation and all other candidate keys of that relation.

Given any admissible state for $B_1$, we can produce a corresponding admissible state for $B_2$ by applying the operation of projection as in the example above. The original $B_1$ state can be recovered by taking the natural join (see Appendix A1 for definition) of $T_1$ and $T_2$ on $S\#$.

We now observe that the schema for $B_2$ has more admissible states than that for $B_1$. Thus, in $B_2$ it is perfectly admissible to have a $S\#$ value appearing in $T_2$ which does not appear in all in $T_1$, or vice versa, as in the $B_2$-state exhibited in Fig. VI.9.

If we now take the natural join of $T_1$ and $T_2$ on $S\#$, we obtain the state (or tabulation) of T exhibited in Fig. VI.10. Although this state is admissible for $B_1$, essential information has been lost.

| $T_1(S\#, P\#)$ | | $T_2(S\#, SC)$ | |
|---|---|---|---|
| u | 1 | u | 'POOLE' |
| u | 2 | v | 'FEISTRITZ' |
| v | 1 | w | 'SWANAGE' |
| z | 3 | | |

FIGURE VI.9 An admissible state for $B_2$.

```
T(S#, P#, SC)
     u        1      'POOLE'
     u        2      'POOLE'
     v        1      'FEISTRITZ'
```

FIGURE VI.10 The natural join of relatons in Fig. VI.9.

An obvious property of the class of admissible states for a given database schema is that, by means of the operations of tuple insertion and tuple deletion, all the admissible states are reachable from any given admissible state. Clearly, the schema for $B_2$ permits insertions and deletions not permitted by the schema for $B_1$. It is accordingly reasonable to say that these schemata are not *insertion-deletion equivalent*.

# 5. Query Equivalence

A useful notion of *query equivalence* of database states can be based on the algebraic view of queries. In this view, retrieval of data is treated as the formation of a new relation from the database relations by some operation of a relation algebra (see [2]).

If $\theta$ is a relational algebra, B is a collection of relations and R is a relation which is derivable from B using operations of the algebra $\theta$ only, then we say (as in [1]) that R is $\theta$-*derivable* from B. Suppose now that we have two databases A,B which at time t are in states $A_t,B_t$ respectively. We say that the database states $A_t,B_t$ are *query-equivalent* providing they are each $\theta$-derivable from the other and $\theta$ is a relationally complete algebra (see [2]). The reasonableness of this definition stems from the fact

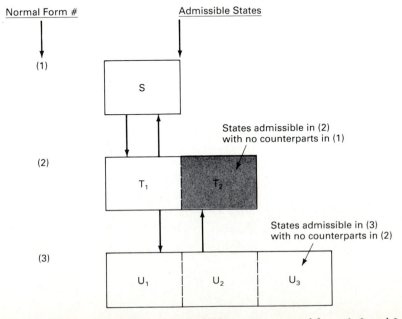

FIGURE VI.11 Admissible states for a database cast in normal forms 1, 2, and 3.

that, if each of the database states $A_t,B_t$ is $\theta$-derivable from the other, then any relation R which is $\theta$-derivable from one must be $\theta$-derivable from the other.

Figure VI.11 summarizes the observations made in Section 4 on admissible states. It also illustrates the fact that the set S of all admissible states for a database cast in first normal form is query-equivalent to a subset $T_1$ of all admissible states when this database is cast in second normal form. Similarly, the set $T_1 \cup T_2$ of all admissible states for this data base cast in second normal form is query-equivalent to a subset $U_1$ of all admissible states when the same database is cast in third normal form.

# 6.  Growth and Restructuring

One of the principal reasons for making application programs interact with an abstract collection of relations instead of their storage representations is to keep these programs from being logically impaired when the storage representations change. Now we wish to consider (but only briefly) what happens to the application programs when the collection of relations is itself changed to conform to a new schema. Simple additions of new database domains and new relations have no effect. Outright removal of a relation R obviously cripples those programs that previously made use of R. Replacement of a relation by *one* of its projections will cripple those programs that previously made use of the attributes now dropped.

The really interesting type of change is replacement of a relation R by two or more of its projections such that R may be recovered by taking the natural join of these projections. We discussed this type of change in Sections 2 and 3 in the context of conversion to second and third normal forms respectively. In the present context of database growth, we call this phenomenon *attribute migration*.

Some of the reasons why attribute migration may accompany database growth are as follows:

1. Through continued acquisition of additional attributes, a relation has become too cumbersome in size and fuzzy in meaning.
2. New controls (e.g., ownership of data, access authorization, recover, etc.) are being introduced.
3. There has been a change in that part of the real world which the database reflects or models.

To illustrate the effect of attribute migration on application programs, consider the splitting of database relation U(E#,JC,D#,M#,CT) into the two projections:

$$U1 = \Pi_{E\#,JC,D\#}(U)$$

$$U2 = \Pi_{D\#,M\#,CT}(U)$$

(See Section 3.1 for the interpretation of U and its attributes.)

We first examine a query and then an insertion. Each is expressed in the database sublanguage ALPHA [3].

> **\*\*Find the contract type (CT) for the employee whose serial number (E#) is 1588. Place result in workspace W.**

$$\underline{GET} \quad W \quad U.CT:(U.E\# = 1588)$$

When U is replaced by the two projections, U1, U2 queries on U must undergo a transformation to make them work as before. If the database system were supplied with a suitable set of substitutions, it could make this transformation automatically. We do not propose to go into the details here but merely state that the resulting transformed query would be:

$$\underline{GET} \quad W \quad U2.CT: \exists U1((U1.D\# = U2.D\#) \wedge (U1.E\# = 1588))$$

The real difficulty arises with insertion and deletion.

> **\*\*Insert from workspace W into the database relation U a tuple for a new employee with serial number 1492 and contract type non-government (n). Values for his jobcode, department number, and manager number are not yet available.**

$$\underline{PUT} \quad W \quad U$$

When database relation U is replaced by U1, U2 and we attempt to transform this insertion to make it work on these projections, we find that the insertion of two new tuples is necessary: one into U1, and one into U2. The insertion into U1 presents no problem because we have a value (1492) for its primary key component (E#). In the case of U2, however, we do not have a value for its primary key component (D#). To cope with this difficulty, the system could temporarily insert a fictitious (but defined) value to represent a department (as yet undetermined) which is assigned to non-government work. Unfortunately, when the total database is considered together with all the possible partially defined associations which may have to be temporarily remembered, the system may require a very large pool of fictitious values to call upon.

We have seen that attribute migration can logically impair an application program. Further, it may be feasible to systematically re-interpret the database requests made by a program P so as to make P work correctly again. This problem is simpler for those programs that avoid insertion and deletion on the relations affected by attribute migration. Whether or not this special case holds, the re-interpretation is likely to cause significant system overhead. Avoidance of attribute migration is accordingly desirable. It is this author's thesis that, by casting the database in third normal form at the earliest possible time and by keeping it that way, an installation will reduce the incidence of attribute migration to a minimum and consequently have less trouble keeping its application programs in a viable state.

# 7.   Conclusion

In Section 1 we introduced the notion of functional dependence within a relation—a notion that is fundamental in formatted database design. Using this notion, two new normal forms were defined. Figure VI.12 summarizes the relationship between the three normal forms introduced by this author. Notice that as a collection of relations is translated from first normal form to second, and then to third, the conditions applied are progressively more stringent.

In the past, design of records (computerized or not) for commercial, industrial and government institutions has been oriented in an ad hoc way to the needs of particular applications. For the large integrated databases of the future, application-independent guidelines for logical record design are sorely needed. This paper is intended to provide such guidelines.

It is also conjectured that physical records in optimal third normal form will prove to be highly economical in space consumed. In some cases a further saving in space can be obtained by factoring (see [2]) relations in third normal form.

Although the three normal forms are query-equivalent in the sense that the set of queries answerable by a collection C in first normal form is transformable into queries yielding the same information from the second and third normal forms of C, there is a difference in information content of the three forms. The second is more informative than the first, and the third is more informative than the second. The increased information lies in the data description (rather than in the data described) as a consequence of the underlying conventions. Like the declarations of redundancies and combinational possibilities within the relational model (see [1]), the normal forms described above tend to capture some aspects of the semantics (minor, of course). Thus, a relational model in second normal form, and more especially, one in third normal form is likely to be more readily understood by people who are not everyday users of the data. It is also likely to be better tuned to the authorization requirements of installations.

Compared with first normal form, the second and third do carry with them the penalty of extra names. In the many databases that have relations of high degree, this

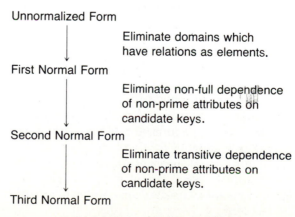

FIGURE VI. 12  Three normal forms.

name penalty will not be nearly as severe as that associated with a complete conversion to nested binary relations.

Some queries will also need to employ more join terms for cross-referencing between relations than might otherwise be the case. This potential burden on the user can be eased by user-declared (and possibly pooled) cross-referencing for heavily used types of queries.

# Acknowledgments

The author is indebted to Claude Delobel of the Conservatoire National des Arts et Metiers, Paris for indicating an inadequacy in the treatment of one-to-one correspondences in an early draft of this paper. Working from this draft, C. J. Date, I. J. Heath and P. Hopewell of the IBM Development Laboratory in Hursley, England have developed some theoretical and practical applications of the third normal form, which will be published soon [4,5]. Their interest in and enthusiasm for the third normal form encouraged the author to produce a more detailed paper than the original version. Thanks are also due to F. P. Palermo and J. J. Rissanen of IBM Research, San Jose for suggesting changes which improved the clarity.

# References

1. E. F. Codd, A relational model of data for large shared data banks, *CACM 13*(6), 377–387, June 1970.

2. E. F. Codd, Relational completeness of data base sublanguages, *Data Base Systems,* Randall Rustin, ed. Englewood Cliffs, N.J.: Prentice-Hall, 1972.

3. E. F. Codd, *A Data Base Sublanguage Founded on the Relational Calculus, IBM Research Report RJ893,* July 1971.

4. C. J. Date, P. Hopewell, File definition and logical data independence, Proc 1971 ACM-SIGFIDET Workshop on Data Description, Access and Control, to be available from ACM HQ, 1972.

# Appendix

## A1.   Basic Definitions

Given sets $D_1, D_2,...,D_n$ (not necessarily distinct), R is a *relation* on these n sets if it is a set of elements of the form $(d_1, d_2,...,d_n)$ where $d_j \epsilon D_j$ for each j = 1,2,...,n. More concisely, R is a subset of the Cartesian product $D_1 x D_2 x...x D_n$. We refer to $D_j$ as the jth *domain* of R. The elements of a relation of degree n are called *n-tuples* or *tuples*. A relation is in *first normal form* if it has the property that none of its domains has elements which are themselves sets. An *unnormalized relation* is one which is not in first normal form.

A database B is a finite collection of time-varying relations defined on a finite collection of domains, say $D_1, D_2 ..., D_p$. Suppose relation R is one of the relations in B and is of degree n. To declare R to a database system we need to cite n of the p database domains as those on which R is defined.

Now, not all these n cited domains need be distinct. Instead of using an ordering to distinguish these n citations from one another (as is common in mathematics), we use a distinct name for each citation and call this the *attribute name* for that particular use of a database domain. Each distinct use (or citation) of a database domain in defining R is accordingly called an *attribute* of R. For example, a relation R of degree 3 might have attributes $(A_1, A_2, A_3)$ while the corresponding database domains are $(D_5, D_7, D_5)$. Attribute names provide an effective means of protecting the user from having to know domain positions.

## A.2  Projection

Suppose r is a tuple of relation R and A is an attribute of R. We adopt the notation r.A to designate the A-component of r. Now suppose A is instead a list $(A_1, A_2, \ldots, A_k)$ of attributes of R. We extend the notation r.A so that, in this case:

$$r.A = (r.A_1, r.A_2, \ldots, r.A_k)$$

When the list A is empty, $r.A = r$.

Let $C = (C_1, C_2, \ldots, C_n)$ be a list of all the attributes of R. Let A be a sublist (length k) of C and r a tuple of R. Then, we adopt the notation $r.\bar{A}$ to designate the (n-k)-tuple r.B where B is the complementary list of attributes obtained by deleting from C those listed in A.

The *projection* of R on the attribute list A is defined by

$$\Pi_A(R) = \{r.A: r \epsilon R\}$$

A more informal definition is given in [1].

## A.3  Natural Join

Suppose R,S are two relations and

$$A = (A_1, \ldots, A_k), \ B = (B_1, \ldots, B_k)$$

are equal-length lists of the attributes of R,S respectively. Suppose that for $i = 1, 2, \ldots, k$ attributes $A_i, B_i$ are comparable: that is, for every $r \epsilon R$, $s \epsilon S$

$$r.A_i = s.B_i$$

is either true or false (not undefined). We say that

$$r.A = s.B$$

if $(r.A_1 = s.B_1)^\wedge \ldots ^\wedge (r.A_k = s.B_k)$

Then, the *natural join* of R on A with S on B is defined by:

$$R*S = \{(r, s.\bar{B}): r \epsilon R \ ^\wedge \ s \epsilon S \ ^\wedge \ (r.A = s.B)\}$$

This definition is the same as that given in [1] except that there is no requirement that

$$\Pi_A(R) = \Pi_B(S)$$

for relations R,S to be joinable. This condition was imposed in [1] solely for the purposes of treating redundancy and consistency.

# Bubble Charting

Bubble charts provide a valuable way to teach users and analysts about data structures. The most elemental piece of data, the *data item* (sometimes also called a *field* or a *data element*), is the atom of data, in that it cannot be subdivided into smaller data types and retain any meaning to users of the data. You cannot split the data item called SALARY, for example, into smaller data items which by themselves are meaningful to end users. In a bubble chart each *type* of data item is drawn as an ellipse:

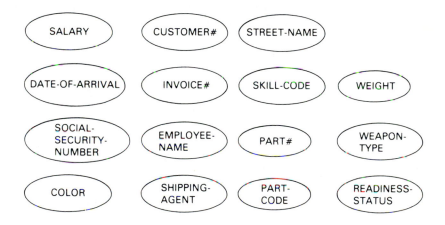

## Associations Between Data Items

A data item by itself is not of much use. For example, a value of SALARY by itself is uninteresting. It becomes interesting only when it is associated with another data item, such as EMPLOYEE-NAME:

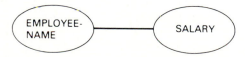

A database, therefore, consists not only of data items but also of associations among them. There are a large number of different data-item types, and we need a map showing how they are associated. This map is sometimes called a *data model*.

# One-to-One and One-to-Many Associations

There are two kinds of links that we shall draw between data items: a one-to-one association and a one-to-many association. A **one-to-one association** from data item type A to data item type B means that *at each instant in time, each value of A has one and only one value of B associated with it.* There is a one-to-one mapping from A to B. If you know the value of A, you can know the value of B.

There is only one value of SALARY associated with a value of EMPLOYEE# at one instant in time; therefore, we can draw a one-to-one link from EMPLOYEE# to SALARY. It is drawn as a small bar across the link:

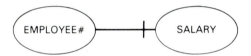

It is said that EMPLOYEE# *identifies* SALARY. If you know the value of EMPLOYEE#, you can know the value of SALARY.

A **one-to-many link** from A to B means that *one value of A has one or many values of B associated with it.* This is drawn with a crow's foot. While an employee can have only one salary at a given time, he might have one or many girlfriends. Therefore, we would draw

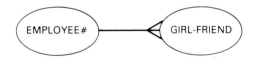

For one value of the data-item type EMPLOYEE# there can be one or many values of the data-item type GIRLFRIEND.

We can draw both of the foregoing situations on one bubble chart:

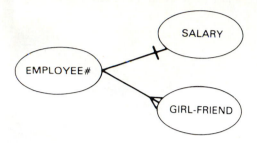

This *synthesizes* the two preceding charts into one chart. From this one chart we could derive either of the two preceding charts. The two preceding charts might be two different user views, one user being interested in salary and the other in girlfriends. We have created one simple data structure that incorporates these two user views. This is what the data administrator does when building a database, but the real-life user views are much more complicated than the illustration above, and there are many of them. The resulting data model sometimes has hundreds or even thousands of data-item types.

---

**Note:**
   Some analysts draw the one-to-one and one-to-many associations as single-headed and double-headed arrows. Thus:

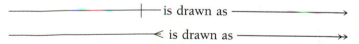

The author has used the single-headed and double-headed arrows in earlier books. These are avoided here because arrows tend to suggest a flow or time sequence and are used extensively for this in other types of diagrams. The one-to-one symbol is extremely important in the processes of normalizing and synthesizing data—the basis of data analysis.

---

# Types and Instances

The terms with which we describe data can refer to *types* of data or to *instances* of that data. "EMPLOYEE-NAME" refers to a type of data item. "FRED SMITH" is an *instance* of this data-item type. "EMPLOYEE" may refer to a type of record. There are many instances of this record type, one for each person employed. The diagrams in this chapter show *types* of data, not instances. A data model shows the associations among *types* of data.

   The bubble chart shows data-item types. There are many occurrences of each data-item type. In the example above, there are many employees, each with a salary and with zero, one, or many girlfriends. The reader might imagine a third dimension to the bubble charts, showing the many values of each data-item type, thus:

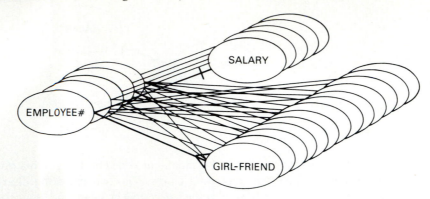

In discussing data we ought to distinguish between types and instances. Sometimes, abbreviated wording is used in literature about data. The words "DATA ITEM" or "RECORD" are used to mean "DATA-ITEM TYPE" or "RECORD TYPE."

## Reverse Associations

Between any two data item types there can be a mapping in both directions. This gives four possibilities for forward and reverse association. If the data-item types are MAN and WOMAN, and the relationship between them represents *marriage*, the four theoretical possibilities are:

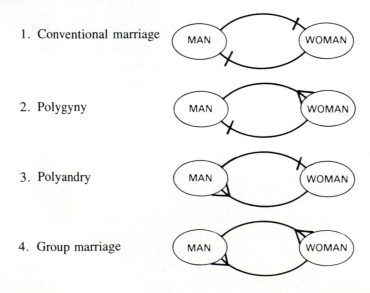

1. Conventional marriage

2. Polygyny

3. Polyandry

4. Group marriage

The reverse associations are not always of interest. For example, with the following bubble chart:

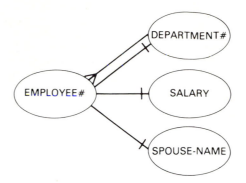

we want the reverse association from DEPARTMENT# to EMPLOYEE# because users want to know what employees work in a given department. However, there is no link from SPOUSE-NAME to EMPLOYEE# because no user wants to ask: "What employee has a spouse named Gertrude?" If a user wanted to ask "What employees have a salary over $25,000?" we might include a crow's-foot link from SALARY to EMPLOYEE#.

# Keys and Attributes

Given the bubble chart method of representing data, we can state three important definitions:

1. Primary key
2. Secondary key
3. Attribute

*A primary key is a bubble with one or more one-to-one links going to other bubbles.* Thus, in Fig. VII.1, *A, C* and *F* are primary keys.

A primary key may uniquely identify many data items. Data items that are not primary keys are referred to as *nonprime attributes.* All data items, then, are either *primary keys* or *nonprime attributes.*

In Fig. VII.1, *B, D, E, G, H* and *I* are nonprime attributes. Often the word "attribute" is used instead of "nonprime attribute." Strictly, the primary key data items are attributes also. EMPLOYEE# is an attribute of the employee.

The names of data-item types that are primary keys are underlined in the bubble charts and drawings of records. We can define a nonprime attribute as follows:

> A nonprime attribute is a bubble with no one-to-one links going to another bubble.

Each primary key uniquely identifies one or more data items. Those that are not other primary keys are attributes.

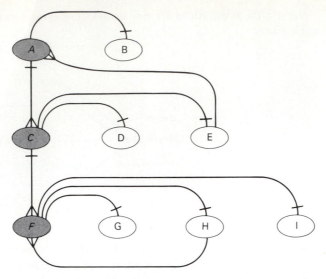

FIGURE VII. 1  A bubble chart showing one-to-one (⊢───┤)
and one-to-many (───<) associations among data-item types.

A *secondary key* does not uniquely identify another data item. One value of a secondary key is associated with one or many values of another data item. In other words, there is a crow's-foot link going from it to that other item.

> A secondary key is a nonprime attribute with one or more crow's-foot links to other data items.

In Fig. VII.1, *E* and *H* are secondary keys.

For emphasis, the following box repeats these three fundamental definitions.

---

A *PRIMARY KEY* is a bubble with one or more one-to-one links going to other bubbles.

A *NONPRIME ATTRIBUTE* is a bubble with no one-to-one link going to another bubble.

A *SECONDARY KEY* is an attribute with one or more one-to-many links going to other bubbles.

---

## Data-Item Groups

When using a database, we need to extract multiple different views of data from one overall database structure. The bubble charts representing these different views of data can be merged into one overall chart. In the bubble chart that results from combining many user views, the bubbles are grouped by primary key. Each primary key is the unique identifier of a group of data-item types. It has one-to-one links to each nonprime attribute in that group.

The data-item group needs to be structured carefully so that it is as stable as possible. We should not group together an ad hoc collection of data items. There are formal rules for structuring the data-item group, which are part of the normalization process (Chapter 9).

## Records

The data-item group is commonly called a *record*, sometimes a *logical record* to distinguish it from whatever may be stored physically. A record is often drawn as a bar containing the names of its data items, as in Fig. VII.2. The record in Fig. VII.2 represents the following bubble chart:

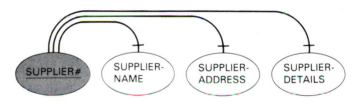

It may be useful to split the SUPPLIER ADDRESS data item into component data items:

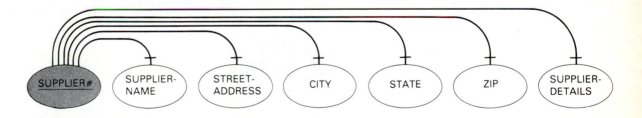

This is useful only if the components may be individually referenced.

Figure VII.3 shows the record redrawn to show that STREET-ADDRESS, CITY, STATE, and ZIP are referred collectively to as SUPPLIER-ADDRESS but are not by themselves a record with primary key.

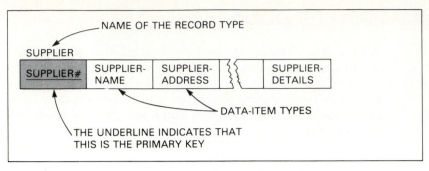

FIGURE VII.2 A drawing of a record.

FIGURE VII.3 The record in Fig. VII.2 redrawn to show the decomposition of SUP-PLIER-ADDRESS. These components do not by themselves constitute a record or data-item group with a primary key.

# Concatenated Keys

Some data-item types cannot be identified by any single data-item type in a user's view. They need a primary key (unique identifier) which is composed of more than one data-item type in combination. This is called a **concatenated key**.

Several suppliers may supply a part and each charge a different price for it. The primary key SUPPLIER# is used for identifying information about a *supplier*. The key PART# is used for identifying information about a *part*. Neither of those keys is sufficient for identifying the *price*. The price is dependent on both the supplier and the part. We create a new key to identify the price, which consists of SUPPLIER# and PART# joined together (concatenated). We draw this as one bubble:

The two data items from which the concatenated key is created are joined with a " + " symbol.

The concatenated key has one-to-one links to the keys SUPPLIER# and PART#. The resulting graph is as follows:

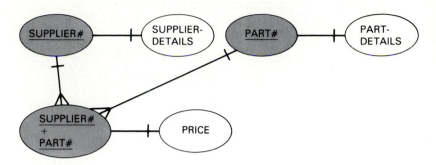

By introducing this form of concatenated key into the logical view of data, we make each data item dependent on one key bubble.

Whenever a concatenated key is introduced, the designer should ensure that the items it identifies are dependent on the whole key, not on only a portion of it.

In practice it is sometimes necessary to join together *more than two* data item types in a concatenated key. For example, a company supplies a product to domestic and industrial customers. It charges a different price to different *types of customers*, and the price varies from one *state* to another. There is a *discount* giving different price reductions for different quantities purchased. The *price* is identified by a combination of CUSTOMER-TYPE, STATE, DISCOUNT and PRODUCT:

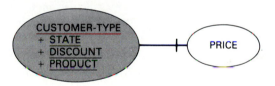

The use of concatenated keys gives each data item group in the resulting data model a simple structure in which each nonprime attrbute is fully dependent on the key bubble and nothing else:

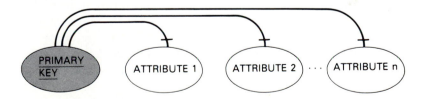

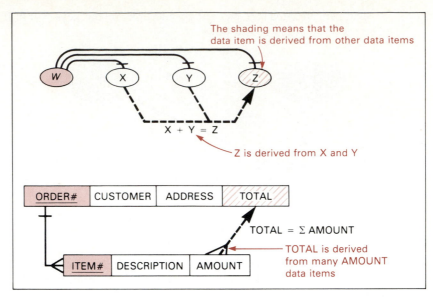

The shading means that the
data item is derived from other data items

X + Y = Z

Z is derived from X and Y

| ORDER# | CUSTOMER | ADDRESS | TOTAL |
|--------|----------|---------|-------|

TOTAL = Σ AMOUNT

TOTAL is derived
from many AMOUNT
data items

| ITEM# | DESCRIPTION | AMOUNT |
|-------|-------------|--------|

FIGURE VII.4  Derived data-item types shown on diagrams of data.

# Derived Data

Certain data items are derived by calculation from other data items. For example, TOTAL-AMOUNT on an invoice may be derived by adding the AMOUNT data items on individual lines. A derived data-item type may be marked on a bubble chart by shading its ellipse. Boldfaced lines or colored lines may be drawn to the derived data-item type from the data-item types from which it is derived. Figure VII.4 illustrates this.

Where possible the calculation for deriving a data item should be written on the diagram, as in Fig. VII.4. Sometimes the computation may be too complex, and the diagram refers to a separate specification. It might refer to a decision tree or table that shows a derived data item.

Derived data items may or may not be stored with the data. They might be calculated whenever the data are retrieved. To store them requires more storage; to calculate them each time requires more processing. As storage drops in cost, it is increasingly attractive to store them. The diagrams initially drawn are *logical* representations of data that represent derived data without saying whether it is stored. This is a later, physical decision.

There has been much debate about whether derived data-item types should be shown on diagrams of data or data models. In the author's view they should be shown. Some fourth-generation or nonprocedural languages cause data to be derived automatically once statements like those in Fig. VII.4 are made describing the derivation.

## THE HOUSE OF MUSIC INC.
### *A Collins Corporation*
Main Office
108 Old Street, White Cliffs, IL 67309
063 259 0003

## SALES CONTRACT

**Contract No.** 7094

| SOLD BY | Mike | DATE | 6/10/83 |
|---|---|---|---|

Name ___ Herbert H. Matlock

Address ___ 1901 Keel Road

City ___ Ramsbottom, Illinois    Zip __ 64736

Phone ___ 063 259 3730    Customer # ___ 18306

REMARKS:

10 yrs. parts and labor on the Piano
1 yr. parts and labor on pianocorder

Delivery Address:

| DESCRIPTION | PRICE | DISCOUNT | AMOUNT |
|---|---|---|---|
| New Samick 5'2" Grand Piano model G-1A | | | |
| # 820991 with Marantz P-101 # 11359 | | | 9500.00 |
| | | | |
| | | TOTAL AMOUNT | 9500.00 |
| | | TRADE IN ALLOWANCE | 2300.00 |
| | | SALES TAX | |
| | | DEPOSIT | 1000.00 |
| | | FINAL BALANCE | 6200.00 |

**PLEASE NOTE:** All sales pending approval by management and verification of trade-in description.

If this contract is breached by the BUYER, the SELLER may take appropriate legal action, or, at its option, retain the deposit as liquidated damages.

Buyer's Signature ___

FIGURE VII.5 A sales contract. The data-item types on this document and their associations are diagrammed in Figs. VII.6 and VII.7.

# Optional Data Items

Sometimes a data-item type may or may not exist. For one value of *A* there may be zero or one value of *B*. This is indicated by putting a "O" on the cardinality indicator:

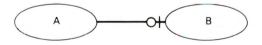

For example:

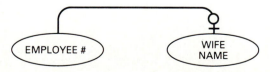

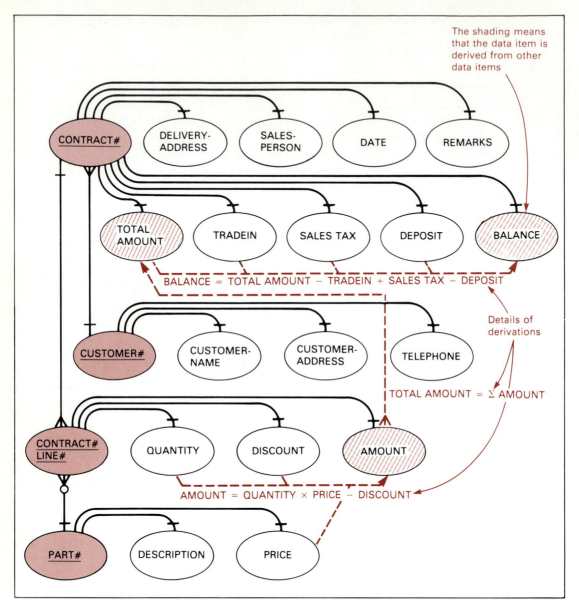

FIGURE VII.6 A data analysis diagram showing the data items on the sales contract of Fig. VII.5 and the associations among them. The diagram is drawn in a more formal style than the others in the chapter for ease of computer representation.

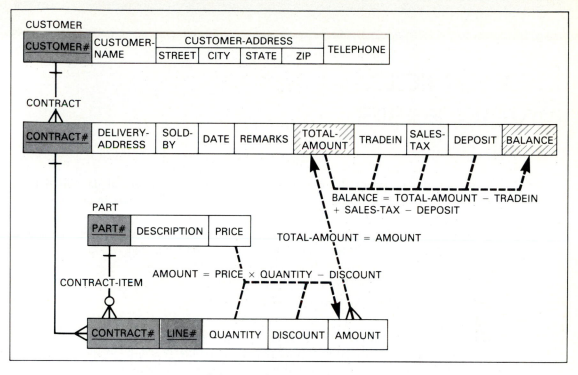

FIGURE VII.7 A record diagram of the data in Fig. VII.6. The derivation expressions could be recorded separately.

If the optional bubble is a nonprime attribute (rather than a primary key), it may be treated like any other nonprime attribute when synthesizing the data model.

Optionality applies to one-to-many associations also:

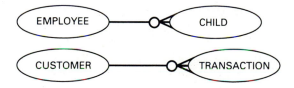

# Data Analysis

When data analysis is performed, the analyst examines the data-item types that are needed and draws a diagram of the dependencies among the data items. The one-to-one and one-to-many links that we have drawn on bubble charts are also drawn between records, as in Fig. VII.4.

Figures VII.5 through VII.7 illustrate data analysis. Figure VII.5 shows a sales contract. The data-item types on this contract are charted in Figure VII.6. The bubble chart of Figure VII.6 is redrawn as a record diagram in Figure VII.7.

# Canonical Synthesis

This appendix describes the use of synthesis to build a **canonical data model**—a minimal, nonredundant, fully normalized representation of the data in an enterprise. We have emphasized that this representation of data needs to be as stable as possible because it is the foundation stone of most future systems. It is the use of a common data model that enables separately built systems to work together.

## Synthesizing Views of Data

The data modeling process takes many separate views of data and *synthesizes* them into a structure that incorporates all of them. The synthesis is done in such a way that redundant data items are eliminated where possible. The same data item does not generally appear twice in the final result. Also, redundant *associations* are eliminated where possible. In other words, a minimal number of lines connects the bubbles in the resulting bubble chart.

The synthesis process is a formal procedure following a formal set of rules. It should be done by computer. This eliminates errors in the process, provides formal documentation that is a basis for end-user discussion and permits any input view to be changed or new views to be added and immediately reflects the effect of the change in the resulting data model.

## Synthesis Illustration

As a simple illustration of the synthesis process, consider the four user views of data shown in Fig. VIII.1. We want to combine those into a single data model.

To start, here is view 1:

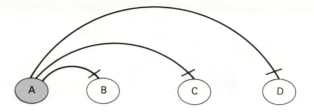

We will combine view 2 with it:

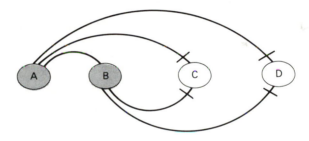

None of the data items above appear twice in the result:

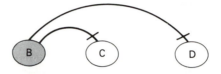

There are, however, some redundant links.

    *A* identifies *B*;

    And *B* identifies *C*;

    Therefore, *A must* identify *C*.

    Therefore, the link *A* ——+ *C* is redundant.

    Similarly, *A* identifies *B* and *B* identifies *D*; therefore, *A must* identify *D*. Therefore, the link *A* ——+ D is redundant. The redundant links are removed, and we have

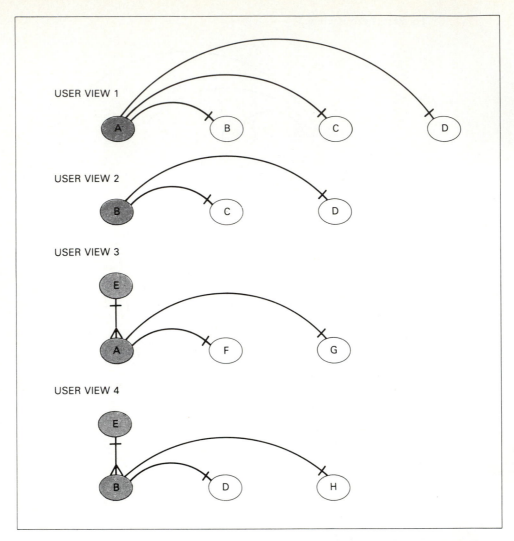

FIGURE VIII.1 Four simple views of data which can be synthesized to form the structure in Fig. VIII.2.

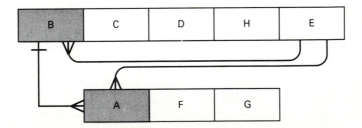

FIGURE VIII.2 The synthesis of the data views in Fig. VIII.1. (Here, *E* is a secondary key pointing to *B* and *A*. These secondary paths could be represented *physically* in a variety of possible ways.)

Now the third view:

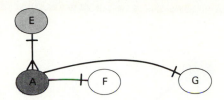

This contains three data items, *E, F* and *G*. When it is merged into the model, we get

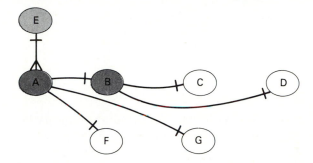

There are no new redundancies; so we will merge in the fourth view:

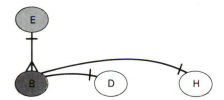

This adds one new data item to the model, *H*:

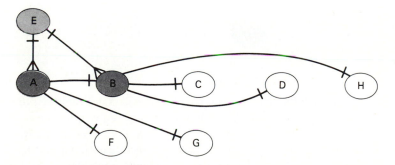

There is now one redundant link.

*A* identifies *B*; *B* identifies *E*; therefore, *A must* identify *E*. We can remove the *A* ——+ *E* link (we cannot change the one-to-many link from *E* to *A*):

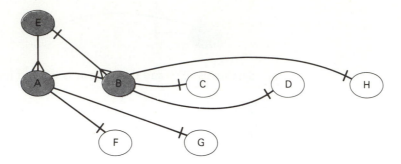

In this resulting structure there are two primary keys: *A* and *B*. (A primary key is a bubble with one or more one-to-one links going to other bubbles.)

We can associate each primary key with the attributes it identifies:

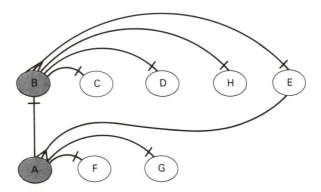

On each linkage between primary keys it is desirable to put the reverse linkage. We should therefore ask: Is the link from *B* to *A* a one-to-one or one-to-many link?

Suppose that it is a one-to-many link. Figure VIII.2, shows the entity records that result from this synthesis. *E*, here, is a secondary key pointing to both *A* and *B*. In old punched-card or batch-processing systems, secondary keys, such as *E*, were the *sort* keys. In on-line systems, secondary key paths such as those from *E* to *A* or *B* are followed by such means as pointers or indices.

# Canonical Data Structures

If we have a given collection of data items and we identify their functional dependencies, we can combine them into a nonredundant model. We combine redundant data items and redundant associations so that no redundancy remains.

*There is one and only one nonredundant model of a given collection of data.* We call this the *canonical model*—the simplest, standard model. Secondary keys may be added to the model later as the need to search the data is identified. If we consider only primary keys and the grouping of the data items in entity records, the resulting model is *independent of how the data are used. We can structure the data independently of their usage.* The structure is inherent in the properties of the data themselves.

We have stressed that procedures—the way people use data—change rapidly in a typical enterprise. The data themselves have a structure that will not change unless new types of data are added. As new types of data are added, the model can grow in a fashion that does not necessitate the rewriting of existing programs (if the database management system has good data independence).

Most structured techniques have analyzed procedures first and then decided what file or database structures are necessary for these procedures. This has resulted in high maintenance costs because the procedures change. In information engineering we analyze the data first and apply various steps to make it stable. Then we look for techniques which enable users to employ data with as little programming effort as possible—techniques that give results *as fast as possible* and techniques that permit fast and easy change to the procedures.

# Canonical Synthesis

The technique we describe takes any number of user views of data and combines them into a minimal set of canonical records with the requisite links between records. We will represent the user views, or application views of data, by means of bubble charts and will combine them, a step at a time, eliminating redundancies. We will include not every possible link between the data item but only those that end users or application programs employ. The method is tedious to do by hand but is easy to do by computer. The input to the process must correctly identify the associations among data items in each user view. *The output is then automatically in fourth normal form.*

The technique can be applied to the narrow perspective of databases designed for a specific set of applications, or to the broader perspective of building enterprise data models. In doing *enterprise* data modeling, the data administrator tries to create a structure representing the inherent properties of the data independently of any one application. This is a big task and needs assistance from many types of end users. It requires multiple reiterations in which the data administrator and the users examine the data to determine whether the model meets their needs now and, as far as they can anticipate, in the future.

# Elimination of Redundancies

In the following grouping of data items, the link from $X$ to $Z$ is *probably* redundant:

If we know that $X \longrightarrow\!\!\!+ Y$ and $Y \longrightarrow\!\!\!+ Z$, this implies that $X \longrightarrow\!\!\!+ Z$ (i.e., there is one value of $Z$ for each value of $X$). In other words, $X$ identifies $Y$; $Y$ identifies $Z$; therefore, $X$ identifies $Z$.

Why did we say that the link from $X$ to $Z$ is "probably" redundant? Is it not *always* redundant? Unfortunately, we cannot be absolutely sure unless we know the meaning of the association. As we have illustrated earlier, it is possible to have more than one association between the same two data items:

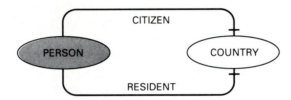

Therefore, before we delete $X \longrightarrow\!\!\!+ Z$, we must examine the meaning of the associations to be sure that $X \longrightarrow\!\!\!+ Z$ is *really* implied by $X \longrightarrow\!\!\!+ Y$ and $Y \longrightarrow\!\!\!+ Z$.

In the following case we could not delete it. An employee has a telephone number:

The employee reports to a next of kin:

The next of kin also has a telephone number:

Combining these gives us

It would not be valid to assume that EMPLOYEE ———+ TELEPHONE# is redundant and delete it. The employee's telephone number is different from the next of kin's and we want both:

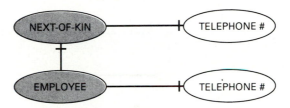

Because TELEPHONE# is an attribute, we can have a separate data item with this name associated with both EMPLOYEE and NEXT-OF-KIN.

The same pattern of associations could have occurred if all the data items in question had been keys.

In this case the links between the three key data items would be left as shown.

Nevertheless, the situation when we have

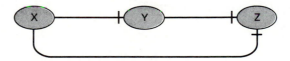

and cannot delete $X$ ———+ $Z$ is the exception rather than the rule. We will use the rule that one-to-one redundancies can be removed, but each time we use this rule we must look carefully too ensure that we have a genuine redundancy.

Sometimes redundancies can be removed in longer strings of links. Thus in the case

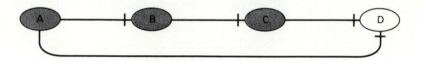

$A \longlongrightarrow D$ is a candidate for removal.

It should be noted that crow's-feet links cannot be removed. There is nothing necessarily redundant in the following:

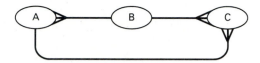

# Candidate Keys

We defined a primary key as a *bubble with one or more one-to-one links leaving it*. There is one exception to this definition—the situation in which we have more than one *candidate key*; more than one data item identifying the other data items in a group:

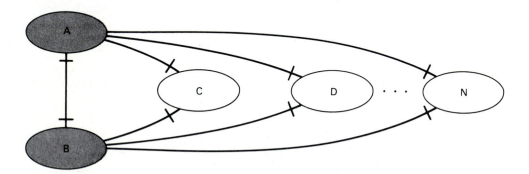

A and B in this case are equivalent. Each identifies the other; hence both identify C, D, ..., N. There is redundancy in this diagram. We could remove $A \longrightarrow C$, $A \longrightarrow D, ..., A \longrightarrow N$. Alternatively, we could remove $B \longrightarrow C$, $B \longrightarrow D, ..., B \longrightarrow N$.

The designer might decide that A is the candidate key that he wants to employ. A, for example, might be EMPLOYEE# and B is EMPLOYEE-NAME. The designer then deletes the links B ———+ C, B ———+ D, . . ., B ———+ N:

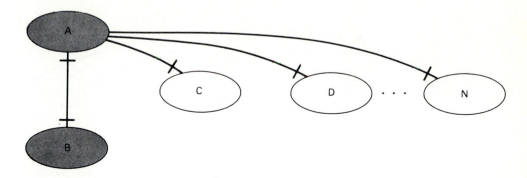

Candidate keys are not as common as this example might suggest. EMPLOYEE-NAME would not normally be represented as identifying EMPLOYEE# because two employees could have the same name. EMPLOYEE# is the unique identifier. Occasionally, there is a genuine A ———+ B relationship that should be left in the graph: for example, EMPLOYEE# ———+ SOCIAL SECURITY#. The designer must make a decision about which redundant links are deleted.

# Transitive Dependencies

The input views to the synthesis process should contain no *hidden* primary keys. In other words, there should be no *transitive dependencies*. The following purchase-order master record contains a transitive dependency:

| ORDER# | SUPPLIER# | SUPPLIER-NAME | SUPPLIER-ADDRESS | ORDER-DATE | DELIVERY-DAY | $-TOTAL |
|--------|-----------|---------------|------------------|------------|--------------|---------|

ORDER# is the key. It might be tempting to diagram this record as

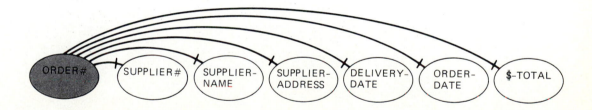

However, SUPPLIER-NAME and SUPPLIER-ADDRESS are identified by SUPPLIER#. The record should therefore be diagrammed as follows:

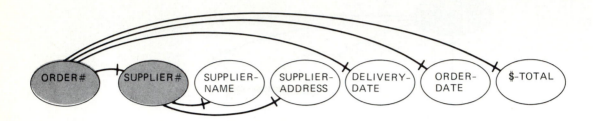

This process of removing transitive dependencies is essentially equivalent to the conversion to *third normal form* discussed in Appendix VI and Chapter 13.

In the design technique discussed in this appendix, transitive dependencies will be removed from a user's view when they are diagrammed, making all the user's attributes directly, not transitively, dependent on a key. This is done before they are fed into the synthesis process.

# Concatenated Keys

As discussed earlier, concatenated keys may be necessary. Price, for example, may be identified by a combination of CUSTOMER-TYPE, STATE, DISCOUNT, and PRODUCT.

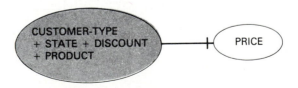

When the modeling process encounters a concatenated key such as this, it *automatically* makes the component data items of the key into data-item bubbles in their own right in the model. In other words, it explodes the concatenated key:

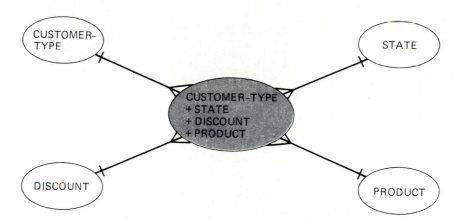

Some of these data items might become keys themselves, for example, PRODUCT; others may remain attributes.

In the final synthesis, those that still remain merely attributes may be deleted because they already exist in the concatenated key. They are deleted if they are not used as separate data items.

## Intersection Data

In some types of database software, data can be related to the *association* between data items. A part, for example, may be supplied by several vendors, each of whom charges a different price for it. The data item PRICE cannot be associated with the PART record alone or with the SUPPLIER record alone. It can only be associated with the combination of the two. Such information is sometimes called *intersection data*—data associated with the association between records.

Figure VIII.3 shows a more complex example of intersection data. Products made by a factory are composed of subassemblies and parts. In the factory database are records called PRODUCT, SUBASSEMBLY and PART. These records are different in composition. They might be linked as shown in the schema of Fig. VIII.3. Associated with each link is a number that tells how many of a given part are in a given subassembly or product, and how many subassemblies are in a product. For example, product 1001 contains 1 of subassembly *X*, 2 of subassembly *Y*, and 4 of part 610. In general, a structure something like that in Fig. VIII.3 gives a *bill of materials* showing a breakdown of the products for manufacturing purposes.

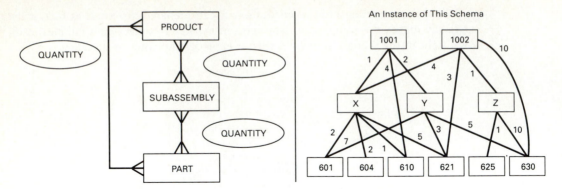

FIGURE VIII.3 A bill-of-materials database. In this illustration there is much intersection data. Extra records (segments) can be created to store intersection data, as in Fig. VIII.5.

Many-to-many associations are often encountered. They are common in the encyclopedia structure, as discussed in Appendix IV. For example:

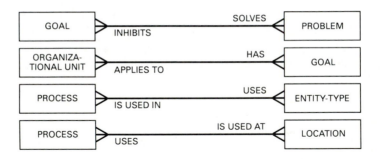

The tools for planning and analysis produce a matrix mapping the two types of data in these cases, as in Fig. VIII.4. The boxes in the matrix contain intersection data. Sometimes, as in Fig. VIII.4, the intersection data consist of only one attribute:

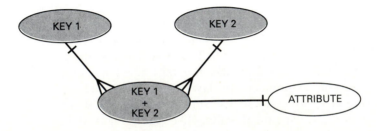

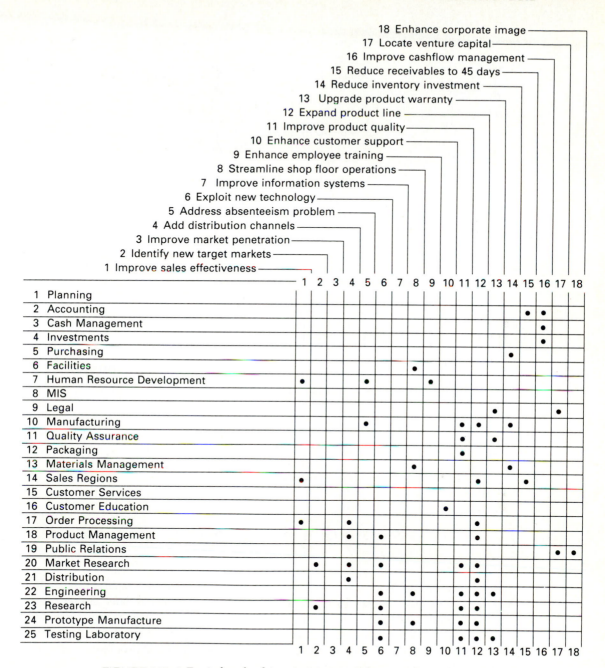

FIGURE VIII.4 Tactical goals of an enterprise mapped against its organizational units.

Two examples of intersection data:

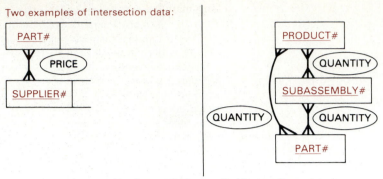

Intersection data could be handled by creating
an exta record (segment) containing the intersection
data and the concatenated key of the records (segments)
associated with it. The keys are shown in red.

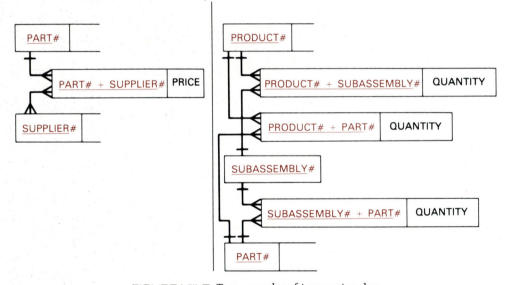

FIGURE VIII.5 Two examples of intersection data.

It is necessary to be cautious with many-to-many associations. Usually, there will be intersection data associated with the pair of data items, sooner or later. If there are no intersection data to start with, they are likely to be added later as the database evolves. If intersection data are associated with records having keys $A$ and $B$, those data are identified by a concatenated key $A + B$. Figure VIII.5 shows two examples of intersection data and how they might be handled.

A data modeling tool may take any many-to-many link and insert a concatenated key:

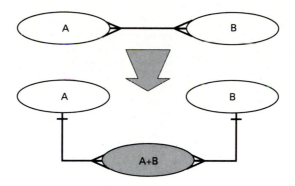

It might ask the analysis to identify possible attributes of the $A + B$ key.

Canonical modeling is an attempt to find the most *stable* data model. It therefore adds to the $A + B$ key rather than risking it being added to later with a possible need to restructure and rewrite programs.

# Two-Way Mapping Between Primary Keys

When the modeling identifies a mapping *between keys* the designer should *always* add the mapping in the opposite direction. This is done when building an entity-relationship model and should be done in the same way during the synthesis process. The design tool should ask the designer to fill in a panel like that in Fig. VIII.6. If the answer indicates that a many-to-many relationship exists, a follow-on window may ask about intersection data.

# Intersecting Attributes

A problem that sometimes exists in the synthesized structure is that an *attribute* may be attached to more than one primary key. In other words, it has more than one one-to-one link pointing to it. This is sometimes called an **intersecting attribute**. It cannot remain in such a state in the final synthesis. An attribute in a canonical model can be owned by only one key. Box VIII.1 illustrates an intersecting attribute and shows three ways of dealing with it. There should be no intersecting attributes on the final canonical graph.

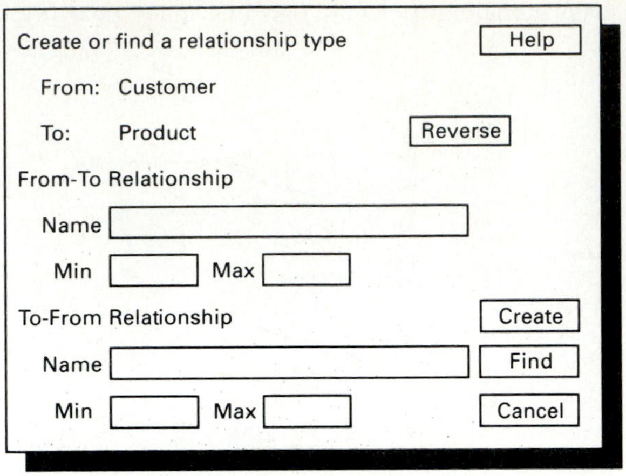

FIGURE VIII.6 A window for the designer to fill in, asking for details of the association between entities or primary keys. The same window is used to find or display a relationship.

## Isolated Attributes

An isolated attribute is an attribute that is not identified by a primary key. It is a bubble with no one-to-one links entering or leaving it, although there will be one-to-many links.

An isolated attribute should be treated in one of the following ways:

1. It may be implemented as a repeating attribute in a variable-length record.
2. It may be treated as a solitary-key—a one-data-item record.

Often, it results from an error in interpretation of the user's data; so the meaning related to it should be carefully checked.

## Record Sequence

In certain user views the *sequence* in which the data are presented to the application program or displayed on a terminal is critical. However, the canonical model does not indicate the sequence in which records are stored. *In general, it is undesirable to state a record sequence in the model because different applications of the data might require the records in a different sequence.*

In a database of book titles, for example, one application might want a logical file of book titles in alphabetical order, another might want them ordered by author, another by Library of Congress number. The different sequencing can be indicated by secondary keys: bubbles with a one-to-many link to BOOKTITLE.

**BOX VIII. 1    Intersecting Attributes Must Be Reorganized**

The following graph contains an intersecting attribute:

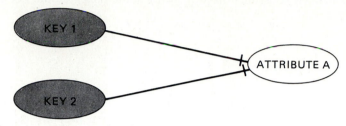

An intersecting attribute can be avoided in one of the following three ways:

1. All but one link to it may be replaced with equivalent links via an existing key:

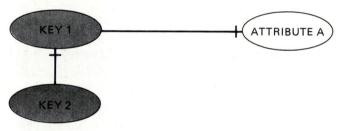

2. Redundant versions of it may be connected to each associated key:

3. It may be made into a key with no attributes:

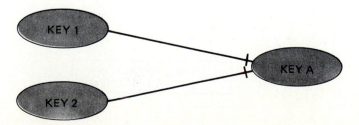

When the model is converted to a physical representation, it is necessary to state the record sequencing. This is a statement that should be part of the physical rather than the logical description of data. Some *logical* data description languages require statements about the order of records. This information must then be added when the canonical model is converted to the software schema. The enthusiasts of *relational* databases stress that the sequencing of the tuples should not be part of the *logical* data description.

# Shipping Example

Now we will examine an example selected to illustrate how intelligent human attention is needed to the *meaning* of the links when they are candidates for deletion. The application relates to the movement of cargo by sea. A company operates a fleet of cargo ships that visit many ports. Box VIII.2 shows views of the data that various

---

## BOX VIII.2   A Shipping Example: Seven Input Views

### Input View 1
Information is stored about each ship. The key is VESSEL#, and access is also required by OWNER.

| VESSEL # | VESSEL-NAME | TONNAGE | DETAILS | COUNTRY-OF-DESTINATION | OWNER | LENGTH | VOYAGE |
|---|---|---|---|---|---|---|---|

### Input View 2
A ship goes on many voyages and stops at many ports. It is necessary to print its itinerary.

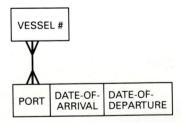

| PORT | DATE-OF-ARRIVAL | DATE-OF-DEPARTURE |
|---|---|---|

## Input View 3

A shipper may have many consignments of goods in transit. They are given a consignment identification number. A list can be obtained, when requested, of what consignment a shipper has in each shipment. Information is also required of shipments to each consignee.

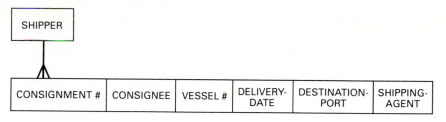

| SHIPPER | | | | | |
|---|---|---|---|---|---|

| CONSIGNMENT # | CONSIGNEE | VESSEL # | DELIVERY-DATE | DESTINATION-PORT | SHIPPING-AGENT |
|---|---|---|---|---|---|

## Input View 4

The fourth user view is the BILL-OF-LADING. A BILL-OF-LADING relates to a given consignment of goods. Large containers are used for shipping the goods. A BILL-OF-LADING relates to goods in one container. If a shipper's goods fill more than one container, a separate BILL-OF-LADING is used for each container.

| BILL-OF-LADING # | SHIPPER | CONSIGNEE | CONSIGNMENT # | SHIPPING AGENT |
|---|---|---|---|---|
| | BILL-OF-LADING-DATE | SAILING-DATE | CONTAINER # | |
| | ORIGINATION-PORT | DESTINATION-PORT | TOTAL-CHARGE | |

| ITEM # | NO-OF-PIECES | COMMODITY-CODE | WEIGHT | CHARGE |
|---|---|---|---|---|

*(Continued)*

BOX VIII.2   Continued

## Input View 5

A shipping agent wants a list of what containers he has in shipment, and what consignments of goods they contain.

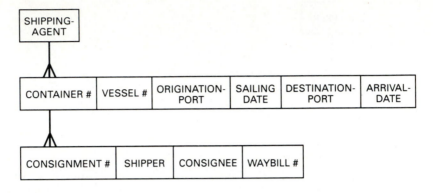

| CONTAINER # | VESSEL # | ORIGINATION-PORT | SAILING DATE | DESTINATION-PORT | ARRIVAL-DATE |

| CONSIGNMENT # | SHIPPER | CONSIGNEE | WAYBILL # |

## Input View 6

Details of the containers are required.

| CONTAINER # | OWNER | TYPE | SIZE | VESSEL-NAME | DESTINATION-PORT | ARRIVAL-DATE |

## Input View 7

For a given voyage of each vessel, a list is required of what containers are to be loaded at each port. Details of the container size, type, and handling instructions are needed for loading purposes. Similarly, a list of what containers should be taken *off* the vessel is needed.

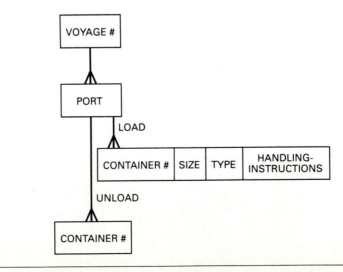

## Input View 1

Input view 1 appears simple, but VOYAGE should not be in the same data group as the other data items. A vessel can go on many voyages. A one-to-many link from VESSEL to VOYAGE is needed.

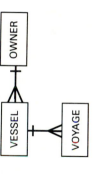

DATA ITEMS:

| Select One: | | | | | | |
|---|---|---|---|---|---|---|
| NAME : | PRIMARY KEY: | CANDIDATE KEY: | FOREIGN KEY: | ATTRIBUTE ONLY: | POSSIBLE ENTITY TYPE: | SEARCH KEY: |

Data items:
VESSEL #
VESSEL-NAME
TONNAGE
DETAILS
COUNTRY-OF-REGISTRATION
OWNER
LENGTH

MORE    ENTER    CANCEL

Owner is marked here as a *foreign key*, so the tool requests that it be linked to VESSEL on the entity-relationship diagram.

(Continued)

699

BOX VIII.3 Continued

## Input View 2

In input view 2 we need to ask: What identifies DATE-OF-ARRIVAL and DATE-OF-DEPARTURE? The stopping of a ship at a port. Is VESSEL # + PORT an adquate key? If you know VESSEL# + PORT, does that identify DATE-OF-ARRIVAL? Not completely, because the vessel stops at the same port many times. VESSEL# + PORT + DATE-OF-ARRIVAL would be a complete key for identifying the itinerary records. In practice, the shipping company gives each voyage a number. The itinerary entries can therefore be identified by VOYAGE# + PORT. VOYAGE# identifies VESSEL#. The view is redrawn as follows:

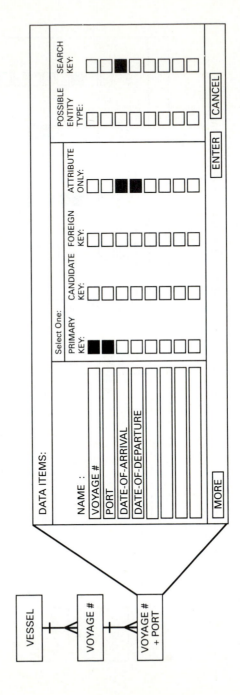

PORT is automatically made an entity. The tool may ask the analyst to enter the primary key of PORT: PORT NAME.

## Input View 3

Input view 3 is straightforward except that we need to ask whether DESTINA-TION-PORT is the same as PORT in view 2. It is. Again, is DELIVERY-DATE the same as DATE-OF-ARRIVAL in view 2? The data administrator decides that these are different dates. DATE-OF-ARRIVAL is the scheduled docking date of the vessel, and DELIVERY-DATE is the estimated date of delivery to the customer.

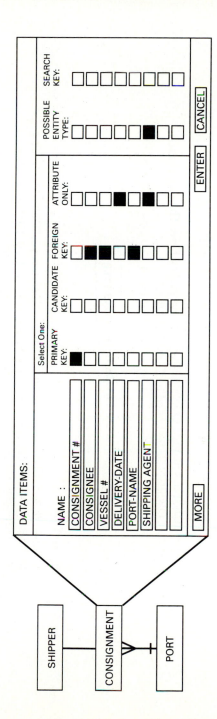

(Continued)

The analyst has marked CONSIGNEE as a foreign key here. The tool requests that the CONSIGNEE be linked to CONSIGNMENT.

### Input View 4

In input view 4 there is a hidden transitive dependency. CONSIGNMENT# identifies CONSIGNEE, SHIPPER, SHIPPING-AGENT, CONTAINER#, ORIGINATION-PORT, DESTINATION-PORT, and SAILING-DATE. It is necessary to ask whether *one* consignment has *one* bill of lading, and vice versa. It is decided that if the consignment is split, there would be more than one bill of lading. Again does one consignment always relate to one container? It is decided that a consignment could be split into two or more containers, and a container can contain multiple consignments.

Both ORIGINATION-PORT and DESTINATION-PORT are the same as PORT in view 2. They can be handled by labeled associations to the entity PORT:

BOX VIII.3  Continued

702

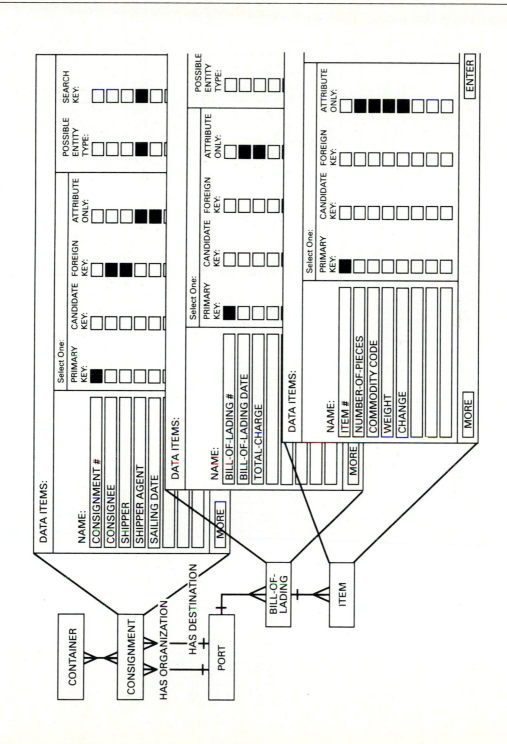

BOX VIII.3 Continued

## Input View 5

View 5 contains the data item WAYBILL#. It is realized that this is called BILL-OF-LADING# in view 4. It is therefore changed to BILL-OF-LADING#.

There is another problem in view 5. CONTAINER# does not, by itself, identify any of the data items that are linked to it. The same container can go on many voyages. To identify VESSEL#, SAILING-DATE, and so on, we need a concatenated key CONTAINER# + VOYAGE#, as follows:

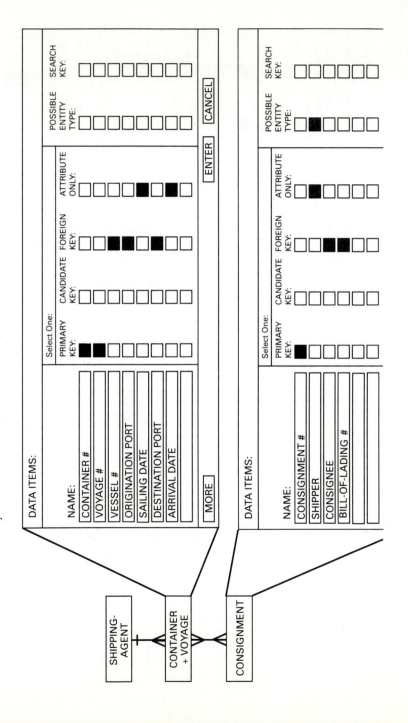

## Input View 6

View 6 mixes up two types of data. Some data are properties of the container, regardless of where it is. Some are properties of the container on this particular voyage. View 6 is split into data items identified by CONTAINER# and data items identified by CONTAINER# + VOYAGE#, as follows:

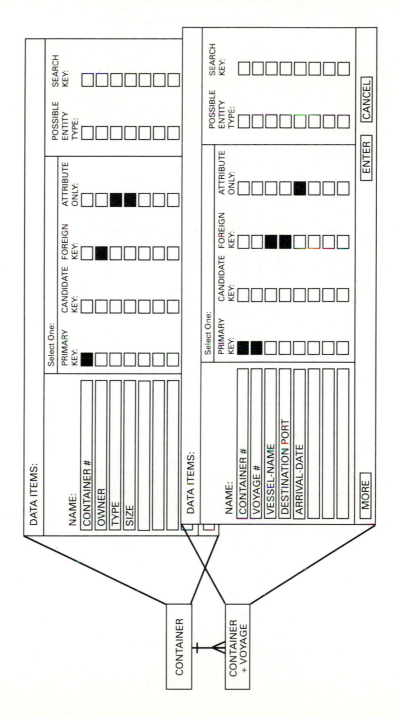

*(Continued)*

BOX VIII.3 Continued

### Input View 7

View 7 also has a problem. A vessel stops at the same port many times. We need VOYAGE# + PORT to identify what containers are to be loaded and unloaded.

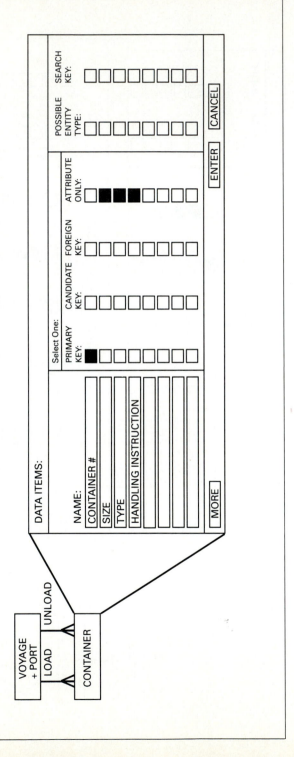

# BOX VIII.4    Synthesis of the Views (produced by Data Designer II)

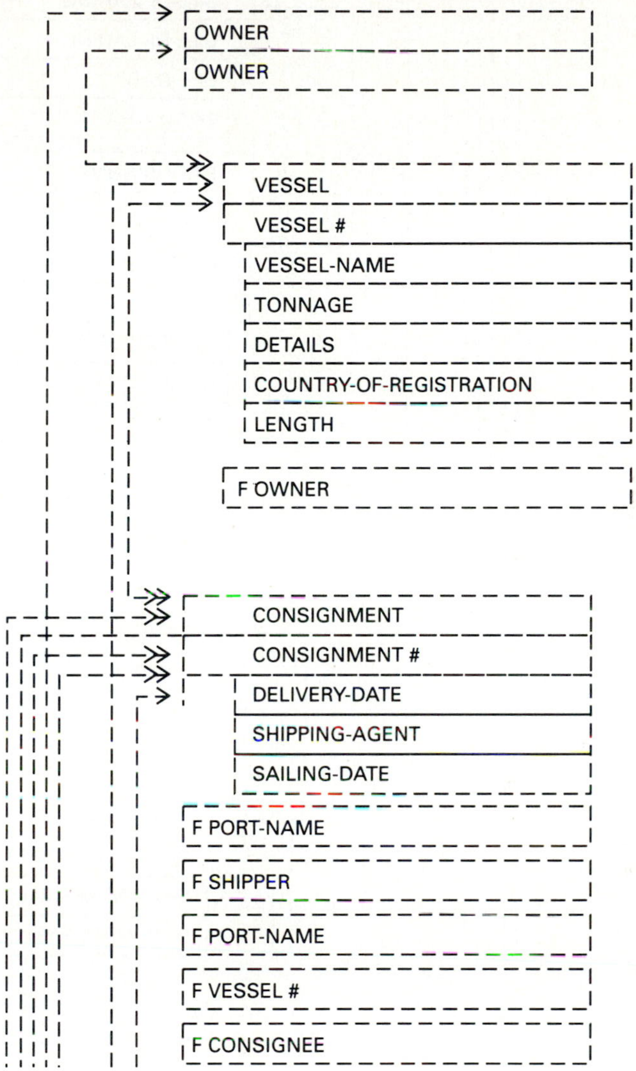

OWNER

OWNER

VESSEL

VESSEL #

I VESSEL-NAME

I TONNAGE

I DETAILS

I COUNTRY-OF-REGISTRATION

I LENGTH

F OWNER

CONSIGNMENT

CONSIGNMENT #

DELIVERY-DATE

SHIPPING-AGENT

SAILING-DATE

F PORT-NAME

F SHIPPER

F PORT-NAME

F VESSEL #

F CONSIGNEE

*(Continued)*

BOX VIII.4    Continued

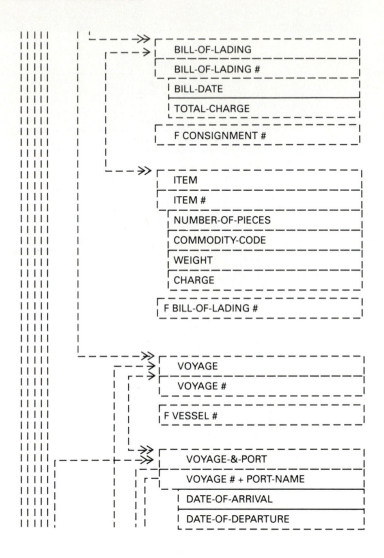

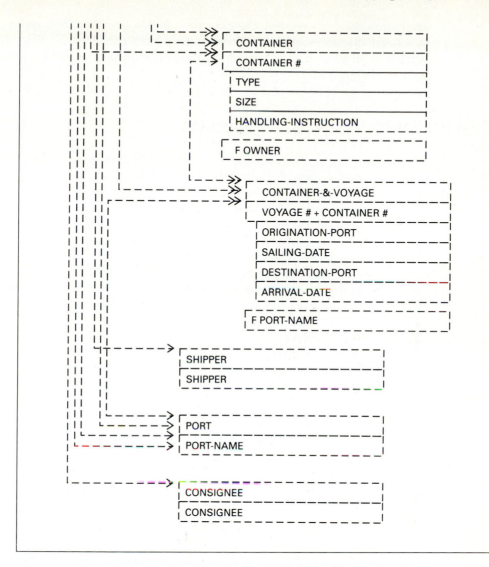

application designers require. The example is *highly* simplified from reality. For ease of tutorial diagramming, many *attributes* have been combined or omitted, and the number of views is small. A real bill of lading typically contains about 65 data items, not the 15 shown here.

# Clarification of User Views

Before attempting to synthesize the views in Box VIII.2, we need to clarify their structure. As is often the case, they are drawn loosely in Box VIII.2 (although not as loosely as often in real life!). The drawings of BOX VIII.2 contain various traps for the unwary. Some of them are incorrect representations of data. Before reading further we suggest that the reader examine BOX VIII.2 looking for misrepresentations of data. We gave BOX VIII.2 to one senior systems analyst, and after trying for a week, he was unable to find some of the misrepresentations in it.

To clarify the input views, they may be drawn as bubble charts. The data administrator or analyst needs to ask the following question for each data item that is synthesized into a data model: On what is it functionally dependent? In different words: What data item (or items) identifies it? The single-headed arrow links between the data items *must* be correct.

Box VIII.3 shows a cleaned-up version of the views being entered into a synthesis tool. In practice, an entity-relationship diagram should exist from an ISP study before the entry of the views, as in Box VIII.3. The views are shown synthesized in Box VIII.4.

# Procedure for Data Use Analysis

The following procedure may be modified with MediaScribe to meet the needs of the particular situation.

Determine what transaction types the database will support.

Establish or extract a data model containing the data for all these transactions.

Add average cardinality to all relationships in the data model.

Determine what the peak hour is.
There may be more than one peak hour for different types of transactions. For example, a peak for interactive transactions may occur at a different time from the peak for batch operations.

For each transaction type:

Determine the number of transactions in the peak hour.
Obtain an action diagram for the transaction.

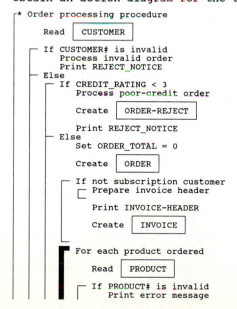

```
* Order processing procedure

    Read   CUSTOMER

    If CUSTOMER# is invalid
        Process invalid order
        Print REJECT_NOTICE
    Else
        If CREDIT_RATING < 3
            Process poor-credit order

            Create   ORDER-REJECT

            Print REJECT_NOTICE
        Else
            Set ORDER_TOTAL = 0

            Create   ORDER

            If not subscription customer
                Prepare invoice header

                Print INVOICE-HEADER

                Create   INVOICE

            For each product ordered

                Read   PRODUCT

                If PRODUCT# is invalid
                    Print error message
```

```
          ┌ Else
          ├ If QTY_ON_HAND < QTY_ORDERED

                 Create │ BACKORDER │

                 Print BACKORDER_NOTICE
          └ Else
                 LINE_ITEM_PRICE = CATALOG_PRICE
                 LINE-TOTAL =QTY_ORDERED * LINE_ITEM_PRICE
                 ORDER_TOTAL = ORDER_TOTAL + LINE_TOTAL

                 Create │ ORDER-PRODUCT │

              ┌ If not subscription customer

                   Create │ INVOICE-PRODUCT │

                   Print INVOICE-LINE


          ORDER_TOTAL = ORDER_TOTAL * [1 - DISCOUNT / 100]
          ORDER_STATUS = 0

          Update │ ORDER │

        ┌ If not subscription customer

             Update │ INVOICE │

             Print INVOICE-TOTAL
```

**Ensure that the action diagram contains all the data accesses.**
**Ensure that the data model supports all the accesses.**
**Print details of access paths on the action diagram.**

```
  ┌* Order processing procedure

       Read │ CUSTOMER │

       ***Access path from Entry to CUSTOMER ****************************************
   ┌ If CUSTOMER# is invalid
        Process invalid order
        Print REJECT_NOTICE
   ├ Else
     ┌ If CREDIT_RATING < 3
          Process poor-credit order
          Print REJECT_NOTICE
     └ Else
          Set ORDER_TOTAL = 0

          Create │ ORDER │

          ***Access path from CUSTOMER to ORDER ****************************
        ┌ If not subscription customer
        ┌ Prepare invoice header

             Print INVOICE-HEADER

             Create │ INVOICE │

             ***Access path from CUSTOMER to INVOICE *************************

        For each product ordered

             Read │ PRODUCT │

             ***Access path from Entry to PRODUCT ****************************
        ┌ If PRODUCT# is invalid
             Print error message
        ├ Else
          ┌ If QTY_ON_HAND < QTY_ORDERED

               Create │ BACKORDER │

               ***Access path from ORDER to BACKORDER *******************
               Print BACKORDER_NOTICE
```

```
                        ─ Else
                              LINE_ITEM_PRICE = CATALOG_PRICE
                              LINE-TOTAL =QTY_ORDERED * LINE_ITEM_PRICE
                              ORDER_TOTAL = ORDER_TOTAL + LINE_TOTAL

                              Create   ┌─────────────────┐
                                       │  ORDER-PRODUCT  │
                                       └─────────────────┘

                                ***Access path from ORDER to ORDER-PRODUCT******************
                              ─ If not subscription customer

                                  Create   ┌───────────────────┐
                                           │  INVOICE-PRODUCT  │
                                           └───────────────────┘

                                    ***Access path from INVOICE to INVOICE-PRODUCT**********
                                    Print INVOICE-LINE


                          ORDER_TOTAL = ORDER_TOTAL * [1 - DISCOUNT / 100]
                          ORDER_STATUS = 0

                          Update   ┌─────────┐
                                   │  ORDER  │
                                   └─────────┘

                          ***Access path from CUSTOMER to ORDER *****************************
                        ─ If not subscription customer

                            Update   ┌───────────┐
                                     │  INVOICE  │
                                     └───────────┘

                              ***Access path from CUSTOMER to INVOICE **************************
                              Print INVOICE-TOTAL
```

```
  ─ Add the mean cardinality of access paths to the diagram
    (automatically).

    ┌* Order processing procedure

          Read   ┌────────────┐
                 │  CUSTOMER  │
                 └────────────┘

          ***Access path from Entry to CUSTOMER ***************************************
          ***Average path cardinality: NA *********************************************
        ─ If CUSTOMER# is invalid
              Process invalid order
              Print REJECT_NOTICE
        ─ Else
            ┌ If CREDIT_RATING < 3
                  Process poor-credit order
                  Print REJECT_NOTICE
            ─ Else
                  Set ORDER_TOTAL = 0

                  Create   ┌─────────┐
                           │  ORDER  │
                           └─────────┘

                  ***Access path from CUSTOMER to ORDER *****************************
                  ***Average path cardinality: 5 ************************************
                ┌ If not subscription customer
                ┌ Prepare invoice header

                    Print INVOICE-HEADER

                    Create   ┌───────────┐
                             │  INVOICE  │
                             └───────────┘

                    ***Access path from CUSTOMER to INVOICE **************************
                    ***Average path cardinality: 5 **********************************

          For each product ordered

              Read   ┌───────────┐
                     │  PRODUCT  │
                     └───────────┘

              ***Access path from Entry to PRODUCT ***************************
              ***Average path cardinality: NA ********************************
            ─ If PRODUCT# is invalid
                  Print error message
            ─ Else
                ┌ If QTY_ON_HAND < QTY_ORDERED

                      Create   ┌─────────────┐
                               │  BACKORDER  │
                               └─────────────┘

                      ***Access path from ORDER to BACKORDER *********************
                      ***Average path cardinality: 0.04*************************
                      Print BACKORDER_NOTICE
```

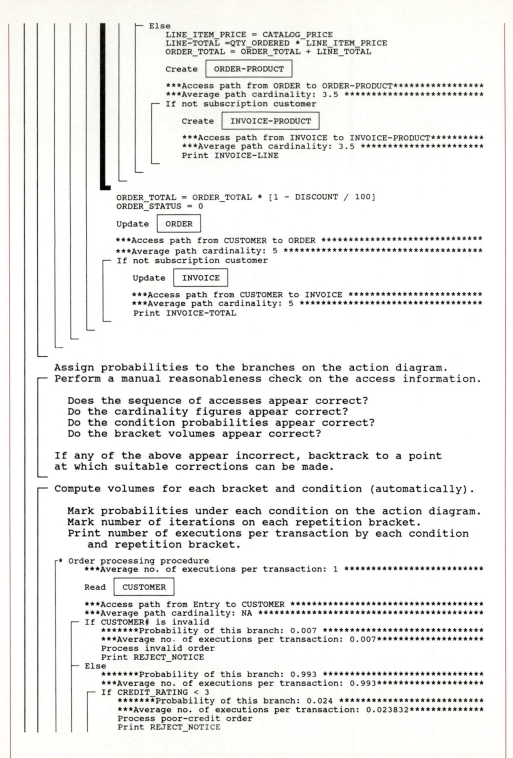

```
          ┌─ Else
          │      LINE_ITEM_PRICE = CATALOG_PRICE
          │      LINE-TOTAL =QTY_ORDERED * LINE_ITEM_PRICE
          │      ORDER_TOTAL = ORDER_TOTAL + LINE_TOTAL
          │
          │      Create  │ ORDER-PRODUCT │
          │
          │      ***Access path from ORDER to ORDER-PRODUCT*****************
          │      ***Average path cardinality: 3.5 **************************
          │   ┌─ If not subscription customer
          │   │
          │   │      Create  │ INVOICE-PRODUCT │
          │   │
          │   │      ***Access path from INVOICE to INVOICE-PRODUCT**********
          │   │      ***Average path cardinality: 3.5 *********************
          │   │      Print INVOICE-LINE

      ORDER_TOTAL = ORDER_TOTAL * [1 - DISCOUNT / 100]
      ORDER_STATUS = 0

      Update  │ ORDER │

      ***Access path from CUSTOMER to ORDER *****************************
      ***Average path cardinality: 5 **********************************
   ┌─ If not subscription customer
   │
   │      Update  │ INVOICE │
   │
   │      ***Access path from CUSTOMER to INVOICE ************************
   │      ***Average path cardinality: 5 *******************************
   │      Print INVOICE-TOTAL
```

Assign probabilities to the branches on the action diagram.
Perform a manual reasonableness check on the access information.

   Does the sequence of accesses appear correct?
   Do the cardinality figures appear correct?
   Do the condition probabilities appear correct?
   Do the bracket volumes appear correct?

If any of the above appear incorrect, backtrack to a point
at which suitable corrections can be made.

Compute volumes for each bracket and condition (automatically).

   Mark probabilities under each condition on the action diagram.
   Mark number of iterations on each repetition bracket.
   Print number of executions per transaction by each condition
      and repetition bracket.

```
 ┌* Order processing procedure
 │    ***Average no. of executions per transaction: 1 **************************
 │
 │      Read  │ CUSTOMER │
 │
 │    ***Access path from Entry to CUSTOMER ***********************************
 │    ***Average path cardinality: NA ****************************************
 │ ┌─ If CUSTOMER# is invalid
 │ │    *******Probability of this branch: 0.007 ****************************
 │ │    ***Average no. of executions per transaction: 0.007*****************
 │ │    Process invalid order
 │ │    Print REJECT_NOTICE
 │ ┌─ Else
 │ │    *******Probability of this branch: 0.993 ****************************
 │ │    ***Average no. of executions per transaction: 0.993*****************
 │ │ ┌─ If CREDIT_RATING < 3
 │ │ │    *******Probability of this branch: 0.024 **************************
 │ │ │    ***Average no. of executions per transaction: 0.023832**************
 │ │ │    Process poor-credit order
 │ │ │    Print REJECT_NOTICE
```

```
Else
    *******Probability of this branch: 0.976 *****************************
    ***Average no. of executions per transaction: 0.969168**************
    Set ORDER_TOTAL = 0

    Create   | ORDER |

    ***Access path from CUSTOMER to ORDER ****************************
    ***Average path cardinality: 5 *********************************
    If not subscription customer
        *******Probability of this branch: 0.3 *************************
        ***Average no. of executions per transaction: 0.2907504**********
        Prepare invoice header

        Print INVOICE-HEADER

        Create   | INVOICE |

        ***Access path from CUSTOMER to INVOICE ************************
        ***Average path cardinality: 5 *********************************

For each product ordered
    ***Average no. of iterations per bracket: 3.5 *****************
    ***Average no. of executions per transaction: 3.392088***********

    Read   | PRODUCT |

    ***Access path from Entry to PRODUCT *************************
    ***Average path cardinality: NA *******************************
    If PRODUCT# is invalid
        *******Probability of this branch: 0.005 ********************
        ***Average no. of executions per transaction: 0.01696044*******
        Print error message
    Else
        *******Probability of this branch: 0.995 ********************
        ***Average no. of executions per transaction: 3.2224836*******
        If QTY_ON_HAND < QTY-ORDERED
            *******Probability of this branch: 0.04 ******************
            ***Average no. of executions per transaction: 0.12889934***

            Create   | BACKORDER |

            ***Access path from ORDER to BACKORDER ********************
            ***Average path cardinality: 0.04*************************
            Print BACKORDER_NOTICE
        Else
            *******Probability of this branch: 0.96 ******************
            ***Average no. of executions per transaction: 3.0935842****
            LINE_ITEM_PRICE = CATALOG_PRICE
            LINE-TOTAL =QTY_ORDERED * LINE_ITEM_PRICE
            ORDER_TOTAL = ORDER_TOTAL + LINE_TOTAL

            Create   | ORDER-PRODUCT |

            ***Access path from ORDER to ORDER-PRODUCT*****************
            ***Average path cardinality: 3.5 *************************
            If not subscription customer
                *******Probability of this branch: 0.3 ************* ***
                ***Average no. of executions per transaction: .92807526*

                Create   | INVOICE-PRODUCT |

                ***Access path from INVOICE to INVOICE-PRODUCT**********
                ***Average path cardinality: 3.5 **********************
                Print INVOICE-LINE


ORDER_TOTAL = ORDER_TOTAL * [1 - DISCOUNT / 100]
ORDER_STATUS = 0

Update   | ORDER |

***Access path from CUSTOMER to ORDER ****************************
***Average path cardinality: 5 *********************************
If not subscription customer
    *******Probability of this branch: 0.3 ************************
    ***Average no. of executions per transaction: 0.2907504**********

    Update   | INVOICE |
```

```
                   ***Access path from CUSTOMER to INVOICE *************************
                   ***Average path cardinality: 5 *********************************
                   Print INVOICE-TOTAL
```

Perform a manual reasonableness check on the volumes.
    Do the figures for "average no. of executions per transaction"
    appear correct?

Compute peak hour volumes for each data access (automatically).

```
* Order processing procedure
    For each order

        Read    CUSTOMER

        ***Average no. of executions per peak hour: 200 ***********************
        If CUSTOMER# is invalid
        Else
            If CREDIT_RATING < 3
            Else

                Create    ORDER

                ***Average no. of executions per peak hour: 193.8336 ************
                If not subscription customer

                    Create    INVOICE

                    ***Average no. of executions per peak hour: 58.15008**********

                For each product ordered

                    Read    PRODUCT

                    ***Average no. of executions per peak hour: 678.4176**********
                    If PRODUCT# is invalid
                    Else
                        If QTY_ON_HAND < QTY_ORDERED

                            Create    BACKORDER

                            ***Average no. of executions per peak hour: 25.79868*
                        Else

                            Create    ORDER-PRODUCT

                            ***Average no. of executions per peak hour: 618.71684 **
                            If not subscription customer

                                Create    INVOICE-PRODUCT

                                ***Average no. of executions per peak hour: 185.61505


                Update    ORDER

                ***Average no. of executions per peak hour: 193.8336 ************
                If not subscription customer

                    Update    INVOICE

                    ***Average no. of executions per peak hour: 58.15008**********
```

Produce a table (automatically) showing the total accesses.
    Transaction Access

```
        ┌──────────────────────────────────────────────────────────┐
        │  Action diagram:  Order Processing Procedure             │
        │  Number of transactions in the peak hour:  200           │
        └──────────────────────────────────────────────────────────┘
```

```
                    Access to buffer, not to physical database (Y) ──────┐
                 Number of references in the peak hour ──────┐            │
                Number of references per transaction ──┐      │            │
              Average path cardinality ──────┐          │      │            │
            Type of access (C,R,U,D) ──┐      │          │      │            │
          Access to ──────┐            │      │          │      │            │
        Access from ──┐    │            │      │          │      │            │
      Number ──┐       │    │            │      │          │      │            │
```

| Number | Access from | Access to | Type | Avg path card. | Refs per trans. | Refs peak hour | Buffer |
|--------|-------------|-----------|------|------|-------|----------|---|
| 1 | Entry | CUSTOMER | R | NA | 1 | 200 | |
| 2 | CUSTOMER | ORDER | C | 5 | 0.969 | 193.834 | |
| 3 | CUSTOMER | INVOICE | C | 5 | 0.291 | 58.150 | |
| 4 | Entry | PRODUCT | R | NA | 3.392 | 678.418 | |
| 5 | ORDER | BACKORDER | C | 0.04 | 0.129 | 25.799 | |
| 6 | ORDER | ORDER—PRODUCT | C | 3.5 | 3.094 | 618.717 | |
| 7 | INVOICE | INVOICE—PRODUCT | C | 3.5 | 0.928 | 185.615 | |
| 8 | CUSTOMER | ORDER | U | 5 | 0.969 | 193.834 | Y |
| 9 | CUSTOMER | INVOICE | U | 5 | 0.291 | 58.150 | Y |
| | Total Number of References: | | | | 9.803 | 1960.532 | |

Determine whether the transaction is response critical.
Make a rough estimate of the transaction response time.
Assess the user's response—time need for the transaction.
Determine whether the database needs to be optimized physically
to achieve this response time.

Produce (automatically) a table aggregating the transaction accesses.
Access Table Consolidating the Accesses of Three Procedures

Action diagram 1:  Order Processing Procedure
Number of transactions in the peak hour:  200

Action diagram 2:  Customer Order Inquiry
Number of transactions in the peak hour:   30

Action diagram 3:  Invoice Follow—up
Number of transactions in the peak hour:  100

```
                  Access Number ──────────────────────┐
                Action Diagram ──────────────────────┐ │
              Number of references in the peak hour ──┐ │ │
            Number of references per transaction ──┐  │ │ │
          Average path cardinality ──────┐          │  │ │ │
        Type of access (C,R,U,D) ──┐      │          │  │ │ │
      Access to ──────┐            │      │          │  │ │ │
    Access from ──┐    │            │      │          │  │ │ │
```

| Access from | Access to | Type | Avg path card. | Refs per trans. | Refs peak hour | Action Diagram | Access Number |
|-------------|-----------|------|------|-------|---------|---|---|
| Entry | CUSTOMER | R | NA | 1 | 200 | 1 | 1 |
| Entry | CUSTOMER | R | NA | 0.99 | 27.9 | 2 | 1 |
| Entry | ORDER | R | NA | 1 | 100 | 3 | 1 |
| Entry | PRODUCT | R | NA | 3.392 | 678.418 | 1 | 4 |
| CUSTOMER | ORDER | C | 5 | 0.969 | 193.834 | 1 | 2 |
| CUSTOMER | ORDER | R | 5 | 4.95 | 148.5 | 2 | 2 |
| CUSTOMER | INVOICE | C | 5 | 0.291 | 58.150 | 1 | 3 |
| ORDER | ORDER—PRODUCT | C | 3.5 | 3.094 | 618.717 | 1 | 6 |
| ORDER | ORDER—PRODUCT | R | 3.5 | 17.325 | 519.75 | 2 | 3 |
| ORDER | ORDER—PRODUCT | R | 3.5 | 3.5 | 350 | 3 | 3 |
| ORDER | CUSTOMER | R | 1 | 1 | 100 | 3 | 2 |
| ORDER | INVOICE | C | 1.8 | 1.8 | 180 | 3 | 7 |
| ORDER | BACKORDER | C | 0.04 | 0.129 | 25.799 | 1 | 5 |
| ORDER | BACKORDER | R | 0.04 | 0.693 | 20.79 | 2 | 4 |

| ORDER | BACKORDER | C | 0.04 | 0.04 | 4 | 3 | 5 |
| ORDER—PRODUCT | INVOICE—PRODUCT | C | 0.96 | 3.36 | 336 | 3 | 6 |
| INVOICE | CUSTOMER | U | 1 | 1 | 100 | 3 | 8 |
| INVOICE | INVOICE—PRODUCT | C | 3.5 | 0.928 | 185.615 | 1 | 7 |

| | Total Number of References: | 3847.473 |

Produce (automatically) a table totaling the transaction accesses.

Total Access Table Consolidating Total Peak Hour Accesses

| Access from | Access to | Number of accesses in the peak hour |
|---|---|---|
| Entry | CUSTOMER | 227.9 |
| Entry | ORDER | 100 |
| Entry | PRODUCT | 678.418 |
| CUSTOMER | ORDER | 342.334 |
| CUSTOMER | INVOICE | 58.15 |
| ORDER | ORDER—PRODUCT | 1488.467 |
| ORDER | CUSTOMER | 100 |
| ORDER | INVOICE | 180 |
| ORDER | BACKORDER | 50.589 |
| ORDER—PRODUCT | INVOICE—PRODUCT | 336 |
| INVOICE | CUSTOMER | 100 |
| INVOICE | INVOICE—PRODUCT | 185.615 |
| | Total Number of References: | 3847.473 |

Note which paths in the data model are heavily loaded.
Determine what can be done to minimize the physical access time
in the DBMS for the most heavily used paths through the data model.

For example:

- Lay out records so that those that are logically together are physically close.

- Lay out records so that a disk access arm does not have to be moved to follow the heavily used path.

- Combine records to minimize physical input/output references for heavily used paths.

- Use physical rather than logical access paths in a DBMS such as IMS.

- Appropriately adjust the use of indices, pointers or hashing.

Reference

James Martin, Information Engineering (a trilogy)
Book III:  Design and Construction, Chapter 14, Box 14.1,
Prentice-Hall, Inc., Englewood Cliffs, New Jersey, 1990 (201—592—2261).

# Procedure for Physical Database Design

> The following procedure may be modified with MediaScribe to meet the needs of the particular situation.

Determine whether the data will be distributed.  (See Chapter 16.)

List and categorize the database procedures that will occur.

Extract a list of the relevant procedures from the encyclopedia. Categorize the procedures by types of data management system needed. The types of data management software may be categorized as follows:

1. File Systems

- These consist of simple data structures.

- They are often designed for one application, as opposed to multiapplication databases.

> good machine efficiency

2. Application Databases

- Database structures are designed to support a narrow group of applications.

> fairly good machine efficiency

3. Subject Databases

- All the data about specific data subjects are stored together.
- One copy, rather than redundant copies, is kept of all data.

> straightforward updating and consistency control

4. Information-Retrieval Systems

- Information is stored for retrieval with multiple, different search parameters.

• Extensive search indices or inverted files are used.

> not appropriate for data that are frequently updated

5. Decision-Support Systems

• These systems support multidimensional data structures that are optimized for highly flexible decision-support activities.

> inefficient or inadequate for high-volume data processing

Categorize the procedures by physical data independence criteria. Programs are categorized into one of the following three groups:

1. Programs written without consideration of physical database design:

• systems with low traffic volumes;
• systems that do not search large bodies of data.

The majority of systems in most installations are of this type.

2. Programs in which the data accesses are adjusted to fit the physical database design:

• programs that are used frequently enough to be worth tuning.

Such programs are tuned by a technician who understands the effects of physical database design.

3. Heavy-duty systems for which the data structures are changed to achieve optimal performance:

• systems with a high throughput (transactions per second);

• systems with a high daily load, which makes it desirable to reduce machine costs;

• systems that search large bodies of data.

Data structures are optimized for a particular application or group of applications.

List the database queries that are likely to be made.

Categorize the queries into one of the following types:

Single-Record Primary-Key Queries
A single record is accessed by means of its primary key.

Multiple-Record Primary-Key Queries
A simple program may be written for handling this type of query.

Anticipated Single-Record Searches

These are queries that require a search of a single logical file. Because they are anticipated, an efficient search index or other search mechanism can be set up.

Anticipated Multiple-Record Queries

These are queries that need a relational JOIN or the equivalent. Because they are anticipated, an efficient mechanism for handling the query can be set up.

Unanticipated Search or JOIN Queries

These queries are more expensive in terms of machine time. They can be extremely expensive with large databases.

Estimate the query volumes.

Determine whether more than one type of DBMS will be needed.

Determine whether the data will be split into separate databases.

Select the DBMS(s).

For each database, do the detailed design.

Obtain data usage information required for the design.
Determine what transaction types the database will support.
Establish or extract a data model containing the data for all these transactions.
Determine average cardinality for all relationships in the data model.
Determine what the peak hour is.
There may be more than one peak hour for different types of transactions. For example, a peak for interactive transactions may occur at a different time from the peak for batch operations.

Perform data-use analysis. (See Appendix IX-1 and Methodology Chart 14-1.

Determine the performance-critical aspects of the design.
Determine which transactions are response-critical.
Note which applications or runs most stress the design.
Produce (automatically) a table totaling the transaction accesses. (See Appendix IX-1 and Methodology Chart 14-1.)

Note which paths in the data model are heavily loaded .
Note which is batch and which is interactive use.

Consider security, auditability, restart, recovery and fallback.
Determine requirements for security.

How is invalid access to the data prevented?
How is unauthorized tampering with the data prevented?
What controls against hackers are needed?
What records should be stored off-site as protection in case of a catastrophe such as fire?
How often should off-site data be renewed?

Determine requirements for auditability.

How are unauthorized uses of the database detected?
How are invalid uses of the data prevented?
What batch or on-line audit programs are needed?

(Auditors' requirements are more complex than most systems analysts analysts realize; so auditors should be involved where appropriate in reviewing the design.)

Determine what accuracy controls are needed.

What accuracy controls does the DBMS software provide?
What additional accuracy controls are needed?
Will hash totals or other totals be used to validate data entry?

Determine the requirements for restart after failure.

How does the system restart after a failure of hardware, software
  or transmission?
What controls prevent data from being invalidated during a failure
  and subsequent restart?
How are partially processed transactions backed out?
Does the DBMS provide automatic backout under all circumstances?
Must additional support be developed?

Determine the requirements for recovery and for rebuilding damaged data.

How are single records reconstructed if accidentally damaged?
How are entire files restored or rebuilt if damaged?
What backup or archival data should be kept for recovery purposes?

Determine the requirements for fallback operation.

When a disk has crashed or a storage unit is inaccessible, does
  the system continue to operate in a mode of lower functionality?
What different fallback modes exist?

Evaluate the design techniques.
Determine what design tools are available for the DBMS selected.

Determine what can be done to minimize the physical access time
in the DBMS for the most heavily used paths through the data model.
For example:

• Lay out records so that those that are logically together
  are physically close.

• Lay out records so that a disk access arm does not have to
  be moved to follow the heavily used path.

• Combine records to minimize physical input/output references
  for heavily used paths.

• Use physical rather than logical access paths in a DBMS such as IMS.

• Appropriately adjust the use of indices, pointers or hashing.

Design the database.

Design is likely to proceed iteratively through the following steps
to converge on an appropriate design:

• Consider the alternate structures available for the DBMS.
• Design the stored record formats.
• Design the record clustering into storage media areas.
• Lay out the data on the storage media.
• Design the access methods.
• Adapt the programs to the design where necessary.

Design the operations facilities.

Design facilities needed for archiving.
Design facilities for reorganization and restructuring.
Design facilities for performance monitoring and tuning.
Design operational interfaces.

Design the implementation facilities.

Generate the database definitions for implementing the database.
Design the database test facilities.
Generate the data needed for testing.

Reference

James Martin, Information Engineering (a trilogy),
Book III:  Design and Construction, Chapter 15, Box 15.1,
Prentice-Hall, Inc., Englewood Cliffs, New Jersey, 1990 (201-592-2261).

# Procedure for Distributed Data Design

The following procedure may be modified with MediaScribe to meet the needs of the particular situation.

The steps listed below assume that, when the higher levels of analysis were done, the locations of functions, processes and procedures were recorded in the repository.

A good distribution design arranges data and programs into clusters so that each cluster has a high level of autonomy and there is a low level of interdependence between clusters.

Determine the procedures and data involved in the design.

- Extract the procedures and entity-types from the repository.
- Generate a matrix mapping procedures and entity-types.
- Validate the matrix to ensure that it is correct and complete.

Determine the locations involved in the design.

- Extract from the repository the locations where the work associated with each procedure is carried out.

- Generate a matrix mapping procedures and locations.

- Validate the matrix to ensure that no locations are missing.

Cluster the procedures into procedure-groups.

- Cluster the procedures into groups that are likely to be carried out at the same location. (We will refer to these as procedure-groups.) Use the procedure/location matrix for this.

- Generate (automatically) a matrix showing procedure-groups and locations.

   Mark the matrix with the locations where the procedure-group is physically performed.

   Mark the matrix with the locations where the procedure PROGRAM may be executed.

Cluster the entity-types into data-structures.

- Cluster the entity-types into entity-relationship structures containing entities that are likely to reside at the same location. (We will refer to these as data-structures.)  Use the entity/location matrix for this.

- Generate a matrix showing data-structures and locations (unfilled at this point).

Generate a matrix mapping procedure-groups and data-structures.

This matrix shows which data structures are accessed by each procedure-group.

Use this matrix to validate the clustering of entities into data-structures and of procedures into procedure-groups.

Mark the matrix with data accesses.
Use CREATE, READ, UPDATE and DELETE codes at the matrix intersections.

Fill in the data-structure/location matrix.

Examine the arguments for multiple distributed copies of data.

For each data-structure:

Decide whether multiple copies of the same data structure can exist.

Determine whether updates can be delayed and batched.

Determine whether the data in the data structure must be kept up-to-date to the second or whether updates can be delayed and batched.  (If updates can be delayed and batched, it is much easier to have multiple replicated copies of the data.)

Mark the possible locations of the data structure on the location/data-structure matrix.

Create a factor table for distribution of PROGRAMS.

List the reasons for centralizing data or decentralizing data. These may include the following:

- The data should be located where the program resides.
- Identical procedures are used at many locations.
- High availability is important.
- The software cannot maintain multiple synchronous copies.
- The data are used at one location only.
- The data are updated by one location only.
- Local users create and own the data.
- Local management is responsible for the data.
- There is local inventiveness in the use of the data.
- Data are highly sensitive to the subunit.
- There can be multiple copies of the data.
- Data transmission is expensive or undesirable.
- Very fast response time is needed.
- A departmental decision-support system is used.
- Data are used by centralized applications.
- Users in distant areas need the up-to-the-second version of the data.
- Users who travel among many locations need the up-to-the-second version of the data.

- Large searches or joins are required.
- Data security is vital.
- Auditability is a major concern.
- Application is maintained centrally.
- The power of a large computer is needed.
- The database is very large.
- Catastrophe protection is vital.
- The data are updated by many people in a department.
- There should be only one copy of the data.

Add to or edit the list of reasons.

List the strength of the reason applied to centralized computing, departmental computing, or personal computing:

Programs should execute on:

|  | Personal computer(s) | Local (shared) computer | Remote computer |
|---|---|---|---|
| **Reason:** | | | |
| Identical procedures used at many locations: | | | |
| High availability important: | | | |
| Etc... | | | |

Create a factor table for distribution of DATA.

List the reasons for centralizing data or decentralizing data.
Add to or edit the list of reasons.

List the strength of the reason applied to centralized data, departmental data or data on a personal computer:

Data structure should reside on:

| Reason: | Personal computer(s) | Local (shared) computer | Remote computer |
|---|---|---|---|
| Identical procedures used at many locations: | | | |
| High availability important: | | | |
| The data are used at one location only: | | | XXXX |
| The data are updated by one location only: | | | XXXX |
| Local users create and own the data: | | | XXXX |
| Local management is responsible for the data: | | | XXXX |
| Local inventiveness in the use of the data: | | | XXXX |
| Data are highly sensitive to the subunit: | | | XXXX |
| There can be multiple copies of the data: | | | XXXX |
| Data transmission is expensive or undesirable: | | | XXXX |
| Very fast response time is needed: | | | XXXX |
| A departmental decision-support system is used: | | | XXXX |
| Data are used by centralized applications: | XXXX | XXXX | |
| Users in distant areas need the up-to-the-second version of the data: | XXXX | XXXX | |
| Users who travel among many locations need the up-to-the-second version of the data: | XXXX | XXXX | |
| Large searches or joins are required: | XXXX | XXXX | |
| Data security is vital: | XXXX | XXXX | |
| Auditability is a major concern: | XXXX | XXXX | |
| Application is maintained centrally: | XXXX | XXXX | |

The power of a large computer is needed:
The database is very large:
Catastrophe protection is vital:
The data are updated
        by many people in a department:
There should be only one copy of the data:

| | |
|---|---|
| XXXX | XXXX |
| XXXX | XXXX |
| XXXX | XXXX |
| XXXX | |
| XXXX | |

Sum the weights in each category.

Decide which of the above reasons should dominate the decision about where the data are placed.

Categorize the data according to type of distribution:

Enter codes into the matrix for type of data distribution.

Categories of Data Distribution   (See reference.)

- Duplicated Data
- Subset Data
- Reorganized Data
- Partitioned Data
- Separate-Schema Data
- Incompatible Data

Codes for indicating types of data distribution:

M:   Mastercopy
V:   Variant (different-schema version at different locations)
D:   Duplicated data (identical data at different locations)
S:   Subset (an extracted subset of a larger database)
R:   Reorganized data
        (e.g., reorganized into a decision-support database)
P:   Partitioned data (same schema, different values)
I:   Incompatible data
T:   Teleprocessing access to data not stored at this location

Categorize the data according to whether multiple copies must have synchronous (up-to-the-second) updates or whether updates can be deferred (e.g., made at night).

Enter codes into the matrix to indicate this.

Codes for indicating synchronous or deferred updates:

DD:   Duplicated data with Deferred updates
SD:   Subset data with Deferred updates
RD:   Reorganized data with Deferred updates
DS:   Duplicated data with Synchronous updates
SS:   Subset with Synchronous updates
RS:   Reorganized data with Synchronous updates

Reference

James Martin, Information Engineering (a trilogy),
Book III:  Design and Construction, Chapter 16, Box 16.1,
Prentice-Hall, Inc., Englewood Cliffs, New Jersey, 1990 (201-592-2261).

# RAD Lifecycle

RAD Lifecycle

> The following procedure may be modified with MediaScribe to meet the needs of the particular situation.

Before the Project Begins

Essentials for Success before the Project Begins

1. The Project Manager must fully understand and be committed to a RAD methodology. (The project leader may manage more than one project).

2. A suitably high-level end-user executive (Executive Owner) must be committed to having the system and paying for it and must be determined to move fast.

3. The methodology should be clearly written, preferably in hyperdocument form, as in this document.

4. A suitable, fully integrated I-CASE toolset must be used, with a repository and the characteristics listed in Chapter 3.

5. The methodology should be customized to take maximum advantage of the toolset used.

6. A trained, experienced RAD Workshop Leader must be available, possibly from a consulting firm.

7. A trained, experienced SWAT Team must be available, possibly from a consulting firm.

Select the tools.

It is desirable to select one toolset and perfect its use. The methodology is highly dependent on a toolset that enables fast, easy design and a rapid cycle of modify-generate-test. The methodology is built around the toolset and adapted to it. Selecting the right toolset is highly critical.

The I-CASE environment should be well established with I.S. professionals well trained in the use of the toolset.

Characteristics (Capabilities) of the I-CASE Toolset

> I-CASE Toolset:  an integrated-CASE toolset with an intelligent central repository (encyclopedia).

The toolset should include the following:

• A complete data-modeling capability, with entity-relationship diagrams and the ability to represent normalized data.

- A complete process-modeling capability with decomposition diagrams, dependency diagrams and data-flow diagrams.

- The ability to display and cluster matrices and map processes against entities, showing how the processes use the entities.

- A versatile screen painter (which can be used very quickly in JAD sessions).

- Ability to link screens and responses into a dialog.

- A versatile report generator (which can be used very quickly in JAD sessions).

- The ability to draw the logic of processes with action (hyper) diagrams.

- The capability of fully checking the consistency and integrity of all of the preceding representations of information.

- The capability of converting the design directly into code that is machine-efficient.

---

The toolset should:

- be interactive;
- be quick and easy to use;
- give the most automated capability for design;
- convert the design directly into code;
- enable code to be generated and tested as quickly as possible;
- give the fastest possible cycle of generate-test-modify, generate-test-modify ...

---

Establish the methodology.

°° Adapt the methodology to the toolset.
Use and tune the methodology.
    The methodology should be applied to many projects and tuned on the basis of experience.

Select and train the practitioners.  (See Chapters 5 and 10.)

Essentials for Success in the Management of SWAT Teams

- Select top-quality, capable team members who are determined to rise to the challenge.

- Choose persons who work well together as a team. Adjust the team if necessary to make it "jell" and be as powerful as possible.

- Allow the team to develop a feeling of uniqueness and team pride.

- Keep successful teams together for many projects, and engender a high level of team spirit.

- Use the most powerful toolset.

- Ensure that the team is motivated for high speed and high quality.

- Use a methodology designed and tuned for high speed and high quality.

- Have the best possible training in the tools and methodology.

- Ensure full end-user participation.

- Structure the work so that each developer has a feeling of achieving something interesting and creative, with frequent closures.

- Establish clear goals and measurements, and rank the teams on how well they meet the goals.

- Ensure that the team keeps metrics of its performance. Allow it to make its own estimates prior to the Construction Phase.

- Employ powerful motivation techniques.

- Provide good SWAT-Team working conditions (Box 10.1).

- Pay attention to avoidance of burnout.

- Make the development process as enjoyable as possible.

- Sweep away any bureaucracy or factors that could slow down the SWAT-Team development.

- Avoid defensive, interfering management; leave the team free to build the system its own way.

RAD Workshop Leader

> a specialist who organizes and conducts the workshops for JRP (Chapter 7) and JAD (Chapter 8).

Human-Factors Expert

> a specialist in human factoring who is responsible for usability testing (Chapter 17).

Data Modeling Expert (Professional)

> a specialist with experience in data modeling, who can create data models rapidly and competently (Chapter 13).

Some professionals have experience in data modeling, are highly skilled at it, and can create correct models quickly. The Data Modeling Expert may be a data administrator or part of the data administration staff.

Initiate the project.

Determine the need for the system.
Write, in one page, the functions of the system.
Establish an Executive Sponsor.

Obtain commitment of the Executive Owner.

Development should not proceed unless a suitably high-level end-user executive is FULLY COMMITTED to having the system built and taking the necessary steps to make end-user managers move rapidly and commit the time needed for development and cutover.

Establish the I.S. team (from the I.S. Community).
Project Manager

> the person responsible for the overall development effort.

In a project with one Construction Team, this person may be the team leader.

Construction Team

> a small team of implementors, highly skilled with the toolset, who build the system -- typically two, three or four people (Chapter 10).

For large projects, there will be multiple Construction Teams (Chapter 12).

°° RAD Workshop Leader  (See separate entry.)
°° Human-Factors Expert  (See separate entry.)
°° Data Modeling Expert (Professional)  (See separate entry.)
Repository Manager

> the executive responsible for the I-CASE repository and its integrity.

A Repository Manager may control what reusable constructs are in the repository. He is particularly important in an environment of Information Engineering (Chapter 21) and reusable design (Chapters 15 and 22).

Customize the methodology for this system.

Select the appropriate variants of the methodology. They are:

Toolset Variants

The technical details are customized to the toolset used because different toolsets have somewhat different capabilities.

Timebox

The timebox variant sets a firm deadline on the Construction Phase. Refinements can be slipped, but the deadline can not (Chapter 11).

Combination of the Requirements Planning and User Design Phases

If the requirements are well known, obvious or simple, it is not necessary to have a separate JRP workshop. The JAD workshop should include the JRP activity.

If the user participants in the JRP and JAD workshops are to be the same, the workshops should be combined. (Usually, however, JRP participants are of a higher level than JAD participants.)

Parallel Development

Complex systems of, say, more than a thousand function points, are split into subsystems on which separate SWAT Teams work independently, with a coordinating model (Chapter 12).

Reusability

Reusable constructs are used to the maximum extent. The lifecycle is managed so that, where it creates new constructs, they are designed to be reusable if possible (Chapter 15).

Data Administration

The lifecycle employs existing data models (Chapter 20).

Information Engineering

The lifecycle is an integral part of an information-engineering methodology (Chapter 21).

Object-Oriented Reusability

An object-oriented approach to information engineering is used to achieve the maximum application-dependent reusability (Chapter 22).

These variants can be used in combination.

Adjust the lifecycle hyperdiagram to show the variants selected.

°° Requirements Planning Phase   (See Methodology Chart 7.)
°° User Design Phase   (See Methodology Chart 8.)
°° Construction Phase   (See Methodology Chart 10-2.)
— Cutover Phase

— Install and adjust the pilot system.
— Perform cutover.   (See Methodology Chart 19.)
— Set up the production procedures.
These include:

- the procedures for normal system operation;
- any manual or paperwork procedures that must accompany the new installation;
- the procedures for restart and recovery;
- the fallback procedures;
- the procedures for security;
- the audit procedures;
- the procedures for phasing out the old system when the new system is running satisfactorily.

Review the preceding procedures with the data center personnel to ensure their understanding.

Review with the end users to ensure their understanding.

— Install the production system environment.

- Install the initial production hardware.

- Confirm that a complete test of the hardware has been successfully completed.

- Coordinate with systems programming administration to schedule the installation.

- Install the software on the production system.

- Test that the software is correctly installed.

- Coordinate with vendors for the ongoing hardware installation at other sites.

— Perform data conversion.

- Execute the data conversion programs.
- Load existing data into the system's database.

- Load manually prepared data, if needed.
- Test the data loading and conversion to verify data quality.
- Review the results to ensure that acceptance test criteria are met.

Implement the new system in production.

- Move the new system to production mode, following the migration plan, possibly running it in parallel with the old system.

- Lock the new software components into the development and test library.

- Phase out the old system as confidence is developed in the new system.

Review the system installation.

- Evaluate the system's performance.
- Determine what system tuning is needed.
- Evaluate user acceptance of the system.
- Determine what improvements are needed in user training.
- Schedule the improvements in training.
- Determine what system modifications are needed.
- Schedule the system modifications.

°° If no modifications are needed, exit.
Else
- Document the adjustments needed.
- Determine the date for installation of the next version.
- Make adjustments.

Expand the pilot to the full system.

Measure the system's performance.
°° Optimize the database design. (See Appendices IX-1 and IX-2.)
Determine what hardware is needed to handle the full load.
Expand the system a stage at a time.
Monitor the system's performance.

# Stability Analysis

## Introduction

There are three main objectives of data modeling:

- to create databases that are as stable as possible (this has a major impact on maintenance costs);
- to ensure that diverse end users can automatically derive information they need;
- to help ensure that separately developed systems will work together.

The structures of databases in use will change in the future, but an objective of their design should be to *minimize those types of change that will cause existing application programs to be rewritten*. It is expensive to rewrite programs—often so expensive that it is avoided or postponed. The data model needs to be a *stable* foundation which serves as the basis for future system design.

The logical structures of data in an enterprise can be made *stable*, whereas the procedures change constantly. Various considerations are needed in data modeling to achieve stable data models. In this appendix we discuss these considerations.

The first step is to employ a computerized tool that synthesizes the views of data into a fully normalized model and makes the coordinated model available to all analysts, developers, and information centers. Given an automated synthesis tool, careful attention is needed to the inputs, and imaginative discussion is needed for the outputs.

The inputs need to come from as many sources as possible to help ensure completeness. Each input needs to be examined to ensure that it represents the data items and functional dependencies correctly. The output needs to be examined to ensure that it contains no anomalies and that it represents future uses of the data as effectively as possible.

The synthesis of views of data is used in conjunction with the entity-relationship diagram established in information strategy planning. The start of the detailed data modeling process is to establish primary keys for the entity types involved in the business area.

# Success in Data Modeling

There are five important rules for success in data modeling:

- Involve the end users at every step in the data-modeling process.
- Employ canonical synthesis with an automated design tool, and ensure that the model is fully normalized.
- Ensure that the users understand and review the data model and data definitions.
- Apply the stability analysis steps listed in this appendix when the data models are being created and reviewed.
- Respond *rapidly* to all end-user criticisms and suggestions about the data models. Fast redesign feedback is essential to keep the end users interested.

Probably the best way to involve end users is to set up committees of interested users to review the inputs and outputs of the modeling process, as described in Chapter 13. Meetings of the user committees should employ a graphics workbench tool with a large-screen projector. As subjects come up for discussion, the relevant portion of the model should be displayed and suggested modifications either entered into the model or recorded for further study. Often there are many last-minute changes to data definitions or associations. These can be appropriately entered into the model ready for the meeting.

Data modeling is done a small step at a time. Views of data are discovered and synthesized into the overall model. The data-modeling and process-modeling parts of business area analysis often proceed hand-in-hand with the process modeling, helping to discover views of data that are added to the overall synthesis. The data model should be accessible online at different locations so that coordination of the data across the enterprise steadily grows. The organization's data are steadily cleaned up, the many inconsistencies removed and documented.

# Thinking About The Future

When the output from the modeling process is reviewed, it is the time to think about the future. If future requirements can be understood at this stage, a better logical design will result, with a lower probability of expensive maintenance later.

The users, systems analysts, and data administrator should examine the output and ask themselves: How might these data be used in the future? Any potential future use should be incorporated provisionally in the model to see whether that use causes changes in the structure of the data-item groups.

Sometimes end users are better at thinking about the future than I.S. professionals because they know their possible applications better. This is not always the case. Sometimes imaginative systems analysts, or a data administrator, are best at thinking up future uses for the data. Often the best way to do it is with a user group meeting with the users, analysts and data administrator all trying to brainstorm future uses of the data.

The user team is asked to play games with the model. They think of things that have not happened or things that were not inputs to the model. Suppose, for example, that a supplier's factory burns down and information is needed for rescheduling. What could be the characteristics of future products? Suppose that new government legislation is enacted. Can the model adapt to change that can be foreseen without enforcing massive rewrites of existing programs? If the model is resiliant to most future changes, it is a *stable* model. We can build stability into the data when there is little or no stability in the business procedures.

The attributes of each entity type should be examined to ask whether the users or analysts can think of possible future attributes. The links between primary keys should be questioned to assess whether a link with "one" cardinality could have "many" cardinality in the future. Thought about future requirements may cause an entity type to be added to the entity-relationship model. Every entity type in the entity-relationship model should be examined to ensure that none are forgotten in the detailed data modeling.

Many enterprises change their organizational structure. The data analysis groups should consider whether possible organizational changes could cause a change in the data model. It is not possible to achieve a data model that will never change, but by applying the steps in the appendix, it can be made as resiliant as possible. To achieve resiliancy, a set of checks should be applied to each input to the synthesis process, and a set of checks should be applied to the output. We discuss these in the remainder of this appendix. Box XI.1 summarizes the steps.

## Input to the Model

Each input data item should be checked to make sure that no data item already in the model has the same name but a different meaning. In some cases an input data item may already exist in the model under a different name: for example, SAILING-DATE and DATE-OF-DEPARTURE. In some cases it may exist in a slightly different form; for example, ETD, EXPECTED-TIME-OF-DEPARTURE, may incorporate the intended SAILING-DATE. Avoiding these situations is part of the process of cleaning up the data.

In some cases the input data can be simplified. For example, it contains DATE-OF-VOYAGE, but this already exists in effect as the first of many dates in the voyage itinerary. There may be no need to have VOYAGE# identifying DATE-OF-VOYAGE when VOYAGE# + PORT already identifies DATE-OF-DEPARTURE.

It *is* desirable to have conventions for naming the data items. This can improve the uniformity of the names and can often help avoid the situation where the same data item has different names in different inputs.

## BOX XI. 1    Steps in Creating Stable Data Models

The data models are a foundation stone on which so much will be built. The foundation needs to be as stable as possible (i.e., it should not change in ways that force application programs to have to be rewritten). The following steps are needed to achieve this:

*STRATEGY*

- Select an encyclopedia/data modeling tool to form the corporatewide repository and coordination tool.
- Determine in an information strategy planning study the information needs of the enterprise. Establish an enterprisewide overview in the form of an entity-relationship model.
- For each business area establish user committees with key persons representing each use of data.

*DATA ANALYSIS*

- Capture all documents that will be derived from the database or will serve as inputs to the database.
- Determine by discussion with the end users what types of data they want to obtain from the database, now and in the future.
- Determine from the systems analysis process whether any new record or document requirements are emerging.
- Examine any existing databases, files or dictionaries that relate to these data.
- Plan whether existing files or databases will coexist with the new database or will be converted. If they will coexist, plan the bridge between the old system and the new.
- Employ a data dictionary to document a description of the meaning of each data item.

*CREATING THE DATA MODEL*

- Employ canonical synthesis, with an automated design tool, and ensure that the model is fully normalized.
- Inspect each input to see whether it can be simplified.
- Do any of the input data items already exist in the model under a different name or in a slightly different form?
- For each input data item, check that no different item in the model has the same name.
- Employ naming convention standards for selecting data-item names.
- Be sure that concatenated keys are correctly represented in the input to the synthesis process.

- Be sure that all attributes entered as input are dependent on the *whole* of the key that identifies them.
- Be sure that the data groups entered as input contain no transitive dependencies (Box VI.2).
- Question the validity of all links that represent business rules, as opposed to the natural inherent properties of the data. Could these rules be changed in the future?
- Question any link between keys with "one" cardinality to ask whether it could become "many" cardinality in the future.

## INSPECTING THE OUTPUT OF THE DATA MODEL

- With the user group, review the data dictionary to ensure that all users agree about the definitions of data items.
- With the user group, review the model to ensure that their data requirements can be derived from it.
- With the user group, brainstorm the possible future uses of the data. For any uses that the model does not serve, create new input to the synthesis process.
- Examine every attribute data item in the model to determine whether it could possibly become a primary key in the future.
- Complete the reverse mapping of any links between keys to identify any possible many-to-many links ($\succ\!\!-\!\!\prec$). The synthesis tool will create an extra concatenated key in the model to take care of any future intersection data (Box VI.3). This can be changed if no intersection data are possible.
- Examine any links that the synthesis process deletes, to ensure that they are truly redundant.
- Examine the effect of exploding any concatenated keys, to see whether the resulting single-field data items need to exist separately in the database.
- If a candidate keys exist in the resulting model, check that they are in fact likely to remain candidate keys in the future.
- Check the treatment of any intersecting attributes to ensure that it is the best of the three possible treatments (Box V.1). Could the intersecting attribute become a primary key in the future?
- Inspect any cycles in the modeling output. Check whether a further link should be added to break the cycle (Box VI.4).
- Use fast (computerized) redesign after any changes are made, in order to maintain the interest of the users.

*Note:* Further considerations for stability are necessary when the database schema and physical representation are designed.

# Caution with Concatenated Keys

Certain circumstances are necessary in creating *input* to the modeling process. First, caution is needed with concatenated keys. There is a big difference between

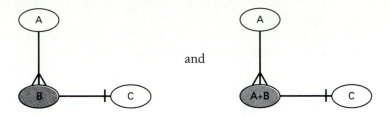

and

It would be incorrect to draw the following:

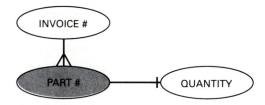

If you know the value of PART#, you do not know the value of QUANTITY. PART# alone does not identify QUANTITY. To know the value of QUANTITY, you need to know both INVOICE# and PART#. QUANTITY therefore needs to be pointed to by a concatenated key INVOICE# + PART#. The following is correct:

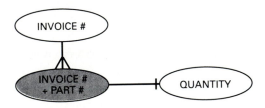

On the other hand,

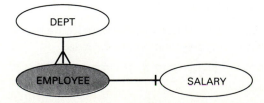

is correct because EMPLOYEE# does (by itself) identify SALARY.

# Reverse Mapping between Keys

For all associations between primary keys, the cardinality in both directions should be entered. For example, in the following case:

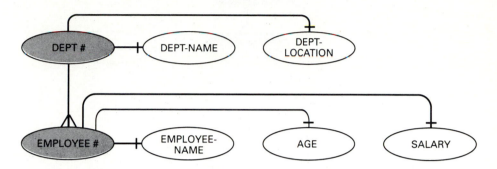

DEPT# and EMPLOYEE# are primary keys. The reverse mapping between them should be entered:

# Dependence on The Whole Key

When attributes are drawn, the user should make sure that they are identified correctly by the primary key that points to them (as above), but they are also dependent on the *entire* concatenated key. Thus, the following is *incorrect*:

PART-DESCRIPTION is identified by only a portion of the concatenated key: PART#. Therefore, a separate key PART# should be drawn:

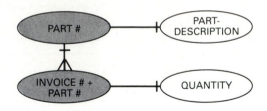

# Avoidance of Hidden Primary Keys

When a data-item group is entered, there may be a hidden primary key in the group. One item entered as an attribute may, in fact, identify some other data item in the group, as in the following:

| ORDER # | SUPPLIER # | SUPPLIER-NAME | SUPPLIER-ADDRESS | ORDER-DATE | DELIVERY-DATE | TOTAL |
|---------|------------|---------------|------------------|------------|---------------|-------|

There is a hidden primary key in this record. SUPPLIER# identifies SUPPLIER-NAME and SUPPLIER-ADDRESS. It should be diagrammed as shown in Box XI.2.

What forces program rewriting is a change in the basic structure of a record. The most common cause of this is that a data item that is an attribute in the record *now* becomes a primary key *later*. It is easy to spot any such data items in the output of a data modeling tool.

---

**BOX XI.2    The Avoidance of Hidden Transitive Dependencies in the Representation of User Views of Data**

The record below, taken from a user's view of data, contains a hidden transitive dependency:

| ORDER# | SUPPLIER# | SUPPLIER-NAME | SUPPLIER-ADDRESS | DELIVERY-DATE | ORDER-DATE | $-TOTAL |
|--------|-----------|---------------|------------------|---------------|------------|---------|

It might be tempting to diagram it thus:

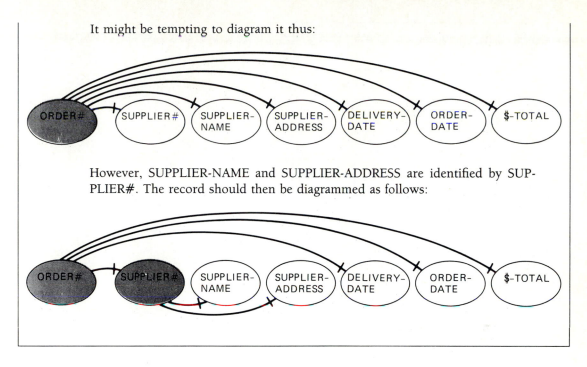

However, SUPPLIER-NAME and SUPPLIER-ADDRESS are identified by SUP-PLIER#. The record should then be diagrammed as follows:

The data administrator, systems analysts and user committee should examine each attribute data item in turn and ask: Could this possibly be used as a primary key in the future? If data items are found that are potential future primary keys, the decision should be made whether to make them primary keys *now* by giving the modeling tool new input views. If they are made into primary keys now, this will possibly save future redesign involving extensive program rewriting.

Let us reexamine our highly simplified model of data for a shipping company. For convenience it is drawn again in a simplified format in Figure XI.1.

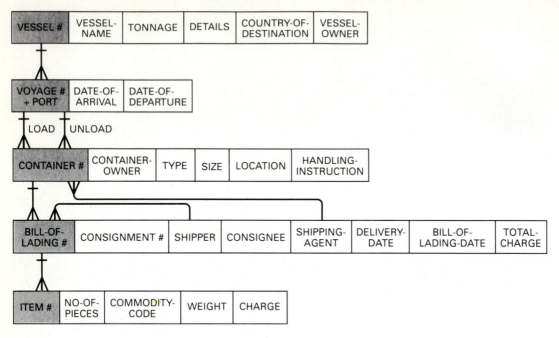

FIGURE XI. 1   The canonical structure for the shipping example developed in Appendix VIII.

We can take each data item that is not by itself a primary key and ask whether it could be used as a primary key in the future:

VESSEL-NAME

This is equivalent to VESSEL#. VESSEL# is used to identify vessels; so there would never be a *separate record* with VESSEL-NAME as its primary key. VESSEL-NAME is a candidate key and may be used for accessing the vessel record.

TONNAGE

No. This would not be used as a primary key at any time. (It could conceivably be used as a secondary key. That does not matter.)

DETAIL

No.

COUNTRY-OF-REGISTRATION

This is an entity type, but no attributes are stored about it.

The data administrator, systems analysts and end-user group should examine each data item in this way. It is generally easy to spot those that might become primary keys in the future. If they are made primary keys now, that will prevent having to restructure that data and rewrite the programs using it in the future. It could save much money and disruption. The modeling process will automatically take care of this if views of data using the key in question are fed to it.

# Dictionary Check

When the foregoing checks are taking place, the dictionary definitions of the data items should be used in conjunction with the model. Users should double check that they really represent the true meaning of the data as employed by the users.

# Intersection Data

With a good database management system, it is possible to add new *attributes* to an existing record without forcing the rewriting of application programs, provided that there is no change in primary keys. It is possible, however, that a new attribute might be needed that relates to an existing *link* rather than to a single key. This is *intersection data*, which we illustrated in Fig. VIII.5.

If a one-to-many link exists between the primary keys, new data can be identified by one or another of the existing primary keys. It can therefore be added to an existing record. If a many-to-many link exists between the primary keys, intersection data cannot be identified by either of the primary keys alone. It needs a concatenated key. This is illustrated in Box XI.3.

The synthesis process should detect any many-to-many links between primary keys and automatically create a concatenated key that combines them, deleting the many-to-many link. This is illustrated in the bottom half of Box XI.3.

Suppose, for example, that a college database was created that recorded information about classes and information about teachers. It contained the following many-to-many link:

It did not consider textbooks.

Sometime later it is necessary to record what textbooks are used. However, the textbook for a class is selected by the teacher. It cannot therefore be identified by the primary key CLASS-TITLE alone. It is identified by the concatenation of CLASS-TITLE and TEACHER:

## BOX XI.3    Intersection Data

The following are examples of intersection data:

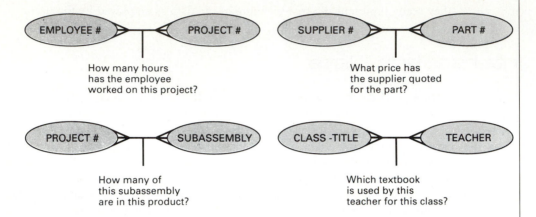

How many hours
has the employee
worked on this project?

What price has
the supplier quoted
for the part?

How many of
this subassembly
are in this product?

Which textbook
is used by this
teacher for this class?

When a many-to-many link exists between two primary keys, it is likely that intersection data will need to be stored, which is keyed by the concatenation of both primary keys. The synthesis process automatically creates these concatenated keys, as follows:

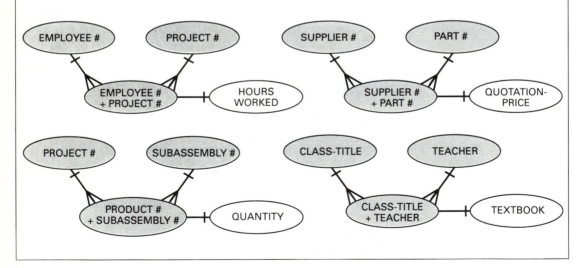

In anticipation of such changes, the modeling process should automatically change each many-to-many link between primary keys and insert the appropriate concatenated key:

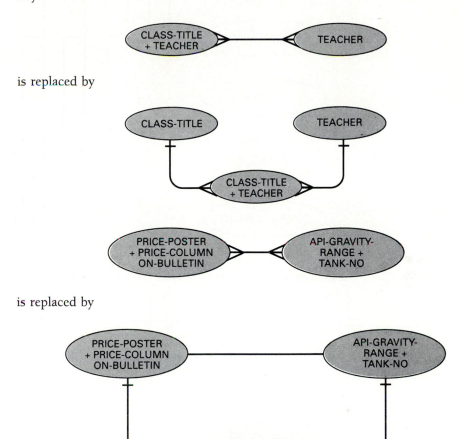

is replaced by

is replaced by

# Candidate Keys

The model may contain some links with a "one" cardinality in both directions. These indicate a *candidate key*. If A identifies B and B identifies A (A ———— B), then A and B are functionally equivalent.

Any such situations should be inspected carefully and the question asked: Are A and B *really* functionally equivalent and likely to remain so in the future?

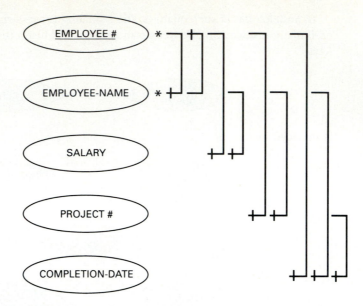

An instance of this record:

| EMPLOYEE # | EMPLOYEE NAME | SALARY | PROJECT # | COMPLETION DATE |
|---|---|---|---|---|
| 120 | JONES | 2000 | X | 17.7.84 |
| 121 | HARPO | 1700 | X | 17.7.84 |
| 270 | GARFUNKAL | 1800 | Y | 12.1.87 |
| 273 | SELSI | 3600 | X | 17.7.84 |
| 274 | ABRAHMS | 3000 | Z | 21.3.86 |
| 279 | HIGGINS | 2400 | Y | 12.1.87 |
| 301 | FLANNEL | 1800 | Z | 21.3.86 |
| 306 | McGRAW | 2100 | X | 17.7.84 |
| 310 | ENSON | 3000 | Z | 21.3.86 |
| 315 | GOLDSTEIN | 3100 | X | 17.7.84 |
| 317 | PUORRO | 2700 | Y | 12.1.87 |
| 320 | MANSINI | 1700 | Y | 12.1.87 |
| 321 | SPOTO | 2900 | X | 17.7.84 |
| 340 | SCHAFT | 3100 | X | 17.7.84 |
| 349 | GOLD | 1900 | Z | 21.3.86 |

FIGURE XI.2 Functional dependencies in the record EMPLOYEE (EM-PLOYEE#, EMPLOYEE-NAME, SALARY, PROJECT#, COMPLETION-DATE). The asterisks indicate the prime data items (members of candidate keys).

It is easy to illustrate candidate keys in textbooks, but in practice they are rare because:

1. In the future, *A* may identify a slightly different set of data items from *B*.
2. Two values of *A* may be identical, whereas the equivalent values of *B* are not. For example, EMPLOYEE# and EMPLOYEE-NAME, shown as functionally equivalent in Fig. VII.2, are not really equivalent candidate keys because two employees might have the same name. Only EMPLOYEE# should be used as the primary key.

The model might contain situations such as the following:

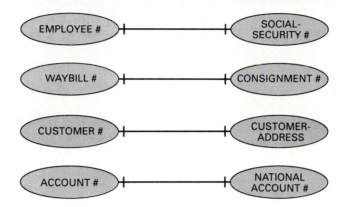

## Cycles in the Model

The one-cardinality links in the model may form a cycle, as in the following case:

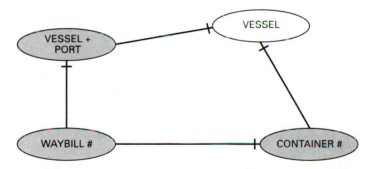

There is often a redundancy in such cycles. They can be simplified by the addition of a cross-link which causes two or more of the links in the cycle to be deleted, thus simplifying the structure. This is illustrated in Box XI.4 The data administrator should examine all such cycles.

# How Large Should User Views Be?

When preparing data for the synthesis process, users and analysts have sometimes worried about how complex one user view should be. They have sometimes had difficulty deciding where one user view starts and where it ends. The answer is: It doesn't matter.

# BOX XI.4    Cycles in The Model

The one-cardinality in the model may form a cycle as in the following cases:

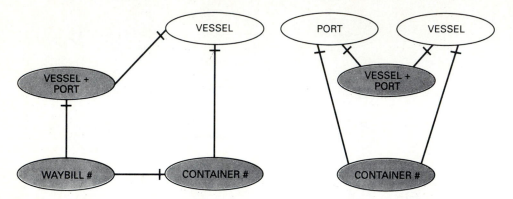

There is often a hidden redundancy in such cycles, which can be broken by adding a cross-link between the data items. For example, in both of the cases above, a link from CONTAINER# to VESSEL + PORT is needed:

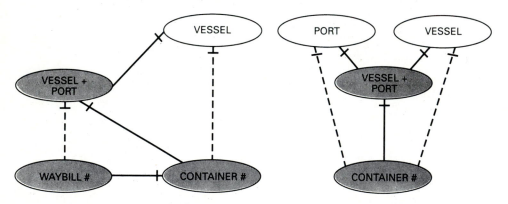

The dashed links are then redundant and automatically removed. A simpler structure results.

The modeling process combines them into a synthesized structure. A complex user view can be entered as multiple separate user views and the end result will be the same. It is often a good idea to do this because it lessens the likelihood of making an error. *Keep the inputs simple.*

For example, the following bubble chart represents the data on the bills that I receive from a nearby hardware store:

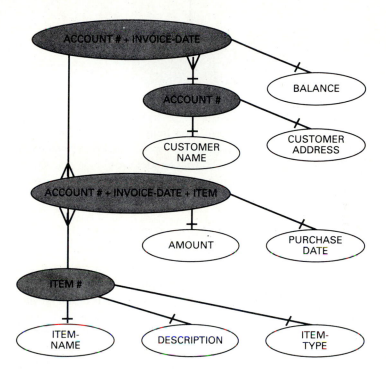

This could be entered in three separate pieces, as follows:

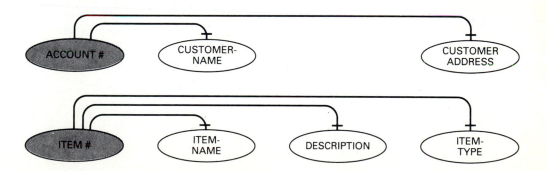

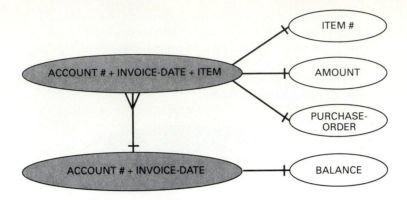

In both cases, ACCOUNT# + INVOICE-DATE + ITEM# would be linked *automatically* to its component data items: ACCOUNT#, INVOICE-DATE, and ITEM#. ACCOUNT# + INVOICE-DATE would be linked *automatically* to ACCOUNT# and INVOICE-DATE. The resulting model would be the same in each case. INVOICE-DATE would not appear as a primary key and, hence, could be deleted.

## Inherent Properties of Data

The intent of the data model is to represent the *inherent* properties of the data. There are two types of inherent characteristics of the links on the bubble chart—those that are *naturally* inherent and those that represent *business rules*.

The *naturally* inherent characteristics include such properties as the following: a branch office can have *many* salespeople; an employee has *one* pension record; a supplier can supply *many* parts; a part has only *one* description.

The *business* rules include such properties as the following: a particular policyholder will be sent all his bills on the same day regardless of how many policies he has; a given flight number is always the same type of plane; a person may have two addresses but not three.

The data administrator should distinguish between the *naturally* inherent properties and the *business* rules. In the case of the latter, he needs to determine how feasible the assumed rule is. Could it change? Should the database be set up so that the policyholder bills *could* be sent out on different days? Should TYPE-OF-PLANE be identified by FLIGHT-NUMBER or FLIGHT-NUMBER + DATE? Often, the data structure can be set up to anticipate changes in the rules.

# Systems for Improved Decision-Making

## Two Types of Systems

A particularly valuable use of computers and networks is to improve the decision-making in an enterprise. Systems that do this are commonly divided into two categories: Executive Information Systems and Decision Support Systems.

### Executive Information Systems (EIS)

Executive Information Systems are targeted at executives or high-level managers who will not do detailed computational analysis of a decision. They are concerned with knowing what is happening, determining when human intervention is needed, having the right information to aid executive decision-making and monitoring the effects of their actions.

The users of such systems often do not type, except for reluctant one-finger pecking at a keyboard; they do not program; they do not learn mnemonics, coded commands or special punctuation.

An Executive Information System must be immediately valuable to the executive and very easy to use.

### Decision-Support Systems (DSS)

Decision-Support Systems are targeted at the manager or staff person who does substantial analysis of facts in order to make better decisions. The computational techniques vary from commonsense business calculations to highly sophisticated operations-research techniques such as trend analysis, linear programming, goal-seeking and optimization techniques.

A wide variety of software is available for Decision-Support Systems [JMPS]. It varies from simple spreadsheet tools to elaborate analytical tools. Most decision-support computation can be done without conventional programming. Some is done using programs written in user-oriented fourth-generation languages. Most decision-support packages have software for generating a variety of chart types so that the results of the computations can be displayed or printed for executives to use. Graphics can be very valuable for exploring complex data and understanding the subtle causes of business phenomena. The purpose of much decision-support computation is to extract the truth from complex data.

The results of decision-support analysis should be made available to executives, and this may be done via Executive Information Systems. It is desirable to integrate these two types of software. (See Box XII.1.)

---

**BOX XII. 1   Contrast between an Executive Information System and a Decision-Support System**

Executive Information System

- brings together the data most valuable for an executive from internal and external sources;
- avoids irrelevant data;
- summarizes, filters and compresses the data;
- makes the data very easy to access without typing;
- presents the data with powerful graphics;
- highlights, with color, information to which the executive's attention should be drawn;
- enables the executive to track critical data to provide monitoring and feedback capabilities.

Decision-Support System

- provides a database of data that has multiple dimensions structured so that two-dimensional slices through the data can be analyzed;
- provides a way to summarize, interrelate and correlate data;
- provides a variety of analysis tools as in Box XII.2;
- provides modeling tools;
- provides "what-if" analysis and modeling;
- provides graphic presentation tools.

---

It is desirable to be able to build decision-making systems quickly and to evolve the decision-making process rapidly so that it meets the company's needs as effectively as possible. As with other systems, tools, methodologies, skilled people and appropriate management are needed. However, the tools and methodologies are different from those needed to build transaction-processing systems.

# Tools

A rich set of tools exists for decision support. Most of these tools operate with a personal computer or workstation on the decision-maker's desk, sometimes connected to a shared database. In many systems, the database for decision-making is a server on a local area network, accessible by many users. Decision-makers often need to communicate with one another while doing decision-support computation. The system may be designed for electronic exchange of information among users while they employ the decisions-support facility.

Decision-making software needs to be integrated with software for database access, electronic mail, printing and publishing and office facilities in general. Many vendors have created this *integrated office* environment.

Decision-Support Systems provide help in accessing data for decision-making, doing analysis and modeling of decisions and making an optimum choice. They help provide understanding of the decision environment and aid human judgment. These packages help their users analyze data, answer "what-if" questions, create financial and other models and, generally, extract the truth from complex data. They range from simple, two-dimensional spreadsheet tools such as LOTUS 1-2-3 to tools that can be used to manipulate data in many dimensions. The higher-level tools incorporate elaborate analysis techniques.

The simplest decision-support tools—the two-dimensional spreadsheet packages— are now familiar to most people with personal computers. At the opposite end of the range are highly sophisticated tools such as EXPRESS [IRI], *System W* [COMSHARE], *AS* (Application Systems) [IBM] and *Metaphor* [METAPHOR], which incorporate many of the techniques of operations research. In the past, financial or business models were created in programming languages. Today they can be created merely by writing business equations and manipulating curves with tools such as JAVELIN [JAVELIN]. Easy-to-use Decision-Support System software brings analysis and modeling techniques to a much broader range of users.

Some tools provide a diversity of analysis techniques, such as regression analysis, correlation, time-series analysis, and forecasting techniques. All of the techniques of operations research can be made easy to use if an appropriate human interface is built into the software. A good tool may guide the user in decision-making techniques and employ sophisticated graphics to make the decision-making process as clear as possible.

Box XII.2 shows the set of tools provided by EXPRESS software.

## BOX XII.2 Set of Tools Provided by EXPRESS

*EXPLORATORY DATA ANALYSIS*

- Mean
- Median
- Standard deviation
- Variance
- Other standard statistical functions
- Scatter plots
- Stem-and-leaf plots
- Box plots
- Normal probability plots

*TIME-SERIES ANALYSIS AND FORECASTING*

- Moving averages
- Moving totals
- Exponential smoothing
- Linear extrapolation
- Compound growth extrapolation
- Linear and compound growth triangles
- Trend curve fitting (including linear exponential, power functions, multiple hyperbolic functions, and S-curves)
- X-11 deseasonalization and forecasting techniques (monthly and quarterly)
- Autocorrelation correction
- Seasonal adjustment (SABL for user-defined periodicity)
- Polynomial distributed lags
- Multiple linear regression
- ARIMA (Box-Jenkins analysis)
- Holt-Winters forecast
- ACCUFOR
- Forecast accuracy measurement testing (actual versus forecast)

*CAUSAL MODELS AND SURVEY ANALYSIS (CROSS-SECTIONAL ANALYSIS)*

- Autocorrelation correction
- Polynomial distributed lags
- Multiple linear regression
- Two-stage least squares
- Leapwise regression (which tests and determines best of all possible models)
- Crosstabs
- Correlation matrices
- Cluster analysis
- Factor analysis
- MONANOVA
- Automatic interaction detector (AID)

*ADVANCED ANALYTICAL TOOLS*

- Linear programming
- Critical path analysis (PERT)
- Risk analysis
- Monte Carlo simulation

Some tools are designed for a specific type of problem, such as job-shop scheduling, calculations that should be done when contemplating taking over another corporation, planning a delivery schedule, financial analysis, assignment of gates at an airport or the management of chaotic processes.

Some tools represent data in a multidimensional fashion. Examples include Decision-Support Systems such as EXPRESS [IRI] and SYSTEM W [COMSHARE]. They provide, in effect, a multidimensional matrix of data so that we are able to examine two dimensions at a time.

For example, suppose that certain variables are mapped against time. The sales revenue of each project that an organization sells, for example, might be mapped against months. To help with market planning, we may choose to project past sales into the future in different ways, with different "what-if" propositions. This gives a three-dimensional array of data, as illustrated in Figure XII.1.

Most Decision Support System languages allow us to explore one two-dimensional slice through the data at a time, as indicated by the shades slice in Figure XII.1.

We might perform calculations, obtain statistics or plot chars from this slice. We might do anything that we can do with two-dimensional spreadsheet software such as LOTUS 1-2-3. On the other hand, we might want to examine a slice relating to one time period, going through several "what-it" propositions, as shown in Figure XII.2.

Product revenue is only one product variable of interest. We might also want to see units sold, price, average order size, average cost of sales, average profit, type of product, age and so on. We might want these variables to be mapped against time periods, as shown in Figure XII.3.

We may not be content with average order size, average cost of sale and average profit on sale. We might want these broken down by type of product and by customer. We might then like to see a histogram of these variables. Now we need more than three dimensions in our representation of data.

It is difficult to draw diagrams with more than three dimensions. To view multi-dimensional data easily, we need a computer. Imagine the shaded slice in Figure XII.3 moving from one time period to another at the press of a key. A computer enables us to deal easily with data in multiple dimensions.

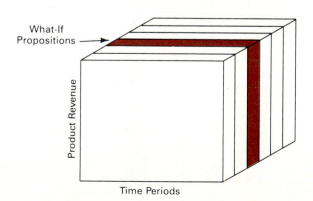

FIGURE XII. 1  Three-Dimensional Array

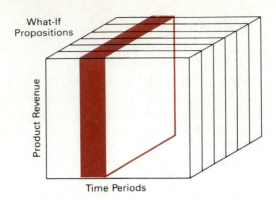

FIGURE XII. 2  Examining One Time Period

SYSTEM W supports the analysis of data up to nine dimensions. Each two-dimensional slice through these data is called a **viewpoint**. The data of a viewpoint can be analyzed or plotted, as with a good spreadsheet tool.

For each slice through multidimensional data, different types of reports may be useful. A Decision-Support System needs a flexible report generator and a business graphics generator with which to display the information. A variety of calculations may be done using the data.

EXPRESS allows its users to state what slice through the data they want to see by using LIMIT statements. This is illustrated in Figure XII.4.

In the top illustration of Figure XII.4, the user says LIMIT PRODUCT TO PENI-CILLIN. This gives a two-dimensional slice through the data. The user then says DISPLAY SALES, and a sales report is displayed. In the second illustration, the user employs two LIMIT statements:

```
LIMIT YEAR TO 1981
LIMIT CUSTOMER TO DISTRICT NEWYORK
```

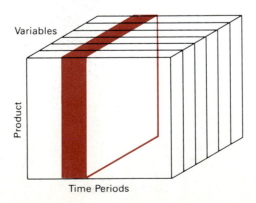

FIGURE XII. 3  Mapping Variables against Time Periods

The product manager can look at the sales totals for that product.

-> LIMIT PRODUCT TO PENICILLIN
-> DISPLAY SALES

PRODUCT PENICILLIN SALES
DOLLAR SALES

| MONTH | WEST | EAST | SOUTH | CENTRAL | TOTAL |
|---|---|---|---|---|---|
| JAN81 | 980,957 | 1,004,613 | 515,221 | 467,683 | 2,968,474 |
| FEB81 | 539,558 | 579,040 | 419,527 | 446,851 | 1,984,976 |
| MAR81 | 527,900 | 639,302 | 339,811 | 401,464 | 1,908,477 |
| APR81 | 478,699 | 498,513 | 351,408 | 369,857 | 1,698,477 |
| MAY81 | 510,750 | 573,416 | 334,904 | 273,907 | 1,692,977 |
| JUN81 | 517,737 | 501,260 | 283,531 | 243,446 | 1,545,974 |
| JUL81 | 484,558 | 529,114 | 249,100 | 227,206 | 1,489,978 |
| AUG81 | 435,095 | 585,827 | 189,950 | 226,606 | 1,437,478 |
| SEP81 | 647,541 | 590,895 | 267,950 | 288,589 | 1,794,975 |
| OCT81 | 652,618 | 692,888 | 319,242 | 279,805 | 1,944,545 |
| NOV81 | 540,578 | 595,727 | 357,235 | 333,405 | 1,826,945 |
| DEC81 | 997,931 | 968,584 | 429,208 | 475,781 | 2,871,504 |
| | 7,313,914 | 7,759,179 | 4,057,087 | 4,034,600 | 23,164,780 |

The New York district manager can look at sales data for the whole year for each customer in the district.

-> LIMIT YEAR TO 1981
-> LIMIT CUSTOMER TO DISTRICT NEWYORK
-> DISPLAY SALES

NEW YORK DISTRICT SALES
DOLLAR SALES

| CUSTOMER | VITA-PLUS | COUGH-OFF | KEN-TRANQ | PENICILLIN | TOTAL |
|---|---|---|---|---|---|
| DAVID | 21,950 | 54,297 | 608,485 | 922,520 | 1,607,252 |
| ACE | 18,988 | 100,825 | 131,642 | 331,601 | 583,056 |
| WILSON | 64,423 | 230,586 | 832,903 | 1,079,243 | 2,207,155 |
| LELISTER | 119,967 | 5,197 | 112,740 | 86,493 | 324,397 |
| MAJOR | 23,001 | 20,949 | 5,281 | 1,684 | 50,915 |
| CLASS | 113,595 | 319,333 | 245,663 | 579,442 | 1,258,033 |
| GLUSCO | 5,195 | 22,972 | 84,422 | 59,334 | 171,923 |
| | 367,119 | 754,159 | 2,021,136 | 3,060,317 | 6,202,731 |

FIGURE XII.4 LIMIT statements in EXPRESS are used to display slices through multidimensional data.

(Continued)

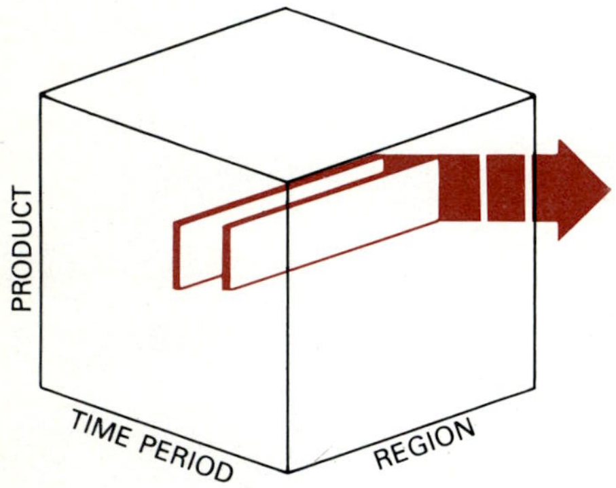

The over-the-counter division manager can produce a monthly report showing the national performance data for each product in that division, plus performance a year ago and the variance.

-> LIMIT MONTH TO CURRENT.MONTH
-> LIMIT PRODUCT TO DIVISION OTC
-> DISPLAY SALES LAG(SALES,12,MONTH) VARIANCE

OTC DIVISION

| PRODUCT | SALES CURRENT MONTH | SALES YEAR AGO | SALES VARIANCE |
|---|---|---|---|
| VITAPLUS | 101,330 | 77,972 | 23,358 |
| COUGHOFF | 1,413,494 | 1,305,945 | 107,549 |
| | 1,514,824 | 1,383,917 | 130,907 |

FIGURE XII.4 (Continued)

REGION

TIME PERIOD

PRODUCT

In the third illustration, the user displays two slices so that he can compare this month's sales with those of a year ago.

The data can be aggregated in various ways. In the third illustration of Figure XII.4. the user says

```
LIMIT PRODUCT TO DIVISION OTC.
```

The products of this division are then displayed.

The user needs help in employing standard types of computation.

A variety of computations need to be done to aid in decision-making. Sometimes fairly elaborate, nested conditions are needed to express the rules that govern the calculations.

Many of the calculations that help in decision-making need standard types of analysis that can be preprogrammed, such as regression analysis, different types of forecasting, sensitivity analysis and a variety of statistical functions. Decision-support software, then, needs the types of facilities listed in Box XII.3 [JMPS].

---

**BOX XII.3   Facilities Needed in Decision-Support Software**

- *Database* that structures data for multidimensional analysis (as in Figure XII.4, but with more than three dimensions).
- *Query language* for querying the multidimensional data.
- *Report generator* with which the user can create reports showing different slices through the data.
- *Spreadsheet manipulator* for manipulating different two-dimensional slices through the data.
- *Graphics generator* that can create charts showing different views of the data.
- *Language* for performing calculations on the data, sometimes with complex nested conditions. A nonprocedural language may be used with which equations or search parameters can be expressed in any sequence.
- *Tools* for:
    Statistical analysis
    Trend analysis
    Financial analysis
    Forecasting
    Goal seeking
    Business modeling
    Other operations research tools.
- *"What-if" exploration*: ability to change data or assumptions and rerun calculations or analyses to explore the effects of changes.
- Ability to *build models* and *store the effects* of alternative strategies.
- *Expert-system tools* that encapsulate the decision-making techniques of experts by the use of rules.

- *User-friendly means* of employing the preceding facilities in such a way that any difficult syntax can be avoided.
- *Communication facilities* for communicating results to other people. People at distant locations should be able to see the same display on their screens and discuss it.

# More Complex Decision-Support System Software

Decision-support software is likely to become far more complex and powerful in the years ahead. It may model very complex processes and use elaborate graphics. In some cases, it will employ the artificial-intelligence technique of **rule-based processing**. This enables many rules to be used to describe the behavior of complex situations. The computer selects and chains together rules to come to conclusions or establish constraints. The rules, for example, might relate to the scheduling of work on a factory floor, the selection of gates for aircraft at a large airport or the choice of dates and venues for public events. Elaborate displays with graphics and windows enable a decision maker to observe the process and interact with it so that the result is a combination of computer processing and human intuition or control. This type of human–computer interaction is valuable for the management of chaotic processes.

An elegant example of this type of decision-support software was built by Texas Instruments to help in the management of airline operations when schedules are disrupted. The decision-maker can see a route map—a worldwide route map if it is a worldwide airline. By pointing at routes or cities, the user can display information about flights, schedules, weather conditions, airplane crews and so on. If an airport closes or a plane is taken out of service, much shuffling of equipment and crews has to take place in an attempt to mimimize the disruption of service. The closing of an airport or loss of equipment can cause a chain reaction of events that ripples through the route map. Using rule chaining, the computer can evaluate consequences and display them. The decision-maker looking at the route map can see the delays highlighted in color. He can make decisions to switch aircraft or cancel certain flights and can observe the effects of these actions. He can try out many possible actions and see their consequences visually, working with the computer to minimize the harmful effects.

Decision-support software such as this may have an expert system built into it. It can give advice to the decision-maker based on expertise captured in the form of rules. During the development lifecycle, the rules may have to be established.

Texas Instruments employs software for building ruled-based decision-support systems called **symbolic spreadsheets**. It does not look like a spreadsheet visually, but it allows symbols and rules to be associated with values of data just as calculations are associated with the values in a spreadsheet.

# The Decision-Support System Lifecycle

It is often important to build decision-support systems quickly. Variants of the RAD lifecycle are used for this purpose, but the tools are usually different from those employed to build operational systems.

In creating decision-support systems, the role of the end user is especially critical. The calculations programmed into the decision-support system should be created largely by the decision-maker. Only the decision-makers who work with the decisions in question understand what calculations they want. I.S. professionals should build a version of the system and train end users how to put their own computations in it and generate the charts and reports they need. I.S. professionals ought to help in selecting and establishing the best software, extracting the necessary data and building the Decision-Support System database.

I.S. professionals may be skilled with decision-making techniques such as forecasting, time-series analysis or use of operations-research tools. In many cases, I.S. professionals work with the users to build the first version of the decision-support system, and then the users expand it to meet their needs and to do subtle investigations of the data in question. Users can be highly creative in their use of Decision-Support System tools. They often build highly complex models that evolve over time.

Decision-support systems vary from very simple ones like spreadsheets to highly elaborate systems. While spreadsheet decision-making can be done with little or no help from I.S., elaborate decision-support systems need careful planning and professional design. The simplest use of decision-support tools is little more than an extension of the calculations the user would have done with a pocket calculator. Elaborate decision-support systems need careful database design and control of development.

Major decision-support systems can be built in stages, as shown in Figure XII.5.

## Stages of Development

The Requirements Planning Stage can be much like that described in Chapter 7. Sometimes it is more intimate because the decision-maker is one person.

When the requirements are well understood, the software should be selected. A criterion of software selection should be that the software enables the system to be created as quickly and automatically as possible. Software with elegant graphics and good presentation techniques is desirable.

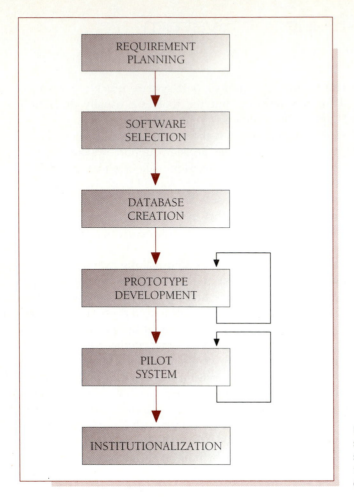

FIGURE XII.5 Major decision-support systems are often built in stages in which a prototype and then a pilot system steadily evolve.

The Requirements Planning Phase should identify the data sources. The data needed for decision making may be external data that are purchased—possibly accessed on-line. The data usually have to be extracted and converted into the format required by the decision-support system (Figure XII.6). Facilities may be established for extracting the data and establishing the decision-support system database on a daily basis.

A prototype should be put to work as early as possible. The prototype may evolve substantially before a fully working system is built. The fully working system (pilot) may be employed by only one user or department and may be enhanced for many months before it is thought appropriate to be institutionalized.

Institutionalizing the system may mean that it has many users and so needs a data network and a different database facility. A staging database may be used, as discussed later. When the system is institutionalized, it needs documentation, training and controlled maintenance.

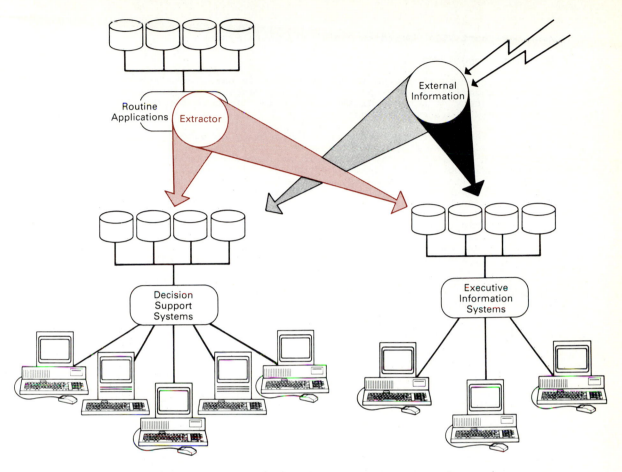

FIGURE XII.6 Data in an executive information system or decision-support system are structured entirely differently from those in routine applications. Some are extracted from routine applications. Some of the data, especially in an executive information system, are extracted from external sources.

The first working version of a decision-support system should be simple and easy to implement. Much is learned from the first working version that may affect the design of the eventual system; so the sooner it is in prototype use, the better. The software selected should permit rapid evolution of the prototype.

# Methodology

Methodology Chart MC-XII gives a suggested methodology for building decision-support systems. These systems differ greatly; so the methodology will need major adjustments under differing circumstances.

Methodology Chart XII:  Building Decision-Support Systems

⌐ Decision-Support Systems

A decision-support system is designed to help users make better
business decisions in a specific area. It requires an
appropriately structured database and a set of tools for doing
decision-support computations.

Decision-support computations should generally be done by
end-users because they understand the business problem they are
trying to solve. They may do this in an innovative, ad-hoc
fashion without specifications. Often, creative investigation of
numerical data is required. Highly complex business models may
result. Evolution through prototyping should occur before the
system is institutionalized.

I.S. professionals should usually design the database and the
means of keeping it up to date. They may select or build the
tools which the end-users employ and guide the end-users in
their use. The choice of decision-support software is critical.

> The procedure given below may be modified with MediaScribe
> to meet the needs of the particular situation.

⌐ Decision-Support-System Procedure

⌐ Initiate the project.   (See Methodology Chart 7.)

⌐ Establish criteria and controls.

Establish the long-term objectives of the development activity.
Establish the objectives of the first working version.

The first working version should be SIMPLE and relatively easy
to implement. Once a working version is fielded, the system will
tend to grow naturally if it useful, with end users extending
its functionality. The long-term potential should be understood
and planned for from the beginning.

Determine how results will be measured or judged.
Establish a budget.
Establish a target date for the first working system.
Establish dates at which progress will be reviewed.
Determine who will assess the progress and with what criteria.

⌐ Determine who will build the system.

Select the I.S. professional developer(s).
Select the end-user developer(s).
Determine what Information Center help is needed.
Determine who, if anyone, will review the results.

⌐ Requirements Planning Phase  (See Methodology Chart 7.)

⌐ Establish the software.

⌐ Select decision-support software.

Determine for which categories of users the system is intended:
        • top management
        • lower management, staff or spreadsheet users

- financial analysts
- general decision analysts

Select a software category suitable for the above user category:
  - Executive Information System (EIS)
  - spreadsheet tool
  - business modeling tool
  - financial analysis tool
  - fourth-generation programming language
  - general decision-support tool

Identify the most appropriate tool within this category.

Ensure that the developers are fully trained in the use of the tools.

Establish the data.

- Determine what data the system needs.

- Establish a data model or extract one from the encyclopedia.

- Determine where the source data comes from.
  (It is often extracted from mainframe production systems.)

- Determine how the source data will be converted or restructured.

Determine whether a staging database will be used.

A staging database is a central repository of data in the DSS format that will be used independently by multiple users.

- Data are extracted from files or transaction databases into the staging database.

- Individual users may extract data from the staging database into their own facilities.

  If so:
    - Select the staging database software.
    - Establish the staging database.
    - Cut over the existing system to run with the staging database.

- Extract the data into the tool that is used.

- Determine how the data in the decision-support system will be kept up to date.

Prototype Evolution

The first prototype should be put to work as early as possible. This can usually be done very quickly with good decision-support software, once the requisite data is established, by a data-processing professional and end user working together. The end-user may then evolve the system to do more sophisticated analysis. Eventually end-users should take over the system, adapting it to help make the most effective decisions.

°° Step-by-Step or Continuous Evolution?  (See Chapter 9.)
If step-by-step evolution

For each prototype iteration:

- Build detailed prototype.  (See Methodology Chart 9.)
- Put the prototype to use.

Brainstorm with decision-makers what features they would like.

Brainstorming is a session in which up to six or so people attempt to produce a stream of creative ideas without inhibition in order to create insight about opportunities or possible solutions to a problem. A rule of a brainstorming session is that there can be no implied criticism for making an impractical or stupid suggestion. The session is intended to generate as many ideas as possible. Negative comments are discouraged. Sometimes a wild or apparently foolish idea turns out to be useful or leads others to think of smart ideas.

The leader of the session keeps the proceedings loose, and fun, persuading the participants to strive for quantity and richness of ideas, not quality or respectability.

After the session, only certain of the ideas will be recorded for possible use.

To facilitate the idea flow, or to restart participants' thinking, the following techniques may be used:

- ANALOGY THINKING:     What problems are analogous to this? How are they solved?

- NATURE THINKING:  How is this or a similar problem solved by nature?

- SCIENCE FICTION THINKING:  If computers were very intelligent, how would they solve the problem?

  Could a similar method be used by a combination of today's computers and intelligent people?

- INVERSION:    How might the opposite of the goal be achieved?

- IMMERSION:    How might you project yourself into the problem?

  See references.

Determine features to be added or changed.

If no need for further iteration, determine target date of next review.

Else, continuous evolution

Build detailed prototype.
Refine the prototype continuously, working with the decision-makers.
Brainstorm possible improvements which might be valuable.

If an acceptable final result is achieved, solidify.

Solidify.

- Conduct usability testing.  (See Chapter 17.)
  Review to ensure that the system is easy to use by potential decision-makers as possible.

- Review to ensure that the business calculations can be easily checked by management.

- Review to ensure that the system can be easily maintained.

- Create the necessary documentation.

Build pilot system.

A pilot system is a fully working system deployed at first with only a small number of users, small number of terminals or a small database. When it is found to be satisfactory, the number of users may be increased and the database expanded.

> A pilot system is a preliminary system in which the functions and design are thought to be understood, but the system is cut over in a limited form so that experience can be gained with it before the full system is cut over.

- Determine what functions of the prototype will be included in the first pilot system.

- Determine how decision-support information will be communicated among separate decision-makers.

- Determine how decision-support information will be communicated with higher management.

- Determine what networking facilities are needed. Will the decision-support facility link to an electronic mail or in-basket facility, for example.

- Determine the nature of the ongoing connection to production databases.

- Determine whether the system should be redesigned or re-architected in order to produce a working pilot.

- Make the necessary design changes.

- Build and debug the pilot.

Install and adjust pilot system.

Phase in system.
Conduct review meeting.

If no modifications needed, exit.

Else

Document adjustments needed.
Determine date for installation of next version.
Make adjustments.

Institutionalize the system.

Determine what locations should use the system.

Determine whether a staging database should be established.

Establish the requisite training.

```
Establish an internal marketing program
to make decision-makers aware of the system.

With some decision-support systems, this step has been particularly
important. It may use:

    •   memos.
    •   giving the system a memorable name and image.
    •   brochures.
    •   articles in the house magazine.
    •   presentations.
    •   film or video.

Expand the system a stage at a time.

Monitor the system performance.
Determine what hardware is needed to handle the full load.
```

# References

[COMSHARE] *System W,* product of Comshare, Inc., P.O. Box 1588, 3001 South State Street, Ann Arbor, Michigan.

[DEBONO70] Edward deBono, *Lateral Thinking: Creativity Step by Step*, Harper and Row, New York, 1970.

[GORDON61] William J. J. Gordon, *Synectics*, Harper and Row, New York, 1961.

[IBM] *AS (Application System),* integrated decision-support-system product, IBM Program #5767-001.

[IRI] *EXPRESS,* product of Information Resources, Inc., 200 Fifth Avenue, Waltham, Massachusetts 02154.

[JAVELIN] *JAVELIN,* product of Information Resources, Inc., 200 Fifth Avenue, Waltham, Massachusetts 02154.

[JMPS] from *The James Martin Productivity Series,* Volume 3: "Financial Analysis and Decision-Support Tools," The Martin Report, Inc., 22 Bessom Street, Marblehead, Massachusetts 01945 (617-639-1958).

[METAPHOR] DIS (Data Interpretation System)-technology-based tool from Metaphor Computer Systems, 1965 Charleston Road, Mountain View, California 94043.

# Index